Health Sciences
Librarianship

MEDICAL LIBRARY ASSOCIATION BOOKS

The Medical Library Association (MLA) features books that showcase the expertise of health sciences librarians for other librarians and professionals.

MLA Books are excellent resources for librarians in hospitals, medical research practice, and other settings. These volumes will provide health care professionals and patients with accurate information that can improve outcomes and save lives.

Each book in the series has been overseen editorially since conception by the Medical Library Association Books Panel, composed of MLA members with expertise spanning the breadth of health sciences librarianship.

Medical Library Association Books Panel

Carol Ann Attwood, AHIP, chair
Barbara Gushrowski, chair designate
Gail Y. Hendler
Megan Curran Rosenbloom
Tracy Shields
Kristen L. Young, AHIP
Lauren M. Young, AHIP
Gabriel R. Rios, board liaison

About the Medical Library Association

Founded in 1898, MLA is a 501(c)(3) nonprofit, educational organization of 4,000 individual and institutional members in the health sciences information field that provides lifelong educational opportunities, supports a knowledgebase of health information research, and works with a global network of partners to promote the importance of quality information for improved health to the health care community and the public.

Books in Series

The Medical Library Association Guide to Providing Consumer and Patient Health Information edited by Michelle Spatz

Health Sciences Librarianship edited by M. Sandra Wood

Health Sciences Librarianship

Edited by M. Sandra Wood

ROWMAN & LITTLEFIELD

Lanham • Boulder • New York • Toronto • Plymouth, UK

Published by Rowman & Littlefield
4501 Forbes Boulevard, Suite 200, Lanham, Maryland 20706
www.rowman.com

10 Thornbury Road, Plymouth PL6 7PP, United Kingdom

British Library Cataloguing in Publication Information Available

Library of Congress Cataloging-in-Publication Data
Health sciences librarianship / edited by M. Sandra Wood.
    pages cm. — (Medical Library Association books)
  Includes bibliographical references and index.
  ISBN 978-0-8108-8812-8 (cloth : alk. paper) — ISBN 978-0-8108-8813-5 (pbk. : alk. paper) — ISBN 978-0-8108-8814-2 (electronic) 1. Medical librarianship. 2. Medical librarianship—United States. 3. Medical libraries—Administration. 4. Medical libraries—United States—Administration. I. Wood, M. Sandra, editor of compilation.
  Z675.M4H43 2014
  026'.61—dc23   2014001391

Printed in the United States of America

Contents

List of Illustrations   xi

List of Tables   xiii

Preface   xv

Acknowledgments   xxi

Editorial Board   xxiii

PART I: The Profession   1

CHAPTER 1. Health Sciences Librarianship in Context   3

James Shedlock

    Introduction   3
    The Health Sciences Library Profession   3
    Health Sciences Librarianship Environments   6
    The National Library of Medicine   10
    Library Organizations   15
    Education for Health Sciences Librarianship   21
    Entering the Health Sciences Library Profession: Job Opportunities
        and the Hiring Process   23
    Professional Involvement and Keeping Current   24
    Summary   26
    Study Questions   27
    References   28

CHAPTER 2. The Health Sciences Environment   30

Gale G. Hannigan and Jonathan D. Eldredge

    Introduction   30
    U.S. Health Care   30
    Health Professionals' Education   39
    Biomedical Research   46
    Health and Global Health   50

Summary   51
Study Questions   52
References   52

CHAPTER 3. EMERGING TRENDS IN HEALTH SCIENCES LIBRARIANSHIP   57
Jonathan D. Eldredge and Gale G. Hannigan

Introduction   57
Trend One: Evidence-Based Practice   58
Trend Two: Active Learning   65
Trend Three: Innovative Research Collaborations   71
Trend Four: Strategies for Adapting New Technologies   75
How to Stay Abreast of Emerging Trends   77
Summary   78
Study Questions   78
References   78

PART II: Collection Services   **85**

CHAPTER 4. COLLECTION DEVELOPMENT IN HEALTH SCIENCES LIBRARIES 87
Holly E. Phillips

Introduction   87
Modern Collection Development   88
Collection Development Policies   90
Putting Policy into Practice   97
Resource Budgets   108
Keeping Current   113
Summary   113
Study Questions   113
References   114

CHAPTER 5. TECHNICAL SERVICES IN HEALTH SCIENCES LIBRARIES   116
Megan Del Baglivo, C. Steven Douglas, and María M. Pinkas

Introduction   116
Acquisitions   116
Collection Organization   119
Summary   139
Study Questions   140
References   141

CHAPTER 6. TECHNOLOGY SERVICES IN HEALTH SCIENCES LIBRARIES 143
Nancy R. Glassman

Introduction   143
Technology Today   143
Planning   145
Security   149

Electronic Health Records   151
Connecting with Patrons   152
Systems   155
Mobile Technologies   158
Emerging Technologies   160
Keeping Current   161
Summary   163
Study Questions   163
References   164

PART III: User Services   **169**

CHAPTER 7. REFERENCE AND INFORMATION SERVICES IN
HEALTH SCIENCES LIBRARIES   171

Marie T. Ascher

Introduction   171
What Is Reference?   171
Reference Functions   172
The Reference Interview and Encounter   173
Types of Users in Health Sciences Libraries   174
Reference Statistics and Transactions   178
Staffing and Scheduling of Reference Service—New Models of Service   183
Virtual Reference Services   191
Summary   192
Study Questions   193
References   193

CHAPTER 8. RESEARCH SERVICES AND DATABASE SEARCHING
IN HEALTH SCIENCES LIBRARIES   196

Lee A. Vucovich

Introduction   196
Information Needs of Biomedical Researchers   197
Searching Biomedical Research Databases   197
Supporting Evidence-Based Practice   210
Conducting Expert Searches   212
Organizing and Managing References   217
Improving Research Services   218
Summary   221
Study Questions   221
References   222

CHAPTER 9. OUTREACH SERVICES IN HEALTH SCIENCES LIBRARIES   226

Michele R. Tennant

Introduction   226
Internal Outreach   226

External Outreach—Outreach to the Community   238
Outreach for Visibility   242
Summary   246
Study Questions   247
References   247

CHAPTER 10. RESEARCH DATA MANAGEMENT AND THE
HEALTH SCIENCES LIBRARIAN   252
Andrew Creamer, Elaine R. Martin, and Donna Kafel

Introduction   252
Background   253
What is RDM?   254
Why Manage Research Data?   255
Common RDM Challenges   258
RDM Services and Roles for Health Sciences Librarians   262
Librarian RDM Skills and Competencies   268
Librarian RDM Tools and Resources   269
Summary   270
Study Questions   271
References   271

CHAPTER 11. INSTRUCTION IN HEALTH SCIENCES LIBRARIES   275
Maureen "Molly" Knapp

Introduction   275
History   275
Generations and Learning   278
Learning Paradigms   279
Disruptive Technology and Health Sciences Instruction   284
Hospital Libraries and Instruction   286
User Education and Instructional Mechanics   286
Instructional Design—Creating Your Class   291
Web-Based Learning   294
Summary   298
Study Questions   298
References   298

CHAPTER 12. ACCESS SERVICES: CIRCULATION, COURSE RESERVES,
AND INTERLIBRARY LOAN IN HEALTH SCIENCES LIBRARIES   303
Everly Brown, Na Lin, and Megan Wolff

Introduction   303
Access Services   303
Circulation Services   304
Course Reserves   308

Interlibrary Loan and Document Delivery   310
Summary   321
Study Questions   321
References   321

CHAPTER 13. CONSUMER HEALTH INFORMATION SERVICES   324

Kay Hogan Smith

Introduction   324
Overview of Consumer Health Information Services   324
Establishing and Managing a Consumer Health Information Service   331
Summary   343
Study Questions   343
References   343

PART IV: Administrative Services   347

CHAPTER 14. LIBRARY ADMINISTRATION IN HEALTH SCIENCES LIBRARIES   349

Diana J. Cunningham

Introduction   349
What Is a Library Administrator or Manager?   350
Some Management Theories or Tools   351
Institutional Organization and Structure   353
Management Competencies   355
Managing the Environment   356
Roles of the Director: Up, Down, and Out   359
Role of Standards and Accreditation   366
Evaluation and Assessment   367
Generating Support   370
Summary   373
Study Questions   373
References   373

CHAPTER 15. PHYSICAL SPACE IN HEALTH SCIENCES LIBRARIES   376

Stewart M. Brower

Introduction   376
Factors in Space Planning and Design   377
Space Needs of Different Types of Health Sciences Libraries   382
Functions and Space Needs of Health Sciences Libraries   385
The Need for Space   399
Summary   400
Study Questions   401
References   401

CHAPTER 16. NEW ROLES AND NEW HORIZONS FOR HEALTH
SCIENCES LIBRARIANS AND LIBRARIES   403

Margaret E. Henderson

   Introduction   403
   Transformation of Health Sciences Librarianship   404
   Expanded Roles in Research   405
   Clinical Librarians and Hospital Libraries   409
   Collaborations   410
   Alternative Roles and Activities   412
   The Changing Health Sciences Library Organization   413
   Summary   414
   Study Questions   415
   References   415

GLOSSARY   419
INDEX   433
ABOUT THE EDITOR AND AUTHORS   443

List of Illustrations

Figure 2.1. Triad Model of Medical Decision Making   35

Figure 2.2. Informatics at the Intersection of Information Science,
Technology, and Specific Subject Domain   45

Figure 4.1. The Long Tail of Information Availability   89

Figure 4.2. Patron Types in Health Sciences Libraries   91

Figure 4.3. NLM Selection Guidelines by Subject   94

Figure 4.4. RLG Conspectus Levels as Defined by IFLA   96

Figure 4.5. Electronic Resources Workflow Flowchart   99

Figure 4.6. Total Expenditures by Type, AAHSL Libraries, 2011–2012   108

Figure 4.7. Total Collection Expenditures by Format, AAHSL Libraries,
2011–2012   111

Figure 5.1. Evolution of Cataloging Standards   123

Figure 5.2. MeSH Subject Authority Record   125

Figure 5.3. MeSH Tree Structures Main Branches   126

Figure 5.4 MeSH Tree Structures Subbranches   126

Figure 5.5. Ben Carson VIAF Authority File   128

Figure 5.6. Outline of the NLM Classification   129

Figure 5.7. Basic Division of MARC Tags for Bibliographic Record   131

Figure 5.8. Example of an OpenURL Using SFX   136

Figure 5.9. Resource Description Framework Triple   137

Figure 5.10. LC Name Authority Record for Florence Nightingale   139

Figure 5.11. Linking Open Data Cloud Diagram: Selection   140

Figure 7.1. Association of Research Libraries (ARL) Service Trends
since 1991   179

Figure 7.2. Total and Electronic Reference Transactions, Mean Values,
2007–2008 to 2011–2012 in AAHSL Libraries   180

Figure 7.3. LibAnswers with RefAnalytics Reference Transactions form
New York Medical College, Health Sciences Library   181

Figure 7.4. Reference Transaction Flowchart, Prior Health Sciences Library,
Ohio State University   189

Figure 8.1. PubMed Publication Trends   197

Figure 8.2. PubMed Search Details   200

Figure 8.3. Result Set Analysis by Journal in Scopus   206

Figure 8.4. Scopus Altmetrics App Example   208

Figure 11.1. Search Process Outlined   288

Figure 13.1. Health InfoNet of Alabama Home Page,
www.healthinfonet.org   338

Figure 13.2. Billboard Promoting both Health InfoNet of Alabama
and Local 2-1-1 Service in Birmingham, 2009   339

Figure 15.1. Blocking   380

Figure 15.2. Modular Design   389

Figure 15.3. Room Scheduler   390

Figure 15.4. Media:Scape Collaboration Furniture   391

Figure 15.5. Examples of Medical Simulators   394

Figure 15.6. Example of a Librarian Office   397

Figure 15.7. Example of a Shared Office   398

Figure 15.8. Multipurpose Room Furniture Plan   399

List of Tables

Table 1.1. A Guide for Seeking Health Sciences Library Positions   24

Table 1.2. Health Sciences Library Journals   26

Table 3.1. EBLIP Levels of Evidence   62

Table 3.2. Types of Active Learning Found in Health Professions Education   68

Table 4.1. Sample Collection Budget of $1 Million   110

Table 5.1. Simple Dublin Core Element Set   133

Table 6.1. Selected Library Technology Journals   161

Table 8.1. Six Steps to a Successful Search   198

Table 8.2. Selected Abstract and Index Databases   203

Table 8.3. Differences between Scopus and Web of Science   206

Table 8.4. The 6S Model   211

Table 8.5. Representative Types of Grey Literature   213

Table 8.6. Selected Reporting Guidelines   215

Preface

The field of library and information sciences, especially health sciences librarianship, continues to be impacted by the rapid social and technological changes of the past decade. Bob Dylan's 1964 song about the times changing is as true today, fifty years after it was written, as it was then. Then, it referred to the social changes of the times—the civil rights movement and social unrest. Today, with the technological changes that have brought the influence of social media to play in libraries, it is equally valid. The difference is that fifty years ago, change was slow to come. Today, change is happening at a lightning pace, and what's useful and a mainstay in how libraries provide services now may be outdated and totally different in the near future.

Health sciences libraries continue to be at the forefront of the profession, adapting to changes not only in the technology arena, but also to rapid advancements in the health care field. The past five years, even, have seen more change and adaptation by health sciences librarians than in the previous ten years. Whereas the Internet was still new in the 1990s and early 2000s, it is now ubiquitous. The transition from print to electronic, although not complete, is virtually here. Virtual health sciences libraries are now the accepted "norm"—users expect to be able to access needed resources anytime, from any place, worldwide, for research, patient care, and educational needs. As new technologies develop to improve access methods and keep data safe, health sciences librarians are adapting and not only using those technologies themselves, but developing new teaching roles to help researchers, clinicians, and students learn how to use these new tools.

At the same time that librarians are adapting to keep up with changes, they are also cognizant that their roles as health sciences librarians are evolving, and that they must become more integrated into the institutions they serve to create a future of collaboration and involvement—one in which they move outside the confines of the library to serve patrons at the point of need, whether as embedded librarians or informationists, as clinical librarians or patient educators, or as course-integrated instructors in the medical curriculum or as simulation laboratory managers. The new roles are limited only by a librarian's abilities, willingness to collaborate with professional colleagues in the health care field, and his or her imagination and drive to succeed.

With every opportunity will come some sense of loss. To add a new service, an old or outdated service may need to be abandoned. For example, as reference statistics have dropped in favor of services provided to patrons as part of new embedded or informationist programs, or are replaced by virtual reference methods in place of in-person visits, the need for a reference desk has diminished, only to be replaced by a single-point-of-service desk. With the move to an electronic collection, print books and journals are rapidly disappearing from libraries, opening up space for new services such as simulation labs, learning commons, and group study rooms equipped with state-of-the-art technologies. Health sciences librarians are embracing these changes in functions and roles while still maintaining their roles as information experts and knowledge managers. These are only a sampling of changes going on right now—and expected for the future.

Health Sciences Librarianship is a comprehensive textbook that is intended for the library science student and new health sciences librarians. The purpose of this text is to provide new librarians with the background and core content needed to handle day-to-day activities and provide quality services in a health sciences library. Health sciences librarians now practice in more than academic health sciences libraries and hospitals—they are located in libraries in general academic and community colleges with health professions educational programs, consumer health libraries, corporate libraries, and more. Although of necessity some general librarianship content is included, *Health Sciences Librarianship* offers core information specific to the needs of practicing health sciences librarians, including real-life examples of programs and services.

This book was written at a time when library functions are changing—roles within the health sciences library are merging or disappearing, only to be replaced by new, emerging roles and job positions with new titles. The book has an overall "classic" approach—technical services versus public services, reference versus access services, and so forth—but in reality, these roles are blurring and blending, depending on the specific library and the institution it serves. And, depending on the size of the library, one or two persons (e.g., in a hospital library) may carry out all roles. However, throughout the book, one theme stands—collaboration. Health sciences librarians are more than service providers; they have become part of the health care team. Libraries and librarians have traditionally collaborated with each other, but new roles are taking the health sciences librarian out of the library and into col-laborative roles within research departments and clinical teams. As this transition continues, the need for possible additional subject-related training and continuing education/professional development is apparent; the Medical Library Association plays an important part in helping librarians keep their skills up to date.

ORGANIZATION

Chapter authors were asked to make their content relevant to academic health sci-ences librarians and hospital librarians, and where appropriate, to other librarians in the health care field. Chapters feature "vignettes"—brief "pearls of wisdom" and statements from practicing librarians relevant to the topic being discussed. Many of the chapters feature sections on keeping current and staying abreast of new tech-nologies, reflecting the volatility of the events shaping the profession. Additionally, each chapter contains Study Questions for use as questions for the reader to assess and think about chapter content, or for use by instructors who might want to assign questions to students. Chapters are extensively documented for readers who want to pursue more subject content.

Health Sciences Librarianship contains sixteen chapters that are organized into four major parts—Part I: The Profession (chapters 1–3); Part II: Collection Services (chapters 4–6); Part III: User Services (chapters 7–13); and Part IV: Administrative Services (chapters 14–16). Although the organization of the book is "traditional," chapter content recognizes that the role of the library and librarians continues to evolve, and the focus is on current and future roles and contributions of health sciences librarians.

Part I: The Profession begins with Chapter 1, "Health Sciences Librarianship in Context," written by James Shedlock. This chapter overviews health sciences librarianship and types of health sciences libraries; the National Library of Medicine and NN/LM; library organizations, with a focus on the Medical Library Association; education for librarianship; job opportunities; and continuing education/professional development, including the Academy of Health Information Professionals.

The second chapter, "Health Sciences Librarianship and Environmental Influences," is coauthored by Gale Hannigan and Jonathan Eldredge. The chapter addresses the health care system, including medical education and health sciences education (nurses, allied health); standards and accreditations; and the library's role. Also included is information about legislation and health sciences research, including translational science and human subjects.

Chapter 3, also written by Jonathan Eldredge and Gale Hannigan, discusses "Trends Affecting Health Sciences Librarianship." The trends selected for this chapter are evidence-based practice, active learning, innovative research collaborations, and strategies for adapting new technologies.

Part II: Collection Services begins with Chapter 4, "Collection Development," which is written by Holly Phillips. The chapter covers modern collection development and creating a collection development policy. Practical applications of using the policy are presented, followed by development of resource budgets.

"Technical Services in Health Sciences Libraries" (Chapter 5) is coauthored by Megan Del Baglivo, C. Steven Douglas, and María Pinkas. Acquisitions, cataloging, classification systems, metadata, and ILS/discovery tools are the topics of this chapter. The emphasis is on the National Library's classification system and Medical Subject Headings (MeSH), and the authors introduce the newer concepts of RDA and Dublin Core.

In Chapter 6, Nancy R. Glassman introduces "Technology Services in Health Sciences Libraries." She covers topics of general interest to all libraries, including planning and security, but she also focuses on topics of special interest to health sciences libraries such as electronic health records. Systems, mobile technologies, and emerging technologies are presented with a focus on use in health sciences libraries. Keeping current is especially important for this chapter.

Part III: User Services begins with Chapter 7, "Reference and Information Services in Health Sciences Libraries"—one of the areas of librarianship that is changing rapidly. Marie Ascher covers the reference interview, types of users and questions typically received in a health sciences library, reference statistics, models of providing reference service including the move toward a single point of service, and virtual reference services. Reference statistics show a downward trend, as health sciences librarians are providing more in-depth services as discussed in Chapter 8, and newer outreach and data management services are introduced, as discussed in chapters 9 and 10.

"Research Services and Database Searching in Health Sciences Libraries" (Chapter 8, by Lee Vucovich) covers information needs of biomedical researchers and focuses on searching the most important biomedical databases (e.g., MEDLINE/ PubMed, CINAHL, Scopus, and Web of Science). She describes the support needed for EBP, involvement of librarians in expert searches, organizing references with a reference manager, and more.

Michele Tennant describes "Outreach Services in Health Sciences Libraries" in Chapter 9. Outreach can occur both within and outside the institution. Some specific outreach efforts within the institution include liaison and embedded librarians, and informationists. Health sciences librarians are already involved in these activities, and these roles are expected to expand. Outside the institution, librarians reach out to members of the community and patients. Marketing is one of the features in a section about outreach for visibility.

Chapter 10, "Research Data Management and the Health Sciences Librarian," is coauthored by Andrew Creamer, Elaine R. Martin, and Donna Kafel, librarians who are involved in the forefront of programs in Research Data Management (RDM) at the University of Massachusetts Health Sciences Library. This thorough discussion of RDM covers everything from reasons to manage research and challenges involved to skills and competencies, tools, and resources librarians need. This field is just opening up and is representative of the new roles health sciences librarians are undertaking.

In Chapter 11, "Instruction in Health Sciences Libraries," Maureen "Molly" Knapp covers the history of instruction, generations of learners that librarians must plan for, learning paradigms, and newer disruptive technologies affecting teaching in health sciences libraries. She covers the various types of user education provided, along with instructional design techniques and web-based learning.

"Access Services: Circulation, Course Reserves, and Interlibrary Loan in Health Sciences Libraries" are the topics covered in Chapter 12. Authors Everly Brown, Na Lin, and Megan Wolff cover a variety of issues related to accessing the library's resources, both physical and electronic: access for the disabled, security, remote storage, e-reserves, interlibrary loan and document delivery, copyright, and newer methods of access such as pay-per-view and purchase on demand (as the interlibrary loan role overlaps with collection development areas).

In Chapter 13, "Consumer Health Information Services," Kay Hogan Smith overviews CHI services, first providing a history of the consumer movement and then describing several active CHI services; she describes the role of the National Library of Medicine in consumer health, along with health literacy. The second part of the chapter discusses how to establish and manage a CHI service, from needs assessment and planning, through policies, staffing, collection development, and evaluation.

Part IV: Administrative Services begins with Chapter 14, "Library Administration in Health Sciences Libraries." Librarians new to the field need to understand what the library director or manager does; librarians looking at moving up to higher level positions also need an understanding of the core functions of the library administrator. In this chapter, Diana Cunningham covers the library director/manager's multiple roles, from working with administration and institutional peers and managing the institutional environment, to managing and mentoring staff, professional networking, and collaboration with colleagues and other libraries. Also included in this chapter are management theories, the role of standards and accreditation, evaluation, and obtaining financial support.

In Chapter 15, "Physical Space in Health Sciences Libraries," Stewart Brower describes technical factors in space planning and space needs of different types of health sciences libraries, and then focuses on the use of space based on library functions (e.g., collections, users, teaching, points of service, staff, and innovative use of space). Included are spaces for new technologies in media, collaborative spaces, library commons, and simulation labs.

In the final chapter of the book (Chapter 16, "New Roles and New Horizons for Health Sciences Librarians and Libraries"), Margaret Henderson discusses the transformation of health sciences librarianship as librarians move into more collaborative roles. Some content from previous chapters is expanded (e.g., informationists and research data management) from a different perspective, but also to emphasize the changing roles and relationships, along with the actual change in the organization of health sciences libraries today.

A Glossary and Index complete the volume.

In a world where researchers and clinicians often believe libraries may not be needed, it is critical for health sciences librarians to make themselves indispensable within the institution (and document the need for their services); to align the library mission with that of its parent institution; proactively to develop new services such as embedded librarians, clinical and research informationists; and to become involved in research data management. All of these roles place the health sciences librarian as a collaborator, not just a provider of services. The times are changing, and health sciences librarians are changing to meet their patrons' new information needs.

Acknowledgments

No book is edited or written alone, without the help of others. I would like to thank the authors of the sixteen chapters of this book (listed in chapter order): James Shedlock, Gale G. Hannigan, Jonathan D. Eldredge, Holly J. Phillips, Megan Del Baglivo, C. Steven Douglas, María M. Pinkas, Nancy R. Glassman, Marie T. Ascher, Lee A. Vucovich, Michele R. Tennant, Andrew Creamer, Elaine R. Martin, Donna Kafel, Maureen "Molly" Knapp, Everly Brown, Na Lin, Megan Wolff, Kay Hogan Smith, Diana J. Cunningham, Stewart M. Brower, and Margaret E. Henderson. Without the expertise and dedication of these highly qualified authors, this book would not have been possible. I would also like to thank the Editorial Board—Ellen Gay Detlefsen, Elaine R. Martin, and Ana D. Cleveland—for their comments and critique. This was truly a collaborative effort.

Editorial Board

Ana D. Cleveland, PhD, regents professor and director, Health Informatics Program and Houston Program, Department of Library and Information Sciences, University of North Texas, Denton, TX

Ellen Gay Detlefsen, PhD, associate professor, School of Information Sciences, the iSchool at Pitt; and training program faculty, Department of Biomedical Informatics, School of Medicine, University of Pittsburgh, Pittsburgh, PA

Elaine Russo Martin, MSLS, DA, director, Lamar Soutter Library, University of Massachusetts Medical School, and associate professor, Department for Family and Community Medicine; and director, National Network of Libraries of Medicine, New England Region, Worcester, MA

PART I

The Profession

CHAPTER 1

Health Sciences Librarianship in Context

James Shedlock

INTRODUCTION

To be successful, the health sciences library student and the young professional just starting a career must understand and appreciate the context in which health sciences librarianship is practiced. The context described here includes the work health sciences librarians are likely to engage in as well as the institutional environment where that work takes place; the ethics of being a health sciences librarian; the culture in which health sciences librarianship is practiced and why this culture makes health sciences librarianship unique and different. The role and services of the National Library of Medicine (NLM) and its relationship to all health sciences librarians is presented along with the impact of library professional organizations. The chapter concludes with a brief discussion of education for health sciences librarianship, securing a professional position, and keeping current while starting a professional career.

THE HEALTH SCIENCES LIBRARY PROFESSION

Today's library profession is broad and expanding; and like the profession as a whole, health sciences librarianship is exploring new areas of practice, especially in developing roles that break from the past and aim toward the future. Overall, the future is bright for librarianship in general and health sciences librarians in particular but not without facing some major challenges.

It is an understatement to say that the flood of information is overwhelming, thanks to the Internet and the web. Society in general is more focused now on producing, using, and dealing with all types of information. Fortunately, a vast array of tools, devices, services, and innovative products focus on connecting, interacting, and relating to this flood of information. Although the tools and services are great to have, now is also the time to possess the skills for managing, organizing, and selecting the information that is worth knowing and preserving. Now is the time for librarians to step forward and lead.

Contrary to reports that libraries are not needed, or may even be dying in this age of information, librarians are seen as valued professionals who can make sense of the flood of information available in a wide range of fields or interests. At the same time, librarians are challenged to demonstrate their value and prove their worth when many individuals and corporate entities see the Internet, the web, and the tools and services to use them as a means to bypass and ignore librarians' professional skills.

Terminology

When referring to librarians and libraries in a health environment, the terms medical and health sciences are almost always synonymous. In publications, the preferred term is health sciences, as in health sciences librarian, rather than medical librarian. Medical librarian, medical library (or libraries), and medical librarianship are often used as a short form. Health sciences librarian as a term is preferred because it encompasses the broader field of health care and biomedical research where health sciences librarianship is practiced. Thus, health sciences librarian can refer to hospital librarians, academic or medical school librarians, nursing librarians, dental librarians, and so on. Also, health sciences is preferred because it refers to the whole range of health disciplines such as medicine, dentistry, nursing, pharmacy, public health, physical therapy, the many allied health disciplines, the areas of biomedical research, health policy, health care administration, and more.

Health Sciences Librarians' Work

Though institutional libraries are not going away, they are changing due to the work of their librarians. The essential work of today's health sciences library involves information discovery, organization and management of information resources, and the support and services deemed necessary to bring user and information together to meet the user's specific and general information needs.

Information discovery is about the search for and identification of answers that solve a user's information problem. In a highly technical and charged health care environment, busy health care professionals and researchers, their students and support staff, are looking for answers amid the ocean of information that is so often at everyone's fingertips. The skill to find answers is and will be highly desired and valuable. Knowing where and how to find answers will be an essential skill of tomorrow's health sciences librarian.

Along with search skills is the equally valued skill to teach and communicate how to do information discovery. A health sciences librarian cannot be physically or virtually available all the time. Users need to fend for themselves. They need basic information literacy to help them understand how to find answers for themselves. The education role of the health sciences librarian is critical in all work environments, and librarians will need the skill to teach effectively and communicate efficiently in order to provide a valued service for users.

Where information resources are of a sufficient number, the skill to manage this collection is needed. Similar to information discovery, the health sciences librarian's skills in identifying, evaluating and analyzing, selecting, and organizing information resources will be required. These activities remain at the heart of what it means to build a library (a collection); and as long as libraries are needed, they require management skills to make them effective for their role within the institution.

Where there is a health sciences library and librarian, there is also the provision of services that support users so they can find answers quickly, obtain the information they need, and learn how best to manage their information needs. In the virtual world, some library services have diminished because they were most often associated with the demands of a physical space and collection. Circulation, for example, is now less about borrowing a physical book than it is about finding it online. The service lies in providing a user-friendly online environment, which means librarians need skills to design and implement online tools (website design, communication forms, search engines, etc.) to support users.

Given the nature of what health sciences librarians do in their professional practice, consider some examples of how this practice is expressed:

- Today's (and tomorrow's) health sciences librarians are assuming the role of **informationists** and **embedded librarians**. These roles are highly specialized positions often found in academic settings to support researchers and graduate students (Shipman et al., 2002; Wheeler and Cogdill, 2013).
- Clinical librarians in academic medical centers and teaching hospitals provide expertise in information discovery and seeking evidence to support patient care (Tan and Maggio, 2013).
- Data services librarians take on roles to organize biomedical data and provide support services that go beyond responsibility for scholarly literature collections (Shaffer, 2013; Martin, 2012).
- Consumer health and patient education roles are expanding and flourishing, often in collaboration with patient educators (Volk, 2007).
- Education and curriculum specialists tackle issues of integrating information literacy and information management into the curricula of health sciences education programs (MacEachern et al., 2012).

A characteristic of the health sciences librarian roles noted above is that they often take place outside the confines of the physical library. Today's and tomorrow's library work now involves librarians working with users in the user's own setting. In other words, health sciences librarians strive to meet users at the point of need. Health sciences librarians do not wait for the user to come to the physical library to present an information problem for solving. Today's health sciences librarians are investigating user needs in their local institution or within their community, anticipating what services will be most responsive to supporting users. Librarians look for the information problems, study and analyze them, and examine what services librarians can provide toward solutions to the problems.

Ethics

The foundation for health sciences librarianship lies in its code of ethics. Two codes are worth mentioning. The code of ethics from the American Library Association (ALA), for example, speaks for the whole profession and states that the code is the basis for ethical decision making. It espouses librarians' values such as support for intellectual freedom, freedom to read, and equanimity of information access. The code guides behavior when values are in conflict. The code is not a list of rules for dictating what behavior to follow in a particular situation or conflict. Key elements of the librarians' ethical code include service to all users, resisting censorship, protecting privacy and confidentiality, respecting intellectual property via the "balance between the interests of information users and rights holders," treating colleagues and others with "respect, fairness and good faith," and separating personal convictions from professional duties (ALA, 2008). The code also states that the profession advances through the maintenance and enhancement of the individual librarian's knowledge and skills through professional development, along with support for the aspirations of potential members.

The Medical Library Association's (MLA) code (see sidebar) reflects similar beliefs, but it is stated in the context of providing health information and related services (MLA, 2010). Differing slightly from the ALA code, the MLA code makes explicit reference to the institutional context of the librarian's work and behavior. For example, a separate paragraph refers to the librarian's leadership role in providing services that meet the needs of the institution. Also, the MLA code calls on the individual librarian to understand and follow the institution's code of ethics including policies related to conflict of interest and disclosure. This reference reflects the trend toward self-policing within the various health professions, which have become more vigilant in advocating to their members a mindfulness of the external influences on decision making.

HEALTH SCIENCES LIBRARIANSHIP ENVIRONMENTS

There are several types of health sciences libraries including academic, hospital, and special. Each has its own unique characteristics but often shares the same features of a common culture of health care.

Types of Health Sciences Libraries

The two dominant types are academic health sciences libraries and hospital libraries. Academic health sciences libraries are dominant because of their size in terms of collections and staffing and their importance to the education of new health professionals. For example, all accredited medical schools are required to have a library (LCME, 2013). Similarly, other health professions require access to a library collection (AACN, 2009; ADA, 2010). Academic health sciences libraries are primarily concerned with the education and research missions of the institution. They exist to support the faculty and students so that these users have the scholarly resources necessary for teaching and learning the basic knowledge of the health profession or conducting research that advances knowledge to improve health.

Hospital libraries are dominant because of their large number. Hospitals themselves are characterized by size and purpose, the primary one being patient care, but they also engage in preventive care and health education, community service, research, and professional and continuing education. Academic medical centers

Goals and Principles for Ethical Conduct

The health sciences librarian believes that knowledge is the sine qua non of informed decisions in health care, education, and research, and the health sciences librarian serves society, clients, and the institution by working to ensure that informed decisions can be made. The principles of this code are expressed in broad statements to guide ethical decision making. These statements provide a framework; they cannot and do not dictate conduct to cover particular situations.

Society

1. The health sciences librarian promotes access to health information for all and creates and maintains conditions of freedom of inquiry, thought, and expression that facilitate informed health care decisions.

Clients

- The health sciences librarian works without prejudice to meet the client's information needs.
- The health sciences librarian respects the privacy of clients and protects the confidentiality of the client relationship.
- The health sciences librarian ensures that the best available information is provided to the client.

Institution

- The health sciences librarian provides leadership and expertise in the design, development, and ethical management of knowledge-based information systems that meet the information needs and obligations of the institution.

Profession

- The health sciences librarian advances and upholds the philosophy and ideals of the profession.
- The health sciences librarian advocates and advances the knowledge and standards of the profession.
- The health sciences librarian conducts all professional relationships with courtesy and respect.
- The health sciences librarian maintains high standards of professional integrity.

Self

- The health sciences librarian assumes personal responsibility for developing and maintaining professional excellence.
- The health sciences librarian shall be alert to and adhere to his or her institution's code of ethics and its conflict of interest, disclosure, and gift policies.

are hospitals affiliated with medical schools and related health sciences schools. Often, the academic medical center is one large unit of the whole university; see the University of Michigan Health System, www.med.umich.edu/index.html, as an example.

At the same time, some stand-alone health sciences universities include their teaching hospital as an equal unit among all the education programs the university supports; see Thomas Jefferson University, www.jefferson.edu, as an example. Other stand-alone teaching hospitals are characterized by their accredited, postgraduate residency and training programs for physicians pursuing specialty education; the Washington Hospital Center, www.whcenter.org, is an example.

Specialized hospitals are similar to these stand-alone teaching hospitals because of the emphasis on specialty education in medicine as well as their focused care; examples include women's health (obstetrical and gynecologic), pediatric care, psychiatric care, orthopedics, and similar specialties. Like the stand-alone teaching hospitals, these types of specialized hospitals often support libraries and librarians depending on their institutional traditions and/or their connections to academic health sciences libraries.

Community hospitals are dominant because of their number (4,973; AHA, 2013). The numbers of beds they are licensed to support often categorizes community hospitals. Community hospitals generally have a library, but these collections and their staff have come under greater scrutiny in

The practice of evidence-based health care in the hospital environment is enhanced by the expertise of a professional librarian. Few health care providers and administrators have the time to learn how to find the highest quality knowledge-based resources and regard the librarian as their partner in providing the best and safest care for patients.

—*Margaret Bandy, MLS, AHIP, FMLA, medical librarian and manager, Library and Knowledge Services, Exempla Saint Joseph Hospital, Denver, CO*

challenging economic times (Thibodeau and Funk, 2009). Formerly, the standards of the Joint Commission on the Accreditation of Healthcare Organizations (now, The Joint Commission or the TJC), www.jointcommission.org, included the requirement to have a hospital library. Over the years this standard has been eliminated in favor of requiring knowledge-based resources but not mandating how a hospital has to provide them. TJC's emphasis now is more on processes and functions needed for safe care rather than on the requirement to have specific departments.

Additional hospital organizations include corporate health systems and clinics (either affiliated with other care organizations or stand alone). Some health systems employ a librarian or several of them to manage the information needs of the whole corporation. The librarian of a health system could be a supervisory manager overseeing several branch libraries and their staff within the corporation, or a single library could serve the whole health system. Generally, clinics refer to small health organizations and do not employ a librarian or maintain a collection. Exceptions include the Mayo Clinic in Rochester, Minnesota, and the Cleveland Clinic in Cleveland, Ohio. Their size and circumstances dictate the presence of large, national libraries.

The third type of health sciences library is the special library. Special libraries encompass all types of health sciences libraries not formally associated with an educational or health care institution. A common thread among special health sciences libraries is a connection to or an interest in health. These special libraries are many and include those serving federal health agencies (the National Library of Medicine, the National Institutes of Health, the Centers for Disease Control and Prevention, etc.) or similar national units (such as the armed forces); pharmaceutical companies and similar businesses engaged in making and/or selling health products (such as health supplies, equipment, devices, tools, implants, etc.) or information services (data analysis, health literacy, publications, etc.); professional societies and organizations (American Hospital Association, American College of Obstetrics and Gynecology); health insurance; consumer health (such as health sciences librarians working in public libraries or similar public agencies); and so on.

Unique and Different: The Culture of Medicine

Besides the different types of institutional support, health sciences libraries are distinguished from other types of librarianship by their culture. This culture is what makes health sciences libraries and librarians unique and different.

Culture is defined "as the shared patterns of behaviors and interactions, cognitive constructs, and affective understanding that are learned through a process of socialization. These shared patterns identify the members of a culture group while also distinguishing those of another group" (CARLA, 2013). Not only do librarians share elements of their own culture (such as defining entry to the profession via a master's degree, protecting the right to read, respecting the freedom to access information, protecting the right to privacy, protecting the confidentiality of user information, etc.) with the health professions, but health sciences librarians participate in the culture of medicine as well. The culture of medicine is characterized primarily by its focus on the patient. In health care, the patient is central. The patient can be defined as that individual who is vulnerable due to a crisis in health. The culture of medicine creates a shared desire to alleviate this crisis through intervention. Other characteristics of this culture include speed and accuracy in defining the intervention, teamwork, authoritativeness of the decisions made to restore the patient's health, individual drive to meet the demands of patient care, and commitment to lifelong learning on the part of members of the health care team in order to maintain standards of quality patient care. The culture of medicine is also described for its "honesty, empathy, altruism, honor and respect. . . . Examples of these elements include the white coat, a shared stylized dress code among physicians; *doctor talk*, a shared language or unique pattern of communication among physicians; and the physician explanatory model, a shared system of beliefs regarding health" (Boutin-Foster, Foster, and Konopasek, 2008: 108).

In contrast is another part of the medical culture that is often criticized, one that the medical profession is trying to correct. This is the culture's tendency toward silence when errors occur, particularly grave errors resulting in severe impairment of the patient and even death. The errors are compounded by the lack of communication on the part of the health professional. The culture is trying to correct itself through better education; in particular, medical school curricula, for example, are now addressing communication skills as a way to mitigate this negative characteristic (AAMC, 2005). The culture of medicine is taught informally and indirectly as part of a medical school's hidden curriculum. This curriculum is most often taught via observation and role modeling by students (Boutin-Foster, Foster, and Konopasek, 2008).

Health sciences librarians learn the culture of medicine the same way students do: through observation and role modeling. They adopt the culture's characteristics as a means of responding to users' needs. Because users need accurate and timely access to health information for patient care, health sciences librarians deliver it in the way users expect it via an emphasis on accuracy, speed, and efficiency. After all, this is what is important for quality patient care. At the same time, health sciences librarians contribute to the culture of medicine by bringing their own culture of service to the health care environment. This, then, is the chief way that health sciences librarians are unique and different: they, too, are members of the health care team who focus on patient care as the ultimate goal for their services. Caring for patients, whether through the work of the actual caregivers or through direct contact with the patient as a health consumer, is the unique aspect of health sciences librarianship. Adding the librarian's service orientation to the patient care focus becomes part and parcel of being a good health sciences librarian.

Health sciences librarians are unique and different in another way as well. Reflecting the culture of medicine's emphasis on lifelong learning, health sciences librarianship is characterized by its emphasis on continuing education. Just as many health professionals require ongoing credentialing of their skills, the health sciences library profession has adopted this same emphasis. The Medical Library Association is well known for its history to formalize its own continuing education program, http://www.mlanet.org/academy/ (Roper, 2006). The current iteration of MLA's recognition for continuing education is membership in the Academy of Health Information Professionals (AHIP), and its purpose is to recognize the health sciences librarian's achievements in maintaining and advancing his or her skills and knowledge; see details later in this chapter.

> Health sciences librarians are unique because they are motivated by the excitement and promise of the health sciences. Health sciences librarians know that these subject domains promote health, save lives, and advance science; and that the librarian's role is to provide systems, services, and resources that link critical information to clinical, scientific, and administrative decision making. Health sciences librarians are obsessive about the timeliness and authoritativeness of information because they know it makes a difference to current and future patients' lives.
>
> —*J. Michael Homan, AHIP, FMLA, director, Mayo Clinic Libraries, Rochester, MN*

THE NATIONAL LIBRARY OF MEDICINE

Simply put, the National Library of Medicine (NLM), www.nlm.nih.gov, is the world's greatest health library. Its greatness is due to several factors including the size of its collections, the prominence of its products (notably MEDLINE/PubMed), and its outward reach to connect users, especially health professionals and researchers, health sciences librarians, and the American public, with the information they need for providing health care, professional education, biomedical research, or personal use. It is important to highlight NLM because of the interdependence that exists between NLM and the country's health sciences libraries and librarians. NLM's existence plays a critical role in the operations of all health sciences libraries and collections and thus impacts on the way health sciences librarians do their work.

NLM's mission is to acquire, organize, and disseminate health information. It receives this mandate from the U.S. Congress and is organized as one of the U.S. National Institutes of Health (NIH). Though it is a U.S. government agency, NLM's mission is global in its impact. Health information is willingly shared in order to improve the health of people regardless of national boundaries.

Because of the size and scope of its collections, NLM is also a publisher, particularly of databases that organize and disseminate information gleaned from its vast collections. NLM's products and related publications fulfill its mission to organize and disseminate health information.

NLM is also known for more than its collections. It is one of the primary innovators in using and developing information technologies to organize and disseminate health information, and not just information available from scholarly publications. NLM is a leader in biomedical research (such as computational molecular biology, the Visible Human Project, human genome resources, and more) and in informatics and health information technology (e.g., medical language systems, communication engineering, telemedicine, digital libraries, and more).

As mentioned, NLM is part of the U.S. Department of Health and Human Services, organized under NIH. It is regarded as a separate institute and as such, it is the public health library of the United States (i.e., its role is to serve the American public). Note that it is not the library of NIH; NIH maintains its own library, http://nihlibrary.nih.gov/, to serve the information needs of all the NIH institutes. NLM's appropriations come from the U.S. Congress and are separately allocated but are reflected in the total NIH budget, http://officeofbudget.od.nih.gov. Its internal organization, www.nlm.nih.gov/about/org.html, reflects the nature of its work and how this work is accomplished. At the heart of what NLM does are the 800 staff persons employed to accomplish this work.

As for NLM's collections, they number nearly 20 million items in FY11 including 1.4 million monographs, 1.4 million bound serials, nearly 20,000 current serial and journal subscriptions, more than 15 million manuscripts, and more than 2 million journal articles from nearly 900 journals in its digital repository, www.nlm.nih.gov/ocpl/anreports/fy2011.pdf. NLM's collections are broad and deep to encompass all areas of health and all formats, www.nlm.nih.gov/tsd/acquisitions/cdm/. The NLM Collection Development Manual defines the boundaries of its collecting activities, guides the NLM staff in its collections decision making, and serves as a guide to other health sciences and research libraries regarding collection development at the local level. NLM's collection is designed to serve health professionals. Although NLM has a commitment to health information for the layperson, primarily through its MedlinePlus products, what NLM collects is the scholarly literature to be used for the education of health care professionals, biomedical research, and clinical care. The NLM staff is also cognizant of its collecting in relation to other national libraries; careful coordination prevents duplication of resources. Collecting in the history of the health sciences is also an important highlight of the NLM collections. This area, along with NLM's preservation activities, makes NLM the library of record for many obscure pieces of literature.

In terms of services, NLM is committed to disseminating its collections as much as possible. After all, NLM is a public good and needs to be shared in order to have a positive effect on improving health. Document delivery is a primary service carried out through the close collaboration with health sciences libraries across the country. Although NLM encourages libraries to share their collections at the local and regional level first, when specific articles or books are not available locally, NLM is the last resort for document delivery. NLM operates the DOCLINE service for effective communication among libraries in the sharing of local, regional, and national resources, www.nlm.nih.gov/docline/ (see Chapter 12 for more information on DOCLINE).

NLM is also known as the producer of several innovative products, primarily databases and related tools, that result from its effort to make the library's collections known to users the world over. The best-known product is MEDLINE and PubMed. MEDLINE/PubMed is the primary database and interface for identifying the biomedical journal literature. This database has a long history of development based on various information technologies developed over time for indexing the most important journal literature from the NLM collections (Dee, 2007). Currently, the database contains 18 million citations from 5,600 current journals and serials dating back to 1946. PubMed, developed at NLM's Lister Hill Center, is freely available so anyone can research and identify current and historic articles in the health sciences. MEDLINE is the foundation database in PubMed; PubMed offers additional citations to what MEDLINE already indexes. These additional citations include in-process citations, out-of-scope articles that are not indexed as part of MEDLINE but are relevant due to their life science content, historic literature not yet indexed with Medical Subject Headings, and other relevant life science literature, www.nlm.nih.gov/pubs/factsheets/dif_med_pub.html. See Chapter 8 for more details.

In addition to MEDLINE/PubMed, NLM produces numerous other databases and tools that are used to identify and use specific resources in the NLM collections; see the current list at wwwcf2.nlm.nih.gov/nlm_eresources/eresources/search_database .cfm.

Of the many databases produced at NLM besides MEDLINE, a few are worth mentioning as examples of the scope of what NLM offers. (Literally, something is there for everyone who has any interest in health literature in the list of databases and research tools at NLM.) MedlinePlus, www.nlm.nih.gov/medlineplus/ (see Chapter 13 for details), is NLM's contribution toward supporting health information for the layperson. This database identifies current and relevant health information from numerous Internet sources. Typical entries include overviews of the disease or condition, its diagnosis and treatment options, specific aspects of the condition, multimedia tools and self-instruction aids, diagrams, the latest research on the disease or condition, information on clinical trials, and more. Many of the links to health topics come from the NIH institutes as well as other authoritative sources. MedlinePlus covers drug information as well, and many entries are now available in the Spanish language.

ClinicalTrials.gov, http://clinicaltrials.gov, was developed by NLM to organize information about available clinical studies regulated by the U.S. Food and Drug Administration (FDA). The goal here is to inform the public about experimental drug studies on life-threatening diseases and conditions and to seek volunteer participation in these studies. Active participation by the public aids clinicians and researchers seeking advances in medicine to improve health.

Another key resource produced at NLM is PubMed Central. This resource is a digital repository of full-text journal articles and other documents in the biomedical and life science literature. Researchers who accept funds from NIH are obligated to deposit their articles in PubMed Central as a condition of receiving financial support; see http://publicaccess.nih.gov/FAQ.htm#753. All PubMed Central material is freely available, and demonstrates NLM and the federal government's commitment to open access for scholarly literature in the health sciences. The premise goes that because the public pays to support the work of the NIH through taxes, then the public has the right to access the results of that effort.

The many resources produced by NLM are too numerous to detail here. Readers are urged to explore the NLM website to review the vast number of resources available to them and to learn the details about how these resources can be searched and used to solve various information problems. Additionally, more information about NLM databases can be found in Chapter 8.

Two divisions/departments at NLM that are worth special mention are the Lister Hill National Center for Biomedical Communications (LHC), www.lhncbc.nlm. nih.gov, and the National Center for Biomedical Information (NCBI), www.ncbi. nlm.nih.gov. The Lister Hill Center is the unit at NLM responsible for biomedical informatics research. The center's website identifies program areas such as consumer health resources, image processing, language processing, and visualization projects.

NCBI's role at NLM concentrates on research related to biomedical and genomic information. NCBI produces databases on molecular biology, biochemistry, and genetics, and the analytical tools necessary to use these resources to their full advantage. As a research unit, NCBI's mission develops new information technologies that aid researchers in the discovery of fundamental knowledge that will impact health and disease. One of NCBI's many innovations is the creation and maintenance of PubMed Central.

A third unit or program at NLM that has a direct connection to the nation's health sciences libraries is the National Network of Libraries of Medicine (NN/LM). NN/LM is one of the remaining legacies of the Medical Library Assistance Act (MLAA). This federal legislation, which provided funds for medical library expansion, was passed in 1965; the initial funding lasted until 1970 (Cummings and Corning, 1971). The purpose of the MLAA was to provide financial support for medical libraries that were falling behind in their effort to keep up with the rapid growth in health literature following the expansion of medical science after World War II. Upwards of $100 million were authorized, but only 39 percent was actually allocated to NLM for all the MLAA programs (Cummings and Corning, 1971). Among the act's major accomplishments, two have had long-lasting impact. One accomplishment was the construction of numerous medical libraries across the country. The MLAA provided $40 million in grants to institutions that allowed them to build physical libraries to support growing print collections of biomedical literature and to house larger numbers of staff to organize those collections and provide information services to their local communities. Eleven library buildings resulted from these MLAA grants (Cummings and Corning, 1971).

The second accomplishment is the regional network of health sciences libraries that is the NN/LM. Originally organized into eleven regions, the MLAA allowed NLM to create regional medical libraries across the country for the purpose of connecting NLM more closely with those health sciences libraries serving the nation's health professionals. The regional network was part of an overall plan to improve communications with users and to speed delivery of medical literature to the point of need. "Regional medical libraries were principally university-based, were selected competitively from libraries with strong collections and well-trained staffs, and a good record of providing medical library services" (Cummings and Corning, 1971: 383). The original plan called for NLM to be at the apex of the new national network. NLM would be the library of last resort for document delivery, and would serve as "the medical indexing and cataloging center. . . . The Regional Libraries are to improve their reference and interlibrary loan services to medical and hospital libraries in a broad geographic area" (Cummings and Corning, 1971: 384). At the most local level would be the academic medical and hospital libraries working directly with health professionals to meet their individual information needs. Bunting (1987) provides a detailed history of the NN/LM.

Given all that NLM does for the country, it is important to address what individual health sciences librarians can do for NLM. Advocating for NLM, especially at the time when its budget is under review, is one way to "testify" to local congressional representatives that NLM is a powerful resource for the American people and worthy of continued funding. Without the necessary financial support for established, vital programs, NLM is unable to maintain consistency in its collections, staffing, services, research efforts, and innovation excellence. Also, financial support is critical for NLM to develop new initiatives. If NLM is to hold its leadership position for advancing health information access and technological innovations, financial support is critical, and it can only come from the U.S. Congress.

At the same time, it is important for health sciences librarians to remember that NLM has many constituencies besides health sciences libraries and librarians. NLM must serve all its users equally including physicians and health professionals, biomedical researchers, students, and the lay public. No one group can demand NLM's attention over any other group. NLM works best by bringing all its users together in

The NLM and NN/LM have been major parts of my professional life. Having grown up as a professional in Baltimore, NLM was just down the road, and I was able to witness firsthand the influence these institutions have on delivering quality health care information. Their constant desire to get needed health information into the hands of individuals, including the general public, to empower their decision making, has made me passionate about health literacy and consumer education.

—Jean P. Shipman, MSLS, AHIP, FMLA, director, Spence S. Eccles Health Sciences Library and MidContinental Region and NLM Training Center, NN/LM, University of Utah, Salt Lake City close collaboration in order to achieve accomplishments that serve as many users as possible.

LIBRARY ORGANIZATIONS

In the context of health sciences librarianship, library organizations play a role by providing a foundation for professional practice. In many ways these organizations are the profession in that they speak for its members and provide the standards, explicit and implicit, by which its members conduct their work in service to their local institutions and communities.

Medical Library Association

The Medical Library Association (MLA), www.mlanet.org, is the premier professional organization for health sciences libraries and librarians. MLA's mission is to "foster excellence in the achievement and leadership of health sciences library and information professionals to enhance the quality of health care, education and research" (MLA, 2013).

MLA consists of several organizational units. Its leadership includes the president, the board of directors, and the executive director. The president and board provide the overall direction for the association. They identify a vision for the association and a strategic plan to realize that vision, and they initiate the programs and services that carry out that plan. The executive director manages the headquarters staff, and together they provide the support for the various association programs, committees, and services; they work to implement the association's strategic plan; and perform day-to-day operations including planning for the annual meeting.

As with any large organization, MLA members volunteer to participate on committees and task forces that are charged to address specific tasks and functions of the association. MLA's organization also includes sections and chapters. Sections reflect the various subject and functional interests of the membership, such as medical informatics, leadership and management, technical services, hospital libraries, dental libraries, history of the health sciences, and many more. Chapters are geographic entities that reflect MLA's work at the regional level (for example, Pacific Northwest, Midwest, New England). Thanks to improvements in communication technologies, the Internet, and social networking, MLA members conduct work throughout the year. However, face-to-face meetings are important, and the MLA annual meeting is the highlight of the year when members gather to conduct official business and do much informal networking. The major goal of the annual meeting is to create the many opportunities for attending members to learn. Above all else, the annual meeting is an educational event. Members come together to learn the latest developments in information discovery, library and collection management, and new services for users; trends and ideas that impact librarians' work; and professional development. The annual meeting is known for its educational programs including continuing education (CE) classes, outstanding speakers with national reputations for excellence in their fields, and meeting with national vendors and companies willing to exhibit and promote products and services of interest to health sciences libraries and librarians. Along with headquarters' staff and the National Program Committee, the sections provide the bulk of the annual meeting's content by organizing invited and contributed papers. Because learning is social, the MLA annual meeting is also known for the opportunity to network with colleagues, greet and catch up with old friends, and make new contacts.

MLA serves its membership with a variety of programs and services. One of MLA's primary programs is professional development through continuing education (CE). Of all the library associations, MLA is known for its efforts to provide CE and to recognize members' achievements in professional development through an established recognition program. MLA's CE program reflects the health sciences librarians' commitment to lifelong learning. This commitment echoes what other health professionals do and reflects the librarians' participation in the culture of medicine. At a typical annual meeting, twenty-five to thirty courses will be offered. In addition, many of the MLA chapters sponsor MLA CE courses at their regional meetings.

Recognition for individual achievement in maintaining a member's professional education resides in membership in the Academy of Health Information Professionals (the Academy; also, AHIP). The Academy has a long history of change and development (Bell, 1996), tracing its origin to MLA's credentialing program that began shortly after World War II. The membership has always been concerned about maintaining educational standards among library staff, and efforts were made to provide the education members needed to work in a health sciences library. MLA provided a certificate verifying achievement. Marshall (1946), Doe (1949), and Darling (1973) also provide details about the history of MLA's education and credentialing programs.

Currently, the Academy, www.mlanet.org/academy/acadfaq.html#8, operates on a volunteer basis. Members are recognized in classes reflecting different levels of achievement, from provisional to emeritus status. The minimum education requirement for Academy membership is a master's degree in library and information science accredited by the American Library Association (ALA) or a postbaccalaureate degree in an accredited field, www.mlanet.org/academy/acadfaq.html. Academy membership recognizes a *credentialed* individual by reflecting the time and effort made toward professional development; MLA does not offer *certification*, which would verify attainment of a minimum standard of measurable competencies.

MLA has also developed specialized educational programs in two areas of health sciences librarianship: consumer health and disaster preparedness. Similar to Academy membership, these specializations provide an individual with additional credentials that indicate education attained, mostly through CE or some other formalized courses, in these two areas.

MLA developed the Disaster Information Specialization, www.mlanet.org/education/dis/, in conjunction with NLM. The specialization is open to any health information professional or any health professional interested in learning more about disaster preparedness. In particular, the specialization provides an opportunity for health sciences librarians to add knowledge and skills to their existing education, credentials, and knowledge base. This specialization offers members two levels of credentials per the number of courses taken. Courses are available in person or online.

The Consumer Health Information Specialization, www.mlanet.org/education/chc/, is similar in purpose and structure. The goal of the consumer health specialization is to aid health sciences librarians who wish to offer more extensive consumer health services. This specialization gives health sciences librarians additional knowledge of resources and other tools that would aid their efforts to work with consumers about health information issues and access.

In addition to education programs for its members, MLA is also known for its advocacy of the profession and related efforts, such as supporting NLM at the time of its budget review. MLA's advocacy efforts reside primarily in its Government Relations Committee and the Joint MLA/AAHSL (Association of Academic Health Sciences Libraries; see more below) Legislative Task Force. As MLA and AAHSL share the same member base, the organizations frequently coordinate responses to national health and information policy issues that affect all health sciences libraries and librarians. The joint Task Force supports NLM at its budget hearings; in addition, other issues have commanded its attention. They include the NIH public access policy on access to funded research results; funding for research conducted by the NIH; other open access and scholarly information policies of publishers and other national organizations; health care reform; copyright rights and intellectual property issues; and many more. More information is available at www.mlanet.org/government/.

Like most professional associations, MLA is committed to sharing the results of its members' research and advancing ideas that promote and improve health information access. MLA has a robust publication program, www.mlanet.org/publications/, anchored by its own professional journal, the *Journal of the Medical Library Association* (*JMLA*). A quarterly publication, *JMLA* maintains a high standard for quality. Articles focus on the latest research about health information access, organization, library management, and trends in services. *JMLA*, which supersedes the *Bulletin of the Medical Library Association*, recently (2013) celebrated one hundred volumes of publication. *JMLA* was one of the first library publications to meet the open access gold standard, www.sherpa.ac.uk/documents/sherpaplusdocs/Nottingham-colour-guide.pdf, when it was included in PubMed Central in 2001, making it totally digital and free to anyone interested in reading it.

MLA News is a newsletter publication that keeps members informed about what is happening within the association and its membership; the *News* is published ten times per year. MLA Focus is a twice-monthly electronic newsletter distributed via

MLA is valuable for many reasons and has been extremely important to me and to my career. The first is that it provides an organizational home and advocate for a library profession focused on "quality information for improved health." The second is the community of practice found at MLA, where members with similar experiences, challenges, and opportunities share strategies for success and innovation. And finally, whether in person, or virtually, through annual, chapter, or section meetings, programming, Listservs, or other opportunities to gather, MLA creates a network of experts, colleagues, and even friends.

—M. J. Tooey, MLS, AHIP, FMLA, associate vice president, academic affairs; executive director, Health Sciences and Human Services Library; and director, National Network of Libraries of Medicine, Southeastern/Atlantic Region, University of Maryland at Baltimore e-mail to its membership and is a much faster way to keep MLA members informed of the latest association business and news. MLA also publishes monographs in conjunction with Rowman & Littlefield Publishing Group. Monographs contribute to the professional literature by addressing topics in a more detailed study that are relevant to the membership, other librarians, and health professionals interested in health information. Practical publications such as BibKits (bibliographies) and DocKits (sample documents) provide helpful resources for the practicing librarian. From time to time, MLA also publishes a variety of standards, guidelines, policy statements, and other publications that promote the health sciences library profession.

Association of Academic Health Sciences Libraries

The Association of Academic Health Sciences Libraries (AAHSL) www.aahsl.org>, is well known in the library profession as the organization for academic health sciences library directors. The association is an institutional membership organization (not personal membership) and is composed of those academic libraries whose parent institutions' medical schools are accredited by and belong to the Association of American Medical Colleges (AAMC) www.aamc.org. The library director is the representative to AAHSL.

AAHSL's mission is to support its members (the directors and by extension, the library staff) as they engage in their efforts to advance health information access and services that support education, research, patient care, and community service. AAHSL conducts several programs and initiatives including benchmarking data, leadership development, advocacy, educational programming, and collaboration.

AAHSL was started in 1977 in order to define closer ties with medical school leadership through participation in the AAMC (Jacobson, 2003). As such, AAHSL is now a member of AAMC's Council of Academic Societies. AAHSL publishes the *Annual Statistics of Medical School Libraries in the United States and Canada* (Shedlock and Byrd, 2003; Byrd and Shedlock, 2003). This compilation of data gleaned from an annual survey covers facets of library collections, budgets, services, and descriptive information. The *Annual Statistics* serves as a major benchmarking tool for library directors and their staff. Survey data are gathered electronically, and a print and electronic publication is produced. Tools in the electronic version allow a reader to compare various peers on a number of data points. Graphic representations of the data are available. Because coverage includes data from the past thirty years or so, retrospective analysis is available for individual libraries or for selected peer groups.

Leadership development is another hallmark of AAHSL's work and accomplishments. Responding to a need to develop future library directors, the Leadership Development Program includes several components forming a continuum of opportunities. The base of the program is an MLA CE course: "Do You Want to Be a Library Director? Knowledge, Skills and Career Paths." The course, generally offered at the MLA annual meetings, is taught by two to three library directors together. It covers the topics of self-awareness and leadership skills for an academic library directorship; financial management, budgeting, and fund-raising roles and responsibilities; political awareness of the library director's role; and general discussion and background such as the director's application process, life-work balance, and other "insider" issues. This CE course provides the means for individuals aspiring to be library directors to assess their readiness for career advancement. In addition to the AAHSL-sponsored CE course, the association offers various scholarships that may be used toward other academic leadership programs relevant to an individual career objective.

At the top of the AAHSL leadership program is the Leadership Fellowship that receives generous support from NLM. This competitive fellowship is a year-long learning opportunity; five or six fellows are selected each year. Central to the fellowship is a mentor relationship where each fellow is matched with a current library director. The highlight of the year is a two-week, on-site visit by the fellow at his or her mentor's library. Here, day-to-day observations are the focus of learning. Fellows and mentors also meet with local library staff to learn the details about library operations, especially budgeting and staffing issues. Fellows observe the director as he or she attends meetings and conducts business with academic medical center leaders. Many opportunities exist to learn about the local library's role with the units it serves. In addition to the two-week visit, the fellowship features additional educational events during the year including conference calls, virtual presentations on a variety of management and self-awareness topics, and additional face-to-face meetings.

Once a directorship is obtained, additional leadership development takes place at the New Directors Symposium. The symposium is offered occasionally to support beginning library directors by discussing relevant topics with presentations by leaders in the profession. AAHSL also promotes leadership development through the Library Director Recruitment Guide, www.aahsl.org/assets/2012/2012_aahsl_recruitguide.pdf. This tool is directed at academic medical center or university library leaders to aid them as they go about recruiting a new health sciences library director. It promotes the skills and knowledge base that health sciences librarians have as they mature in their career path toward library directorships.

Like MLA, AAHSL is known for its role in advocating for the health sciences library profession. As noted above, AAHSL works with MLA on the Joint Legislative Task Force. AAHSL is also involved in advocating for open access and other scholarly communication issues. Its Scholarly Communications Committee keeps the membership informed about issues that require attention. The committee is also responsible for the Scholarly Communications Toolkit that provides resources, guidance, and ideas on how best to promote open access and other communication issues to users.

AAHSL meets annually at the AAMC's annual meeting. In this way, AAHSL is seen as part of the effort to improve medical education via better information access and new services to meet the needs of students and faculty. Here, AAHSL provides its own programming for the directors. These annual workshops and other educational events touch on timely and relevant topics. AAHSL committees have a chance to hold face-to-face meetings, and members can network with colleagues to advance the association's vision and strategic plan. AAHSL also contributes to the AAMC's overall educational programming through sponsorship of the Matheson Lecture in collaboration with the AAMC's Group on Information Resources (GIR), www.aamc.org/members/gir/. The Matheson Lecture is named for Nina L. Matheson, former director of the Welch Medical Library at Johns Hopkins University in Baltimore. Matheson was a leader in medical library science and medical informatics and was instrumental, along with John A. D. Cooper, former president of the AAMC, in writing a report that pushed for the redevelopment of medical libraries as information management centers in academic medical centers through the use of the latest advances in information technologies. This report, www. aahsl.org/index.php?option=com_content&view=article&id=78:matheson-cooper-report&catid=19:site-content, was instrumental in gaining support from NLM to finance implementation of the report's ideas through the IAIMS (integrated advanced information management systems) grants (Goldstein, 1983). The Matheson Lecture invites leading national speakers to the AAMC annual meeting to present topics related to information access, management, systems development, and more. The Matheson Lecture presents an opportunity for AAHSL and the GIR to share its programming with all attendees of the AAMC annual meeting.

Special Libraries Association

The Special Libraries Association (SLA), www.sla.org, is another library organization that appeals to some health sciences librarians. SLA is generally perceived as the organization that supports one-person libraries and solo librarians. Because special libraries tend to be single units within a larger organization, the special librarian is often the only information professional within the parent institution. As such, the librarian lacks a support group of peers to aid the mission of the library; thus, the larger SLA provides that support. SLA is organized in a fashion similar to MLA: It has both subject-oriented groups (SLA calls them divisions) and geographic-oriented chapters. SLA also organizes informal caucuses that represent a special topic or interest and cuts across divisions.

In terms of subject interest, SLA offers a connecting point for those librarians with a broad interest in the biological sciences, allied technology interest, pharmaceutical and medical device industry, and similar special interests. SLA's Biological and Life Sciences Division, http://dbiosla.org, and its related Medical Section, http://dbiosla.org/medicalsection/, provide an alternative home for health sciences librarians.

American Library Association

The American Library Association (ALA), www.ala.org, generally speaks for the library profession as a whole. Its main constituents are public and academic librarians, public library trustees, and library suppliers and vendors. Its main concern is advocacy and lobbying. The ALA Washington, DC, office tracks national issues that have potential impact on libraries and librarians. Through its Committee on Accreditation (COA), ALA maintains the standards for accrediting library science education programs; these standards are located at www.ala.org/groups/committees/ala/ala-coa. In addition, ALA is the leading voice for intellectual freedom, defends the right to read and argues strenuously against censorship, and addresses other important issues such as copyright. ALA promotes diversity within the library profession through various programs and initiatives. Above all else, ALA promotes equitable access to information for all.

Because AAHSL only speaks for academic medical school libraries that are connected to AAMC-accredited medical schools, ALA, along with some MLA sections, provides a home for other academic health sciences libraries and librarians who work in colleges and universities that do not have a medical school. This ALA home is the Health Sciences Interest Group, located within the Association of College and Research Libraries (ACRL), www.ala.org/acrl. This group "provides an opportunity for academic librarians with health sciences responsibilities to have a place in ACRL to network, share information, ask questions, and work on special projects relevant to the academic health sciences" (ALA, ACRL, 2013). ACRL's Health Sciences Interest Group is an alternative and complementary home to the many MLA sections focused on health subjects (nursing, pharmacy, allied health, public health, etc.).

American Medical Informatics Association, EDUCAUSE, ASIS&T

Additional organizations that may be of interest to health sciences librarians are the American Medical Informatics Association (AMIA), www.amia.org; EDUCAUSE, www.educause.edu; and the Association for Information Science & Technology (ASIS&T), www.asis.org. AMIA is the leading organization for health informaticians, those health professionals engaged in research, education, and developing applications that use information systems and other computer-based applications in health care. AMIA publishes a highly respected namesake journal and holds annual spring and fall education conferences that advance the informatics profession. EDUCAUSE is committed to addressing information technology (IT) issues in higher education. It is an institution-based membership aimed at colleges and universities, the corporations that serve their IT needs, as well as other associations, agencies, and nonprofit organizations that are engaged in IT issues at the college or university level. EDUCAUSE is known for its national and regional education conferences that address the latest trends in information technologies and their applications in higher education. ASIS&T is the Association for Information Science and Technology. Generally, ASIS&T is perceived as a research association whose primary focus is "new and better theories, techniques, and technologies to improve access to information" (ASIS&T, 2013). ASIS&T attracts students and new librarians whose career focus is on research in how information is used and accessed. For the health sciences librarian, ASIS&T has a Health Informatics Special Interest Group (SIG).

Other Library Organizations

In addition to the national organizations, many other national, regional, and local groups foster collegiality and professional support. The Regional Medical Libraries of the NN/LM maintain lists of statewide health sciences library associations and other library groups and consortia. Consult these lists for regional and local library associations in your area.

EDUCATION FOR HEALTH SCIENCES LIBRARIANSHIP

The foundation for any librarian position is the master's degree in library and/or information science from an ALA-accredited library science program. As noted above, the degree's course work provides instruction in the core elements of librarianship:

ethics, philosophy, history, organization of scholarly materials, building and acquiring resources appropriate for the community to be served, the design and implementation of services needed by users, understanding and using information technologies as a tool for information access and delivery, and the overall management of the library and its staff. Additional course work provides instruction for the specialization the student wishes to pursue.

To pursue a specialization in librarianship, the student takes the required core courses and any others available that are related to the specialization choice. For health sciences librarianship, MLA tracks the library science programs that offer such courses at www.mlanet.org/education/libschools/.

One way to extend the value of health sciences librarianship courses is through available internships or course assignments for the student to experience the day-to-day work life in a health sciences library. Internships and special course projects that get students out of the classroom and into real-life library situations provide students with experiences that put theory into practice and test their understanding of the course instruction. Supervised by practicing librarians and in collaboration with the student's faculty adviser, internships can enhance the student's overall experience of what it means to be a librarian and to practice the profession. Often, students will be brought into a library situation to assist on a project or tackle a defined project under the supervision of a library director, department head, or some other supervising librarian. Students should expect to be told the goals of the project, what is expected of them while "on the job," and any other expectations for finishing a project. Often, a student will be introduced to other aspects of the local library so that he or she gets the full experience of what real, everyday library work is all about. Students generally are not compensated for an internship. Besides the experience, students will get a grade for their work in place of compensation. The student generally would meet with the supervising librarian and/or library team and interview for the internship, thus also gaining some experience in interviewing. During the interview, goals and expectations should be clearly discussed; if the student is unclear about expectations, the student should discuss them immediately with the supervising librarian as well as with his or her student adviser.

What about a librarian who already possesses the library science master's degree and is interested in moving into health sciences librarianship? One option is for the librarian to contact a local library science education program offering a specialization in health sciences librarianship and check whether it is possible to earn a certificate in the desired specialization. Failing that option, the librarian could take any available health sciences library courses for credit (in person or online) and gain the basic knowledge base about health sciences librarianship. If the librarian already has experience working with resources that relate to the health sciences, for example, life science literature or health administration, more familiarity with health sciences librarianship can be gained by learning about the field independently. Reading the health sciences librarianship literature, purchasing or browsing through books about the issues facing health sciences librarianship, taking continuing education courses, attending local or regional conferences, and other options would build the librarian's knowledge base about health sciences librarianship.

For health professionals who already possess appropriate degrees in the health sciences and desire to change careers and move into library work, the options are many. The health professional could pursue the master's degree in library science and earn the credentials to enter the job market as a librarian. Another option is to apply for available informationist positions. Many academic health sciences libraries and some hospital libraries are now actively searching to hire individuals who have a knowledge base in the health sciences and can apply that knowledge base to the library's services. Depending on the library's particular needs, a health professional could qualify and successfully compete for this type of library position without possessing a master's degree in library science. Once a position is attained, the new "librarian" could expand his or her knowledge base using some of the options mentioned above, such as reading the literature, taking CE courses, and attending library conferences and similar education events. In effect, these options create an apprenticeship model for entering the profession but lack the MLS credential.

A related topic that students often raise about becoming a health sciences librarian is the need for a science background (undergraduate degree) or a second master's degree in a health discipline. In the past, having additional degrees or specialized experiences aided getting a health sciences librarian position, but they were not required. What was important was the desire to learn the basic concepts of the health sciences and the language and terminology of the health professions. Today, when the job market is more competitive, additional course work or related work experience is a plus. However, even today when health sciences libraries seek specialists to fill their ranks, formal course work is not always required (Anton and Twose, 2012).

The informationist program has proven to be a key ingredient in the success of the NIH Library over the past ten years. With expertise in both information management and biomedical research, these individuals spend approximately three-quarters of their time as embedded members of research and clinical teams across NIH. Their dual expertise enables them to provide information solutions at the time and place of need. Looking to the future, we anticipate a growing reliance on information professionals who possess expertise in an area of biomedical research as well as biomedical researchers who have acquired informatics or information management expertise.

—*Keith W. Cogdill, PhD, AHIP, director, National Institutes of Health Library, Division of Library Services, Office of Research Services, Bethesda, MD*

ENTERING THE HEALTH SCIENCES LIBRARY PROFESSION: JOB OPPORTUNITIES AND THE HIRING PROCESS

Once the master's degree in library and information science has been earned, new professionals start the job hunt. This hunt is similar across the whole library profession: identifying open positions, writing application letters, going on interviews and hoping for an offer. What separates the job hunt for health sciences library positions is the same characteristic that makes the health sciences library position unique—a focus on the literature and culture of medicine and health care. Candidates for open health sciences library positions will stand out from their peers by their specialization in course work, internships, related on-the-job experiences, and any credential or connection to the world of health care. Almost all open health sciences library positions are going to request some evidence of that connection.

Table 1.1 summarizes some guidance in approaching the job hunt for new members of the health sciences library profession. These same tips would be appropriate to follow for those individuals who want to move up in their career.

Table 1.1. A Guide for Seeking Health Sciences Library Positions

To Do	Action
Gather new job announcements	Sources include: MLA, www.mlanet.org/jobs/index.html; SLA, http://careercenter.sla.org/jobs; ALA, http://joblist.ala.org. For academic jobs, see *Chronicle of Higher Education* Job Center, http://chronicle.com/section/Home/5. See mentor for inside information (see below).
Study job announcements	Analyze announcements for experience and knowledge. Match your skill set to job requirements via self-assessment of knowledge and skills: Which skills are missing for the job that is most appealing? Which skills are the weakest and which the strongest?
Test decision to apply	Find a mentor. A mentor will counterbalance any self-assessment; double-check application letters and resumes; offer tips on how to locate prospective positions; provide inside knowledge about prospective employers; and supply general advice, encouragement, and counsel when starting the job search.
Consider mobility	Ask yourself: Am I willing to go where the jobs are located? Can I relocate, and if yes, what geographic areas appeal to me?
Apply for a position	Do research: learn as much about the position, the library, and the parent institution as possible. Craft a well-written application or cover letter. Market your skills specific to the job that is announced. Market any additional skills that may be relevant to the library; do not repeat what is in your resume or CV; make your application letter stand out.
Interview	Be yourself. If presenting to the search committee or library staff, polish your teaching and presentation skills. Don't forget to interview those you will work with. Ask relevant questions for information not covered anywhere else. Follow up with a thank-you note, other relevant questions, if necessary, or ask if a decision has been made about the job.
Follow above ideas for planning a career move	Advance your career after two or three years by seeking challenges in new positions and/or in new locales.

PROFESSIONAL INVOLVEMENT AND KEEPING CURRENT

Once a position has been obtained, the new health sciences librarian can begin to get involved in the health sciences library profession. Getting involved starts with becoming a member of MLA, its sections and chapters, and other local or regional health sciences library associations (e.g., Metropolitan Detroit Medical Library Group; Health Sciences Librarians of Illinois). In addition, membership in the other national library organizations mentioned above should be considered as well. The issue of whether to join more than one national organization will depend on what a young professional can afford in terms of dues, time commitments, and the focus of his or her interests.

Getting involved in a professional association will mean keeping current with relevant issues facing the profession and the association. Reading the journals, newsletters, and other digital media that emanate from the organization will be critical to understanding those issues. Reading the professional literature beyond the publications of one organization will also broaden an understanding of professional issues, along with providing ideas for improving the daily practice of library and information services, using technology to improve professional practice, discussing ethical issues, and more. See Table 1.2 for a list of some journals important to health sciences librarianship.

Social media is another means of keeping current. Twitter, Facebook, LinkedIn, and e-mail lists form the bulk of the communication means for connecting to colleagues. These connections address many professional and work-related topics as well as purely social conversations. MEDLIB-L, www.mlanet.org/discussion/medlib_l_faq.html, is the e-mail discussion list sponsored by MLA for anyone interested in health sciences libraries. The list covers a range of topics including ideas for handling difficult reference questions and search problems, difficult to obtain interlibrary loan documents, announcements of various sorts (including job openings), professional issues, and MLA-related activities.

Getting involved in the profession also means volunteering. Professional organizations survive and advance on the work of their members' volunteer efforts on committees, task forces, or other groups. Much of a professional association's work is handled electronically through e-mail, other social media, and the occasional conference call. Volunteers also come together at the association's annual meeting to conduct the association's business in person, to conclude the work of the previous year and/or to set the agenda of goals and objectives for the coming year. Not every volunteer can be accommodated with a national committee appointment. To get started in association work, volunteer for service on local or regional committees and within the parent institution. By gaining this experience at the local and regional level, young professionals show their commitment to the profession and demonstrate skills obtained through this work. In time, these skills will transfer to national appointments.

Another way to get involved professionally is writing for publication. Various outlets are available, from national journals to association newsletters, internal newsletters, blogs, and lists. Writing for publication is topic-specific and shows the author's skills in communication. Writing for publication is one of the most direct ways of contributing to the library profession: it's the author, through the medium, sharing his or her ideas and views with the profession.

Getting involved is rewarding. A great deal of satisfaction comes from accomplishing goals that advance the profession. Association work also tests and develops leadership skills. Working with groups can be frustrating when action is

Table 1.2. Health Sciences Library Journals

Journal Title	Publisher	Date Started
Health Information and Libraries Journal	Blackwell Science	2001
Journal of Electronic Resources in Medical Libraries	Taylor & Francis	2004
Journal of Consumer Health on the Internet (formerly *Health Care on the Internet*)	Taylor & Francis	1997
Journal of eScience Librarianship	University of Massachusetts Medical School	2012
Journal of Hospital Librarianship	Taylor & Francis	2001
Journal of Medical Internet Research	JMIR Publications	1999
Journal of the Canadian Health Libraries Association	National Research Council of Canada	2006
Journal of the European Association for Health Information and Libraries	European Association for Health Information and Libraries	2005
Journal of the Medical Library Association (formerly *Bulletin of the Medical Library Association* and other iterations)	Medical Library Association	1898
Medical Reference Services Quarterly	Taylor & Francis	1982
National Network	Hospital Library Section, Medical Library Association	1990
NLM in Focus	National Libraries of Medicine Office of Communications and Public Liaison	2004
NLM Technical Bulletin	National Library of Medicine	1977
Watermark, Newsletter of the Archivists and Librarians in the History of the Health Sciences Section	Archivists and Librarians of the History of the Health Sciences Section, Medical Library Association	1992

desired, but the patience and compromise that are learned are important to the young professional. These lessons often are relevant to working with users and colleagues back home at the library. Volunteering in an association also builds a young professional's network of contacts and connections to colleagues and demonstrates leadership skills. Such networks and skill development are important for aiding career advancement.

SUMMARY

This chapter discusses the contexts for the practice of health sciences librarianship as it is rarely practiced alone or in isolation of users, colleagues, or supporting institutions. Using education, experience, and professional development as a knowledge base, along with familiarity with the ethical principles of the health sciences library profession, the health sciences librarian enters the profession through a position in a range of health-related institutions and businesses: from academic medical centers to community hospitals to special libraries and information centers. The local institution impacts the everyday practice of the health sciences librarian through its mission and role in society. The health sciences librarian responds by building collections and services that meet local needs. The details of how this is done are contained in the remaining chapters.

The practice of health sciences librarianship relies heavily on networks of libraries and librarians, especially the National Network of Libraries of Medicine. NLM plays a critical role in supporting the life of every health sciences librarian and library through its collections, services, products, and technological innovation, and the support is mutual. Health sciences librarians work to keep NLM strong so it can support information access at the most local and fundamental level—improving health and healing disease.

The professional associations, especially the Medical Library Association, are also fundamental to the practice of health sciences librarianship. Professional associations provide the collegiality among practitioners so there is a mutual reliance on the membership for sharing ideas and experience in how best to move the practice of health sciences librarianship forward.

Above all else, the context of patient care makes the practice of health sciences librarianship unique and different. Each health professional, including librarians, develops the mind-set of the patient is first. This is part of the culture of medicine. Further, collaboration among health professionals working together to improve health and heal disease assures better patient care.

All of these contexts impact the nature of health sciences librarianship and are part of what makes the health sciences library profession unique among peers. The nature of health care in the United States is constantly changing, and the health sciences library profession will change with it. The future is bright but not without its challenges.

STUDY QUESTIONS

1. Select a role in a health sciences library—informationist, data librarian, technology manager, and so forth—and review its origin by finding articles that describe its activities and academic preparation for it.
2. Discuss the culture of medicine and how health sciences librarians relate to it. Speak with experienced health sciences librarians and ask their opinion about this culture and how they experience it, especially as it affects the work they do. Ask health sciences librarians how they think they are different from other librarians.
3. Examine in detail the products and services of the National Library of Medicine. Considering your potential interests in an area of practice and examine NLM's products and services that would impact you the most. Pick one product or service and describe it, especially how it affects your future work. Then, examine

NLM's products and services that you think would affect you the least in your future role. Provide a report that compares the two.

4. Study the history of the NN/LM. Debate this question: Is the Regional Medical Library (RML) program relevant in today's economy and with advances made in information technologies, networking, Internet access, and more? What do you think is the role of the NN/LM in the future?

REFERENCES

AACN (American Association of Colleges of Nursing). 2009. "Standards for Accreditation of Baccalaureate and Graduate Degree Nursing Programs." American Association of Colleges of Nursing. Amended April 2009. www.aacn.nche.edu/ccne-accreditation/standards09.pdf.

AAMC (Association of American Medical Colleges). 2005. "Recommendations for Clinical Skills Curricula for Undergraduate Medical Education." See Appendix A: Communication Skills. https://members.aamc.org/eweb/upload/Recommendations%20for%20Clinical%20 Skills%20Curricula%202005.pdf.

ADA (American Dental Association). 2010. "Accreditation Standards for Dental Education Programs." ADA Commission on Dental Accreditation. Adopted August 6, 2010. www.ada. org/sections/educationAndCareers/pdfs/predoc_2013.pdf.

AHA (American Hospital Association). 2013. "Fast Facts on U.S. Hospitals." January 3. www. aha.org/research/rc/stat-studies/fast-facts.shtml.

ALA (American Library Association). 2008. "Code of Ethics of the American Library Association." American Library Association. Amended January 22, 2008. www.ala.org/advocacy/ proethics/codeofethics/codeethics.

ALA (American Library Association), ACRL (Association of College and Research Libraries). 2013. "Health Sciences Interest Group." Accessed August 3. www.ala.org/acrl/aboutacrl/ directoryofleadership/interestgroups/acr-ighs.

Anton, Blair, and Claire Twose. 2012. "Hiring an Informationist: An Interview with Blair Anton and Claire Twose, William H. Welch Medical Library, Johns Hopkins University School of Medicine, Baltimore, MD." *MLA News* 52, no. 10 (November–December): 7.

ASIS&T (American Society for Information Science and Technology). 2013. "About ASIS&T." Accessed August 7. www.asis.org/about.html.

Bell, Jo Ann H. 1996. "History of the Medical Library Association's Credentialing Program." *Bulletin of the Medical Library Association* 84, no. 3 (July): 320–33.

Boutin-Foster, Carla, Jordan C. Foster, and Lyuba Konopasek. 2008. "Physician, Know Thyself: The Professional Culture of Medicine as a Framework for Teaching Cultural Competence." *Academic Medicine* 83, no. 1: 106–11.

Bunting, Alison. 1987. "The Nation's Health Information Network: History of the Regional Medical Library Program, 1965–1985." *Bulletin of the Medical Library Association* 75, no. 3 supplement (July): 1–62.

Byrd, Gary D., and James Shedlock. 2003. "The Association of Academic Health Sciences Libraries Annual Statistics: An Explanatory Twenty-Five Year Trend Analysis." *Journal of the Medical Library Association* 91, no. 2 (April): 186–202.

CARLA (Center for Advanced Research on Language Acquisition). 2013. "What Is Culture?" www.carla.umn.edu/culture/definitions.

Cummings, Martin M., and Mary E. Corning. 1971. "The Medical Library Assistance Act: An Analysis of the NLM Extramural Programs, 1965–1970." *Bulletin of the Medical Library Association* 59, no. 3 (July): 375–91.

Darling, Louise. 1973. "The View Behind and Ahead: Implications for Certification." *Bulletin of the Medical Library Association* 61, no. 4 (October): 375–86.

Dee, Cheryl Rae. 2007. "The Development of the Medical Literature Analysis and Retrieval System (MEDLARS)." *Journal of the Medical Library Association* 95, no. 4 (October): 416–25.

Doe, Janet. 1949. "The Development of Education for Medical Librarianship." *Bulletin of the Medical Library Association* 37, no. 3 (July): 213–20.

Goldstein, Rachael K. 1983. "Roles for the Library in Information Management. Introduction." *Bulletin of the Medical Library Association* 71, no. 4 (October): 404.

Jacobson, Susan. 2003. "Present at the Creation: The Founding and Formative Years of the Association of Academic Health Sciences Libraries." *Journal of the Medical Library Association* 91, no. 2 (April): 149–54.

LCME (Liaison Committee on Medical Education). 2013. "Functions and Structure of a Medical School: Standards for Accreditation of Medical Education Programs Leading to the M.D. Degree, June 2013." Liaison Committee on Medical Education. June. www.lcme.org/functions.pdf.

MacEachern, Mark, Whitney Townsend, K. Young, and Gurpreet Rana. 2012. "Librarian Integration in a Four-year Medical School Curriculum: A Timeline." *Medical References Services Quarterly* 31, no. 1 (January–March): 105–14.

Marshall, Mary Louise. 1946. "Training for Medical Librarianship." *Bulletin of the Medical Library Association* 34, no. 4 (October): 247–65.

Martin, Elaine Russo. 2012. "What Do Data Librarians Do?" *Journal of eSciences Librarianship* 1, no. 3: 115–17.

MLA (Medical Library Association). 2010. "Code of Ethics for Health Sciences Librarianship." Medical Library Association. Revised 2010. www.mlanet.org/about/ethics.html.

———. 2013. "About the Medical Library Association: Our Mission)." Accessed August 3. www.mlanet.org/about/mission.html.

Roper, Fred W. 2006. "The Medical Library Association's Professional Development Program: A Look Back at the Way Ahead." *Journal of the Medical Library Association* 94, no. 1 (January): 8–18.

Shaffer, Chris J. 2013. "The Role of the Library in the Research Enterprise." *Journal of eSciences Librarianship* 2, no. 1: 8–15.

Shedlock, James, and Gary D. Byrd. 2003. "The Association of Academic Health Sciences Libraries Annual Statistics: A Thematic History." *Journal of the Medical Library Association* 91, no. 2 (April): 178–85.

Shipman, Jean P., Diana J. Cunningham, Ruth Holst, and Linda A. Watson. 2002. "The Informationist Conference: Report." *Journal of the Medical Library Association* 90, no. 4 (October): 458–64.

Tan, Maria C., and Lauren A. Maggio. 2013. "Expert Searcher, Teacher, Content Manager, and Patient Advocate: An Exploratory Study of Clinical Librarian Roles." *Journal of the Medical Library Association* 101, no. 1 (January): 63–72.

Thibodeau, Patricia, and Carla J. Funk. 2009. "Trends in Hospital Librarianship and Hospital Library Services: 1989 to 2006." *Journal of the Medical Library Association* 97, no. 4 (October): 273–79.

Volk, R. M. 2007. "Expert Searching in Consumer Health: An Important Role for Librarians in the Age of the Internet and the Web." *Journal of the Medical Library Association* 95, no. 2 (April): 203–7.

Wheeler, Terrie R., and Keith W. Cogdill. 2013. "What Is an Informationist and What Do Informationists Do? An Interview with Terrie R. Wheeler and Keith W. Cogdill, AHIP, NIH Library, National Institutes of Health, Bethesda, MD." *MLA News* 53, no. 1 (January): 7, 9.

CHAPTER 2

The Health Sciences Environment

Gale G. Hannigan and Jonathan D. Eldredge

INTRODUCTION

Health sciences librarians practice in the context of the larger health care environment. In the United States, health care is a huge and complex enterprise that ranges from the level of individual patient care to the management of multibillion dollar research efforts and organizations. It is important to understand this environment because the context affects what health sciences librarians do every day, and changes in the environment will influence the future development of the profession.

This chapter covers various aspects of the health care environment including how health care is organized and delivered in the United States, the education of health professionals, and the biomedical research process. People write entire books about each of these topics; this chapter makes no attempt to be comprehensive. Rather, the goal is to provide enough information so that a student in a library/information program or health sciences librarian new to the field will have a basic understanding of the unique and interesting situation that is health care today, with some appreciation of how it evolved and the important contributions librarians make.

U.S. HEALTH CARE

Those interested in the history of health care in the United States may wish to read sociologist Paul Starr's Pulitzer Prize-winning *The Social Transformation of American Medicine: The Rise of a Sovereign Profession and the Making of a Vast Industry* (1982). A *New York Times* review praised it as "a brilliant blend of sociological, political, economic and cultural analysis covering two centuries of American experience" (Geiger, 1983). The narrative, which ends in the early 1980s, sets the stage for contemporary times in which hospitals, once community institutions, are owned by big corporations that employ physicians, once independent practitioners. As Starr noted, we now have a thriving medical-industrial complex.

Health sciences librarians work in this context. Even though they may not be directly involved in patient care, they are committed to the ultimate goal of improving health and health care. Health sciences librarians believe that a patient's well-being may be at the source of every question and that the information they provide may make an important difference in that person's care.

The Business of Health Care

U.S. health care is big business. According to the U.S. Department of Commerce,

the United States has the largest healthcare services market in the world, representing a significant portion of the U.S. economy. In 2010, the healthcare services industry accounted for approximately $1.75 trillion in revenues and employed over 14 million people, or nine percent of the U.S. workforce. The U.S. Bureau of Labor Statistics estimates that growth in the industry will yield 3.2 million new jobs between 2008 and 2018. Jobs in home healthcare services and diagnostic laboratories are expected to grow at the fastest pace—up to 40 percent over the next 10 years. (U.S. Department of Commerce, 2013)

Debate continues over the role of government in health care. Health care is not considered one of the rights that all U.S. citizens have, although the issue has been on and off the national agenda for a century. Most Americans get health insurance coverage through their workplace. Medicare and Medicaid are both popular and expensive government programs for specific groups (i.e., people sixty-five and older and people with low income, respectively). The U.S. Department of Veterans Affairs (VA) manages the country's largest integrated health care system. According to a report by the Bureau of Labor Statistics, "approximately 31 percent of individuals are covered by public sources, mostly Medicare and Medicaid, while employers cover 55.3 percent of individuals. About 16 percent of Americans—nearly 50 million individuals—were uninsured in 2010" (Mauersberger, 2012). "Coverage" does not imply free insurance or care. Employees usually must contribute substantially to their employer-sponsored plan as well as make co-payments for services; and some—often, expensive—services may be denied coverage. Employer-sponsored coverage is typically significantly less expensive than private coverage. People are uninsured because they are not employed, they cannot afford private coverage, their employer does not offer coverage, or they choose not to enroll.

U.S. health care is expensive. No other country spends a greater percentage of its **gross domestic product (GDP)** on health care than the United States. The latest data available from the Organisation for Economic Co-operation and Development (OECD) show U.S. health care at 17.7 percent of GDP, followed by the Netherlands at 11.9 percent, France at 11.6 percent, and Germany at 11.3 percent (OECD, 2013). The United States also spends more per capita on health care than any other country. In 2011, health care costs grew 3.9 percent to $2.7 trillion, or $8,680 per person, on average (Centers for Medicare & Medicaid Services, 2011). It cost a private industry employer $2.12 per hour worked to provide health benefits, more than twice as much as it did in 2001 (Mauersberger, 2012).

Dollars spent on health care do not guarantee better health. For several years, health status indicators have shown that other countries spending far less of their GDP on health care outrank the United States. In fact, U.S. rankings declined during the past fifty years for basic health indicators such as life expectancy at birth. The United States ranks thirty-fourth for 2011, dropping around twenty-five places since the early 1950s, with life expectancy now at 78.5 years, compared to 83.4 years for Japan (Bezruchka, 2012). Infant mortality in the United States is estimated at 5.9 deaths per 1,000 live births, worse than forty-nine other countries including Hungary, Cuba, and Belarus, and more than twice the rate of Japan at 2.17 (Central Intelligence Agency, 2013). Some of the relative decline can be attributed to the overall improvement in health worldwide. Meanwhile, the United States has not kept pace.

A common explanation had been that, in the United States, some people get the best care in the world and others almost none at all and that the rankings are a result of the average outcomes of two very different health systems. But that argument apparently no longer holds true. A recent and disturbing report, *U.S. Health in International Perspective: Shorter Lives, Poorer Health*, measured Americans' health status against sixteen peer countries. On average, Americans don't live as long as their counterparts and, by age fifty, are in generally poorer health. Although lower socioeconomic status contributes to poorer health, it does not account for the differences; "that is, Americans with healthy behaviors or those who are white, insured, college-educated, or in upper-income groups appear to be in worse health than similar groups in comparison countries" (National Research Council and Institute of Medicine, 2013: 3).

All of these factors contributed to yet another push for national health care reform to control costs and provide better access to health care. After acrimonious debate, Congress passed the **Patient Protection and Affordable Care Act (PPACA)** on March 23, 2010 (Public Law 111–148. 111th Congress, 2010), also referred to as the Affordable Care Act. This complex legislation has many, many aspects, but a major goal is that, by 2014, all Americans will have access to affordable health insurance options. The time line for implementation can be found at Key Features of the Affordable Care Act at www.healthcare.gov/law/timeline/. It is estimated that thirty million previously uninsured citizens will be covered, but speculation continues about how successful the PPACA will be in terms of addressing access to health care, preventing fraud, reducing costs, and improving health (Doherty, 2010).

Public librarians and consumer health librarians have a role to play in making people aware of the provisions of the PPACA and new services associated with its implementation. In June 2013, the American Library Association and U.S. Department of Health and Human Services announced an agreement to disseminate information, especially an "apples-to-apples comparison among competing insurance plans," with the National Network of Libraries of Medicine committing to work to raise public awareness and support "health insurance literacy" (Eberhart, 2013).

Quality of Health Care

In 2000, the Institute of Medicine (IOM) issued a report suggesting that as many as 98,000 people die from preventable errors each year in U.S. hospitals (Kohn, Corrigan, and Donaldson, 2000). A subsequent IOM report elaborated on the problem:

The delivery of care often is overly complex and uncoordinated, requiring steps and patient "handoffs" that slow down care and decrease rather than improve safety. These cumbersome processes waste resources; leave unaccountable voids in coverage; lead to loss of information; and fail to build on the strengths of all health professionals involved to ensure that care is appropriate, timely, and safe. (Institute of Medicine, 2001: 28)

The report recommends four changes in the environment to improve the health care delivery system: apply evidence to practice; use information technology, which includes the development of an information infrastructure; align payment methods with quality improvement goals; and prepare the workforce for the future transformation of health care delivery.

In the specific area of patient safety, librarians have found ways to participate in and contribute to their institution's efforts to develop a culture of safety. For example, hospital librarians have become members of patient safety teams, providing information support and often hosting team meetings in the library. The lack of health literacy is a threat to patient safety and, increasingly, librarians are developing the skills to create and deliver information resources at a level that is appropriate for patients and consumers. The American Medical Association recognizes the importance of health literacy and an informed patient, stating: "It is neither just nor fair to expect a patient to make appropriate health decisions and safely manage his or her care without first the information needed to do so" (American Medical Association Foundation, 2007: 15). Even more fundamental to health sciences librarianship, the quality evidence-based information that librarians provide to clinicians supports the current best practices and helps avoid health care errors. The Medical Library Association's *Role of Health Sciences Librarians in Patient Safety Position Statement* (MLA, 2009) offers many strategies librarians can employ to become more involved in this important endeavor.

Influences on Health Care

The quality of health care is both a personal and national issue. The National Research Council recommends that educators as well as accreditation, licensing, and certification organizations ensure that students and working professionals develop and maintain proficiency in five core areas: delivering patient-centered care, working as part of interdisciplinary teams, practicing evidence-based medicine, focusing on quality improvement, and using information technology (Greiner and Knebel, 2003).

Delivering Patient-Centered Care

Time and again, leaders remind us that the individual should be at the center of health care. "Patient-centered care" is a MEDLINE (PubMed) Medical Subject Heading (MeSH) defined as the "design of patient care wherein institutional resources and personnel are organized around patients rather than around specialized departments" (Sherer, 1993: 14). Another source defines it as "care that is respectful of and responsive to individual patient preferences, needs, and values" (Institute of Medicine, 2001: 6). Patient-centeredness encompasses interpersonal, clinical, and structural aspects of health care. This complexity argues for a systems approach, involving all components of the health care system, in order to deliver patient-centered care (Greene, Tuzzio, and Cherkin, 2012). The **patient-centered medical home (PCMH)** has become a popular model to improve the delivery of health care. The PCMH concept strengthens the role of a single, primary care point of contact and emphasizes the coordination of health care around the needs of the patient (Epperly, 2011).

The U.S. population continues to age, and by 2050, one in five Americans will be sixty-five years old or older. Society and health care professionals will need to respond to the needs of more people with chronic diseases. The number of children born either to teenage or older mothers continues to trend upward, resulting in more at-risk infants. The population is also growing more diverse. The percentage of the population of Hispanic or Latino origin is expected to increase, rising from about one in seven persons in 2000 to almost one in three persons by 2050; the Asian population is expected to grow by 23.7 million during the same time period, an increase of 220 percent (Shrestha and Heisler, 2011). The different ways in which various ethnic groups use health care services, and their particular risks for specific diseases, must be incorporated into modifications in health care delivery.

People who are socially disadvantaged experience poorer health and poorer health care. Mounting evidence documents disparities by race, ethnicity, socioeconomic status, and gender. For example, minorities experience disproportionately high rates of end-stage renal disease but are less likely to receive live donor kidney transplants (Purnell, Hall, and Boulware, 2012). Racism may be associated with the prevalence of hypertension (Brondolo et al., 2011). Women may experience heart disease differently from men; those therapies based on clinical trials with mostly male participants might not be as effective for females (O'Callaghan, 2009). Teasing out specific causes of these disparities challenges even the most sophisticated researchers. Improved cultural humility at both the individual and institutional levels is needed (Saha, Beach, and Cooper, 2008).

A current model of medical decision making consists of the triad of medical knowledge, clinical expertise, and patient preference (see Figure 2.1). Librarians can affect all three points of the triad. Health sciences librarians obviously play a key role in locating medical knowledge. Librarians at one health sciences library created a What Your Patient Reads tool to provide clinicians with short summaries of media health reports supplemented by references to related evidence-based literature, thus assisting busy clinicians in keeping abreast of what their patients might have recently read or heard (Shaw-Daigle, Giles-Smith, and Raynard, 2011). For patients to have a preference and fully participate in their own health care, they need information, and health information on all subjects and of all degrees of quality is readily available on the Internet and through mass media. Patient and consumer health librarians have the expertise to assess users' information needs and level of comprehension in order to guide patients to the most appropriate and authoritative resource. Chapter 13, "Consumer Health," goes into detail about consumer health, health literacy, and library services to support these important efforts.

Genomic medicine that informs personalized medicine is a reality (Ginsburg and Willard, 2009). Genetic information adds to the amount and complexity of information that should be considered in the treatment of an individual patient,

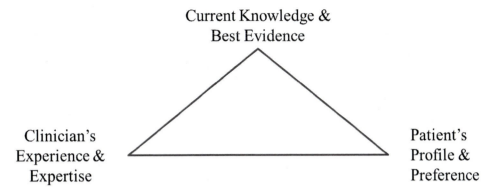

Figure 2.1. Triad Model of Medical Decision Making. Each component should contribute; the "weight" of the contribution depends on the specific decision.

and health sciences librarians will need to hone their knowledge of the field and skills in searching to find more patient-specific information. Genetic counseling is another rapidly developing field; librarians will be asked to locate and provide appropriate information for both professionals and their patients. Lyon et al. (2004) describe a curriculum for practicing librarians designed to increase their bioinformatics competencies; the twelve-week course covers resources and concepts related to molecular biology and genetics.

Working as Part of Interdisciplinary Teams

In the last half of the twentieth century, the health care environment became more complex and compartmentalized as specialization increased among providers. It is not surprising that errors occur when information and care are not coordinated. The IOM report on patient safety noted that

> the decentralized and fragmented nature of the health care delivery system (some would say "nonsystem") also contributes to unsafe conditions for patients, and serves as an impediment to efforts to improve safety. Even within hospitals and large medical groups, there are rigidly-defined areas of specialization and influence. When patients see multiple providers in different settings, none of whom have access to complete information, it is easier for something to go wrong than when care is better coordinated. (Kohn, Corrigan, and Donaldson, 2000: 3)

The traditional hierarchical culture of medicine may have worked when one doctor coordinated the total care of a patient, but those days are gone. Multiple physicians and other health professionals all have specific roles to play in an individual patient's care. This is especially true in the hospital setting, which is a complex 24/7 organization. Health care is a group effort, and members of the group need to be able to work as a team, understanding and appreciating each other's roles for the benefit of the patient.

Workforce issues and health care delivery trends also contribute to the need for cross-disciplinary coordination and cooperation. A current projection is for 90,000 fewer physicians by 2020 at a time when the population will have grown and aged (Kirch, Henderson, and Dill, 2012). One response is to establish more medical schools and to increase enrollment at existing medical schools. Nonphysician practitioners, including nurse practitioners and physician assistants, continue to fill new and important roles. The expected increase in home-based health care will drive the demand for home health workers, social workers, and many others. All of these people must be able to work together effectively.

Librarians are often seen as neutral parties who can help others come together to collaborate. As trusted professionals, librarians may be recruited to participate on interdisciplinary teams, often in coordinator roles. Expert communications skills and the ability to get to the heart of an issue or question, in addition to knowledge of the organization as a whole, make librarians valuable contributors in teamwork. For example, multidisciplinary teamwork has been a hallmark of cancer care. Librarians embedded in clinical teams at a major cancer center describe using Web 2.0 tools to enhance communication and collaboration among team members (Damani and Fulton, 2010).

The Interprofessional Education Collaborative (IPEC), which consists of a partnership of six associations (the American Association of Colleges of Nursing, the American Association of Colleges of Osteopathic Medicine, the American Association of Colleges of Pharmacy, the American Dental Education Association, the American Association of Medical Colleges, and the Association of Schools of Public Health), convened an expert panel in 2009. Subsequently, it published *Core Competencies for Interprofessional Collaborative Practice*, which outlines the future directions of health professions education (Schmitt et al., 2011). The endorsed competencies address values/ethics for interprofessional practice; knowing each other's roles/responsibilities; effective communication with patients, families, and other health professionals; and teamwork. These competencies are meant to help guide curriculum development so that future health care professionals are more adept in working together effectively. Librarians working in academic environments can expect to participate in interdisciplinary education and should advocate for the librarian's role as a full member of the health care team.

> Sometimes it is content expertise, searching skills, knowledge of new technology, or willingness to try new things that enables librarians to be effective members of teams. Figure out what is needed with the group you have and run with it.
>
> —*Stephanie Fulton, MSIS, AHIP, executive director, Research Medical Library, The University of Texas MD Anderson Cancer Center, Houston*

It should be noted that the "health care team" and users of health sciences library services encompass other people besides traditional health professionals. Hospital administrators, lawyers, researchers, students, mental health and social work practitioners, hospital chaplains, clerks, facilities managers, janitorial staff, and others—all may look to the librarian for assistance with their work or personal information needs.

Practicing Evidence-Based Medicine

Evidence-based practice (EBP) is discussed in great detail elsewhere in this book (see chapters 3 and 11). Evidence-based practice requires that practitioners incorporate the best current scientific evidence into decision making. This implies that a practitioner knows or can locate the current best evidence and, because of the evolving nature of research, requires that a practitioner must also be a lifelong learner. A practitioner needs to incorporate the most current and valid information into decisions about the care of a specific patient. Librarians play a key role in teaching the skills of lifelong learning and evidence-based practice, as well as participate in the development of EBP tools and, of course, apply EBP principles in their own profession. Many health sciences librarians teach the question formulation, searching, and critical appraisal skills of evidence-based practice. This role requires librarians who are not only expert in searching the literature, but also able to evaluate the quality of studies that are retrieved and understand how the information in a given article might apply to a specific patient question.

Focusing on Quality Improvement

Quality health care is the overall goal of organizational efforts to improve health care. Quality Improvement (QI) methodologies offer systematic approaches to processes and outcomes designed to achieve that goal and measure progress. As incremental changes are made in complex systems, measures are taken of their effects across the entire system. For instance, adherence to a particular practice guideline for diabetes control (a process) is measured in conjunction with the resulting health status of diabetics such as incidence of kidney failure or retinopathy (outcomes). Potential adverse effects, costs, and inconvenience to patient and provider must also be monitored. Several QI methodologies that come from business and industry are applicable to systems in general, including health care. Methodologies often used include Plan-Do-Study-Act (PDSA) cycle, Six Sigma, Failure Modes and Effects Analysis, and Root Cause Analysis. All of these techniques are highly dependent on data acquisition and analysis (Varkey, Reller, and Resar, 2007; Schriefer and Leonard, 2012).

Economic incentives are used to influence the quality of care. For example, a Medicare reimbursement penalty for hospitals with high readmission rates is prompting hospitals to maintain better communication with patients after discharge (Hansen et al., 2011). The fee-for-service economic model rewards procedures more than it rewards cognitive effort and prevention. Repeat testing (e.g., echocardiography) of Medicare patients is an example of this and contributes to unnecessary costs and effort.

Over the years, Marshall and colleagues have conducted studies to determine the impact of library and information services on patient care, which is the "bottom line" issue in terms of the value of these services in the clinical setting. Her most recent multisite study indicates that the information clinicians sought for a patient care incident was of high quality, contributed to patient care, and saved time (Marshall et al., 2013). Three-quarters of the health professionals surveyed (n = 10,303) "said they definitely or probably handled some aspect of the patient care situation differently as a result of the information" (Marshall et al., 2013: 41). It should be noted that in most cases, clinicians neither came to the library nor consulted a librarian, demonstrating the important trend toward librarians providing user-friendly, remote access to information. On the other hand, when asked if they found the information they needed, only 59 percent responded, "Completely." This suggests the continuing need for librarians to offer direct search services, teach clinicians better search strategies, and contribute to the development of resources that are easier to use.

Using Information Technology

The information revolution starting in the second half of the twentieth century continues, and it prompts changes in health care. Information technology helps to create as well as to manage the overwhelming amount of data and information generated by research and practice. Information technology makes possible online education and the incorporation of simulation in the health professional curriculum. However, health information technology's effect on reducing costs and improving care has been hard to demonstrate. As is the experience with information technology in general, new technologies enable entirely new activities, making it difficult to compare current status with the past. Digital medical imaging, telehealth, and e-mail between provider and patient did not exist before computers made them possible. New tools and new opportunities for using them continue to become available. How new technologies and applications improve the quality of health care requires considerable research and even new methods of study.

After almost fifty years of effort, the "holy grail" of health information technology—the electronic health record (EHR)—became a reality. There still is not one national system, not every practitioner uses an EHR system, and different EHR systems aren't necessarily able to share information. Even so, EHRs are now part of the health care landscape.

The American Recovery and Reinvestment Act of 2009 (ARRA) allocated billions of dollars to encourage the adoption of EHRs. National goals include the ability to exchange health information among systems while protecting the privacy of electronic health information, first addressed by the Health Insurance Portability and Accountability Act of 1966 (HIPAA). The law also supports the development of a national health information infrastructure, overseen by the Office of the National Coordinator for Health Information Technology (ONCHIT) (Burke, 2010).

An EHR is more than the computerization of written records ("charts"), which historically provided documentation about patients and communication among practitioners. Some EHRs incorporate information resources, decision-support aids, and data analysis, and also allow for data mining, making it feasible to gather the data required to track quality improvement efforts. Health Information Exchanges (HIE) promise the ability to access health information about individuals as people move among various health care systems. Currently, an emergency room physician treating an unconscious person probably has no information about that person's health history. Patients who seek services from different organizations in the same city will not have a complete record at any one of them; dental records, for example, are not typically part of an individual's medical record (Downing et al., 2009). Information shared internationally could help not only travelers who fall ill away from home, but enhance the ability to track trends and detect patterns of disease worldwide (Vest, 2012). Patients' access to their own health information should further the goal for informed patient participation in their health care. Access to an individual's lifetime health information could help reduce unnecessary duplication of tests, avoid errors due to lack of coordination and communication, and reduce costs.

The technical challenges to implement effective EHRs and HIEs are formidable. Even greater challenges are issues related to policy, incentives to cooperate, protocols and standardization, and the appropriate design and use of the systems as they are built (Williams et al., 2012). Financial incentives are being used to prompt the adoption of EHRs designed to achieve specific goals. For example, the federal government provides financial support for the implementation of electronic health records systems that demonstrate evidence of "meaningful use." Organizations must show that their electronic records systems incorporate key features such as electronic drug prescribing (Galbraith, 2013; Wright et al., 2013). EHRs are among the many health information technologies changing the face of health care today, and it is likely that the electronic health record will become the framework to organize much of the information used for personal and public health (Yasnoff, Sweeney, and Shortliffe, 2013; Friedman, Wong, and Blumenthal, 2010).

If that is true, and the EHR becomes the focal point of information for clinical care, personal and public health, librarians need to be involved. Many EHRs include or link to commercial "point-of-care" resources that libraries support. At the University of Pittsburgh, health sciences librarians developed a clinical information tool, embedded in the medical center's electronic records system, that makes it easy for users to search across multiple resources for a specific type of information such as diagnosis or patient education (Epstein et al., 2010). At Vanderbilt University, clinicians using the EHR "can submit clinical questions to information professionals, have the option of linking the question directly to a patient's chart, and can specify the urgency of the request and the desired turnaround time for the response" (Giuse, Williams, and Giuse, 2010: 221). But the fact that many EHRs provide access to point-of-care resources and links to other library resources does not diminish the value of the many clinical librarians who support patient care teams and understand the context of the questions that come up.

> Although EHRs are promoted as the major method of handling physician inquiries into care, current data show that physicians often don't consult information resources, either because they don't believe they will find an answer or don't have the time. Librarians on rounds can help identify information needs, pursue the answers to clinical questions, and provide information that allows physicians to achieve a higher quality of care.
>
> —*Julia M. Esparza, MLS, AHIP, clinical medical librarian/associate librarian, LSUHSC—Shreveport, LA*

HEALTH PROFESSIONALS' EDUCATION

Chapter 11 covers current and future roles of librarians in the education of health professionals. Chapter 3 discusses significant trends that affect health sciences education. This section provides some background about the education of health professionals in the United States. Medical education dominates the discussion because medicine has been the dominant profession in the health sciences. The education of physicians has a long tradition and embodies strong cultural beliefs. Some have likened the medical school curriculum to a graveyard to which things are added but nothing is removed. Discussions about reform often dominate curriculum committee meetings, but innovation is often prompted from outside influences, such as accrediting organizations. Still, encouraging pockets of education reform are found at certain medical schools. For example, McMaster University introduced **problem-based learning (PBL)** in the medical school curriculum in 1969; since then, many schools have adopted some variation of PBL. Changes in medical education affect the education of other health professionals. Health sciences librarians are increasingly involved in teaching health professional students, so it is important to know about the evolution and current direction of educational programs.

A Brief History of Health Professional Education in the United States

In a 1910 article published in *The Atlantic* magazine, Abraham Flexner describes the development of American medicine from primarily an apprenticeship, perhaps with additional training in Europe (Flexner, 1910a). Eventually, the apprenticeship model was displaced, but many independent medical schools provided no clinical facilities. For the most part, facilities were poor, and the educational content was minimal. The *Atlantic* article, written for the general public, appeared the same year as Flexner's most cited contribution to medical education, a survey of medical schools requested by the American Medical Association's Council on Medical Education and sponsored by the Carnegie Foundation (Flexner, 1910b). The survey results and conclusions, popularly known as the Flexner Report—and still referred to in curriculum committees—called for reform in medical education, including recommendations requiring college-level training, applying the scientific method to learning and medical practice, and strengthening state regulation of medical licensure.

The Flexner Report prompted considerable change in medical education. Today, it is typical for a postbaccalaureate student to complete four years of medical school, pass national licensure exams, and finish three or more years of **residency training** before becoming eligible for testing and certification by one of many specialty boards. Numerous subspecialty fellowship programs train physicians for unique roles, such as members of transplantation teams.

The education of other health professionals followed a similar course, from apprenticeship models to more formal, academic training. Today's nurse has an associate degree or bachelor of science in nursing, and there are advanced degrees (master of science in nursing, doctor of nursing practice). Nurse practitioners have an advanced degree plus specialized training to practice is a variety of health care settings. For pharmacists, the PharmD is the accepted degree for professional practice, and there is current debate about residency requirements for pharmacists; some residencies are available in specialized areas such as pain management and palliative care. Most dentists have completed four years of college and four years of dental school, resulting in a DDS or DMD degree. With advanced training, dentists can specialize in a variety of areas such as oral and maxillofacial surgery, pediatric dentistry, and dental public health. These core health professionals take care of humans. Veterinary medicine covers all other animals. Postundergraduate four-year programs lead to a DVM degree, with postgraduate opportunities for specialization; veterinarians also contribute to food safety, the understanding and control of global pandemics, and biomedical research.

Allied health encompasses other health professionals who work with patients. According to the Association of Schools of Allied Health Professions, these, "to name a few, include dental hygienists, diagnostic medical sonographers, dietitians, medical technologists, occupational therapists, physical therapists, radiographers, respiratory therapists, and speech language pathologists" (ASAPH, 2013). Many of these fields existed early in the 1900s, with practitioners' education based in hospitals and universities. The Allied Health Professions Personnel Training Act of 1966 unified and recognized the importance of the allied health professions and provided funds to increase the number of allied health schools in the United States within the academic environment. The 1970 Health Training Improvement Act allocated funds to strengthen the quality of allied health education (Lecca, Valentine, and Lyons, 2003). Entry into many of these fields is quite competitive; education is often at the baccalaureate level, with opportunities for advanced degrees and specialization, including doctoral-level degrees for practice, such as the DrOT (doctor of occupational therapy), OTD (doctorate of occupational therapy), and the DPT (doctor of physical therapy).

Most practitioners take care of individual patients. Public health professionals are concerned with the health of entire populations and the prevention of disease; examples of these activities include health promotion, sanitation, vaccination programs, and environmental health studies. Founded in 1872, the American Public Health Association (APHA) unsuccessfully advocated for the inclusion of public health principles in the education of health professionals early in the twentieth century. A few medical schools offered postgraduate programs in public health, but public health was not part of the basic medical school curriculum. The first degree programs in public health emphasized research, leaving the actual practice of public health to others who had little or no formal training in the field. By the 1950s, only ten schools conferred MPH degrees (Ruis and Golden, 2008).

In 1988, the Institute of Medicine published *The Future of Public Health*. This comprehensive review of the state of public health pointed to the lack of formal training and appropriate education for public health practitioners: "most public health workers have no formal training in public health, and their need for basic grounding may not be appropriately met by the degree programs appropriate to prepare people for middle and upper-level positions" (Institute of Medicine, 1988: 16). A renewed emphasis on population health, the need for appropriate formal education of public health workers, and the importance of public health's analytic methods in understanding disease and biomedical research resulted in an increase in the number of schools of public health and public health workforce training programs.

Public health and medicine, two professions that were largely estranged from one another during most of the twentieth century, have begun to combine their efforts to promote health. Medical school programs that combine the MD and MPH degrees are slowly gaining popularity. In 2010, the Association of American Medical Colleges (AAMC) and the Centers for Disease Control and Prevention (CDC) cosponsored a conference titled Patients and Populations—Public Health in Medical

Education. The *American Journal of Preventive Medicine* devoted an entire supplement in 2011 to papers presented at the conference; many describe progress in the integration of public health into the medical school curriculum (Maeshiro, Koo, and Keck, 2011). Other health professions also are realigning with public health in mutually beneficial ways.

For most of the nineteenth century, medicine lacked basic and lifesaving tools, such as anesthesia and antibiotics, and knowledge such as germ theory. Advances in public health practices extended the average life expectancy during the twentieth century (Centers for Disease Control and Prevention, 1999). Medicine in the twentieth century saw the rise of effective use of pharmaceuticals, successful organ transplantation, and amazing imaging modalities, among many other advances. The education of health care professionals necessarily became increasingly scientific, specialized, and credentialed. In general, health professionals are now graduates of accredited academic programs who have studied the scientific foundations of their field as well as had patient care experience before becoming eligible to take a licensing examination and practice.

Modern Efforts in Health Sciences Educational Reform

Acquiring medical knowledge and skill has always been a challenge. "Life is short, and the art is long" is a quote attributed to Hippocrates. Post–World War II saw a tremendous increase in scientific discovery. Widespread use of information technology since the mid-1900s greatly expanded the amount of information and knowledge available. What health sciences students need to know and how they can best learn it have been the impetus of debate for decades.

As noted above, the Flexner Report and its recommendations set the stage for medical education in the twentieth century. Ironically, Flexner's report was used to support the emphasis of scientific research in medicine, but his own words describe more an integration of the scientific approach and the practice of medicine. This quote, from the 1910 report, could appear today in an article about the importance of lifelong learning:

> The progress of science and the scientific or intelligent practice of medicine employ, therefore, exactly the same technique. To use it, whether in investigation or in practice, the student must be trained to the positive exercise of his faculties; and if so trained, the medical school begins rather than completes his medical education. . . the teacher . . . seeks to evoke the attitude, and to carry him through the process, of the thinker and not of the parrot. (Flexner, 1910b: 55)

In 1910, Flexner criticized the almost exclusive use of didactic lectures in medical schools. Traditionally, students spend many hours in lecture to first learn basic sciences, after which they are allowed to see patients and acquire clinical skills. In 1984, the Association of American Medical Colleges issued *Physicians for the Twenty-First Century. The GPEP Report: Report of the Panel on the General Professional Education of the Physician and College Preparation for Medicine* (AAMC, 1984). Among many recommendations, the panel addressed reducing scheduled time and lecture hours, promoting independent learning and problem solving, and incorporating information sciences.

An underlying theme of educational reform is that it is impossible to learn all of medicine in medical school. This problem was recognized by many observers during the 1950s and 1960s. As just one example, former dean of the Medical School at Harvard University Sydney Burwell told his dinner audience, "My students are dismayed when I say to them, 'Half of what you are taught as medical students will in 10 years have been shown to be wrong. And the trouble is, none of your teachers knows which half'" (Pickering, 1956).

The volume of information has become far more overwhelming, and the knowledge base continuously changes as the result of updated research. What a student learns as fact in lecture may no longer be true a few years later in practice. Entirely new fields, such as genomics and molecular medicine, evolve during a professional's life span. All health professionals must continuously learn, which means that they must master the skills of lifelong learning in order to remain current in their professional practice. The emphasis on EBP underscores the need for lifelong learning skills. Librarians' involvement in EBP was mentioned earlier in this chapter and is further discussed in chapters 3 and 11.

Since the *GPEP Report* and other calls for educational reform appeared, curriculum committees have struggled with attempts to improve and evaluate educational programs that incorporate the skills and behaviors of problem solving and self-directed learning. At the same time, debate continues about what constitutes necessary and fundamental knowledge. Many medical schools cut back on the number of lectures and incorporated alternative methods for learning that are less passive and more active. Chapter 3 addresses active learning in more detail.

Forty years later, much has been attempted, but many of the major problems related to knowledge acquisition identified in the *GPEP Report* remain. A recent study found that, at one medical school, faculty assigned 29,239 pages of reading over a seventy-one-week period. The authors estimated it would take students twenty-eight to forty-one hours per week to read the assigned material once (Klatt and Klatt, 2011). A 2005 review of studies relating medical knowledge and health care quality to years in practice and physician age concluded that performance decreased with increasing years in practice, indicating a lack of continuous learning by practitioners (Choudhry, Fletcher, and Soumerai, 2005).

In addition to the need to keep up to date with current knowledge, there is widespread agreement that health professionals must be skilled clinicians, competent communicators, productive team members, sensitive to cultural context, ethical professionals, and good stewards of resources. To address all of these goals poses an enormous challenge. In 1978, the World Health Organization (WHO) issued a report titled *Competency-Based Curriculum Development in Medical Education*. The report explained the core problem facing medical schools:

> On the one hand, there is a legitimate expectation that graduates will be proficient in the latest and most advanced techniques for preserving health and managing disease. This expectation is coupled with the belief that a thorough foundation in the basic and clinical sciences is a fundamental prerequisite for achieving that goal. On the other hand, concern for assuring academic quality in these sciences must not divert attention from the competence required to meet the real health needs of people. It is a rare school that has seemed successful in resolving this dilemma. (McGaghie et al., 1978: 11)

For most of the twentieth century, health sciences education consisted of a set curriculum including lectures, laboratories, and clinical experience; assessment was primarily in the form of written standardized tests and observation of clinical performance. The WHO report identified three possible approaches to curricula change:

> The most common method of curriculum change has been to revise content while preserving the subject-centred structure. Two major alternatives also demand a wider hearing. The first is an integrated programme model where learning and teaching attempt to fuse formerly separate medical disciplines by using, for example, organ systems or medical problems as the organizing structure. The second arranges learning and teaching around the functional elements of medical practice. Because the emphasis is on learning how to practise medicine, not on accumulating knowledge about medical practices, it is called competency-based. (1978: 13)

Competency-based education is a concept that reframes what it means to complete an educational program. Objective demonstration of specified knowledge and skills by students is emphasized. In a recent systematic review of competency-based education literature in the health sciences, Frank et al. propose the following definition:

> Competency-based education (CBE) is an approach to preparing physicians for practice that is fundamentally oriented to graduate outcome abilities and organized around competencies derived from an analysis of societal and patient needs. It deemphasizes time-based training and promises greater accountability, flexibility, and learner centredness. (2010: 636)

As a clinical librarian working closely with resident physicians, I find the Accreditation Council for Graduate Medical Education (ACGME) Core Competencies are closely tied to library information concepts. Specifically, the Practice-Based Learning and Improvement (PBLI) competency encourages skill development in locating and appraising evidence, which is what medical librarians teach.

—*Sarah Knox Morley, MLS, AHIP, clinical services librarian, University of New Mexico, Health Sciences Library & Informatics Center, Albuquerque*

Forty years of discussion have led to the adoption of core competencies, or measurable outcomes, for each of the various clinical professions. Competencies are broadly defined with input from professional associations and accreditation, licensing, and certification agencies. Conceivably, in the future, students will move through a curriculum individually by demonstrating competencies rather than attending courses and taking exams as a group.

As educators began to address lifelong learning-related competencies, they looked to librarians as experts in teaching these skills. Other chapters in this book delineate the many ways librarians participate as members of curriculum committees and instructors. Eldredge and colleagues (2012) inventoried library/informatics competency statements of various health professions, https://repository.unm.edu/handle/1928/15363, as an aid for librarians who want to integrate skills training into the various curricula.

Mention of library/informatics competencies leads naturally to a discussion of health care informatics, a relatively new field that intersects with library and information science.

Health Care Informatics

Information, information technology, and information management are essential tools for implementing needed changes in health care. The impact of computer and telecommunications technology on the growth, organization, dissemination, and use of information cannot be underestimated; this ongoing revolution in information is both exciting and unsettling. The term informatics broadly labels a multidisciplinary field that encompasses the study and use of information and information technology. It helps to think of informatics as the intersection of information science and computer science, technology, and a specific discipline, as illustrated in Figure 2.2. Friedman (2013) recently proposed other models to help define what informatics is—and what it isn't. This is a discipline that relates to library and information science, and it is important that health sciences librarians be aware of health informatics initiatives and conversant with practitioners in this emerging field.

Different disciplines use and organize information differently. For example, the historian, who relies on historic records and primary sources, might spend weeks thoroughly poring over correspondence, source documents, or local news sources. Contrast this approach to that of the health practitioner, who requires speedy retrieval of current research information. The resulting informatics activities in the field of history differ considerably from the activities in health sciences informatics. Health care informatics includes many different topics and activities, a few of which are discussed, with examples.

Librarians and informaticians are both concerned with the fundamentals of information organization and exchange. Developing standardized vocabularies, improving information retrieval, identifying technical protocols for electronic transfer and reuse of information are of interest to both fields, although the kinds of items each

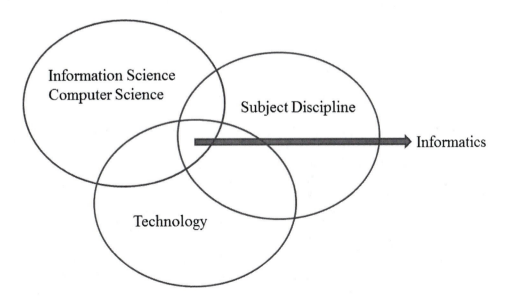

Figure 2.2. Informatics at the Intersection of Information Science, Technology, and Specific Subject Domain.

focuses on may differ. Librarians have mostly dealt with published materials; health informatics specialists often work with health information in the form of records, registries, images, and so forth.

Electronic health records systems, discussed earlier in the chapter, continue to be a focus of informatics activity with new initiatives related to optimizing the use of what had previously existed in separate records consisting of pieces of paper. For example, computerized records can show trend data for a patient's laboratory results, and can provide the clinician, researcher, and institution with an overview of performance in treating a specific disease in many patients.

Medical imaging technology provides digitized visual information that can be enhanced, interpreted, and combined with other information, including other images. In addition to opening a new window to anatomy, physiology, and disease process, how images are generated, interpreted, organized, and repurposed is a developing field in itself.

Students in the health professions now interact with simulated patients and use decision aids. People who design these simulations and decision aids must incorporate a knowledge base, technical expertise, human factors, and a deep understanding of what these systems can and cannot achieve in terms of affecting learning and behavior.

The Internet is radically changing how people relate and learn. People use the Internet to find health information, share their experiences with others via social media, and send e-mail to their health care providers. Health informatics research seeks to understand the impact of these online activities.

Information science is integral to the field of informatics. Library practice intersects with many aspects of informatics practice, including in the areas of education, information management, and information dissemination. Health sciences librarians should participate in the growing field of health informatics; they can do so by learning more about it and collaborating as appropriate. In their book, *Health Informatics for Medical Librarians*, Cleveland and Cleveland (2009) provide a more in-depth description of the ways in which librarians can and should be involved.

BIOMEDICAL RESEARCH

The Research Process

Research constitutes much of the literature and information in the biomedical and health sciences and forms the basis of evidence in evidence-based practice. Most of this research is categorized as either "basic science (bench) research" or "clinical investigation." It is easy to think of clinical investigation as research involving humans, and basic science research as everything else (e.g., cellular level processes, animal studies). This dichotomy is an oversimplification. Public health researchers often conduct community-based research. Health care research also encompasses the study of education, economics, and other topics. Social sciences methodologies often apply. Traditionally, the research process typically follows a standard process including establishing a question or hypothesis; reviewing the literature; designing a study using valid methods; collecting and analyzing data; and reporting results, preferably in a peer-reviewed journal. Newer methods, especially those used in community-based research, employ more iterative investigative designs, gather qualitative as well as quantitative input, and involve those studied as full participants in the process rather than as just subjects of study.

Animal studies often precede studies involving humans for safety and efficacy reasons. Clinical research studies involving human experimentation (e.g., testing a new drug or procedure) are called clinical trials and categorized by phases as follows:

- Phase I: Researchers test a new drug or treatment in a small group of people for the first time to evaluate its safety, determine a safe dosage range, and identify side effects;
- Phase II: The drug or treatment is given to a larger group of people to see if it is effective and to further evaluate its safety;
- Phase III: The drug or treatment is given to large groups of people to confirm its effectiveness, monitor side effects, compare it to commonly used treatments, and collect information that will allow the drug or treatment to be used safely;
- Phase IV: Studies are done after the drug or treatment has been marketed to gather information on the drug's effect in various populations and any side effects associated with long-term use (U.S. National Library of Medicine, 2008).

Research is an ongoing conversation resulting in new knowledge. The volume of research information can be overwhelming. According to a recent PubMed search, nearly 4,000 articles were published about the cause of rheumatoid arthritis in just the past five years. Not all of those articles reported research, not all of the research reported was necessarily valid, and not all of the results of the valid research are applicable in the clinical setting. But some results could have significant impact. How to identify these is a goal of translational research.

"Translational research" describes the efforts to make important results of research available to benefit human health. "Big science" identifies large-scale projects requiring significant funding, often at the national or international level. "E-science" refers to collaborative efforts requiring access to large data sets. Chapter 3 explores these topics further.

Funding

The National Institutes of Health (NIH), www.nih.gov, is the world's largest funding source for biomedical research. Researchers applying for funding will ask librarians to identify the literature relevant to their grant proposals because investigators must describe existing knowledge and demonstrate the importance of the proposed study. Funding announcements often give researchers no more than a matter of weeks to prepare an entire research proposal and logistical plan. Funding deadlines are firm; requests for literature searches are often urgent. A grant proposal's literature review contributes to a researcher's success or failure in securing funds, and health sciences librarians can play a vital role in this process.

Research involving humans and other animals is highly regulated. The Federal Wide Assurance (FWA) for the Protection of Human Subjects, www.hhs.gov/ohrp/assurances/assurances/filasurt.html, mandates adherence to established ethical principles. The Federal Animal Welfare Act (AWA) regulates "treatment of animals in research, exhibition, transport, and by dealers" (USDA, 2013). Plans for research must be approved by an Institutional Review Board (IRB) for studies involving humans and by an Institutional Animal Care and Use Committee (IACUC) for studies involving animals. These institutional review committees protect subjects from harm, physical and psychological. Many journals require authors to include a statement about prior institutional approval of their research in their manuscripts.

Institutions that conduct research using animals may appoint a librarian to search for information about alternatives to animal models, methods for reducing animal pain or stress, and techniques for improving animal well-being. Keefer and Westbrook (1995–1996) wrote about the role of the librarian in this context.

Publication

An important component of the research process is the dissemination of results. A core role of librarians has been to collect and make available authoritative health sciences knowledge, much of it in journal form.

John Shaw Billings directed the U.S. Surgeon General's Library from 1865 to 1895; he was intimately involved in the formation of what later became the National Library of Medicine (NLM). In 1879, he published *Index Medicus*, the first comprehensive index of journal articles in the library's collection (Chapman, 1994). Billings could hardly have imagined that *Index Medicus* would evolve into today's MEDLINE database. The 1880 *Index Medicus* volume contains an estimated 22,248 citations (Greenberg and Gallagher, 2009); in 2013, MEDLINE included more than nineteen million citations (U.S. National Library of Medicine, 2013).

Research publication and its dissemination continue to evolve. Electronic access to full-text articles and electronic-only publications are two major changes in format. The open access movement promotes free access to electronic publications, greatly increasing the availability of content. The NIH now requires NIH-funded researchers to deposit resulting publications in PubMed Central, a free digital archive of published biomedical and life sciences journal literature managed by the National Library of Medicine. In institutions with a wealth of electronic resources, the role of librarian as mediator of access to the literature at the individual level may have decreased, but the librarian's role in making available and managing electronic resources at the institutional level has become increasingly complex, important, and visible.

Research reports follow the fairly standard format of purpose, background, literature review, methods, and results. Busy clinicians do not have enough time to read all of the research reports pertinent to their practice. For much of the twentieth century, the narrative review article attempted to summarize the causes, diagnoses, and treatments for a disease or cluster of diseases. Journal editors solicited recognized experts to write narrative review articles as a way to update textbook information, and readers appreciated narrative reviews because they summarized and interpreted complicated aspects of diseases. But narrative reviews on the same disease frequently contradicted one another, and they offered few clues as to what literature the authors had consulted and how the authors had reached their conclusions. A different type of review, called a **systematic review**, has become more highly regarded and prevalent.

Systematic reviews summarize the current best evidence. They are valuable because they identify relevant studies that address a similar question, apply rigorous methods of selection, organize the results, and provide a current answer to a specific question based on the best scientific evidence at the time (Mulrow and Cook, 1998). The completed systematic review guides clinicians in making evidence-based decisions. Librarians have a definite role in the comprehensive identification of relevant studies needed for systematic reviews (Harris, 2005). The Institute of Medicine's (IOM) standards for systematic reviews recommend that authors "work with a librarian or other information specialist trained in performing systematic reviews to plan the search strategy" (Eden et al., 2011: 8).

Meta-analyses combine the results of similar research studies with identical or near-identical data sets to increase the statistical strength of the combined results. A meta-analysis relies upon the compatibility, or homogeneity, of the data sets (Rosenthal, 1991). Sometimes a systematic review includes a meta-analysis (the statistical combination of data sets). Unfortunately, this practice has led some to incorrectly equate "meta-analysis" with "systematic review," when, in fact, not all systematic reviews include this special form of data synthesis. Examples of each of these types of articles on the same topic can be found in the sidebar (shown in MEDLINE/PubMed format).

Most research publications report the summarized results of analyzed data. The original data, often acquired with considerable effort and expense, typically languish in a computer or file cabinet. Electronic files enable researchers more easily to

EXAMPLES OF TYPES OF ARTICLES

Research Report

Lewin MH, Bailey N, Bandaletova T, Bowman R, Cross AJ, Pollock J, Shuker DE, Bingham SA. Red meat enhances the colonic formation of the DNA adductO6-carboxymethyl guanine: implications for colorectal cancer risk. Cancer Res. 2006 Feb 1;66(3):1859-65.

Traditional/Narrative Review

Fraser GE. Vegetarian diets: what do we know of their effects on common chronic diseases? Am J Clin Nutr. 2009 May; 89(5):1607S-1612S.

Systematic Review

Streuling I, Beyerlein A, Rosenfeld E, Schukat B, von Kries R. Weight gain and dietary intake during pregnancy in industrialized countries—a systematic review of observational studies. J Perinat Med. 2011 Mar; 39(2):123-9.

Systematic Review with Meta-analysis

Huang T, Yang B, Zheng J, Li G, Wahlqvist ML, Li D. Cardiovascular disease mortality and cancer incidence in vegetarians: a meta-analysis and systematic review. Ann Nutr Metab. 2012; 60(4):233-40.

reuse and share these data, which can be repurposed or combined with other data to contribute to further analyses and research. Librarians are becoming involved in supporting researchers through data management and data curation initiatives (Gore, 2011). E-science was mentioned above, and chapters 3 and 10 go into more detail about those roles.

HEALTH AND GLOBAL HEALTH

Two other topics deserve attention in a chapter about the health care environment. They are health and global health.

Health

Health is more than the absence of disease. According to the WHO, "health is a state of complete physical, mental and social well-being and not merely the absence of disease or infirmity" (WHO, 1948). Health care in the United States has been primarily focused on disease. The movement to incorporate public health into the medical school curriculum, discussed earlier in this chapter, is an acknowledgment of this imbalance.

The Healthy People project is an interagency effort to improve the nation's health through health promotion and disease prevention. For more than thirty years, the project has developed health objectives and measured progress in areas such as risk behaviors, screening, and social indicators. Healthy People 2020 identifies approximately 600 objectives with 1,200 measures. Statistics from census sources and surveys are available at the national, state, and county levels for health indicators such as poverty, water quality, and mental health (HealthyPeople.gov, 2013). These objectives guide the development of state and community plans.

Health promotion and disease prevention go hand in hand. The Centers for Disease Control and Prevention (CDC), www.cdc.gov/, collects and disseminates a wealth of information about the nation's health. According to the CDC, "four modifiable health risk behaviors—lack of physical activity, poor nutrition, tobacco use, and excessive alcohol consumption—are responsible for much of the illness, suffering, and early death related to chronic diseases" (CDC, 2009: 5). The U.S. Preventive Services Task Force (USPSTF) is an independent panel of experts that reviews scientific evidence and develops recommendations about preventive health care services, including screening and counseling (U.S. Preventive Services Task Force— www.uspreventiveservicestaskforce.org/). USPSTF's goal is "to make accurate, up-to-date, and relevant recommendations about preventive services in primary care" (U.S. Preventive Services Task Force, 2013).

Global Health

U.S. health care and health exist in the context of world, or global, health. AIDS, the 2003 SARS epidemic, and the H1N1 influenza in 2009 got international attention and response. People, animals, food—and disease—travel more quickly than ever before. Approximately 70 percent of emerging and reemerging infections originate in or are transmitted by animals (One Health Initiative, 2013a). WHO member countries are required to report potential public health emergencies of international concern that might lead to the spread of disease (WHO, 2005).

One Health is an international initiative with the vision of "improving the lives of all species—human and animal—through the integration of human medicine, veterinary medicine and environmental science" (One Health Initiative, 2013b). Notably, in 2013, the Medical Library Association (MLA), the International Congress on Medical Librarianship (ICML), the International Conference of Animal Health Information Specialists (ICAHIS), and the International Clinical Librarian Conference (ICLC) joined together in a meeting titled "One Health: Information in an Interdependent World" to underscore global information interdependency.

The Medical Library Association is an active participant in Librarians without Borders, an international effort to address information inequity. MLA's Librarians without Borders program provides training in information retrieval and "helps provide medical information for healthcare personnel responding to epidemics and natural and man-made disasters anywhere in the world" (MLA, 2013).

Epidemics, human-made catastrophes such as war, and natural disasters such as earthquakes threaten health and well-being and require coordinated, international response. Data collection and analysis, research that results in new knowledge, and information that is organized and disseminated to address immediate needs are critical components of the many complex systems involved in health and health care today. The National Library of Medicine has taken a lead in this area with its Disaster Information Management Research Center (DIMRC), with acknowledgment of the various roles librarians and libraries can assume in times of crisis.

> One Health: Information in an Interdependent World was an opportunity to bring together the world's health sciences librarians to focus on a theme encompassing the information aspects of human and animal health, public health, environmental health, climate change, food safety/production, and international policy in a federated international meeting format. The information connotation of the "one health" theme sought to emphasize interdisciplinary and international collaboration and global interdependencies in all health-related areas.
>
> —*J. Michael Homan, MA, AHIP, director of libraries, Mayo Clinic and Mayo Clinic College of Medicine, Rochester, MN*

SUMMARY

The intent of this chapter was to provide a realistic overview of today's health care environment. By all accounts, U.S. health care is in crisis. On the positive side, the health care field is growing and getting a lot of attention. As information specialists, health sciences librarians make important contributions in many ways, as will be illustrated in the following chapters.

Despite discouraging statistics, political wrangling, and limited resources, efforts continue to improve health—individually, nationally, and worldwide. The opportunity to participate in such an important endeavor is a privilege. Understanding the health sciences environment enhances a librarian's ability to meet the information needs of practitioners, students, and researchers and to become a valued and productive member of the health care team.

STUDY QUESTIONS

1. Select a health care topic that interests you. Go to http://PubMed.gov and access the MeSH Database. Identify the MeSH term that has a definition that matches your topic. Click on the link under your MeSH term to reveal a detailed display with subheadings. Click one subheading. It will be immediately combined with the MeSH term. Run your search. In three separate steps, filter your search by clinical trial, a narrative review article, and a systematic review article related to that topic. How do the references differ from one another when using these three different filters? Read the abstracts. Describe how these articles differ in their stated objectives. (Hint: Use PubMed's Filters feature.)
2. Reflect on your own professional education. Compare and contrast characteristics of health professional education described in this chapter with your experience.
3. Think about you or a family member's recent experience with the health care system. What kind of information was involved? Was it easy for the patient to understand and use the information provided? Where did the patient or family seek information beyond what was provided by the health professional? How satisfactory was the experience from the point of view of trying to make informed decisions?

REFERENCES

AAMC (American Association of Medical Colleges). 1984. "Physicians for the Twenty-first Century. Report of the Project Panel on the General Professional Education of the Physician and College Preparation for Medicine." *Journal of Medical Education* 59, no. 11 (pt. 2) (November): 1–208.

American Journal of Preventive Medicine. 2011. 41, no. 4 (supplement 3, October).

American Medical Association Foundation. 2007. *Health Literacy and Patient Safety: Help Patients Understand. Reducing the Risk by Designing a Safer, Shame-Free Health Care Environment.* Chicago: AMA. www.ama-assn.org/ama1/pub/upload/mm/367/hl_monograph.pdf.

ASAHP (Association of Schools of Allied Health Professions). 2013. "Definition of Allied Health." Accessed August 11. www.asahp.org/definition.htm.

Bezruchka, Stephen. 2012. "The Hurrier I Go the Behinder I Get: The Deteriorating International Ranking of U.S. Health Status." *Annual Review of Public Health* 33 (April): 157–73.

Brondolo, Elizabeth, Erica E. Love, Melissa Pencille, Antoinette Schoenthaler, and Gbenga Ogedegbe. 2011. "Racism and Hypertension: A Review of the Empirical Evidence and Implications for Clinical Practice." *American Journal of Hypertension* 24, no. 5 (May): 518–29.

Burke, Taylor. 2010. "The Health Information Technology Provisions in the American Recovery and Reinvestment Act of 2009: Implications for Public Health Policy and Practice." *Public Health Reports* 125, no. 1 (January–February): 141–45.

CDC (Centers for Disease Control and Prevention). 1999. "Ten Great Public Health Achievements—United States, 1900–1999." *MMWR Morbidity and Mortality Weekly Report* 48, no. 12 (April 2): 241–43.

———. 2012. "Chronic Disease Prevention and Health Promotion." Last updated August 12. www.cdc.gov/chronicdisease/overview/index.htm.

———. National Center for Chronic Disease Prevention and Health Promotion. 2009. The Power of Prevention. Chronic Disease . . . the Public Health Challenge of the 21st Century. www.cdc.gov/chronicdisease/pdf/2009-power-of-prevention.pdf.

Centers for Medicare & Medicaid Services. 2013. "National Health Expenditure Data. NHE Fact Sheet Historical NHE, including Sponsor Analysis, 2011." Last modified January 3. www.cms.gov/Research-Statistics-Data-and-Systems/Statistics-Trends-and-Reports/NationalHealthExpendData/NHE-Fact-Sheet.html.

Central Intelligence Agency. 2013. *The World Factbook 2013–14*. www.cia.gov/library/publications/the-world-factbook/rankorder/2091rank.html.

Chapman, Carleton B. 1994. *Order out of Chaos: John Shaw Billings and America's Coming of Age*. Boston: Boston Medical Library.

Choudhry Niteesh, K., Robert H. Fletcher, and Stephen B. Soumerai. 2005. "Systematic Review: The Relationship between Clinical Experience and Quality of Health Care." *Annals of Internal Medicine* 142, no. 4 (February 15): 260–73.

Cleveland, Ana D., and Donald B. Cleveland. 2009. *Health Informatics for Medical Librarians*. New York: Neal-Schuman Publishers.

Damani, Shamsha, and Stephanie Fulton. 2010. "Collaborating and Delivering Literature Search Results to Clinical Teams Using Web 2.0 Tools." *Medical Reference Services Quarterly* 29, no. 3 (July–September): 207–17.

Doherty, Robert B. 2010. "The Certitudes and Uncertainties of Health Care Reform." *Annals of Internal Medicine* 152, no. 10 (May 18): 679–82.

Downing, Gregory J., Scott N. Boyle, Kristin M. Brinner, and Jerome A. Osheroff. 2009. "Information Management to Enable Personalized Medicine: Stakeholder Roles in Building Clinical Decision Support." *BMC Medical Informatics and Decision Making* 9 (October 8): 44. www.biomedcentral.com/content/pdf/1472-6947-9-44.pdf.

Eberhart, George M. 2013. "The Prescription for Finding Healthcare Information." *American librariesmagazine.org* (blog). www.americanlibrariesmagazine.org/blog/prescription-finding-healthcare-information.

Eden, Jill, Laura Levit, Alfred Berg, and Sally Morton, eds. 2011. *Finding What Works in Health Care: Standards for Systematic Reviews*. Washington, DC: National Academies Press.

Eldredge, Jonathan D., Sarah K. Morley, Ingrid C. Hendrix, Richard D. Carr, and Jason Bengtson. 2012. "Library and Informatics Skills Competencies Statements from Major Health Professional Associations." *Medical Reference Services Quarterly* 31, no. 1 (January–March): 34–44.

Epperly, Ted. 2011. "The Patient-Centred Medical Home in the USA." *Journal of Evaluation in Clinical Practice* 17, no. 2 (April): 373–75.

Epstein, Barbara A., Nancy H. Tannery, Charles B. Wessel, Frances Yarger, John LaDue, and Anthony B. Fiorillo. 2010. "Development of a Clinical Information Tool for the Electronic Medical Record: A Case Study." *Journal of the Medical Library Association* 98, no. 3 (July): 223–27.

Flexner, Abraham. 1910a. "Medical Education in America. Rethinking the Training of American Doctors." *The Atlantic*. June 1. www.theatlantic.com/magazine/archive/1910/06/medical-education-in-america/306088/.

———. 1910b. *Medical Education in the United States and Canada. A Report to the Carnegie Foundation for the Advancement of Teaching*. Bulletin no. 4. Boston: Updyke. www.carnegiefoundation.org/sites/default/files/elibrary/Carnegie_Flexner_Report.pdf.

Frank, Jason R., Rani Mungroo, Yasmine Ahmad, Mimi Wang, Stephanie De Rossi, and Tanya Horsley, Jr. 2010. "Toward a Definition of Competency-based Education in Medicine: A Systematic Review of Published Definitions." *Medical Teacher* 32, no. 8: 631–37.

Friedman, Charles P. 2013. "What Informatics Is and Isn't." *Journal of the American Medical Informatics Association* 20, no. 2 (March–April): 224–26.

Friedman, Charles P., Adam K. Wong, and David Blumenthal. 2010. "Achieving a Nation-wide Learning Health System." *Science Translational Medicine* 2, no. 57: 57cm29. http://stm.sciencemag.org/content/2/57/57cm29.full.

Galbraith, Kyle L. 2013. "What's So Meaningful about Meaningful Use?" *Hastings Center Report* 43, no. 2 (March–April): 15–17.

Geiger, H. Jack. 1983. "An Overdose of Power and Money." *New York Times Book Review*, January 9. www.nytimes.com/books/98/12/06/specials/starr-medicine.html.

Ginsburg, Geoffrey S., and Huntington F. Willard. 2009. "Genomic and Personalized Medicine: Foundations and Applications." *Translational Research: The Journal of Laboratory and Clinical Medicine* 154, no. 6 (December): 277–87.

Giuse, Nunzia B., Annette M. Williams, and Dario A. Giuse. 2010. "Integrating Best Evidence into Patient Care: A Process Facilitated by a Seamless Integration with Informatics Tools." *Journal of the Medical Library Association* 98, no. 3 (July): 220–22.

Gore, Sally A. 2011. "e-Science and Data Management Resources on the Web." *Medical Reference Services Quarterly* 30, no. 2 (April–June): 167–77.

Greenberg, Stephen J., and Patricia E. Gallagher. 2009. "The Great Contribution: *Index Medicus, Index-Catalogue*, and IndexCat." *Journal of the Medical Library Association* 97, no. 2 (April): 108–13.

Greene, Sarah M., Leah Tuzzio, and Dan Cherkin. 2012. "A Framework for Making Patient-Centered Care Front and Center." *The Permanente Journal* 16, no. 3 (Summer): 49–53.

Greiner, Ann C., and Elisa Knebel, eds., and Committee on the Health Professions Education Summit. National Research Council. 2003. *Health Professions Education: A Bridge to Quality.* Washington, DC: National Academies Press. www.nap.edu/catalog/10681.html.

Hansen, Luke O., Robert S. Young, Keiki Hinami, Alicia Leung, and Mark V. Williams. 2011. "Interventions to Reduce 30-Day Rehospitalization: A Systematic Review." *Annals of Internal Medicine* 155, no. 8 (October 18): 520–28.

Harris, Martha R. 2005. "The Librarian's Roles in the Systematic Reviews Process: A Case Study." *Journal of the Medical Library Association* 93, no. 1 (January): 81–87.

HealthyPeople.gov. 2013. "Home page." Last updated July 30. www.healthypeople.gov/2020/default.aspx.

Institute of Medicine. 1988. *The Future of Public Health.* Washington, DC: National Academies Press.

Institute of Medicine. Committee on Quality of Health Care in America. 2001. *Crossing the Quality Chasm: A New Health System for the 21st Century.* Washington, DC: National Academies Press.

Keefer, Elaine, and Fred Westbrook. 1995–1996. "The Role of the Librarian in the Work of the Institutional Animal Care and Use Committee (IACUC)." *Animal Welfare Information Center Newsletter* 6, no. 2–4. www.nal.usda.gov/awic/newsletters/v6n2/6n2keefe.htm.

Kirch, Darrell G., Mackenzie K. Henderson, and Michael J. Dill. 2012. "Physician Workforce Projections in an Era of Health Care Reform." *Annual Review of Medicine* 63: 435–45.

Klatt, Edward C., and Carolyn A. Klatt. 2011. "How Much Is Too Much Reading for Medical Students? Assigned Reading and Reading Rates at One Medical School." *Academic Medicine* 86, no. 9 (September): 1079–83.

Kohn, Linda T., Janet M. Corrigan, and Molla S. Donaldson, eds. 2000. *To Err Is Human: Building a Safer Health System.* Washington, DC: National Academies Press. www.nap.edu/catalog.php?record_id=9728.

Lecca, Pedro J., Peggy Valentine, and Kevin Lyons, eds. 2003. *Allied Health: Practice Issues and Trends in the New Millennium.* New York: Haworth Press.

Lyon, Jennifer, Nunzia Bettinsoli Giuse, Annette Williams, Taneya Koonce, and Rachel Walden. 2004. "A Model for Training the New Bioinformationist." *Journal of the Medical Library Association* 92, no. 2 (April): 188–95.

Maeshiro, Rika, Denise Koo, and C. William Keck. 2011. "Patients and Polulations: Public Health in Medical Education." *American Journal of Preventive Medicine* 41, no. 4 (suppl. 3, October): A1-6, S145-S318.

Marshall, Joanne Gard, Julia Sollenberger, Sharon Easterby-Gannett et al. 2013. "The Value of Library and Information Services in Patient Care: Results of a Multisite Study." *Journal of the Medical Library Association* 101, no. 1 (January): 38–46.

Mauersberger, Brian. 2012. "Tracking Employment-Based Health Benefits in Changing Times." U.S. Department of Labor. Bureau of Labor Statistics. Compensation and Working Conditions. January 27. www.bls.gov/opub/cwc/cm20120125ar01p1.htm.

McGaghie, William C., George E. Miller, Abdul W. Sajid, and Thomas V. Telder. 1978. *Competency-Based Curriculum Development in Medical Education: An Introduction.* Geneva: World Health Organization. http://whqlibdoc.who.int/php/ WHO_PHP_68.pdf.

MLA (Medical Library Association). 2009. *Role of Health Sciences Librarians in Patient Safety Position Statement.* www.mlanet.org/government/positions/patient-safety.html.

———. 2013. "Librarians without Borders." Accessed July 29. www.mlanet.org/resources/global/.

Mulrow, Cynthia, and Deborah Cook, eds. 1998. *Systematic Reviews: Synthesis of Best Evidence for Health Care Decisions.* Philadelphia: American College of Physicians.

National Research Council and Institute of Medicine. 2013. *U.S. Health in International Perspective: Shorter Lives, Poorer Health. Panel on Understanding Cross-National Health Differences among High-Income Countries,* edited by Steven H. Woolf and Laudan Aron. Committee on Population, Division of Behavioral and Social Sciences and Education, and Board on Population Health and Public Health Practice, Institute of Medicine. Washington, DC: National Academies Press. https://download.nap.edu/catalog.php?record_id=13497.

O'Callaghan, Kathryn M. 2009. "Solutions for Disparities for Women with Heart Disease." *Journal of Cardiovascular Translational Research* 2, no. 4 (December): 518–25.

OECD. (Organisation for Economic Co-operation and Development). 2013. "Health Policies and Data. OECD Health Data 2013—Frequently Requested Data." Accessed July 26. www.oecd.org/els/health-systems/oecdhealthdata2013-frequentlyrequesteddata.htm.

One Health Initiative. 2013a. "One Health Initiative Will Unite Human and Veterinary Medicine." Accessed July 29. www.onehealthinitiative.com/index.php.

———. 2013b. "Vision Statement." Accessed July 29. www.onehealthinitiative.com/mission.php.

Pickering, G. W. 1956. "The Purpose of Medical Education." *British Medical Journal* 2, no. 4985 (July 21): 113–16.

Public Law 111–148. 111th Congress. 2d sess. 2010. Patient Protection and Affordable Care Act. March 23. www.gpo.gov/fdsys/pkg/PLAW-111publ148/pdf/PLAW-111publ148.pdf.

Purnell, Tanjala S., Yoshio N. Hall, and L. Ebony Boulware. 2012. "Understanding and Overcoming Barriers to Living Kidney Donation among Racial and Ethnic Minorities in the United States." *Advances in Chronic Kidney Disease* 19, no. 4 (July): 244–51.

Rosenthal, Robert. 1991. *Meta-Analytic Procedures for Social Research,* rev. ed. Newbury Park, CA: Sage Publications.

Ruis, A. R., and Robert N. Golden. 2008. "The Schism between Medical and Public Health Education: A Historical Perspective." *Academic Medicine* 83, no. 12 (December): 1153–57.

Saha, Somnath, Mary Catherine Beach, and Lisa A. Cooper. 2008. "Patient Centeredness, Cultural Competence and Healthcare Quality." *Journal of the National Medical Association* 100, no. 11: 1275–85.

Schmitt, Madeline, Amy Blue, Carol A. Aschenbrenner, and Thomas R. Viggiano. 2011. "Core Competencies for Interprofessional Collaborative Practice: Reforming Health Care by Transforming Health Professionals' Education." *Academic Medicine* 86, no. 11 (November): 1351.

Schriefer, Jan, and Michael S. Leonard. 2012. "Patient Safety and Quality Improvement: An Overview of QI." *Pediatrics in Review* 33, no. 8 (August): 353–59.

Shaw-Daigle, C., L. Giles-Smith, and M. Raynard. 2011. "What Your Patient Reads: Creating a Value-Added Tool for Physicians." *Medical Reference Services Quarterly* 30, no. 3 (July–September): 213–20.

Sherer, Jill L. 1993. "Putting Patients First: Hospitals Work to Define Patient-Centered Care." *Hospitals* 67, no. 3 (February 5): 14–24, 26.

Shrestha, Laura B., and Elayne J. Heisler. 2011. *The Changing Demographic Profile of the United States.* Congressional Research Service. March 31. www.fas.org/sgp/crs/misc/RL32701.pdf.

Starr, Paul. 1982. *The Social Transformation of American Medicine.* New York: Basic Books.

U.S. Department of Commerce. 2013. "The Health and Medical Technology Industry in the United States. The U.S. Healthcare Industry." SelectUSA. Accessed July 26. http://selectusa .commerce.gov/industry-snapshots/health-and-medical-technology-industry-united-states.

U.S. National Library of Medicine. 2008. "FAQ. ClinicalTrials.gov-Clinical Trial Phases." Last updated April 18. www.nlm.nih.gov/services/ctphases.html.

———. 2013. "Fact Sheet MEDLINE®." Last updated February 20. www.nlm.nih.gov/pubs/ factsheets/medline.html.

U.S. Preventive Services Task Force. 2013. "Home page." Accessed September 5. www .uspreventiveservicestaskforce.org/.

USDA (U.S. Department of Agriculture). 2013. "Animal Welfare Act." National Agricultural Library. Last modified August 9. http://awic.nal.usda.gov/government-and -professional-resources/federal-laws/animal-welfare-act.

Varkey, Prathibha, M. Katherine Reller, and Roger K. Resar. 2007. "Basics of Quality Improvement in Health Care." *Mayo Clinic Proceedings* 82, no. 6 (June): 735–39.

Vest, Joshua R. 2012. "Health Information Exchange: National and International Approaches." *Advances in Health Care Management* 12: 3–24.

WHO (World Health Organization). 1948. "WHO Definition of Health." (Preamble to the Constitution of the World Health Organization as adopted by the International Health Conference, New York, June 19–22, 1946; signed on July 22, 1946, by the representatives of sixty-one states (Official Records of the World Health Organization, no. 2, p. 100) and entered into force on April 7, 1948). www.who.int/about/definition/en/print.html.

———. 2005. *The International Health Regulations. IHR Brief no. 1.* www.who.int/ihr/ ihrbrief1en.pdf.

Williams, Claudia, Farzad Mostashari, Kory Mertz et al. 2012. "From the Office of the National Coordinator: The Strategy for Advancing the Exchange of Health Information." *Health Affairs* 31, no. 3 (March): 527–36.

Wright, Adam, Stanislav Henkin, Josuhua Feblowitz, Allison B. McCoy, David W. Bates, and Dean F. Sittig. 2013. "Early Results of the Meaningful Use Program for Electronic Health Records." *New England Journal of Medicine* 368, no. 8 (February 21): 779–80.

Yasnoff, William A., Latanya Sweeney, and Edward H. Shortliffe. 2013. "Putting Health IT on the Path to Success." *JAMA* 309, no. 10 (March 13): 989–90.

CHAPTER 3

Emerging Trends in Health Sciences Librarianship

Jonathan D. Eldredge and Gale G. Hannigan

INTRODUCTION

Health sciences librarians need to be proactive leaders who are skilled in detecting trends that affect the profession, envision roles for librarians within those trends, and seize opportunities related to those trends in a timely fashion. Health sciences librarians today enjoy many exciting professional roles because their colleagues during earlier eras were able to leverage emerging trends effectively. This chapter identifies and describes trends currently influencing health sciences librarianship. These trends likely will have an impact on health sciences librarianship for at least the coming decade. These trends might be partially embedded in the environment described in Chapter 2 that already has been affecting health sciences librarianship for a number of years. Trends covered in this chapter differ because they are still in highly formative states with limited certainty about their shape and their eventual place in the more established environment. For now, health sciences librarians can only ascertain that they will be part of the future environment.

The noun "trend" refers to a "general direction in which something is developing or changing" (Stevenson and Lindberg, 2010: 1846). It might reflect "an inherent tendency or general drift" or "a prevailing tendency or inclination" or possibly "the general movement over a sufficiently long period of time" (Gove, 1993). Four centuries ago the noun "trend" denoted the rounded bend of a stream or river, suggesting the diversion of water in a certain direction (OED online, 2013). Nowadays a trend indicates that groups of people in society are either aspiring to move or are actually moving in a general direction.

This chapter does not seek to predict the future of health sciences librarianship. Futurists might forecast events based upon one or more current trends (Taleb, 2012; Sheffield, Alonso, and Kaplan, 1994). But futurists also are engaging in educated guesses about the distant future (Conway, 1992). The future has a tendency to bring volatile changes or barely discernible movements that few could have ever foretold based on current developments. In the library profession, F. W. Lancaster predicted that by 1985 libraries would be working with largely paperless systems with the elimination of paper soon to follow (Lancaster, 1982; Lancaster, 1977). Lancaster's futuristic vision took forty years to reach some resemblance of his prediction, although for many years librarians miscalibrated their planning efforts prematurely based on the time line of Lancaster's predictions. Booth and Brice drolly noted, "Prediction is difficult, especially the future" (2007: 89). Three seminal volumes on futurism document, in sobering detail, the pitiful record of futurists to predict the future (Schnaars, 1987; Gardner, 2011; Silver, 2012).

In contrast to the futurist approach, this chapter pursues the more modest goal of outlining those few trends that will continue to influence health sciences librarianship in the foreseeable future. Trends analysis has captured the attention of health sciences librarians outside the United States in recent years (Murphy, 2011; Browne et al., 2012; Dollfus et al., 2012; Haglund et al., 2012; Beverly and Rodriguez-Jimenez, 2013). In the United States, there have been revealing research results about past trends, although even past trends can be challenging to identify and measure (Funk, 2013; Gore et al., 2009; McGowan, 2012; Howard, 2011; Goetz, 2012). Hundreds of trends unfolding in the world today are not covered in this chapter because they likely will have only a minor, or peripheral, bearing on health sciences librarianship (Herron, 2013). Whether same-sex marriage will become the law of the land or whether health care reform succeeds might interest us personally, for instance, but this legislation probably will have little effect upon how we manage health sciences libraries. This chapter focuses upon the following trends based on their potential to affect health sciences librarianship over the coming decade:

- Evidence-Based Practice
- Active Learning
- Innovative Research Collaborations
  - Big Science
  - E-Science
  - Translational Sciences
- Strategies for Adopting New Technologies

TREND ONE: EVIDENCE-BASED PRACTICE

Fifteen or twenty years ago this chapter on trends would have highlighted continuous quality improvement and strategic planning as trends capable of affecting health sciences librarians within the coming decade. Today, these two former trends are firmly established in the environment described in Chapter 2. **Evidence-based practice (EBP)** clearly represents the most important trend that will affect health sciences librarians during the coming decade. To date, EBP has not quite become part of the environment for a number of reasons. First, despite its popularity and the fact that health professionals frequently invoke EBP, its actual implementation has been far more uneven than everyday conversations might suggest. For one, it has not been institutionalized or codified completely within even its profession of origin: medicine. Second, within medicine many physicians have not adapted EBP thoroughly in their practices. Third, some health professions outside of clinical medicine have not accepted or implemented EBP as widely. Those health professions that have accepted it, moreover, have not necessarily codified or institutionalized it comprehensively.

EBP represents the most significant social phenomenon unfolding in the health sciences professions today. EBP "refers to a sequential process employed by professionals to reach informed decisions. EBP offers a process for reconciling the need to make sound decisions with the exponential growth of applied research-based knowledge" (Eldredge, 2008: 242). Many professions both inside and outside the health sciences subscribe to an EBP approach, although health professionals tend to be some of EBP's strongest adherents. All forms of EBP seem to share two core elements: 1) a sequential process that leads to a decision and 2) the recognition that not all evidence will be equally valid or appropriate. The sidebar displays the five steps in the EBP process. All forms of EBP seem to rely heavily upon authoritative information as the basis for most evidence.

Many other authors have described and elaborated on EBP elsewhere. This chapter instead will briefly describe the ways that this current trend offers opportunities for health sciences librarians. Then, the chapter describes the profession-specific version of EBP, known as Evidence-Based Library and Information Practice (EBLIP).

Health sciences librarians can be involved with the EBP process in collaboration with members of another health sciences profession in the first, second, and third steps of the specific profession's process. Librarians are experts at formulating focused, answerable questions in the first EBP process step. Librarians also excel in searching for authoritative evidence, the second EBP step. Health sciences librarians even can assist in the EBP process by filtering by article type in order to facilitate the third EBP step, **critical appraisal**, in the process.

Health sciences librarians have been involved in these first three steps of the five-step EBP process for at least a decade. Librarians primarily have served and have been best known in their capacities as expert bibliographic database searchers. Librarians normally are members of teams conducting systematic reviews that synthesize vast numbers of research studies on a focused clinical question (Beverley, Booth, and Bath, 2003; Harris, 2005). Librarians additionally are involved in creating or improving upon authoritative EBP information resources such as PubMed, the Cochrane Library, and point-of-care tools such as DynaMed that bring evidence to the bedside. Librarians also serve as instructors who train either health care providers or students in health professions degree programs to become self-sufficient

THE EVIDENCE-BASED PRACTICE (EBP) PROCESS

The EBP process consists of five steps:

1. Formulate an answerable question on an important issue
2. Search for the best available evidence to answer the question
3. Critically appraise the evidence
4. Make a decision and apply it
5. Evaluate one's performance (Eldredge, 2012a: 140)

searchers for answering their basic EBP questions. Librarian involvement in EBP frequently appears as a featured topic in the leading health sciences library journals and at the Medical Library Association (MLA) annual meetings. It is safe to assume that health sciences librarians will continue to pursue and deepen these central roles in collaboration with other health professions, thereby propelling this trend.

Evidence-Based Library and Information Practice (EBLIP)

Evidence-based library and information practice (EBLIP) represents librarianship's version of EBP. EBLIP follows the same sequential process as other forms of EBP as presented earlier in the sidebar. A recent overview of EBLIP defined it this way:

> EBLIP provides a sequential, structured process for integrating the best available evidence into making important decisions. The practitioner applies this decision-making process by using the best available evidence while informed by a pragmatic perspective developed from working in the field, critical thinking skills, an awareness of different research designs, and modulated by knowledge of the affected user population's values or preferences. (Eldredge, 2012a: 139)

Step One

Questions are the "driving force" behind the EBLIP process (Davies, 2011). The first step of question formulation resembles other forms of EBP, except that since 2008 librarians have begun to take an innovative approach to this step in the process. Two separate teams of librarians during 2008 with no knowledge of one another, one in Sweden (Maceviciute and Wilson, 2009) and the other in the United States under the auspices of the Medical Library Association (MLA), uniquely employed the **Delphi method** for identifying the most important and answerable EBLIP questions facing the profession. The U.S. team surveyed through multiple iterations the MLA leadership and researchers to identify the top-ranked questions (Eldredge, Harris, and Ascher, 2009). They repeated the process in 2011. Beginning in 2012, they organized more than 200 volunteers into fifteen teams charged with conducting systematic reviews on the best available evidence on answering those top-ranked fifteen questions (Eldredge et al., 2012; Eldredge et al., 2013). When completed, these systematic reviews will be helpful for practitioners trying to make decisions by anticipating many of the practitioners' important EBLIP questions. No other known health profession has embarked on such a systematic method for addressing EBP questions.

Step Two

The second EBLIP step involves finding the best available evidence. This step normally begins with a review of the published evidence via bibliographic databases such as PubMed. For example, a researcher can use an evidence-based approach to trends analysis and thereby search the published literature for evidence on trends. This chapter reflects this strategy for analyzing trends. To use one example related to this chapter, PubMed offers excellent coverage of education related to the health sciences. There are two major approaches to searching for information about trends in PubMed. First, the searcher can select a Medical Subject Heading (MeSH) term such as "Education" and pair it in the MeSH database with the subheading "trends." The narrower MeSH term "Professional Education" in the hierarchy of major and minor MeSH terms might be more focused. By selecting even a narrower MeSH term such as "Pharmaceutical Education," the search will be even more specific. The second approach to searching PubMed entails identifying a leading medical school-related education journal such as *Academic Medicine*. The Single Citation Matcher feature in PubMed allows a user to enter the journal title *Academic Medicine* and enter the truncated term "trend*" in the article title line.

Three other bibliographic databases that index articles on trends will be of potential interest to health sciences librarians. Cumulative Index to Nursing and Allied Health Literature (CINAHL) represents an essential supplement to health sciences professions journals not indexed in MEDLINE. CINAHL has education subject headings related to various professions that can be combined with the subject term "Trend Studies." The bibliographic databases Library and Information Science Abstracts (LISA) and Library, Information Science & Technology Abstracts (LISTA) lack the robust subject heading systems of a database such as MEDLINE, and they do not offer a specific trend-related subject heading as does CINAHL. Instead, searchers in these databases need to select types of sectorial library headings such as "Health Care Libraries," "Medical Libraries," or "Hospital Libraries." Or, they might possibly search by a library specialty such as "Library Instruction." These subject terms can then be combined with the truncated term "trend*" to construct a search. For trends related to more general subjects in education, a user needs to perform a keyword search using the truncated term "trend*" in an education subject database such as Education Research Complete.

The second step in this instance of health professions education also involves searching the large **grey literature** connected with national associations charged with establishing competencies. The Association of American Medical Colleges and the National League for Nursing, to cite only two examples, have extensive publications consisting of some books and many more reports. Some of these publications either address directly or allude to current trends. The national or regional conference programs include speeches, contributed papers, and posters that offer information on trends. These grey literature sources sometimes include abstracts that are readily accessible even when the original texts no longer exist.

Local sources of evidence sometimes can supplement or inform searches of the published and grey literatures. Libraries collect various forms of data for internal management use or for comparative statistical reports such as the Association of Academic Health Science Libraries' *Annual Statistics of Medical School Libraries in the United States and Canada* (Squires, 2013). Local sources might include the results of surveys of key library constituencies or from focus groups held at the university, hospital, or research institute that the library serves. The institution's strategic plan, SWOT (Strengths, Weaknesses, Opportunities, or Threats) analyses, annual reports, and public affairs communications also might inform the search for needed evidence. Local sources often serve promotional rather than applied research purposes, so the EBLIP practitioner must view these data sources with some skepticism.

Health sciences librarians wishing to search for authoritative published evidence in the second EBLIP step are fortunate to have their leading peer-reviewed journals of *Journal of the Medical Library Association, Medical Reference Services Quarterly*, and *Health Information and Libraries Journal* indexed in MEDLINE. The open access peer-reviewed journal *Evidence Based Library and Information Practice*, http://ejournals .library.ualberta.ca/index.php/EBLIP, can be directly searched via its website. Beyond these four journals, however, health sciences librarians will need to search in less-developed bibliographic databases such as LISA and LISTA as indicated above. Health sciences librarians likely will need to search in the extensive grey literature that serves as a repository for much of the knowledge base for the profession (Harvey and Wandersee, 2010; Alberani and Pietrangeli, 1995). The second step has been aided since 2006 by the "Evidence Summaries" published as regular features (Koufogiannakis, 2006; Kloda, Koufogiannakis, and Mallan, 2011) in every issue of *Evidence Based Library and Information Practice*. These evidence summaries examine significant research publications and "translate" them for application by everyday practitioners.

Step Three

Critical appraisal in the third EBLIP step involves sorting through all of the available evidence gathered during step two. Critical appraisal establishes which of the possibly many multiple pieces of identified evidence even has relevance to the question. Regardless of the quality of any evidence found, if the evidence does not address the question formulated in step one, it must be placed aside.

EBLIP has its own three types of questions: prediction, intervention, and exploration. When reviewing the relevant evidence to answer the question, all information varies in its quality. EBLIP, like the broader EBP movement, adheres to the view that not all evidence is equal in quality. Evidence, thus, can be ranked in a hierarchy from highest to lowest quality in what are known as the **levels of evidence**. The first two question types generally require quantitative forms of evidence at the higher levels whereas the third type, exploration, considers evidence from the realms of qualitative research under certain circumstances. Table 3.1 lists the levels of evidence by the three types of EBLIP question.

Table 3.1. EBLIP Levels of Evidence

Prediction	Intervention	Exploration
Systematic review	Systematic review	Systematic review
Meta-analysis	Meta-analysis	Summing up
Prospective cohort study	Randomized controlled trials	Comparative study
Retrospective cohort study	Prospective cohort study	Qualitative studies
Survey	Retrospective cohort study	Survey
Case study	Survey	Case study
Expert opinion	Case study	Expert opinion
	Expert opinion	

Copyright © Jonathan Eldredge. November 4, 2013

Systematic reviews are the highest level of evidence perched at the uppermost level in each column on Table 3.1. **Systematic reviews** answer a narrowly focused question based on all of the best available evidence in order to enable practitioners to make sound decisions. The team documents the systematic review process in sufficient detail that any colleague could replicate the systematic review process and reproduce a similar result. Replicability supports much of the applied research in any profession (Starr, 2009; Casedevall and Fang, 2010). The team that assembles systematic reviews analyzes all of the best available evidence using the levels of evidence as a guide in order to identify the highest quality evidence for answering the question. Thirty-nine systematic reviews on librarianship are currently in existence (Koufogiannakis, 2012), with others under development. The levels of evidence serve as a guide rather than a strict prescription for critical appraisal. The quality of an individual research study takes precedence within the levels of evidence. A research design such as a randomized controlled trial (a type of experiment) that resides near the top of the levels of evidence in answering an intervention question, for example, might have too few participants. This small population might constrain its reaching statistical significance. Or, this otherwise high-level evidence type might have flaws in the details of the design or its implementation. In such an instance, another research design deployed to answer the same question such as a high-quality cohort study, a popular type of observational research design, might be more appropriate.

Step Four

The third EBLIP step involves a determination of the quality of the evidence itself. This aspect of step three leads directly into step four. Do the authors offer a logical argument based on generally accepted evidence? Do they use sound research methods to support their views? Professional judgment, therefore, plays an important role in appraising the best available evidence in order to make a sound decision in the fourth step of the process. The needs of the user populations that rely upon the specific health sciences library need to be consulted and their interests given a central role in making any major decision.

The definition of EBLIP quoted at the beginning of this section references the importance of practical experience, critical thinking skills, and knowledge of user populations. These characteristics become paramount in the fourth decision-making step. EBLIP guides making sound decisions, which ultimately results in making a change; and, change often frightens people. The EBLIP definition, particularly when it mentions professional experience and knowledge of a user population, implies the presence of professional values in making a decision. The former president of the Association of College and Research Libraries made the following observation about the library profession's values and the inevitability of change:

> In times of change, people and institutions seek stability. I believe that stability can come from our values: not from the way we do things, but by the beliefs we hold as immutable. By reaffirming, by changing when necessary, but most of all, by understanding those values most critical to us and our profession, we can move into the future with confidence. (Hisle, 1997: 764)

The comedian Jon Stewart has quipped bitingly, "If you don't stick to your values when they're being tested, they're not values: they're hobbies" (Stewart, 2013). Many factors, including personal biases, can influence making decisions in step four of the EBLIP process. Interested readers should review the chapter on evidence-based practice in the 2008 textbook edited by Wood for further information and guidance on cognitive biases in the fourth decision-making step (Eldredge, 2008).

Step Five

The fifth step in the EBLIP process might follow the decision immediately. Far more likely, it will occur in the future when enough evidence based on past decisions accrues to make an evaluation. The fifth step involves evaluating professional performance as an EBLIP practitioner. This fifth reflective step normally happens weeks, months, or years after the preceding four steps. This evaluation step might occur in three domains, or loci: the individual, institutional, and professional. The individual health sciences librarian might reflect on how well her or his practice integrates the best available evidence into making decisions. Librarians as members of a library or its parent institution might ask the same question. These parent institutions' libraries then might elaborate further to ask if their organization supports applied research to produce high-quality evidence. Librarians and possibly others at the institution might reflect upon the kinds of data they normally collect about its operations because certain data might represent another source of evidence for supporting practice decisions. The profession via one of its national associations might evaluate its performance in a number of formal and less formal ways. Editorials or commentaries published in professional journals can make recommendations on future research or practice directions. Professional associations might encourage teams to conduct systematic reviews on the leading EBLIP questions as in the case of MLA during early 2013. A professional association such as MLA also might articulate a research policy or sponsor continuing education courses on topics related to furthering EBLIP. The EBLIP process begins anew each time the professional association poses a question and calls upon its membership to find an answer in order to make an important decision.

EBLIP in Action

The trends identified and described in this chapter are the products of an EBLIP approach. Each identified trend emerged from an EBLIP process adapted to the topic instead of the usual use as a decision-making resource. Many health sciences librarians describe themselves as EBLIP practitioners. Interested readers can pursue the subject of EBLIP in greater detail by browsing the journals *Evidence Based Library and Information Practice* and *Hypothesis*. The international Evidence-Based Library and Information Practice conferences occur on odd-numbered years in countries such as Australia, Canada, Sweden, the UK, and the United States.

Origins

EBP emerged from modest, grassroots origins. EBP formally began in 1991 with the publication of a one-page commentary in the *ACP Journal Club* titled "Evidence

Based Medicine" (Guyatt, 1991). This one-page article gave a label to the aspirational goals that had been emerging for at least a decade among geographically separated clusters of physicians and clinical epidemiologists. Another article by Goldman et al. (1990) lamented the need for evidence rather than experience alone to support everyday clinical practice. The time seemed ripe for a momentous change within medicine. Within a matter of just a few years, many physicians were discussing evidence-based medicine (EBM). Very quickly, a vocal and intelligent opposition arose to counter the enthusiasm of EBM's advocates. Some critics claimed that EBM would destroy professional autonomy for physicians through the promulgation of "cookbook medicine." A spirited debate raged for almost a decade. EBM advocates nimbly adapted and integrated changes into EBM based upon some of the substantive criticisms.

EBLIP emerged in 1997 from similarly modest origins as EBM. During the early years, EBLIP derived the inspiration for its process and the concept of levels of evidence from EBM. Librarians and other information professionals quickly realized that the types of questions sometimes called for forms of evidence outside the realm of mainstream medicine. The "Exploration" column in Table 3.1 on p. 62, for example, represents a unique approach to managing decision making for library and information practice.

TREND TWO: ACTIVE LEARNING

Institutions of higher education involved with training future health professionals generally resist curricular change as evidenced by the history of curricular reform outlined in Chapter 2. Consequently, health professions education programs have been slow to incorporate educational innovations.

Perhaps surprisingly, **active learning** currently represents the most significant innovation taking root in health professions education. Active learning represents one sustained trend in health professions education that will likely affect health sciences librarians in coming decades of the twenty-first century. Active learning, like EBP, emerged from modest origins. Many health professions educators are discussing active learning now, but misapprehensions still surround active learning. This section begins by defining active learning, describes its origins, and then outlines the ways that health sciences librarians can seize upon this trend.

Experiential Education

The American educator John Dewey (1859–1952) introduced the revolutionary idea that education naturally flows from experience and therefore formal education should incorporate elements of actual experience or simulate experience, whenever possible. Until the diffusion of Dewey's ideas, educators conceived of education as a mechanical process of oral transmission from the teacher to the passive student, possibly supplemented by assigned readings or drills. Dewey proposed that educators build upon students' existing experiences. Educators should furthermore design learning encounters either to resemble actual experience or to include relevant experiences to facilitate learning (Dewey, 1963; 2009).

The American education system largely ignored Dewey's ideas. Elementary and secondary education, whether public or private, remained largely uninfluenced by Dewey. Higher education in the United States largely persisted in promulgating the transmission model of education with the student positioned as the passive receptacle of the instruction. A few individual educators were excited by Dewey's ideas. Dewey founded the University of Chicago Laboratory School in 1896 where his ideas have flourished up to the present, www.ucls.uchicago.edu/about-lab/index. aspx. Beginning in the 1960s, several small liberal arts colleges such as Antioch, Beloit, Colorado, and Oberlin began to incorporate Dewey's ideas about experiential learning. Meanwhile, some private and public secondary schools began to introduce experiential learning. Some educators conducted progressively more and more rigorous evaluations of experiential learning at all levels of the educational system. The mounting evidence was compelling: Experiential education yields better learning. News of these research results spread. A decade later even a conservative bastion of higher education such as Dartmouth College unveiled its "Dartmouth Plan" (Widmayer, 1972; Newman and Fisher, 1974; and "Dartmouth Plan," 1974), which closely resembled the Beloit Plan. Even the established University of Michigan featured experiential learning in some courses.

David Kolb incorporated many of Dewey's and other experiential educators' ideas into a comprehensive theory of educational cycles. Kolb's theory also included the growing body of evidence to support experiential learning. Kolb's 1984 work noted that genuine learning followed a cycle consisting of a learner having a concrete experience and reflective observation about that experience, abstracting concepts from the experience, and finally actively experimenting to generate and interpret new learning experiences. At the time of publication of Kolb's book, elementary and secondary school teaching included limited experiential learning. Many in higher education still remained skeptical about experiential learning. A 1995 article titled "From Teaching to Learning" (Barr and Tagg, 1995) served as a sentinel event in changing many faculty members' views in American higher education. The health professions educational institutions were slow to change, but they have begun to embrace experiential learning.

Problem-Based Learning

In 1969, a new medical school opened at McMaster University in Hamilton, Ontario. At the time no one could have imagined that this fledgling medical school eventually would change medical education worldwide. McMaster pioneered a new method of medical education called **problem-based learning (PBL)**. At McMaster, students clustered in small groups led by a faculty member and worked through simulated patient cases intended to teach them the basic sciences pertinent to becoming a physician. PBL students engaged in a lot of self-directed learning, oftentimes involving students' pursuit of library research. Students did not attend many lectures (Neville and Norman, 2007). Ten years later, PBL spread to the United States to the recently-opened medical school at the University of New Mexico. PBL in New Mexico was strongly linked to the training of primary care physicians in rural or frontier areas. PBL in New Mexico largely resembled PBL at McMaster with some local variations (Eldredge, 1993). Twenty years later, PBL had diffused, albeit, modestly to other medical schools. Resistance to PBL persisted. In 1999, a chapter on PBL declared that "the current debate over the effectiveness of . . . PBL in medical education continues with no apparent end in sight" (Eldredge and Rhyne, 1999: 407). In the same volume, Sayre (1999) identified PBL as only one form of active learning and outlined ways that other forms, particularly those involving new information technology, might serve health professions education.

The conservative U.S. medical education establishment adamantly resisted the adoption of PBL for many years. Medical education generally changes at a deliberate pace (Friedman, 2012; Hoover, 2005). In time, a growing research evidence base suggested that PBL equaled traditional curricula in preparing medical students for their licensure exams. The evidence suggested something else: Students graduating from PBL programs were happier with their educational experiences and tended to perform well in certain clinical skills areas. As broader acceptance arrived, PBL eventually became a more standardized educational experience within U.S. medical schools. A majority of medical schools in the United States and numerous other medical schools worldwide now include PBL elements within their curricula (Schmidt et al., 2009).

Active Learning Takes Root

PBL represents one of perhaps a dozen specific pedagogical approaches known by the overarching name of active learning. The phrase "active learning" encompasses just about any learning method that avoids students assuming the role of passive receptacle for transmitted content. Table 3.2 lists and describes some of the types of active learning approaches found today in health professions education. The Office to Support Effective Teaching at the University of New Mexico offers a helpful resource, www.unm.edu/~oset/UsingActiveLearning.html, for both understanding and applying active learning approaches. Team-based learning, as one currently popular variant of active learning in medical education, shifts the burden of studying prior to and after class with plenty of incentives to ensure that students learn the material and work effectively in teams (Michaelsen, 2008).

Some health sciences librarians have used active learning techniques for at least the past decade. Active learning appears to work, provided the instructor follows certain core principles:

1. Students need to apply any skills or content they are expected to learn;
2. Students must be held individually accountable for all required assignments or work, as measured by assessment exercises such as graded tests;
3. Students must be given clear instructions about what they are expected to accomplish;
4. Students must be given incentives to both perform individually and to learn cooperatively with other students.

Instructors who use active learning might need to invest as much as tenfold attention to instructional design in advance compared to traditional lecturing.

Table 3.2. Types of Active Learning Found in Health Professions Education

The following examples of active learning techniques can be used alone or in various combinations in accordance with the instructional design of the learning experiences.

Type	Description
Assignment Questions	The instructor directs students to answer or to be able to answer several questions related to an assignment. For example, the instructor might require students to answer three questions about a book chapter assigned for reading.
Audience Response System	Sometimes called "clickers," these devices allow students to vote on questions or select their individual choices on a multiple-choice question displayed by the instructor. Some systems use students' cell phones.
Debate	Students are instructed ahead of class to prepare for debating a position on an issue.
First-Day Question	The instructor asks a series of questions that lead students to consider the rationales for the instructor's organizing the course content in a certain way. Stimulates student motivation in the course by engaging them in the reasons for organizing the course.
Formative Assessment	The instructor asks students to take a quiz or complete some other exercise representing only a small percentage of the total grade. Students experience less anxiety, and the instructor can provide feedback to assure that students recognize their strengths and weaknesses prior to an assessment representing a larger percentage of the overall course grade.
Games	Games have been proven to augment interest and accelerate learning, provided the games do not trivialize the content and are closely integrated with course learning objectives. Most games nowadays are computer-based experiences, although students often respond well to games in face-to-face classes.
JITT	JITT means "just in time teaching" that involves students conveying to their instructor in advance what points confuse them after students have completed an assignment outside of class. JITT enables the instructor to adjust the next class session to explain any confusing points. This website provides some guidance and examples: http://jittdl.physics.iupui.edu/jitt/.
Large Group Sessions	Large group sessions need not be exclusively lecture-based.
Opening Question	As students walk into the classroom they are presented on the board, screen, or a handout with an opening question. This helps the students to focus upon the subject more quickly to ease any transition. An opening question might be: "Why are question formulation skills important for your success as a future physician?"
Oral Presentations	Individuals or groups of students are asked to present on a narrow topic before the entire class.
Problem-Based Learning	Problem-based learning (PBL) attempts to teach fundamental biological mechanisms in the context of solving simulated clinical cases. Students discuss the patient's problems while identifying and researching areas where they lack the needed information. Evidence suggests that students learn fundamental information and retain it better within a clinical context. Meanwhile, students can practice identifying learning needs and finding information.

(Continued)

Table 3.2. (*Continued*)

Type	Description
Random Selection	Students in the classroom are divided up using existing boundaries such as rows or tables into clearly-demarcated sections of the classroom. When no existing features are available, the instructor can create boundaries with ribbon or colored string. The students are randomized into groups that the instructor will call upon to answer a posed question or to report on an assignment.
Reflective Closing	These experiences allow students to synthesize and commit to long-term memory what they have learned within a class session or even within a segment of a course. The first type might ask, "What have we learned today?" The second type might ask, "What is the most important thing you have learned in the Evidence-Based Practice course thus far?"
Rubrics	Rubrics offer a time-tested technique for lending global consistency to feedback on student performance. Rubrics isolate discrete components of educational activities for ease of assessment. Rubrics define and describe these components and link them to a range of student performance levels on the discrete tasks. The four elements in rubrics consist of 1. A task description; 2. Scales of potential student achievement levels (examples: does not meet, meets expectations, exceeds expectations); 3. Component parts of the activities; 4. Descriptions of achievement levels that are reached through incremental stages.
Self-Knowledge Exercises	Students are asked to engage in an activity that will enable them to learn more about themselves in relation to their learning pursuits. It can be a written exercise or an online experience. The Felder-Silverman Index of Learning Styles serves as just one example: www4.ncsu.edu/unity/lockers/users/f/felder/public/Learning_Styles.html. One author witnessed a colleague who once described to students different information-seeking strategies as categorized by breed of dog: pointers, retrievers, and so forth, and asked students to describe their style in terms of one of the dog breeds.
Self-Reflection	The instructor asks students to reflect on some aspect of the course content or to synthesize disparate content. Self-reflection can occur either within the class time or outside of class.
Service Learning	Students provide a noncompensated service to a real-life working environment as a learning experience about the working world. Employers gain the benefits of the student's service, and the students receive valued experience. Service learning experiences by higher education institutions were pioneered by Antioch, Beloit, and Northeastern during the 1960s and 1970s. Since then, this technique has become far more codified and popularized in higher education.
Silence	After posing a question to the class, the instructor resists the temptation to answer it or to call on a student to answer it. Instead, the instructor remains silent, except possibly to repeat the question. The instructor then transitions to another exercise or proceeds with the class content, knowing that as it unfolds the session will eventually answer the unanswered question.
Student Peer Assessment	Student peer assessment (SPA) involves students evaluating the work of other students, oftentimes in highly-structured environments. SPA often measures unambiguous observable behavior or completion of course assignments. Students' evaluation of their peers' performance normally represents a formative rather than a summative assessment activity for these peers.

(*Continued*)

Table 3.2. Types of Active Learning Found in Health Professions Education (*Continued*)

Type	Description
Surveys	Surveys can be conducted by a show of hands, votes on an audience response system, or via an online survey tool.
Team-Based Learning	Teams of students are asked to master clearly defined knowledge or skills. Individuals as well as groups of students earn their grades through tests and exams, taken alone and as a group.
Think-Pair-Share	The instructor asks a focused question and then asks students to think about how they would answer the question. After a minute or two of quiet self-reflection, students are asked to pair up with a neighbor to compare their respective answers in order to come up with a synthesized answer. Variations of this technique might include students writing their answers to the question individually prior to sharing in pairs. Sometimes triads or even larger groups discuss the question, although this might lead to some individuals dominating the discussion.
Thought Question	The instructor asks students to reflect alone about a focused question posed to the entire class. The instructor might couple this technique to "Think-Pair-Share," but sometimes simply the quiet moment of reflection alone engages student learning.
Visualization	The instructor guides the students through a simulated situation and models desired thinking or behavior in the imagined scenario.

Active learning represents a major trend unfolding in health sciences education. Health sciences librarians need to keep two aspects of active learning in mind. First, librarians need to ask how active learning techniques will change the ways that students use libraries. Some of the techniques outlined in Table 3.2 offer the potential to increase use of library services and resources. Second, health sciences librarians involved in library instruction need to employ active learning techniques if that has become the principal method of student learning in the curriculum. Fortunately, library instruction with its emphasis upon skills development and applying knowledge aligns well with active learning techniques. For example, health sciences librarians often teach database classes involving hands-on application of the searching techniques. A recent study of library instruction in academic libraries serving medical schools pointed to the

Active learning is one of the most important trends in medical education today. It represents a return to and focus on what we have learned from education research. It has long been recognized that learners are not passive recipients of knowledge from teachers but that they must be actively involved in the process. The emphasis on active learning is aimed at making the classroom a place for learners to participate and engage with the subject material.

—*Craig Timm, MD, senior associate dean for education and professor of internal medicine and cardiology, University of New Mexico School of Medicine, Albuquerque* preponderance of health sciences using active learning techniques (Eldredge et al., 2013).

TREND THREE: INNOVATIVE RESEARCH COLLABORATIONS

Health sciences librarians serve multiple constituencies simultaneously: educators, students, researchers, clinicians, and members of the broader community outside the parent institution. Members of these constituencies frequently have overlapping roles: clinicians conducting research, educators pursuing literature reviews for manuscripts, and students completing assignments involving their searches for the latest research evidence. Librarians nowadays generally forget that the earliest librarians' roles were existentially intermingled with the roles of the earliest researchers. Before professional librarianship became established during the early twentieth century, some research institutions selected highly-respected researchers as directors of their libraries. Harvard University surprised nearly everyone in 1995 when it selected world-class researcher and faculty member Sidney Verba instead of a professional librarian to direct its libraries, thereby reminding many of these past practices (Hafner, 2005).

Of course, most health sciences libraries today are led by professional librarians. Health sciences librarians, most notably in the realm of collection resources management, universally pursue providing access to the best research-based information resources for their users with an almost religious zeal. Researchers similarly feel passionate about ensuring access to the most authoritative research-based information resources. Over the past two decades, these similarly inclined parties sometimes have clashed on the best means to accomplish their common goal. Researchers want access to the best resources, namely journals, in their own subject disciplines. Their sentiments run deep with regard to protecting and advocating for their specific subject areas. Meanwhile, librarians must satisfy multiple research disciplines, all clamoring for their specific subject coverage, while serving broad institutional values of appropriately allocating underfunded budgets and advocating against publisher incursions on researchers' intellectual property rights.

These high-profile conflicts have obscured the deeply shared values held among both librarians and researchers for providing access to the best research-based evidence. This section describes three overlapping areas where librarians and researchers are forging new productive partnerships: **big science**, **e-science**, and the **translational sciences**. For health sciences librarians, the translational sciences appear to be the most noteworthy element in this trend.

Big Science

"Big science" describes large-scale projects requiring significant funding, often at the national or international level, conducted by teams of researchers in pursuit of a major goal. Big science has been occurring for many years yet involving only a limited number of projects. The NASA initiative to transport humans to the surface of the moon and return them safely to earth served as an early instance of big science during the 1960s. The robotic exploration of Mars, the space shuttles, and the international space station were other big science descendants of the race to the moon. The War on Cancer, for example, initiated by the National Cancer Act of 1971, prompted a massive infusion of research dollars into cancer research. The Human Genome Project, with origins in the Department of Energy and the National Institutes of Health (NIH) during the 1980s, became a fifteen-year international quest. Over the past two decades, multiple institutions have pursued various epidemiologic or clinical treatment initiatives in accordance with the big science pattern.

Health sciences research, despite these noteworthy examples of big science, traditionally has involved a single principal investigator at only one institution. Early exceptions consisted of cancer researchers who conducted multisite clinical trials. Lately, U.S. government requests for funding research proposals have shifted emphasis toward collaborations among multiple research teams at different institutions. This new development has changed the very complexion of much of the funded research.

Big science requires extensive information support. This requirement also provides for novel ways for researchers and librarians to collaborate. The NIH's National Library of Medicine developed information resources to support the Human Genome effort, including GenBank, www.ncbi.nlm.nih.gov/genbank/, an annotated collection of all publicly available DNA sequences. GenBank itself is part of an international collaboration to exchange sequencing information. Health sciences librarians naturally network among themselves, so oftentimes those librarians can quickly serve as ready partners in emerging research collaborations among multiple institutions. Librarians at their respective institutions need to be proactive in networking so their involvement with this emerging trend can be taken into account in the planning stages of funded projects involving multiple institutions.

E-Science

Big science has a huge appetite for computing power to facilitate real-time collaboration among multiple institutions. The term "e-science" refers to the use of networked, high-powered computers to support any research endeavor requiring extensive data support. E-science serves both big science and other research projects whenever these involve computation or large file sets. As just one example, e-science provides the information infrastructure to store and network medical images requiring massive file sizes in order to ensure high-quality resolution for those images.

Large data sets eventually raise questions about who can access these resources because they are often funded by taxpayers' dollars. Researchers likely have an ethical obligation to share their data sets with others despite continued resistance by many researchers (Ohno-Machado, 2012). Questions naturally arise about continued accessibility over the coming decades, as other researchers subsequently want to review, possibly manipulate, or even merge these huge data sets with other huge data sets through meta-analyses. The U.S. National Science Foundation already has promulgated rigorous standards for all submitted research project proposals to include a detailed data management plan. NIH similarly requires data plans for grant submissions for more than $500,000. For more information, see Chapter 10, which deals with research data management.

These requirements placed on funded research projects offer possible opportunities for unique collaborations between health sciences librarians and researchers. Librarians are skilled at adapting to broad institutional needs, so there are variations across the United States on how librarians are meeting requirements for data management plans. At some universities librarians embed themselves in projects with large data sets in order to make their expertise available, as needed, by researchers. Other librarians are providing metadata tags for data sets. Shaffer (2013) has noted, however, that there is little consensus nationwide on what roles librarians should pursue. Meanwhile, job opportunities for librarians with skills related to research data management seem to be proliferating (Hyams, 2012). Health sciences librarians at the University of Massachusetts Medical School have helped design and implement a full data-management curriculum that can be adapted to training health sciences researchers at other institutions (Piorun, Kafel, Leger-Hornby et al., 2012).

Translational Sciences

Translational sciences seek to incorporate useful research results into relevant health care practices. The translational sciences might represent the most productive area for health sciences librarians to collaborate with their researcher colleagues for reasons outlined below. The history of the emergence of the translational sciences as a major trend contrasts with the evidence-based practice and active learning trends. Several commentaries published during 2003 in high-profile peer-reviewed journals alerted the clinical community to the problem of relevant research findings taking far too long to reach patient care, at potentially great emotional and financial cost to patients (Rosenberg, 2003; Lenfant, 2003; Nathan and Wilson, 2003). The example of aspirin taking seventeen years from the first randomized controlled trial demonstrating its preventive effects against myocardial infarction until its first-ever appearance in a clinical practice guideline characterizes the kinds of delays that can happen on the lengthy journey from research to practice (Elwood et al., 1973; Jacobi, 1997).

Health sciences librarians are discussing both the translational sciences and EBP extensively these days. The discussions often overlap, so at times it becomes disorienting for outsiders to distinguish EBP from the translational sciences. It might help to use mechanistic metaphors to draw a distinction. EBP seeks to extract or "pull" out

Translational science encompasses everything from basic laboratory research, to clinical implementation and care, to improved quality of life for the community. Today's health sciences libraries stand ready to support a wide variety of information needs along this spectrum by facilitating interdisciplinary collaboration, by enhancing evidence-based research and care, and by providing top-notch expertise and resources to their campus and their community. The concepts emphasized by the CTSA Consortium and translational science centers can provide a practical framework for libraries—enabling them to better leverage existing strengths and consider dynamic new initiatives to support the evolving information needs of their partners.

—*Kristi L. Holmes, PhD, director,*
Galter Health Sciences Library,
Northwestern University, Chicago, IL

evidence in the knowledge base of a specialty or discipline, no matter how deeply embedded or seemingly hidden in the remote corners in that knowledge base. Any valid and relevant evidence then becomes integrated into decision making as part of professional practice. Conversely, the translational sciences seek to "push" research evidence into the realms of professional practice so it can be readily apparent for making decisions. Both EBP and the translational sciences strive to improve professional practice, yet they employ radically different methods, infrastructures, and orientations.

The translational sciences seemed to be following the same trajectory as the two previously discussed trends of EBP and active learning: beginning as a modest proposal and stirrings of a modest, grassroots social movement within the profession. As the phrase "translational science" gained currency in the medical literature, however, NIH gave translational sciences a tremendous boost in late 2007 when it announced a new initiative for funding the establishment of clinical and translational sciences centers across the United States (U.S. Department of Health and Human Services, 2007). Suddenly, academic health sciences across the nation began competing for Clinical and Translational Sciences Awards. The announcement outlined the purposes of the new awards:

> The Clinical and Translational Science Award (CTSA) initiative assists institutions to create an integrated academic home for clinical and translational science that has the resources to train and advance multi- and interdisciplinary investigators and research teams with access to innovative research tools and information technologies that apply new knowledge and techniques to patient care. Clinical and Translational Science Awards (CTSAs) will attract basic, translational, and clinical investigators; community clinicians; clinical practices; networks; professional societies; and industry to develop new professional interactions, programs, and research projects. Through innovative advanced degree programs, CTSAs will foster a new discipline of clinical and translational science that will be much broader and deeper than its separate components. (NIH, 2007)

Today, sixty institutions are participating in Clinical and Translational Sciences Awards. Most define translational sciences as the process through which the results of research, whether laboratory or clinic-based, eventually become part of everyday professional practice in the community. Type I translational science refers to laboratory or clinical research migrating from "bench to bedside," whereas Type II translational science refers to the migration into the widespread practice known as "bedside to community" (Kroth, Phillips, and Eldredge, 2009). Sometimes these types are broken down further into four rather than two discrete phases. Other countries, including Australia, Canada, Costa Rica, Japan, and the United Kingdom, now have government initiatives in the translational sciences that in some ways resemble the United States (Kroth, Phillips, and Eldredge, 2010).

Collaborations with the Translational Sciences

MLA sponsored the formation of a Translational Sciences Collaboration Special Interest Group in 2010. This nascent group recognizes that translational sciences encompasses far more than NIH's sixty centers across the United States. This recently formed group identified, through a nominal group technique at its first meeting in Minneapolis during 2011, several top-ranked areas where librarians are collaborating with translational sciences researchers. They include guidance on plagiarism and copyright, integration of the library into the CTSA, teaching in the informatics courses in the CTSA graduate program, assigning a librarian as a liaison to the CTSA to work with translational scientists, facilitating systematic reviews, collaborating on compiling dynamic directories of researchers and their research interests (example: VIVO), intellectual property guidance, and serving on administrative committees (Eldredge, 2011). A year later, the Translational Sciences Collaboration Special Interest Group determined through a facilitated discussion that health sciences librarians needed to be proactive by volunteering and being involved in the CTSA, to be organized and prepared for any emerging opportunities to collaborate, remain focused on integrating library and informatics instruction into CTSA graduate programs, exceed expectations, persist and adhere to long-range goals to be involved in the CTSA, and be flexible (Eldredge, 2012b). Health sciences librarians also might find an evolving role as advocates for open access publication with translational research (Eldredge, Kroth, and Phillips, 2011). Librarians may see opportunities to work in this area because translational research involves evaluation, management, and dissemination of information (Cleveland, Holmes, and Philbrick, 2012).

A conference in 2010 and another one in 2013 related to librarians' roles in the translational sciences brought out some of the aforementioned themes. Participants at the 2010 Evidence-Based Scholarly Communications Conference focused on the need to correctly identify core faculty members engaged in translational research because these individuals often traverse traditional disciplinary boundaries. Participants also noted the need for librarians to facilitate digital archiving in repositories and share practices that work in one setting that might be transferable to other environments (Kroth, Phillips, and Eldredge, 2010). The 2013 CTSA Community Engagement Strategic Planning Workshop reiterated the previous inventories, with a special emphasis upon the following foci: Every CTSA has its unique personality and priorities so "one size does not fit all"; CTSAs are becoming more focused and stable, which creates opportunities for more in-depth collaboration with libraries; translational researchers tend to collaborate most heavily with health sciences librarians through in-depth research consultations, research output, and tracking; and CTSA graduate students need to be trained in library/informatics skills (NN/LM, South Central Region, 2013). For more information on the translational sciences, see Chapter 9.

TREND FOUR: STRATEGIES FOR ADAPTING NEW TECHNOLOGIES

More than one hundred years ago, sponge divers off the Greek island of Antikythera discovered remnants of an ancient shipwreck. Strewn across the ocean floor were statues, vases, and a mysterious heavily oxidized bronze object. Archaeologists eventually detected small metal gears and inscriptions on the object but otherwise could not identify its purpose or functions. Derek de Solla Price examined it with the help of radiographs during the 1970s. He determined that the object was a computerized calendar from 100 BC (Freeth, 2009; Wright, 2007). Western civilization would not invent anything else like it for almost another 2,000 years.

The secrets of the Antikythera computer would remain undecipherable until more modern three-dimensional X-ray computerized tomography and new ways of lighting revealed its interior contents. The sophistication of the ancient computer defied preconceptions of ancient technology. The computer could predict the correct movements and positions of the sun, moon, and five planets for any given date (Lobell, 2007; Freeth et al., 2006; Curry, 2009). It even could predict lunar and solar eclipses on nineteen- and seventy-six-year cycles (Yan and Lin, 2012). To date, no one has determined the primary or even the secondary purposes of this ancient computer. Clearly, it was not widely known in ancient Greece, and it was used only by a very select group of academics.

In contrast, any new information technology in the twenty-first century presents the possibility of becoming widely known within a matter of months. Often overlooked is the fact that only a small percentage of that new information technology actually becomes used, however. As Haymes has noted, "The dirty little secret of technology in education is that a lot of it doesn't get used effectively—or at all" (2008: 68). He outlines three prerequisite conditions for new technology to even have a chance of becoming accepted: properly calibrating user expectations, ease of use, and its proving essential to user productivity. Another observer has suggested conversely that new information technology tends not to be accepted by users when it changes users' relationship to time, space, or others in their lives (Thompson, 2012). Spotting new trends in the information technology world represents a fairly simple task. The online newsletter *Campus Technology*, the journal *Educause Review*, and other serials are helpful for identifying possible information technology trends (McCrea, 2013). The real challenges appear to be identifying *desirable* information technology and appropriately *adapting* it so it will be adopted by health sciences library users.

The **Hype Cycle**, www.gartner.com/technology/research/hype-cycles/, has become a popular conceptual framework for organizations to track the emergence, peak, decline, and eventual plateau of successful new information technology adaptation (Ringrose, 2013). The Hype Cycle reveals that even information technologies that become widespread fail to deliver their initial hyped promises (Jun, 2012b). When information technology companies introduce a new product, the initial burst of enthusiastic customer early adoption declines precipitously.

Jun and others have used the Hype Cycle to study the rate of adoption of numerous new technologies such as software applications ("apps"), cloud computing (Cruz Marta et al., 2011), and hybrid cars (Jun, 2012a). Readers might detect the resemblance between the graphic Hype Cycle and Rogers's verbally descriptive Diffusion of Innovation model that has been employed since the 1960s as a means for understanding technology adaptation (Rogers, 2003). The Hype Cycle and the Diffusion of Innovation models focus primarily on successful technologies, whereas the broader world of information technology adaptation can be characterized as volatile and chaotic.

This volatile information technology environment disrupts creation of any long-term or resource-intensive investments of effort in developing new resources.

Information technology professionals as well as health sciences librarians instead are using strategies for adopting new technologies. The new **minimum viable product (MVP)** strategy represents one such approach. MVP has several synonyms or close equivalents: lean product development, launch-and-learn, and proof-of-concept. MVP provides a framework for developing a modestly scaled information technology application quickly and without seeking high levels of perfection. The popular yet volatile technology DropBox, for example, represents an MVP production approach to new technology (Kirsner, 2013; Ries, 2011). MVP seeks to determine, from the producer perspective, whether users might want or need an information resource. As one author explains, "So, start with something simple that lets you determine whether there are any customers . . . you shouldn't solve the whole problem at once. Solve a simple piece that shows you whether . . . it's worth going further" (Patil, 2013: 1). Some of the conditions that tend to encourage MVP are a strong project manager, responsibility-based planning and control, and rapid prototyping (Hoppmann et al., 2011). As it turns out, the organizational culture also plays a major role in supporting an MVP approach (Iqbal and Najafi, 2011). The MVP even has been applied to public sector administration. There, the key elements consist of "minimizing the use of resources, a customer-driven interpretation of the concept of value, the re-engineering of processes in the effort of eliminating those without real added-value" (Poddighe, Lombrano, and Inniello, 2011).

The library and informatics professions pursue the same MVP and equivalent approaches to adapting new technology, although within the literature they tend to label the approach as "proof-of-concept" (Wong, 2012; Lindlar, 2010; Miranda, Gualtieri, and Coccia, 2009). Ten or twenty years ago health sciences libraries were inclined to build elaborate information technology plans. The National Library of Medicine tended to fund large-scale technology projects involving extensive planning. This might have been an artifact of the mainframe computer era when such planning was more appropriate to the technology. Health sciences libraries in the twenty-first century, like many public sector entities, are generally under-resourced for their ambitious missions. MVP and its equivalents such as proof-of-concept make a great deal of sense, pragmatically, as a means to adapt new information technology without burdening health sciences libraries with major investments of personnel and budget resources.

HOW TO STAY ABREAST OF EMERGING TRENDS

The trends identified and described in this chapter should serve readers well for the coming decade. Readers can remain abreast of emerging trends by consulting several sources. Using the specific database search techniques described previously in this chapter for finding sources in MEDLINE/PubMed, LISA, and LISTA offers a high-yield strategy. A new emerging issues column in the *MLA News* provides a recent additional resource for interested readers (Shedlock and Attwood, 2012). Most importantly, readers now equipped with the evidence-based skills described in this chapter can appraise trends critically in order to make sound judgments on relevance and impact of emerging trends.

SUMMARY

This chapter provides an overview of four major trends capable of influencing health sciences libraries both in the present and for the coming decade. The trends of evidence-based practice (EBP), active learning, innovative research collaborations, and strategies for keeping abreast of new technologies emerge from an evidence-based review of many more potential trends. The evidence-based methodology enables readers to obtain and appraise critically the evidence to determine if these trends will have the same effect on their specific health sciences library.

STUDY QUESTIONS

1. Select an area of interest within health sciences librarianship such as data management, library instruction, or reference consultancy. Using the EBP process, work through the following questions:
   - What EBLIP questions come to mind in your area?
   - How would you find authoritative evidence to make a decision in this subject area?
   - Once you have collected your evidence, how would you apply the levels of evidence to make a decision?
2. Discuss with at least one colleague how active learning might impact your area(s) of health sciences librarianship.
3. Distinguish between big science, e-science, and the translational sciences.
4. EBP and the translational sciences have similar goals. Contrast their respective approaches.
5. Describe the Hype Cycle using an example of information technology with the potential to affect health sciences libraries.

REFERENCES

Alberani, Vilma, and P. D. De Castro Pietrangeli. 1995. "Grey Literature in Information Science: Production, Circulation and Use." *INSPEL* 29, no. 4: 240–49.

Barr, Robert B., and John Tagg. 1995. "From Teaching to Learning: A New Paradigm for Undergraduate Education." *Change* (November–December): 13–25.

Beverley, Catherine A., Andrew Booth, and P. A. Bath. 2003. "The Role of the Information Specialist in the Systematic Review Process: A Health Information Case Study." *Health Information and Libraries Journal* 20, no. 2 (June): 65–74.

Beverly, Berry, and Teresa M. Rodriguez-Jimenez. 2013. "International Trends in Librarianship. Part 5 Latin America and the Caribbean." *Health Information and Libraries Journal* 30, no. 1 (March): 76–82.

Booth, Andrew, and Anne Brice. 2007. "Prediction Is Difficult, Especially the Future: A Progress Report." *Evidence Based Library and Information Practice* 2, no. 1: 89–106.

Browne, Ruth, Kaye Lasserre, and Jill McTaggert et al. 2012. "International Trends in Health Sciences Librarianship: Part 1—the English Speaking World." *Health Information and Libraries Journal* 29, no. 3 (March): 75–80.

Casadevall, Arturo, and Ferric C. Fang. 2010. "Reproducible Science." *Infection and Immunity* 78, no. 12 (December): 4972–75.

Cleveland, Ana D., Kristi L. Holmes, and J. L. Philbrick. 2012. "'Genomics and Translational Medicine for Information Professionals': An Innovative Course to Educate the Next Generation of Librarians." *Journal of the Medical Library Association* 100, no. 4 (October): 303–5.

Conway, Hobart McKinley. 1992. *A Glimpse of the Future: Technology Forecasts for Global Strategists.* Norcross, GA: Conway Data.

Cruz Marta, Fernando, Ana-Maria Ramalho Correia, and Fátima Trindade Neves. 2012. "Supporting KMS through Cloud Computing: A Scoping Review." *CISTI (Iberian Conference on Information Systems & Technologies)* (July): 825–30.

Curry, Andrew. 2009. "2,000 Year-Old Astronomical Computer." *Discover* 30, no. 1 (January): 61.

"Dartmouth Plan." 1975. *Dartmouth Alumni Magazine* (April): 26–28.

Davies, Karen Sue. 2011. "Formulating the Evidence Based Question: A Review of the Frameworks." *Evidence Based Library and Information Practice* 6, no. 2: 75–80.

Dewey, John. 1963. *Experience and Education.* New York: Collier Books.

———. 2009. *Democracy and Education.* Lexington, KY: Feather Trail Press.

Dollfus, Helmut, Bruno Bauer, Ghislaine Decleve et al. 2012. "International Trends in Health Science Librarianship: Part 2—Northern Europe." *Health Information and Libraries Journal* 29, no. 2 (June): 166–71.

Eldredge, J. D. 1993. "A Problem-based Learning Curriculum in Transition." *Bulletin of the Medical Library Association* 81, no. 3 (July): 310–15.

Eldredge, Jonathan D. 2008. "Evidence-Based Practice." In *Introduction to Health Sciences Librarianship*, edited by M. Sandra Wood, 241–69. New York: Routledge.

———. 2011. "Results of Nominal Group Technique on Frequency of Activities." Unpublished document from the Medical Library Association Annual Meeting Translational Sciences Collaboration Special Interest Group, Minneapolis, May 15.

———. 2012a. "The Evolution of Evidence Based Library and Information Practice, Part I: Defining EBLIP." *Evidence Based Library and Information Practice* 7, no. 4 (December): 139–45.

———. 2012b. "Facilitated Discussion on Educational Roles of Libraries in CTSAs." Unpublished document from the Medical Library Association Annual Meeting Translational Sciences Collaboration Special Interest Group, Seattle, May 21.

Eldredge, Jonathan D., Marie T. Ascher, Heather N. Holmes, and Martha R. Harris. 2012. "The New Medical Library Association Research Agenda: Final Results from a Three-Phase Delphi Study." *Journal of the Medical Library Association* 100, no. 3 (July): 214–18. doi:10.3163/1536-5050.100.3.012.

———. 2013. "Top-Ranked Research Questions and Systematic Reviews." *Hypothesis* 24, no. 2 (Winter): 19–20.

Eldredge, Jonathan D., Martha R. Harris, and Marie T. Ascher. 2009. "Defining the Medical Library Association Research Agenda: Methodology and Final Results from a Consensus Process." *Journal of the Medical Library Association* 97, no. 3 (July): 178–85. doi:10.3163/1536-5050.97.3.006.

Eldredge, Jonathan D., Karen M. Heskett, Terry Henner, and Josephine P. Tan. 2013. "Current Practices in Library/Informatics Instruction in Academic Libraries Serving Medical Schools in the Western United States: A Three-Phase Action Research Study." *BMC Biomedical Education* 13, no. 1 (September 4): 119. www.biomedcentral.com/1472-6920/13/119.

Eldredge, Jonathan D., Philip J. Kroth, and Holly E. Phillips. 2011. "The Translational Sciences: A Rare Open Access Opportunity." *Journal of the Medical Library Association* 99, no. 3 (July): 193–95.

Eldredge, Jonathan D., and Robert L. Rhyne. 1999. "Building Foundations for Effective Library Skills in Medical Education." In *Handbook on Problem-Based Learning,* edited by Jocelyn Rankin, 407–32. Chicago: Medical Library Association (Forbes Custom Publishing).

Elwood, Peter C., Archibald L. Cochrane, and Michael. L. Burr et al. 1974. "A Randomized Controlled Trial of Acetyl Salicylic Acid in the Secondary Prevention of Mortality from Myocardial Infarction." *British Medical Journal* 1, no. 5905 (March 9): 436–40.

Freeth, Tony. 2009. "Decoding an Ancient Computer." *Scientific American* 301, no. 6 (December): 76–83.

Freeth, T., Y. Bitsakis, and X. Moussas et al. 2006. "Decoding the Ancient Greek Astronomical Calculator Known as the Antikythera Mechanism." *Nature* 444, no. 7119 (November 30): 587–91.

Friedman, Charles P. 2012. "Educating Health Professionals in the Era of Ubiquitous Information." Paper presented at the University of New Mexico School of Medicine, December 17.

Funk, Mark E. 2013. "Our Words, Our Story: A Textual Analysis of Articles Published in the *Bulletin of the Medical Library Association/Journal of the Medical Library Association* from 1961 to 2010." *Journal of the Medical Library Association* 101, no. 1 (January): 12–20. doi:10.3163/1536-5050.101.1.003.

Gardner, Dan. 2011. *Future Babble: Why Expert Predictions Are Next to Worthless and You Can Do Better.* New York: Dutton.

Goetz, Thomas. 2012. "How to Spot the Future." *Wired Magazine* 20, no. 5 (May): 153–61.

Goldman, Lee, Francis E. Cook, and John Orav et al. 1990. "Research Training in Clinical Effectiveness: Replacing 'In My Experience . . .' with Rigorous Clinical Investigation." *Clinical Research* 38, no. 4 (December): 686–93.

Gore, Sally A., Judith M. Nordberg, Lisa A. Palmer, and M. E. Piorun. 2009. "Trends in Health Sciences Library and Information Science Research: An Analysis of Research Publications in the *Bulletin of the Medical Library Association* and *Journal of the Medical Library Association* from 1991 to 2007." *Journal of the Medical Library Association* 97, no. 3 (July): 203–11. doi:10.3163/1536-5050.97.3.009.

Gove, Philip Babcock, editor in chief. 1993. "Trend." *Webster's Third New International Dictionary.* Springfield, MA: Merriam-Webster, 2438.

Guyatt, Gordon H. 1991. "Evidence-Based Medicine." *ACP Journal Club* 114, no. 2: A-16.

Hafner, Katie. 2005. "At Harvard, a Man, a Plan and a Scanner." *New York Times,* November 21.

Haglund, Lotta, Karen J. Buset, Hanne M. Kristiansen, Tuulevi Ovaska, and Jeannette Murphy. 2012. "International Trends in Health Librarianship: Part 3—the Nordic Countries." *Health Information and Libraries Journal* 29, no. 3 (September): 247–51.

Harris, Martha R. 2005. "The Librarian's Roles in the Systematic Review Process: A Case Study." *Journal of the Medical Library Association* 93, no. 1 (January): 81–87.

Harvey, Sally A., and Janene R. Wandersee. 2010. "Publication Rates of Abstracts of Papers and Posters Presented at Medical Library Association Annual Meetings." *Journal of the Medical Library Association* 98, no. 3 (July): 250–55.

Haymes, Tom. 2008. "The Three-E Strategy for Overcoming Resistance to Technological Change." *Educause Quarterly* 31, no. 4 (October–December): 67–69.

Herron, David. 2013. "On the Makings of the EAHIL Workshop 2013 Stockholm, Sweden." *Journal of the European Association for Health Information and Libraries* 9, no. 3: 10–13.

Hisle, W. Lee. 1997. "Facing the New Millennium." *College & Research Libraries News* 58, no. 11 (December): 764–65.

Hoppmann, Joern, Eric Rebentisch, Uwe Dombrowski, and Thimo Zahn. 2011. "A Framework for Organizing Lean Product Development." *Engineering Management Journal* 23, no. 1 (March): 3–15.

Hoover, Eddie L. 2005. "A Century after Flexner: The Need for Reform in Medical Education from College and Medical School through Residency Training." *Journal of the National Medical Association* 97, no. 9 (September): 1232–39.

Howard, Jennifer. 2011. "Citation by Citation, New Maps Chart Hot Research and Scholarship's Hidden Terrain." *The Chronicle of Higher Education*, September 11.

Hyams, Elspeth. 2012. "Trends: What's Hot, What's Not?" *Cilip Update* (February): 28.

Iqbal, Farrukh, and Azadeh Najafi. 2011. "Towards a Lean Perspective in Product Development: A Case Study of a Global Company in Sweden." *Interdisciplinary Journal of Contemporary Research in Business* 3, no. 1 (July): 313–27.

Jacobi, Judith. 1997. "An Aspirin a Day: Advice that Makes Sense." *American Journal of Health-System Pharmacy* 54, no. 17 (September 1): 1949–50.

Jun, Seung-Pyo. 2012a. "A Comparative Study of Hype Cycles among Actors within the Socio-Technical System: With a Focus on the Case Study of Hybrid Cars." *Technological Forecasting and Social Change* 79, no. 8 (October): 1413–30.

———. 2012b. "An Empirical Study of Users' Hype Cycle Based on Search Traffic: The Case Study on Hybrid Cars." *Scientometrics* 91, no. 1: 81–99.

Kirsner, Scott. 2013. "A Promising Intern and a Missed Opportunity." *Boston Globe* (August 5): G1, G4.

Kloda, Lorie A., Denise Koufogiannakis, and Katrine Mallan. 2011. "Transferring Evidence into Practice: What Evidence Summaries of Library and Information Studies Research Tell Practitioners." *Information Research* 16, no. 1 (March): Paper 465. http://informationr.net/ir/16-1/paper465.html.

Kolb, David A. 1984. *Experiential Education: Experience as the Source of Learning and Development*. Englewood Cliffs, NJ: Prentice Hall.

Koufogiannakis, D. 2006. "Small Steps Forward through Critical Appraisal." *Evidence Based Library and Information Practice* 1, no. 1: 81–82.

———. 2012. "LIS Systematic Reviews [blog]. http://lis-systematic-reviews.wikispaces.com/Welcome.

Kroth, Philip J., Holly E. Phillips, and Jonathan D. Eldredge. 2009. "Leveraging Change to Integrate Library and Informatics Competencies into a New CTSC Curriculum: A Program Evaluation." *Medical Reference Services Quarterly* 28, no. 3 (July–September): 221–34.

———. 2010. "Evidence-Based Scholarly Communication: Information Professionals Unlocking Translational Research." *Evidence Based Library and Information Practice* 5, no. 4: 108–14.

Lancaster, Frederick W. 1977. *The Dissemination of Scientific and Scientific Information: Toward a Paperless System* (University of Illinois Graduate School of Library Science Occasional Papers Number 127). Urbana: University of Illinois Graduate School of Library Science.

———. 1982. "The Evolving Paperless Society and Its Implications for Libraries." *International Forum on Information and Documentation* 7, no. 4: 3–10.

Lenfant, Claude. 2003. "Clinical Research to Clinical Practice—Lost in Translation?" *New England Journal of Medicine* 349, no. 9 (August 28): 868–74.

Lindlar, Michelle. 2010. "Digitalization and Digital Preservation Projects at the German National Library of Medicine (ZB MED)." *Journal of the European Association for Health Information and Libraries* 6, no. 2: 7–9.

Lobell, Jarrett A. 2007. "The Antikythera Mechanism." *Archaeology* 60, no. 2 (March/April): 42–45.

Maceviciute, E., and T. D. Wilson. 2009. "A Delphi Investigation into the Research Needs in Swedish Librarianship." *Information Research* 14, no. 4, Paper 419. http://informationr.net/ir/14-4/paper419.html.

McCrea, Bridget. 2013. "6 Higher Ed Tech Trends to Watch in 2013." *Campus Technology* (January 15): 1–2.

McGowan, Julie J. 2012. "Evolution, Revolution, or Obsolescence: An Examination of Writings on the Future of Health Sciences Libraries." *Journal of the Medical Library Association* 100, no. 1 (January): 5–9. doi:10.3163/1536-5050.100.1.003.

Michaelsen, Larry K., Dean X. Parmelee, Kathryn K. McMahon, and Ruth E. Levine, eds. 2008. *Team-Based Learning for Health Professions Education: A Guide to Using Small Groups for Improving Learning.* Sterling, VA: Stylus.

Miranda, Giovanna F., Francesca Gualtieri, and Paolo Coccia. 2009. "The Web 2.0 Revolution in Library and Information Services." *Journal of the European Association for Health Information and Libraries* 5, no. 1: 3–7.

Murphy, Jeannette. 2011. "Trend Spotting—Whither Health Science Librarianship?" *Health Information and Libraries Journal* 28, no. 4: 321–25.

Nathan, David G., and Jean D. Wilson. 2003. "Clinical Research and the NIH—A Report Card." *New England Journal of Medicine* 349, no. 19 (November 6): 1860–65.

Neville, Alan J., and Geoff R. Norman. 2007. "PBL in the Undergraduate MD Program at McMaster University: Three Iterations in Three Decades." *Academic Medicine* 82, no. 4 (April): 370–74.

Newman, Andrew J., and Melanie Fisher. 1974. "Education in the Round." *Dartmouth Alumni Magazine* (June): 18–21.

NN/LM, South Central Region. 2013. "Communities and Their Assets: Community Asset Mapping for CTSA Community Engagement: CTSA Community Engagement Strategic Planning Workshop." San Antonio, TX, February 22.

OED Online. 2013. "Trend, n." Oxford University Press. Accessed March 17. www.oed.com/view/Entry/205544?rskey=6ReEpM&result=1.

Ohno-Machado, Lucila. 2012. "To Share or Not to Share: That Is Not the Question." *Science Translational Medicine* 4, no. 165 (December 19): 1–4.

Patil, D. J. 2013. "Data Jujitsu: The Art of Turning Data into Product." *O'Reilly Radar* (January 26): 1–13.

Piorun, Mary, Donna Kafel, Tracey Leger-Hornby, Siamak Najafi, and Elaine R. Martin. 2012. "Teaching Research Data Management: An Undergraduate/Graduate Curriculum." *Journal of eScience Librarianship* 1, no. 1: 46–50.

Poddighe, Francesco, Alessandro Lombrano, and Mario Ianniello. 2011. "Lean Production and One-Stop Shop for Municipal Services." *Public Administration & Management* 16, no. 1: 1–20. www.spaef.com/articleArchives.php?journal=PAM.

Ries, Eric. 2011. "How DropBox Started as a Minimal Viable Product." *Techcrunch* (October 19): 1–7.

Ringrose, Fergal. 2013. "Hype Cycle of Files." *TVB Europe* (August): 4.

Rogers, Everett M. 2003. *Diffusion of Innovations*, 5th ed. New York: Free Press.

Rosenberg, Roger N. 2003. "Translating Biomedical Research to the Bedside." *JAMA: Journal of the American Medical Association* 289, no. 10 (March 12): 1305–6.

Sayre, Jean Williams. 1999. "Active Learning Models in Medical School Curricula." In *Handbook on Problem-Based Learning*, edited by Jocelyn Rankin, 31–43. Chicago: Medical Library Association (Forbes Custom Publishing).

Schnaars, Steven P. 1989. *Megamistakes: Forecasting and the Myth of Rapid Technological Change.* New York: Free Press.

Schmidt, Henk G., Henk T. van der Molen, Wilco W. R. te Winkel, and Wynand H. F. W. Wijnen. 2009. "Constructivist, Problem-Based Learning Does Work: A Meta-Analysis of Curricular Comparisons Involving a Single Medical School." *Educational Psychologist* 44, no. 4: 227–49.

Shaffer, Christopher J. 2013. "The Role of the Library in the Research Enterprise." *Journal of eScience Librarianship* 2, no. 1: 8–15.

Shedlock, James, and Carol Ann Attwood. 2012. "Turning Points: Opinions about Emerging Issues in Health Sciences Librarianship." *MLA News* 52, no. 8 (September): 1, 8.

Sheffield, Charles, Marcelo Alonso, and Morton A. Kaplan, eds. 1994. *The World of 2044: Technological Development and the Future of Society*. St. Paul, MN: Paragon House.

Silver, Nate. 2012. *The Signal and the Noise: Why So Many Predictions Fail—but Some Don't*. New York: Penguin Press.

Squires, Steven J., ed. 2013. *2011–2012 Annual Statistics of Medical School Libraries in the United States and Canada*, 35th ed. Seattle: Association of Academic Health Sciences Libraries.

Starr, Susan. 2009. "Making the Case: Solutions for Tough Times." *Journal of the Medical Library Association* 97, no. 2 (April): 73–74.

Stevenson, Angus, and Christine A. Lindberg, eds. 2010. "Trend." *New Oxford American Dictionary*, 3rd ed. New York: Oxford University Press, 1846.

Stewart, Jon. 2013. "Values." Accessed October 26. www.goodreads.com/quotes/133424 -if-you-don-t-stick-to-your-values-when-they-re-being.

Taleb, Nassim. 2012. *Antifragile: Things that Gain from Disorder*. New York: Random House, 135–36; 390–91.

Thompson, Clive. 2012. "The Rules of Panic." *Wired* 20, no. 11 (November): 70.

U.S. Department of Health and Human Services. National Institutes of Health. 2007. Institutional Clinical and Translational Science Award (U54). Accessed October 26, 2013. http:// grants.nih.gov/grants/guide/rfa-files/RFA-RM-08-002.html.

Widmayer, Charles E. 1972. "The Dartmouth Plan." *Dartmouth Alumni Magazine* (January): 18–19.

Wong, Shun Rebekah. 2012. "Which Platform Do Our Users Prefer: Website or Mobile App?" *Reference Services Review* 40, no. 1: 103–15.

Wright, M. T. 2007. "The Antikythera Mechanism Reconsidered." *Interdisciplinary Science Reviews* 32, no. 1: 27–43.

Yan, H-S, and J-L Lin. 2012. "Reconstruction Synthesis for the Unexplained Feature of the Lunar Subsystem of the Antikythera Mechanism." *Proceedings of the Institution of Mechanical Engineers, Part C: Journal of Mechanical Engineering Science* 226, no. 4 (April): 1053–67.

PART II

Collection Services

CHAPTER 4

Collection Development in Health Sciences Libraries

Holly E. Phillips

INTRODUCTION

This chapter covers the current state of collection development in the health sciences in terms of patron expectations, collection development policies, licensing, resource evaluation, budgeting, and setting priorities. Although health sciences libraries come in many types, basic collection development principles and practices should be understood and implemented based on the local context and patron needs.

Collection development is the art of understanding and meeting user information needs through careful assessment of the population served, evaluation and acquisition of resources in a variety of formats to serve those needs, and ongoing maintenance and care of the collection, including deselection. Collection development is ultimately a creative endeavor and is limitlessly fulfilling for the library professional. It is the ability to anticipate, organize, present, and sustain a curated set of scholarship designated for a population with specific needs.

The collection development librarian needs a varied skill set. Duties include setting acquisition and deselection guidelines; allocating budgets; establishing relationships with colleagues, patrons, and vendors; evaluating resources usage statistics; keeping current with information delivery trends; monitoring expenditures and renewals; scheduling vendor visits; training internal employees on new or updated resources; and finding time to read reviews and select quality materials.

Although the population served and scope of resources provided is unique, the collection development process in health sciences libraries is similar to that in other library types. Massive technological and information delivery changes in recent years have shifted collection priorities, stretched budgets, and required updated skills training. The best way forward is to stay current with the library and health care environment trends, determine and communicate collection priorities, pick up practical resource management skills, and set an effective budget with room for innovation.

MODERN COLLECTION DEVELOPMENT

Over the past two decades librarians supporting all disciplines, regardless of library type, have incorporated some degree of electronic resource collection development and management into their traditional print collection development practices and workflows. The past five years have brought even more advances in resource platforms, delivery mechanisms, and end-user technology. Changes in scholarly communication (e.g., institutional repositories, open science, data management), the rapidity of information sharing through social media, and a greater number of online courses have also caused librarians to further reassess how to meet the patron information demands when and where they need it. In an era of severe budget reductions and return on investment scrutiny, collection development librarians' skill sets have necessarily expanded to include activities not traditionally associated with the role, such as arguing the need for a curated collection or mining the large amount of usage data in conjunction with dollars spent to evaluate patron interest and cost effectiveness.

Understanding the larger library, technology, health care, and research settings is essential in anticipating resource needs and expectations. The very essence of collection development is anticipating and fulfilling information basics. Major library and technology changes will now be briefly presented and will be addressed throughout the chapter.

Content Growth, Disaggregation, Disintermediation, and Technology

Librarians' traditional approach to collection development has been to acquire and make available to the libraries' patron base the potentially useful major works, journals, and locally relevant material in specific topic areas. More recently, globalization and technological advances have led to information proliferation. The discoverability of the breadth and depth of information in a topic area, along with the general sense of "information is free on the Internet," means patrons are finding and requesting more resources. The concept of the long tail is helpful in picturing the impact of consumer demand (Anderson, 2006). The dark gray section (left side) of Figure 4.1 depicts what most libraries can afford to have onsite in a particular subject and the light gray portion (right side) represents the remaining information on the subject.

The long tail of resources is growing longer, and library users are in a position to demand more from the tail (Gregory, 2011). In a sense, selection has moved to users' fingertips; if they locate information that fits their needs and find the source even remotely useful, they will want libraries to acquire it or provide access to the item, especially in fast-paced biomedical research libraries (Clark, Levine, and Shane, 2013).

Technology has enabled content growth; at the same time, it has brought about significant change in how information is bundled and how information requests can be fulfilled. Consumers are increasingly purchasing unbundled content. Interlibrary loan is a form of **disaggregated content**. The patron requests the most applicable article or chapter rather than purchasing the entire work for access to only a few relevant sections.

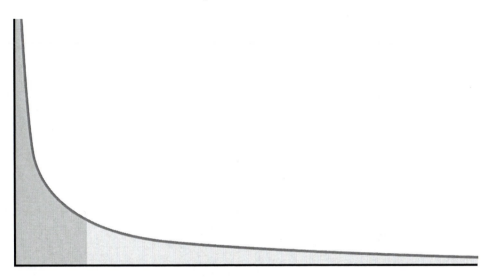

Figure 4.1. The Long Tail of Information Availability. Source: Hay Kranen (http://haykranen.nl), from Wikipedia (http://en.wikipedia.org/wiki/File:Long_tail.svg).

Patrons are becoming more accustomed to immediate and **disintermediated** access, which has resulted in reduced interaction between the knowledgeable selector and the consumer. In the past, a librarian would carefully select the most relevant high-quality materials. Instead of looking through numerous books on a topic, the patron would be presented with fewer, but perhaps better, items. Now, the long tail and immediate, seamless access to anything electronic further clouds how libraries can keep up with users' daily life experience. The phrases "point-of-need rather than just-in-case" and "find it, get it" are commonly heard in collection development circles. In this model the library no longer develops a collection. Rather, it acts as the acquisitions partner fulfilling the patron's information request in as little time as possible with little to no contact with a librarian.

In the past five years, the publishing world has either created or adapted to massive technological advances in how people retrieve and review publications. Since the release of the first Kindle in November 2007, an impressive array of e-book readers and operating systems have come and gone. Additionally, early personal digital assistants (PDAs) and later smartphones and tablets ushered in a new era of device specific mobile applications (or apps).

Publishers and libraries have embraced e-readers, tablets, and smartphones. As these technologies become more robust and publishers create platform-specific content that is optimized for mobile access, the long tail of information resources will also apply to delivery methods. For example, electronic medical textbooks gained in popularity after color e-readers and the iPad became available. Now, it is possible to purchase personal iPad editions of popular texts such as *Harrison's Principles of Internal Medicine* in a variety of ways (e.g., see www.inkling.com). Use of portable devices in a variety of health sciences content delivery environments is well-documented in the medical literature; for an example, see Mickan et al. (2013).

Social media and review sites such as Faculty of 1000, http://f1000.com/, expand the ways in which people communicate and learn about resources, also increasing the demand for new and specialized content. Social media "share this" links permeate publisher offerings. The vast amount of information sources and ease of finding content through intuitive interfaces will push libraries to be more nimble in procuring resources.

COLLECTION DEVELOPMENT POLICIES

Health sciences libraries represent a subset of library types; therefore, many of the standard library collection development principles also apply to health sciences libraries. Consider the similarities of health sciences libraries to other library types. Like general academic libraries, most publicly funded academic health sciences libraries are open to the public in addition to the institution's students, faculty, and researchers. Thus, if a consumer health section is developed, thought must be given to reading level and varieties of language spoken in the immediate community. Hospital libraries are special libraries for health care providers but often have a strong patient education focus and are considered a vital part of patient care. Hospital libraries, like public libraries, may allow materials to circulate, necessitating multiple copies of high-demand resources.

Talk to your experts to gather knowledge from them to apply to the strategy. They know what they need and how they need it. Sitting down with them face-to-face will not only provide the librarian with a deeper understanding of the topics the collection hopes to cover and services to deliver it, but the conversations will build lasting relationships with those experts for both the individual librarian and the library.

Lorri Zipperer, MA, cybrarian and editor, Zipperer Project Management, Albuquerque, NM

Unlike public or general academic libraries that cover a multitude of topics, health sciences libraries have a focused selection area and relatively defined set of clientele. Health sciences libraries must strive to maintain the collection focus and balance user priorities. To achieve this, librarians should carefully assess the user population. Figure 4.2 is a simple Venn diagram of typical health sciences library patron types. In this figure, all the patron area circles are the same size. Each library, with its own user population, can draw a version of this diagram where the size of the circle indicates the relative importance and focus of a constituency.

Academic libraries may reduce the patient/consumer circle in favor of research and education. The clinical care circle may shrink if the teaching hospital has a separate library. Hospital libraries may accentuate clinical care and patient/consumer resources. The research minded on the hospital staff may need to affiliate with other institutions to conduct in-depth studies. Before setting any policies or purchasing directions, the librarian should know the patron base. Reviewing the organizational mission, clinical model, research portfolio, and educational

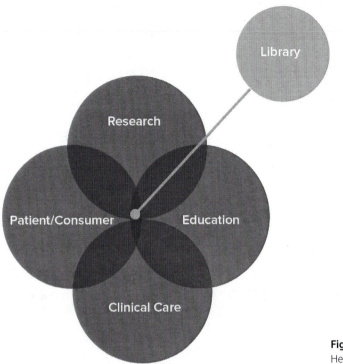

Figure 4.2. Patron Types in Health Sciences Libraries.

programs complete with student enrollment and library fund sources can aid this exercise.

Collection development policies provide a general framework for how a library prioritizes selection, management, and access to the collection. A policy contains a general description of the collection areas and strengths, organizational priorities, and selection and deselection guidelines. Above all, it serves as a communication tool between the library staff and the patrons so both parties are aware of expectations and redress in the case of potential censorship or dispute. A collection policy can direct internal workflows, but the posted collection policy is ultimately a public document, not a procedure manual.

Well-written policies take time and careful thought. Numerous articles and books have been written about creating policies; and the relative merits of having a collection policy for print, electronic resources, historical medical books, and more (Anderson, 1996; Biblarz, 1992; Clark, Levine, and Shane, 2013; Clement and Foy, 2011; Demas and Miller, 2012; Futas, 1995; Hoffman and Wood, 2005; Mangrum and Pozzebon, 2012; Picket et. al, 2011; Schleicher, 2010; Snow, 1996). Traditional collection development policies follow a similar format and use a conspectus approach developed by the Research Libraries Group (RLG). The RLG Conspectus is a system used to apply a uniform approach to collection strength and collecting intensities by subject. The RLG method has been adapted by a variety of library associations but is not consistently applied across libraries. However, it offers a useful approach to defining collection scope and emphasis.

The International Federation of Library Associations and Institutions (IFLA) issued a brief, freely available, "Guidelines for a Collection Development Policy Using the Conspectus Model" in 2001 (IFLA, 2001). It is a good starting place for those interested in learning more about collection policy models and the conspectus approach. The guide outlines essential policy sections, elements, and definitions to describe collection strength and intensity.

Although daunting, each library should adopt only the pieces that make sense in relation to library size, patron interaction, and budget. A policy for an academic library versus a small hospital library may have similar structure but vary significantly in level of detail. It is possible that no policy is the right action. Or, perhaps, a complete rethinking of the policy process and how decisions are documented is necessary (Douglas, 2011).

Although no policy, or even a limited one, might be appropriate for a library, proper attention is now given to the traditional policy development approach. The information is general in nature but includes tips relative to the health sciences environment based on the many excellent health sciences library policies available online.

HEALTH SCIENCE LIBRARY POLICY EXAMPLES

- Drexel University Health Sciences Libraries: www.library.drexel.edu/files/about_documents/HSCollDev2007.pdf
- National Library of Medicine: www.nlm.nih.gov/tsd/acquisitions/cdm/index.html
- Ohio State University Health Sciences Library: https://hsl.osu.edu/resources/collection-development-policy
- University of Colorado Anschutz Medical Campus Health Sciences Library: https://hslibrary.ucdenver.edu/policies/collection
- University of Maryland Health Sciences and Human Services Library: www.hshsl.umaryland.edu/about/policies.cfm
- University of Michigan Taubman Health Sciences Library: www.lib.umich.edu/taubman-health-sciences-library/collection-policies-um-health-sciences-libraries-medicine-nursing-and-pharma

Policy Sections

Introduction

The *introduction* should set the stage for the reader—both for internal selectors and for the community of users. It firmly states the library mission and history, the user population it serves, a description of the programs or activities the collection supports, an overview of material types collected complete with budget priority settings, and collection intensity information.

If a library does not have a *mission* statement, then the individuals or team tasked with constructing the policy should develop one. Knowing why a library exists and its purpose is central to understanding the collection. A mission statement need not be lengthy. For example, see the Drexel University Health Sciences Libraries mission:

The Drexel University Health Sciences Libraries are committed to providing quality information services to support the education, research, and clinical programs of Drexel University's College of Medicine, Nursing and Health Professions, and School of Public Health. The Libraries aim to provide users with a collection of materials, in multiple formats, that reflects their changing needs as well as the dynamic nature of the field of biomedical literature, embracing new technologies in order to serve its clientele most efficiently. (Drexel University Health Sciences Libraries, 2007)

The mission clearly states that the library provides health-related services, resources, and products in the best format possible to a diverse group. This alone tells the reader that the library is unlikely to collect material unrelated to health sciences. It also recognizes that it serves more than students and clinicians.

The library *history* adds a depth of understanding but is not essential. If a library started from a large donation or in a specific field, the history would explain why, for example, the library is named for an individual or why it contains a large historical section within a particular subject area. The history can be central to the library identity; therefore, caution should be exerted in weeding or making other significant collection changes. The collection development policy may be the only official document that covers the library's history and is therefore a significant and interesting addition to the record—one that potential donors may even find intriguing (see https://hsl.osu.edu/resources/collection-development-policy#Introduction for the history of The Ohio State University Health Sciences Library).

The *user population* in the policy can be described in both qualitative and quantitative terms. For brevity, the library could mention the major user groups in broad strokes. Or, armed with organizational fact books, it could present exact numbers in each constituency and weight selection priorities accordingly. Important concepts to convey are primary clientele and how the library provides access to off-site, public, or any other special group. Health sciences libraries often serve geographically independent sites such as clinics, teaching hospitals, health centers, or groups of individuals. Include all relevant constituencies up to and including library consortiums or National Network of Libraries of Medicine (NN/LM) partnerships (see University of Maryland HS/HSL Policy, www.hshsl.umaryland.edu/about/policies.cfm).

To further identify priorities, include an accounting of areas or *programs served*. A hospital or special library can refer to certain patient or research populations (e.g., a library within a children's hospital or a pharmaceutical research organization). Educational institutions can range from a stand-alone medical school to numerous schools, colleges, and programs with a diverse research portfolio. Degrees offered and research agendas change over time, so regular assessment is encouraged. Alternately, provide a link to an institutional course description and degrees offered web page.

Collection areas, complete with subject listings and material types, comprise the remaining policy sections. At this juncture in the policy, only make quick reference to any unusual or frequently asked resource questions. For example, it is worth notifying the user if the library is online only and has no browsing or print collection.

General and Narrative Statements

The *general and narrative statements* address any policies or characteristics the library finds important to share with the user group and sets collection parameters for the library staff. Statements can include information about which library position(s) is responsible for collection decisions for new or historic materials, gifts, suggested purchases, how constituent groups are or are not involved in selection (e.g., Faculty Library Committee), and how collection-related complaints are resolved. Other areas often covered are languages collected, publication date, geographic area, subject areas or formats not collected or collected heavily, funding constraints, collaborative collection development partners, and materials in storage. Descriptions of the general collection and historical collection (if applicable) belong here as well as collection policy revision frequency.

Subject Profiles

The *subject profiles* are the heart of the collection policy. Health sciences libraries subjects are often consistent with the National Library of Medicine's (NLM) Medical Subject Headings (MeSH) or NLM Classification schedule.

The *Collection Development Manual of the U.S. National Library of Medicine*, www .nlm.nih.gov/tsd/acquisitions/cdm/, employs the MeSH terms in most cases (see Figure 4.3). The *Manual* is a useful reference point for a new health sciences library collection development policy. Each subject category is subdivided into a definition, discussion, scope, emphasis, and special considerations.

The definition briefly describes the subject area in terms of the study, branches or fields of medicine, or related areas. The discussion interprets the definition for areas in need of further clarification and context. The scope and emphasis establish the level of collection intensity (more on this next in the Collection Depth Indicator section). Finally, the special considerations subdivision presents additional local or format information of use to the selector. Related topics have "see also" references. Librarians writing in-depth collection policies should refer to the *Manual* for framework ideas and inspiration.

Figure 4.3. NLM Selection Guidelines by Subject. Source: National Library of Medicine (www.nlm .nih.gov/tsd/acquisitions/cdm/subjects.html#1084571), 22.

Collection Depth Indicators

As previously noted, the RLG Conspectus, and its variations as adopted by other practitioner groups such as the Association of Research Libraries (ARL), is a system used to apply a uniform approach to collection strength and collecting intensities by subject. Application of the Conspectus can be done in a simple table format (see Drexel and Taubman libraries, links in sidebar on p. 92) or in narrative form (see NLM, which mostly collects at one primary level, link in Figure 4.3).

The RLG Conspectus as adopted by IFLA is displayed in Figure 4.4 (IFLA, 2001). To apply the Conspectus levels, each subject is evaluated based on the health sciences library's relative commitment to direct funds and collection efforts to the subject area. The decision to use one level over another is local and can be viewed from a qualitative or quantitative lens.

Qualitative aspects to consider include historical significance to the institution or geographic area (e.g., tuberculosis in New Mexico); library mission (e.g., NLM's mandate to collect comprehensively in scholarly biomedical literature); research specialty or supporting infrastructure (e.g., existence of a complete animal care facility); or special population served (e.g., Veteran's Administration hospitals). The sections on library mission, history, clientele, and programs provide the support and rationale for the Conspectus level granted to a subject.

Quantitative measures to review are internal circulation, interlibrary loan (ILL), and electronic usage data within an area. Data show which areas are trending high and which are experiencing a decline in usage. Collection analysis by funds spent per area, average publication date of a section, and size relative to other parts of the collection all provide additional information regarding collection trends and breadth and depth of a collection.

Although useful, librarians should use data judiciously. For example, health sciences libraries typically favor current information. A collection analysis in a library with a historical collection will show many older publication dates. If a librarian is reviewing average publication date, the statistics will be skewed toward an older average. The librarian should know what part of the collection is responsible and why and, depending on the nature of the inquiry, should use an alternate evaluation method to regulate the analysis. Similarly, material cost varies by subject. For instance, nursing materials generally cost less than medical materials. A straight cost review across subjects can reveal discrepancies that are due to price variation rather than selection preference. The baseline and underlying assumptions are critical to a well-reasoned investigation.

Due to rapid availability of materials and scope, very few health sciences libraries outside of NLM collect at the "comprehensive level." Stand-alone medical schools may collect at the "study or instructional support level," whereas large academic centers with Clinical Translational Science Awards may assign "research level" to numerous subject areas. Children's hospitals may consider gerontology and geriatrics to be out of scope or at the "minimal information level." Specialty libraries may have select areas at "research level" and only other relevant areas at "basic information level." Again, the levels applied by a library are based on local facts and figures.

Score	Description
0	**Out of Scope: Library does not intentionally collect materials in any format for this subject.**
1	**Minimal Information Level: Collections that support minimal inquiries about this subject and include:** • A very limited collection of general materials, including monographs and reference works. • Periodicals directly dealing with this topic and in-depth electronic information resources are not collected. The collection should be frequently and systematically reviewed for currency of Information. Superseded editions and titles containing outdated information should be withdrawn. Classic or standard retrospective materials may be retained.
2	**Basic Information Level: Collections that serve to introduce and define a subject, to indicate the varieties of information available elsewhere, and to support the needs of general library users through the first two years of college instruction include:** • A limited collection of monographs and reference works. • A limited collection of representative general periodicals. • Defined access to a limited collection of owned or remotely-accessed electronic bibliographic tools, texts, data sets, journals, etc. The collection should be frequently and systematically reviewed for currency of information. Superseded editions and titles containing outdated information should be withdrawn. Classic or standard retrospective materials may be retained.
3	**Study or Instructional Support Level: Collections that provide information about a subject in a systematic way, but at a level of less than research intensity, and support the needs of general library users through college and beginning graduate instruction include:** • An extensive collection of general monographs and reference works and selected specialized monographs and reference works. • An extensive collection of general periodicals and a representative collection of specialized periodicals. • Limited collections of appropriate foreign language materials, e.g. foreign language learning materials for non-native speakers or foreign language materials about a topic such as German history in German. • Extensive collections of the works of well-known authors and selections from the works of lesser-known authors. • Defined access to an extensive collection of owned or remotely-accessed electronic resources, including bibliographic tools, texts, data sets, journals, etc. The collection should be systematically reviewed for currency of information and for assurance that essential and important information is retained, including significant numbers of classic retrospective materials.
4	**Research Level: A collection that contains the major published source materials required for doctoral study and independent research includes:** • A very extensive collection of general and specialized monographs and reference works. • A very extensive collection of general and specialized periodicals. • Extensive collections of appropriate foreign language materials. • Extensive collections of the works of well-known authors as well as lesser-known authors. • Defined access to a very extensive collection of owned or remotely accessed electronic resources, including bibliographic tools, texts, data sets, journals, etc. • Older material that is retained and systematically preserved to serve the needs of historical research
5	**Comprehensive Level: A collection in a specifically defined field of knowledge that strives to be exhaustive, as far as is reasonably possible (i.e., a "special collection"), in all applicable languages includes:** • Exhaustive collections of published materials. • Very extensive manuscript collections. • Very extensive collections in all other pertinent formats. • A comprehensive level collection may serve as a national or international resource.

Figure 4.4. RLG Conspectus Levels as Defined by IFLA.

Deselection

Deselection, also known as weeding, is a necessary part of collection maintenance, especially in health sciences libraries where resource currency is paramount. Weeding should be done regularly and according to general rules set forth in the collection policy and internal procedures. Factors to consider when weeding print monographs are age of material, usage, physical condition, duplication in electronic format, editions (choose how many to keep), accuracy of information, and local or historical value (e.g., retention in perpetuity of all monographs written by institutional authors); Clark, Levine, and Shane (2013) provide more information. Print journal factors to consider are availability in electronic format, usage, completeness of holdings and length of run, language other than English, subject matter, subject matter expert recommendations, and local or historical value. Other physical items such as anatomical models or audiovisual holdings should be evaluated on physical condition, accuracy, format (e.g., move from VHS to CD to DVD), and usage. Keep in mind that space considerations often prompt quick action, so regular and judicious weeding should be conducted and, if available, criteria for off-site or shared storage considered.

Weeding is still viewed through the physical collection lens. Most new collection additions are electronic, so consider adding a section addressing electronic resource deselection. Evaluation criteria for books, journals, and databases are usage (see section on COUNTER statistics later in this chapter), faculty recommendation for alternate resource or platform, unsupportable cost increase, new editions, and overlap with other package content, to name a few. Finally, how a library will review free electronic resources should be included. Free resources are easy to add but can degrade easily (e.g., broken links) and add clutter that reduces the visibility of core resources.

> Weeding projects for book collections are good and necessary. Do what you think is best for the collection and the library. Faculty will not mind too much, and the students will appreciate it. Weed as often as you see fit.
>
> *Jeffrey G. Coghill, CAS-HSL, AHIP, MLS, MA, head of outreach at East Carolina University; and director, Eastern AHEC Library Services, Greenville, NC*

At this point, the library has compiled a collection development policy. However, a policy is never complete. It is informational, puts forth an ideal set of guidelines, and is a communication tool. It also lays the groundwork for evaluating, purchasing, and licensing content. As librarians practice the art of collection development, their work informs the policy and vice versa.

PUTTING POLICY INTO PRACTICE

A well-written and well-conceived collection policy is only a framework. It guides decisions and serves as an internal and external communication tool, but the practice of evaluating, licensing, purchasing, preserving, and withdrawing or deselecting resources takes considerable time and effort. Many fortunate collection development librarians work closely with an acquisitions librarian or team. Once the item is selected (or deselected), the details are handled by others in the organization. However, in many health sciences libraries, the librarian is either solo or is part of a small department so she or he must also manage the acquisition process. One benefit to shepherding the entire process is learning the mechanics of e-resource management, which becomes another decision point when deciding to purchase a resource.

Consider the differences between print and electronic acquisition and management in Figure 4.5 from the Digital Library Federation (Jewell et al., 2004). In this deceptively simple workflow (for more in-depth analysis visit the DLF site), the similarities stop after the first step. The ability to use resources on a trial basis and gather feedback from colleagues and patrons starts a separate electronic resource process that includes licensing, technical evaluation, business negotiation, implementation, and finally maintenance and review. Before delving into the evaluation of resources by material type, it is worth briefly reviewing the particular pieces of the e-resource workflow that may assist with supporting collection development.

General Electronic Resource Licensing Considerations

Electronic resources require a unique set of evaluation criteria. Questions regarding terms of use in the areas of user access, sharing, **perpetual access**, platform requirements, legal issues, and provision of service are paramount. Each aspect is typically present in the accompanying license. Before negotiating or accepting a trial of a resource, librarians should create a set of nonnegotiable terms. Several areas will be discussed below. See the Liblicense Model License Agreement and Commentary at http://liblicense.crl.edu/licensing-information/model-license/ to view a model license.

Authorized Use and Users

The online nature of electronic resources means user access can be potentially unlimited. Librarians should review each license for publisher restrictions or cost model for authorized users and concurrent users.

An authorized user is anyone who, according to the license, is allowed to access the resource. Publishers are particularly interested in the number of full-time equivalent (FTE) student, staff, and faculty. FTE often sets the number of authorized users and thus the price. For public institutions, off-site access may be restricted to employees and students whereas any walk-in user, regardless of affiliation, has access while on-site. Walk-in use is fairly common and is acceptable to most publishers, thus should be negotiated for if applicable. Affiliation must be defined at the health sciences library site level in order to ensure proper access to a range of patrons including contract providers, preceptors (community-based educators), temporary researchers, and other categories of essential users.

Concurrent use refers to the number of users who can access the same platform, database, resource (e.g., book or article) at the same time. A variety of concurrent use models exist. Some resources provide access to all users at the same time, whereas others limit access to a specific book or database to a preset number.

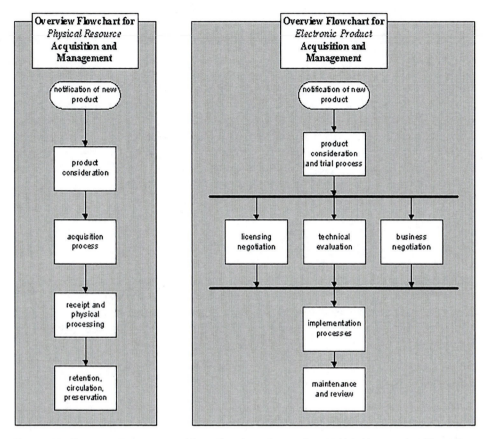

Figure 4.5. Electronic Resources Workflow Flowchart. Source: http://old.diglib.org/pubs/dlf102/dlf102 .htm#dlfermi0408appb.

When the limit is reached, new users are blocked until a seat is available. The library can negotiate numbers, and therefore cost, on a database or book-by-book basis depending on its anticipated use. Some licenses restrict concurrent users regardless of individual items available on the platform. If a library pays for five concurrent users to a book platform that has thirty books, only five users can access any of those thirty books at one time. This last model creates problems when a professor assigns a chapter to an online book, and the chapter and all other titles are unavailable while a limited number of students review the chapter. Unlimited use is best but can be expensive.

Sharing

Details to consider under sharing are Fair Use and ILL transactions. **Fair Use** falls under U.S. copyright law, www.copyright.gov/fls/fl102.html, and refers to the ability to use published material for education, scholarly work, or research. Information about printing, downloading, and copying should be addressed in the license.

Health sciences libraries serving academia should review course reserves and course packs terms.

No licensing standard exists for ILL (Lamoureux and Stemper, 2011). Most licenses allow for ILL, but some restrict how the information is shared and with what user groups. Health sciences librarians should take time to review license restrictions. Moreover, although most electronic journal articles can be provided, electronic books prove difficult. Lending is per chapter, and some e-book aggregators do not allow ILL. As with all things regarding e-resources, publishers and librarians are continuously looking to strike a balance between payment and access. Some enterprising librarians are experimenting with group licensing that will allow sharing among the group (Duke, 2013); others are researching the move from ILL to other delivery methods such as CCC's Get It Now Service (Jarvis et al., 2013). Chapter 12 covers ILL in more depth.

Although no standard license exists, the Shared Electronic Resource Understanding (SERU) is a NISO best practice that offers an alternative to the standard license agreement. It is not a legal document, "rather, the SERU statements describe a set of commonly agreed-upon expectations for using and providing electronic resources" (NISO SERU Standing Committee, 2012: 1). The library and publisher join a registry; and if both parties accept the SERU statements, resource access is granted immediately. Key acquisition aspects such as cost and access duration are still negotiated separately, but SERU is a promising step toward reducing the time spent negotiating licenses.

Delivery and Access

Electronic resources are delivered through online networks to a subscriber site. Access on-site is controlled by the institution's computer and server IP addresses. **Remote access** refers to the ability of authorized users to use the resource in question off-site. Remote access is typically achieved through the use of a proxy server, VPN, Shibboleth, Athens, or other authentication schemes such as passwords or public keys (more about these topics in chapters 6 and 12).

Perpetual access is the right to have ongoing, permanent access to the licensed material after the license has been discontinued. Publishers vary greatly on how they provide perpetual access, so diligent consideration of provision terms is essential. Most often, the publisher will continue to host the material on its site for a small "platform fee." The library simply links to the years (journals) or items (books) for which they paid. Other publishers supply a disc or hard drive with purchased content. However, without the platform to host the material, it is of little use to most organizations. Be sure to keep careful purchase records, as journals change publishers, and the library may need to negotiate perpetual access with a new vendor.

Legal Issues

Key legal considerations are indemnification and governing law. **Indemnification** is the agreement to hold one party harmless from claims alleged from a third party. Typically state governments and organizations do not allow libraries to indemnify the content provider. Indemnifying the publisher or aggregator would allow a third party to sue the state in cases of user copyright infringement or access abuse.

Governing law sets the legal jurisdiction in the event of a dispute and is another area where states and parent organizations may have strict rules. State institutions typically require license issues be adjudicated in the institution's home state, not the publisher's home state.

This is a cursory overview of key license issues. Knowing potential nonnegotiable license issues ahead of evaluation and potential purchase saves time and advises the content provider to take care on insisting on overly restrictive rules. When starting at a new institution, take a generic license to the legal department for review and advice. Similarly, speak with library colleagues about walk-ins, ILL practices, and use of course reserves, among other license issues. Any nonnegotiable terms should be included in the Collection Development Policy for reference and general communication.

Consortial Licensing

According to the 2011–2012 Association of Academic Health Science Libraries (AAHSL) data, consortial spending accounted for 29 percent of an academic health sciences library's collection expenditures (Squires, 2013). Health sciences libraries consortiums range from agreements with other hospitals libraries, the home academic institution, the state, or the region. For example, the SCAMeL (South Central Academic Medical Libraries) Consortium, www.tulane.edu/~scamel/, has a long history of consortial licensing of electronic resources. Whether or not a resource is available through a consortial deal may affect the pricing enough to determine the acquisition. During, or even before, a resource trial, the librarian should check with consortial partners to discover if a vendor arrangement is available or if there is interest in requesting a vendor quote. Regular communication with consortial members is essential after entering into a consortial agreement in order to monitor usage, product satisfaction, and group financial status to make sure the product has ongoing support.

Electronic Resource Product Evaluation

On average, electronic resources represent approximately 49 percent of an AAHSL member library's collection expenditures (Squires, 2013). Therefore, health sciences libraries often follow standard electronic resource evaluation criteria. Sometimes it is included in the collection policy (see University of Maryland policy, www.hshsl. umaryland.edu/about/policies.cfm); at other times it is an internal checklist the resource selectors manage.

Beyond the boilerplate licensing topics addressed in the previous section, health sciences librarians should use standard evaluation questions for content, usability, and technical support. Carrigan, Higa, and Tobia (2008) present useful tables with digital resource characteristics and questions to consider.

- Content should be evaluated for currency, authority, accuracy, uniqueness, and scope/coverage.

- Usability considerations include ease of use, navigation, searching functionality, printing/saving/e-mail/video capabilities, stability, response time, and integration capabilities.
- Technical support questions cover vendor-supplied support topics such as timeliness of problem resolution, availability of COUNTER (Counting Online Usage of Networked Electronic Resources)-compliant usage statistics (www.project-counter.org), training offerings, ease of branding, and other administrative tasks.
- Library technical support concerns relate to local authentication systems, security policies and practices, and technical demands of the content (e.g., downloads) or access restrictions (barriers for guest or remote access).

These tables are still useful in today's context and are worth seeking out. Additional topics and questions based on market and technological changes are provided in the sidebar.

Statistics

A key component of any electronic resource offering is the availability of reliable usage data. Most publishers and vendors are COUNTER-compliant, meaning standardized usage reports are obtainable through the administrative module. The benefit of COUNTER-compliance is the ability to merge and compare all resource usage across vendors so that librarians can easily generate and apply cost-per-use and other metrics in collection decisions. Some manual gathering of data is still necessary, but a variety of products and services based on COUNTER and SUSHI (Standardized Usage Statistics Harvesting Initiative) protocol, www.niso.org/workrooms/sushi/, are available to assist in gathering and analyzing the data.

Trials

Resource trials are an excellent way to gauge interest for a product or journal title. Most vendors make resources available either via IP address or username and password. The vendor may even have promotional material—in both print and electronic images—to assist with promoting a trial. A simple survey with between three and five questions and a section for comments will aid in collection and collation of feedback. Record the results and decision in your Electronic Resource Management (ERM system; if the purchase is not completed, it is likely a repeat request will arise. Products change and improve, so a baseline will help in the next evaluation.

Journal Evaluation

Journal management is perhaps the most complex area of collection development and especially important for health sciences libraries. Some libraries continue to collect print journals for key areas or for a browsing collection, but electronic is typically preferred for its instant and ubiquitous availability.

In the print world, the criteria to include a title in the collection centered on whether or not a user has requested a title, the number of ILL requests in a predetermined period of time, indexing in relevant sources such as PubMed or CINAHL, and cost. The library would then order the title for delivery. These base criteria still

ELECTRONIC RESOURCE EVALUATION CONSIDERATIONS

Smartphones and tablets

1. Are applications ("apps") available? For iPhone/iPad, Android, other devices?
2. Is there a mobile interface?
3. Is the information available off-line via the app?
4. How is authentication managed?

Technological and social media advances

1. What is possible via APIs (Application Programming Interfaces) (e.g., embedding video or images in websites)?
2. Are widgets available for integration with resource guides (e.g., LibGuides) or websites?
3. Do they have social media sharing capabilities?
4. What is the customized user experience (e.g., MyFolder, highlighting, bookshelf, notes, etc.)?
5. Is there seamless integration with a variety of bibliographic management tools (e.g., Serials Solutions)?

Health sciences-specific questions

1. Has the resource provider successfully integrated its product at other sites? Can it provide references?
2. Is the resource evidence-based? Which system of evidence does it use, http://en.wikipedia.org/wiki/Evidence-based_medicine#Assessing_the_quality_of_evidence?
3. What other "value-added" features are available, such as calculators, patient education, drug information, and so forth?
4. Does the resource provide video of instruction or lab protocols? Is there lag time, and what is the quality of the video?
5. Can the user manipulate 3-D images?
6. Are CME/CNE credits offered through the product? If so, is there a link with the local CME office or is accreditation provided through a third party?

Library discoverability and vendor support

1. Is the resource compatible with discovery tools (EBSCO Discovery, Encore, Primo, Summon, WorldCat Local, etc.)?
2. Is the vendor current with industry statistical standards (COUNTER), and are the statistics harvestable (SUSHI)?
3. Is the vendor current with other industry standards such as SERU, ONIX, or other collaborative standards?
4. Are catalog records available for no cost or minimal cost with purchase? How often are records updated, and do they supply records with MeSH?

apply, but now the librarian must consider a number of additional factors when acquiring electronic journals such as licensing terms, consortial availability, overlap with other resources, embargo periods, and whether to purchase the title individually or within a package.

For a historical perspective, Frazier (2001) offers an insightful discussion of the "big-deal" journal packages. Although many librarians express the desire not to participate in large packages, little evidence shows that this is happening, and participation in packages is actually increasing (Bosch and Henderson, 2012). A complicating factor is the growth in full-text subject databases that have acquired the rights to offer full text of scholarly journals along with citation information. Immediate access to the full text through a database is great for the user, but what does it mean for the collection development librarian?

The main issues related to full text from a variety of sources are overlap and embargo. **Overlap** refers to having access to the same title from more than one provider. A library may have four instances of a journal from four providers, but each platform offers different dates. This could be due to a historical purchase from another vendor, two databases with the same full text, and a current publisher subscription. More often than not, all access points are needed to make a full date range available. **Embargo** is the time lapse between now and when journal content access begins. For example, many providers have a one-year rolling embargo. If today is August 1, 2013, then your access is from a point in the past up to July 31, 2012. If the journal is highly regarded by the user community—such as the *New England Journal of Medicine* or *Lancet*—a current subscription should be purchased.

THE FUTURE OF PRINT

Libraries are still a hybrid print and electronic environment; however, they are no longer the single local repository of a broad base of published knowledge. As electronic availability of publications becomes more ingrained and reliable, libraries must plan how to manage or deconstruct their legacy print collections. Certainly, libraries with facility and space issues will look to reduce the physical imprint. Space concerns in health sciences libraries are often discussed in the literature (Ludwig, 2010), at medical library conferences (Ryan, Hart, and Steelman, 2012), and on social media (Kraft, 2013). One study estimates the cost of open stack storage to be $141.89 per book versus $28.77 per book in high-density storage (Lewis, 2013); thus, retention of "just in case" print titles may not be a cost-effective strategy. Libraries without acute space needs or budgetary pressure may prefer to repurpose square footage into student collaboration sites. Lewis offers an in-depth, current, and insightful handling of this topic.

Aspects to examine when deconstructing a print collection are preservation, local content, storage issues, and secure long-term access to the content. The librarian must methodically and judiciously deselect titles for disposal and set rigorous criteria for what remains or is included in off-site, high-density, or a regionally shared print repository. Depending on the geographic location, a health sciences library may need to seek out nonhealth science partners to achieve reasonably priced and accessible storage. Reliability of digital libraries with preservation goals, such as PubMed Central, www.ncbi.nlm.nih.gov/pmc/ (host of the *Journal of the Medical Library Association: JMLA*); or JSTOR, www.jstor.org/, must be evaluated before choosing to withdraw titles based on long-term availability online.

Fortunately, overlap and embargo assessment help is available through ERM systems. ERM systems are useful collection development tools in other areas such as cost analysis and managing license and vendor information.

Publishers have geared packages and databases for health sciences. One package may be perfect for some libraries whereas others, especially large academic libraries, may find significant overlap with other products already available. In addition to overlap, careful evaluation of a cost-per-use package is needed. For example, Lippincott, Williams, and Wilkins (LWW) is the exclusive provider of the LWW Total Access Package with more than 250 medical and nursing journals. Although the package may seem expensive at the outset, many of the journals are highly regarded and frequently used. It may be better to purchase the whole package even when some titles are underused. Again, a fully implemented ERM can assist in overlap and cost-per-use analyses. Finally, some publishers can set up a debit account or tokens with the library that allow seamless patron access to articles while the library is charged for the use (Hosburgh, 2012).

Monograph Evaluation

Monographs for health sciences are available in print and electronic format. Many subject areas have essential texts (e.g., Longo's *Harrison's Principles of Internal Medicine*, 18th ed.; DiPiro's *Pharmacotherapy: A Pathophysiologic Approach*, 8th ed.; Lewis's *Medical-Surgical Nursing*, 9th ed., etc.). Print formats are still desirable for users who like to view complex matter and visual aids, especially color images, in printed form. Electronic books are popular as they are easily portable, and many reading devices are color capable. Both formats have advantages and disadvantages from the patron perspective. Few health sciences libraries can offer texts in both formats, so communication with the user population is key.

Print books can be purchased on an "as-needed" basis or can be acquired through an approval plan. An **approval plan** is a customized profile of subject areas, publisher and format preferences, and depth of collection (e.g., standard, research, etc.) in each subject area. For example, a library that serves a medical school would set up minimal selection in an area such as veterinary science, but it might choose to have comprehensive coverage in the field of pulmonology or surgery. The approval plan vendor selects appropriate titles and ships them to the library without further librarian intervention. Depending on how the plan is set up, the books come in for further evaluation or in **shelf-ready** condition.

The advantages of e-books: They cannot be mis-shelved, stolen, hidden for future use, or damaged with coffee; they do not require labels, book stamps, or barcodes. However, some e-books do not have page numbers, making it difficult for some class assignments; others do not print well. Rules about simultaneous users can drive librarians crazy; and ability to highlight, bookmark, and make notes varies widely and can be very frustrating to students. Encourage them to use a universal platform such as Amazon's Cloud Reader, which does NOT require buying a Kindle.

Jean L. Siebert, BS pharmacy, MLS, MBA, AHIP, collection manager/reference librarian, Health Sciences Library, Robert C. Byrd Health Sciences Center, West Virginia University, Morgantown

Patron-driven acquisition (PDA) is a recent form of shared collection development. The library works with an e-book provider or vendor to populate the online catalog with bibliographic records of books within the approval plan scope, but these titles are not currently part of the collection. Patrons are able to see the record and are unaware of whether the book is available. After a certain set of limits on access is exceeded, like user clicks, the book is automatically purchased and available for patron use. The vendor charges the library, and the book becomes part of the regular collection. This type of acquisition allows the collection to develop on an "as-needed" rather than a "just-in-case" basis. Arguably, the collection is more relevant when users choose the material instead of the library hoping that what is on the shelf is satisfactory. Lorbeer (2013) and Clark, Levine, and Shane (2013) provide more information about the pros and cons of this practice.

The main criteria for health sciences monograph selection are authority, quality, relevancy, and currency. It is not general practice to supply textbooks to individuals, although some libraries purchase print or electronic access to test preparation books and core texts such as *Harrison's* or *Adams and Victor's Principles of Neurology* for their students. Core e-books will require multiple concurrent users in packages such as Access Medicine.

The most widely used resource for health sciences collection development is Doody's Core Titles (DCT), www.doody.com/dct/, and Doody's Review Service (DRS), www.doody.com/DEJ/. Both are subscription or cost-based and provide a wealth of information gathered and written by health sciences librarians and content experts across basic science, clinical medicine, nursing, allied health, and other health science-related areas. All reviews follow strict evaluation guidelines. DCT provides information on the top books or software titles in 121 disciplines. DRS contains more than 25,000 reviews in 140 specialties. Both services are organized by subject, contain Brandon/Hill indicators, and are easily gathered or exported for individualized use.

Database Evaluation

As with monographs, core databases are available for the health sciences in major topic areas. Standard index and abstract databases by area are MEDLINE

BEFORE DOODY'S: HISTORY OF BRANDON-HILL

The initial "Selected List of Books and Journals for the Small Medical Library" was published in the *Bulletin of the Medical Library Association* in 1965; and from its onset, this series of selection guides was heavily used and highly valued by librarians, nurses, health care practitioners, and publishers. The Small Medical Library list was followed in 1979 by the "Selected List of Nursing Books and Journals" and by the "Selected List of Books and Journals in Allied Health Sciences" in 1984. In 2001, the publications were made available on the Internet, promoting unrestricted access. It was always the instruction of Alfred Brandon and Dorothy Hill, the original authors, that the selected lists would not be published under their names without their direct involvement, which is why they retained copyright of the lists. With the retirement of Dorothy Hill in 2004, this long-standing project drew to a close, http://library.mssm.edu/brandon-hill/index.shtml.

for biomedical literature, CINAHL for nursing, and International Pharmaceutical Abstracts (IPA) for pharmacy. In addition to indexes and abstracts, there are a number of full content resources, drug resources such as Lexi-Comp or Micromedex, specialty databases such as VisualDX, exam preparation resources such as ExamMaster, full clinical decision support tools such as UpToDate (Wolters-Kluwer), DynaMed (EBSCO), or Nursing Reference Center (EBSCO). A full treatment on the content and searching techniques within these tools is provided in Chapter 8.

Often the content is available for licensing via a number of vendors. Although the base content may be similar (e.g., CINAHL via EBSCO or Ovid), each vendor adds its own unique value. A parallel trial of vendor offerings will help the librarian determine which product fits best in the local setting. The decision to purchase from one vendor over another may be influenced by having more than one database from the same provider, which will facilitate training, create a seamless user experience while searching across a platform, and can result in a cost reduction. Ask about special educational deals. For example, some drug information vendors will allow IP-restricted access to certain buildings where instruction takes place. Other factors to evaluate are concurrent user cost, pricing structure (per FTE, research band, or number of people in a specific discipline), overlap of "value-added" content such as patient handouts or drug information, electronic health record integration, drug formulary compatibility, and continuing education offerings. The ideal selection may be based on integration and augmentation with local systems and services rather than cost alone.

Free Resource Evaluation

Free resources are easily discoverable with today's ERM systems from vendors such as EBSCO, Ex Libris, and Serials Solutions. Lists such as the Directory of Open Access Journals: DOAJ, www.doaj.org/, are available

Librarians are well-suited to evaluate and promote health-related mobile apps and resources to their users. Librarians should review their website statistics to identify which mobile devices are most commonly used among their primary user groups to decide which platforms to focus on (e.g., iOS and Android). They should be familiar with the electronic resources they have already purchased and the corresponding mobile apps (e.g., DynaMed, UpToDate, and EBSCO). Librarians should also understand the distinctions between native apps and mobile apps, and which ones would be most appropriate under various circumstances. Although they are evaluated in app stores, mobile medical apps are not typically evaluated for content accuracy, only for the presence of malware, so it is important that librarians evaluate content for themselves and educate their users accordingly. At a minimum, mobile app and electronic resource selection criteria should include the operating system, user community, formal reviews, whether the information is evidence-based, whether content has been plagiarized or infringes on another's copyright, and the cost. Speaking knowledgeably about mobile apps and devices is an excellent way for librarians to enhance their authority and open the door for promoting additional services.

Jon Goodell, MA, AHIP, reference and outreach librarian, University of Arkansas for Medical Sciences Library, Little Rock

for selection alongside paid resource packages. Many excellent journals are available, such as titles from BioMed Central; however, be selective. Free resources can obscure access to core health sciences resources. Free collections should be weeded just like paid content. Resources managed through an ERM are perhaps more stable than independently added links, but all require routine evaluation. Whether made available through the ERM or the catalog, they need regular attention.

RESOURCE BUDGETS

Over the past five years, libraries have experienced extreme budgetary challenges and few library budgets have grown; indeed, most have shrunk or at the very least remained constant. Resources and personnel are the two largest areas of most health sciences library budgets (see Figure 4.6); therefore, the collection development librarian is often responsible for administering a third or more of the overall library budget. Naturally, the recent funding volatility affects collection budgets in total initial appropriations. Personnel costs are difficult to modify, so the collection budget may possibly be tapped to cover unexpected midyear rescissions. Careful financial planning, complete with contingencies, is essential to offset unexpected funding modifications.

The library resource budget is one of the most important guiding documents used in collection development. It sets the parameters of expenditure, usually based on the concepts and priorities set forth in the collection development policy. Spending expectations or legal requirements may exist depending on the type of library and

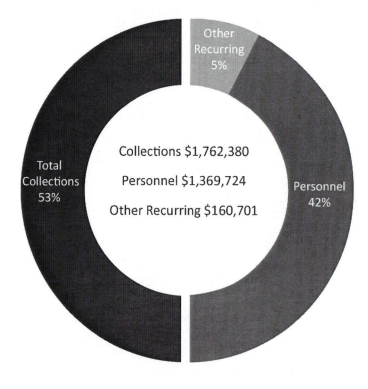

Collections $1,762,380

Personnel $1,369,724

Other Recurring $160,701

Other Recurring 5%

Total Collections 53%

Personnel 42%

Figure 4.6. Total Expenditures by Type, AAHSL Libraries, 2011–2012. Source: Steven J. Squires, ed. 2013. *2011–2012 Annual Statistics of Medical School Libraries in the United States and Canada*, 35th ed. Seattle: AAHSL.

the funds dedicated to the collection. Knowing the larger organizational mission, funding sources, and fiscal climate will assist in proper planning and anticipating larger priority or funding shifts.

Budget Types

According to Gregory, library collection budgets "typically fall into one of four general categories: (1) an object of expenditure, or line-item budget; (2) a lump-sum budget; (3) program budget; or (4) a formula budget" (2011: 103). The size, type, and standard accounting rules of the parent organization may determine which of these four categories are applied to the library, and the library may choose to implement any of the four methods to the collection as appropriate.

The line-item budget is a line-by-line listing of expenditure areas and funds allocated to that area. The specificity of allocation is up to the librarian, but it could range from high-level categories such as monographs, serials, or databases to very specific purposes such as monographs for physician assistant program students. Broad categories allow greater flexibility, whereas precise categories can be more restrictive and may require more reallocations during the year. Libraries with distributed collection development typically use smaller categories or "mini-budgets" and assign the amounts to subject selectors. It is the responsibility of the collection development librarian to ensure proper adherence to the totals so any midcourse corrections can be made.

A lump-sum budget is the total amount of funds assigned to the library for use. Although this type of allotment carries the greatest amount of flexibility from meeting any demands of the parent organization, it is not a practical approach to thoughtful resource acquisition. The collection development and acquisitions librarians, in consultation with other library personnel, would likely distribute the lump sum into a line item or other priority-based grouping.

The program budget is an attempt to relate the cost of an activity to the funds allocated to carry out the activity. In the case of acquiring library resources, a program budget would start at zero each year and only be as large as the cost of the essential resources purchased to meet the library mission. Library missions rarely change unless the institutional mission changes, so most program budgets would remain similar in content if not overall cost.

Finally, the formula budget is developed using objective data to calculate fund distribution. The data could be student enrollment by program, research overhead dedicated to the library, or types and frequency of health care practiced. For example, a large university library that serves several colleges might give the greatest collection weight to the College of Nursing, which has the largest enrollment, or the College of Medicine, which brings in greater research dollars. Under this model each location will be funded differently.

Funding Sources

The funding source may determine how the yearly funds are allocated to the library and how they can be spent. General collection dollars (sometimes referred to as Instruction & General in academic libraries) are the least restrictive. Endowed spending accounts, foundation accounts, gifts, and receipts from any local, state, or federal bonds are examples of fund sources that may be one time or recurring and may also have restrictions on their use. For example, special state funding may have a time limit (e.g., two years) and may only be used for certain types of expenditures (e.g., capital vs. noncapital). Endowments have companion spending accounts, but the amount varies based on the financial markets; expenditures may be limited to a certain subject area or donor requirement. It is essential to know all the funding sources that comprise the collection budget and to make assurances that each fund is spent in a timely and appropriate manner.

Budget Planning and Monitoring

Once a budgeting method is identified, the librarian allocates dollar figures to categories. Table 4.1 is an example of a simple budget strategy for a collection budget of $1 million. The sample budget uses the concept of recurring and non-recurring expenses to account for platform charges or other ongoing annual costs for purchased items such as e-books or perpetual journal access. Allocations based on enrollment or other data-driven, decision-making techniques may require more involved methods such as breaking out journal, book, and database expenditures by strategic priorities or subject area. Special funds (endowments, bonds) might require a similar but separate tracking mechanism.

Journal Budgets

Journal subscriptions are the largest collection expense for health sciences libraries (see Figure 4.7). Staying informed about serial trends and likely inflation increases enables the librarian to plan for potential cuts. Every April the *Library Journal*

Table 4.1. Sample Collection Budget of $1 Million

Category	Budget (recurring)	Budget (nonrecurring)	TOTAL
Print journals		2,000	2,000
Electronic journals	683,000		683,000
Print monographs		50,000	50,000
Electronic monographs (+PDA*)	10,000	30,000	35,000
Databases	150,000		150,000
Bibliographic utilities	40,000	10,000	50,000
Binding		12,000	12,000
Freight/postage**		5,000	10,000
Other (anatomical models, DVDs, etc.)		8,000	8,000
TOTAL	$883,000	$117,000	$1,000,000

*PDA—patron driven acquisition.
**Includes ILL shipping costs.

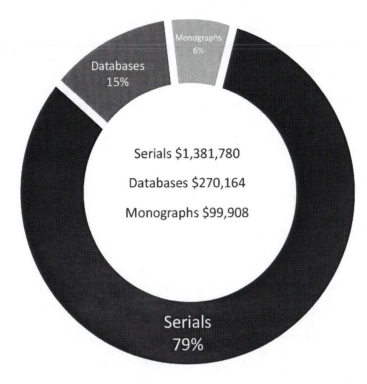

Serials $1,381,780

Databases $270,164

Monographs $99,908

Monographs 6%

Databases 15%

Serials 79%

Figure 4.7. Total Collection Expenditures by Format, AAHSL Libraries, 2011–2012. Source: Steven J. Squires, ed. 2013. *2011–2012 Annual Statistics of Medical School Libraries in the United States and Canada,* 35th ed. Seattle: AAHSL.

publishes an article written by experts in the acquisition and subscription delivery field that presents inflation estimates overall and by subject area. Journals in the science, technology, and medicine (STM) fields regularly carry the highest cost subscriptions and the highest rate of inflation year to year, so budgets can change significantly year to year without adding any new titles.

Database Budgets

Databases are the next largest expense in the collection budget. Although the U.S. government provides the major biomedical citation database, MEDLINE/PubMed, at no cost, the growth in the variety of specialty, point-of-care, and multiformat databases (e.g., books, journals, images, guidelines, drug information, etc.) ensures increased expenditures in this area. If finances allow, set aside an assessment line to trial databases on a one- or two-year rotation.

Monograph Budgets

Individual or packaged electronic books are purchased in a variety of ways including onetime purchase or annual subscription. Providers of one-time purchases can charge annual hosting fees that should be added to the recurring budget line. As discussed earlier, libraries are increasingly offering e-books via patron-driven acquisition (PDA). Librarians assign PDA providers a fund amount so patrons cannot overspend the amount ascribed to electronic monographs in the budget.

Print and Binding Budgets

Electronic resources were 49 percent of academic health sciences library collection expenditures in 2012 (Squires, 2013). Obviously print books and journals are still a vital part of a library. Some titles are not available electronically, or the library may choose to have a title on-site as an extended study or browsing option for patrons. The print portion of the budget is the easiest to rearrange if budget numbers are insufficient in other areas. Print journals, and less often print books, require setting aside funds for preservation and binding. Binding is another area that can be suspended if the need arises. However, caution should be exercised in raiding these lines on a regular basis lest the book collection become outdated and the unbound print journals be damaged or lost.

Bibliographic Utility Budgets

For budgeting purposes, bibliographic utilities (e.g., OCLC) and other services (e.g., ILL software, ERM) should be considered fixed costs. A small library can manage without some of these standard tool sets but will spend the money in staff time. A well-managed ILS or ERM brings other value-added components such as overlap analysis or other reports that can assist with collection management. Balancing the need for tools versus resources is delicate but should be evaluated before reducing or growing the budget line. Although some libraries pay for bibliographic utilities from the collection budget, other libraries choose to pay for them from the technology, cataloging, or general budget.

Budgeting for "Other"

"Other" encompasses a range of possibilities from new tools (e.g., XML or metadata software), to memberships that come with journals, and other miscellaneous expenses such as supplies or specialized equipment used for processing collections. Sometimes maintenance for compact shelving or security gates is included in the collection budget if viewed as expenditures on the collection. This category can also include anatomical models, media, or additional infrequent spending areas.

Monitoring Budgets

Careful tracking of expenditures is necessary to ensure proper disbursement of funds. In a small library, the librarian may serve as the accountant and track encumbrances and payments on a single spreadsheet. Larger organizations may have accountants in addition to a number of acquisitions staff who track purchases through Integrated Library Systems (ILS) acquisition modules, Electronic Resources Management (ERM) systems, and in the organizational Enterprise Financial System (e.g., Banner, PeopleSoft). Most organizations will require allotment of capital and noncapital expenditures (owned vs. rented) for centralized accounting and insurance purposes. Librarians should take time to learn the key terms, cycles, accounting methods, and data reports available in each system and what reports are required from the parent organization.

Setting Priorities

Budgeting requires flexibility and a keen awareness of resource details. Regardless of budget size, the collection development librarian should track the budget to ensure priority expenditures are paid for and gauge the need to halt those purchases that can be varied if needed. The priority expenditures are those resources ranked as high priority for the collection. For example, if a point-of-care database is integrated with the Electronic Health Record (EHR) of the clinical care arm of the enterprise, then it should be considered a priority, and therefore a fixed cost. Purchase of non-recurring materials such as print monographs can be suspended or delayed. In a severe crisis, recurring items can be canceled in descending priority order.

It is possible to have additional collection funds available near fiscal year end. A prioritized list of nonrecurring expenditures is useful in this event. Funds can be put toward resources such as monographs, anatomical models, or could be used by technical services to purchase modules for the integrated library system (catalog) or services such as authority control work.

KEEPING CURRENT

It takes time and experience to become adept in any or all collection development areas. One way to learn more or stay current is to review the many resources available to a collection development librarian. An excellent place to start is the MLA Collection Development Section "Resources for Librarians" list, http://colldev.mlanet.org/resources/. The list contains information about Listservs, conferences, resource review locations, and more. In addition to this resource, a general familiarity with Open Access terms and mandates (see Sherpa/Romeo, www.sherpa.ac.uk/romeo/, and Sherpa/Juliet, www.sherpa.ac.uk/juliet/) is recommended.

SUMMARY

This chapter covers the current state of collection development in the health sciences in terms of collection development policies, licensing, resource evaluation, and budgeting. The most important thing to remember is the information needs of the patron base. Regular and clear communication with constituents about resource needs and with the support team (librarians, vendors, and professional colleagues) will make for a successful career as a health sciences collection development professional.

STUDY QUESTIONS

1. Consider the Venn diagram in Figure 4.2. What other groups could be included? Think of a health sciences library and create a diagram that reflects the user population. Consider how you would describe these users in a collection policy.
2. Choose five health sciences subjects from MeSH. Apply Conspectus levels to the subjects based on a real or imagined library. Explain the rationale for the assigned level.

3. You are in charge of licensing for a hospital library. Which license terms are non-negotiable, and why are they not negotiable?

4. Evaluate an electronic resource using the criteria in the Electronic Resource Evaluation sidebar. If available to you, compare two similar products such as DynaMed and UpToDate or AccessMedicine and Stat!Ref. Which would you choose based on the criteria and why? What other questions would you ask?

REFERENCES

Anderson, Chris. 2006. *The Long Tail: Why the Future of Business Is Selling Less of More*. New York: Hyperion.

Anderson, Joanne S. 1996. *Guide for Written Collection Policy Statements/Subcommittee to Revise the Guide for Written Collection Policy Statements, Administration of Collection Development Committee, Collection Management and Development Section, Association for Library Collections & Technical Services*, 2nd ed. *Collection Management and Development Guides: no. 7*. Chicago: American Library Association.

Biblarz, Dora. 1992. "The Conspectus as a Blueprint for Creating Collection Development Policy Statements." *Acquisitions Librarian* 4, no. 7: 169–76.

Bosch, Steven, and Kittie Henderson. 2012. "Coping with the Terrible Twins." *Library Journal* 137, no. 8: 28–32.

Carrigan, Esther, Mori Lou Higa, and Rajia Tobia. 2008. "Monographic and Digital Resource Collection Development." In *Introduction to Health Sciences Librarianship*, edited by M. Sandra Wood, 97–126. Binghamton, NY: Haworth Information Press.

Clark, Ann Marie, Beth Levine, and Douglas Shane. 2013. "Collecting for the Platypus—Acquisition and Collection Management in the Arnold Library." *Journal of Hospital Librarianship* 13, no. 1: 11–22.

Clement, Susanne K., and Jennifer M. Foy. 2011. *Collection Development in a Changing Environment: Policies and Organization for College and University Libraries*. CLIP Note 42. Chicago: ACRL.

Demas, Samuel, and Mary E. Miller. 2012. "Rethinking Collection Management Plans: Shaping Collective Collections for the 21st Century." *Collection Management* 37, no. 3/4: 168–87.

Douglas, C. Steven. 2011. "Revising a Collection Development Policy in a Rapidly Changing Environment." *Journal of Electronic Resources in Medical Libraries* 8, no. 1: 15–21.

Drexel University Health Sciences Libraries. 2007. "Collection Development Policy." www.library.drexel.edu/files/about_documents/HSCollDev2007.pdf.

Duke, Judy. 2013. "NovaNet Libraries Test E-Book Sharing." *Advanced Technology Libraries* 42, no. 2 (February): 7.

Frazier, Kenneth. 2001. "The Librarians' Dilemma: Contemplating the Costs of the 'Big Deal.'" *D-Lib Magazine* 7, no. 3. www.dlib.org/dlib/march01/frazier/03frazier.html.

Futas, Elizabeth. 1995. *Collection Development Policies and Procedures*, 3rd ed. Phoenix: Oryx Press.

Gregory, Vicki L. 2011. *Collection Development and Management for 21st Century Library Collections: An Introduction*. New York: Neal-Schuman Publishers.

Hoffmann, Frank W., and Richard J. Wood. 2005. *Library Collection Development Policies: Academic, Public, and Special Libraries*. Lanham, MD: Scarecrow Press.

Hosburgh, Nathan. 2012. "Getting the Most Out of Pay-Per-View: A Feasibility Study and Discussion of Mediated and Unmediated Options." *Journal of Electronic Resources Librarianship* 24, no. 3: 204–11.

IFLA (International Federation of Library Associations and Institutions). Section on Acquisition and Collection Development. 2001. *Guidelines for a Collection Development Policy Using the Conspectus Model*. The Hague: IFLA.

Jarvis, Christy, Jean P. Shipman, Joan M. Gregory, Amy Birks, and Camille Salmond. 2013. "No Subscription? No Problem!: A Trial Implementation of CCC's Get It Now Service." Poster for the Annual Meeting of the Medical Library Association, Boston, May 7.

Jewell, Timothy D., Ivy Anderson, Adam Chandler et al. 2004. *Electronic Resource Management Report of the DLF ERM Initiative*. Washington, DC: Digital Library Federation.

Kraft, Michelle. 2013. "What Is the Biggest Thing in Medical Libraries?" *The Krafty Librarian* (blog). August 26. http://kraftylibrarian.com/?p=2439.

Lamoureux, Selden D., and James Stemper. 2011. "White Paper: Trends in Licensing." *Research Library Issues* 275: 19–24.

Lewis, David W. 2013. "From Stacks to the Web: The Transformation of Academic Library Collecting." *College & Research Libraries* 74, no. 2: 159–76.

Lorbeer, Elizabeth R. 2013. "A Demand-Driven Future." *Against the Grain* 25, no. 2: 24–26.

Ludwig, Logan. 2010. "Health Sciences Libraries Building Survey, 1999–2009." *Journal of the Medical Library Association: JMLA* 98, no. 2 (April): 105–34.

Mangrum, Suzanne, and Mary Ellen Pozzebon. 2012. "Use of Collection Development Policies in Electronic Resource Management." *Collection Building* 31, no. 3: 108–14.

Mickan, Sharon, Julie K. Tilson, Helen Atherton, Nia Wyn Roberts, and Carl Heneghan. 2013. "Evidence of Effectiveness of Health Care Professionals Using Handheld Computers: A Scoping Review of Systematic Reviews." *Journal of Medical Internet Research* 15, no. 10: e212.

NISO SERU Standing Committee. 2012. "SERU: A Shared Electronic Resource Understanding." Baltimore: National Information Standards Organization (NISO).

Pickett, Carmelita, Jane Stephens, Rusty Kimball, Diana Ramirez, Joel Thornton, and Nancy Burford. 2011. "Revisiting an Abandoned Practice: The Death and Resurrection of Collection Development Policies." *Collection Management* 36, no. 3: 165–81.

Ryan, Mary L., J. K. Hart, and Susan C. Steelman. 2012. "Re-positioning the Library for the Future: Repurposing, Relationships & Renovations." Paper presented at the SCC/MLA Annual Conference, Lubbock, TX, October 16.

Schleicher, Mary C. 2010. "Assembling Selection Criteria and Writing a Collection Development Policy for a Variety of Older Medical Books." *Journal of Hospital Librarianship* 10, no. 3: 251–64.

Snow, Richard. 1996. "Wasted Words: The Written Collection Development Policy and the Academic Library." *Journal of Academic Librarianship* 22, no. 3: 191–95.

Squires, Steven J., ed. 2013. *2011–12 Annual Statistics of Medical School Libraries in the United States and Canada*, 35th ed. Seattle: Association of Academic Health Sciences Libraries.

CHAPTER 5

Technical Services in Health Sciences Libraries

Megan Del Baglivo, C. Steven Douglas, and María M. Pinkas

INTRODUCTION

Technical services departments play an important role in the health sciences library by acquiring and organizing information resources so that users can find the information they need. Much of the work technical services librarians and staff do is highly specialized and invisible to the average library patron. In fact, the work may even be done by the main library on a university campus or by a contract vendor for stand-alone libraries. Most health sciences librarians will be more involved with collection development (see Chapter 4), the process of selecting resources to meet the needs of the library's users, than with technical services. But the processes are complementary, and a basic understanding of the underlying precepts is important to all who are entering the library profession.

As in the rest of the field, changes in technology are driving changes in technical services. The broad move from print to electronic resources has changed the way acquisitions departments work. Where formerly acquisitions staff purchased print monographs and managed print journals, they are increasingly licensing electronic journals, e-books, and databases. These new formats also lend themselves to innovative methods of acquisition. This change has had a major effect on the way librarians organize information as well, resulting in far-reaching and evolving changes to international bibliographic standards. Resource Description and Access (RDA) has replaced the old standard, the Anglo-American Cataloging Rules (AACR2), and as web and local resources become more important, new types of metadata are being developed that will continue to improve resource discovery.

ACQUISITIONS

Acquisitions, simply put, is the process in which resources chosen for the library are ordered and paid for. This requires that acquisitions personnel have a good relationship with the library's collection development staff, their larger institution's purchasing and accounts payable departments, and with the various vendors of library resources. This can be a complex process, and larger libraries may rely on the acquisitions module of their library management system either alone or in conjunction with an electronic resources management system. Smaller libraries may find that using spreadsheets and tickler files suffices. In either case, it is the acquisition staff's responsibility to order, pay for, and receive the library's information resources while staying within budget.

The acquisitions process begins when collection development selectors choose resources to add to the library's collection. Acquisitions personnel often have a role to play in this decision making by providing information on possible sources and pricing. The resource is then ordered. Sometimes this can be simply accomplished by placing an order online or by phone. Often, however, library purchases can involve complex negotiations. Electronic books, journals, and databases, for example, almost always require that the library or its parent institution sign a license. This legal document spells out the obligations of the provider and the terms under which the resource can be used. In some institutions designated library personnel have negotiating and signatory authority. In others, however, this authority resides with another office in the institution—most often the legal or purchasing department. In any case, acquisitions staff need to work closely with the selectors to make sure the license meets the library's needs and to represent the library to the vendor and other offices in the institution.

Payment can also be simple or complex. The use of credit cards to pay for low-cost purchases is becoming more prevalent, but more expensive items and packages often have to be submitted to the institution's purchasing and accounts payable departments. In either case, it is important that acquisitions staff know and closely follow all of their institution's procurement policies and procedures. It is also crucial to keep meticulous financial records to help those responsible for collection oversight keep close track of the budget.

Acquisitions staff also need to work closely with cataloging staff during this process. In most library management systems, a catalog record or other metadata is needed before an order is placed. This may be provided by the vendor, obtained from another source by cataloging or acquisitions personnel, or even created. For electronic resources, it is important to keep those who are responsible for creating and maintaining access points aware of new purchases and renewals. And all print journals and books must be physically processed and made available to the user. Acquisitions in libraries, then, requires not only financial skills, but also coordination between selectors within the library, the purchasing and legal departments of the institution, and external vendors of library resources.

Monograph Acquisitions

Books are a small but important part of the health sciences library collection. Health sciences monograph collections tend to rely heavily on core textbook titles, whereas journal subscriptions provide access to the most current research. Traditionally, larger libraries have depended on the services of book distributors to provide most of their monographs. These companies represent multiple publishers and provide additional bibliographic services that simplify the work of book collection development and acquisitions. One of the most important services they provide are approval plans. Under these plans, the library provides a profile—most often based on LC or NLM classification—of the subject areas it is interested in collecting. The book distributor then chooses new books that meet these parameters as they are published and presents them for the library's consideration. In the past, the actual books were shipped to the library, reviewed by selectors, and either added to the collection or returned to the distributor. Currently, electronic approval plans have gained in popularity. In this case, the distributor supplies an electronic file with detailed bibliographic information that selectors use to choose books for acquisition or further review, thus saving the costly and time-consuming shipping of books back and forth. Many book distributors also include electronic books on their approval plans.

Book distributors also provide standing order and firm order services. Some titles are so important for the collection that selectors know in advance that they will want the next edition. When a standing order for a title is set up, the distributor automatically ships new editions, ensuring that the library receives them in a timely fashion. In the cases where books not in the approval plan profile are needed, the library places an order for them on an individual basis. These are called firm orders because they are not contingent on review and selection like books presented on the approval plan. Those libraries fortunate enough to have a credit card can also order books directly over the Internet from online vendors. This is particularly useful for small libraries and for more rapid receipt of materials. Although book distributors provide important services and greater efficiency, it often takes longer for them to process orders and ship books than the major online book vendors. In fact, libraries that only order a few books may find this method more convenient than using a book distributor.

Electronic editions of books are increasingly available, and requests for them are growing. Acquiring these books is often more complicated than the straightforward purchase of a print edition. First, most providers and publishers of e-books require that the library or its parent body sign a license. And the methods of acquisition are often complicated as well. Several e-book providers work with multiple publishers to provide electronic books for purchase, either as individual titles or collections. These are most often onetime purchases, but they may require an annual service charge if you want the provider to host them. To get e-books from several important health sciences imprints, however, it is necessary to deal directly with the publishers. Some publishers sell their books on an à la carte basis at a onetime cost. Other publishers and providers will sell their titles only in packages of related titles. And some publishers will only license their books on a subscription basis, where the library pays an annual fee for access to the book or book collection. Each method has advantages and disadvantages. The à la carte onetime purchase of e-books is the easiest to manage, but the price paid is often more expensive than the same title in print. Collections often provide a discount on a per-book-basis, but the chance is that titles will be included that the library would not have selected. In the subscription model, the publisher or vendor provides the most recent edition of the titles selected, but earlier editions are no longer available unless the library also purchases them in another format. Another model that many libraries are exploring is demand-driven acquisitions (DDA). In these programs, a library provides access to many e-books through its catalog and other discovery systems, but only the books that patrons actually use are purchased. The acquisitions staff has to work closely with the collection development staff to make sure that book purchases meet users' needs, remain within budget, and are in the format most useful to the library's patrons.

Serials and Database Acquisitions

Journal subscriptions make up the bulk of most medical libraries' expenditures, particularly in academic health sciences libraries. Just as book distributors help with the acquisition of monographs, serials agents greatly simplify the time-consuming ordering and maintenance of journal subscriptions. These agents place orders and pay for subscriptions on an annual basis and then bill the library. Because even the smallest library will subscribe to journals from multiple publishers, these services, which significantly decrease the journal acquisitions workload, are widely used. Serials agents maintain extensive bibliographic databases, providing a single point for acquisitions staff to locate publication information and pricing on journals of interest to the library. Bulk renewal services greatly simplify the annual task of renewing, canceling, and adding journals titles to meet the library's changing budget and information needs. If problems arise with a print subscription, a serials agent will place a claim with the publisher for missing issues and even supply them from its own stock. And agents greatly simplify the maintenance of electronic journal subscriptions as well, providing information on licensing terms and claim services. When access to an e-subscription is lost—something that happens all too often—serials agents are able to contact the correct person at the publisher quickly to troubleshoot and provide proof of payment.

Like journals and some electronic books, databases are a subscription product. However, to subscribe to most databases, the library must most often work directly with the publisher or provider. Managing database subscriptions, then, often calls into play the entire acquisitions skill set: a strong knowledge of the marketplace, good negotiation skills, scrupulous record keeping, and good relationships with stakeholders in the library, other offices in the larger institution, and providers of library resources.

COLLECTION ORGANIZATION

Resources Management and Access: Overview

The primary purpose of all collection organization activities is to facilitate discovery of resources by the user. "Connecting users with the information they seek is one of the pillars of our profession" (Vaughan, 2011: 5).

The development of the **MARC (MAchine Readable Cataloging)** record in the late 1960s facilitated the sharing of bibliographic data leading to an increase in **copy cataloging**, adapting an existing catalog record for a resource with local modifications. This is the most common type of cataloging done today. In 1995, in response to a growing need for "cooperative venues that promised to produce more cataloging that would be better, cheaper, and faster" (Wiggins, 1998), the

Program for Cooperative Cataloging (PCC) was formed. The PCC has an extensive and varied membership of representatives from a wide variety of libraries including the Library of Congress (LC) and the National Library of Medicine (NLM). Two of the four major programs within the PCC's directorship are **BIBCO (Monographic Bibliographic Record Program)** and **CONSER (Cooperative Online Serials Program)**, the members of which contribute a large number of authoritative bibliographic records available for sharing. Other responsibilities include creating and maintaining standards, providing documentation on guidelines and procedures, and offering workshops and training material (LC, 2013).

As early as the mid-1970s, specialized software and hardware were developed to support bibliographic processing associated with the MARC record. The 1980s witnessed an expansion of the vendor marketplace for these systems as more libraries continued to automate their cataloging activities. Competition led to the development of additional software features such as acquisitions and budget management, circulation, authority control capability, and an **OPAC (Online Public Access Catalog)**. This type of coordinated software package is called an **integrated library system (ILS)**. Initially, these were complex, proprietorial products offered by large library service vendors on a contractual basis for a specified number of years. Although the number of vendors has been reduced somewhat due to mergers and acquisitions, many are still in operation today. However, within the past decade **open source** competitors have entered the field, providing libraries with an alternative to the commercial vendors. Both have advantages and disadvantages. Commercial products are expensive and may offer limited customization options, but, in large part, installation and continued maintenance responsibilities rest with the vendor. Open source systems freely share their code but require technically skilled library staff to install and maintain. However, open source software can be considerably modified to meet local needs.

More recently, some commercial vendors have released a new type of product termed "discovery services." These tools challenge the traditional OPAC in providing single, "Google-like" searches that return result lists that incorporate all formats of relevant resources with a granularity to the article level. As these services have matured, a trend is growing to move away from the ILS, separating the "front-end" discovery layer (user interface) from the "back end" (resource processing functions). Breeding calls the latter "library service platforms" (Breeding, 2013: 20). Functions associated with these back-end products include acquisition and budget, metadata management, circulation, and electronic resources management (ERM).

Cataloging procedures have had to adapt to the evolving nature of information delivery. The significant shift has been from purchasing print in favor of online counterparts, originally for journals and more recently for books. With the development of tools such as A–Z lists and **link resolvers**, libraries now have more options with regard to providing access to their holdings than just the OPAC. Both of the newer products rely on linking capability, with the former providing users with quick and seamless connectivity to online resources. The latter can function either at the title or article level within the catalog or database. Search criteria for A–Z lists may include title, words in title, subject, and International Standard Serial Number (for journals) and International Standard Book Number (for books). Clicking on a link in a hit list takes a user to an e-journal or e-book home page with full-text content. Maintaining holdings data is accomplished through an administrative site whereby single titles or entire packages can be activated or deactivated with a single click. Information about print resources may also be accommodated. A variety of vendors offer A–Z products, and they have become a standard library tool.

Formally cataloging all resources and maintaining records for a large ILS may not always be the most efficient use of time or funds for smaller operations. Hospital libraries, in particular, tend to have minimum staff, limited budgets, and support a narrowly focused user population with specialized requirements. Depending upon organizational needs, tracking resources may simply be accomplished through the use of spreadsheet, database, or reference management software with access to on-line holdings provided via an A–Z list on a web page on the facility's intranet. An-other option is to purchase MARC records from vendors or publishers and download them into automated systems developed specifically for small library operations that include an OPAC.

Traditional cataloging practices are currently in a state of transition. Every aspect of organizing and providing access to resources is undergoing a complete transformation driven by technological changes and the emergence of the **Semantic Web**. AACR2, the cataloging standard used by librarians for decades, has been superseded by RDA; and BIBFRAME, a new framework initiative, is well under way to replace MARC. Departmental staffing requirements have changed as well. The migration from print to online collections has reduced physical processing activities (labeling, bindery, journal issue check-in, claiming) and increased the tasks associated with the digital environment.

Due to the physical space and time constraints that can exist in busy hospital libraries, hospital librarians (often solo) are faced with extra challenges. We have migrated most of our journal collection from print to online and have used many computerized tools to deliver resources (A–Z lists, link resolvers) at multiple access points to physicians and hospital staffs. Other tools (serial agents, DOCLINE, EFTS) have been crucial in expediting the hospital librarian's workload.

Cynthia Phyillaier, MSLS, medical librarian, Holy Cross Hospital, Silver Spring, MD

These include troubleshooting connectivity problems, communicating with content providers and vendors, and attending to maintenance issues for tools such as A–Z lists, link resolvers, and discovery systems. Therefore, today's resources management staff must possess a high degree of flexibility and technical skill.

The medical library cataloger must be prepared to take on a technical role as libraries transition from mostly print to mostly electronic collections. Catalogers need to be actively involved with the development and handling of electronic resource collections, and be prepared to discuss and evaluate the differences and issues that affect retrieval and relevancy. Catalogers must also seek to establish the philosophy of the library concerning the presentation of the electronic materials. Catalogers need to promote awareness of issues that are involved with the chosen philosophy. If a library chooses the philosophy that all available materials will be made available to patrons, then everyone involved in this decision must be aware that the cataloging role becomes that of managing the data input into the catalog, and that the data loads will be huge and very little quality control will be available. If the library philosophy chosen is to present only materials within the scope of the medical library, the cataloger will have more ability for quality control, but the manual work required for selection and control may be beyond the time available to the cataloger. (Perkins, 2009: 220)

Due to the growing influence of web-based technology, **bibliographic control** is no longer the sole purview of the library profession, but it has become a process integrated into the wider information universe. **Metadata** is an umbrella term used by many communities involved with processing descriptive, structural, and administrative data and related activities across the web. Many within the profession feel that "cataloging" has outlived its usefulness as an appropriate term for the functions associated with organizing resources and related information for identification, search, and retrieval. Instead, "metadata management," "metadata services," or a variation thereof are more indicative of the current environment.

Cataloging Standards

The process of organizing library resources for identification and access has traditionally been known as cataloging. The deceptively simple term represents more than 150 years of creating and maintaining rules and standards that govern bibliographic control, also known as information organization. The profession has long recognized the value of applying established practices and consistent terminology to facilitate finding, selecting, and retrieving library holdings. Until recently the standard for bibliographic description and related processes has been the *Anglo-American Cataloging Rules (AACR2)*, published jointly by the American Library Association (ALA), the Canadian Library Association (CLA), and the Chartered Institute of Library and Information Professionals (CILIP). Figure 5.1 illustrates the evolution of cataloging rules from the beginning of the twentieth century.

Over the past two decades, the maturation of the Internet and the emergence of new formats for resources (CDs, DVDs, streaming video, digital) have had a considerable impact on the cataloging process. A revision of AACR2 (termed AACR3) began in 2004, but it was abandoned in favor of a completely new initiative titled **RDA: Resource Description and Access**.

RDA is the current cataloging standard encompassing all types of content and media. In June 2010, the RDA guidelines were published online as the "RDA Toolkit" (ALA, 2010) and tested throughout that fall by the U.S. national libraries and twenty-six participating partners. Adjustments were made to the guidelines based upon the test results, and full implementation of RDA by LC, NLM, and several major international libraries occurred in March 2013. All authority work through the **Name Authority Cooperative Program (NACO)** transitioned at the same time.

Like any new set of rules, it will take time to become accustomed to RDA; some of us remember when AACR2 was implemented. Change may be difficult at first, but we will all adapt. As we move ahead with new discovery tools, RDA with the concepts of FRBR and FRAD will be integrated into a more effective means of retrieving information.

Wilma Bass, MSLS, head—Unit 3, Cataloging Section, National Library of Medicine, Bethesda, MD

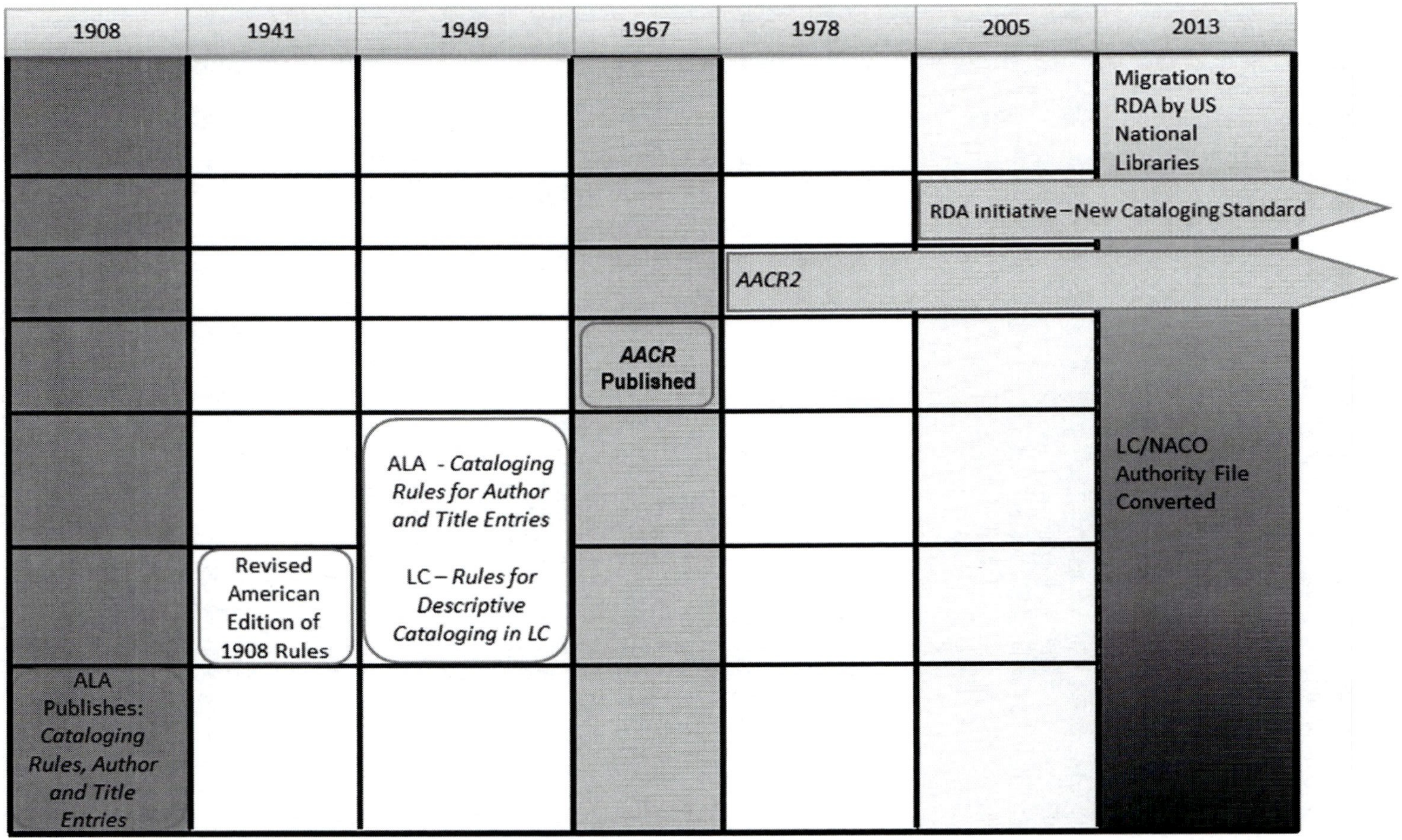

Figure 5.1 — Evolution of Cataloging Standards (timeline)

1908	1941	1949	1967	1978	2005	2013
						Migration to RDA by US National Libraries
					RDA initiative – New Cataloging Standard	
				AACR2		
			AACR Published			
		ALA - Cataloging Rules for Author and Title Entries / LC – Rules for Descriptive Cataloging in LC				
	Revised American Edition of 1908 Rules					
ALA Publishes: Cataloging Rules, Author and Title Entries						LC/NACO Authority File Converted

Figure 5.1. Evolution of Cataloging Standards. Copyright © María M. Pinkas and Thom Pinho.

The RDA Toolkit is continuously updated and includes links to AACR2, mapping to MARC from RDA, and other useful features.

It is worth noting that some RDA decisions are advantageous to the needs of scientific/medical literature. For example, with AACR2 a rule of three was instituted for including author names in a bibliographic record. If a record represented more than three authors, only one would be included and "et al." would be appended after that name. With RDA, all names of those responsible for a work are present in the bibliographic record. In a professional environment where cooperative work among many is common, identifying all authors and linking them to their other publications is very important.

Implementation of RDA by individual libraries is a local decision. No plans are afoot to retrospectively convert AACR2 records to conform to the new guidelines; therefore, records in either version will coexist for the foreseeable future. However, for those who participate in cooperative cataloging efforts, adjustments to their online systems have been essential for appropriate display of data in their local catalogs.

Authority Control: MeSH

During the process of cataloging, access points such as subject headings, proper names, and titles are assigned according to a standard known as **authority control**. This is the practice of consistently using the same unique term or name for all synonyms and variations (including pseudonyms). Cross-references or entry terms provide links between non-authoritative headings and the established form. The purpose is to retrieve works by the same author, regardless of the form used in the resource, or that have the same subject. A list, or thesaurus, of authorized subject terms is called a **controlled vocabulary**. The most common authority thesaurus for subjects in the health sciences library profession is the National Library of Medicine's **Medical Subject Headings (MeSH)**.

Authority records are created for each established term and name. Although they are similar in structure to bibliographic records, they differ considerably in content. Each **authority record** represents a person, corporate body, common title, or subject that may be an access point for searching. "When a new authority record must be made, considerable checking in reference and other sources, as well as considerable consultation is often required to arrive at the decisions that are ultimately registered in it. Authority work, therefore, has long been regarded as the most time-consuming and costly aspect of cataloging" (Chan, 2007: 28).

An authority record contains:

1. The preferred name, or the preferred title, or the normalized subject term;
2. Variant access points ("see references" in AACR2); and
3. Authorized access points for related entities ("see also references" in AACR2).

For example, in MeSH, "Drug Therapy" is the preferred term for "The use of drugs to treat a disease or its symptoms. One example is the use of antineoplastic agents to treat cancer." Terms such as Chemotherapy and Pharmacotherapy are "entry terms" or variant access points, but the subject term that is authorized is "Drug Therapy." MeSH authority records such as the one in Figure 5.2 exist to show the authorized

National Library of Medicine - Medical Subject Headings

2013 MeSH

MeSH Descriptor Data

Return to Entry Page

Standard View. Go to Concept View; Go to Expanded Concept View

MeSH Heading	Drug Therapy
Tree Number	E02.319
Annotation	general only: prefer / drug ther with disease term: Manual 19.7+, 19.8.26; note entry term CHEMOTHERAPY: prefer specific chemical or chemical group, e.g., chemotherapy of lymphoma = LYMPHOMA / drug ther + ANTINEOPLASTIC AGENTS / ther use, not DRUG THERAPY
Scope Note	The use of DRUGS to treat a DISEASE or its symptoms. One example is the use of ANTINEOPLASTIC AGENTS to treat CANCER.
Entry Term	Chemotherapy
Entry Term	Pharmacotherapy
Entry Term	Therapy, Drug
See Also	Medication Errors
See Also	Pharmacologic Actions
Allowable Qualifiers	AE CL CT EC ES HI IS MO MT NU PX SN ST TD UT VE
Entry Version	DRUG THER
Date of Entry	19990101
Unique ID	D004358

Figure 5.2. MeSH Subject Authority Record. Source: U.S. National Library of Medicine, National Institutes of Health. 2013. "Medical Subject Headings: MeSH Browser (2013 MeSH)" (www.nlm.nih.gov/mesh/MBrowser .html). Search: Drug Therapy.

MeSH heading, the "scope note," the "entry terms" or variant access points, and "see also" references among others.

MeSH is organized in a hierarchical arrangement termed a "tree structure." At the highest level are very broad terms such as "Anatomy" or "Psychiatry and Psychology." Figure 5.3 shows the sixteen main branches of the MeSH tree structure as they appear on the NLM website.

More-specific headings such as "Back" and "Lumbosacral Region" are found at deeper points within the hierarchy, as can be seen in Figure 5.4.

Additionally, a considerable number of nonauthorized entry terms link to the most appropriate established heading. For example, a search on "Vitamin C" will produce a reference to the authorized term "Ascorbic Acid." MeSH is also used for indexing articles from the journals within the MEDLINE/PubMed database. The thesaurus is available free from NLM at www.nlm.nih.gov/mesh/.

MeSH Tree Structures

MeSH headings are organized in a "tree" with 16 main branches:

A. Anatomy

B. Organisms

C. Diseases

D. Chemical and Drugs

E. Analytical, Diagnostic and Therapeutic Techniques and Equipment

F. Psychiatry and Psychology

G. Phenomena and Processes

H. Disciplines and Occupations

I. Anthropology, Education, Sociology and Social Phenomena

J. Technology, Industry, Agriculture

K. Humanities

L. Information Science

M. Named Groups

N. Health Care

V. Publication Characteristics

Z. Geographicals

Figure 5.3. MeSH Tree Structures Main Branches. Source: U.S. National Library of Medicine, National Institutes of Health. 2013. "Medical Subject Headings (MeSH®) in MEDLINE®/PubMed®: A Tutorial" (www.nlm.nih.gov/bsd/disted/meshtutorial/meshtreestructures/index.html).

MeSH Tree Structures

Each branch has many levels of sub-branches, and each heading has a position in the hierarchy.

Anatomy
    Body Regions
        Torso
            Back
                Lumbosacral Region
                Sacrococcygeal Region

Figure 5.4. MeSH Tree Structures Subbranches. Source: U.S. National Library of Medicine, National Institutes of Health. 2013. "Medical Subject Headings (MeSH®) in MEDLINE®/PubMed®: A Tutorial" (www.nlm.nih.gov/bsd/disted/meshtutorial/meshtreestructures/02.html).

The **Library of Congress Subject Headings (LCSH)**, as the most commonly used general subject thesaurus among academic libraries, can be used in conjunction with MeSH in the same bibliographic record. This is common practice in OCLC MARC records and thus is an option in larger academic health sciences libraries that use this cataloging utility.

Controlled vocabularies are also an important tool for describing resources in institutional repositories and digital archives. This is particularly true in today's web-based linked data environment. Some organizations have creatively used established headings for local purposes. For instance, the Fred Hutchinson Cancer Research Center's Arnold Library used MeSH in its drop-down menu of subjects in its institutional repository Authors@FHCRC, http://authors.fhrc.org/.

For the subject drop-down menu in our repository at FHCRC, we selected specific branches of MeSH and then adapted and simplified them to meet local/institutional needs.

Ann Marie Clark, MLS, director, Arnold Library, Fred Hutchinson Cancer Research Center, Seattle, WA

Name authority records are to personal names what subject authority records are to topical terms. Publications by the same author often bear variant forms of the name. A middle initial can be added or omitted or a name completely changed as the result of marriage or divorce. Transcriptions from a language that has a different alphabet may vary. In order to group works by the same author, an established form is created (termed *preferred name* in RDA) with links to alternate forms (*variant access points*). The name authority thesaurus most used by libraries in the cataloging environment is LC's Name Authority Records or NARs. Since March 2013, all new LC NARs follow RDA guidelines based on FRAD. LC's authority records are freely available for use at http://authorities.loc.gov/.

The Library of Congress has been active in creating authority records with a unique URL link. In so doing, the data can be used in the web environment. One example of this is the **Virtual International Authority File (VIAF)**, http://viaf.org. Websites such as *Wikipedia* can link to the authority data for an author in the VIAF from its article about that author.

Use of name authority records in the health sciences fields are important because the names of authors often appear in the form of initial or initials of first and middle names plus surname in some publications, and full names in others. Or, in some cases, the preferred professional name may be different than the full name. Authority records can provide a way to link all of the works of a researcher or a known personality in a scientific field.

One example of this is the neurosurgeon Ben Carson, pioneer in the successful separation of conjoined twins joined in the head. Although his full name is Benjamin Solomon Carson, because his preferred name is Ben Carson, this is the one used in his name authority records internationally. Thanks to this, information on him and works by him or about him are linked on the web. Carson, Benjamin S. appears as a variant form of his name in the Library of Congress Name authority File. Figure 5.5 shows the Virtual International Authority file evidencing that he is internationally identified as Carson, Ben.

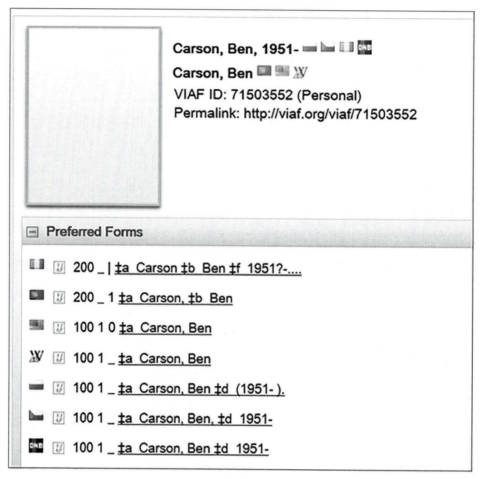

Figure 5.5. Ben Carson VIAF Authority File. Source: VIAF (Virtual International Authority File). Accessed July 25, 2013 (http://viaf.org/viaf/71503552/). © 2013 OCLC Online Computer Library Center, Inc. Image used with OCLC's permission. VIAF is a trademark/service mark of OCLC Online Computer Library Center, Inc.

National Library of Medicine Classification System

Classification schemes are alphanumeric or numeric hierarchical codes that represent topics and subtopics. Originally, they were used to assign a unique shelf location for each resource within a library according to subject, author, or type of publication and to facilitate browsing.

The NLM Classification System was designed to be used in coordination with the Library of Congress Classification System (LCC). LCC was originally developed to address the specific needs of the Library of Congress. Therefore, the detail bias is toward subjects related to history, politics, and other social sciences. Conversely, the National Library of Medicine's classification scheme emphasizes health- and biomedical-related

---

Outline of the NLM Classification

Preclinical Sciences:

- QS Human Anatomy
- QT Physiology
- QU Biochemistry. Cell Biology and Genetics
- QV Pharmacology
- QW Microbiology and Immunology
- QX Parasitology
- QY Clinical Pathology
- QZ Pathology

Medicine and Related Subjects:

- W General Medicine. Health Professions
- WA Public Health
- WB Practice of Medicine
- WC Communicable Diseases
- WD Disorders of Systemic, Metabolic or Environmental Origin, etc.
- WE Musculoskeletal System
- WF Respiratory System
- WG Cardiovascular System
- WH Hemic and Lymphatic Systems
- WI Digestive System
- WJ Urogenital System
- WK Endocrine System
- WL Nervous System
- WM Psychiatry
- WN Radiology. Diagnostic Imaging
- WO Surgery
- WP Gynecology
- WQ Obstetrics
- WR Dermatology
- WS Pediatrics
- WT Geriatrics. Chronic Disease
- WU Dentistry. Oral Surgery
- WV Otolaryngology
- WW Ophthalmology
- WX Hospitals and Other Health Facilities
- WY Nursing
- WZ History of Medicine. Medical Miscellany
- 19th Century Schedule

Figure 5.6. Outline of the NLM Classification. Source: U.S. National Library of Medicine, National Institutes of Health. 2013. "NLM Classification 2013" (www.nlm.nih.gov/class/OutlineofNLMClassificationSchedule.html).

subjects. Classes and subclasses within the LC schedules are reserved exclusively for use by NLM. These include subclasses QS-QZ in the Q schedule, which relate to preclinical sciences, and the entire Class W with twenty-seven subclasses representing medicine and related subjects. NLM reverts to using LCC for all material in its collection that does not fall within either medicine or the preclinical sciences. Figure 5.6 shows the first letters of the NLM Classification System and their captions.

Since 2002, the "National Library of Medicine Classification" has been published only in electronic format and is updated annually. Beginning in 2006, it has been downloadable in PDF form as well. It is available from NLM at www.nlm.nih.gov/class/.

Metadata

The term "metadata" was reportedly created by Jack E. Myers in 1969 and first used in print in 1973 in a product brochure (Greenberg, 2005). Commonly defined as "data about data," the actual meaning of the word has grown in complexity along with its popularity over the past four decades. The use of the term was initially understood to be limited to digital material, but it has evolved to encompass all types of resources regardless of format. The **National Information Standards Organization (NISO)** describes metadata as "structured information that describes, explains, locates, or otherwise makes it easier to retrieve, use, or manage an information resource" (NISO, 2004: 1).

NISO divides metadata into three main categories depending upon its purpose. Information about a resource such as author, title, and publisher is called **descriptive metadata**. **Structural metadata** is used to identify and organize related files such as chapters in a book (compound objects) for display in logical sequence and to enable flexible navigation throughout the entire resource. The third category is **administrative metadata**, among the subcategories for which are rights management and preservation. The former includes information on copyright and restrictions on use and reproduction, whereas the latter relates to those technical aspects of a digital object that will facilitate the transition to new technologies of the future, critical for maintaining perpetual access (NISO, 2004). Many different "communities" (libraries, archives, museums, scientific organizations, government agencies, e-commerce) work with metadata. Consequently, the number of categories and definitions can differ depending upon the specialized interests of a particular group. "These distinctions, while useful, can be somewhat artificial and it is important to realize that they are not absolutely distinct or mutually exclusive. The same piece of metadata, such as creator, digital file format, or digital file size, for example, can serve both descriptive and administrative functions at the same time" (Miller, 2011: 12).

MARC/BIBFRAME/Dublin Core

It is important to emphasize that RDA (and its predecessor, AACR2) and MARC are two different standards that work together. The former governs what and how content should be entered into the record; the latter is the "carrier," facilitating data transmission, extraction, and display.

The MARC format has been a bibliographic standard for more than four decades. Few, if any, technologies have withstood the test of time as well as the MARC record, which is testament to its adaptability and efficacy. Henriette Avram and her team at the Library of Congress began working on a project to develop a machine-readable bibliographic data model in 1965. Within seven years MARC had become an American National Standards Institute (ANSI) standard (Rather and Wiggins, 1989).

The format underwent several revisions throughout the years with the current version, MARC 21, established in 1998, the result of harmonizing USMARC and the Canadian, CAN/MARC. Today, there are five MARC 21 standards: Bibliographic, Authority, Holdings, Classification, and Community Information. All share the same basic structure, some elements of which are associated with communication protocols and other machine processing tasks. However, the majority of the MARC record is comprised of triple digit tags (fields), single character alpha or numeric subfields, and indicator codes. The first two contain textual content associated with the resource being described; indicators, where applicable, usually affect indexing and display.

Figure 5.7 is a list of the tags for the bibliographic standard that are divided into numerical blocks of one hundred, each associated with a general type of data. For example, the 2XX fields (titles, edition, imprint) include the 245 (Title Statement), 246 (Varying Form of Title), 250 (Edition Statement), and the 260 (Publication, Distribution, etc.), among others. Each tag has a variety of valid subfields that more specifically define type of content. Therefore, subfield "a" in the 260 contains the place of publication or distribution; subfield "b" is reserved for the name of publisher, distributor, and so forth. Delimiters such as a double dagger (‡) are used to separate one subfield from another. Punctuation marks are required between some subfields, which makes for an extremely "cluttered" record to the uninitiated human eye.

The adoption of a machine-readable format for processing bibliographic data gave rise to "bibliographic utilities," organizations that maintain repositories of MARC records that are downloadable directly from the utility site to library computers for local processing. Today, **OCLC** is the leading provider with more than 290 million records in its global catalog (OCLC, 2013). However, a relative newcomer, SkyRiver, made its debut in late 2009, promising a more cost-effective alternative. As of 2013, it maintained a database of 40 million unique titles (SkyRiver, 2013). Additional sources of MARC records include book distributors and library service companies as well as some publishers who offer them for their publications, although the quality can vary significantly.

The MARC standards were developed specifically for libraries for sharing and processing data associated with their resources. However, with the continuous evolution of the web as an information gateway, libraries no longer have a monopoly on bibliographic control. New technological initiatives, formats, and concepts demand more flexibility in structure; the ability to identify relationships and to accommodate different material formats; and interoperability in a shared machine-readable environment. In May 2011, the Library of Congress embarked on a project to analyze the critical components of a new bibliographic framework based on RDF (Resource Description Framework) and linked data principles (LC, 2011). Another impetus for developing a replacement resulted from testing the new RDA cataloging standards in MARC records. Some libraries participating in the test

0XX   Control information, numbers, codes
1XX   Main entry
2XX   Titles, edition, imprint (in general, the title, statement of responsibility, edition, and publication
          information)
3XX   Physical description, etc.
4XX   Series statements (as shown in the book)
5XX   Notes
6XX   Subject added entries
7XX   Added entries other than subject or series
8XX   Series added entries (other authoritative forms)

Figure 5.7. Basic Division of MARC Tags for Bibliographic Record. Source: Library of Congress, "Understanding MARC" (www.loc.gov/marc/umb/um01to06.html).

expressed concern that the full benefits of RDA could not sufficiently be realized through MARC. In May 2012, LC announced that it had contracted with Zepheira, an open data services company, to create a contemporary bibliographic framework model (LC, 2012a); and within six months the *Bibliographic Framework as a Web of Data: Linked Data Model and Supporting Services* document was released (LC, 2012b). Termed BIBFRAME, testing of the model began in early 2013. Test partners include LC, NLM, the British Library, Deutsche Nationalbibliotek, George Washington University Library, Princeton Library, and OCLC (LC, 2012c). The document introduction states:

> It is important to remember that this model, like MARC, must be able to accommodate any number of content models and specific implementations, but still enable data exchange between libraries. It needs to support new metadata rules and content standards that emerge, including the newest library content standard—RDA (Resource Description & Access). The BIBFRAME model must therefore both broaden and narrow the format universe for exchange of bibliographic data. (LC, 2012b: 5)

Work on BIBFRAME will continue, and it is expected to change over time. Meanwhile, the MARC standard will remain active for the foreseeable future. However, its certain destiny is to be replaced by a more adaptable, interoperable, and relationship-oriented structure.

A recent trend in libraries is the development of **institutional repositories** or digital archives to preserve and expose their organizations' intellectual and/or historical material. One of the most important metadata schemes supporting these web-based endeavors is **Dublin Core**. It was developed in the mid-1990s as a generic uncomplicated method by which to tag documents for search and retrieval across the Internet. All activities related to DC are currently managed by the **Dublin Core Metadata Initiative (DCMI)**. The initial set of fifteen "core" elements (Dublin Core Metadata Element Set or DCMES) was the result of a combined effort by OCLC and the National Center for Supercomputing Applications (NCSA) at a meeting in 1995 in Dublin, Ohio (hence the name Dublin Core) (DCMI, 2013) and became an ANSI/NISO standard in 2007.

Table 5.1 lists the elements with their descriptions. Eventually, the original set of fifteen, termed Simple Dublin Core, was supplemented with three additional elements and the assignment of attributes that further refine some of the existing ones. The second group is called Qualified Dublin Core.

The scheme is among the most popular metadata standards by virtue of its ease of use, syntax independence, ability to be combined with controlled vocabularies such as LCSH and MeSH, and for metadata harvesting purposes.

The **Open Archives Initiative Protocol for Metadata Harvesting (OAI-PMH)**, probably the most commonly used method of harvesting cultural heritage metadata as of this writing, requires that all participants provide a set of simple Dublin Core metadata for every digital resource, even when they also have and/or provide metadata in other, more complex formats. (Miller, 2011: 56)

Digital collection management software such as OCLC's CONTENTdm and the open source, DSpace, use the DC scheme as a base structure. Catalogers become

Table 5.1. Simple Dublin Core Element Set

Element Label	Description
Contributor	An entity responsible for making contributions to the resource
Coverage	The spatial or temporal topic of the resource, the spatial applicability of the resource, or the jurisdiction under which the resource is relevant
Creator	An entity primarily responsible for making the resource
Date	A point or period of time associated with an event in the life cycle of the resource
Description	An account of the resource
Format	The file format, physical medium, or dimensions of the resource
Identifier	An unambiguous reference to the resource by means of a string conforming to a formal identification system
Language	A language of the resource
Publisher	An entity responsible for making the resource available
Relation	A related resource
Rights	Information about the rights held in and over the resource
Source	A related resource from which the described resource is derived
Subject	The topic of the resource
Title	A name given to the resource
Type	The nature or genre of the resource

Source: Adapted from Dublin Core Metadata Initiative "Dublin Core Metadata Element Set, Version 1.1" (issued June 14, 2012), http://dublincore.org/documents/dces/.

familiar with Dublin Core because their specialized skills in authority control are particularly valuable for **digital curation** of repository and archival material.

Discoverability

In the precomputer, print-centric environment, the physical card catalog with its limited search capability was the sole tool available for identifying a library's holdings. The flexible indexing the OPAC provided extended search capability by offering options such as keyword and Boolean functionality. However, in today's digital environment, the information within the catalog reflects only a portion of a library's collection. Ordinarily, these are resources that have been formally cataloged at the title level (monographs, journals, audiovisual media). A significant amount of remotely or locally hosted material such as licensed e-journal literature, data from abstracting and indexing resources, and content within institutional repositories and digital archives is often not included in the OPAC (Vaughan, 2011). Therefore, in addition to the catalog, users must access a variety of other tools such as A–Z lists and databases in order to find resources.

Discovery interfaces have recently been developed that address the "compartmentalized" nature of library content. A type of interface known as a **web-scale discovery system** offers large, centralized, preaggregated indexes capable of maintaining data for all of a library's resources regardless of format or source. A single search retrieves all relevant material, even to the article level, and may include open access publications and repository content as well. These interfaces are usually independent of back-end systems, capable of extracting the catalog data for the centralized index and using link resolver technology to access subscribed full-text content.

Web-scale discovery systems refer to "a class of products that index a vast number of resources in a wide variety of formats and allow users to search for content in the physical collection, print and electronic journal collections, and other resources from a single search box" (Hoy, 2012: 323). This is accomplished by preharvesting content from all library sources, which facilitates deep indexing and a high degree of granularity in search results. Another definition for web-scale discovery provided by Vaughan is "a service capable of searching across a vast range of pre-harvested and indexed content quickly and seamlessly" (Vaughan, 2011: 6). These systems have also developed highly confidential and complex formulas to rank results according to the relevancy of search criteria.

Another aspect of the functionality of these tools is that both the content provider and the library must subscribe to these proprietary resources. Web-scale discovery vendors contract with "partners" in order to use their content and/or metadata. Information about these agreements becomes important in selecting a discovery system because they can have a significant effect on access. In its considerations, a health sciences library must weigh how much in-scope content the discovery tool being assessed actually provides.

It should be noted that the suitability of these tools for use in medical and other specialty libraries has been questioned due to the large number of results returned for each search. Hoy points out that "users in these types of libraries are interested in a specific set of resources, and data from outside that group of resources is little more than noise" (Hoy, 2012: 326). Nevertheless, user expectations are based upon familiarity with web searches. Web-scale discovery systems are similar in their use of a single search box and lengthy result lists ranked by relevancy. However, the major difference between the two is that the latter returns quality content, the majority of which the library subscribes to or purchases.

Early providers of these new discovery systems include Summon from Serials Solutions, Primo Central from Ex Libris, the EBSCO Discovery Service, OCLC's WorldCat Local, and Innovative Interfaces Encore Synergy.

Students and faculty want fast, comprehensive searches that will mine the full range of the library's licensed resources. With Discovery, users get a simple, Google-like search of all our quality electronic and print content. The robust metadata assure targeted, relevant search results, and the preindexing from discovery assures fast retrieval.

Stephanie Ferreti, MLS, associate director, Medical Library, Philadelphia College of Osteopathic Medicine, Philadelphia, PA

Link Resolvers

Within a decade after Herbert Van de Sompel and Patrick Hochstenbach of Ghent University, Belgium, first discussed experimenting with link resolvers (Van de Sompel and Hochstenbach, 1999), the technology had become an indispensable tool for users to access digital content seamlessly from across the spectrum of services and resources offered by libraries (OPAC, aggregator database, discovery tool, etc.). This is referred to as "reference linking" (Caplan, 2001: 16). The heart of a link resolver is the knowledge base (KB), a customizable database of sources (such as journals, books, dissertations) and their associated targets, which are the vendors offering full-text versions. The content providers are responsible for supplying the data for the KB; and it is common, especially with journal titles, for a source to have multiple targets. A library customizes the knowledge base by activating only those vendors through which it has licensed content. Additionally, in the case of journals, dates of access may be maintained locally as subscriptions are canceled, digital back files purchased, or other adjustments are made that alter the range of available full-text volumes. The KB is continuously updated with information from the content providers to reflect a multitude of possible modifications such as the migration of a target to a new service platform or changes in publisher or journal title. The variety of content may range from books and journals to newspaper articles, dissertations, book chapters, patents, and more.

Link resolvers have revolutionized literature research. They close the gap between finding references to needed information and being able to read full text of the article. This saves the searcher both time and effort. A link to our library's resolver appears with each citation in a database, so the full text is just a click or two away. Our patrons love it!

Rena Sheffer, MLS, electronic journals coordinator, University of Arkansas for Medical Sciences, Little Rock

Another component of link resolver functionality is the OpenURL, which is based upon the OpenURL framework, a "protocol for extraction and transmission of metadata elements" (Ferguson and Grogg, 2004: 17). When the user clicks on the resolver icon from a reference source (such as a database, OPAC, discovery tool), it creates an OpenURL composed of the local link server address (base URL) and the metadata associated with the requested material extracted directly from the source. The metadata can vary, but ordinarily it includes standard bibliographic elements such as ISBN or ISSN, date, title, and for journals, volume, issue, and pages, which are critical for article-level access.

Figure 5.8 is an example of an OpenURL via the SFX link resolver. The base URL is the local server address with the remainder of the string, or descriptor, containing embedded metadata necessary for accessing the full-text article.

The third component is the resolver software, which deconstructs, or parses, the URL into the server address and metadata, and automatically compares the latter against the locally maintained KB. A link or links are created to only those targets for which the library has licensed content. These are then displayed to the user in a resolver menu (Trainor and Price, 2010). The menu itself may also be customized to include additional sources or services such as links to the OPAC, Google Scholar, interlibrary loan, and export options to reference management tools such as RefWorks.

Because the metadata in the OpenURL and within the knowledge base are crucial for successful linking, any inaccuracies or incomplete data will result in a broken link. Indeed, error rates of close to 30 percent have been reported (Trainor and Price, 2010). The causes of failures vary, but often the problem rests with the content providers for supplying poor metadata either from the source or in the KB

Example of an OpenURL Using SFX

http://sfx.university.edu/hs?sid=OVID:medline&id=pmid:22782414&id=doi:10.1001%2Fjama.2
012.7379&issn=0098-7484&isbn=&volume=308&issue=2&spage=143&pages=143-
4&date=2012&title=JAMA&atitle=Eliminating+the+use+of+partially+hydrogenated+oil+in+fo
od+production+and+preparation.&aulast=Dietz&pid=%3Cmonth%3E<p18/>%3C%2Fmonth%3
E%3Cauthor%3EDietz+WH%2CScanlon+KS%3C%2Fauthor%3E&%3CAN%3E22782414%3
C%2FAN%3E%3CDT%3EJournal+Article%3C%2FDT%3E

BaseURL: http://sfx.university.edu/hs

Descriptor Metadata:

Origin:	Ovid Medline
Journal:	JAMA
ISSN:	0098-7484
Year:	2012
Volume:	308
Issue:	2
Start Page:	143
Pages:	143-144
Title:	Eliminating the use of partially hydrogenated oil in food productions and preparation
Author:	Dietz WH
Author:	Scanlon KS

Figure 5.8. Example of an OpenURL Using SFX.

target. Efforts are currently under way to work with publishers to improve the quality of the data used in link resolvers. KBART (Knowledge Bases and Related Tools) and IOTA (Improving OpenURLs Through Analytics) are two initiatives that address metadata inconsistencies. The former is a combined endeavor by the UKSG (United Kingdom Serials Group) and NISO that is focused on best practice guidelines for standardizing metadata in the KB. Journal-related recommendations were issued in 2010 (Glasser, 2012). IOTA is sponsored by NISO and operates by analyzing patterns from log files (provided by vendors and libraries), comparing OpenURL quality, identifying problems, and recommending improvements to content providers (Glasser, 2012).

In addition to commercially available link resolver products such as Serials Solutions' 360 Link, Ex Libris's SFX, and EBSCO's LinkSource, which are system independent, a number of locally developed tools work within specific sets of databases. An example is NLM's PubMed LinkOut service, which works with the Entrez databases including PubMed, PubMed Central, the National Center for Biotechnology Information (NCBI), and other relevant sources (NCBI, 2012). Libraries participating in LinkOut maintain their local online holdings via LinkOut's KB and may also add an icon for their own link resolver service (called an "outside tool"). Print holdings are accommodated in LinkOut as well, by automatically harvesting the SERHOLD (SERials HOLDings) data from the DOCLINE service or by uploading a text file.

PubMed users associated with participating libraries are alerted to the availability of full-text access via the display of the LinkOut icon for online, print, or both formats.

Linked Data and the Semantic Web

The adoption of new standards such as RDA and BIBFRAME will significantly affect the processing of bibliographic content and its relationship to the digital information universe. The profession has a long history of using technology to facilitate and enhance the processing of resource-related data and search and retrieval functionality. However, the rapid growth and popularity of the web has outpaced the proprietary systems and associated standards most libraries currently use. This has resulted in limiting the exposure of bibliographic metadata to within the library community, creating what is commonly called an "information silo."

The Semantic Web is the vision of Tim Berners-Lee, the inventor of the web and director of the World Wide Web Consortium (W3C), "an international community that develops open standards to ensure the long-term growth of the Web" (W3C, 2013). In a 2001 article, he stated, "The Semantic Web is not a separate Web but an extension of the current one, in which information is given well-defined meaning, better enabling computers and people to work in cooperation" (Berners-Lee, Hendler, and Lassila, 2001: 37). This concept is predicated on the development of web technology with the structure, protocols, and definitions to accurately identify and retrieve data according to search criteria. The important distinction between the current environment and the Semantic Web is that the former functions at the document level whereas the latter is at the data level. In order for an automated system to operate successfully at this degree of granularity requires metadata to be appropriately contextualized so that a machine can recognize and disambiguate terms, names, places, and many other types of information.

Resource Description Framework (RDF) is the underlying structure for labeling metadata for the Semantic Web. Figure 5.9 is the graphical representation of the basic "unit," which is called a triple (or statement). The subject "node" and object "node" are connected via a relationship (predicate or property). In terms of bibliographic data, "author name" can be substituted for "subject," "title" can be

Figure 5.9. Resource Description Framework Triple. Source: Graham Klyne and Jeremy J. Caroll, eds., "Resource Description Framework (RDF): Concepts and Abstract Syntax," World Wide Web Consortium Website, February 10, 2004, 3.1 Graph Data Model (www.w3.org/TR/rdf-concepts/). Accessed February 10, 2013. Copyright ©2004 World Wide Web Consortium (Massachusetts Institute of Technology, European Research Consortium for Informatics and Mathematics, Keio University). All Rights Reserved. www.w3.org/consortium/Legal/2002/copyright-documents-20021331.

substituted for "object," and "is author of" can be substituted for "predicate" or, Florence Nightingale—is author of—Notes on Nursing. The concept is to connect two pieces of information by virtue of their relationship to one another.

However, the proper name, Florence Nightingale, is a textual string as is much of the data within web documents. Computers require more specific designations in order to distinguish a name from a title or recognize that variations of a name denote the same individual. Attaching a unique identifier to structural terms, data values, and properties provides automated systems with a "tool" with which to establish meaningful connections in a search across the web and return accurate results. This is the "simple" concept of **linked data**. Currently, the unique identifier is a URL (Uniform Resource Locator), a form of URI (Uniform Resource Identifier) that also includes location information, typically assigned by the organization responsible for maintaining the data set. Both the DCMI and LC have been active in establishing Semantic Web-compliant lists of metadata.

Figure 5.10 is part of LC's authority record for Florence Nightingale. Note the identifier begins with "http://id.loc.gov" indicating the source (location) and ending with a unique alphanumeric code for LC's established form of the name.

Returning to the RDF triple example, substituting LC's unique identifier http://id.loc.gov/authorities/names/n79103647 for "Florence Nightingale" and similar identifiers for property and title provide an automated system with the means by which to recognize and match metadata from across the web. In order for this process to be successful, however, the metadata has to exist in the appropriate form in the Semantic Web environment and be freely available for use as linked open data (LOD). At present, a significant number of registries house data sets established by a wide variety of different information communities. Among the sites associated with library-related data are the Open Metadata Registry (RDA, FRBR, FRAD, FRSAD) and vocab.org (FRBR) (Coyle, 2012). Additionally, the Linked Data Cloud, http://linkeddata.org, is a continually expanding project to facilitate connections and sharing across the web with contributions from a large and diverse number of participants.

Figure 5.11 is a section of a diagram of the cloud that Richard Cyganiak and Anja Jentzsch created and maintain. The entire graphic may be viewed at http://lod-cloud.net/.

This is an extremely brief and simplistic explanation of a complex subject. The Semantic Web as Berners-Lee envisioned does not yet exist. Currently, an astounding number of organizations, communities of interest, and initiatives are associated with Semantic Web-related activities. The linked data environment is in a constant state of change with the ultimate outcome yet to be determined. Although a great deal of work remains to be done, progress has been made with regard to library-related bibliographic and structural metadata standards and Semantic Web compliance. The W3C Library Linked Data Incubator Group, composed of experts from different sectors of the profession, released a final report in 2011 with recommendations for increasing "global interoperability." They include establishing Semantic Web-compliant protocols and standards for bibliographic data; designing automated systems that incorporate elements that facilitate the sharing of, and mapping to, existing vocabularies and URIs; library professional organizations participating

Nightingale, Florence, 1820-1910

[Florence Nightingale (1820-1910) was a British nurse, statistician, and social reformer.]

URI(s)
- http://id.loc.gov/authorities/names/n79103647

Instance Of
- MADS/RDF PersonalName
- MADS/RDF Authority
- SKOS Concept

Scheme Membership(s)
- Library of Congress Name Authority File

Collection Membership(s)
- Names Collection - Authorized Headings
- LC Names Collection - General Collection

Variants
- フローレンスナイチンゲール, 1820-1910

Exact Matching Concepts from Other Schemes
- http://viaf.org/viaf/sourceID/LC%7Cn+79103647#skos:Concept

Sources
- found: Her Notes on nursing ... 1860.
- found: Britannica online, via WWW, May 9, 2012 (Florence Nightingale; b. May 12, 1820 in Florence, Italy; d. Aug. 13, 1910 in London, England; philosopher of modern nursing, statistician, and social reformer; raised at Lea Hurst in Derbyshire and Embley Park in Hampshire; managed nursing of British and allied forces during Crimean War at Scutari; est. Nightingale School of Nursing in London, 1860; set up training for midwives and nurses in workhouses; awarded Order of Merit, 1907)

General Notes
- [Florence Nightingale (1820-1910) was a British nurse, statistician, and social reformer.]

Figure 5.10. LC Name Authority Record for Florence Nightingale.

in ongoing Semantic Web development efforts; and cultivating discussions regarding open data, rights, and preservation issues (W3C Library Linked Data Incubator Group, 2011).

Certainly the RDF-based BIBFRAME Initiative, the adoption of RDA as the new content standard, and the processing of authority values and element properties with unique identifiers are significant steps toward transitioning bibliographic metadata currently stored in information silos to exposure in a shared, interoperable web environment.

SUMMARY

Just as rapid evolution in technology has affected many areas of library work, it continues to drive changes in technical services. As health sciences libraries move to an almost exclusively digital environment, resources are increasingly licensed rather than purchased outright. Although this complicates the acquisitions process, it also provides exciting new methods to build collections such as the demand-driven acquisition of e-books. This change also has had a profound effect on the way librarians organize information and make it available to users. Cataloging standards are

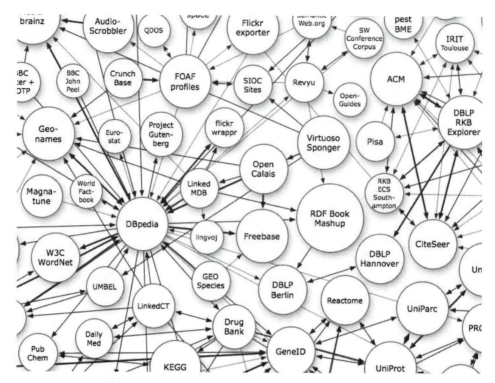

Figure 5.11. Linking Open Data Cloud Diagram: Selection. Source: Richard Cyganiak and Anja Jentzsch (http://linkeddata.org/).

changing to adapt to the new and emerging environment, and systems increasingly link and share information with one another to lead library users to information as seamlessly as possible. The hallmark of an efficient technical services operation is often its invisibility. Indeed, technical services are often outsourced to another library or outside contractor. Although patrons aren't usually interested in how the systems work behind the scenes, a basic knowledge of technical services is important for those entering the profession.

STUDY QUESTIONS

1. What is demand-driven acquisition, and how does it benefit the library?
2. What is the difference between licensing and purchasing a resource?
3. What are the issues to be considered when deciding whether or not to formally catalog a library's resources?
4. What is authority control and what is its purpose?
5. What is MeSH?
6. Provide a definition of a web-scale discovery system.
7. Discuss the importance of linking technology to libraries both currently and in the future.

REFERENCES

ALA (American Library Association), Canadian Library Association, and CILIP. 2010. *RDA Toolkit.* June. www.rdatoolkit.org/news/archive/201006.

Berners-Lee, Tim, James Hendler, and Ora Lassila. 2001. "The Semantic Web." *Scientific American* 45, no. 5 (May): 34–43.

Breeding, Marshall. 2013. "Tech Review and Forecast for 2013." *Computers in Libraries* 32, no. 10 (December): 19–22.

Caplan, Priscilla. 2001. "A Lesson in Linking." *Library Journal netconnect.* (Fall): 16–18.

Chan, Lois Mai. 2007. *Cataloging and Classification: An Introduction,* 3rd ed. Lanham, MD: Scarecrow Press.

Coyle, Karen. 2012. "Linked Data Tools: Connecting on the Web." *Library Technology Reports* 48, no. 4 (May/June): 15–26.

DCMI (Dublin Core Metadata Initiative). 2013. "History of the Dublin Core Metadata Initiative." Accessed February 26. http://dublincore.org/about/history/.

Ferguson, Christine L., and Jill E. Grogg. 2004. "OpenURL Link Resolvers." *Computers in Libraries* 24, no. 9 (October): 17–24.

Glasser, Sarah. 2012. "Broken Links and Failed Access: How KBART, IOTA, and PIE-J Can Help." *Library Resources & Technical Services* 56, no. 1 (January): 14–23.

Greenberg, Jane. 2005. "Understanding Metadata and Metadata Schemes." *Cataloging & Classification Quarterly* 40, no. 3/4: 17–36.

Hoy, Matthew B. 2012. "An Introduction to Web Scale Discovery Systems." *Medical Reference Services Quarterly* 31, no. 3 (July–September): 323–29. *Academic Search Premier,* EBSCOhost.

LC (Library of Congress). 2011. "Transforming Our Bibliographic Framework: A Statement from the Library of Congress." May. www.loc.gov/marc/transition/news/framework-051311.html.

———. 2012a. "The Library of Congress Announces Modeling Initiative." May. http://loc.gov/marc/transition/news/modeling-052212.html.

———. 2012b. "Bibliographic Framework as a Web of Data: Linked Data Model and Supporting Services." November. www.loc.gov/marc/transition/pdf/marcld-report-11-21-2012.pdf.

———. 2012c. "Bibliographic Framework as a Web of Data: Linked Data Model and Supporting Services." *News and Announcements.* November. www.loc.gov/marc/transition/news/bibframe-112312.html.

———. 2013. "Program for Cooperative Cataloging." Accessed March 4. www.loc.gov/aba/pcc/.

Miller, Steven J. 2011. *Metadata for Digital Collections.* New York: Neal-Schuman Publishers.

NCBI (National Center for Biomedical Information). 2012. "Welcome to LinkOut." February. www.ncbi.nlm.nih.gov/books/NBK3805/#Public.Examples_of_LinkOut.

NISO (National Information Standards Organization). 2004. *Understanding Metadata.* Bethesda, MD: NISO Press. www.niso.org/publications/press/UnderstandingMetadata.pdf.

OCLC (Online Computer Library Center). 2013. "World Facts and Statistics." Accessed February 23. www.oclc.org/us/en/worldcat/statistics/default.htm.

Perkins, Heather. 2009. "The Effect that Electronic Collections Has on Cataloging." *Journal of Hospital Librarianship* 9, no. 2: 218–20.

Rather, Lucia J., and Beacher Wiggins. 1989. "Henriette D. Avram: Close-up on the Career of a Towering Figure in Library Automation and Bibliographic Control." *American Libraries* 20, no. 9 (October): 855–59.

SkyRiver Technology Solutions. 2013. "Frequently Asked Questions." Accessed February 23. http://theskyriver.com/faqs.

Trainor, Cindi, and Jason Price. 2010. "Rethinking Library Linking: Breathing New Life into OpenURL." *Library Technology Reports* 46, no. 7 (October): 5–35.

Van de Sompel, Herbert, and Patrick Hochstenbach. 1999. "Reference Linking in a Hybrid Library Environment." *D-Lib Magazine* 5, no. 10 (October). www.dlib.org/dlib/october99/van_de_sompel/10van_de_sompel.html.

Vaughan, Jason. 2011. "Web Scale Discovery: What and Why? *Library Technology Reports* 47: Web Scale Discovery Services, no. 1 (January). *MasterFile Premier*.

W3C (World Wide Web Consortium). 2013. "Home Page." Accessed March 15. www.w3.org/.

W3C (World Wide Web Consortium) Library Linked Data Incubator Group. 2011 "W3C Incubator Group Report 25." October. www.w3.org/2005/Incubator/lld/XGR-lld-20111025/.

Wiggins, Beacher. 1998. "The Program for Cooperative Cataloging." June. http://research archive.calacademy.org/research/informatics/taf/proceedings/wiggins.html.

CHAPTER 6

Technology Services in Health Sciences Libraries

Nancy R. Glassman

INTRODUCTION

Technology impacts just about every function in a library, from the most ordinary to the highly complex. In this era of big data and shrinking physical space, librarians rely on technology for fast, reliable access to provide the most relevant information and services to their patrons. Technologies found in most types of libraries run the gamut from integrated library systems (ILS), proxy servers, link resolvers, websites, e-resources, public access computers, and printers, to the networks that connect them.

Technology is advancing so rapidly that any textbook discussion of the topic runs the risk of becoming outdated even before it is published. This chapter will provide an overview of selected technology services that impact libraries, focusing on aspects that are unique to health sciences libraries. The aim is to provide the reader with a sense of the issues involved with managing technology. Technologies used for outreach to patrons, such as communications and educational tools, will be discussed. A variety of technology resources used to provide and secure access to resources will also be covered. New opportunities for health sciences librarians to share their unique technology expertise with their parent institutions, such electronic health record integration and mobile computing, will be introduced. Technology plans, the key to coordinating all of these services, will also be reviewed. Finally, the chapter will provide some suggestions for keeping up with emerging technology trends.

TECHNOLOGY TODAY

Typical health sciences library patrons, such as clinicians, researchers, administrators, and students, do not necessarily work during standard business hours and are often located off-site. An emergency medicine resident seeks information to help diagnose a patient presenting with an unusual rash in the early hours of the morning. A postdoc running a twenty-four-hour experiment in a cell biology lab takes advantage of some downtime to put the finishing touches on an article he or she hopes to submit for publication. A nursing student spending a semester working in an outreach program in Ethiopia needs information on etiology of tropical diseases. A medical student spends a holiday weekend at home studying exam questions for the Boards on a mobile device. Patrons need and expect reliable access to e-resources around the clock, including weekends and holidays, and potentially from around the world. Library resources are often needed for urgent patient care, so system downtime is not an option.

Not all health sciences libraries have the same technology requirements. For example, due to the **Health Insurance Portability and Accountability Act (HIPAA)** regulations, computer and network security is of paramount importance in patient care settings, affecting the types of technology services a library can provide and the way patrons use them. Although security is still a major concern for a library in an organization focusing on basic research and not involved in patient care, the network security level might not be quite as restrictive.

Librarians' responsibilities and involvement in providing technology services vary widely even between health sciences institutions. Small hospital libraries, for example, usually do not have their own information technology (IT) staff and must work closely with their institution's IT department. Some large, academic health sciences libraries have their own IT staff. Other libraries might actually be part of the IT department. Some institutions do not have their own IT staff, but they outsource the management of all IT services to outside contractors.

Although librarians do not need to be experts on all things technical, a certain degree of "technical literacy" goes a long way. Understanding the basics of technology enables librarians to discern future trends from passing fads. Whether communicating with patrons, colleagues, administrators, vendors, or IT professionals and technicians, librarians must be familiar with the technologies used in the library as well as in the parent institution.

In any exploration of the use of technology in libraries, one fact holds true: Technology is always changing. As new technologies emerge, many old ones are rendered obsolete and fade away. This evolution is plain to see by reviewing the literature of health sciences librarianship. In his Janet Doe lecture presented at the 2013 Annual Meeting of the Medical Library Association, Mark Funk (2013) explored changes in the field of librarianship over the course of forty years, from 1961 through 2010, through a textual analysis of the *Bulletin of the Medical Library Association* and *Journal of the Medical Library Association*. Terms such as audiovisual, CD-ROMs, and PDAs have given way to digitization, web, and mobile computing, clearly indicating a shift in focus has moved beyond physical material toward ubiquitous online access and services.

MEDLARS Then and Now

The history of the National Library of Medicine's MEDLARS system illustrates the evolution of library technology during the past half century (U.S. National Institutes of Health, 2005). Established in 1964, MEDLARS was designed to speed access to biomedical information, primarily in print tools such as *Index Medicus*. In 1971, the introduction of MEDLINE heralded faster online access to the MEDLARS database, opening up new opportunities for clinical use. Searches were primarily conducted by librarians via dial-up modems. In 1996, the user-friendly, PC-based software Grateful Med made it possible for individuals in the health community to run their own searches for even faster access to clinical information. Free, web-based access to MEDLINE became available in 1998 with the introduction of PubMed. Taking advantage of the new wireless technology and personal data assistants (PDAs), PubMed on Tap was launched in 2003 (Fontelo et al., 2003). PubMed on Tap has since evolved into PubMed4Hh (PubMed for Handhelds), which is available as both a mobile-friendly website and downloadable app.

Understanding the Past to Predict the Future

Nearly a decade ago, the National Library of Medicine's director, Donald Lindberg, and deputy director, Betsy Humphreys, envisioned the medical library in 2015 asking, "What will happen to medical libraries in the post-Google world?" (Lindberg and Humphreys, 2005: 1067). Because of their keen understanding, not only of the state of medical libraries, but also of health care and science, their predictions proved to be spot on. They understood not only the importance of easy access to information from a variety of devices and potentially from great distances, but also that the information must connect to related knowledge, such as protocols and clinical alerts. In addition, Lindberg and Humphreys (2005) emphasized the continued importance of the "library as place," pointing out that space formerly used to house the print collection might be repurposed for group study and classroom space.

How Technology Fits

It takes a combination of technologies to run a library. Networks allow for sharing and transferring data. A variety of communications tools enable librarians to connect with patrons at anytime or almost anywhere. Systems help make information findable. Public computers and related equipment encourage patrons to visit the library. Teaching tools help librarians instruct groups of patrons, on-site or at remote locations, and mobile devices and resources allow patrons to access information at the point of need. Integration of library resources into the **electronic health record (EHR)** is another way health sciences libraries extend their reach to the point of care. Careful planning is the key to keeping all of these functions running like a well-oiled machine.

PLANNING

"Fail to plan. Plan to fail." This old saying sums up the importance of thoughtful library planning. Obviously, no crystal ball can foretell exactly what a library or its parent institution will need, or what new technologies will emerge in the coming years. No one can predict for certain the state of the economy or specifics of a library's budget in the future. Short- and long-term planning are the keys to the effective use of existing library technologies as well as the implementation of new ones. Planning is a process; once a plan has been developed, it must be reviewed and reassessed on a regular basis. Often overlooked, documentation of systems and processes, technical training for staff, and disaster planning should be factored into a technology plan.

Technology Plans

Technology plans can be developed as part of a library's strategic plan, or as a freestanding document. Either way, the plan should be written with the library's mission as well as the parent institution's mission in mind. The plan should focus on what needs to be accomplished over a period of several years and how these accomplishments will be achieved (Cohn and Kelsey, 2010). A technology plan serves many purposes. It can help librarians develop partnerships with departments in the organization working toward similar goals. It also demonstrates to administrators that librarians are proactive and forward thinking. Grant and funding applications often require evidence of a technology plan. Even when they are not required, a good plan will enhance the application process and be useful in project implementation. A plan will help gauge whether current technologies are providing the library with an adequate return on investment (ROI).

Cohn and Kelsey (2010) divide a technology plan into five main sections.

1. The summary highlights the plan's recommendations.
2. The background is comprised of a description of the library including its mission statement.
3. An overview of the current state of technology in the library includes an inventory of equipment and software.
4. The plan outlines goals and objectives for improving library resources and services including a budget.
5. Finally, the evaluation establishes criteria that will be used to measure the plan's success. Regular review and reassessment should be built into the plan.

An inventory of the current state of a library's technology includes all hardware, software, and electronic resources that library staff and patrons use. Serial numbers, model numbers, version numbers, and date acquired should be recorded. In addition to looking within the library, it is worthwhile to explore technologies currently in use in the parent institution. For example, if a school of nursing plans to provide tablet computers to incoming students, librarians can take advantage of this opportunity to collaborate with nurse educators to support the tablets.

Needs assessments, using a variety of methods, will guide the planning process.

- Observations of patrons and staff using technology tools (students and staff walking around the institution with their eyes glued to their smartphones provide a clue to librarians that mobile resources would be in demand).
- Direct feedback through interviews and focus groups.
- Print or online surveys.
- Usage logs and statistics provide a treasure trove of information, including which resources are used and how they are being used.

- Input and opinions from stakeholders, such as professional and support staff in the library, patrons, board members, advisory committee members, and "friends" groups.

To support the evolving information needs of biomedical researchers and health sciences students, Chen and colleagues (2011) realized they had to make better use of available technologies. To achieve this goal, they created a series of objectives divided into three categories—creating knowledge, using knowledge, and sharing knowledge—and developed their technology strategies accordingly.

Once the library's goals and objectives have been identified, it is important to plan how these initiatives will be paid for. At minimum, ballpark pricing should be estimated. If the proposed technology improvements are beyond a library's budget, it might be necessary to seek funding opportunities. Partnering with "Friends of the Library" or Institutional Advancement departments is one option to search for funds. Applying for technology improvement awards is also a great idea. The National Network of Libraries of Medicine site, http://nnlm.gov/funding/, lists previously funded projects. For example, a number of recent projects involved support for mobile devices.

Although not a lot of literature discusses technology planning in health sciences libraries, other resources are available. OCLC's WebJunction, www.webjunction.org/explore-topics/tech-planning.html, offers a wide variety of resources. Although it is geared primarily toward public libraries, many of the tools could easily be adapted for a health sciences library. Kenefick and Werner (2012) observed how the five principles of the U.S. Department of Education's National Education Technology Plan 2010, www.ed.gov/sites/default/files/netp2010.pdf, could be adapted to the unique needs of the populations that hospital librarians serve.

Planning for Obsolescence

Planning for the future includes keeping an eye on the past. As existing technologies are replaced by newer, more efficient ones, important sources of information are at risk of being left behind. Many a researcher has been frustrated when searching for information, only to find that it had been stored in an obsolete file format or on a medium the library no longer has the hardware to support. What can be done with floppy disks or Zip disks, audiotapes, 16mm movie reels, or even VHS cassettes? Digitization of these types of material for long-term storage should be included in a technology plan.

Technology Training

An important part of technology planning is training—for both staff and patrons. A training agenda should be in place for new library hires. The training plan should include an assessment of their current technology skills and experience. Existing staff will require training when new systems are acquired or when existing systems are updated. Occasional review sessions are beneficial as well. Cross-training staff, especially on mission-critical resources, is essential (Lynn, FitzSimmons, and Robinson,

2011). Redundant staffing might seem like a waste of effort, but it prevents services from coming to a standstill when a particular staff member leaves or is unavailable (Cunningham, 2010). Online and in-person training opportunities are offered from organizations such as the Medical Library Association, www.mlanet.org/education/, and the National Network of Libraries of Medicine, http://nnlm.gov/training/. Online sessions are often recorded for "on-demand" viewing. Many local library organizations and consortia offer continuing education opportunities. Massive open online courses (MOOCs) on technology topics offer free or low-cost learning opportunities of potential interest to librarians (Goodell, 2013).

Documentation

Knowledge is power. With regard to technology services, power should not be allowed to rest in the hands of an individual. Library services cannot come to a standstill due to the unavailability of a single staff member. Documentation of systems processes is an often overlooked but essential aspect of technology planning. Documentation should be reviewed and updated on a regular basis. Processes should be clearly outlined, and contact information for relevant technical support and staff should be listed. Documentation should be kept in an easy-to-find and accessible location.

Backup Plans

A popular expression among IT help-desk staff is: "There are two types of people in this world—those who back up—and those who will." That is to say, it only takes one computer crash or a lost or stolen laptop to bring home the importance of backing up irreplaceable data. Instituting backup plans for servers, for public access computers, and for staff computers *before an accident occurs* is crucial. Many questions must be addressed when reviewing a backup plan, starting with the location of the servers that must be backed up. Are the servers located in the library or in a data center? How are they being backed up? What media are being used—CDs, tapes, network? Who is responsible for the media? Is a copy kept in a safe location off-site? Is redundancy built into these systems? For example, if one hard drive fails, in a redundant system another server will automatically perform the same function. How often are backups done? Backup schedules might be determined based on how frequently data on a system is updated. A system, such as an ILS, which is constantly in flux, requires daily backups. Questions to ask when preparing a backup plan include:

- Is there a plan for restoring from a backup?
- Has the backup ever been tested? Many people run backups for years without ever knowing if the backup is capable of fully restoring a system.
- In the case of systems that are hosted on a vendor, how are backups run?
- Will the vendor provide the library with a copy of its own data?

A backup plan must also consider secure disposal of backup media, particularly if patron data are involved. Just tossing an old tape or CD in the trash when it reaches its end of life is not sufficient. Security is a major concern for everyone who uses the Internet. The stakes are particularly high at hospitals and academic medical centers.

Disaster Plans

Technology must factor in heavily to a library's disaster plan. Disasters come in many forms: power failures, storms, fires, floods, epidemics, to name but a few. It is important to be aware of emergency situations that are likely to occur in the area where the library is located. Particularly in a health care setting, where information for patient care is at stake, procedures must be in place to make sure that technology remains functional and can be easily restored from backups, no matter the nature of the disaster. A library emergency response plan usually has two parts: disaster management, to deal with the immediate impact of a disaster; and service continuity, to deal with a disaster's long-term effects (Yeh, McMullen, and Kane, 2010). The plan should include:

1. Contact information for key personnel from the parent organization.
2. Library staff contact information and responsibilities.
3. A communication plan, possibly including social media for sending alert information.
4. A service continuity plan, describing how services will be maintained and who is responsible. Services include online resources; proxy/remote access; interlibrary loan; the library's website; and library e-mail, chat, or text messaging service. If servers are located on-site, it is important to make sure emergency power sources are available.
5. A prioritized list of collections and equipment to recover.

The National Network of Libraries of Medicine has created a single-page Pocket Response Plan (PReP) to help libraries create a plan that can easily be stored on- and off-site. Another important aspect of disaster planning involves establishing partnerships with other libraries. In the event of a service disruption, partner libraries can assist in maintaining services on behalf of the affected library (NN/LM, 2013).

SECURITY

Due to their unique circumstances, hospitals and their libraries have special technology needs. Hospital libraries with IT staff of their own are few and far between. Often, a single librarian fills all the roles, with the aid of a few support staff (Ennis, 2009). Computer and network security are of vital importance to hospitals and have implications for librarians. This is because of two things: the Health Insurance Portability and Accountability Act of 1996 (HIPAA) regulations and electronic health records (EHR). HIPAA protects the privacy of individually identifiable health records and sets national standards for the security of electronic health information (U.S. Department of Health and Human Services, 2013). As defined by the Health Information Management Systems Society (2013), an EHR is a "longitudinal electronic record of patient health information generated by one or more encounters in any care delivery setting."

The focus on security is not unique to clinical settings. An emerging area of concern for academic institutions is protecting and maintaining strict data privacy and security standards for research data generated by faculty and students (Johnson, Butler, and Johnston, 2012).

Firewalls

Firewalls play an important role at the institutional level, particularly in hospital networks. In accordance with HIPAA's Privacy and Security Rules, hospital network administrators are required to lock down networks as tightly as possible to control all traffic flowing in and out to protect patient health information. Security measures include blocking access to certain types of websites, such as shopping and social media sites, which can prevent librarians from using social media platforms to advertise their resources and services. Firewalls can be configured to restrict or permit access to certain network ports. A port is an application/process specific standard that allows traffic to flow from one system to another (Blansit, 2009). For example, websites generally use port 80, so most firewalls allow traffic to flow (Mitchell and Ennis, 2010). Proxy servers may require additional ports, and many integrated library systems make use of numerous ports to perform various functions. For example, **FTP** uses ports 20 or 21.

Internet security is a priority at our hospital. Access to websites classified as shopping, social networking, sports, and entertainment is restricted from computers on the hospital network. My monthly training sessions for first-year residents include a YouTube video. Recently, I discovered that access to this video had been blocked. I contacted the service desk and justified my access to the video. Access was immediately restored. As an alternative, I can connect my iPad or laptop through the hospital's separate Wi-Fi network, which has fewer restrictions. Although experiences like this can be frustrating, patient information must be secure.

Marie Elias, MLS, AHIP, associate librarian,
Montefiore Medical Center, Bronx, NY

Z39.50 usually uses port 210. In addition, **IP addresses** for important resources such as DOCLINE might have to be added to firewall configuration settings as a "trusted site" (U.S. National Library of Medicine, 2012). Health sciences librarians must understand the rules in place at their institutions (Mitchell and Ennis, 2010). Before implementing a new system, or even upgrading an old one, it is essential to learn which network ports must be opened. Sharing this information with network administrators will help to avoid complications. When requesting changes to firewall setting, librarians should be as specific as possible and be prepared to explain why these changes are necessary.

To further protect patient information, hospitals often create separate networks or network zones for public, administrative, and patient data (Stephenson et al., 2012). Public networks can provide a more open environment, while confidential information remains secure.

Intranets

Many institutions use an intranet to provide access to secure information. An intranet allows sections and departments within an organization to collaborate and share resources from within the institution's firewall. An intranet might include news about the institution, policies, staff directories, and departments such as the library and human resources (Herbert, 2013).

Intranets are very useful to patrons working on site, but without remote access they can be a source of frustration for people at other locations. Virtual private networks (VPNs) are used by many organizations in order to allow authorized users secure access to an institution's intranet from off-site. When a patron connects to a network via a VPN, he or she is considered to be "on-site" and will have access to most, if not all, of the resources available from within the hospital (Wink and Killingsworth, 2011).

Authentication

A virtual private network is just one way of providing authorized access to restricted resources and is usually managed at the institutional level. Proxy servers, such as OCLC's EZproxy, www.oclc.org/ezproxy.en.html/, are used by many libraries to allow off-site users access to IP-authenticated resources. Proxy servers can be linked to a library's integrated library system or an institutional directory for ease of patron authentication (Barton and Mak, 2012). Proxy servers sometimes cannot accommodate high bandwidth resources such as videos and might have to be configured to work with patrons' personal firewalls.

Additional authentication methods include Athens, www.openathens.net/; and Shibboleth, www.internet2.edu/shibboleth/, which provide users with single sign-on capabilities, thus reducing the number of passwords to remember and avoiding some of the pitfalls of proxy servers (Blansit, 2007). Athens and Shibboleth are usually managed at the institutional level.

Remote desktop software allows users to log on to their institution's computers from off-site. Once connected, it is as if they were sitting in their office, lab, or dormitory (Blansit, 2007). Remote desktop is also a powerful tool for librarians who manage technology services. Problems occurring during weekends and off hours can sometimes be remedied by connecting to the institutional network from a desktop computer at home in order to reboot a server or restart a process (avoiding an unexpected trip to the office).

ELECTRONIC HEALTH RECORDS

Electronic Health Records (EHRs) consolidate patient information, such as treatment, tests, lab results, prescriptions, and billing into a single record that can be accessed by all of the patient's health care providers. By simplifying record keeping, the EHR's goal is to reduce costs, reduce errors, and in the long run, improve patient care. With an EHR, physicians, nurses, pharmacists, and other health professionals all use the same patient information (Bushhousen, 2013).

As hospitals and health care systems implement EHRs, librarians have been exploring ways to collaborate. In some cases, librarians are partnering with health care providers to append information to the record for the patient at the time of discharge as well as for the provider. The creation of an "info" button on the EHR would allow for context-sensitive linking to evidence-based resources.

Upon learning that many physicians found it difficult to search for medical information through the library's link on the hospital's intranet, librarians at the South East Area Health Education Center (AHEC) Medical Library knew it was time to take action. AHEC librarians worked with the IT department to integrate the AHEC Digital Library into the hospital's electronic medical record (EMR). Because of the EMR's tightly controlled security settings, logins and passwords for individual resources could be removed, simplifying access even further. Once the integration was completed, this new access method was heavily marketed around the hospital and was met with a positive response. EMR integration increased the library's visibility at the hospital and increased physicians' respect for librarians and the services they provide (Flake, 2010).

In academic settings, librarians are collaborating with other departments to train medical students in the efficient use of EHRs (Gomes, Linton, and Abate, 2013). Clinical librarians, in particular, participate in teaching and creating self-paced tutorials.

An important component of EHR implementation is the use of Clinical Decision Support Systems (CDSS), which are designed to improve clinical decision making at the point of care. CDSSs provide several functions. They alert physicians about routine tests that should be done for a particular patient, provide warnings about test results that are outside the normal range, and warn about potential drug interactions. A CDSS can also assist with making a diagnosis and prognosis (Moore and Loper, 2011).

> The library has integrated content with our hospital's Electronic Health Record (EHR) for many years. When the hospital transitioned to a new EHR system, we were well positioned to advocate for clinical content at the point of care. Working closely with the clinical integration team, we facilitated communication between vendors, technical support, and the information systems staff, showcasing the library staff as "team players" during a stressful time for the institution. Ongoing access to the EHR allows us to troubleshoot problems with the clinical content integration and appreciate the workflow of our users at the point of care.
>
> *Dina McKelvy, MLS, AHIP, library manager*
> *for automation and planning,*
> *Maine Medical Center, Portland*

CONNECTING WITH PATRONS

Communication

In their role providing information services to patrons, health sciences librarians use a variety of communication channels. Some patrons might be working from distant locations—at a clinic across town or on the other side of the globe.

Nontraditional work or study schedules present an obstacle to contacting the library during regular business hours. To reach patrons, technology offers librarians a number of options—some in real time, others asynchronously.

Voice-over IP

Voice-over IP (VoIP) allows users to talk to each other over the Internet, instead of telephone lines, and is accessible from many parts of the world. Some VoIP services include video conferencing as well. Many VoIP services, such as Skype, are available at low or no cost, require minimal equipment, and can be used from mobile devices. During an exploration of new services to offer, librarians at the University of North Carolina at Chapel Hill asked scientists to suggest potential new service areas. One surprising but easy-to-implement suggestion was consultations with librarians via Skype (Vaughan et al., 2013).

E-mail

In addition to sending and receiving messages, a few things can be done to enhance e-mail functionality. Setting up mailing lists for groups of staff members and groups of patrons offers a quick way to share information with groups of individuals. Prewritten messages that answer frequently asked questions can be saved and reused as needed, making it easy to answer frequently asked questions. E-mailing news and updates on topics such as health policy to hospital administrators on a regular basis is one way hospital librarians use e-mail to increase the library's visibility and highlight services and resources (Sostack, 2012).

Virtual Reference

Traditional methods of communication are just too slow for many "digital natives." Newer, quicker communications tools continue to gain traction. Short Message Service (SMS) text messaging is very popular among mobile device users. Web-based SMS management services, some of which are designed specifically for libraries, allow multiple librarians to monitor queues. Other useful features include "canned messages" to answer frequently asked questions, an archive of transactions, and usage statistics reports.

Many library websites are now sporting chat widgets. As with text messaging, chat is a fast and easy way for patrons to connect with librarians. Some chat services allow patrons to remain anonymous. Chat services designed specifically for libraries usually offer canned messages, archived transactions, usage statistics, and the ability to "transfer" a patron from one librarian to another. Many chat services allow patrons to leave a message or search a knowledge base when the queue is not being monitored. Librarians at the Claude Moore Health Sciences Library provide an example of the innovative use of an instant messaging service for communication with patrons and also among library staff. Upon noticing a steady decrease in questions asked at the reference desk, librarians decided to explore more efficient approaches to providing reference services. Instead of sitting at the reference desk waiting for patrons, the library now offers "on-demand" reference services using Libraryh3lp,

http://libraryh3lp.com, open source instant
messaging software. When a patron at the
service desk requires reference assistance, a
staff member contacts a librarian "on call"
through a specially configured queue in Li-
brary3lp. Patrons can also click on a link on
the library's website to chat with a librarian.
Even though librarians still work in shifts
to monitor queues, this service model allows librarians extra time to pursue other
projects (Horne, Ragon, and Wilson, 2012).

Not every communication method fits
the culture of every library or institution.
When possible, it is beneficial to explore
the available options and select the ones
that best match patron needs. If a particular
method of communication is not heavily
used, it should be evaluated and perhaps
discarded.

Technology, such as our new chat
service, has increased our reach
and improved customer service options that enable busy clinicians, faculty,
and health sciences students to find
answers to their questions much more
easily, efficiently, and quickly. Although
traditional reference methods are now
woven creatively into encounters that
mostly happen online, our value to
those we serve has increased, allowing
us to devise new services and retrain
staff to gain more opportunity than
ever before.

Gail Y. Hendler, MLS, associate provost
and director, Health Sciences Library,
Loyola University, Chicago, IL

Technology Supporting Education

Technology has had a profound effect on education. Even as classrooms and
lecture halls are outfitted with increasingly sophisticated tools and gadgets, more
and more teaching and learning takes place outside the traditional classroom environment. Because libraries are often learning resource centers for their institutions,
health sciences librarians should be familiar with tools and technologies to enhance
education in traditional and nontraditional settings.

"Smart" classrooms are becoming increasingly common. In addition to classroom management software, a smart classroom might be equipped with interactive
whiteboards, allowing groups to collaborate on projects (Brigham, 2013). Audience response systems, which might consist of small "clicker" devices, or an app or
website for participants' smartphones, give instructors real-time feedback on their
presentations (Bandyopadhyay, 2013; Connor, 2011).

As schedules get tighter and responsibilities increase, people find it more difficult
to attend training sessions in person. Recorded online tutorials provide an alternative training venue that can be customized for specific populations. The nursing
librarian at Michigan State University used online tutorials to introduce students to
the library services and to increase their information literacy skills using screen recording software that had been licensed by her library. And it came with the advantage of in-house training and support. Equipment, especially microphones, had to
be tested for sound quality. The tutorials were comprised of a combination of screen
captures and PowerPoint presentations. Few participants provided feedback to the
brief assessment survey embedded into the tutorial; a later survey was e-mailed to
nursing students and faculty (Schroeder, 2010).

Librarians at the University of Saskatchewan took an innovative approach to using screen capture software to evaluate web-based tutorials on the use of databases

such as PsycINFO. Participants were given five minutes to conduct a PsycINFO search on the topic of their own choosing. After searching, participants watched a video tutorial. After watching the video, participants were given five minutes to rerun their searches. Both pre- and post-video tutorial searches were recorded using screen capture software. The librarians were then able to analyze the recordings. Screen capture technologies were used to create and evaluate the effectiveness of the tutorials (Boden, Neilson, and Seaton, 2013).

Although recorded training sessions are very convenient, many patrons still prefer the human touch. To accommodate patrons' diverse learning styles, many librarians will "take the show on the road." Because many of their rural hospital affiliates lack training facilities of their own, librarians from the University of Saskatchewan Health Sciences Library have developed a portable computer lab. Their kit fits into a custom travel case and contains laptops (with accessories), an LCD projector, and a wireless broadband router. Before visiting a site, librarians consult with local IT staff to make arrangements to set up the equipment and necessary network configurations (Neilson, 2010).

SYSTEMS

A number of systems work together to make a library tick; for example: integrated library systems (ILS), proxy servers (remote access), link resolvers, discovery tools, electronic resources management systems, interlibrary loan (ILL) and document delivery, websites (internal and external), and library intranet for staff file sharing and communication. Because they are essential functions of the library, these systems require routine attention and planning for upgrades or renovation. Familiarity with exam schedules and grant deadlines is helpful for scheduling system maintenance. Reviewing a system's usage logs can help to identify times that will impact the fewest patrons. When acquiring new systems or upgrading old ones, it is essential to consider where they will be housed. Infrastructure is important and sometimes overlooked. Servers need reliable electrical power sources and climate control. For systems that are hosted in-house, a hardware replacement schedule should be built into the library's technology plan. Many hardware suppliers recommend a three- to five-year replacement cycle. A growing number of system vendors now offer "hosted" services, eliminating the need for a library to purchase and maintain its own hardware. If a hosted solution is chosen, it is important to be certain that the institution's network is configured to handle the required traffic.

Integrated Library Systems

For many libraries, the ILS acts like a central nervous system providing functions needed by library staff to manage the collection and patron database and also providing an interface (OPAC) that allows patrons to search the catalog and check out material (Breeding, 2012). Selecting the right ILS is not an easy decision, particularly in recent years, because fewer options are available. Libraries that are part of larger organizations with more than one library might not have much of a say in the final selection.

Academic health sciences libraries that share an ILS with their parent institution (i.e., a university library system) face unique challenges. Health sciences libraries are traditionally organized using the National Library of Medicine's (NLM) subject headings (MeSH) and call number scheme, whereas universities usually follow the Library of Congress (LC). Librarians must work together and with their ILS vendor in order for these two systems to exist in tandem. One solution, used by the Harrell Library at Penn State University, Hershey, was to configure dynamic links, which offered patrons the option to search the catalog using either MeSH or LC headings (Brennan, 2011).

In recent years, health sciences libraries have started moving toward open source ILS. A number of factors have played into this decision. In some cases, heightened network security measures have made it difficult for proprietary ILS vendors to access library servers in order to perform maintenance and upgrades. Libraries with sufficient IT staff of their own prefer the flexibility to manage and maintain their own system (Morton-Owens, Hanson, and Walls, 2011). Smaller libraries that do not have sufficient IT staff to run their own servers have taken advantage of the power of consortia to move toward **open source** systems (Genoese and Keith, 2011).

Web-Scale Discovery

Federated search engines were introduced and had a brief moment in the spotlight during the early 2000s. Their popularity soon faded as patrons and librarians became frustrated with their slow response times and unreliable search results and relevancy rankings. New discovery services featuring the added bonus of allowing libraries to add their own content from catalogs and institutional repositories are promising one-stop searching with greater speed and accuracy than ever before (Thompson, Obrig, and Abate, 2013; Hallyburton and Marcus, 2012).

Implementation of a new service such as a web-scale discovery service is a complex process that should be carefully planned. Librarians at the Himmelfarb Health Sciences Library of George Washington University set an implementation schedule allowing ample time for configuration, testing by staff, and usability testing with a small group of patrons before their new discovery system was made available to all patrons. A few issues were of particular concern to librarians: 1) the discovery service did not have a health sciences focus; 2) concerns about the accuracy of relevancy ranking; 3) the decision whether to limit to health sciences resources or to include peripheral databases as well (which could skew rankings) (Thompson, Obrig, and Abate, 2013).

Web-scale discovery services can be expensive additions to a library's technology toolkit. Librarians on a tight budget have to explore less costly options. When faced with financial constraints, librarians at Western Carolina University devised a search web page using resources at hand: a multidatabase search box using EBSCO's Search Box Builder to search health sciences databases, a link to USA.gov for government documents, and the library's catalog. Although not as seamless as a true web-based discovery service, it was a convenient workaround for students and faculty (Hallyburton and Marcus, 2012).

Link Resolvers

Up-to-date journal literature is vital for biomedical research, and patrons expect this access to be quick and seamless (Crum, 2011; Kosteniuk, Morgan, and D'Arcy, 2013; Connaway, Dickey, and Radford, 2011). Although bibliographic databases including MEDLINE/PubMed display links to publishers' websites, the path to full text is not always straightforward. Patrons trying to access full-text links from off-site may face roadblocks when following links to journals requiring IP authentication. Link resolvers simplify this process using the **OpenURL** standard to link a citation from an e-resource to the citation's full text (Price and Trainor, 2010). In essence, OpenURL is a set of parameters within a URL. These parameters can be configured to allow off-site access to authorized users (Cecchino, 2008). To provide links to local holdings from PubMed's Abstract display, libraries can register OpenURL-based link resolvers with the National Center for Biotechnology Information (NCBI). Two options exist for implementing this OpenURL service: Linkout and Outside Tool. The Linkout option allows users to limit search results based on library holdings. Outside Tool works with a library's link resolver to connect patrons to full text, appropriate holdings in the library's catalog, and to interlibrary loan forms with the citation information already entered (NCBI, 2012).

Websites

As collections continue to shift from print to online, the library's website is becoming the main access point for many patrons. In fact, many librarians view their website as a "virtual branch" whether the website is available to the outside world on the Internet or just within the institution's intranet. Faced with the loss of space, librarians at Michigan State University created a "Health Sciences Digital Library" website, pulling together relevant electronic resources, services, and contact information for the health sciences librarians. The website provided information for patrons to connect with librarians via instant messaging, Skype, e-mail, or telephone. It also included course-specific research guides and instructional videos (Kendall, 2012).

Usability is a key consideration when designing, or redesigning, a website. The first step in designing a usable website is to understand the site's users and their needs (what they currently use the site for, as well as what they would like the site to do) (Rosario, Ascher, and Cunningham, 2012; Graham et al., 2012). In designing their first mobile-friendly website, librarians at New York Medical College divided the process into three sections: 1) planning, which included a needs-assessment survey; 2) usability testing, which involved recruiting participants to test a prototype; and 3) site design, which involved designing, testing, and launching the site (Graham et al., 2012).

Web 2.0

Web 2.0 technologies, such as blogs, wikis, podcasts, RSS feeds, and social bookmarking, have brought new levels of interactivity between librarians and users. In a survey of medical libraries and other health care organizations, Chu et al. (2012)

found that most libraries were using Web 2.0 applications to foster information sharing, promote existing services, foster knowledge sharing, and to improve teaching
and learning. Being early adopters of new technologies has the potential to garner
good publicity for a library. For example, from their experience using wikis and other
Web 2.0 tools to create knowledge bases for clinicians and students, librarians at the
University of Texas MD Anderson Cancer Center are viewed as being on the cutting
edge of new technologies (Damani and Fulton, 2010). Encouraging patron feedback
and discussion is useful, guiding collection development and library services. Ranking and reviews for items in the library catalog can give a sense of how resources are
being used. Along with Web 2.0, social media have taken off in a big way. Many
libraries have cultivated a presence on Facebook and Twitter, using the platforms to
reach out to users. Although it is interesting and fun to explore these new platforms,
they might not be an option for hospital librarians due to network restrictions.

A part-time solo hospital librarian seized an opportunity when her institution
planned a new initiative to strengthen its nursing education program. In collaboration with a clinical nurse specialist and the education department, she developed an
interactive website for the initiative using a free online service. The success of this
website demonstrated the librarian's skills at gathering and organizing information
in an easy-to-use interface, solidifying her standing as an integral member of the
education department (Egan, 2012).

MOBILE TECHNOLOGIES

Use of mobile devices, particularly tablets, by the public has been increasing at
lightning speed. In a 2012 survey conducted by the Pew Internet & American Life
Project, 31 percent of cell phone owners used their phones to look for health or
medical information online (Fox and Duggan, 2012). A growing number of patrons
are accessing their libraries via mobile devices as well (Rainie, 2012). These trends
can be viewed as opportunities for consumer health libraries.

Mobile computing is making a huge impact on medical education and medical
practice. Students, researchers, and clinicians are using smartphones, tablets, and
e-readers to enhance their studies and research endeavors, and for use at the point
of care.

After having been banned from classrooms for many years, mobile devices are
now being welcomed—for educational purposes. They can be used as presentation
tools and can function as classroom response systems (Garner, 2011). The 2013 *Horizon Report* identified tablet computing as a key trend in higher education, because
they allow users to "seamlessly load sets of apps and content of their choosing,
making the tablet itself a portable personalized learning environment" (Johnson
et al., 2013).

Librarians are exploring ways to support these endeavors, including training,
licensing mobile content, creating mobile-friendly websites and apps, and lending
devices (Bushhousen et al., 2013). There are several ways to find out what types
of devices patrons are using when visiting a library's website (Le Ber et al., 2013).
A simple, web-based survey will give an idea if the response rate is reasonable;
another way to find out how users are accessing the library's website is to look

at web log analytic reports (Rosario, Ascher, and Cunningham, 2012). Most web analytics indicate which operating system and browser types are being used to access the website.

Mobile devices come in a variety of shapes and sizes. To accommodate the smaller screens, librarians are creating websites optimized for small screens (Grabowsky and Wright, 2013). In many cases, these websites were pared-down versions of the library's main website, containing only the features that would be easily used on a smaller screen (Graham et al., 2012). Some sites automatically redirect mobile users to the mobile-optimized site. Others give mobile users the option to link to the mobile site from the library's website (Bengtson, 2012). Responsive web design incorporates innovations in HTML5 and CSS3 to create scalable websites that are automatically optimized, no matter the size of the screen (Hoy, 2011; Prince, 2013a). Websites created using responsive design principles offer users all of the features of the main website, displayed in a way that is attractive and legible on any device, from a small phone screen to a large LCD screen.

Libraries with technical expertise have created their own apps, which are customized to include the features needed by the mobile users and can be downloaded from the various app stores. Advantages of a mobile app are that patrons do not necessarily have to be connected to the Internet in order to use it, and it is a visible reminder of the library right on their home screen. However, apps are not without their disadvantages. They have to be designed differently not only for each operating system, but also for different versions of an operating system. For example, when a new version of the iOS or Android system becomes available, the app will have to be tested and possibly updated as well. Mobile websites are "device agnostic," meaning that they will display on any device with a web browser and do not have to be updated every time an operating system changes (Schnell, 2012).

Mobile tools that are popular among patrons of health sciences libraries include drug references, evidence-based medicine tools, diagnostic tools, medical calculators, dictionaries of eponyms, and e-textbooks. The multimedia capabilities and high screen resolution for images have made mobile devices very attractive to users. Many e-resources licensed by libraries are offering mobile-optimized websites or apps. This has proven to be challenging on a number of fronts. For example, the variety in authentication models is wide; in many cases, users must create usernames and passwords to be able to use the mobile tools. Some vendors do not offer their mobile resources to institutional subscribers (Mihlrad and Glassman, 2012).

In order to introduce patrons to their collection of mobile resources, some libraries have implemented mobile device lending programs (Thompson, 2011; Capdarest-Arest, 2013). In order to do this, it is important to configure the devices with the appropriate security settings and to have a procedure to restore the devices to their original settings when they are returned. Staff needs to be trained to look for damaged or missing parts. Patrons must understand the loan and fine policies. Librarians at the University of Utah worked with faculty to design a course providing third-year medical students with hands-on experience using iPads in the practice of medicine. They further supported the course with an iPad-lending program (Lombardo and Honisett, 2014).

Librarians are using Wi-Fi-enabled tablets to help patrons on the go, around campus, at the point of care, on rounds, or at case conferences. The tablets are used to highlight new or existing apps and to find answers to questions as soon as they arise (Lee and Gleason, 2012). But using mobile devices at the point of care has drawbacks. Wi-Fi is not always available, and concern about microbial contamination is growing (Ustan and Cihangiroglu, 2012; Morris, Moore, and Shaunak, 2012).

Librarians also connect to mobile users through services such as chat reference and text messaging. This allows patrons to ask questions as they arise. Quick Response (QR) codes are square "bar codes." Using a reader app, patrons can scan the codes and be directed to a website, telephone number, or e-mail address. QR codes have been used in health sciences libraries for such things as room reservations, workshop signup, and linking to resources (Ohigashi Oasay, 2011).

The medical college gave iPads to all incoming first-year students in fall 2013. Thankfully, they included the library staff in the planning. This also means we have to be on our game. We have to be able to demonstrate how to access and use library resources via mobile devices. It has been an exciting journey of discovery for all involved.

Max Anderson, MLIS, assistant library director for educational technology, Rush University/McCormick Educational Technology Center, Chicago, IL

EMERGING TECHNOLOGIES

New technologies emerge from unexpected places; implications for libraries are not always apparent at first glance. What seems promising at first might end up as a flash in the pan. (On the other hand, it could be a technology that is ahead of its time—who remembers the Apple Newton?) Here are three technologies that health sciences librarians have already begun exploring.

The era of ubiquitous computing is here. Technology users are no longer bound to their desktop or laptop computers for accessing information. Tablets and smartphones are already commonplace. Will wearable technologies, such as Google Glass and smart watches, be adopted by health professionals for clinical and research purposes? Websites must seamlessly scale to fit any size display. Innovations such as HTML5 and responsive web design enable librarians to provide resources for patrons, no matter how they access it (Bengtson, 2012; Prince, 2013a).

Although cloud computing is not exactly a brand-new technology, some aspects of it could affect health sciences librarians. Libraries that had previously maintained their own servers in-house might explore migrating to a hosted platform, having implications for staffing and space allocation. On the other hand, libraries lacking staff to maintain their own servers might be able to provide services that would have been impossible before. HIPAA concerns will have a large impact on the way this plays out in health sciences libraries (Hoy, 2012).

Three-dimensional printers build three-dimensional objects based on digital designs. Although they have been used in industry for many years, easy-to-use and reasonably priced 3-D printers are now on the market (Hoy, 2013). Could a health sciences library use a 3-D printer as a marketing tool? Would researchers and clinicians come to the library to create models of bones or molecules?

KEEPING CURRENT

Change is the only constant in the world of technology. Keeping up with trends and innovations is a daunting but essential task. Librarians should be aware of technology innovations that could affect them or their patrons (Prince, 2012; Prince, 2013b). No single, go-to source contains all the technology news. In addition to the many resources by and for librarians, a great deal can be learned by exploring technology trends from other perspectives.

Resources for Librarians

Browsing library journals is a good place to start (see Table 6.1). Most general interest library journals include technology-related articles. Most journals offer some form of alerting service, usually via RSS feed or e-mail. Database automatic alerts can also be set up based on search strategies using technology terms of interest.

Keeping abreast of new and emerging technologies that might be helpful in libraries is vital. This was demonstrated to us when a student "complained" that, unfortunately, our laptop loan service was not available after the circulation desk closed, but the twenty-four-hour space remained open. His comment spurred us to look for a solution, which resulted in our acquiring a laptop kiosk to dispense laptops in the twenty-four-hour room via insertion of a university identification card. The borrower returns the laptop to the machine, which then resets the laptop. There is no charge for this service.

Linda M. G. Katz, MS, AHIP,
former associate director (retired),
Health Sciences Partnerships, Drexel
University Libraries, Philadelphia, PA

Local and national meetings and special-interest groups provide a treasure trove of information. New ideas are often introduced during poster sessions. The informal nature of poster sessions allows participants to share ideas and learn from each other's experiences.

Some library organizations have sections or special-interest groups (SIGs) that focus on technology. The Library Information Technology Association (LITA), a division of the American Library Association (ALA), www.ala.org/lita/, is very active. LITA offers many ways to learn about technology, including publications, meetings, workshops, and discussion groups. The Medical Informatics Section (MIS) of the Medical Library Association (MLA), www.medinfo.mlanet.org/, focuses on technologies involved with health care. MIS presents a session on technology trends each

Table 6.1. Selected Library Technology Journals

Journal	URL
Computers in Libraries	www.infotoday.com/cilmag/default.shtml
Information Technology and Libraries	http://ejournals.bc.edu/ojs/index.php/ital/index
Journal of Electronic Resources in Medical Libraries	www.tandfonline.com/toc/werm20/current#.Un6mwRAlhi8
Library Hi Tech	www.emeraldinsight.com/journals.htm?issn=0737-8831
Library Technology Reports	www.alatechsource.org/ltr/index

year at MLA's annual meeting. Many groups communicate through e-mail discussion lists, or Listservs. Although active participation is encouraged, a great deal can be learned from just "lurking" (i.e., following the discussions without contributing).

A number of tech-savvy librarians write their own blogs. Although blogs tend to reflect an author's personal opinions, they are very useful for gaining insight into the implications of technology trends. The Krafty Librarian blog, http://kraftylibrarian.com, by Michelle Kraft focuses on topics of interest to health sciences librarians, many of which are technology related.

Social Media

In addition to following and connecting with friends, social media (e.g., Twitter, LinkedIn, Facebook, Google+, etc.) are an easy—and sometimes fun—tool for learning about technology news. Many technology-oriented individuals, organizations, and publications share and discuss trends and innovations. Topic-specific searches using keywords or hashtags make it easy to follow trends. The social media world is very interactive. Participants are usually quick to answer questions and share their own experiences. One example of social media in action is the weekly #medlibs Twitter chat. In 2012, a group of medical librarians began holding weekly Twitter chats, http://medlibschat.blogspot.com/, to discuss a wide variety of topics of interest. Participants take turns moderating the conversation. A different topic is discussed each week; the chat is open to everyone. Transcripts of previous chats are archived.

Education and Nonprofit Organizations

EDUCAUSE, www.educause.edu/, is a nonprofit organization that focuses on the use of technology to improve higher education. EDUCAUSE hosts in-person and online conferences and events, produces a variety of publications, and has a strong social media presence. In addition to covering a wide range of higher education topics, EDUCAUSE also has a section that focuses on topics of interest to librarians. In collaboration with the New Media Consortium, EDUCAUSE publishes *The Horizon Report*, an annual report that describes how educators are adapting emerging technologies (Johnson et al., 2013).

The technology interests of educational and nonprofit organizations are very similar to those of libraries. TechSoup, www.techsoup.org, is a nonprofit organization that helps other nonprofits with technology issues. Its resources include newsletters, webinars, how-to guides, and forums. TechSoup also helps qualifying organizations acquire discounted and donated software and hardware.

Technology Websites and Publications

It is exciting to discover applications for new technologies before they have found their way into mainstream library use. Following general-interest technology news offers the potential for getting one step closer to the cutting edge. Many technology industry publication subscriptions are free. Magazines such as *Wired* and websites such as ReadWriteWeb, http://readwrite.com/, highlight emerging technology trends in popular culture.

Newspapers and News Websites

The business sections of many newspapers view technology trends from a very different perspective—the investor. This can provide useful insights into new technologies on the horizon, even before the implications for health care or librarianship are obvious.

Many newspapers, news broadcasts, or news websites have columns or section devoted specifically to technology. In addition, it is worthwhile to keep an eye out for technology innovations in unexpected areas. Creative uses of new technologies in the areas of art, design, travel, sports, and so forth can spark innovative ideas for libraries.

Diversification is the key to keeping up with technology trends. As with technology in general, it is not necessary to be an expert on every new trend. A general awareness enables librarians to identify new technologies that could be beneficial to them and their patrons.

SUMMARY

The rate at which technology evolves is overwhelming. Keeping up with developments seems all but impossible. But that is what makes it such an exciting time to be a librarian. More opportunities are available to explore than ever before.

Technology is the means to an end, and not the end itself. When exploring the implementation of new technologies in a health sciences library, it is vital to ask these questions:

- Who will benefit?
- What is the desired outcome?
- Where will users access it?
- When will it be tested, launched, evaluated?
- Why is this project being undertaken?
- How will it be supported? (Also, how will it be paid for?)

Careful planning and ongoing training are required, not only to keep services running smoothly, but also to stay on par with patrons' needs and expectations. Technology-savvy librarians have a lot to offer their parent organizations, and can use their skills and expertise to forge new collaborations with stakeholders—increasing the value and visibility of the library.

STUDY QUESTIONS

1. In what ways might a hospital library's technology plan differ from an academic library's plan?
2. How does HIPAA compliance affect health sciences librarians?
3. Why is it important to be knowledgeable about technology? What resources would you use to keep up to date with technology trends?

4. What are some ways to train and engage staff in the use of new hardware or software tools?
5. If you were to implement a mobile device lending program, what types of apps and resources would you include? What procedures would you use for checkin and checkout?
6. Can technology be used as a tool to connect with other departments or divisions in an organization? Give some examples.

REFERENCES

Bandyopadhyay, Aditi. 2013. "Measuring the Disparities between Biology Undergraduates' Perceptions and Their Actual Knowledge of Scientific Literature with Clickers." *Journal of Academic Librarianship* 39, no. 2: 194–201. doi:10.1016/j.acalib.2012.10.006.

Barton, Joshua, and Lucas Mak. 2012. "Old Hopes, New Possibilities: Next-Generation Catalogues and the Centralization of Access." *Library Trends* 61, no. 1: 83–106.

Bengtson, Jason. 2012. "The Art of Redirection: One Library's Experiences and Statistical Results From the Deployment of Mobile Redirect Script." *Journal of Hospital Librarianship* 12, no. 3: 191–98. doi:10.1080/15323269.2012.692228.

Blansit, B. Douglas. 2007. "Beyond Password Protection." *Journal of Electronic Resources in Medical Libraries* 4, no. 1–2: 185–94. doi:10.1300/J383v04n01_17.

———. 2009. "Firewalls: Basic Principles and Some Implications." *Journal of Electronic Resources in Medical Libraries* 6, no. 3: 260–69. doi:10.1080/15424060903167377.

Boden, Catherine, Christine J. Neilson, and J. X. Seaton. 2013. "Efficacy of Screen-Capture Tutorials in Literature Search Training: A Pilot Study of a Research Method." *Medical Reference Services Quarterly* 32, no. 3 (July–September): 314–27. doi:10.1080/02763869.2013.806863.

Breeding, Marshall. 2012. "Managing Mission-Critical Infrastructure: Libraries Tend Toward a State of Inertia in Respect to Their Automation Systems, Even in the Face of Increasing Frustration with Its Capabilities Relative to Their Current Requirements." *Computers in Libraries* 32, no. 8 (October): 30–33.

Brennan, David P. 2011. "Accessing Medical Subject Content Using Dynamic Links in the ILS." *Journal of Electronic Resources in Medical Libraries* 8, no. 4: 339–47. doi:10.1080/1542 4065.2011.626344.

Brigham, Tara J. 2013. "Smart Boards: A Reemerging Technology." *Medical Reference Services Quarterly* 32, no. 2 (April–June): 194–202. doi:10.1080/02763869.2013.776903.

Bushhousen, Ellie. 2013. "Electronic Health Records and Hospital Librarians." *Journal of Hospital Librarianship* 13, no. 1: 66–70. doi:10.1080/15323269.2013.745368.

Bushhousen, Ellie, Hannah F. Norton, Linda C. Butson et al. 2013. "Smartphone Use at a University Health Science Center." *Medical Reference Services Quarterly* 32, no. 1 (January–March): 52–72. doi:10.1080/02763869.2013.749134.

Capdarest-Arest, Nicole. A. 2013. "Implementing a Tablet Circulation Program on a Shoestring." *Journal of the Medical Library Association* 101, no. 3 (July): 220–24. doi:10.3163/1536-5050.101.3.013.

Cecchino, Nicola J. 2008. "Full-Text Linking Demystified." *Journal of Electronic Resources in Medical Libraries* 5, no. 1: 33–42. doi:10.1080/15424060802093377.

Chen, Kuan-nien, Hao-chang Sun, Wen-chuan Lin, and Pei-chun Lin. 2011. "Into the Future: Three Keys to Success for Medical Libraries." *Journal of Hospital Librarianship* 11, no. 4: 348–57. doi:10.1080/15323269.2011.611105.

Chu, Samuel K. W., Matsuko Woo, Ronnel B. King, Stephen Choi, Miffy Cheng, and Peggy Koo. 2012. "Examining the Application of Web 2.0 in Medical-Related Organisations." *Health Information and Libraries Journal* 29, no. 1: 47–60. doi:10.1111/j.1471-1842.2011.00970.x.

Cohn, John M., and Ann L. Kelsey. 2010. *The Complete Library Technology Planner: A Guidebook with Sample Technology Plans and RFPs on CD-ROM*. New York: Neal-Schuman Publishers.

Connaway, Lynn Sillipigni, Timothy J. Dickey, and Marie L. Radford. 2011. "'If It is Too Inconvenient I'm Not Going after It': Convenience as a Critical Factor in Information-Seeking Behaviors." *Library & Information Science Research* 33, no. 3: 179–90. doi:http://dx.doi.org/10.1016/j.lisr.2010.12.002.

Connor, Elizabeth. 2011. "Using Cases and Clickers in Library Instruction: Designed for Science Undergraduates." *Science & Technology Libraries* 30, no. 3: 244–53. doi:10.1080/0194262X.2011.592787.

Crum, Janet A. 2011. "An Availability Study of Electronic Articles in an Academic Health Sciences Library." *Journal of the Medical Library Association* 99, no. 4: 290–6. doi:10.3163/1536-5050.99.4.006.

Cunningham, Kay. 2010. "The Hidden Costs of Keeping Current: Technology and Libraries." *Journal of Library Administration* 50, no. 3: 217–35. doi:10.1080/01930821003634955.

Damani, Shamsha, and Stephanie Fulton. 2010. "Collaborating and Delivering Literature Search Results to Clinical Teams Using Web 2.0 Tools." *Medical Reference Services Quarterly* 29, no. 3 (July–September): 207–17. doi:10.1080/02763869.2010.494476.

Egan, Laurel. 2012. "The Librarian as a Member of the Education Department Team: Using Web 2.0 Technologies to Improve Access to Education Materials and Information." *Medical Reference Services Quarterly* 31, no. 3 (July–September): 330–35. doi:10.1080/02763869.2012.698192.

Ennis, Lisa A. 2009. "The Art of Talking Tech: Strategies for Effective Communication with Information Technology Departments." *Journal of Hospital Librarianship* 9, no. 2: 210–17. doi:10.1080/15323260902820628.

Flake, Donna. 2010. "No Password Required—A Case Study of Integrating the Library's Electronic Resources Into the Hospital's Electronic Medical Record." *Journal of Hospital Librarianship* 10, no. 4: 402–9. doi:10.1080/15323269.2010.514670.

Fontelo, Paul, Michael Ackerman, George Kim, and Craig Locatis. 2003. "The PDA as a Portal to Knowledge Sources in a Wireless Setting." *Telemedicine Journal and e-Health* 9, no. 2: 141–47. doi:10.1089/153056203766437480.

Fox, Susannah, and Maeve Duggan. 2012. *Mobile Health 2012*. Pew Research Center, November 8. http://pewinternet.org/Reports/2012/Mobile-Health.aspx.

Funk, Mark E. 2013. "Our Words, Our Story: A Textual Analysis of Articles Published in the *Bulletin of the Medical Library Association/Journal of the Medical Library Association* from 1961 to 2010." *Journal of the Medical Library Association* 101, no. 1 (January): 12–20. doi:10.3163/1536-5050.101.1.003.

Garner, Michael. 2011. "Presenting with an iPad." *Journal of Electronic Resources in Medical Libraries* 8, no. 4: 441–48. doi:10.1080/15424065.2011.626359.

Genoese, Lisa, and Latrina Keith. 2011. "Jumping Ship: One Health Science Library's Voyage from a Proprietary ILS to Open Source." *Journal of Electronic Resources in Medical Libraries* 8, no. 2: 126–33. doi:10.1080/15424065.2011.576605.

Gomes, Alexandra W., Anne Linton, and Laura Abate. 2013. "Strengthening Our Collaborations: Building an Electronic Health Record Educational Module." *Journal of Electronic Resources in Medical Libraries* 10, no. 1: 1–10. doi:10.1080/15424065.2012.762202.

Goodell, Jon. 2013. "Massive Open Online Courses." *MLA News* 53, no. 9 (October): 19.

Grabowsky, Adelia, and Melissa Wright. 2013. "Connecting with Health Science Students and Faculty to Facilitate the Design of a Mobile Library Website." *Medical Reference Services Quarterly* 32, no. 2 (April–June): 151–62. doi:10.1080/02763869.2013.776882.

Graham, Jamie, Stephen Maher, Dorothy Moore, and Emily Morton-Owens. 2012. "Taking the Library to the Clinic: Building Mobile Services for a Medical Library." *Reference Librarian* 53, no. 3: 326–45. doi:10.1080/02763877.2012.679856.

Hallyburton, Ann, and Elizabeth Marcus. 2012. "Maximize Discovery and Minimize Cost." *Journal of Electronic Resources in Medical Libraries* 9, no. 1: 1–12. doi:10.1080/15424065.2 012.651574.

Healthcare Information and Management Systems Society. 2013. *Electronic Health Records 2012–2013*. Accessed September 28. www.himss.org/library/ehr/?navItemNumber=13261.

Herbert, Paul. 2013. "The NHS Lanarkshire Intranet site (FirstPort) and Its Effectiveness as a Knowledge Management Tool." *Health Information and Libraries Journal* 30, no. 1: 72–75. doi:10.1111/hir.12014.

Horne, Andrea S., Bart Ragon, and Daniel T. Wilson. 2012. "An Innovative Use of Instant Messaging Technology to Support a Library's Single-Service Point." *Medical Reference Services Quarterly* 31, no. 2 (April–June): 127–39. doi:10.1080/02763869.2012.670557.

Hoy, Matthew B. 2011. "HTML5: A New Standard for the Web." *Medical Reference Services Quarterly* 30, no. 1 (January–March): 50–55. doi:10.1080/02763869.2011.540212.

———. 2012. "Cloud Computing Basics for Librarians." *Medical Reference Services Quarterly* 31, no. 1 (January–March): 84–91. doi:10.1080/02763869.2012.641853.

———. 2013. "3D Printing: Making Things at the Library." *Medical Reference Services Quarterly* 32, no. 1 (January–March): 93–99. doi:10.1080/02763869.2013.749139.

Johnson, Larry, Samantha Adams Becker, Michelle Cummins, Victoria Estrada, Alex Freeman, and Holly Ludgate. 2013. *NMC Horizon Report: 2013 Higher Education Edition*. Austin, TX: New Media Consortium.

Johnson, Layne M., John T. Butler, and Lisa R. Johnston. 2012. "Developing E-Science and Research Services and Support at the University of Minnesota Health Sciences Libraries." *Journal of Library Administration* 52, no. 8: 754–69. doi:10.1080/01930826.2012.751291.

Kendall, Susan K. 2012. "Strategies of Health Sciences Librarians Working Without a Traditional Health Sciences Library." *Journal of Hospital Librarianship* 12, no. 4: 363–71. doi:10.1080/15323269.2012.719192.

Kenefick, Colleen, and Susan E. Werner. 2012. "Lessons From the National Education Technology Plan." *Journal of Hospital Librarianship* 12, no. 4: 384–90. doi:10.1080/15323269.2012.719195.

Kosteniuk, Julie G., Debra G. Morgan, and Carl K. D'Arcy. 2013. "Use and Perceptions of Information Among Family Physicians: Sources Considered Accessible, Relevant, and Reliable." *Journal of the Medical Library Association* 101, no. 1 (January): 32–37. doi:10.3163/1536-5050.101.1.006.

Le Ber, Jeanne M., Nancy T. Lombardo, Amy Honisett, Peter Stevens Jones, and Alice Weber. 2013. "Assessing User Preferences for E-Readers and Tablets." *Medical Reference Services Quarterly* 32, no. 1 (January–March): 1–11. doi:10.1080/02763869.2013.749101.

Lee, Angela, and Ann Whitney Gleason. 2012. "Tablet Mania: Exploring the Use of Tablet Computers in an Academic Health Sciences Library." *Journal of Hospital Librarianship* 12, no. 3: 281–87. doi:10.1080/15323269.2012.692226.

Lindberg, Donald A., and Betsy L. Humphreys. 2005. "2015—the Future of Medical Libraries." *New England Journal of Medicine* 352, no. 11: 1067–70. doi:10.1056/NEJMp048190.

Lombardo, Nancy T., and Amy Honisett. 2014. "One Tool for Many Tasks: Integrating iPads into the Third-Year Learning Experience." *Medical Reference Services Quarterly* 33, no. 1 (January–March): 17–28.

Lynn, Valerie A., Marie FitzSimmons, and Cynthia K. Robinson. 2011. "Special Report: Symposium on Transformational Change in Health Sciences Libraries: Space, Collections, and Roles." *Journal of the Medical Library Association* 99, no. 1 (January): 82–87. doi:10.3163/1536-5050.99.1.014.

Mihlrad, Leigh, and Nancy R. Glassman. 2012. "Institutional Access to Mobile Resources." *Journal of Electronic Resources in Medical Libraries* 9, no. 1: 77–86. doi:10.1080/15424065.2011.651383.

Mitchell, Nicole, and Lisa A. Ennis. 2010. "Scaling the (Fire)Wall." *Journal of Hospital Librarianship* 10, no. 2: 190–96. doi:10.1080/15323261003681588.

Moore, Mary, and Kimberly A. Loper. 2011. "An Introduction to Clinical Decision Support Systems." *Journal of Electronic Resources in Medical Libraries* 8, no. 4: 348–66. doi:10.1080/15424065.2011.626345.

Morris, Thomas C., Luke S. Moore, and Sunil Shaunak. 2012. "Doctors Taking a Pulse Using Their Mobile Phone can Spread MRSA." *BMJ* 344: e412. doi:10.1136/bmj.e412.

Morton-Owens, Emily G., Karen L. Hanson, and Ian Walls. 2011. "Implementing Open-Source Software for Three Core Library Functions: A Stage-by-Stage Comparison." *Journal of Electronic Resources in Medical Libraries* 8, no. 1: 1–14. doi:10.1080/15424065.2011.551486.

NCBI (National Center for Biotechnology Information). 2012. "LinkOut Help: Implementing OpenURL-based Services in PubMed." Last updated September 17. www.ncbi.nlm.nih.gov/books/NBK3808/#lib.Implementing_OpenURLbased_Services_i.

NN/LM (National Network of Libraries of Medicine). 2013. "NN/LM Emergency Preparedness & Response Toolkit." Last updated August 8. http://nnlm.gov/ep/.

Neilson, Christine J. 2010. "Have Computers, Will Travel: Providing On-site Library Instruction in Rural Health Facilities Using a Portable Computer Lab." *Medical Reference Services Quarterly* 29, no. 1 (January–March): 1–9. doi:10.1080/02763860903484897.

Ohigashi Oasay, Luree H. 2011. "QR Codes in the Library." *Journal of Electronic Resources in Medical Libraries* 8, no. 3: 294–301.

Price, Jason S., and Cindi Trainor. 2010. "Chapter 4: The Future of OpenURL Linking." *Library Technology Reports* 46, no. 7: 27–33.

Prince, J. Dale. 2012. "Keeping Up with Technology: Sources for Mid- to Long-Term Planning." *Journal of Electronic Resources in Medical Libraries* 9, no. 4: 300–307. doi:10.1080/15424065.2013.735129.

———. 2013a. "HTML5: Not Just a Substitute for Flash." *Journal of Electronic Resources in Medical Libraries* 10, no. 2: 108–12. doi:10.1080/15424065.2013.792561.

———. 2013b. "Keeping Up with Technology: Some Resources." *Journal of Electronic Resources in Medical Libraries* 10, no. 1: 52–64. doi:10.1080/15424065.2012.762222.

Rainie, Lee. 2012. "Smartphone Ownership Update: September 2012." Pew Research Center, September 11. www.pewinternet.org/Reports/2012/Smartphone-Update-Sept-2012.aspx.

Rosario, Jovy-Anne, Marie T. Ascher, and Diana J. Cunningham. 2012. "A Study in Usability: Redesigning a Health Sciences Library's Mobile Site." *Medical Reference Services Quarterly* 31, no. 1: 1–13. doi:10.1080/02763869.2012.641481.

Schnell, Eric. 2012. "The Mobile Medical Library—Is There an App for That?" *Journal of Electronic Resources in Medical Libraries* 9, no. 2: 147–54. doi:10.1080/15424065.2012.680318.

Schroeder, Heidi. 2010. "Creating Library Tutorials for Nursing Students." *Medical Reference Services Quarterly* 29, no. 2 (April–June): 109–20. doi:10.1080/02763861003723135.

Sostack, Maura. 2012. "Virtual Hospital Libraries." *MLA News* 52, no. 1 (January): 15.

Stephenson, Priscilla L., Teresa R. Coady, Janet M. Schneider, and Dorothy P. Sinha. 2012. "E-Readers: New Opportunities for Hospital Patients and Staff." *Medical Reference Services Quarterly* 31, no. 2 (April–June): 219–24. doi:10.1080/02763869.2012.671662.

Thompson, JoLinda L., Kathe S. Obrig, and Laura E. Abate. 2013. "Web-Scale Discovery in an Academic Health Sciences Library: Development and Implementation of the EBSCO Discovery Service." *Medical Reference Services Quarterly* 32, no. 1: 26–41. doi:10.1080/02763869.2013.749111.

Thompson, Sara Q. 2011. "Setting Up a Library iPad Program: Guidelines for Success." *College & Research Libraries News* 72, no. 4: 212–36.

U.S. Department of Health and Human Services. 2013. "Health Information Privacy." Accessed September 29. www.hhs.gov/ocr/privacy/.

U.S. National Institutes of Health. 2005. "The NIH Almanac—Organization: National Library of Medicine." Last reviewed June 21. www.nih.gov/about/almanac/archive/2003/organization/NLM.htm.

U.S. National Library of Medicine. 2012. "DOCLINE—Connecting to DOCLINE from Behind a Firewall or Proxy Server." Last reviewed January 27. www.nlm.nih.gov/services/doc_firewall.html.

Ustun, Cemal, and Mustafa Cihangiroglu. 2012. "Health Care Workers' Mobile Phones: A Potential Cause of Microbial Cross-Contamination between Hospitals and Community." *Journal of Occupational and Environmental Hygiene* 9, no. 9: 538–42. doi:10.1080/15459624.2012.697419.

Vaughan, K. T. L., Barrie E. Hayes, Rachel C. Lerner et al. 2013. "Development of the Research Lifecycle Model for Library Services." *Journal of the Medical Library Association* 101, no. 4 (October): 310–14. doi:10.3163/1536-5050.101.4.013.

Wink, Diane M., and Elizabeth K. Killingsworth. 2011. "Optimizing Use of Library Technology." *Nurse Educator* 36, no. 2: 48–51. doi:10.1097/NNE.0b013e31820b4e01.

Yeh, Felicia, Karen D. McMullen, and Laura T. Kane. 2010. "Disaster Planning in a Health Sciences Library: A Grant-Funded Approach." *Journal of the Medical Library Association* 98, no. 3 (July): 259–61. doi:10.3163/1536-5050.98.3.016.

PART III

User Services

CHAPTER 7

Reference and Information Services in Health Sciences Libraries

Marie T. Ascher

INTRODUCTION

The success and quality of a library are dependent not only on its collections and information resources provided, but also on the quality of its services. Central to the practice of reference service is a strong service ethic that connects library users with the information they need. Reference service or "information services" primarily refers to the professional public services activities librarians carry out in order to unite the user with the right information. Reference service is a core professional service of any staffed library, traditionally emanating from the library's reference desk where users would visit or call to ask their questions, or maybe even write letters. Today, these traditional modes of contacting the reference librarian are being supplemented with or replaced by newer technologies such as e-mail, chat (IM) reference, and text (SMS) reference. And more frequently, librarians are employing new models of offering reference services—"embedding," "roving," "rounding," "triaging," and making house calls—while using new technologies to offer information services well beyond the walls of the library. Essentially reference service is provided every time a librarian answers a question, sends a document, or helps a library user at the point of need—whether that occurs in the library or outside, at the reference desk or in the halls of the hospital. This chapter will discuss all of these methods of connecting users with the information they need via what is still referred to as reference services, or more currently information services.

WHAT IS REFERENCE?

Reference service can best be understood in terms of the base unit of service, the "reference transaction." Several definitions of reference transaction have been set forth. The Reference and User Services Association (RUSA) of the American Library Association defines reference transactions as:

information consultations in which library staff recommend, interpret, evaluate, and/ or use information resources to help others to meet particular information needs. Reference transactions do not include formal instruction . . . (RUSA, 2008)

The Association of Research Libraries (ARL) definition is similar:

an information contact that involves the knowledge, use, recommendations, interpretation, or instruction in the use of one or more information sources by a member of the library staff. (Kyrillidou, Morris, and Roebuck, 2013)

Implicit in both of these definitions is a librarian possessing the skills necessary to recommend and interpret information sources and provide some consultation and informal instructional guidance on their use. Reference librarians are often directly involved in a library's instructional and outreach programs and are almost always responsible for database/literature searching as well, functions that are covered in other chapters of this book.

REFERENCE FUNCTIONS

In his seminal article on reference, Green (1876) introduced the four primary functions of the reference librarian:

1. Instructing on the use of the library.
2. Answering patron queries.
3. Aiding in the selection of resources.
4. Promoting the library in the community.

The reference librarian as question-answerer is what most people think of when they think of the professional librarian, and reference librarian positions are what most library school graduates still aspire to upon graduation (Ard et al., 2006). The image of the librarian at the reference desk is an enduring one. The values of librarians are also enduring, and like stewardship of collections and resources, a commitment to service is of primary importance. It is through reference service that the librarian delivers information to the user and adds value to the library's collection of resources. Michael Gorman (2000) names several characteristics of importance to the provision of public service: Librarians should be approachable, knowledgeable, and comprehensible. Not only should the librarian be pleasantly approachable, but the space in which the librarian works should be approachable. The librarian should be knowledgeable about the collections of his or her library, and also other libraries, and importantly, how to conduct a **reference interview** to understand the true needs of the user. Comprehensibility refers to the ability of a librarian to speak in clear and direct, easy-to-understand language.

The American Library Association (ALA) Reference and User Services Association (RUSA) has gone so far as to codify behavioral guidelines for the provision of reference service broken into these broad categories (2013): 1. Visibility/Approachability; 2. Interest; 3. Listening/Inquiring; 4. Searching; and 5. Follow up. RUSA provides a lot of detail for each of these categories. In a nutshell, the provision of the highest level reference service in a health sciences library requires:

- Question negotiation skills: the ability to conduct a successful reference interview.
- Interpersonal skills: approachable, communicative, pleasant, engendering trust, ability to explain and instruct.
- Knowledge of library collections: major journals in a field; bibliographic databases such as PubMed, Embase, Scopus, CINAHL, Dynamed, UpToDate, and so forth, and how to use them expertly; major reference works, particularly drug references and major textbooks, in all available formats.
- Familiarity with the subject discipline: be able to speak the language, pronounce the words, understand the concepts, know about current advances in medicine and public health. Procure a second master's degree or certification if possible. Some health sciences librarians have backgrounds in related fields, and some procure a degree in a field such as public health or health administration after beginning work as a professional health sciences librarian. This knowledge becomes invaluable in speaking the language with users.
- Accuracy and timeliness.
- Dexterity and technical savviness.

THE REFERENCE INTERVIEW AND ENCOUNTER

Core to the skill sets necessary to providing reference service is the ability to conduct a reference interview. Every library science student learns this, but research has shown that a reference interview actually occurs in only about half of all reference encounters (Ross, Nilsen, and Radford, 2009), so it is reiterated here. The reference interview is the conversation that occurs between the librarian and user, in which the librarian asks questions aimed at determining the type and amount of information needed and how it is to be used. This information negotiation is necessary because it helps the user to articulate the question, to define his or her need, and to convey it to the librarian. The reference interview also adds value to the reference transaction because the user's original question cannot always be taken at face value as the true question and information need. By using probing techniques aimed at garnering trust, the librarian will understand what the user really needs and how he or she can be assisted. To conduct a successful reference interview, the librarian must be patient and adept at asking the right questions that get to the essence of the information need. In the health care setting, understanding the user's information need is especially important because of implications for patient care, translational science, and research studies (i.e., obtaining grant funding). An understanding of medical terminology and concepts, and even correct pronunciations, can be very important. The librarian needs to be able to ask the right questions and demonstrate intelligence about the subject in order for the user to seek assistance.

A service-oriented reference librarian is focused on one goal: getting the user the information he or she needs. Without a reference interview, it is difficult to fully understand what that is. The interview needn't be extensive and may only take the form of a few questions and validation. Other times, a more elaborate conversation is required, along with thorough information gathering in order to understand the subject, the context, the way in which the information will be used, and how much information is desired. Does the user want comprehensive information or just a few pieces of good-quality information or "best evidence?" All librarians, new and veteran, should read *Conducting the Reference Interview* (Ross, Nilsen, and Radford, 2009) to appreciate the value and understand the techniques involved in the reference interview.

The reference interview should occur regardless of the mode of communication, whether it is face-to-face, via telephone, or via other digital means (Straw, 2000). A user may send a list of keywords for a librarian to search instead of sending the search request as an articulated topic or searchable question. This can lead to the librarian searching too broadly, not broadly enough, or for the wrong thing entirely. In medicine, it can sometimes be useful during the reference interview to use the components of the PICO (Patient, Intervention, Comparison, Outcome) format to facilitate the structuring of a request into a fully articulated question—rather than that list of keywords. Another method of getting the requester to articulate the question better is to say, "If I could get you the perfect article to answer this question, what do you think it would look like?" This technique might elicit some articulation of study design and hypothesis.

It can be difficult to provide a reference interview using e-mail where the communication is **asynchronous** and delayed and without interpersonal physical cues. However, the disadvantages related to asynchronous reference interviewing may be offset by the luxury of time to give thoughtful response and to perform some preliminary research before responding, which would likely not occur when a waiting library user is standing at the reference desk or otherwise present (Tibbo, 1995). Well-designed web forms (and paper forms for in-person requests) should try to collect the information gained during a reference interview, but a conversation is always going to be preferable if possible. The RUSA Behavioral Guidelines (2013) do take remote technologies for reference into consideration and should be reviewed. The behaviors mention reinforced interpersonal behaviors, such as maintaining "word contact" with users on the other end of a chat reference session so they know you are still there—even while you are looking up something for them.

TYPES OF USERS IN HEALTH SCIENCES LIBRARIES

Every library will have a different mix of users, depending on the type of health sciences library: a community hospital library; a hospital with university ties, which means residents on staff (commonly referred to as "house staff") and medical students rotating through their clerkships; an academic health sciences library, which includes students from various programs, medical students, clinical and nonclinical medical faculty, basic sciences research faculty, residents, fellows, and postdocs. Hospital libraries may have all of the above, depending on their university affiliation(s), plus a full array of clinical staff including attending physicians, nurses, physical therapists, nutritionists, social workers, and others. All of these users approach the reference desk with different information needs. The following broad examples demonstrate the types of information needs these populations may present.

Students

Students (medical students, nursing students, graduate students, undergraduate students, etc.) are a diverse group. They usually are completing assignments based upon a curriculum and may need assistance with a search strategy, sometimes presenting with the classic "I need about ten articles on a subject" type of transaction. In response to this type of request, the librarian should work with the student to articulate the topic and any subtopics and how the information will be used, recommending a few databases to search and assisting in the development of a logical search strategy. As part of the reference interview, the librarian should ascertain what background information and other data will be useful to include in a final project. For instance, statistical information related to disease incidence and prevalence is valuable for developing rationale in a paper. Students often tend to view their information requests very narrowly. Librarians can work with them to more fully develop their topic. This is an opportunity for a "teachable moment." Be aware that most current students are not likely to come to the library for assistance and will search Google and *Wikipedia* for references instead (Judd and Kennedy, 2011). However, these encounters do still occur at the desk with some frequency. And when they do, it is the responsibility of the librarian to out-Google Google.

Upper level students, such as PhD students, will likely have a higher level of information literacy and ability to use various interfaces, but it is the duty of the librarian to ascertain their skill level and work with these students accordingly. These students may have more intense research needs and require greater assistance; however, their library use is often modeled after that of their faculty adviser.

Faculty members have a tendency to overestimate their students' information literacy (Lampert, 2005), a misconception that computer literacy translates to information literacy. As a result, students aren't regularly referred to the library to seek information, nor are the librarians regularly involved in the development of research assignments. The students who come to the library for reference assistance tend to be two types: the student who needs the highest amount of feedback and assurance; and the student who really does not know where to begin his or her project. In all cases, interactions with students should be as instructional as possible. The librarian should not just hand a student those ten desired articles. The student and the librarian should work in collaboration to define and articulate the topic, to identify the types of information needed, to select databases, devise search strategies, and select and assess articles retrieved—in an effort to reinforce **information management competencies**. Graduate students in a research methods class at New York Medical College School of Health Sciences and Practice are required to schedule and attend consultations (in person or other) with a reference librarian, a project that has been well-received by the students and has improved their information management competencies. The project is seen as valuable and sustainable by the librarian and faculty member involved (Ascher and Liberatos, 2013).

Examples of the types of actual reference/research questions that a reference librarian might get from a health sciences student:

- "I'm doing a paper on X. My instructor says I need five to seven articles."
- "I've been asked to find one good article like this one."
- "I need to do a paper on a famous physician in history. My instructor says I can't use websites. I've actually never had to use the library."
- "I am writing a paper and would like to learn how to use RefWorks or EndNote for doing my references."
- "I need review materials for the USMLE Step 1 exam. Do you have any?"
- "Do you have a medical dictionary online?"
- "Do you have a scanner?"

Residents and Fellows

Residents and fellows in medical programs are most likely to make contact with the librarians when they have patient questions, need to present at morning report, or are in a research month. These information needs won't regularly culminate in a reference transaction in the library, but if the librarian is immediately available, such as a clinical librarian rounding with residents, the library can see an increase in reference transactions. For academic librarians who want to work with residents who are not coming to the library, it is crucial to go to them, whether via orientations or instructional sessions, to market library services and encourage residents to ask questions, or to attend morning report or other activities of the departments. It is crucial that the librarian provide evidence of skill and competence in order to gain their confidence and entice them to use reference services.

Residents are a special type of library user. Having gone through medical school and begun the practice of medicine, they are at this point aware of some of their inadequacies in terms of information management. This is an opportunity point for providing instruction and reference service. Sometimes they may forget the librarians are there. Don't let them. Be present and visible. Residents are practicing medicine for the first time, making clinical decisions, learning the utility of evidence-based medicine, and perhaps publishing research for the first time. Many are eager at this point to skillfully use the resources of the library more than ever before. That being said, whereas transactions with students tend to be instructional, librarians are more likely to provide complete search services for residents and fellows in support of patient care. But consultations and instructional opportunities are still desirable.

Examples of the types of questions that a reference librarian might get from a medical resident:

- "I am writing a case report for publication. I have never published a paper before and I need to do a literature review."
- "I need to present a patient case tomorrow and need information."
- "What are the differential diagnoses for X condition?"

- "How do I get remote access to library resources?"
- "What resources do you have available for use on my smartphone?"
- "What journals do you have available on X specialty?"
- "How do I know I've done a good search?"

Faculty

As the university's most stable occupants, faculty members develop working relationships with librarians, particularly where strong liaison programs are in place. In addition to liaisons, libraries are serving faculty via informationist and embedded librarian programs (discussed in Chapter 9), and research data management programs (discussed in Chapter 10).

The faculty members are the researchers, educators, and administrators in the university. Their requests may have to do with their research, although in those areas directly related to their own research specialty they generally establish mechanisms to keep themselves up-to-date with developments in the literature, many eschewing the library in favor of their own habits. Conversations with faculty about how they access information and use the library are crucial and eye-opening. Sit down with faculty. Have them show you how they use the library. Don't overestimate their abilities, yet be respectful of established working procedures.

Examples of the broad range of types of questions that a reference librarian might get from faculty in a health sciences university:

- "Do you have these journals?" [Hands the librarian a list.]
- "What tools are used to measure competencies in medical students?"
- "I'm doing a lecture on this topic. Could you help me get started with getting articles?"
- "I can't log in."
- "I need to get permissions to use figures from this article. How do I do that?"
- "Where are your drug reference books?"
- "Do you have 'the green journal'?" [Uses lingo.]

Clinicians

Depending on the type of health sciences library, clinicians may also be faculty, but clinicians will have information needs particular to patient care, and the research assistance of a librarian can be potentially critical in the prevention of clinical errors. For the sake of brevity, all clinicians are grouped into one category for discussion. The following examples of questions are adapted from a classification of clinicians' information needs presented at an American Medical Informatics Association (AMIA) Symposium (Allen et al., 2003):

- "What is the beeper number for Dr. Smith in Radiology?"
- "What is the normal value for this calcium result or other laboratory test?"
- "What does this abbreviation mean?"
- "What is the definition of this term?"

- "What other tests may be associated with this radiology report?"
- "How do these two drugs interact?"
- "What is the correct dosage for this patient?"
- "How do you calculate a patient's anion gap?"
- "What are the different potential causes of coffee-ground emesis?"
- "What patient information is available about this condition or procedure?"

Administrative Staff

The final broad category in this noncomprehensive list is administrative staff. This staff is more involved with the management of a health care facility and may have questions such as:

- "What is the Joint Commission standard for health literacy?"
- "How many inpatient beds are in each of the hospitals in Orange County?"
- "Where can I locate information on 'value based purchasing'?"

REFERENCE STATISTICS AND TRANSACTIONS

It is no secret that the number of reference transactions libraries are reporting is universally down. Data are reported by member libraries to the Association of Research Libraries (ARL) and to the Association of Academic Health Sciences Libraries (AAHSL) annually, and the downward trend continues. Figure 7.1 depicts a 65 percent drop in reference transactions since 1991, according to the statistics ARL collected, a decrease greater than in any other library service area. Likewise, Figure 7.2 illustrates the statistics AAHSL collected, where a downward trend in reference transactions persists. Electronic transactions have increased, but not enough to counter the overall decline.

The overall number of reference transactions is reported to be declining in libraries everywhere because users either are bypassing the library entirely or using resources remotely. Some evidence shows that the decrease is largely in directional questions, whereas ready reference questions may be approximately stable, and in-depth reference transactions have increased (De Groote, Hitchcock, and McGowan, 2007). No doubt, users are more and more likely to use library resources from a remote location and bypass the librarian in the conduct of their research, thus changing the nature of reference service. Further information is needed to understand what libraries are and are not considering reference transactions in terms of reporting data. Are questions asked during instructional sessions considered reference questions? Are questions asked in the hospital corridor added to reference statistics collection forms? Are questions that come in from the chief resident via the librarian's personal e-mail counted? Do librarians need to develop new behaviors in order to elicit questions from a new type of library user? Reference service is not dead, but it may need to change to meet new realities. How reference service is evaluated and enumerated is likewise under consideration. The following section presents current practices in reference statistics collection in health sciences libraries.

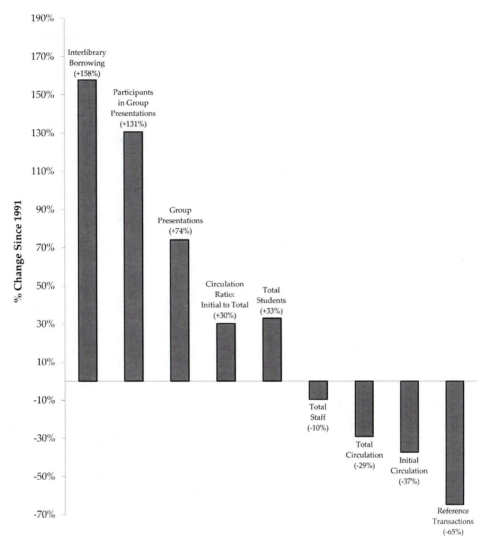

Figure 7.1. Association of Research Libraries (ARL) Service Trends since 1991. Source: Steven J. Squires, ed. 2013. *2011–2012 Annual Statistics of Medical School Libraries in the United States and Canada*, 35th ed. Seattle: AAHSL.

Statistics and Evaluation

How is reference service evaluated? Most of the data collected are quantitative, and several methods exist for collecting reference statistics and data. The traditional method was via a tally sheet kept at the reference desk and/or other service point. The tally sheet may or may not have spaces to record time of day, type of user, whether the question came via phone or in person, or the user's program affiliation. The sheet may also be used only periodically during sample weeks instead of recording every day throughout the year. Examples of 2002

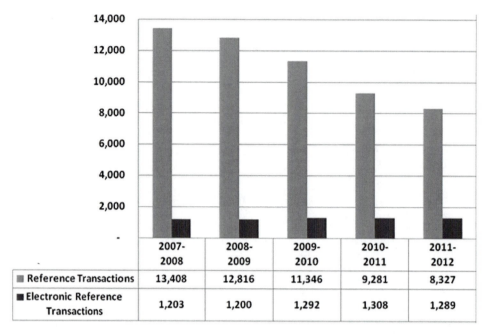

	2007-2008	2008-2009	2009-2010	2010-2011	2011-2012
■ Reference Transactions	13,408	12,816	11,346	9,281	8,327
■ Electronic Reference Transactions	1,203	1,200	1,292	1,308	1,289

Figure 7.2. Total and Electronic Reference Transactions, Mean Values, 2007–2008 to 2011–2012 in AAHSL Libraries. Source: Steven J. Squires, ed. 2013. *2011–2012 Annual Statistics of Medical School Libraries in the United States and Canada*, 35th ed. Seattle: AAHSL.

then-state-of-the-art reference desk activity sheets can be seen in an ARL Spec Kit from that year (Novotny, 2002).

Many libraries surely still record their reference statistics on paper tally sheets rather than using commercially available web-based options such as LibAnswers from SpringShare, http://www.springshare.com/libanswers/, and DeskTracker, www .desktracker.com/. Some libraries have created homegrown systems, or use software such as Microsoft Excel, Microsoft Access, or Survey Monkey (Vardell, Loper, and Vaidhyanathan, 2012) to record their reference statistics. The more information that can be collected, the more can be understood about the current nature of reference work and how librarians are interacting and providing service and value to their intended users. Online systems allow users to add transactions from anywhere and can generate reports on transactions that were previously difficult to generate. The forms required in an online system may generate more robust information, but sometimes they require more effort to complete than the old tally sheet. For instance, if a faculty member comes to the desk and asks about holdings on one journal and then two more, on a tally sheet that would probably be recorded as three ready reference transactions—using three hash marks—as the interaction consisted of three lookups. Will the librarian enter this three times in a longer online form? That can be pretty tedious and time consuming.

The reference staff at the New York Medical College (NYMC) Health Sciences Library add all transactions to a form in LibAnswers with RefAnalytics from

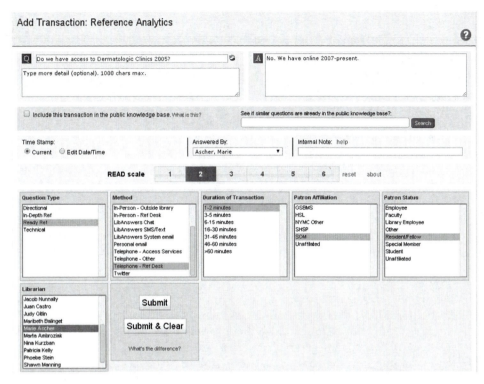

Figure 7.3. LibAnswers with RefAnalytics Reference Transactions form New York Medical College, Health Sciences Library.

SpringShare. This form is shown as Figure 7.3. It includes data not previously collected on a paper tally sheet, including the question and answer itself, the name of the librarian answering, the READ score (see below), question type, point of service, duration of transaction, user status and affiliation, extra notes, and the ability to add a transaction to the public knowledge base. This system produces extremely robust data for immediate and future analysis, but the concern is that when a librarian is busy at the desk, some transactions may be lost due to lack of time to record them.

Note that NYMC librarians are expected to enter reference transactions regardless of the point of service. This includes questions that come in via their own e-mail accounts, Twitter and Reference, SMS text messages, chat (IM), or in person inside or outside the library, making the whole library and campus count, and wherever the librarian is part of the service provided by the library. Moving service away from the reference desk has radically changed the way health sciences reference service is provided. Different models of providing reference will be covered later in the chapter.

Types of Reference Transactions

Reference service is largely evaluated by an analysis of the number and nature of reference transactions that occur within a library setting. Discussion of level of service is generally about reference statistics going up or, more frequently in recent years, going down. Analysis looks at the number and types of questions received, by whom, how, and where, and in some cases libraries measure how successful the transactions were. Several locally defined classification schemes can be used to look at the reference transactions that occur in the library. At New York Medical College Health Sciences Library, classification is by type of questions, a variation on the traditional Katz Classification:

1. **Directional questions** are not true reference questions. They don't require any lookup. They may ask where some facility is in the library, where to locate a staff member, or have a question about library policies. Examples: "What are the library's hours this Friday?," "Where can I find a hole punch?," or "What is the library director's phone number?"

2. **Technical questions** may be related to the library's proxy server, hospital firewalls, wireless access, software, or equipment. These are not content-based. Examples: "I am having trouble logging in to access resources remotely.", "Can you help me scan this item?", or "How do I create a new text box in Power-Point?"

3. **Ready reference questions** are generally quick lookups of holdings or discrete facts. Ready reference questions can usually be answered in fewer than five minutes. Examples: "Do you have the *American Journal of Obstetrics and Gynecology?*" or "What is the generic name for Vicodin?"

4. **In-depth questions** generally take more time and require more resources than ready reference questions. They usually require some selection of resources and often involve the development of a search strategy and/or training on the use of electronic databases or indexes. Examples: "I need the best research that has been conducted on the topic of VBAC in the last two years. How will I find it?" or "I need to write a paper on Margaret Sanger."

5. **Consultations** are usually prescheduled meetings between a user and a librarian and can either be seen as one-on-one (or small-group) training or as scheduled in-depth reference transactions. Consultations are usually scheduled for bigger in-depth reference questions related to a research project or topic. Consultations may be individual or small group. In reporting to external bodies for annual statistics such as the AAHSL and ARL, consultations are counted as reference transactions, and that is how they will be discussed in this chapter. Some libraries offer reference service only in the form of consultation.

In addition to tracking the type of question, often libraries collect other data on reference transactions such as date, day of week, time of day, mode of delivery/ location, time spent, user status, difficulty, and who answered the question. An Association of Research Libraries study published as a *SPEC Kit* in 2002 revealed dissatisfaction by librarians with the traditional types of data collected to evaluate research transactions; librarians felt that the quantitative data collected did not adequately address the level of work being performed (Novotny, 2002). One result of these sentiments was the development of the READ (Reference Effort Assessment Data) Scale. The READ Scale is a six-point scale that seeks to measure effort (i.e., the amount of work as well as the amount of expertise required to successfully respond to a reference query [Gehrlich, Karr, and Berard, 2010]). Recently the READ Scale has been integrated into LibAnswers virtual reference software Springshare, which may help popularize it.

Another classification scheme, developed by Debra Warner (2001), uses levels to indicate category of the transaction:

Level I = non-resource based transactions
Level II = skill-based transactions
Level III = strategy-based transactions
Level IV = consultations

The rationale behind this system was that it allows for consistent **triage** from a **single-service point** desk in a **tiered reference service**. Theoretically, Level I and II questions should be answerable by trained nonlibrarians. This is how it was applied at the San Jose State University (SJSU) library (Meserve et al., 2009) following the experiences at East Carolina University Health Sciences Library. At SJSU, they found 60–80 percent of Level I and II questions were being answered by librarians during initial assessment. Then they trained staff to recognize and handle Level I and II questions, and that number dropped to roughly 30–40 percent.

STAFFING AND SCHEDULING OF REFERENCE SERVICE— NEW MODELS OF SERVICE

The reference desk is something of a controversial topic in the library world—a dinosaur. With competing priorities, new modes of providing service, and a decline in reported number of transactions at the reference desk, staffing and scheduling of reference service is not as straightforward as providing a set of shifts for librarians to "work the desk." However, scheduled reference desk time is still a common practice in many libraries that maintain a reference desk. Scheduling designated reference time in a health sciences setting depends on the type of library and size of the professional staff. Hospital libraries with one or two librarians are not likely to have scheduled reference desk time. More frequently, academic health sciences libraries are restructuring their reference desks in favor of a combined or single service point with access services/circulation or more of a tiered reference model of service or triage service, where reference questions received at the service point at the library entrance are referred back to the most appropriate (subject or skill expert) reference librarian. Other libraries promote roving reference where the librarians are encouraged or scheduled to make rounds of the library rather than staying at a desk. Another model is the **embedded librarian** or **informationist**, who acts as part of a department outside the library. Embedded librarians and informationists are discussed in Chapter 9 of this book.

Several logical reasons exist for changing the way reference service is offered. First, with a decrease in the number of questions that come to the reference desk, as mentioned previously in this chapter, the cost-effectiveness of staffing a desk is questionable. At a small liberal arts university, Ryan (2008) calculated an average cost of $7.09 per reference question, including directional questions (directions to another campus building or room) and machine-related transactions (paper jams and toner refill help)—which accounted for nearly half of the questions in her study. It is possible that in smaller specialized health sciences libraries with decreasing reference transactions, this cost per transaction may be even higher. Secondly, evidence shows that a large percentage of the questions asked at the reference desk can be handled by trained nonprofessionals. In alternate reference service models, the librarian is freed from the reference desk to offer service where the users are or to maintain office hours for scheduled in-depth reference consultations (Schulte, 2011; Tennant et al., 2012).

Who is providing frontline service then? How are student helpers, staff, and paraprofessionals trained to handle reference questions, and how well are they doing? Various new reference models are explored below.

Reference Service Points and Models of Service

For the most part, health sciences libraries are set up like any other library in terms of service points and the way reference services are offered. Reference librarians are eager to help users wherever and however they can, whether it be via the traditional reference desk, by phone, or whether the librarian roves the library, halls or hospital, or receives queries via e-mail or chat, text, or social media. As a result, the current trend is to offer all or many of these as ways for the library user to communicate with the librarian, each with its unique set of opportunities and challenges.

Reference service comes via several models (Tyckoson, 2001). The old-school, traditional model of reference service involves the reference librarian working at a desk answering all types of questions, with the librarian doing all of the work to find the answers on behalf of the library user. Contrast this with a teaching model in which the librarian serves to instruct the user rather than answering questions. A tiered reference model—or **Brandeis model** (Nassar, 1997)—places graduate students at the primary service point answering the majority of questions, reserving reference librarians for research consultations and in-depth questions. **Virtual reference services** use digital technologies to provide reference service. Most libraries offer a combination of all of these models dependent on the requester and the nature of the request. For instance, in a health sciences library, the librarian is likely to provide answers to a busy clinician but will require that a student submit to instruction. In libraries with strong liaison programs, a consultation request will be scheduled with the appropriate liaison. And in today's world, almost any of these activities can happen using digital technologies. This section may draw some distinctions between the different service models with the understanding that most libraries, including health sciences libraries, offer some form of all of these.

The Reference Desk and the Traditional Model of Reference

The reference desk is the traditional home of reference and information services, the place where librarians have traditionally worked while waiting for users to approach and ask their questions. In a seminal *Library Journal* article, Samuel Swett Green, a pioneer of reference work, describes the interaction between the librarian and the reader like a business transaction: the "librarian should be as unwilling to allow an inquirer to leave the library with his question unanswered as a shopkeeper is to have a customer go out of his store without making a purchase"; users should be met with "something of the cordiality displayed by an old-time inn-keeper" (1876: 79–80). But he cautioned that librarians "give them as much assistance as they need, but try at the same time to teach them to rely upon themselves and become independent" (80). This may sound quaint, yet is still solid advice for the provision of reference service at the desk and beyond. A librarian at the desk has the opportunity to work with a user who explicitly has come to the desk for help, wanting information, whether it is the answer to a specific factual question or help with references for an assignment. A reference interview is conducted, and the librarian ascertains how best to meet the user's information need, whether by locating an answer online or in the library's collection, or by instructing the user on the use of library resources and databases. The librarian, given the time, has the opportunity to explore the topic with the user and build a relationship that will lead to continued use of and mastery of the library.

This model of reference,—and the reference desk in particular—has been challenged over the past several decades as libraries have been eliminating the desk as the point of service in favor of freeing up librarians to offer other types of service such as outreach and instruction—also worthy activities most often carried out by the same professionals (Meldrem, Mardis, and Johnson, 2005). That said, many librarians find value in what the reference desk offers to the library user: convenience, immediate access to a professional librarian, and therefore the best chance of getting to the answer quickly by working with the most qualified staff from the start.

This section will address alternatives and supplements to the reference desk for reference services, but first it will identify some characteristics currently understood to make for a good reference desk design. A reference desk or any public service information desk should include these characteristics, as adapted from Ahlers and Steiner (2012):

- Be approachable with a smaller footprint and minimal storage space. Gone are the days of the monolithic reference desk with tall counters behind which the librarian is almost invisible to the user.
- Be positioned near the entrance to the library or in a prominent visible spot in the library.
- Be clearly labeled. Library users should understand that this is the place to get answers to their questions or help with their research.
- Be located near public computer terminals or a computer lab.
- Enable proximity and eye-level contact between librarian and user.
- Accommodate both seated consultation and standing interactions.

In other words, not only the reference librarian, but also the space in which the reference librarian is situated, should be welcoming and conducive to open and congenial exchange of information and assistance. The reference librarian who may bring other work out to the desk to handle when no users are present will have to adapt to and welcome potential interruptions. This can be more challenging than it may appear at face value, but given additional responsibilities and competing priorities the librarian at the reference desk must serve the user first. The user is the customer and should never be compelled to say, "Sorry for interrupting you." (Users will anyway, but only to be polite. The librarian should never make them feel as if they are interrupting or a bother.)

To Reference Desk or Not to Reference Desk?

Users are no longer required to physically come to the library to use the resources of the library; likewise, it follows that they are not compelled to come to the library to meet with the librarian to ask questions about the use of those resources. Hence the falling off of reference questions asked at the reference desk (and overall). A study by De Groote, Hitchcock, and McGowan (2007) at the University of Illinois at Chicago Library of the Health Sciences demonstrated via quantitative and qualitative means a steady decrease in reference questions beginning in 1997–1998 when the majority of the library's information resources were becoming available online. Their reference model before the time of the study was a frontline information desk staffed by paraprofessionals who could answer directional and ready reference questions. More in-depth questions were triaged to a research consultation office where professional librarians offered service and instruction. Due to decreased numbers of questions, they changed to a single shared reference desk staffed simultaneously by paraprofessionals and librarians. One of the main findings of this study was that overall questions decreased, but research consultation/in-depth questions increased. This occurred after instituting the single-service reference desk, which in this case meant bringing the librarian out to a visible public service point. This trend toward fewer overall questions but more in-depth questions appears to be a trend in other health sciences libraries as well.

The Single-Service Desk

The single-service desk has been a major trend in libraries, particularly academic libraries, including academic health sciences

When our library closed its reference desk three years ago, our very experienced information desk supervisors—some with library school coursework—needed minimal training to triage questions for the new on-call reference service. A dedicated phone line relieves information desk staff of the need to remember phone numbers, schedules, and subject/function expertise of individual subject specialist librarians. The scheduled on-call professional reference and instruction librarian completes the in-depth portion of reference interviews that started on the information desk; and works on grants, collection management, and other projects between calls.

Nancy Schaefer, MLIS, AHIP, reference and instruction librarian, UF Health Science Center Library, Gainesville, FL

libraries, over the past two decades (Moore, McGraw, and Shaw-Kokot, 2001; Murphy et al., 2008; Schulte, 2011). The rationale usually relates to freeing up librarians to do more consulting and instructing and meeting with users at the point of need, along with reducing user confusion about which desk to go to, and the aforementioned dropping reference statistics and budget constraints. In a single-service desk, the functions of reference and access services may be merged with broadened responsibilities, requiring cross-training (Moore, McGraw, and Shaw-Kokot; Murphy et al.).

Triage, Tiered, and On-Call Service

When libraries switch to a single-service desk, they may opt to triage reference questions by having librarians "on call" (Murphy et al., 2001; Allegri and Bedard, 2006; Schulte, 2011). This is similar to the Brandeis model referrals from graduate students or other staff at a service desk at the front of the library.

Several considerations need to be taken into account when planning a single-service point or triage type of arrangement:

- Who staffs the desk? Is it staffed by librarians and nonlibrarians (e.g., paraprofessionals and students) simultaneously?
- Do librarians at a single-service desk assume some traditionally nonprofessional roles such as circulation and user registrations?
- Does the single-service point employ a triage model where questions are triaged from the desk staff to the librarians?
- Are librarians "on call," and what does that look like? (Murphy et al., 2008)
- What is the method for referral?
- How are the frontline staff trained to ascertain the need to triage? (Allegri and Bedard, 2006)
- What kinds of questions are your currently employed nonlibrarian staff equipped to answer?
- How much training will be needed? (Schulte, 2011)
- How will staff morale be affected?
- What is the evidence for any alternative model of service over the other?
- What is unique about any particular institution that would make one model more appropriate than another?
- How does the library assure a consistent level of service?

The Duke University Medical Center Library switched to a single-service desk with on-call librarians in 2002–2003 (Murphy et al., 2008). Coincidentally, they had administered their first **LibQUAL+ survey** one month before the planning of the project began. LibQUAL+ is designed to identify gaps in services between users' expectations and perceptions of the library's facilities, resources, and services. The survey was repeated in 2007, along with other assessments, and results were consistent with previous levels of satisfaction with staff courtesy, readiness, and abilities as well as with the referral process. Even resistant staff members were increasingly convinced that the new reference model worked.

The effect of remote users, who rarely if ever actually come to the library, is multiplied in academic health sciences libraries, which are more likely to have a larger remote community of users as they support students, residents, fellows, faculty clinicians, and community preceptors at disparate clinical sites. These remote users are rarely seen at the library's reference desk. Yet at most libraries with a reference desk, the desk continues to be the place where most reference questions are asked (De Groote, Hitchcock and McGowan, 2007).

No matter which route a library chooses to take with its reference desk, it is clear is that there is no one way to deliver reference services. Keeping a reference desk does not mean that other more progressive outreach services, instruction, and digital services will not be offered; they will be offered *in addition to* reference desk service. The question becomes one of workload and staff burnout. Outreach and instruction are also crucial aspects of library service, depending on the nature of the institution, and will be described in detail in other chapters. Other means of delivering reference service are described below.

Consultation Services

A **consultation** is a scheduled in-depth research assistance session that may include searching, instruction, in-depth assistance, assistance with references, or some combination thereof. Consultations are scheduled with reference librarians, often **liaison** librarians who have or are developing subject specialization with the departments they serve. Consultations are a traditional library service often supplemental to the reference desk where the user has an information need that is extensive enough that it requires the librarian to be away from the desk where other users might simultaneously need reference service. Libraries may have dedicated consultation rooms, or librarians may take consultations in their offices, in multipurpose training and computer rooms, or as "house calls" in faculty offices (Tennant et al., 2012). A consultation provides the opportunity to work with the library user one-on-one without interruption. Consultations can also occur via remote technologies using products such as Adobe Connect , GoToMeeting, WebEx, or other services that offer co-browsing and screen sharing capabilities (Ascher and Liberatos, 2013).

As noted above, at one point the University of Illinois at Chicago Library of the Health Sciences offered something of a triage-to-consult service, which meant on-demand, unscheduled consultations as well as those scheduled (De Groote, Hitchcock and McGowan, 2007). Likewise, the "on-call" model at Duke can be seen as as-needed reference consultation. Some libraries such as Ohio State University's Prior Health Sciences Library (Schulte, 2011) went from a single-service information desk to an on-call model to no longer offering walk-in reference service at all. Theirs is currently a consult-only service with close ties to their liaison program. Figure 7.4 illustrates the process of the reference transaction beginning at the information desk where nondirectional questions are either referred by paraprofessional staff to Basic Reference (answered by paraprofessionals) or to the appropriate subject specialist liaison, who works with the user in consultation. Evaluation of this program showed a substantial increase in the number of reference transactions taking more than thirty minutes and an overall increase in the number of reference questions answered.

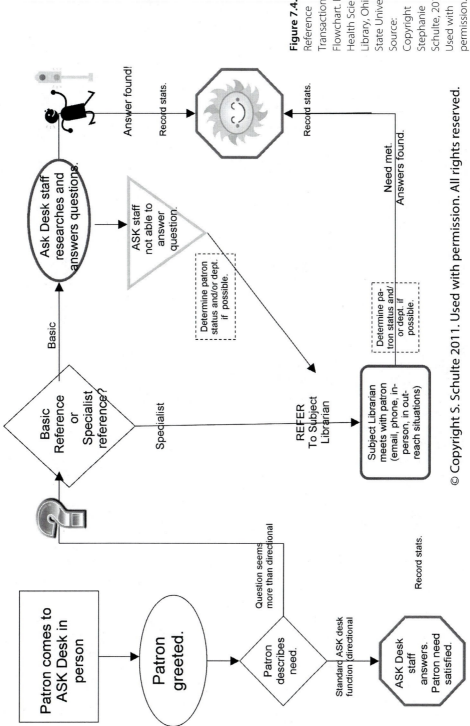

Figure 7.4.
Reference Transaction Flowchart. Prior Health Sciences Library, Ohio State University. Source: Copyright Stephanie Schulte, 2011. Used with permission.

Roving Reference

> The more freely a librarian mingles with readers, and the greater the amount of assistance he renders them, the more intense does the conviction of citizens, also, become, that the library is a useful institution.—Samuel Swett Green, 1876

Roving or "roaming" reference (Smith and Pietraszewski, 2004) isn't a particularly new idea. It requires that the reference librarian step out from behind the reference desk—if there is one—and walk through the library offering assistance to users. Many users don't like to ask for help when they walk into the library, even if they don't know how to use the library. Perhaps it makes them appear unknowledgeable and embarrassed. So they may head into the stacks on their own or may be sitting at a computer terminal in a lab struggling with the plethora of databases available to them. A roving librarian may be able to offer assistance at that point of need. It doesn't hurt for a librarian to step into a computer lab and ask quietly if anyone is in need of assistance. Librarians may even leave the confines of the library itself and offer assistance in other areas where students gather to study or even in research labs.

Often roving librarians are equipped with mobile technologies when they rove, so they may have iPads or other tablet computers available in case a lookup in the stacks becomes necessary. These have been found to be useful tools for roving reference service and other newer models of mobile reference (Tennant et al., 2012; Lee and Gleason, 2012). The roving reference model allows the librarian to ascertain the ways in which the library is being used by going to little-visited areas of the library and recording information about usage. But beware: One finding of a pilot study involv-

Our hospital library hasn't had a reference/circulation desk in about four years. It is rare that someone comes into the library and asks for help; they almost always call, page, or e-mail. In that respect, my job is very much the same as it was ten years ago in that I have a conversation (reference interview) with the person to find out what he or she wants. How I handle it depends on the question. If it is something I can do quickly or while I'm on rounds, I will (from my iPad); but the occasional request requires more, and I will work on those when I have time to be in my office or at least some place stationary. So I am still doing the same work; but instead of sitting at a desk, waiting for someone to come in and ask, I am doing rounds (or whatever) and I address their need from wherever I happen to be—which is usually not in the library. We haven't done stats for years. Admin doesn't care about stats. They want to know how the library is saving them money.

Heather N. Holmes, MLIS, AHIP,
clinical informationist, Summa
Health System, Akron, OH

ing roving reference service at Texas A&M was the need for librarians to be sensitive to demonstrating welcoming behavior versus intruding upon a quiet study area appearing like a monitor policing the building (Smith and Pietraszewski, 2004). In hospital libraries, clinical librarians regularly rove and also go on rounds with physicians to provide reference service.

VIRTUAL REFERENCE SERVICES

Over the past several decades, virtual reference services have increased and are now nearly ubiquitous. Virtual reference or digital reference services refer to electronic tools that are used to offer services to library users who do not walk into the library. Of course, since the advent of the telephone, libraries have offered reference via telephone, often as a separately scheduled function of the reference staff. A ringing telephone in a quiet reading room is sometimes considered unwelcome, and library staff may be unable to answer telephone calls during a busy reference shift. With decreasing numbers at the reference desk, this is rarely a problem anymore. However, depending on the location of the telephone and the reference desk, noise can still be a problem. Librarians providing instructional help via telephone may irritate studying library users.

Similarly, e-mail is a fairly popular way of delivering reference service, both via direct contact in the librarian's inbox (particularly in situations where the librarian has developed a relationship with a library user, such as in a liaison role) or through e-mail-based systems; or via the library's institutional e-mail account, which is likely publicized on the library web page and promotional materials. E-mail reference was the first medium that allowed the librarian to receive reference queries away from the desk or phone. The librarian must remember with e-mail that the reference interview is still important, and the transaction may need to evolve to a telephone call or in-person conversation if the information request is unclear. Also, when conducting reference transactions via e-mail, keep in mind that professionalism should be maintained with regard to proper address, correct spelling, grammar, and the use of a signature file (Straw, 2000).

The benefits of e-mail include ease of use and ubiquity. Another benefit is that the communication is asynchronous, so it gives the librarian time to evaluate and research a request before responding. The downside of e-mail is that e-mail messages can get lost either in a spam filter or in the overwhelming volume of e-mail received every day. Straight e-mail can be ignored accidentally for some time so conversations may be slow going. Also, it is sometimes difficult to communicate asynchronously and without visual cues from the library user.

Synchronous Digital Reference Service

Telephone, voice mail, and e-mail generally are not what is meant by digital reference. Digital reference refers mostly to synchronous technologies over the Internet. The benefit is real-time immediate interaction using services such as chat or instant messaging, and text reference. In addition, asynchronous virtual reference systems are also available.

By 2004, 27 percent of academic health sciences library provided a combination of chat and e-mail reference services (Dee, 2005). Today, almost all health sciences libraries, including hospital libraries, are using some form of synchronous chat reference. Many libraries now use free chat services such as Zoho Chat, https://chat.zoho.com/, or Trillian, www.trillian.im/, to conduct chat reference. Others use Springshare's proprietary LibAnswers service for their chat reference. LibAnswers has a synchronous chat module, as well as an asynchronous Ask the Library module that includes e-mail, text reference, and Twitter integration. The benefit of using a system such as this is it removes the need to pull statistics from disparate places as they are all aggregated into one analytics system called RefAnalytics. Other libraries have implemented text reference service using products such as Google Voice, www.google.com/voice, or Mosio's Text a Librarian, www.textalibrarian.com/.

Although libraries have eagerly implemented these services, chat reference, and even more so, text reference, have been slow to gain broad acceptance by users at academic health sciences libraries. A recent presentation at ALA's annual meeting described a twenty-four-hour text reference program at Virginia Commonwealth University that was defined as "successful" with just six text messages per day (Doherty and Peacemaker, 2013). Moreover, although social media, particularly Facebook and Twitter, are seen as having potential for the conduct of reference activity, they are not a major contributor yet. This may change in the near future. Research in this area is needed in health sciences libraries.

> The use of text messaging as a point of contact for our reference service has been underwhelming. It is the lowest method of contact from our users, garnering only about 120 incoming texts in a two-year period.
>
> *Heather L. Brown, MA, AHIP, associate professor and head of access services, McGoogan Library of Medicine, University of Nebraska Medical Center, Omaha*

SUMMARY

The core values and services references librarians provide have in many ways stayed the same over the years, with adaptation based upon the needs and information-seeking behaviors of our users. The library exists for its users, and the function of the library is to serve those users. Sometimes, in reference, that means librarians provide a user with a direct answer to his question. Other times librarians teach users to find the information themselves. Librarians use a variety of methods to provide reference service, whether in person, at a desk, roving the stacks of the library, via a tiered service, or working as embedded informationists (covered elsewhere). Decisions about what reference services to provide and how to provide them should be determined by what works to serve the information needs of users based on library staff availability and user preferences. Not one size will fit all. Health sciences librarians should conduct research to determine how well some of the newer methods are working and affecting reference and information service currently offered to their users. Librarians also need to investigate ways to go beyond

> Gauging the value of reference assistance? It is not about answering questions. It is about connecting people to information . . . and doing so easily. It is about demystifying skills for success in a world of information overload. It is about building confidence that knowledge is that added edge of smartness. And it is our continued challenge to assess its value to our institutions.
>
> *Danuta A. Nitecki, PhD, dean of libraries and professor, College of Computing & Informatics, Drexel University, Philadelphia, PA*

enumerating reference transactions in favor of other methods of evaluating reference service.

STUDY QUESTIONS

1. Name some characteristics that a reference librarian should possess. Which of these do you think are the most important and why?
2. Dr. Daniels approaches you in the hall and tells you he needs the most significant articles related to infertility written in the past three years. How do you respond to him? (Hint: You do not nod and say, "Okay, great!")
3. Which type of library users do you think offer the greatest challenge to the librarian? Why do you think so? How would you need to prepare yourself to work with each different type of user?
4. How are current means of collecting reference statistics limited? What types of statistics would be most useful in evaluating the level of and the value of reference service in health sciences libraries?
5. How are reference statistics used to influence how service is offered and staffed?
6. Which model of reference service do you think would work best in a large academic health sciences library? How about a small hospital library with one librarian? Why?

REFERENCES

Ahlers, Deborah, and Heider Steiner. 2012. "The Approachable Reference Desk." *College and Research Libraries News* 73, no. 2 (February): 70–73.

Allegri, Francesca, and Martha Bedard. 2006. "Lessons Learned from Single Service Point Implementations." *Medical Reference Services Quarterly* 25, no. 2 (Summer): 31–47.

Allen, Mureen, Leanne M. Currie, Mark Graham, Suzanne Bakken, Vimla L. Patel, and James J. Cimino. 2003. "The Classification of Clinicians' Information Needs While Using a Clinical Information System." *AMIA Symposium Proceedings.*

Ard, Allyson, Susan Clemmons, Nathan Morgan et al. 2006. "Why Library and Information Science? The Results of a Career Survey of MLIS Students Along with Implications for Reference Librarians and Recruitment." *Reference & User Services Quarterly* 45, no. 3, (April): 236–48.

Ascher, Marie T., and Penny Liberatos. 2013. "Addressing Information Management Competency Attainment through Consultations: An Effective and Sustainable Strategy?" Poster presented at the annual meeting of the Medical Library Association, Boston, May 7.

Dee, Cheryl R. 2005. "Digital Reference Service: Trends in Academic Health Science Libraries." *Medical Reference Services Quarterly* 24, no. 1 (Spring): 19–27.

De Groote, Sandra L., Kristin Hitchcock, and Richard McGowan. 2007. "Trends in Reference Usage Statistics in an Academic Health Sciences Library." *Journal of the Medical Library Association* 95, no. 1 (January): 23–30.

Doherty, Teresa, and Bettina Peacemaker. 2013. "24 Hour In-House Text Service." Contributed paper presented at the annual meeting of the American Library Association, Chicago, June 3.

Gehrlich, Bella Karr, and G. Lynn Berard. 2010. "Testing the Viability of the READ Scale (Reference Effort Assessment Data): Qualitative Statistics for Academic Reference Services." *College & Research Libraries* 71, no. 2 (March): 116–37.

Gorman, M. 2000. *Our Enduring Values: Librarianship in the 21st Century*. Chicago: American Library Association.

Green, Samuel Swett. 1876. "Personal Relations Between Librarians and Readers." *Library Journal* 1 (November): 74–81.

Judd, Terry, and Gregor Kennedy. 2011. "Expediency-Based Practice? Medical Students' Reliance on Google and Wikipedia for Biomedical Inquiries." *British Journal of Educational Technology* 42, no. 2 (March): 351–60.

Kyrillidou, Martha, Shaneka Morris, and Gary Roebuck, eds. 2013. *ARL Statistics 2011–2012*. Washington, DC: Association of Research Libraries.

Lampert, Lynn. 2005. "'Getting Psyched' About Information Literacy: A Successful Faculty-Librarian Collaboration for Educational Psychology and Counseling." *The Reference Librarian* 43, no. 89–90: 5–23.

Lee, Angela, and Ann Whitney Gleason. 2012. "Tablet Mania: Exploring the Use of Tablet Computers in an Academic Health Sciences Library." *Journal of Hospital Librarianship* 12, no. 3 (July): 281–87.

Meldrem, Joyce A., Lori A. Mardis, and Carolyn Johnson. 2005. "Redesign Your Reference Desk: Get Rid of It!" In *Currents and Convergence: Navigating the Rivers of Change, Proceedings of the 12th National Conference of the Association of College and Research Libraries in Minneapolis, MN*, 305–11. Chicago: Association of College and Research Libraries.

Meserve, Harry C., Sandra E. Belanger, Joan Bowlby, and Lisa Rosenblum. 2009. "Developing a Model for Reference Research Statistics: Applying the 'Warner Model' of Reference Question Classification to Streamline Research Services." *Reference & User Services Quarterly* 48, no. 3 (March): 247–58.

Moore, Margaret Eilene, Kathleen A. McGraw, and Julia Shaw-Kokot. 2001. "Preparing Staff to Work at a Single Service Desk." *Medical Reference Services Quarterly* 20, no. 1 (March): 79–86.

Murphy, Beverly, Richard A. Peterson, Hattie Vines et al. 2008. "Revolution at the Library Service Desk." *Medical Reference Services Quarterly* 27, no. 4 (September): 379–93.

Nassar, Anne. 1997. "An Evaluation of the Brandeis Model of Reference Service at a Small Academic Library." *The Reference Librarian* 27, no. 58: 163–76.

Novotny, Eric. 2002. *SPEC Kit Number 268: Reference Service Statistics & Assessment*. Washington, DC: Association of Research Libraries.

Ross, Catherine S., Kirsti Nilsen, and Marie L. Radford. 2009. *Conducting the Reference Interview: A How-To-Do-It Manual for Librarians*, 2nd ed. New York: Neal-Schuman Publishers.

RUSA (Reference and User Services Association). 2008. "Definitions of Reference. Approved January 14. http://www.ala.org/rusa/resources/guidelines/definitionsreference.

———. 2013. "Guidelines for Behavioral Performance of Reference and Information Service Providers." May 28. http://www.ala.org/rusa/resources/guidelines/guidelinesbehavioral.

Ryan, Susan M. 2008. "Reference Transactions Analysis: The Cost-Effectiveness of Staffing a Traditional Academic Reference Desk." *Journal of Academic Librarianship* 34, no. 5 (September): 389–99.

Schulte, Stephanie J. 2011. "Eliminating Traditional Reference Services in an Academic Health Sciences Library: A Case Study." *Journal of the Medical Library Association* 99, no. 4 (October): 273–79.

Smith, Michael M., and Barbara A. Pietraszewski. 2004. "Enabling the Roving Reference Librarian: Wireless Access with Tablet PCs." *Reference Services Review* 32, no. 3: 249–55.

Squires, Steven J., ed., 2013. *2011–2012 Annual Statistics of Medical School Libraries in the United States and Canada*, 35th ed. Seattle: Association of Academic Health Sciences Libraries.

Straw, Joseph E. 2000. "A Virtual Understanding: The Reference Interview and Question Negotiation in the Digital Age." *Reference & User Services Quarterly* 39, no. 4 (June): 376–79.

Tennant, Michele R., Beth Auten, Cecilia E. Botero et al. 2012. "Changing the Face of Reference: Adapting Biomedical and Health Information Services for the Classroom, Clinic, and Beyond." *Medical Reference Services Quarterly* 31, no. 3 (July–September): 280–301.

Tibbo, Helen R. 1995. "Interviewing Techniques for Remote Reference: Electronic Versus Traditional Environments." *American Archivist*, 58, no. 3 (Summer): 294–310.

Tyckoson, David A. 2001. "What Is the Best Model of Reference Service?" *Library Trends* 50, no. 2 (September): 183–96.

Vardell, Emily, Kimberly Loper, and Vedana Vaidhyanathan. 2012. "Capturing Every Patron Interaction: The Move from Paper Statistics to an Electronic System to Track the Whole Library." *Medical Reference Services Quarterly* 31, no. 2 (April–June): 159–70.

Warner, Debra. 2001. "A New Classification for Reference Statistics." *Reference and User Services Quarterly* 41, no. 1 (September): 51–55.

CHAPTER 8

Research Services and Database Searching in Health Sciences Libraries

Lee A. Vucovich

INTRODUCTION

Health sciences librarians support biomedical and clinical researchers in both academic medical centers and hospital libraries to meet a wide and constantly evolving range of researcher needs (Jaguszewski and Williams, 2013; Auckland, 2012). Some of the services librarians currently provide to biomedical and clinical researchers include:

- Expert search assistance to answer questions, research topics, and write literature reviews
- Organization and management of PDFs and citations
- Locating and understanding publication metrics
- Assistance with understanding and complying with regulations such as the NIH Public Access Policy

Librarians may also be asked to collaborate on such issues as information literacy, scholarly communication, copyright issues, and data management, and to use their reference skills in support of interdisciplinary research (Jaguszewski and Williams, 2013). Versatile health sciences librarians continue to embrace the new roles supporting the research enterprise discussed elsewhere in this book to meet these needs. Learn more about the roles of informationists and embedded librarians in Chapter 9. Research data management is explored in Chapter 10.

This chapter reviews the biomedical databases and resources that provide the foundation health sciences librarians use to meet these evolving information needs, and the expert search techniques necessary to use them well. Specialized searches, including searches to support **evidence-based health care**, **systematic reviews**, and Institutional Animal Use and Care Committees, and an overview of resources used to organize and manage an individual's PDF library and references are included. Librarians supporting researchers must be willing to develop expertise required to deliver comprehensive and precise result sets, confidence to evaluate results, flexibility to stay current with constant interface enhancements and new tools, and the enthusiasm to incorporate these into their work.

INFORMATION NEEDS OF BIOMEDICAL RESEARCHERS

Studies have shown that biomedical researchers choose to conduct their own searches and often start with research databases. Their preferred information sources in the digital age are journal articles, preferably those available online, web sources, colleague recommendations, and textbooks, often online (Allan et al., 2012; Kosteniuk, Morgan, and D'Arcy, 2013; Niu et al., 2010; Grefsheim and Rankin, 2007; Hemminger et al., 2007).

The number of journals and articles published annually continues to escalate.

PubMed, the gold standard free biomedical database, added more than one million articles in 2012, which continues the trend of the past twenty years, as shown in Figure 8.1.

MEDLINE/PubMed only indexes 5,639 of the approximately 28,100 active scholarly peer-reviewed journals published worldwide in 2012. Therefore, it is no surprise that scientists think that time is a significant barrier to their ability to find, appraise, and organize the articles they need for research and grants (Auckland, 2012).

SEARCHING BIOMEDICAL RESEARCH DATABASES

Researchers prefer to initiate searches for articles themselves and consider themselves competent searchers (Hemminger et al., 2007). Therefore, they often only consult librarians for complex searches such as those needed for extensive literature

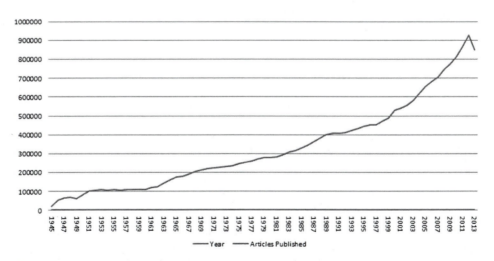

Figure 8.1. PubMed Publication Trends.

reviews, complicated clinical questions, or when their searches do not provide the desired results.

Communication with the researcher about these searches is essential. After the reference interview, as discussed in Chapter 7, the librarian may send examples of the citations provided by different searches or databases to the researcher to review before running the search. The librarian should document the search strategy, the dates the searches were performed, and other information the researcher may need. Result sets can be shared with the researcher via e-mail of links from the databases, a bibliography written by the librarian, or through shared libraries in bibliographic software.

Table 8.1 details the steps most librarians perform when searching for articles. It is necessary to understand the structure of each database, the **controlled vocabulary** if used, and the symbols used for **truncation** and **proximity operators** if these are available. In biomedicine, for example, often both the generic and trade names of drugs need to be searched. Genes also have multiple names that may or may not be included when using the subject headings provided by the database's thesaurus.

Librarians and others have created online guides, www.libguides.com, and videos, www.youtube.com. These can be particularly useful when beginning to explore an unfamiliar resource, but as databases update their interfaces often, it remains necessary to use database help files. Most of the databases mentioned in this chapter now also offer short, current instructional videos on their websites.

The most relevant research databases specific to the health sciences are introduced below. Many others are useful for targeted searches in various disciplines. Websites of content providers such as Ovid, www.ovid.com, and EBSCO, http://ebscohost .com/academic, are a good source for more detailed information about the databases they provide.

Table 8.1. Six Steps to a Successful Search

---

1. Start with a well-defined question or clearly defined topic.

2. Identify key concepts and think of synonyms for each concept.

3. Know how much and what type of information is needed.
   Consider books and e-books for background information.
   Use research database(s) for journal articles and studies.

4. Build search statements with the Boolean operators AND, OR, and NOT.
   Combine synonyms into a search string with OR.
   Use AND with concepts to narrow your search and OR to broaden it.
   The PubMed Tutorial has a good explanation of Boolean operators.

5. Choose the right databases and resources to search.

6. Each database is searched differently. Use the search tips or help files in the database to search it efficiently.
   Some have a thesaurus (controlled vocabulary) and some use keywords only.
   Some have filters for language, patient age, publication type, date, and so forth.
   Check for phrase searching, truncation symbols, and proximity operators.

Additionally, in response to the growing number of smartphone and tablet users, most of these databases offer subscribers smartphone and tablet apps, mobile websites, or both. Links to these apps and sites are available on each resource's web page and in the app store for the mobile device the user owns.

PubMed

PubMed, www.pubmed.com, is a free database provided by the National Center for Biotechnology Information (NCBI) at the National Library of Medicine (NLM). It contains more than 23 million citations to journal articles from more than 5,600 medical and scientific journals. PubMed includes citations from the MEDLINE database (U.S. National Library of Medicine, 2013b), plus:

- In-process and "ahead-of-print" citations that have not yet been indexed for MEDLINE
- Pre-1966 citations that have not yet been updated with current MeSH
- Citations to author manuscripts of articles written by NIH-funded researchers
- Citations to most books on the NCBI bookshelf

PubMed citations may contain links to the full-text articles located in PubMed Central, www.ncbi.nlm.nih.gov/pmc/, and to publisher websites and library e-journal collections.

Health sciences librarians usually start searching for research and clinical topics in MEDLINE, often using PubMed. PubMed is the most widely used free database for biomedical literature (Lu, 2011; Nourbakhsh et al., 2012). Many other vendors also provide interfaces for searching MEDLINE. Ovid MEDLINE and EBSCO MEDLINE with Full Text are examples of platforms for searching MEDLINE that are often purchased by health sciences libraries.

MEDLINE is NLM's bibliographic database of biomedical and life science articles, covering the years 1946 forward (1946–1966 is the OLDMEDLINE subset). All MEDLINE records are indexed with NLM's controlled vocabulary, Medical Subject Headings (MeSH), to assist users in searching. Updated annually, MeSH includes more than 23,000 descriptors (subject headings and qualifiers) arranged in both hierarchical and alphabetical order as well as a database of Supplementary Concept terms and more than 213,000 additional entry terms (U.S. National Library of Medicine, 2013a). The MeSH browser, www.nlm.nih.gov/mesh/MBrowser.html, is an online vocabulary lookup aid designed to help the end user quickly locate MeSH descriptors and their place(s) in the hierarchy, scope notes, allowable qualifiers, and so forth. The MeSH browser is useful for librarians developing a search strategy, but it does not link to PubMed, so librarians can use the MeSH database, discussed below, to build searches.

Searching PubMed

Users search PubMed by entering terms in the PubMed search box. PubMed uses automatic term mapping to match the user-entered keywords to MeSH headings. This means the terms are searched as both keyword and subject headings, allowing all of PubMed to be searched. The translated search for the user-entered query "pathophysiology migraine headache" is displayed in the Search Details box shown in Figure 8.2.

Alternatively, searchers needing more precise searches can use the MeSH database, www.ncbi.nlm.nih.gov/MeSH, to locate and select appropriate MeSH terms and qualifiers to build the search and then send it to PubMed. The Filters sidebar can be used to narrow search results by categories including ages, publication date, article type, and many more.

Users can construct more complex searches using field tags on the Advanced Search page. The search history and advanced search builder located on the Advanced Search page are used to combine key concepts. Hospital librarians use expertise in PubMed to perform the complex clinical searches frequently requested of them.

Health sciences librarians need to be proficient PubMed or MEDLINE searchers. NLM offers comprehensive online training to librarians wanting to improve their PubMed searching skills, www.nlm.nih.gov/bsd/disted/pubmed.html. Librarians can complete the self-paced PubMed Tutorial or select some of the short animated tutorials on specific topics offered on the site.

Special Queries

PubMed provides a set of filtered search strategies (also called hedges) that have been optimized for sensitive/broad or specific/narrow retrieval. Available from the PubMed home page, these results are limited to specific topics and should not be used for a comprehensive search. Each search query page links back to the hedge

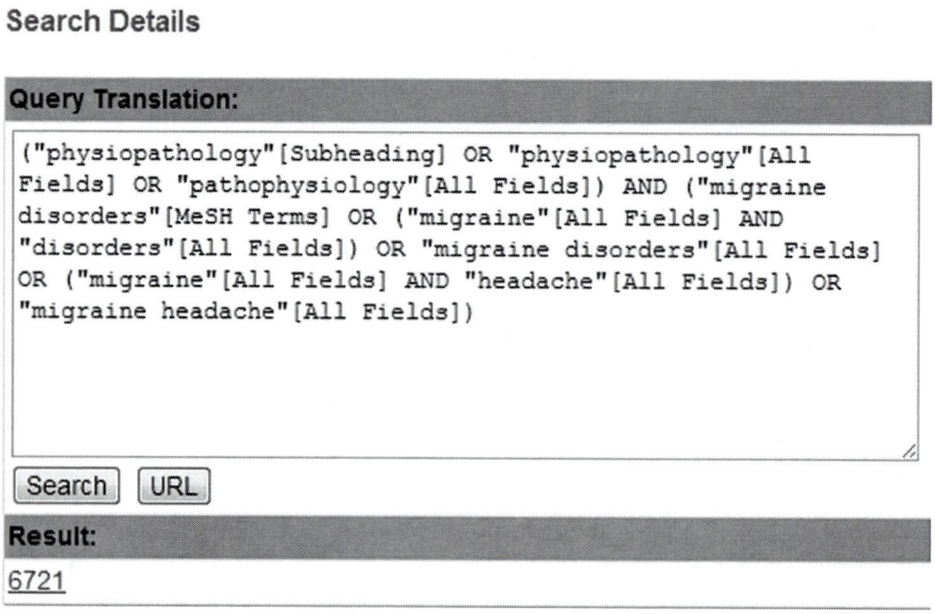

Search Details

Query Translation:

```
("physiopathology"[Subheading] OR "physiopathology"[All
Fields] OR "pathophysiology"[All Fields]) AND ("migraine
disorders"[MeSH Terms] OR ("migraine"[All Fields] AND
"disorders"[All Fields]) OR "migraine disorders"[All Fields]
OR ("migraine"[All Fields] AND "headache"[All Fields]) OR
"migraine headache"[All Fields])
```

[Search] [URL]

Result:

6721

Figure 8.2. PubMed Search Details.

and references supporting it. Health sciences librarians should become familiar with the following special queries.

Clinical Queries include results to systematic reviews and meta-analyses, limited by study type (choice of etiology, therapy, diagnosis, prognosis, or clinical prediction guidelines), and by several medical genetics topics conveniently arranged in columns on a single result page.

Special-Topics Queries contain various topics and subjects. For example, Health Services Research (HSR) Queries provide specialized PubMed searches on health care quality and costs. Both hospital librarians and those working in academic medical libraries see many of these questions. Topics include outcomes assessment, process assessment, qualitative research, quality improvement, costs, appropriateness, and economics.

Comparative Effectiveness Research is conducted to "improve health outcomes by developing and disseminating evidence-based information to patients, clinicians, and other decision-makers, responding to their expressed needs, about which interventions are most effective for which patients under specific circumstances" (NICHSR, 2013). In other words, this research informs health care decisions by

Surgeons are often enthusiastic users of hospital library services. The hospital where I worked did bariatric surgery, so a typical question from one of my surgeons might be, "What is the optimal length of the roux limb in gastric bypass surgery?" On PubMed, I might start with this search strategy: "Anastomosis, Roux-en-Y/methods AND gastric bypass AND (length [tw] OR short [tw] OR shorter [tw] OR long [tw] OR longer [tw])." Use of text words brings up some miss-hits, but I notice this interesting article title, "Short versus long Roux-limb length in Roux-en-Y gastric bypass surgery for the treatment of morbid and super obesity: a systematic review of the literature." A quick search of the Cochrane Library retrieves the same reference.

Carolyn Holmes, MLIS, reference librarian, library associate, Lister Hill Library, University of Alabama at Birmingham (formerly hospital librarian at Baptist Health System in Birmingham)

providing evidence on the effectiveness, benefits, and harms of different treatment options (AHRQ, 2013).

The types of studies using this research are evolving and cover a wide range of study designs. The Comparative Effectiveness Special-Topic page provides a set of queries to guide the librarian or researcher in specialized research on comparative effectiveness. It includes filters for published literature in PubMed and for work still in progress in the ClinicalTrials.gov and NLM's Health Services Research Projects in Progress (HSRProj), wwwcf.nlm.nih.gov/hsr_project/home_proj.cfm, databases.

PubMed Health

PubMed Health, www.ncbi.nlm.nih.gov/pubmedhealth/, is an evolving resource from NCBI and NLM for consumers and clinicians on clinical effectiveness, designed to answer the question "What works?" in medicine and health care. It provides summaries and full text of selected, current systematic reviews, grouped for consumers and clinicians, and concurrently searches PubMed for systematic reviews. As this new resource usually ranks at the top of Google searches for diseases and some medications, medical librarians need to be aware of the content and purpose of PubMed Health and how comparative effectiveness research can be used in medical decision making (Miles, 2011).

PubMed Derivatives

To meet the perceived need for automated search tools that will help researchers search the growing MEDLINE database efficiently and accurately, groups from academia and business can use the MEDLINE database and *Entrez Programming Utilities* to develop new tools to enhance PubMed searches (Lu, 2011). These tools provide different search options and often present results clustered by concept or ranked by different relevancy parameters.

NCBI maintains a website, www.ncbi.nlm.nih.gov/CBBresearch/Lu/search, that lists the properties for many such free tools and includes a tool selector. Some of these may be of much value for researchers in different areas, especially in basic research. Here are two examples:

- GoPubMed, www.gopubmed.org/web/gopubmed/, provides an **ontology**-based PubMed search. Gene Ontology and MeSH headings are used to sort the result set. GoPubMed also includes robust statistics including authors, journals, and institutions relating to the search.
- Quertle, www.quertle.info/, is a **semantic** search engine that allows searching for meaningful relationships between search concepts. It searches PubMed, PubMed Central (PMC), TOXLINE, NIH RePorter (for grants), and more. Libraries can arrange for their holdings to be linked to the records retrieved.

PubMed Central (PMC)

Launched by NLM in 2000, PubMed Central, www.ncbi.nlm.nih.gov/pmc/, is a free digital archive of full-text biomedical and life science articles. It is a repository for journal literature deposited by participating publishers and is the designated repository for papers and author manuscripts submitted in compliance with the NIH Public Access Policy. The NIH Public Access Policy implements a law that ensures that the public has access to the published results of NIH funded research (U.S. National Library of Medicine, 2013b). More than 2.6 million articles were archived as of early 2013. Each has a corresponding record in PubMed.

The public can search PubMed Central directly from its website using similar search strategies to PubMed. The papers are linked to PubMed records, and searchers can find them in PubMed with the free full-text filter. Search engines such as Google Scholar also search the articles and provide full text to users.

CINAHL

CINAHL, www.ebscohost.com/biomedical-libraries/the-cinahl-database, the Cumulative Index to Nursing and Allied Health Literature, is a fee-based core resource to support nursing research for patient care, process improvement, and nursing education. It also supports research and patient care in the allied health professions.

EBSCO markets several different versions of CINAHL with increasing amounts of content and attached full-text articles. CINAHL indexes 3,000 journals from 1981 forward, but all CINAHL Plus (and CINAHL Complete) versions include indexing for at least 4,800 journals back to 1937. In addition, CINAHL Plus provides Evidence-Based Care Sheets and Quick Lessons that provide concise overviews of diseases and conditions and outline treatment options. CINAHL is primarily a database of journal articles, but it also includes pamphlets, government documents, dissertations, and books about nursing and allied health.

Like PubMed, citations in CINAHL are indexed with a controlled vocabulary, called CINAHL Headings. Subject terms and subheadings can be located and searches built within the database. Searches can be combined with Boolean operators and limited with a large number of CINAHL limiters, including publication type, peer-reviewed articles, age groups, clinical queries, evidence-based practice, and many more. Result sets obtained can be further narrowed in many ways. It does not contain automatic term mapping, but CINAHL offers truncation and proximity operators and either relevance or date sorting.

Other Research Databases

Like PubMed and CINAHL, the databases listed in Table 8.2 are abstract and index databases extremely useful in finding literature supporting health sciences researchers. They are available through several vendors and in different versions, so coverage may vary.

Health sciences librarians should have a working knowledge of the research databases available in other disciplines that would support literature retrieval for researchers studying topics in hospital administration and management, bioengineering, drug development, or public health. Some of these databases are ABI Inform and other business databases, Agricola, International Pharmaceutical Abstracts (IPA), Compendex, and PAIS International. These databases are available through

Table 8.2. Selected Abstract and Index Databases

Database	Scope	Coverage	Source of Indexing Terms
Biological Abstracts http://wokinfo.com/ products_tools/specialized/ ba/	Biology 4,200 journals	1969–present, archive from 1929	Biosis Index
EMBASE www.embase.com/ www.embase.com	8,000 biomedical, international, and pharmacological journals 2000 journals not in MEDLINE	1947–present	EMTREE
PsycINFO www.apa.org/psycinfo/	Behavioral sciences and mental health. Journals, books, dissertations. 2,500 journals	1597–present, comprehensive from the 1880s	Thesaurus of Psychological Index Terms

commercial vendors. Searchers use them to identify additional studies to supplement their searches in the biomedical databases.

Drug Databases

The following two authoritative and comprehensive drug resources are widely used by hospitals, staff health care providers, and in some pharmacy, medical, and nursing schools and their libraries. Drug information from these and similar providers is integrated into many point-of-care tools, including those discussed later in this chapter.

Micromedex, www.micromedex.com/, is a suite of full-text drug information databases that includes authoritative, peer-reviewed, evidence-based drug information about investigational and nonprescription drugs. Mobile apps are available.

Lexicomp Online, www.lexi.com/, is a suite of databases providing comprehensive drug, disease, and clinical information including drug monographs. A robust mobile app, Lexi-Drugs, is available.

Many libraries also license either Natural Medicines Comprehensive Database, http://naturaldatabase.therapeuticresearch.com/, or Natural Standard, www.natural standard.com/, to provide evidence-based information on dietary supplements and complementary, alternative, and integrative therapies.

Epocrates, www.epocrates.com/, and Micromedex Drug Information, http://truven health.com/products/drug_information.aspx, both offer current and comprehensive full-text drug information as free smartphone apps for use at the point of care. The blog iMedicalApps, www.imedicalapps.com/, has timely reviews of this rapidly evolving field, and includes both of these products in its recommendations for the twenty best free iPhone apps (Husain, 2013).

Cochrane Library

The Cochrane Library, www.thecochranelibrary.com/, is an online collection of six databases containing research on the effectiveness of health care treatments and interventions and a seventh that provides details about the Cochrane Collaboration. Although all are important, librarians most often use:

- Cochrane Database of Systematic Reviews: Cochrane Reviews are rigorous, systematic reviews of research in health care and health policy, created by members of the Cochrane Collaboration. Intervention reviews assess the benefits and harms of intervention and are widely used as evidence in making clinical decisions. Cochrane Reviews also include diagnostic test and methodology reviews. Many consider Cochrane Reviews to be the gold standard for clinical evidence.
- Cochrane Central Register of Controlled Trials (CENTRAL) includes details of articles identified by Cochrane Collaboration authors, primarily from MEDLINE and Embase and other published and unpublished sources.
- Database of Abstracts of Reviews of Effects (DARE): DARE contain abstracts of systematic reviews that have been quality-assessed. Each abstract includes a summary of the review together with a critical commentary about the overall quality. Focused primarily on systematic reviews that assess the effects of health

care interventions and delivery and organization of health services, DARE is freely available online through the Centre for Reviews and Dissemination, www.crd.york.ac.uk/CRDWeb/SearchPage.asp.

Librarians and patients who do not have access to the Cochrane Library can get much useful information from Cochrane summaries, http://summaries.cochrane. org. These include the full plain language summary of each review and provide links to the abstract and full review as well as related topic summaries. Users can also retrieve Cochrane summaries and abstracts using search engines, PubMed Health, and many point-of-care tools.

Scopus and Web of Science

Scopus and Web of Science are online abstract and index databases of peer-reviewed literature that also include bibliographic information (references and forward citations) for the articles they contain. For that reason, they are known as abstract and citation indexes. Both are interdisciplinary, but librarians in academic health sciences libraries often use them for both their citation metrics and their interdisciplinary content.

Scopus and Web of Science are similar in structure and organization. Neither provides a thesaurus or controlled vocabulary, but both rely instead on author-defined keywords. Scopus includes MeSH and EMTREE terms in their keywords to facilitate retrieval; Web of Science includes KeywordsPlus, index terms in which the terms are derived from the titles of articles in the reference list.

Both include author affiliations for all article authors and both offer comprehensive author profiles with links to coauthors. Both provide tools to sort and refine searches. Each also offers analysis tools that group and graph search results by author, publication year, institution, source title, subject category, and language.

However, Scopus and Web of Science do not index the same content. Because their content is so different, citation counts and analyses vary between databases (see Table 8.3). Neither is all-inclusive and both offer unique citations (Jacso, 2005; Burnham, 2006; Shariff et al., 2012; Anders and Evans, 2010). These databases are relatively expensive, so few institutions offer both. Health sciences librarians most often use these databases for the three main purposes of subject searching, tracking a single article, and assisting authors with metrics to measure their productivity.

Both databases are interdisciplinary, so researchers who are interested in subjects that cross disciplines may be able to collect articles with one search as they begin their research. The international scope Scopus brings can also be valuable in some fields. Another reason to perform a subject search in Scopus or Web of Science is that result sets can be sorted by relevancy or times cited. This helps to prevent overlooking older articles in identifying the **seminal** articles on the topic. Through the analysis tools users can identify potential collaborators and publication trends to decide where to submit an article. Figure 8.3 shows the number of articles published each year in Scopus in six selected journals for the search "TITLE-ABS-KEY (probiotics AND [allergies OR hypersensitivity])."

Often researchers want to see who is citing their work. Scopus and Web of Science records for a single article include the number of, and links to, articles that have

Table 8.3. Differences between Scopus and Web of Science

Scopus: www.elsevier.com/online-tools/scopus
- Scope: Life sciences, physical sciences, health sciences, social sciences, and humanities
- Coverage: 20,500 journal titles (including open access journals), trade publications, book series, articles in press, conference papers
  - International; more than half of SciVerse Scopus content originates from Europe, Latin America, and the Asia Pacific region
  - 100 percent MEDLINE coverage
  - Dates: –present; complete citation information began in 1996
- Availability: Elsevier
- Website: www.scopus.com

Web of Science: http://thomsonreuters.com/products_services/science/science_products/a-z/web_of_ science/
- Scope: sciences, social sciences, arts, and humanities
  - Coverage: 12,000 journals, conference proceedings, and MEDLINE are available
    - 1,600 regional journals recently added
    - Dates: back files to 1900 available
  - Availability: Thomson Reuters Web of Knowledge platform
  - Website: http://webofknowledge.com/

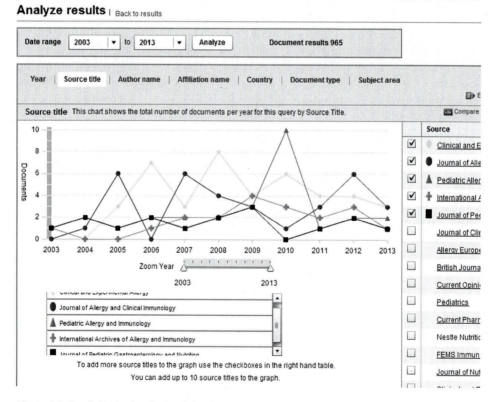

Figure 8.3. Result Set Analysis by Journal in Scopus.

cited the article after its publication. Authors using either database can easily set citation alerts to e-mail them whenever the work is cited in either database.

The articles in the reference list, also included in the record, can be used to identify additional resources on the topic. Reviewing articles in the reference list plus those citing the article of interest allows the user to move forward and backward in time to follow the progress of the research from prior influences to future developments.

In academic institutions, investigators ask librarians for assistance in finding metrics commonly used to measure productivity. Each database generates an author details page for every author in the database. Content includes institution, subject areas, coauthors, and a list of their documents with the current number of times cited for each. Both databases create graphs and charts grouping the documents in different ways.

The h-index (Hirsch, 2005) is one metric commonly used, despite its limitations, to measure the productivity and impact of a scientist's work. The h-index is based on a list of articles ranked in descending order by the times cited. The value of h is equal to the number of papers (N) in the list that have N or more citations. A scholar with an h-index of eleven has published eleven papers, each of which has been cited in other papers at least eleven times.

Both Scopus and Web of Science databases include the h-index for authors. Because the content provided is different, the h-indexes are usually different between databases. Librarians should help investigators understand the metrics as well as locate them.

Altmetrics, an emerging field, measures the impact of articles shared via social media and is being discussed to complement citation analysis (Kwok, 2013). Figure 8.4 shows the Scopus Altmetrics app for the article "Myths, Presumptions, and Facts about Obesity" (Casazza et al., 2013), retrieved seven months after the article was published. Altmetrics can demonstrate the early impact of an article before it is widely cited in the peer-reviewed literature. In fact, according to a 2011 study, tweets can predict highly cited articles within the first three days of publication (Eysenbach, 2011).

Journal Citation Reports (JCR)

Librarians are often asked where to find Journal Impact Factors (JIF). Proposed by Eugene Garfield (Garfield, 2006), the Journal Impact Factor is one of the metrics available in Web of Knowledge's JCR, http://wokinfo.com/products_tools/analytical/jcr/, and remains the standard for ranking journal influence and prestige. The JIF is defined as the average number of times articles from the journal published in the past two years have been cited in the JCR year. JCR is highly selective about the titles included in the database, so all journals do not have a JIF.

To find impact factors, JCR may be searched by journal title, or users can browse a list of journals ranked by impact factor within a subject category. Impact factors vary widely across disciplines so should only be compared within a subject area. Despite considerable controversy over their use and misuse, impact factors remain an indicator of a journal's prestige. Librarians use the JIF for journal selection and to assist authors to decide where to submit manuscripts for publication, but using it to evaluate individual performance is highly controversial (Baethge, 2012).

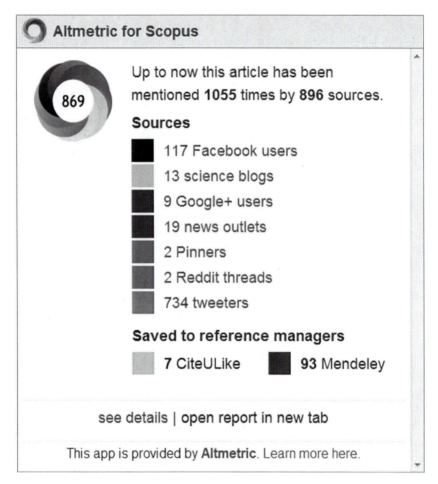

Figure 8.4. Scopus Altmetrics App Example.

JCR includes other metrics for journal evaluation, including the Eigenfactor, www.eigenfactor.org. Available free online, the Eigenfactor ranks the influence of the journals included in JCR much as Google's PageRank **algorithm** ranks the influence of web pages. The scores can be compared across disciplines.

Scopus Journal Analytics

Scopus includes the SJR or Scimago Journal Rank metric with the database. Also available freely online, www.scimagojr.com/journalrank.php, SJR is another competing indicator of scientific prestige. SJR uses methodology inspired by Google page rank but uses a different algorithm than the Eigenfactor. SJR ranking includes journals that are not included in JCR. Scopus also provides the SNIP (Source-Normalized Impact per Paper) metric. SNIP measures contextual citation impact by weighting citations based on the total number of citations in a subject field.

Full-Text Search Engines

For librarians without the financial resources to license multiple or expensive research databases, using free online tools offers an inviting alternative, especially to complement or enhance a PubMed search. Others find that the time to learn a new database is a barrier and prefer alternatives that allow them to leverage their online search skills. Google Scholar is a search engine used frequently in biomedical reviews reported in the literature. Because full-text databases are organized to retrieve and rank results very differently than the abstract and indexing databases, librarians need to understand how best to use their strengths.

Full-text search engines search the complete full text of all articles in their index, and using very different algorithms, as described below, relevancy rank the result set. They do not include controlled vocabulary, so synonyms or truncation must be used for a comprehensive search. Often the relevancy algorithms bring older articles to the top of the result list, which makes it easy to identify important articles on the topic. However, as science and medicine develop study-by-study, searchers should be certain that they see the latest articles as well, especially if a recent systematic review or meta-analysis exists on the topic.

It is necessary to note that not all full-text articles are available free. Newer articles often link back to the publisher website for purchase. These resources may offer partnerships with libraries to provide links to library-licensed full-text articles for their users. Examples of web search engines indexing full-text articles are PubMed Central and Microsoft Academic Search.

Google Scholar

Google Scholar (GS), www.scholar.google.com, searches across many disciplines for scholarly research publications. This content includes "articles, theses, books, abstracts and court opinions, from academic publishers, professional societies, online repositories, universities and other web sites" (Google Scholar, 2013). It includes PubMed records and the full text of PMC papers. Although Google Scholar does not disclose its source list, it derives its content from a subset of Google that looks "scholarly in content or format" and adds articles and documents supplied by the types of partner agencies listed above. Finally, citations extracted from the reference list of previously indexed documents are included (Walters, 2011).

Although studies have been done comparing searches in Google Scholar with those completed in PubMed, the results have been inconclusive (Anders and Evans, 2010; Gehanno, Rollin, and Darmoni, 2013; Mastrangelo et al., 2010; Nourbakhsh et al., 2012; Shariff et al., 2013). Google Scholar seems to have sensitivity and vast coverage, but concerns remain about the lack of reliable advanced search functions and its changing content. It is probably best to use Google Scholar to locate relevant papers quickly when beginning a search, and to complement searches of PubMed and other research databases.

For example, because Google Scholar searches the full text of entire articles, it will find articles in which the topic is mentioned in the methodology section but not in title, abstract, or MeSH term. This is useful for finding test instruments, named surgical procedures, some medical devices, and new genes and pathways that have various names and no associated MeSH descriptors. Google Scholar can also be used as a "backdoor" to PubMed for a difficult search. The librarian can look up relevant articles retrieved from Google Scholar in PubMed, and identify both the MeSH terms for a future PubMed search and additional related articles.

Google Scholar ranks sources according to relevance using a different algorithm than Google. According to the website, Google Scholar "aims to rank documents the way researchers do, weighing the full text of each document, where it was published, who it was written by, as well as how often and how recently it has been cited in other scholarly literature" (Google Scholar, 2013). Librarians need to be sure they have found the most current evidence. Google Scholar offers a date range search in the left sidebar, allowing relevant results during that range to be displayed. Alternatively, a user can choose to see a date sort for all results from the past one year.

Like Scopus and Web of Science, Google Scholar tracks forward citations in its index for the items in its database. Users can click on the "cited by" link under the article to see other articles in Google Scholar that have used this article in their bibliographies. This is another way to track any developments in the research reported in older articles.

Authors can set up a profile page with their articles that also displays a citation chart and h-index. Comparisons of Google Scholar, Scopus, and Web of Science metrics in the literature have confirmed that each finds unique citations, but questions remain about Google Scholar's metadata and content sources. The h-indexes vary across these three resources as well (De Groote and Raszewski, 2012; Patel et al., 2013).

For librarians supporting authors at institutions without the citation and abstract indexes, Google Scholar can be used to generate article lists with citation counts and h-indexes and other productivity metrics. Publish or Perish (POP), www.harzing.com/pop.htm, is a free program that imports the raw data from Google Scholar and analyzes it. It allows authors to select the imported articles, ensuring accuracy.

SUPPORTING EVIDENCE-BASED PRACTICE

Research for busy health care providers in the clinical setting usually means finding the evidence to make or confirm a clinical decision. Searching the literature and then critically appraising the results takes a significant amount of time. This is one of the barriers physicians report to practicing evidence-based medicine as many questions are answered during the patient visit (Graber et al., 2008; Chisholm and Finnell, 2012). It is not surprising that studies have shown that the information source physicians and residents use most often to answer questions is colleagues (Ndosi and Newell, 2010; Kosteniuk, Morgan, and D'Arcy, 2013; Allan et al., 2012). To solve this problem, providers have developed evidence-based, online point-of-care tools. These tools filter and preappraise evidence to identify studies of high quality, provide summaries and references, and update the content frequently. Many clinicians use these point-of-care tools to answer some of the most common questions on a wide range of topics.

The 6S model is a hierarchy of preappraised evidence used to guide clinical decision making (DiCenso, Bayley, and Haynes, 2009). In this model, the health care provider starts at the top and drills down until he or she finds the answer (see Table 8.4).

At the top of the hierarchy are clinical decision-support systems (CDSSs.) A CDSS is "any electronic system designed to aid directly in clinical decision making, in which characteristics of individual patients are used to generate patient specific assessments or recommendations that are then presented to clinicians for consideration" (Bright et al., 2012). Alerts and reminders in **computerized provider order entry (CPOE)** systems and informational retrieval tools, such as "Info buttons" embedded in the electronic health record, are examples of systems that provide targeted information based on the patient (Kawamoto et al., 2005). Bright and colleagues concluded that significant research is still required to promote widespread use of CDSSs and to improve their clinical effectiveness. Hospital librarians should follow this trend as more hospitals begin to provide information through CDSSs.

For physicians without a CDSS or with questions that it does not answer, the next step is to look for summaries. These include background summaries that incorporate current preappraised evidence-based information about specific clinical problems. DynaMed and UpToDate are two online point-of care tools that provide these summaries. Current, evidence-based practice guidelines are also examples of summary-based evidence.

DynaMed, https://dynamed.ebscohost.com/, is EBSCO's evidence-based, clinical reference tool. It includes clinically organized summaries for more than 3,200 topics and is updated daily, through a process called Systematic Literature Surveillance overseen by DynaMed editors. DynaMed summaries include links to PubMed articles, links to evidence-based guidelines, and patient handouts.

UpToDate, www.uptodate.com, is Wolters Kluwer's evidence-based clinical decision support resource designed for use at the point of care. UpToDate covers more than twenty specialties and includes more than 10,000 topic reviews, each of which

Table 8.4. The 6S Model

◆ **Systems**
Computerized decision support systems

◆◆ **Summaries**
Evidence-based clinical practice textbooks and guidelines

◆◆◆ **Synopses of Syntheses**
Evidence-based abstracts of high-quality systematic reviews

◆◆◆◆ **Syntheses**
Systematic reviews

◆◆◆◆◆ **Synopses of Studies**
Evidence-based abstracts of high-quality individual studies

◆◆◆◆◆◆ **Studies**
Original articles published in journals, not preappraised

Adapted from DiCenso, Bayley, and Haynes, 2009.

answers multiple clinical questions. The summaries begin with a brief summary and recommendations section, and include graphs and tables and references linked to PubMed.

Several studies have evaluated the use of these and other tools. Both DynaMed and UpToDate are well respected, but they have their differences. Therefore, health care providers should not rely on only one tool for decision making (Prorok et al., 2012; Isaac, Zheng, and Jha, 2012; Ketchum, Saleh, and Jeong, 2011; Banzi et al., 2011; Campbell and Ash, 2006).

UpToDate and DynaMed are designed for busy health care providers to find quick answers. Guidelines, on the other hand, can be difficult to find. The National Guideline Clearing House, www.guideline.gov, is a freely accessible comprehensive source of guidelines. Librarians searching for guidelines should be sure that the guidelines are current and evidence-based. Other guidelines can be found in some databases and through MEDLINE searches.

Librarians are more involved as clinicians move down the hierarchy in the 6S model. They use resources such as DARE and Evidence Updates, http://plus.mcmaster.ca/evidenceupdates/, a free online database of summaries of studies and systematic reviews. They locate meta-analyses and systematic reviews using the Cochrane Library, PubMed, and other research databases. Hospital librarians are often asked to find the evidence to answer the more specific and difficult questions that cannot be answered using the 6S model.

CONDUCTING EXPERT SEARCHES

Finding Grey Literature

Librarians can use their expert searching skills to support researchers in finding useful and appropriate unpublished research referred to as grey literature. According to the definition presented during the 12th International Conference on Grey Literature, Prague, 2010, grey literature comprises

document types produced on all levels of government, academics, business and industry in print and electronic formats that are protected by intellectual property rights of sufficient quality to be collected and preserved by library holdings or institutional repositories but not controlled by commercial publishers, i.e., where publishing is not the primary activity of the producing body. (Schopfel, 2010)

However, grey literature may include "non-conventional, fugitive and sometimes ephemeral" publications (New York Academy of Medicine, 2013).

Grey literature is noteworthy because it often contains information vital to research, yet it is not indexed in the major databases. It may be more current than published material. For example, ongoing research is shared at conferences, yet less than half of all studies, and about 63.1 percent of randomized or controlled clinical trials, initially presented as abstracts or summaries at professional meetings, are subsequently published in full as peer-reviewed journal articles. Positive results were associated with full publication (Scherer, Langenberg, and von Elm, 2007).

Grey literature is also significant because including it can reduce publication bias. Systematic reviews, for example, will overestimate treatment effects if only studies with significant results are published (Hopewell et al., 2007; Jannot et al., 2013). Clinical Trials databases therefore often provide essential information from unpublished studies. Table 8.5 gives examples of different types of grey literature.

Finding grey literature can be challenging. When published online, it is often located deep within the hidden web, but a growing amount is found on scientists' personal websites and institutional repositories. The following resources and strategies offer a good starting point:

Grey literature is an essential supplement to the peer-reviewed literature. In some ways, it is superior as grey lit is more likely to tell the "real story" behind a scientific process than the airbrushed scholarly work. These days, grey literature includes blogs and tweets. Make sure your search strategy is comprehensive.

Marcus Banks, MLIS, director, library/
academic and instructional innovation,
Samuel Merritt University, Oakland, CA

- New York Academy of Medicine Grey Literature Report, www.greylit.org/, includes selected new grey literature publications in health services research and public health topics. Reports are archived and can be browsed or searched.
- Grey Matters, www.cadth.ca/en/resources/grey-matters, is a practical search tool for evidence-based medicine. CADTH's free online interactive checklist of resources contains links to many ongoing clinical trials sites.
- Use Scopus or Web of Science to scan reference lists for pertinent documents
- Try a specialized search engine. Examples:
  - Science.gov, www.science.gov. Searches more than fifty-five databases and more than 2,100 selected websites from thirteen federal agencies, and mines the hidden web
  - Mednar, http://mednar.com/mednar/ Searches the deep web
- For medical interventions, check clinical trials registries, including ClinicalTrials .gov

Table 8.5. Representative Types of Grey Literature

Blogs and tweets
Census, economic, and other data sources
Conference proceedings and abstracts
Databases of ongoing research
Electronic networks, such as Listserv archives
Informal communications including e-mail, chat transcripts, and meeting minutes
Newsletters
Preprints of e-journal articles
Registered clinical trials
Research reports, completed and uncompleted
Technical reports
Theses and dissertations
White papers

Collaborating on Systematic Reviews

A systematic review attempts to collate all empirical evidence that fits pre-specified eligibility criteria to answer a specific research question. It uses explicit, systematic methods that are selected with a view to minimizing bias, thus providing more reliable findings from which conclusions can be drawn and decisions made. (Higgins and Green, 2011: sect. 1.2.2)

The sheer number of studies, reviews, and systematic reviews is exploding. According to a study published in 2010, seventy-five trials and eleven systematic reviews are published daily, and the numbers are growing (Bastian, Glasziou, and Chalmers, 2010). Because medical decisions should be based on all the information available about what causes a disease or the best way to prevent, diagnosis, or treat it, rather than upon a single study (Moher et al., 2007), clinicians practicing evidence-based medicine rely upon systematic reviews and meta-analyses as they are considered the highest level of evidence. Although they are comprehensive and the methodology is rigorous, these studies and reviews are actually of varying quality (Moher et al., 2008; Yuan and Hunt, 2009). The importance of a thorough search cannot be overemphasized. If studies with inconclusive or negative results are not included, perhaps because they are unpublished, treatments may seem to be more effective to readers of the medical literature than they actually are (Jannot et al., 2013).

Librarians in increasing numbers are contributing their skills to teams conducting systematic reviews. The Cochrane methodology, considered the gold standard in systematic reviews (Meerpohl et al., 2012), includes identification of relevant studies from a number of different sources (including unpublished sources).

Clearly, a librarian's expertise with expert searching, including searching the grey literature, would support the comprehensive search strategies quality systematic reviews require. The Institute of Medicine recognized this, and in its report *Finding What Works in Health Care: Standards for Systematic Reviews* included the standard that the researcher should work with a librarian trained in systematic reviews to develop the search and peer review the search strategy. It also provided clear recommendations of the databases and resources that need to be searched for studies (Eden et al., 2011). In an article on methodology for systematic reviews and meta-analysis, Crowther and colleagues also advised, "the help of an experienced librarian is invaluable and is strongly recommended" (Crowther, Lim, and Crowther, 2010: 3141).

The librarian, as active collaborator on a systematic review team, can fill other roles in the process. As expert searcher on the team, he or she can collaborate on forming the research question and exclusion criteria, then formulate and document the searches. In the role of organizer and analyzer, the librarian must have the skills to manage the articles and keep accurate records, then write the search methodology (Dudden and Protzko, 2011; McGowan and Sampson, 2005). Most journals and reporting guidelines require documented, reproducible, search strategies as part of their methodology.

Librarians supporting systematic reviews should use recommended reporting guidelines, such as PRISMA for systematic reviews (Moher et al., 2009). The Equator Network defines reporting guidelines as statements that provide advice on how to report research methods and findings. Usually in the form of a checklist, flow diagram or explicit text, they specify a minimum set of items required for a clear and transparent account of what was done and what was found in a research study, reflecting in particular issues that might introduce bias into the research. (Equator Network, 2013)

Librarians should work with the research team to ensure the standards for the appropriate guidelines, shown in Table 8.6, are adhered to throughout the project.

Librarians collaborating on systematic reviews are rewarded by the sense of accomplishment from contributing to guidelines for improving health outcomes, building relationships with researchers, and expanding their professional expertise. Often they are coauthors on the papers resulting from the review.

Supporting Institutional Animal Care and Use Committees

The Institutional Animal Care and Use Committee (IACUC), www.iacuc.org/aboutus.htm, is a self-regulating entity that, according to U.S. law, must be established by institutions that use laboratory animals for research or instructional purposes to oversee and evaluate all aspects of the institution's animal care and use program. Similar animal care committees are mandated worldwide. Researchers planning to use animals for scientific purposes must complete an animal use protocol and submit it to the IACUC for approval prior to commencement of the study.

The U.S. Animal Welfare Act regulations require that the principal investigators consider alternatives to procedures that cause more than momentary pain or distress to the animals. Thus, searches for animal alternatives are required for most animal use protocols. These searches are based on the 3Rs described in the book *The Principles of Humane Experimental Technique* (Russell and Burch, 1959). These are:

Table 8.6. Selected Reporting Guidelines

Reporting Guidelines	Type of Review
CONSORT: Consolidated Standards of Reporting Trials www.consort-statement.org/	Randomized Controlled Trials
PRISMA: Preferred Reporting Items for Systematic Reviews and Meta-Analyses www.prisma-statement.org/statement.htm	Systematic Reviews and Meta-Analyses
MOOSE: Meta-analysis of Observational Studies in Epidemiology www.equator-network.org/reporting-guidelines/meta-analysis-of -observational-studies-in-epidemiology-a-proposal-for-reporting -meta-analysis-of-observational-studies-in-epidemiology-moose -group/	Meta-Analyses of Observational Studies
equator: Enhancing the Quality and Transparency of Health Research www.equator-network.org/index.aspx?o=1032	Links to reporting requirements for all study types

- Replacement: Methods that avoid using animals, such as in vitro, cell culture, tissue culture, models, and simulations
- Reduction: Strategies for using fewer animals, such as shared control groups, and consultation with a statistician
- Refinement: Modifications in experimental procedures to enhance animal well-being or minimize pain and distress such as the use of analgesics and analgesia

Librarians support animal welfare at their institutions in various ways. Some serve formally or informally on their institutions' IACUCs. Others provide training for the biomedical researchers, through consultations, workshops, and provision of online resource guides. Many libraries provide services where the IACUC librarian conducts a thorough, comprehensive animal alternatives search for the investigator to use in his or her protocols. These activities are usually quite rewarding.

Animal alternatives searches are complex and must be highly specific. The following is a short list of respected online resources for animal alternative searches. These are good starting points for a librarian interested in developing these skills.

- National Library of Medicine. "Altbib: Bibliography on Alternatives to Animal Testing," http://toxnet.nlm.nih.gov/altbib .html

    Access to MEDLINE/PubMed citations relevant to animal alternatives. Includes topic area PubMed searches, a bibliography, and news.

Because literature searching in support of systematic reviews requires a specialized set of skills and knowledge to create thorough search strategies across numerous resources, it provides a great opportunity for librarians to be members of the research team that includes coauthorship. That coauthorship of librarians with other health professionals in nonlibrary journals holds the promise of increasing visibility and promoting the value of librarianship across the biomedical sciences. Even though librarians' contributions warrant authorship and most researchers offer it, not all researchers are aware of the value or realize they should offer authorship. It is important to speak up for yourself.

I find being part of research teams very rewarding, but I have also discovered that the process from beginning to publication can take a long time. I just received word that a project I started on three years ago was accepted for publication. It will be the first published systematic review in which I will be included as an author.

Susan Fowler, MLIS, clinical librarian, Bernard Becker Medical Library, Washington University School of Medicine in St. Louis, MO

- Animal Welfare Information Center. USDA National Agriculture Library. "Alternatives," http://awic.nal.usda.gov/alternatives

    Information on methods and sources available to reduce, refine, or replace animals used in teaching, testing, and research.
- Johns Hopkins Bloomberg School of Public Health. "Altweb: Resources: Search for Alternatives," http://altweb.jhsph.edu/resources/searchalt/index .html

    Global clearinghouse for information on alternatives to animal testing.

- CCAC. "Three Rs Microsite," http://3rs. ccac.ca/en/

    Information on replacement, reduction, and refinement alternatives for animal use in science. Includes step-by-step strategy guide for 3R searches.
- UCDavis University Libraries. "UC-Davis Center for Animal Alternatives Information," www.lib.ucdavis.edu/dept/animalalternatives/

    Portal of information for information about animal alternatives.

ORGANIZING AND MANAGING REFERENCES

Researchers need to store, organize, and retrieve their references to write journal articles, literature reviews, theses and dissertations, class lectures, and grant applications. They also must review the journal literature to stay current in their fields. Although some researchers print journal articles to read, many store the PDFs digitally and want an easy way to manage their PDF libraries. Many people who read articles online or on tablets want to highlight and annotate the PDFs, and to have both these notes and the original papers be searchable. Investigators commonly use bibliographic software, called reference managers, for these purposes. Most reference managers:

In order to put forth a good-faith effort to alleviate animal pain and distress and eliminate unnecessary animal use, researchers must be trained to appropriately conduct "3R" literature searches. As a librarian and IACUC nonvoting member, too often I have reviewed literature searches that improperly use Boolean operators, search only with research method acronyms, and retrieve zero relevant citations. Researchers need a librarian's expertise, and I encourage librarians to become involved with their institution's animal committee; it is a role in which we can truly make an impact.

Melissa Ratajeski, MLIS, AHIP, RLAT,
reference librarian, Health Sciences
Library System, University of Pittsburgh,
Pittsburgh, PA

- Collect references from different sources including article databases, library catalogs, e-book collections, and websites
- Make it easy to organize the references and associated PDFs
- Allow annotations and notes to be added to references and/or PDFs
- Insert citations in footnotes, in-text citations, and bibliographies
- Format the document according to the proper reference style, and reformat automatically when needed
- Provide a means to share references with colleagues and collaborators
- Allow synchronization of references across multiple platforms and computers

To manage research and PDF libraries, the software should:

- Attach PDFs of articles to references
- Store and index images and other files
- Find full-text articles for references in the library
- Import PDFs into the library and find the metadata to index them
- Offer an intuitive interface and options for organization including tagging
- Provide the ability to read, annotate, and highlight PDFs within the software

Librarians providing research services should understand reference managers and how to use them. Popular proprietary reference managers include EndNote, Reference Manager, RefWorks, and Papers. Free, open source options are also available. Some of the most popular are Zotero, Mendeley, and CiteULike. Each of these offers different functionality (Zhang, 2012).

Many serious researchers will choose EndNote because it has no limit to the number of references that can be stored and includes more than 5,000 professionally created bibliographic styles. Others choose Zotero or Mendeley for ease of importing references found online and options to share references with public or private groups online, despite the community managed style options. Additional space can be purchased for each.

CiteULike, often referred to as a social bookmarking site for researchers, is a similar tool in that it allows researchers an easy way to store, organize, and publicly share papers they are reading online. As with Mendeley, people can search CiteULike to see what others have saved on a topic of interest, possibly finding other valuable papers. However, citations must be exported to other reference managers to build in-text citations and bibliographies in different output styles.

IMPROVING RESEARCH SERVICES

Both libraries and product vendors are experimenting with new ways to connect users to the information they need. Here are three trends that bear watching.

Web-Scale Discovery Systems

A web-scale discovery system (WSDS) is "a preharvested central index coupled with a richly featured discovery layer that provides a single search across a library's local, open access, and subscription collections" (Hoeppner, 2012: 7). Central indexes typically include full-text journal articles and book chapters, full-text articles from open source collections and digital repositories, full text and abstracts from some databases such as MEDLINE, and records from library catalogs.

Searchers can use a WSDS to perform simple, keyword searches of library print and electronic collections. WSDSs rank results by relevancy and provide facets so users can narrow their searches and focus results. Because the content in a vendor's index is dependent upon agreements with publishers and database vendors, the results a user will retrieve vary widely depending on the WSDS used and the decisions librarians make upon implementation. Four vendors who currently offer popular WSDSs are:

- EBSCO Discover Service (EDS), www.ebscohost.com/discovery
- Ex Libris Primo, www.exlibrisgroup.com/category/PrimoOverview
- OCLC's WorldCat Local (WCL), www.oclc.org/worldcatlocal
- Serials Solutions Summon, www.serialssolutions.com/en/services/summon/

Many academic libraries are using WSDSs, but fewer health sciences libraries have implemented them. Health sciences librarians need to balance advantages of WDSSs, such as the ease of use and the integration of a large number of resources, with disadvantages pertinent to medical researchers. For example, some relevancy algorithms return many older articles and may return articles lower on the strength-of-evidence pyramid before a well-written systematic review. Too many out-of-scope results may be retrieved from the massive index. Furthermore, if a WSDS only returns results from a library's full-text collection, clinicians and researchers may miss key papers that could change a clinical decision or research proposal (Hoy, 2012; Thompson, Obrig, and Abate, 2013). Librarians need to work closely with users and vendors to provide WSDSs that meet the distinctive needs of health sciences libraries.

E-Book Portals

Books are used for background information to answer clinical questions and in research. Studies show that e-books are heavily used in the health sciences and accepted by most users, although some still prefer print. Reference and pharmaceutical topics are the types of e-books users preferred most, and students, postdoctoral fellows, researchers, and clinical physicians are among the heaviest e-book users (Folb, Wessel, and Czechowski, 2011; Hartel and Cheek, 2011). As more users read articles and book chapters on tablets and e-readers, comfort with and use of online books should continue to grow. Currently, models that vendors and libraries use to provide e-books to users are evolving and in a state of flux. Users seem to prefer finding books and chapters through discovery tools and websites rather than library catalogs (Folb, Wessel, and Czechowski, 2011). The following representative commercial products provide intuitive semantic searches of e-book collections integrated with multimedia and other content.

- AccessMedicine, www.accessmedicine.com, is McGraw-Hill's online resource that provides medical students, residents, clinicians, and researchers with seventy-five textbooks prominent in medical education. It includes thousands of images, video and audio files, linked drug information, a differential diagnosis tool, and case studies. Books can be browsed individually, and chapters retrieved using keyword topic searches. Result sets are narrowed by clinical categories such as diagnosis, etiology, or pathophysiology. McGraw-Hill has other collections in the series with similar integrated content, including Access-Surgery and AccessEmergencyMedicine.

- ClinicalKey, www.clinicalkey.com, is Elsevier's new "clinical insight engine," replacing MD Consult. Although it is marketed as a point-of-care tool, Clinical Key contains primary content rather than preappraised summaries like DynaMed and UpToDate, making it useful for research and education in addition to clinical care. The resource integrates all of Elsevier's surgery and medical textbooks (more than 1,000), recent (past five years) articles from more than 500 journals, MEDLINE records, more than 13,000 medical and surgical videos, and millions of images. Simple keyword searches produce a results list that can be narrowed by study type, clinical specialty, and type of content. Individual books can be browsed, and book chapters are included in the results lists for subject searches.

Representative other biomedical e-book portals include Stat!Ref, www.statref
.com/; EBSCO eBooks, www.ebscohost.com/ebooks; eBrary, www.ebrary.com; and
SpringerLink eBooks, www.springer.com/librarians/e-content/ebooks.

Tools for Staying Current

Faculty of 1000: Post Publication Peer-Review

F1000Prime, http://f1000.com/prime, is a subscription-based directory of top
articles in medicine and biology recommended by 10,000 experts (or "faculty")
worldwide. The experts rate each article and explain why it is noteworthy. Readers can nominate articles, and comments are included after the evaluations. These
recommendations and comments constitute a searchable database covering forty
faculties (subjects) to which approximately 1,500 new recommendations are added
monthly.

Libraries can add links to F1000 reviews on PubMed records, making it easy for
users to identify these articles and read the evaluations. E-mail alerts to saved F1000
searches help users to identify relevant articles on topics of interest.

Beyond E-Mail Alerts: Other Alerting Tools

The research databases reviewed in this chapter provide e-mail alerts to saved
searches. Many journals send tables of contents via e-mail to registered users. Currently, many users are coping with the profusion of peer-reviewed literature and
overflowing e-mail boxes by also looking for articles recommended by colleagues
or experts. New products are being developed to simplify this process for users, but
the field is evolving so rapidly that it simply must be watched. Librarians can recommend these new strategies and tools in consultations or post about them in blogs,
tweets, or newsletters.

Evidence Updates, http://plus.mcmaster.ca/evidenceupdates/, is a free database
of citations from 120 major medical journals, prerated for quality and clinical relevance. These articles, provided by the BMJ group and McMaster Evidence, support
evidence-based clinical decisions. Clinicians can register for e-mail alerts for one or
more specialties or search the database online.

Medscape, www.medscape.com, offered by WebMD, is a free website for clinicians. Medscape Today News provides news across all disciplines from Medscape
News, Reuters, the FDA, and more. It includes Specialty sites that provide targeted
articles, including conference presentations. Clinicians can subscribe to Topic Alert
Newsletters via e-mail for specific specialties, including cross-disciplinary ones such
as Business of Medicine or Genomic Medicine, or alternatively, browse articles using
free apps for their tablets or smartphones.

As mentioned earlier, researchers use reference management tools such as CiteU-
Like and Mendeley to see papers others have deemed to be important. Researchers
also use social media to identify articles of interest. They blog and tweet references
to new research and articles, and these are often reviewed informally online. Others
use Facebook for this purpose.

Finally, apps are being developed to make it easy to browse journal tables of contents and read articles from open access and library-licensed journals on an individual's tablet or smartphone. Examples include Docphin, www.docphin.com/; Docwise, http://docwi.se; Read by QXMD, www.qxmd.com/apps/read-by-qxmd-app; and Browzine, http://thirdiron.com/browzine/. Although these platforms have some difficulties, particularly in providing content from aggregators, they offer great promise in helping users stay current with the newest articles in their areas of research.

SUMMARY

Librarians serving the research community must have excellent searching skills, know the best databases for a topic, and understand how to use them effectively. PubMed (MEDLINE) for biomedicine and CINAHL for nursing are the databases typically used to initiate searching, but for comprehensive results, other research databases such as Embase, Scopus, or PsycINFO should be consulted. Full-text search engines such as Google Scholar can be useful in expanding searches beyond database searches. The citation databases Web of Science and Scopus can be used to trace the evolution and future development of the research reported in a paper, as well as in locating metrics.

As expert searchers, librarians can participate on research teams creating systematic reviews or in supporting investigators performing IACUC or animal alternative searches, and contribute in other ways as well. They must understand the importance of grey literature and how to find it. In the clinical setting, librarians need to provide point-of-care tools and assistance in finding answers to the more complex clinical questions preappraised evidence cannot answer.

The sheer volume of new information published annually can seem overwhelming. Health sciences librarians should also assist researchers in organizing their PDFs and references and in using new and traditional tools to keep up with the literature.

STUDY QUESTIONS

1. You are asked to help locate current research on the prevention of eating disorders in teenagers.
   a. Which two databases would you search and why?
   b. List your search strategy for one database.
   c. Look at your result set. Did you find articles to answer the question? Did you need to expand or focus your searches to make them useful?
2. Discuss the advantages and disadvantages of using point-of-care tools such as DynaMed and UpToDate to answer clinical questions.
3. A retired physician requests current research articles about the outcomes of deep brain stimulation in Parkinson's disease. He needs full-text articles freely available to the public.
   a. Where would you search?
   b. What search strategy did you use? Include any limits or filters you applied.

4. List the pros and cons of initiating a search for a literature review on a biomedical question in Google Scholar.
5. Based on your experience in collecting references and writing papers, what features would you look for in a reference manager? Which of the reference managers mentioned in this chapter might you use, and why?

REFERENCES

AHRQ (Agency for Healthcare Research, and Quality). 2013. *What Is Comparative Effectiveness Research/AHRQ Effective Health Care Program.* September 16. www.effectivehealthcare.ahrq.gov/index.cfm/what-is-comparative-effectiveness-research1/.

Allan, G. Michael, Victoria Ma, Sarah Aaron, Ben Vandermeer, Donna Manca, and Christina Korownyk. 2012. "Residents' Clinical Questions: How Are They Answered and are the Answers Helpful?" *Canadian Family Physician Médecin de Famille Canadien* 58, no. 6: e344–e351.

Anders, Michael E., and Dennis P. Evans. 2010. "Comparison of PubMed and Google Scholar Literature Searches." *Respiratory Care* 55, no. 5: 578–83.

Auckland, Mary. 2012. *Re-skilling for Research: An Investigation into the Role and Skills of Subject and Liaison Librarians Required to Effectively Support the Evolving Information Needs of Researchers.* RLUK. Research Libraries UK. www.rluk.ac.uk/files/RLUK%20Re-skilling.pdf.

Baethge, Christopher. 2012. "Impact Factor—a Useful Tool, but Not for All Purposes." *Deutsches Ärzteblatt international* 109, no. 15: 267–69. doi:10.3238/arztebl.2012.0267.

Banzi, Rita, Michela Cinquini, Alessandro Liberati et al. 2011. "Speed of Updating Online Evidence Based Point of Care Summaries: Prospective Cohort Analysis." *BMJ (Clinical Research ed.)* no. 343: d5856. doi:10.1136/bmj.d5856.

Bastian, Hilda, Paul Glasziou, and Iain Chalmers. 2010. "Seventy-Five Trials and Eleven Systematic Reviews a Day: How Will We Ever Keep Up?" *PLoS Medicine* 7, no. 9. doi:10.1371/journal.pmed.1000326.

Bright, Tiffani J., Anthony Wong, Ravi Dhurjati et al. 2012. "Effect of Clinical Decision-Support Systems: A Systematic Review." *Annals of Internal Medicine* 157, no. 1: 29–43. doi:10.7326/0003-4819-157-1-201207030-00450.

Burnham, J. F. 2006. "Scopus Database: A Review." *Biomedical Digital Libraries* 3, no. 1: 1.

Campbell, Rose, and Joan Ash. 2006. "An Evaluation of Five Bedside Information Products Using a User-centered, Task-oriented Approach." *Journal of the Medical Library Association* 94, no. 4 (October): 435–41, e206–e207.

Casazza, K., K. R. Fontaine, A. Astrup et al. 2013. "Myths, Presumptions, and Facts about Obesity." *New England Journal of Medicine* 368, no. 5: 446–54. doi:10.1056/NEJMsa1208051.

Chisholm, Robin, and John T. Finnell. 2012. "Emergency Department Physician Internet Use During Clinical Encounters." *American Medical Informatics Association Annual Symposium Proceedings* no. 2012: 1176–83.

Crowther, Mark, Wendy Lim, and Mark A. Crowther. 2010. "Systematic Review and Meta-analysis Methodology." *Blood* 116, no. 17: 3140–46. doi:10.1182/blood-2010-05-280883.

De Groote, Sandra L., and Rebecca Raszewski. 2012. "Coverage of Google Scholar, Scopus, and Web of Science: A Case Study of the H-Index in Nursing." *Nursing Outlook* 60, no. 6: 391–400. doi:10.1016/j.outlook.2012.04.007.

DiCenso, Alba, Liz Bayley, and R. Brian Haynes. 2009. "ACP Journal Club. Editorial: Accessing Preappraised Evidence: Fine-tuning the 5S Model into a 6S Model." *Annals of Internal Medicine* 151, no. 6: JC3-2, JC3-JC3.

Dudden, Rosalind F., and Shandra L. Protzko. 2011. "The Systematic Review Team: Contributions of the Health Sciences Librarian." *Medical Reference Services Quarterly* 30, no. 3 (July–September): 301–15. doi:10.1080/02763869.2011.590425.

Eden, Jill, Laura Levit, Sally Morton, and Alfred Berg, eds., Research Committee on Standards for Systematic Reviews of Comparative Effectiveness; and Institute of Medicine. 2011. *Finding What Works in Health Care: Standards for Systematic Reviews*. Washington, DC: National Academies Press.

Equator Network. 2013. *Reporting Guidelines*. September 15. www.equator-network.org/.

Eysenbach, Gunther. 2011. "Can Tweets Predict Citations? Metrics of Social Impact Based on Twitter and Correlation with Traditional Metrics of Scientific Impact." *Journal of Medical Internet Research* 13, no. 4: e123. doi:10.2196/jmir.2012.

Folb, Barbara L., Charles B. Wessel, and Leslie J. Czechowski. 2011. "Clinical and Academic Use of Electronic and Print Books: The Health Sciences Library System E-book Study at the University of Pittsburgh." *Journal of the Medical Library Association* 99, no. 3 (July): 218–28. doi:10.3163/1536-5050.99.3.009.

Garfield, Eugene. 2006. "The History and Meaning of the Journal Impact Factor." *Journal of the American Medical Association* 295, no. 1: 90–93. doi:10.1001/jama.295.1.90.

Gehanno, Jean-François, Laetitia Rollin, and Stefan Darmoni. 2013. "Is the Coverage of Google Scholar Enough to be Used Alone for Systematic Reviews?" *BMC Medical Informatics and Decision Making* 13: 7. doi:10.1186/1472-6947-13-7.

Google Scholar. 2013. "About." Google.com. Accessed October 27. http://scholar.google.com/intl/en-US/scholar/about.html.

Graber, Mark A., Bradley D. Randles, John W. Ely, and Jay Monnahan. 2008. "Answering Clinical Questions in the ED." *American Journal of Emergency Medicine* 26, no. 2: 144–47. doi:10.1016/j.ajem.2007.03.031.

Grefsheim, Suzanne F., and Jocelyn A. Rankin. 2007. "Information Needs and Information Seeking in a Biomedical Research Setting: A Study of Scientists and Science Administrators." *Journal of the Medical Library Association* 95, no. 4 (October): 426–34. doi:10.3163/1536-5050.95.4.426.

Hartel, Lynda J., and Fern M. Cheek. 2011. "Preferred Book Formats in an Academic Medical Center." *Journal of the Medical Library Association* 99, no. 4 (October): 313–17. doi:10.3163/1536-5050.99.4.011.

Hemminger, Bradley M., Dihui Lu, K. T. L. Vaughan, and Stephanie J. Adams. 2007. "Information Seeking Behavior of Academic Scientists." *Journal of the American Society for Information Science and Technology* 58, no. 14: 2205–25.

Higgins, Julian P. T., and Sally Green, eds. 2011. *Cochrane Handbook for Systematic Reviews of Interventions Version 5.1.0*. Updated March 2011. www.cochrane-handbook.org/.

Hirsch, Jorge E. 2005. "An Index to Quantify an Individual's Scientific Research Output." *Proceedings of the National Academy of Sciences of the United States of America* 102, no. 46 (November 15): 16569–72.

Hoeppner, Athena. 2012. "The Ins and Outs of Evaluating Web-Scale Discovery Services." *Computers in Libraries* 32, no. 3: 6–10.

Hopewell, Sally, Steve McDonald, J. Clarke Mike, and Matthias Egger. 2007. "Grey Literature in Meta-analyses of Randomized Trials of Health Care Interventions." *Cochrane Database of Systematic Reviews* (2). doi:10.1002/14651858.MR000010.pub3.

Hoy, Matthew. 2012. "An Introduction to Web Scale Discovery Systems." *Medical Reference Services Quarterly* 31, no. 3 (July–September): 323–29. doi:10.1080/02763869.2012.698186.

Husain, Iltifat. 2013. "The 20 Best Free iPhone Medical Apps for Healthcare Professionals, Edition 3." *iMedicalApps* (blog). September 16. www.imedicalapps.com/2013/06/free-iphone-medical-apps-physicians/.

Isaac, Thomas, Jie Zheng, and Ashish Jha. 2012. "Use of UpToDate and Outcomes in US Hospitals." *Journal of Hospital Medicine: An Official Publication of the Society of Hospital Medicine* 7, no. 2: 85–90. doi:10.1002/jhm.944.

Jacso, P. 2005. "As We May Search—Comparison of Major Features of the *Web of Science, Scopus,* and *Google Scholar* Citation-based and Citation-enhanced Databases." *Current Science* 89, no. 9: 1537–47.

Jaguszewski, Janice M., and Karen Williams. 2013. *New Roles for New Times: Transforming Liaison Roles in Research Libraries.* Washington, DC: Association of Research Libraries. www .arl.org/storage/documents/publications/NRNT-Liaison-Roles-final.pdf.

Jannot, Anne-Sophie, Thomas Agoritsas, Angèle Gayet-Ageron, and Thomas V. Perneger. 2013. "Citation Bias Favoring Statistically Significant Studies was Present in Medical Research." *Journal of Clinical Epidemiology* 66, no. 3: 296–301. doi:10.1016/j.jclinepi.2012.09.015.

Kawamoto, Kensaku, Caitlin A. Houlihan, E. Andrew Balas, and David F. Lobach. 2005. "Improving Clinical Practice Using Clinical Decision Support Systems: A Systematic Review of Trials to Identify Features Critical to Success." *BMJ (clinical research ed.)* 330, no. 7494. doi:10.1136/bmj.38398.500764.8F.

Ketchum, Andrea M., Ahlam A. Saleh, and Kwonho Jeong. 2011. "Type of Evidence behind Point-of-care Clinical Information Products: A Bibliometric Analysis." *Journal of Medical Internet Research* 13, no. 1. doi:10.2196/jmir.1539.

Kosteniuk, Julie G., Deborah G. Morgan, and Carl K. D'Arcy. 2013. "Use and Perceptions of Information among Family Physicians: Sources Considered Accessible, Relevant, and Reliable." *Journal of the Medical Library Association* 101, no. 1 (January): 32–37. doi:10.3163/1536-5050.101.1.006.

Kwok, Roberta. 2013. "Research Impact: Altmetrics Make Their Mark." *Nature* 500, no. 7463: 491–93.

Lu, Zhiyong. 2011. "PubMed and Beyond: A Survey of Web Tools for Searching Biomedical Literature." *Database: The Journal of Biological Databases and Curation* no. 2011. doi:10.1093/database/baq036.

Mastrangelo, Giuseppe, Emanuela Fadda, Carlo R. Rossi, Emanuele Zamprogno, Alessandra Buja, and Luca Cegolon. 2010. "Literature Search on Risk Factors for Sarcoma: PubMed and Google Scholar May Be Complementary Sources." *BMC Research Notes* no. 3: 131. doi:10.1186/1756-0500-3-131.

McGowan, Jessie, and Margaret Sampson. 2005. "Systematic Reviews Need Systematic Searchers." *Journal of the Medical Library Association* 93, no. 1 (January): 74–80.

Meerpohl, Joerg J., Florian Herrle, Gerd Antes, and Erik von Elm. 2012. "Scientific Value of Systematic Reviews: Survey of Editors of Core Clinical Journals." *PloS One* 7, no. 5. doi:10.1371/journal.pone.0035732.

Miles, Alisha. 2011. "PubMed Health." *Journal of the Medical Library Association* 99, no. 3 (July): 265–66. doi:10.3163/1536-5050.99.3.018.

Moher, David, Jennifer Tetzlaff, Andrea C. Tricco, Margaret Sampson, and Douglas G. Altman. 2007. "Epidemiology and Reporting Characteristics of Systematic Reviews." *PLoS Medicine* 4, no. 3: e78. doi:10.1371/journal.pmed.0040078.

Moher, D., A. Tsertsvadze, A. C. Tricco et al. 2008. "When and How to Update Systematic Reviews." *Cochrane Database of Systematic Reviews* (1): MR000023. doi:10.1002/14651858.MR000023.pub3.

Moher, David, Alessandro Liberati, Jennifer Tetzlaff, Douglas G. Altman, and the Prisma Group. 2009. "Preferred Reporting Items for Systematic Reviews and Meta-Analyses: The PRISMA Statement." *PLoS Medicine* 6, no. 7 doi:10.1371/journal.pmed.1000097.

Ndosi, M., and R. Newell. 2010. "Medicine Information Sources Used by Nurses at the Point of Care." *Journal of Clinical Nursing* 19, no. 17/18: 2659–61. doi:10.1111/j.1365-2702.2010.03266.x.

New York Academy of Medicine. 2013. *What is Grey Literature?* September 16. www.greylit. org/about.

NICHSR (National Information Center on Health Services Research, and Health Care Technology). 2013. *NLM Resources for Informing Comparative Effectiveness* [Applications, Forms, Registrations]. U.S. National Library of Medicine. September 16. www.ncbi.nlm.nih.gov/pubmed/http://www.nlm.nih.gov/nichsr/cer/cerqueries.html#definition.

Niu, Xi, Bradley M. Hemminger, Cory Lown et al. 2010. "National Study of Information Seeking Behavior of Academic Researchers in the United States." *Journal of the American Society for Information Science and Technology* 61, no. 5: 869–90.

Nourbakhsh, E., R. Nugent, H. Wang, C. Cevik, and K. Nugent. 2012. "Medical Literature Searches: A Comparison of PubMed and Google Scholar." *Health Information and Libraries Journal* 29, no. 3: 214–22. doi:10.1111/j.1471-1842.2012.00992.x.

Patel, Vanash M., Hutan Ashrafian, Alex Almoudaris et al. 2013. "Measuring Academic Performance for Healthcare Researchers with the H Index: Which Search Tool Should Be Used?" *Medical Principles and Practice: International Journal of the Kuwait University, Health Science Centre* 22, no. 2: 178–83. doi:10.1159/000341756.

Prorok, J. C., E. C. Iserman, N. L. Wilczynski, and R. B. Haynes. 2012. "The Quality, Breadth, and Timeliness of Content Updating Vary Substantially for 10 Online Medical Texts: An Analytic Survey." *Journal of Clinical Epidemiology* 65, no. 12: 1289–95. doi:10.1016/j.jclinepi.2012.05.003.

Russell, William Moy Stratton, and Rex Leonard Burch. 1959. *The Principles of Humane Experimental Technique.* London: Methuen Publishing.

Scherer, Roberta W., Patricia Langenberg, and Erik von Elm. 2007. "Full Publication of Results Initially Presented in Abstracts." In *Cochrane Database of Systematic Reviews*, 2, no. 2. doi:10.1002/14651858.MR000005.pub3.

Schopfel, Joachim. 2010. *Towards a Prague Definition of Grey Literature.* GreyNet, Grey Literature Network Service. www.opengrey.eu/item/display/10068/700015.

Shariff, S. Z., S. A. Bejaimal, J. M. Sontrop et al. 2013. "Retrieving Clinical Evidence: A Comparison of PubMed and Google Scholar for Quick Clinical Searches." *Journal of Medical Internet Research* 15, no. 8: e164. doi:10.2196/jmir.2624.

Shariff, Salimah Z., Jessica M. Sontrop, Arthur V. Iansavichus et al. 2012. "Availability of Renal Literature in Six Bibliographic Databases." *Clinical Kidney Journal* 5, no. 6: 610–17. doi:10.1093/ckj/sfs152.

Thompson, Jolinda, Kathe Obrig, and Laura Abate. 2013. "Web-Scale Discovery in an Academic Health Sciences Library: Development and Implementation of the EBSCO Discovery Service." *Medical Reference Services Quarterly* 32, no. 1 (January–March): 26–41. doi:10.1080/02763869.2013.749111.

U.S. National Library of Medicine. 2013a. *Fact Sheet Medical Subject Headings (MeSH®)* [Fact Sheets]. U.S. National Library of Medicine. www.nlm.nih.gov/factsheets/mesh.ht.

———. 2013b. *Fact Sheet MEDLINE, PubMed, and PMC (PubMed Central): How Are They Different?* [Fact Sheets]. U.S. National Library of Medicine. September 16. www.nlm.nih.gov/pubs/factsheets/dif_med_pub.html.

Walters, William H. 2011. "Comparative Recall and Precision of Simple and Expert Searches in Google Scholar and Eight Other Databases." *Portal: Libraries and the Academy* 11, no. 4: 971–1006.

Yuan, Y., and R. H. Hunt. 2009. "Systematic Reviews: The Good, the Bad, and the Ugly." *American Journal of Gastroenterology* 104, no. 5: 1086–92. doi:10.1038/ajg.2009.118.

Zhang, Yingting. 2012. "Comparison of Select Reference Management Tools." *Medical Reference Services Quarterly* 31, no. 1 (January–March): 45–60. doi:10.1080/02763869.2012.641841.

CHAPTER 9

Outreach Services in Health Sciences Libraries

Michele R. Tennant

INTRODUCTION

Chapter 9 covers library outreach, an activity that has multiple meanings and little consistent definition among the libraries that practice it (Fama et al., 2005; Carter and Seaman, 2011). The term "outreach" may describe services to users external to the institution—for example, to nonaffiliated health care providers, hospitals, or health care consumers (McGowan, 2000). Outreach services may also be provided to those within a library's home institution, whether students, faculty, staff, administrators, laboratory researchers, or clinicians (Fama et al., 2005). Two major components of outreach are generally considered: "services offered by libraries" and "promotion of these services" (Carter and Seaman, 2011).

For the purposes of this chapter, the term "outreach" will be used to describe reaching out to clients (internal or external) to meet an information need and/or promote the library's resources, services, or existence, with the intent of developing a long-term relationship with those clients. A variety of methods for internal outreach performed by health sciences liaison/**embedded librarians** and **informationists** (both clinical and basic science) will be discussed. Internal outreach to less traditional and/or newer entities, such as offices of research and clinical and translational science institutes, will also be introduced. External outreach will be illustrated with examples of health-related outreach to senior citizens, dental public health care practitioners, health care consumers, high school students, and patients. Information on funding such endeavors is introduced. Finally, the chapter ends with a discussion of promotional outreach, the importance of a strong marketing plan, and attributes of successful outreach programs.

INTERNAL OUTREACH

Liaison Librarian Programs

Liaison librarian programs are frequently seen in academic health sciences libraries. The cornerstone of liaison services is the personal connection that the liaison makes to individuals, academic units, and programs, emphasizing two-way communication between library patrons and the liaison (Shedlock, 1983). In liaison programs, a specific librarian is usually responsible for a specific user population—perhaps segmented by discipline (nursing), rank (faculty member), cohort (second-year medical student), role (clinical versus basic science), or other distinction. That specific librarian is responsible for communication, and depending on the liaison model, one or more (or perhaps all) services for those constituents. One specific contact/service provider makes it easy for clients as they are not required to identify multiple contacts (this staff member for ILL, this librarian for instruction, another for consultations, and so forth), and facilitates the liaison's development of close professional relationships with clients, a key for success. Potential benefits to clients are clear; likewise, benefits to the library and librarians are also apparent. In a well-designed and strategic liaison program, information dissemination is a two-way street, with clients learning about library services and resources from the liaison, and liaisons learning about clients' information needs, academic unit culture, new academic programs, and client expectations of the library. Liaison programs provide libraries visibility, and can engender positive feelings and support.

A number of liaison librarian program models exist, with a primary difference between them being the level of subject expertise exhibited by the liaison. The importance of subject specialization has been debated in detail (Pratt, 1991; Ryans, Suresh, and Zhang, 1995), as has the question of whether adequate subject expertise can be learned on the job and through continuing education courses, or whether liaisons must have formal training in the disciplines they serve. In any case, a number of activities may be undertaken to increase liaisons' subject knowledge, such as joining appropriate subunits of the Medical Library Association and attending local seminars (Cataldo et al., 2006).

The University of Florida's Health Science Center Libraries (UFHSCL) is an example of a well-planned and implemented liaison librarian program that relies heavily on subject expertise and has evolved over time with changing circumstances of clients and the library. Developed out of the library's strategic plan, the program was meant to be the "unifying theme" for library services and communication (Tennant et al., 2001). Liaisons are assigned to a particular academic unit or group of subject-related patrons, with the expectation that this will facilitate the provision of focused, customized, subject-specific services; the development of close professional relationships with clients; and learning by the liaison about client information needs, unit politics, priorities, and culture. At the UFHSCL, liaisons provide all of the subject-specific information services for their assigned units—all teaching, consultations, and collection development, with an emphasis on course-integrated instruction. By 2001, more than fifty potential liaison activities were identified for the program: traditional services, such as providing instruction and collection development for liaisons' assigned units; as well as "softer" activities, such as supporting best practices and developing close relationships with clients (Tennant et al., 2001). Over the years the program has evolved, with two liaisons being funded by academic units for some time period, and with "functional liaisons" being added in the areas of basic biomedical sciences, consumer health and community engagement, and clinical and translational research. These functional liaisons work with clients from any unit on campus in need of support in these areas (Tennant et al., 2012).

Alternatively, a "facilitator model" liaison program was developed by librarians at the University of Texas Southwestern Medical Center Library. The primary role of these liaisons is to "facilitate communication between their departments and the library" (Crossno et al., 2012: 172). Because many of the liaisons in this model are not librarians or subject experts, an extensive training series was developed and ran the gamut from basic reference skills and technology support, to library policies and procedures, an understanding of campus culture, and leadership and time management skills. Aside from the level of subject specialization, this model differs from that of Tennant et al. (2001, 2006) in that liaisons develop one point of contact per assigned unit, rather than communicating with all members of that unit. The facilitator model, with liaisons concentrating on communication rather than subject expertise or expert information skills, may be feasible in smaller libraries including those in hospitals, which often have difficulty fielding a liaison program due to lower staff sizes. These libraries may also benefit from providing liaison services solely to limited segments of an institution—for example, those that most need them, or those with which partnerships would be most beneficial. Choices should be "strategic" and "symbiotic" (Livingston, 2003).

Some liaison librarians are "embedded" in the workplace of their clients—academic departments, research laboratories, administrative suites, or perhaps the clinic. Embedded librarians may or may not have strong subject expertise, but they are expected to develop strong professional relationships with the groups in which they are embedded. Liaison librarians at the Welch Medical Library (Johns Hopkins University) were placed in "touchdown suites" in research and clinical venues, providing information services where researchers, clinicians, and patients needed them—the clients' environment, not the library. Such venues included the Hopkins Population Center and an oncology clinic (Oliver, 2005). Librarians at the Arizona Health Sciences campus were embedded into a new research building (Bio5) with the aim of taking advantage of the synergy around the interdisciplinary inhabitants—a wide variety of basic scientists (Freiburger and Kramer, 2009). Researchers from areas as diverse as agriculture, the basic sciences, engineering, medicine, and pharmacy shared Bio5, and it was expected that increased levels of research collaboration and synergy would produce intense information needs. Word of mouth soon led to librarians embedded in the Colleges of Pharmacy, Public Health, and Nursing. Conversely, the first embedded librarians, those in Bio5, moved back to the library, as basic science researchers were far less interested in consultation or searching services.

Liaison and embedded librarian services can be quite time-consuming, especially when liaisons are responsible for all services provided to a particular constituency; constituencies are large and/or varied; or liaisons are well-integrated into the framework of the units, serving on various committees, attending seminars, and participating in unit meetings and social events (Schulte, 2011). Increases in instructional workload and other duties may offset the advantages of any time saved via subject specialization. Successes in instruction may lead to more classes and assignments, and visibility often creates more in-office client questions. Because liaison programs often result in clients contacting liaisons directly and a subsequent reduction in reference desk questions, some libraries have closed or restructured their reference desks to provide liaisons with the time and mobility necessary to get out of the library, serve clients where they live, and integrate more fully into the activities of their assigned units (Lubker et al., 2010; Schulte, 2011; Tennant et al., 2012). See Chapter 7 for discussion of the reference desk.

Informationists/Information Specialists in Context (ISIC)

Informationists (also known as information specialists in context, or ISICs), provide the ultimate in outreach to clients, in that they are often sited in the context of the work (clinical, research, administrative, or educational settings), and provide highly specialized and customized information services. In some ways these professionals combine what is most unique and successful from subject-specific liaison and embedded librarian programs, with the added feature, by definition, of having both extensive information and domain knowledge.

Davidoff and Florance proposed this new model of health information delivery in 2000. Several factors provided impetus for the informationist concept: Clinicians in general do not possess expert literature searching skills, and even if they did, they have little time to search for or filter the disparate biomedical literature. Clinicians rarely ask librarians or other information professionals for assistance. The disconnect between these facts and the information gaps that occur in the clinic provide an impediment to patient care. The informationist concept was built on the previous work of clinical rounding librarians (Lamb, 1982; Lipscomb, 2000). Although informationist programs at different institutions have a number of characteristics in common (Rankin, Grefsheim, and Canto, 2008), the specific tasks performed among informationists are variable, as those tasks need be determined by the context in which the informationist find himself or herself (Whitmore, Grefsheim, and Rankin, 2008). In order for the informationist concept to be adopted widely, a number of issues must be resolved, including formal training needs, credentialing, reporting structure, funding, liability, and clinician and health system buy-in (Sathe, Jerome, and Giuse, 2007). In 2002, the Informationist Conference was hosted by the Medical Library Association (MLA) and funded by and held at the National Library of Medicine (NLM) (Shipman et al., 2002). Participants and speakers from numerous fields—health care workers (physicians, nurses, pharmacists), biomedical researchers, librarians and library school educators, administrators, government agencies, potential funders—discussed over two days many of the issues listed above, and attended presentations by practicing informationists. Following the conference, an MLA Task Force on the concept was formed, and a consultant study and final report were produced (Giuse, Sathe, and Jerome, 2006).

The informationist program at the National Institutes of Health (NIH) Library was developed in 2001. This library exists to serve the information needs of clinicians, researchers, and administrators who work at NIH, and is separate from NLM (although both reside on the NIH campus in Bethesda, Maryland). This program was "designed to integrate information services, not just resources, into the work environment" (Cooper, 2011: 190) and to "increase the return on investment of the larger labs [at NIH]" (Shedlock and Attwood, 2013: 9), and it has been a model for implementing informationist methodologies. Initially created to work with clinical teams, the program has evolved to meet the needs of basic science researchers and administrators, with subsequent roles expanding from clinical rounding and expert searching to **bioinformatics** analysis and database development among others (Whitmore, Grefsheim, and Rankin, 2008). Subject-specific informationists are embedded into research and clinical teams, whereas those with cross-cutting domain knowledge (such as expertise in bioinformatics) serve the entire institute. Unlike liaison librarians, who are assigned to a department but generally work with individual faculty members or students, the informationists at the NIH library, by definition, work as a member of a team and are matched with them based on educational background (clinical or science) and/or interest of the informationist.

Informationists at the NIH Library keep researchers up-to-date on the literature and provide evidence that can change clinical practice or the direction of laboratory research. Clients' time savings, facilitated by the informationists, were key to program success, given how time-limited clinicians and researchers are. The fact that the informationist becomes part of the clinical or research team, often embedded in the workplace of the practitioner, is another key to the success of the program. This integration allows the informationist to learn more about the science, culture, tools, and information needs of the team, and facilitates the creation of training and services to meet those information needs in context (Robison, Ryan, and Cooper, 2009).

Two informative studies endeavored to identify distinctions between informationist services and those of other information professionals. A systematic review of the literature and subsequent coding of 113 articles helped determine how far the informationist concept had penetrated the literature, what attributes were exhibited in model programs, education and training needs, success factors, challenges, and other characteristics (Rankin, Grefsheim, and Canto, 2008). Four attributes were identified as defining for informationist programs:

- "Formal training in both information science and a subject domain expertise." On-the-job training alone is not sufficient, but instead requires formal degree programs, practical experience (such as using bioinformatics tools in a research laboratory), or additional training through workshops or participation in graduate level courses.
- "Deep understanding of work culture." Informationists understand the culture of the group with which they are working—for example, how medicine is performed, how basic scientists use the scientific method, preferred modes of communication, and information seeking-behavior of clinicians and researchers.
- "In-context work as a team member and/or expert consultant." The work that is done by the informationist is part of a collaborative team effort.
- "Critical appraisal and literature synthesis and/or complex bioscience data analysis." Informationists are expected to not only find relevant information, but also be able to appraise, synthesize, apply, and analyze that information.

A second study used a logic model to assess whether the informationist role was new and distinct from the "general medical librarian (GML)" (Cooper, 2011). A number of differences between the two roles were identified in the NIH setting. Apparent differences included education/training (more generalist for GML, subject-specific and ongoing for informationists); locus of service (inside [GML]) versus outside (informationist) the library; role (GML) or lack thereof (informationists) in acquiring materials, or in critical appraisal and synthesis of the literature

(GML no, informationist yes). Levels of ongoing client interactions, working across specialties versus deeply in one or a handful of specialties, and characteristics of deliverables all lent credence to differences between general medical librarians and informationists.

The Eskind Biomedical Library at Vanderbilt University Medical Center provides a model of clinical informationist services: reaching out to clinicians, providing information services as part of a clinical rounding team, answering questions at morning report, providing expert searching and critical appraisal and synthesis of the literature. As an expert, the informationist identifies and solves information needs. All four attributes of "classic informationist programs" are apparent at Vanderbilt: Informationists have a large skill set with deep knowledge in terms of information seeking and concepts of clinical medicine; they are expert searchers who are able to critically appraise the literature and synthesize for clinicians the information that they find; they understand completely the culture and environment in which they work; and they serve as fully contributing members of the health care team. An essential component of the development of the program at Vanderbilt was "understanding the vital importance of participating in an environment to comprehend it" (Giuse et al., 2005: 250)—the ultimate in outreach to clinicians. Library administration has made the commitment to place its informationists squarely within the clinical realm, not as an "extra" activity, but as a priority that is supported and funded (Plutchak, 2002). Integration of informationists into the clinical team at Vanderbilt is further evidenced by the fact that informationists have access to the electronic patient record, and queries from clinicians come directly to the informationists through this system. Being privy to such patient information allows the informationist to locate information specific to the patient's case (Giuse et al., 2005).

Outreach to basic biomedical science researchers can be challenging. Such researchers are major constituents of academic health centers and research institutes, often outnumbering their clinical research counterparts and sometimes bringing in the highest level of research dollars to the institution. Basic science researchers have extensive information needs, and it might be expected that they are an obvious and willing audience for library outreach and use. However, numerous investigations have shown these researchers to be less likely to use or consider using the library than would be expected. Scientists are trained to be skeptics and may trust their own work more than that of librarians (Grefsheim, Franklin, and Cunningham, 1991).

> I participate in walking rounds going from room to room, and I am considered part of the health care team. I carry an iPad; and although some questions are easily addressed at the point of care, others are more complex and require extensive literature searches after formal rounds. These efforts have a direct impact on patient care and treatment decisions, and expand outreach to our clinical staff. Participating in clinical rounding is exciting and challenging, especially in the neuro and trauma ICUs because of the uniqueness and complexity of patients' illnesses/injuries; and often the timeliness of information provision is critical.
>
> *Gretchen Kuntz, MSW, MLIS, director, Borland Health Sciences Library, University of Florida-Jacksonville*

Information-seeking behaviors are consistent; these researchers infrequently use the library's website, advanced search features of databases, or physical space; rely on their colleagues and what they learn at professional meetings to meet their information needs; do not know what services are provided by their home libraries; believe that their graduate students learn from their peers or mentors and do not need library instruction; and are not interested in such instruction for themselves (Grefsheim and Rankin, 2007). Researchers' and information professionals' assumptions regarding the role of libraries in accessing information do not match. Although librarians consider the library to be the center of the information universe, basic sciences researchers often think of the library as the last resort, used only when they cannot find information from their desktop or through colleagues at their home institution or elsewhere, when doing so would be too expensive, or when starting work in a new field. For example, two years after implementation of the University of Vermont's Dana Medical Library's liaison program, interactions with clinical departments had increased more than 50 percent, but no change was observed among the basic science departments (Haines et al., 2010).

Over the past several decades, basic biomedical science research has become increasingly molecular. The **"omics"**—genomics, proteomics, metabolomics, and others are primary sciences that require the use of fact-based databases and analysis tools. Computational methods are used to make sense of data and solve biological problems. This research requires the use of resources that go beyond the literature and into the realm of sequence, structure, expression, and other biological data. Many of these databases and tools are freely available over the web (such as GenBank or BLAST), but numerous others are commercial products that require licensing. Library-based support for such basic science research often includes database instruction, data retrieval and analysis consultations, and providing access to resources. Although such support is often referred to as library-based "bioinformatics" support, the majority of clients using these services are not bioinformaticians or bioinformaticists (who build the tools), but instead researchers from other disciplines, such as molecular biology, biochemistry, physiology, and genetics, who need to use the tools to generate hypotheses and conduct research.

Prior to the mid-1990s, most library outreach to basic biomedical researchers was related to literature searching and resources. One of the earliest instances of library-based bioinformatics support began in 1995, when the University of Washington's Health Science Library hired a PhD biologist, Stuart Yarfitz, to provide molecular biology information services (Yarfitz and Ketchell, 2000). Yarfitz immediately performed a thorough information needs assessment through survey and researcher focus groups, as a key to success would be the development of researcher-centered, value-laden services. Through the assessment, it became clear that researchers had numerous information needs but were unaware of many of the bioinformatics-related resources available to them. Yarfitz developed a full-service library-based molecular biology program, which included advanced consultation services, database and analysis tools skills training, graduate level courses, a web-based Molecular Biologist Toolkit, and accessible networked biological information resources. In order to reach out to this challenging client base, Yarfitz introduced the program through letters to department chairs, gave presentations at numerous basic science departmental meetings, and developed an electronic mailing list of more than 400 basic science researchers. A number of other libraries embraced these specialized services as a means to perform outreach to the basic biomedical science research community; these programs were described in a special issue of the *Journal of the Medical Library Association*, published in July 2006.

Developing collaborations with other institutional units is an excellent strategy for performing outreach to researchers, as the synergy between libraries and other research support units (e.g., genome centers and biotechnology cores) can foster relationships and facilitate the creation and coordination of services. Careful planning between units can create complementary rather than competitive services and can fill existing service gaps, and shared user contacts can broaden the user group of each entity. Information professionals working with researchers should think broadly about potential partners and collaborators: computational biology groups; life sciences departments and institutes; sequencing cores; supercomputing centers; and biomedical informatics and bioinformatics departments. "Visibility is key to building collaborations" (Lyon et al., 2006: 330) and can be gained through a number of potential activities, including hosting courses from the National Center for Biotechnology Information (NCBI), using liaison librarian relationships, participating in relevant journal clubs, and heavily publicizing the library's courses and services.

Outreach to researchers should begin before programs have been designed or are in place, as buy-in by key stakeholders and clients is essential for success. The University of Pittsburgh Health Sciences Library System identified relevant stakeholders, including faculty leaders from basic research, computational biology, bioinformatics, and human genetics to join their planning committee (Epstein, 2006), thus paving the way for the program's success. Pittsburgh's molecular biology and genetics information service includes training workshops, graduate course lectures, bioinformatics consultation services, a molecular biology

In today's big data/genomic era, it is logical that a common-use facility such as a library would include bioinformatics databases and software in its collection. Libraries have the infrastructure in place to offer hands-on training, consultations, and online tutorials. We have spent more than ten years performing outreach and building our service to support a broad spectrum of users— postdocs, students, techs, clinicians, tenured faculty—whom we reach through a weekly e-mail announcement, a blog, our website, and by word-of-mouth. It is a challenge to keep up-to-date with all that is happening in the bioinformatics world—we are learning along with our researchers.

Carrie Iwema, PhD, MLS, AHIP, information specialist in molecular biology; and Ansuman Chattopadhyay, PhD, head, Molecular Biology Information Service, University of Pittsburgh Health Sciences Library System, Pittsburgh, PA

web portal, and licensing of software and databases (Chattopadhyay et al., 2006). This program has been so successful that it now employs two specialists in molecular biology resources.

A number of other such library-based bioinformatics programs have been successful enough in their outreach to researchers to warrant the employ of more than one bioinformationist, including the Becker Medical Library at Washington

University in St. Louis Medical School, Harvard Medical School's Countway Medical Library, and the University of Southern California's Norris Medical Library. These programs tend to provide advanced services and employ, for the most part, bioinformationists with advanced degrees in science or medicine, with or without a library degree. Although some questions remain about the degree requirements necessary to provide advanced and full-service bioinformatics support (Epstein, 2006; Geer, 2006), evidence suggests that librarians with disparate educational backgrounds can perform varying but useful levels of bioinformatics, molecular, and genetic information support (Osterbur et al., 2006). The literature contains a number of papers that provide information on training programs and strategies for librarians and other information professionals interested in performing outreach and providing services to basic science researchers (Helms et al., 2004; Cleveland, Holmes, and Philbrick, 2012).

The work of bioinformationists and clinical informationists described above represents only the tip of the opportunity iceberg when health sciences library administration decides to pursue outreach to researchers through the use of informationists. The National Institutes of Health have begun offering "administrative supplements" for informationist services in support of preexisting research grants. NLM (2013) has made available the list of funded projects for 2012, and the activities performed by informationists are far-ranging and substantive. These activities include improving data workflows, enhancing databases through the addition of GIS (geographic information systems) data, assisting with systematics reviews, applying metadata, capturing medical billing information, and digital interview recordings, to name a few.

Additional Populations for Internal Outreach

The discussions above regarding liaison/embedded librarians and informationists have concentrated on major user groups, such as teaching faculty, students, clinicians, and basic science researchers. Given the numerous and diverse information needs at typical academic health centers, research institutions, hospitals, and corporations, the array of client groups that can be approached for outreach is endless. The following section illustrates just a few of these specific groups.

Basic Science Graduate Students

Graduate students in the basic biomedical sciences have a number of responsibilities—taking courses; performing original laboratory research; writing theses, dissertations, and journal articles; taking preliminary, qualifying, and final oral/written examinations; and in some disciplines, teaching laboratories or undergraduate courses. As such, they have intense information needs and are prime candidates for library outreach. These students are learning the skills that they will use for the rest of their careers, including locating, managing, and synthesizing the literature. Basic biomedical science is intensely molecular in nature, so these students require bioinformatics resources, just as their research mentors do (Yarfitz and Ketchell, 2000; Tennant, 2005; Chattopadhyay et al., 2006). Because many PhD programs in these disciplines do not require a master's degree, PhD students may be matriculating fresh from their undergraduate program and cannot be assumed to be any more skilled than their MS colleagues in literature searching, information or data management, or use of molecular analysis tools and resources. Mentors' attitudes toward libraries, as described above, can serve as an impediment to outreach efforts (Tomaszewski, 2012), as students generally learn from their mentors or others in the laboratory.

Outreach to these students is much simpler if the graduate program in question has students enter as a single cohort and students take orientations and some core courses together; this generally means that one point of contact may exist for the program, perhaps a high-level educational administrator or a faculty member serving as director of the program. For example, at the University of Florida the majority of PhD students in the basic biomedical sciences are admitted as a cohort into the College of Medicine's Interdisciplinary Program in Biomedical Sciences. The basic sciences librarian was integrated into orientation, literature and NCBI database instruction, and consultation at the academic program planning stage (Tennant, 2005).

Librarians at the Dana Medical Library at the University of Vermont restructured their freestanding walk-in instructional program to make it more attractive to basic science graduate students, who do not matriculate as a single cohort and are traditionally difficult to reach. Based on faculty input, librarians developed a series of interrelated workshops on databases and skills needed by research scientists (O'Malley and Delwiche, 2012). Evaluation of the series identified the sessions that graduate students found most useful (literature searching, PubMed, EndNote, scholarly publishing), and underscored the importance of faculty buy-in and assistance in marketing efforts.

Research Postdoctoral Associates

A postdoctoral associate (postdoc) is a researcher who has completed the PhD and performs research, usually in the laboratory of a specific, more senior researcher (**principal investigator, or PI**). Much of the actual research product created at universities is created by postdocs. Most postdocs have two major responsibilities, performing the research related to the interests of the laboratory's PI and, very often, running the lab on a day-to-day basis. Postdocs rarely have instructional responsibilities, and, as such, their primary information needs revolve around their research, laboratory administration, and finding funding or a position so that they may become PIs. The biomedical sciences employ large numbers of postdocs, so outreach and service to postdocs fall under the purview of the health sciences librarian. Postdoc assignments are considered apprenticeships—this is a time of intense learning for the associate, and, thus, an intense period of information need. In terms of scientific information, postdocs have the same needs, and often library perceptions, as their PIs.

Few studies of the information needs or information-seeking behavior of postdoctoral associates exist. Science PhD students and postdocs at Georgia State University were surveyed to explore their information needs and perceptions of the library (Tomaszewski, 2012). Results of this study paralleled those described above for faculty in the basic biomedical sciences—most respondents did not know the name of their science librarian; the majority had never communicated with their librarian; and respondents received their literature searching assistance primarily from their major adviser and colleagues, but very rarely from librarians. Results of a national survey of postdocs suggested that postdoctoral associates lack an understanding of what traditional resources and services are available at their home libraries (McCrillis et al., 2012). Bioinformatics, data management, and statistical analysis were identified as major areas of information need, with identifying funding opportunities and potential research collaborators deemed "challenging." These results suggest that libraries reaching out to postdoctoral associates should expand their visions of "core" information needs and services, a theme that echoes the information needs of basic science researchers in general. Because postdocs get little experience teaching but may need to teach extensively when they become professors, librarians should consider potential contributions to preparing postdocs for this role. Although postdocs traditionally have been a difficult group to identify and reach, the recent creation of postdoctoral affairs offices on academic campuses facilitates outreach to this population.

Clinical and Translational Science Researchers/Institutes

As described in chapters 3 and 10, the Clinical and Translational Research (CTR) community comprises a diverse workforce with numerous information needs related to clinical, basic, and translational science; community health and engagement; and administration. As such, it is an obvious community for library outreach. A robust organizational scheme of fourteen Key Function Areas (KFA) serves as national and local priorities for institutions that have received Clinical and Translational Science Awards (CTSA). Current and potential library support for KFAs includes a number of activities: offer intensive information consultation and expert literature search, coordinate vendor training and provide library-based information workshops, provide basic bioinformatics and biostatistics support, locate national resources within the CTSA consortium, serve on campus-wide committees and workgroups related to regulatory knowledge and responsible conduct of research, perform systematic reviews, assess research impact, and serve on community engagement leadership teams, among others (Holmes et al., 2013: 328–29).

Collaboration is an essential component of clinical and translational science research, as such research is characterized by an interdisciplinary team-based approach. Health sciences librarians can facilitate researcher collaboration through a number of means: bring researchers together using

Libraries can not only support collaboration, but through outreach efforts, parlay it into significant partnerships for libraries; collaboration support has been identified as a priority area for the library. We connect people on campus and help them identify needed expertise or resources through the published literature or research representation platforms such as VIVO. We offer training to help people efficiently use these tools. We keep aware of trends and resources in the larger scholarly ecosystem of "team science." Finally, social network analysis and visualizations allow us to assist groups to understand their own patterns of collaboration.

Kristi L. Holmes, PhD, director,
Galter Health Sciences Library,
Northwestern University, Chicago, IL

the "Collaborating with Strangers" (CoLAB) method, an approach similar to "speed dating" (DeFarber, 2012); support researcher profile systems such as SciVal or VIVO (Garcia-Milian et al., 2013); run seminar series and other events (Tennant, 2005; Lyon et al., 2006); create research networking visualizations to help characterize collaboration (Hunt, Whipple, and McGowan, 2012); and create space in the library for collaboration (Adamson and Bunnett, 2002).

Another area in which librarians and informationists are reaching out to clinical and translational science researchers is through the assessment of research impact and dissemination. CSTA-funded institutions must track the impact of research performed with CTSA support, and many of the tools used and skill sets required to do so fall under the purview of health sciences libraries. Therefore, outreach to clinical and translational science administrators involved in tracking and evaluation makes sense. The staff at the Becker Medical Library has developed a model to assess the impact of research, which may be modified for use at other institutions (Sarli, Dubinsky, and Holmes, 2010). Partnering with administrators on impact studies represents a prime example of a library providing a transformative outreach service.

Our campus ICTS Tracking and Evaluation (T&E) Team represents an interdisciplinary team of statisticians, evaluation specialists, social scientists, clinical investigators, public health investigators, a librarian, a bioinformaticist, and project/business managers—all contributing unique perspectives. Outreach efforts related to impact include capturing publication data, reconciling author variants, identifying bibliometric analyses to use for publication data, and assisting with development of survey instruments to capture qualitative data. Working toward a common goal for our campus as a member of the T&E Team is a rewarding experience and has far surpassed any expectation of what I imagined myself doing as a librarian.

Cathy C. Sarli, MLS, AHIP, scholarly communications specialist, Becker Medical Library, Washington University, St. Louis, MO

Outreach to Committees, Task Forces, and Work Groups

Medical librarians have a long history of service on college-level curriculum committees, a partnership that provides information assistance to clients, keeps committee members apprised of resources and services available in the library, provides librarians with an understanding of client information needs and how they might be supported, and improves library visibility (Francis and Fisher, 1997). Such advantages can ensue through outreach to many types of committees in the academic health center, hospital, research institute, or other venue. Liaison librarians in particular have a number of opportunities to become involved in the work of their academic units.

Committees related to research regulation, such as Institutional Review Boards (IRB) and Institutional Animal Care and Use Committees (IACUC), are especially attractive targets for library outreach. These committees are intended to protect humans and animals during the research process, and members of these committees have a number of information needs. The research librarian at the Ohio State

Medical Center supports two IRBs (Cheek, 2010). One, the Clinical Scientific Review Committee (CSRC), provides required review of the science contained in protocols prior to submission to the Cancer IRB. Although she performs a number of other activities including instruction, this librarian's primary contribution to the committee is to complete comprehensive literature searches to support the protocols that are submitted to the Cancer IRB. As a voting member of the CSRC, she reads the submitted protocols as would a nonscientist and evaluates the reading levels of the informed consent documentation. Librarians at Eastern Virginia Medical School provide expert and comprehensive literature searches and quality filtering of articles to support the reviews of IRB members. Having a librarian performing outreach to the IRB resulted in numerous benefits to the library, including a better understanding of the research occurring at the institution, high profile visibility, and strengthened quality control for searches (Robinson and Gehle, 2005).

I became involved with the Nursing Research Council through an invitation to provide instruction and am now a voting member. The council is involved with the production of new knowledge at the hospital and oversees the nursing fellowship program, a journal club, and other activities. I provide quarterly sessions introducing hospital nurses to evidence-based and other library resources. I am a member of the College of Nursing Writing Support Group, which provides feedback to faculty and student authors preparing manuscripts for publication. I have developed these relationships serendipitously, by being available and contributing ideas when invited to participate.

Beth Auten, MSLIS, MA, AHIP,
liaison librarian, UF Health Science
Center Library, Gainesville, FL

Offices of Research, Research Compliance, Conflict of Interest, and Similar Venues

The NIH Public Access Mandate is an excellent opportunity to provide outreach services to an institutional office of research or research compliance; a number of models exist, with some libraries submitting manuscripts for researchers, whereas others provide instruction or consultations on the process (Keener and Sarli, 2010; Rosenzweig et al., 2011). Librarians are developing workshops and LibGuides to walk researchers through the PubMed Central submission process. Following NIH's announcement that the Institutes would begin withholding grant funding for noncompliant PIs, stakeholder interest in partnering with the library is at an all-time high.

EXTERNAL OUTREACH—OUTREACH TO THE COMMUNITY

Opportunities for information outreach to external populations abound. The need for health information is universal—all people need such information at some point in their lives, either for themselves or for a family member or friend. Improving health literacy and health information literacy are two ways that NIH and NLM seek to improve the nation's health and decrease the disparities that can affect populations based on race, age, gender, geographic location, class, or economic status. Following are examples of exemplary outreach projects targeted to specific populations—senior citizens, dental public-health professionals, health care consumers, high school students, and patients. It is important to note that the examples cited below are just a snapshot of the possibilities for external outreach. In and of itself, outreach to clinicians provides opportunities to work with physicians, nurses, public health practitioners, and many professions—at academic health centers, hospitals, clinics, freestanding offices, and other venues. Likewise, numerous possibilities for working with patients and consumers exist, many of which can be found in this textbook in Chapter 13, "Consumer Health Information Services."

Librarians at the University of Minnesota Health Sciences Libraries developed a model health literacy educational program for senior citizens. Adults age sixty-five and over account for almost four of ten hospital stays, and use approximately one-third of prescription and over-the-counter medications in the United States, although they comprise about 12 percent of the population. Unfortunately, they also score quite low (3 percent) in health literacy proficiency (Aspinall, Beschnett, and Ellwood, 2012). Librarians collaborated with the Minnesota Health Literacy Partnership (a community-based organization) and Boutwells Landing Senior Living to create the Health Literacy Program for Minnesota Seniors (HeLP MN Seniors). Funded by the Greater Midwest Region National Network of Libraries of Medicine (NN/LM), the intent of the project was to develop an evidence-based training program to improve the health literacy status of these Minnesota seniors. Focus groups were held prior to the development of the workshops in order to understand the current health literacy and information needs of the seniors. The information intervention included two workshops, one on communicating with clinicians and the second on authoritative health websites and how to evaluate health-related information. Finally, an outcomes assessment questionnaire was used to determine success of the project and identify any needed modifications to the interventions. The outreach team identified seniors' information concerns (quality, quantity, complexity, time constraints), where seniors get their information (clinicians, pharmacists), and types of questions they have (drug costs, interactions, and side effects). Following the workshops, an outcomes-assessment survey indicated that more than 90 percent of respondents felt more empowered to ask questions at their visit with their doctor. The information identified through initial focus groups, pre-/posttests, and the final survey provided evidence-based insights to modify the intervention and the tools.

When the NIH announced that it would delay grant funding for noncompliant PIs, UF's CTSI was concerned and called an emergency meeting with the administration of sponsored research and research compliance. They included me in that meeting as their "go-to" person on scholarly communication and bibliographic issues. I am an integral part of the university's plans for PI compliance and have worked closely with the director of research compliance to identify noncompliant faculty and to provide training and consultation services. This continuing relationship with the office of research should prove to be extremely valuable to the libraries in the future.

Jennifer A. Lyon, MS, MLS, AHIP,
clinical research librarian, UF Health
Science Center Library, Gainesville, FL

Sometimes outreach efforts are targeted at facilitating information skills improvement of health care providers. For example, dentists, dental hygienists, and promotores (community health workers) were targeted in the SMILE (Sharing MedlinePlus for Information Literacy Education) project (Gaines, Levy, and Cogdill, 2011). Librarians at the University of Texas Health Science Center at San Antonio partnered with the San Antonio Metropolitan Health District and the Gateway Community Health Center to provide large-group training sessions and one-on-one consultations for these dental public health professionals. Resources covered included PubMed, MedlinePlus, MedlinePlus en Espanol, and Loansome Doc; current awareness through blogs, RSS feeds, and the PHPartners.org website; and using the library's document delivery services—with the goal of increasing the clinicians' information-seeking skills and use of technology to access information. Focus groups and a survey were used to determine the baseline skill set and assess the dental professionals' information needs. Participants increased their ability to use blogs, PubMed, and MedlinePlus. In addition to providing information to these clinicians, the project team learned a number of lessons, including the need to emphasize to clinicians the time saved and efficacy of using information for clinical decision making.

Modern tools, such as geographic information systems (GIS) can be used to identify priorities for outreach (Socha et al., 2012). Combining geographic information with census data, librarians from the Preston Medical Library in Knoxville, Tennessee, identified areas that could benefit from extra outreach. This library hosted a free telephone-based Consumer and Patient Health Information Service, in which consumers requested materials over the phone and were mailed information packets at the appropriate literacy level. Using data on requests back to 1998 (indexed with MeSH) and requesters' zip codes, the librarians cross-referenced the requests with the known prevalence of disease in particular geographic locations, and from those data, determined whether the number of requests for information were higher or lower than expected. If lower, the area could be targeted as a focus for outreach. The librarians also compared census data on poverty, age, and ambulatory disabilities to requests for information. They found that the counties with the highest rates of poverty had made no requests for information, with similar results for those with high ambulatory disability, providing them with a roadmap for future outreach efforts.

Librarians at the Health Science and Human Services Library (HS/HSL) at the University of Maryland have taken on outreach with a different population—high school students. Funded by a NLM Resource Grant to Reduce Health Disparities, Project SHARE (Student Health Advocates Redefining Empowerment) is a teen health advocacy program, http://guides.hshsl.umaryland.edu/SHARE/. Focusing on students from the Vivien T. Thomas Medical Arts Academy (VTTMAA), an underserved high school in west Baltimore, this innovative project encompassed three goals: 1) To empower high school students as "community health advocates"; 2) To promote improved health and reduce health disparities in Baltimore neighborhoods; and 3) To develop a replicable student health advocacy program. Librarians developed a health promotion curriculum aligned with standards including those in *Healthy People 2020* (U.S. Department of Health and Human Services, 2013a), *National Health Education Standards* (CDC, 2013), and *National Partnership for Action to End Health Disparities* (U.S. Department of Health and Human Services, 2013b).

Students participated in numerous training sessions to help them build the capacity and skills that they need to become health advocates in their communities, including workshops on advocacy, health literacy and policy, locating and evaluating health information, outreach campaigns, personal health records, presentation skills, and learning how to create a poster for presentation. Librarians assisted students in the creation of posters, which were presented in the spring. During the summer, students used what they learned in the classroom to develop and implement health promotion events for the community. Librarians worked closely with students on their public speaking, writing, and poster presentation skills, essential communication skills for their efforts as health advocates. The Project SHARE librarians developed this curriculum and provided all classroom instruction, arranged for guest speakers, took students on field trips to relevant venues, and provided health information outreach around Baltimore. A similar project, focusing on high school students in Alabama, was recently completed by health sciences librarians from the University of South Alabama (Rossini, Burnham, and Wright, 2013).

Outreach directly to patients is another opportunity for health sciences librarians. The UFHSCL's Community Engagement and Consumer Health Librarian participated in an NN/LM-funded project to work with patients in an academic health center's Internal Medicine clinic. Spending four hours per week in the waiting room of the clinic, the librarian met individually with patients, providing them with quality health information and helping them formulate questions for their doctors (surprisingly, not all patients realized that asking clinicians questions is allowed). Preparatory work for the project was extensive, with the librarian laying the groundwork for buy-in by both clinic workers (clinicians and administrators) and patients. Because

It is amazing to see students make the connections between social determinants of health and health disparities. I have grown as a teacher and as a person, and I am proud to be a part of these students' lives. One of the teachers said she can tell which students are in SHARE because they are more outspoken and use research to back up their statements. SHARE has created a strong platform for further library outreach activities. Several students used the word "love" to describe the project. A student from the first cohort has used her experience to win two scholarships.

Anna L. Tatro, MLS, outreach librarian,
Health Sciences and Human Services Library,
University of Maryland, Baltimore

Building relationships with users can lead to extraordinary collaborations. I collaborated with medical faculty on two grants to provide information services to patients in a university clinic's waiting room. Patients are genuinely appreciative of the information provided and of the service, even when they do not have questions. Faculty and residents had questions they would not have bothered to ask if they had to call or come to the library. Being in the clinic provides an opportunity to interact with faculty and residents as colleagues and enables them to see librarians as active participants in the health care team.

Linda Butson, MLS, MPH, AHIP,
community engagement and consumer
health librarian, UF Health Science
Center Library, Gainesville, FL

the intervention took place in the clinic and was being pursued as a research project, the librarian was required to submit the protocol to the institution's IRB-01, the IRB to which clinical protocols are submitted. The opportunity for this project came about through a longtime professional relationship with a College of Medicine faculty member, one that was initiated through a simple reference question.

Clearly, such external outreach projects take time and money; it is not surprising that the majority of projects described above were externally funded. NLM is working toward the elimination of health disparities between minority and majority populations; one method to address this goal is to make available freely accessible high-quality health information (U.S. National Library of Medicine, 2009). NN/LM is dedicated to "advancing the progress of medicine and improving the public health through access to health information" (NN/LM, 2012) and supports a number of activities related to outreach. Funding opportunities are offered on a regional basis, with awards available for a variety of project types—outreach to health professionals or the community, health literacy, and hospital library promotion, among others, depending on the region. Awards can range from $1,000 to $50,000 depending on award type and regional priority. A recent study of the impact of outreach projects supported by NN/LM confirmed that such projects do improve access to health care information for both the general public and clinicians (Huber et al., 2011). NN/LM websites also provide information on planning and evaluating outreach projects and tips on writing grants and proposals.

OUTREACH FOR VISIBILITY

In the above examples, the purpose of outreach was to bring identified needed information services to clients within and outside the institution, whether traditional services (database instruction, search services), or newer ones, such as support for bioinformatics, assessing research impact, or facilitating collaboration. However, sometimes outreach is primarily designed to bring visibility to the library, engage the community, encourage use of the library and its resources and services, emphasize the library's role as intellectual and cultural center of the institution, and demonstrate its centrality to all aspects of institutional life.

Although most libraries dedicate some level of staff time to library promotional activities, the method and support vary greatly. A national survey of promotional outreach services at academic libraries reveals that almost half of responding libraries make use of an outreach position, the majority of which were .5 or less FTE (Carter and Seaman, 2011). Most of these positions were held by librarians, rather than marketing or public relations professionals. About one in five reporting libraries uses an outreach committee for such promotional work, spending an average of seven hours per week on outreach. About one-quarter of respondents report having a dedicated budget for outreach; little correlation was observed between the size of an institution and the size of its outreach budget, nor did large private institutions report greater funding than their smaller public counterparts. This study concludes that the limited FTE and funding dedicated to outreach, in combination with the fact that few libraries report working from an outreach plan, mission statement, or articulated goals, suggests that in many academic institutions, promotional outreach is not afforded sufficient support to be effective. Limited support may be, in part, the result of the difficulty of evaluating and quantifying the actual impact that promotional outreach has. Although this study does not address which models of promotional outreach are most effective, the work focuses on a number of questions that are ripe for further research.

Although the literature shows little evidence that events and exhibits are effective long term, many libraries use them for promotional purposes (Carter and Seaman, 2011). Because of this popularity, it has been suggested that coursework related to exhibit design, organization, and planning should be integrated into library school curricula (Dutka, Hayes, and Parnell, 2002). Health sciences libraries are fortunate in having NLM as a natural partner in these endeavors. In 2002, NLM implemented the Traveling Exhibit Program, www.nlm.nih.gov/hmd/about/exhibition/about-us. html, which adapts selected NLM exhibits for loan to external institutions. Evidence does exist that exhibits and events can increase the number of library users in the short term, although whether these increases represent lasting relationships is less clear. When the Coates Library at Trinity University hosted the NLM exhibit *Franken- stein: Penetrating the Secrets of Nature*, the library reported increased gate counts not only during the exhibit period, but in the following year as well (MacAlpine, 2005).

Auten and colleagues (2013) describe their experiences hosting four NLM exhibits: *Rewriting the Book of Nature: Charles Darwin and the Rise of Evolutionary Theory*; the Frankenstein exhibit noted above; *Opening Doors: Contemporary African American Academic Surgeons*; and *Harry Potter's World: Renaissance Science, Magic and Medicine*. The team developed for each exhibit a series of events tied to exhibit theme and content. Events such as film screenings, lectures by subject matter experts from on and off campus, panels of students and clinicians, and even a suture clinic were hosted by the library, bringing in current library users as well as potential new users from the academic health center, the university at large, and the local community. More than 300 persons participated in the opening reception for the Harry Potter exhibit, enjoying numerous activities: wand making, magic demonstrations, a Quidditch team meet-and-greet, and refreshments including pumpkin pasties and butter beer. These event series facilitated the development of numerous partnerships and collaborations with individual faculty from throughout campus (more than a dozen departments or programs), as well as with entities that funded or hosted elements of the series—the campus Genetics Institute, local chapter of the National Medical Student Association, the Honors College, a local art museum, and the public library. Results of event exit surveys suggested that attendees expanded their vision of what the library had to offer and expected to use the library more in the future.

In recent years, librarians on some campuses have worked to develop a more "participatory culture" to engage with students, teach them information literacy skills, and bring them into the library. Because "today's students are critical thinkers, collaborators, and creators" (Johnson et al., 2011: 2), it has been suggested that they learn best in environments that allow them to be active participants and problem solvers, and that libraries can benefit from taking part in such culture through student-organized campus-wide alternate reality games, such as Humans vs. Zombies (HvZ). In HvZ, one student is designated to be a zombie, and can "infect" other game participants just by tagging them. Non-zombies work together through a series of missions to try to survive the zombie outbreak. Numerous health-related tie-ins can be created for the enterprising health sciences library, such as a mission involving a brain pathology laboratory and related library activities (Norton et al., 2012).

Marketing and Communication

The goals of marketing and promotion of any service are to develop long-term relationships and repeat business. A key aspect of marketing communication is to match the media used for promotion to the audience that the library is trying to reach. For example, several studies have demonstrated that basic science researchers prefer to be contacted via e-mail (Crossno et al., 2012; Tomaszewski, 2012). Although a health sciences librarian who is trying to reach these researchers would likely devise a number of strategies to do so, the primary strategy would be through e-mail. Once the primary strategy is determined, it is then essential to understand everything possible about that strategy (e.g., will the client's e-mail system allow for attachments, or must the information be included in the text of the e-mail instead?) Both the mode of information delivery and the message need to be well-planned, as different constituencies have different preferences for formality of language, and different needs, such as literacy levels. Because of such client diversity, marketing can be challenging—"to market successfully, a clear definition and understanding of target audiences must be paired with appropriately selected media and specifically tailored messages" (Conley and Tucker, 2005: 48).

In preparing for the NLM exhibits and event series described above, the UFHSCL exhibits team developed a three-level "segmented" marketing communications plan, including more than forty promotional activities. Identified market segments included clients of the academic health center, the entire campus, and the local community. More finely tuned divisions were identified with each exhibit or event, matching clients with theme (Auten et al., 2013). The literature provides a number of ways to promote services, resources, and events, including media outlets (local radio, television, newspaper); targeted and mass e-mails; flyers; posters; stories in newsletters (electronic and print) and institutional publications (e.g., the alumni magazine); presentations in classes, department, or college meetings; poster presentation at research days; word of mouth; library web pages and LibGuides (Wakeham, 2004; Conley and Tucker, 2005; Carter and Seaman 2011).

New technologies make it possible for libraries to market their services and develop relationships with their clients in ways previously impossible. Librarians at the Lister Hill Library of the Health Sciences at the University of Alabama at Birmingham have made use of social networking tools—Facebook, Pinterest, blogs, Twitter, and YouTube—to build relationships and promote library services and events (Vucovich et al., 2013). These librarians evaluated the use of such tools for outreach and determined that for their users, the time and manpower involved were worth the effort. An important consideration is that multiple modes of social media are required to meet client preference and need. In Tomaszewski's (2012) study of science postdoctoral associates and PhD students, 84 percent reported using Facebook and 46 percent texted; few respondents were Twitter users. Although the study did not address whether respondents were interested in receiving library information via these tools, the high percentage of respondents using social networking tools makes this an avenue to investigate.

Characteristics of Successful Outreach

Successful outreach programs share a number of characteristics, regardless of client type, location, or whether intended to provide information services or promote the library.

- Needs Assessment

It is essential to understand the needs of the community to which outreach is targeted; without this understanding, it is very difficult to develop useful interventions or attract clients to the service. Understanding customer needs has been cited as the most important success factor for outreach (Fama et al., 2005). Needs assessment must be relevant; otherwise, "meaningful objectives will not be identified, and imagined outcomes may not be realized (or actual outcomes may be overlooked)" (Rambo et al., 2001: 405). Taking a client-centered approach to services and programming, rather than a library-centered approach, will align services and programming with actual needs, can help customize programming to specific populations, and will facilitate prioritizing among multiple potential projects. It is no coincidence that many of the well-regarded and long-standing outreach programs and projects described in this chapter started with needs assessment.

- Relationship Building

The development of trusted professional relationships can lead to client buy-in, increased usage of services, champions who can influence others, and collaboration. Building relationships and networking has been cited as the second most important factor in successful outreach projects (Fama et al., 2005). Lining up champions (e.g., deans or associate deans) who view librarians as contributing partners is an essential element of success (Freiburger and Kramer, 2009). Developing sustainable partnerships can facilitate the creation of library programming and funding for that programming (Auten et al., 2013).

- Alignment of Goals

It is highly desirable to align outreach efforts to the strategic goals of the library and the mission of the institution in which the library resides, as doing so facilitates support from the home institution and keeps the outreach program focused on the essentials (Fama et al., 2005). For example, external outreach to health care providers statewide may seem like a superfluous goal for a university health sciences library during these times of budget constraints. However, such services may align tightly with the core principles of a land-grant institution—service to the state (McGowan, 2000). Bringing in key stakeholders at the planning stage ensures an understanding of institutional missions and goals, facilitating such alignment. Sharing goals, rather than foisting unwanted, unneeded, or unaligned services on customers, can foster the sustainable partnerships cited above (Rambo et al., 2001).

- Evaluation

Evaluation of outreach services is essential to identifying whether an intervention has been successful, for understanding what attributes contributed to this success or failure, and for informing planning of future outreach endeavors. Again, it is no coincidence that so many of the successful outreach projects described in this chapter include an evaluation component, and that results of the evaluation are used subsequently to modify the intervention. NLM makes available a number of guides for successful outreach and evaluation planning and implementation (Burroughs and Wood, 2000; Olney and Barnes, 2006).

- Mobility

Visibility is an important key to successful outreach, and the ability to go where the clients are can be an important factor in being visible. An emphasis on librarians getting out of the library to facilitate relationship building and service integration was a common theme at the recent Banbury Conference on the future of academic science and health science libraries (Feltes et al., 2012). Providing mobile devices (tablets and smartphones) to librarians, informationists, and other key staff can be a powerful means of ensuring mobility, the ability to work from any location, and facilitate integration into clients' territory (Tennant et al., 2012).

- Skills

Clearly, librarians and informationists performing outreach services must possess expert-level information skills; no amount of promotion will be effective if the person doing the work does not possess the skill set. But a number of other provider characteristics contribute to the success of outreach. In particular, liaison/embedded librarians, informationists, and other outreach specialists must have excellent oral communication and interpersonal skills, good interviewing skills, the ability to develop close professional relationships, the willingness to be visible, an understanding of the culture of the assigned unit, and real interest in providing service to that unit (Shedlock, 1983; Tennant et al., 2001; Freiburger and Kramer, 2009; Shedlock and Attwood, 2013).

SUMMARY

This chapter has introduced numerous examples of librarians and informationists providing outreach to their clients, both within and external to their institutions. New roles include teaching bioinformatics resources and assessing impact complement traditional searching, instruction, and reference services. Health sciences librarians and informationists provide outreach in the library, the laboratory, and the clinic, and work closely with researchers, clinicians, patients, the public—anyone with a health-related information need. Outreach provides visibility for the library and its information providers, demonstrating relevance and increasing usage. Successful outreach programs have a number of attributes in common—they are based on user needs and are designed to align to these needs and institutional mission. They rely on relationship building and collaboration, and are evaluated frequently and adjusted as needed. The examples of successful outreach programs and activities described in this chapter give a snapshot of the here and now, and may serve as a jumping-off point for future exploration. Possibilities for outreach in health sciences librarianship abound.

STUDY QUESTIONS

1. What are the key differences between liaison librarians, embedded librarians, and informationists?
2. Describe the differences between the information needs and information-seeking behaviors of clinicians and basic science researchers. How might you match outreach services to those needs and behaviors?
3. Identify programs, academic units, committees, task forces, advisory boards, regulatory offices, or other entities within the health sciences on your campus that would benefit from library outreach.
   a. What kinds of outreach activities might be appropriate for each?
   b. Why would these activities be appropriate for these entities?
   (Note, if your institution does not encompass the health sciences, use another major unit on your campus.)
4. You have an idea for providing library outreach services to a community health organization.
   a. What steps would you take in the planning process to ensure that the interventions you are planning will be used by and useful to these clients?
   b. How will you align these interventions with your institution's mission and goals, as well as with those of the community health organization?
   c. What steps would you take post-intervention to determine whether the intervention should be sustained, reworked, or abandoned?
5. How might you use outreach services to bring clients into the library/promote services in a hospital library? An academic health sciences library? A health sciences program housed in a public library?

REFERENCES

Adamson, Martha C., and Brian P. Bunnett. 2002. "Planning Library Spaces to Encourage Collaboration." *Journal of the Medical Library Association* 90, no. 4 (October): 437–41.

Aspinall, Erinn E., Anne Beschnett, and Alisha F. Ellwood. 2012. "Health Literacy for Older Adults: Using Evidence to Build a Model Educational Program." *Medical Reference Services Quarterly* 31, no. 3 (July–September): 302–14.

Auten, Beth, Hannah F. Norton, Michele R. Tennant et al. 2013. "Using NLM Exhibits and Events to Engage Library Users and Reach the Community." *Medical Reference Services Quarterly* 32, no. 3 (July–September): 266–89.

Burroughs, Catherine M., and Fred B. Wood. 2000. *Measuring the Difference: Guide to Planning and Evaluating Health Information Outreach.* Bethesda, MD: National Library of Medicine.

Carter, Toni M., and Priscilla Seaman. 2011. "The Management and Support of Outreach in Academic Libraries." *Reference & User Services Quarterly* 51, no. 2 (Winter): 73–81.

Cataldo, Tara Tobin, Michele R. Tennant, Pamela Sherwill-Navarro, and Rae Jesano. 2006. "Subject Specialization in a Liaison Librarian Program." *Journal of the Medical Library Association* 94, no. 4 (October): 446–48.

CDC (Centers for Disease Control and Prevention). 2013. "National Health Education Standards." Atlanta: CDC. www.cdc.gov/HealthyYouth/SHER/Standards/Index.htm.

Chattopadhyay, Ansuman, Nancy Hrinya Tannery, Deborah A. L. Silverman, Phillip Bergen, and Barbara A. Epstein. 2006. "Design and Implementation of a Library-based Information Service in Molecular Biology and Genetics at the University of Pittsburgh." *Journal of the Medical Library Association* 94, no. 3 (July): 307–13, E192.

Cheek, Fern M. 2010. "Research Support in an Academic Medical Center." *Medical Reference Services Quarterly* 29, no. 1 (January–March): 37–46.

Cleveland, Ana D., Kristi L. Holmes, and Jodi L. Philbrick. 2012. "'Genomics and Translational Medicine for Information Professionals': An Innovative Course to Educate the Next Generation of Librarians." *Journal of the Medical Library Association* 100, no. 4 (October): 303–5.

Conley, Kathleen, and Toni Tucker. 2005. "Matching Media to Audience Equals Marketing Success." *College & Undergraduate Libraries* 12, no. 1–2 (January): 47–64.

Cooper, I. Diane. 2011. "Is the Informationist a New Role? A Logic Model Analysis." *Journal of the Medical Library Association* 99, no. 3 (July): 189–92.

Crossno, Jon E., Claudia H. DeShay, Mary Ann Huslig, Helen G. Mayo, and Emily F. Patridge. 2012. "A Case Study: The Evolution of a 'Facilitator Model' Liaison Program in an Academic Medical Library." *Journal of the Medical Library Association* 100, no. 3 (July): 171–75.

Davidoff, Frank, and Valerie Florance. 2000. "The Informationist: A New Health Profession?" *Annals of Internal Medicine* 132, no. 12 (June 20): 996–98.

DeFarber, Bess. 2012. "Collaborating with Strangers." Gainesville: University of Florida, George A. Smathers Libraries. www.uflib.ufl.edu/communications/colab/home.html.

Dutka, Andrew, Sherman Hayes, and Jerry Parnell. 2002. "The Surprise Part of a Librarian's Life: Exhibition Design and Preparation Course." *College and Research Libraries News* 63, no. 1 (January): 19–22.

Epstein, Barbara A. 2006. "A Management Case Study: Challenges of Initiating an Information Service in Molecular Biology and Genetics." *Journal of the Medical Library Association* 94, no. 3 (July): 245–47.

Fama, Jane, Donna Berryman, Nancy Harger et al. 2005. "Inside Outreach: A Challenge for Health Sciences Librarians." *Journal of the Medical Library Association* 93, no. 3 (July): 327–37.

Feltes, Carol, Donna S. Gibson, Holly Miller, Cathy Norton, and Ludmila Pollock. 2012. "Envisioning the Future of Science Libraries at Academic Research Institutions." Cold Spring Harbor, NY. http://ufdc.ufl.edu/l/IR00002101/00001.

Francis, Barbara W., and Clarissa C. Fisher. 1997. "Librarians as Liaisons to College Curriculum Committees." *Medical Reference Services Quarterly* 16, no. 2 (Summer): 69–74.

Freiburger, Gary, and Sandra Kramer. 2009. "Embedded Librarians: One Library's Model for Decentralized Service." *Journal of the Medical Library Association* 97, no. 2 (April): 139–42.

Gaines, Julie K., Linda S. Levy, and Keith W. Cogdill. 2011. "Sharing MedlinePlus®/MEDLINE® for Information Literacy Education (SMILE): A Dental Public Health Information Project." *Medical Reference Services Quarterly* 30, no. 4 (October–December): 357–64.

Garcia-Milian, Rolando, Hannah F. Norton, Beth Auten et al. 2013. "Librarians as Part of Cross-Disciplinary, Multi-Institutional Team Projects: Experiences from the VIVO Collaboration." *Science & Technology Libraries* 32, no. 2: 160–75.

Geer, Renata C. 2006. "Broad Issues to Consider for Library Involvement in Bioinformatics." *Journal of the Medical Library Association* 94, no. 3 (July): 286–98, E152–55.

Giuse, Nunzia B., Taneya Y. Koonce, Rebecca N. Jerome, Molynda Cahall, Nila A. Sathe, and Annette Williams. 2005. "Evolution of a Mature Clinical Informationist Model." *Journal of the American Medical Informatics Association* 12, no. 3 (May–June): 249–55.

Giuse, Nunzia B., Nila Sathe, and Rebecca Jerome. 2006. "Envisioning the Information Specialist in Context (ISIC): A Multi-center Study to Articulate Roles and Training Models." Chicago: Medical Library Association. http://cec.mlanet.org/2008-may/isic_final_report_feb06.pdf.

Grefsheim, Suzanne F., Jon Franklin, and Diana Cunningham. 1991. "Biotechnology Awareness Study, Part 1: Where Scientists Get Their Information." *Bulletin of the Medical Library Association* 79, no. 1 (January): 36–44.

Grefsheim, Suzanne F., and Jocelyn A. Rankin. 2007. "Information Needs and Information Seeking in a Biomedical Research Setting: A Study of Scientists and Science Administrators." *Journal of the Medical Library Association* 95, no. 4 (October): 426–34.

Haines, Laura L., Jeanene Light, Donna O'Malley, and Frances A. Delwiche. 2010. "Information-seeking Behavior of Basic Science Researchers: Implications for Library Services." *Journal of the Medical Library Association* 98, no. 1 (January): 73–81.

Helms, Alison J., Kevin D. Bradford, Nancy J. Warren, and Diane G. Schwartz. 2004. "Bioinformatics Opportunities for Health Sciences Librarians and Information Professionals." *Journal of the Medical Library Association* 92, no. 4 (October): 489–92.

Holmes, Kristi L., Jennifer A. Lyon, Layne M. Johnson, Cathy C. Sarli, and Michele R. Tennant. 2013. "Library-based Clinical and Translational Research Support." *Journal of the Medical Library Association* 101, no. 4 (October): 326–35.

Huber, Jeffrey T., Emily B. Kean, Philip D. Fitzgerald et al. 2011. "Outreach Impact Study: The Case of the Greater Midwest Region." *Journal of the Medical Library Association* 99, no. 4 (October): 297–303.

Hunt, Joe D., Elizabeth C. Whipple, and Julie J. McGowan. 2012. "Use of Social Network Analysis Tools to Validate a Resources Infrastructure for Interinstitutional Translational Research: A Case Study." *Journal of the Medical Library Association* 100, no. 1 (January): 48–54.

Johnson, Margeaux, Melissa J. Clapp, Stacey R. Ewing, and Amy Buhler. 2011. "Building a Participatory Culture: Collaborating with Student Organizations for Twenty-first Century Library Instruction." *Collaborative Librarianship* 3, no. 1: 2–15.

Keener, Molly, and Cathy C. Sarli. 2010. "Public Access Policy Support Programs at Libraries: A Roadmap for Success." *College & Research Libraries News* 71, no. 10 (November): 539–42.

Lamb, Gertrude E. 1982. "A Decade of Clinical Librarianship." *Clinical Librarian Quarterly* 1, no. 1: 2–4.

Lipscomb, Carolyn E. 2000. "Clinical Librarianship." *Bulletin of the Medical Library Association* 88, no. 4 (October): 393–96.

Livingston, Jill. 2003. "The Benefits of Library Liaison Programs for Small Libraries: An Overview." *Medical Reference Services Quarterly* 22, no. 1 (Spring): 21–30.

Lubker, Irene M., Margaret E. Henderson, Catharine S. Canevari, and Barbara A. Wright. 2010. "Refocusing Reference Services Outside the Library Building: One Library's Experience." *Medical Reference Services Quarterly* 29, no. 3 (July–September): 218–28.

Lyon, Jennifer A., Michele R. Tennant, Kevin R. Messner, and David L. Osterbur. 2006. "Carving a Niche: Establishing Bioinformatics Collaborations." *Journal of the Medical Library Association* 94, no. 3 (July): 330–35.

MacAlpine, Barbara M. 2005. "Frankenstein @ Our Library—Monstrous Opportunities for Marketing." *College & Undergraduate Libraries* 12, no. 1/2: 101–17.

McCrillis, Aileen, Alisa Surkis, Dorice Vieira, Pauline S. Beam, and Tina O'Grady. 2012. "Survival and Success Beyond Grad School: Improving Library Services to Postdoctoral Researchers." Contributed paper presented at the annual meeting of the Medical Library Association, Seattle. May 22.

McGowan, Julie J. 2000. "Health Information Outreach: The Land-grant Mission." *Bulletin of the Medical Library Association* 88, no. 4 (October): 355–61.

NN/LM (National Network of Libraries of Medicine). 2012. "National Networks of Libraries of Medicine." Bethesda, MD: NNLM. http://nnlm.gov/.

Norton, Hannah F., Beth Auten, Linda C. Butson et al. 2012. "Zombie Pathology Lab: Using Health Information Resources during a Zombie Outbreak." Poster presented at the Quad Chapter Meeting of the Medical Library Association, Baltimore. October 14. http://ufdc .ufl.edu/IR00001216/00001.

Oliver, Kathleen Burr. 2005. "The Johns Hopkins Welch Medical Library as Base: Information Professionals Working in Library User Environments." In *Library as Place: Rethinking Roles, Rethinking Space*. Washington, DC: Council on Library and Information Resources. www .clir.org/pubs/reports/pub129/pub129.pdf.

Olney, Cynthia A., and Susan Barnes. 2006. *Planning and Evaluating Health Information Outreach Projects*, Booklets 1–3. Seattle: National Network of Library of Medicine, Pacific Northwest Region; Bethesda, MD: National Library of Medicine.

O'Malley, Donna, and Frances A. Delwiche. 2012. "Aligning Library Instruction with the Needs of Basic Sciences Graduate Students: A Case Study." *Journal of the Medical Library Association* 100, no. 4 (October): 284–90.

Osterbur, David L., Kristine Alpi, Catharine Canevari et al. 2006. "Vignettes: Diverse Library Staff Offering Diverse Bioinformatics Services." *Journal of the Medical Library Association* 94, no. 3 (July): 306, E188–91.

Plutchak, T. Scott. 2002. "The Informationist-Two Years Later." *Journal of the Medical Library Association* 90, no. 4 (October): 367–69.

Pratt, Gregory F. 1991. "Liaison Services for a Remotely Located Biotechnology Research Center." *Bulletin of the Medical Library Association* 79, no. 4 (October): 394–401.

Rambo, Neil, Joan S. Zenan, Kristine M. Alpi, Catherine M. Burroughs, Marjorie A. Cahn, and Jocelyn Rankin. 2001. "Public Health Outreach Forum: Lessons Learned." *Bulletin of the Medical Library Association* 89, no. 4 (October): 403–6.

Rankin, Jocelyn A., Suzanne F. Grefsheim, and Candace C. Canto. 2008. "The Emerging Informationist Specialty: A Systematic Review of the Literature." *Journal of the Medical Library Association* 96, no. 3 (July): 194–206.

Robinson, Judith G., and Jessica Lipscomb Gehle. 2005. "Medical Research and the Institutional Review Board: The Librarian's Role in Human Subject Testing." *Reference Services Review* 33, no. 1: 20–24.

Robison, Rex R., Mary E. Ryan, and I. Diane Cooper. 2009. "Inquiring Informationists: A Qualitative Exploration of our Role." *Evidence Based Library and Information Practice* 4, no. 1 (January): 4–16.

Rosenzweig, Merle, Anna Ercoli Schnitzer, Jean Song, Scott Martin, and Jim Ottaviani. 2011. "National Institutes of Health Public Access Policy and the University of Michigan Libraries' Role in Assisting with Depositing to PubMed Central." *Journal of the Medical Library Association* 99, no. 1 (January): 97–99.

Rossini, Beverly, Judy Burnham, and Andrea Wright. 2013. "The Librarian's Role in an Enrichment Program for High School Students Interested in the Health Professions." *Medical Reference Services Quarterly* 32, no. 1 (January–March): 73–83.

Ryans, Cynthia C., Raghini S. Suresh, and Wei-Ping Zhang. 1995. "Assessing an Academic Library Liaison Programme." *Library Review* 44, no. 1: 14–23.

Sarli, Cathy C., Ellen K. Dubinsky, and Kristi L. Holmes. 2010. "Beyond Citation Analysis: A Model for Assessment of Research Impact." *Journal of the Medical Library Association* 98, no. 1 (January): 17–23.

Sathe, Nila A., Rebecca Jerome, and Nunzia Bettinsoli Giuse. 2007. "Librarian-perceived Barriers to the Implementation of the Informationist/Information Specialist in Context Role." *Journal of the Medical Library Association* 95, no. 3 (July): 270–74.

Schulte, Stephanie J. 2011. "Eliminating Traditional Reference Services in an Academic Health Sciences Library: A Case Study." *Journal of the Medical Library Association* 99, no. 4 (October): 273–79.

Shedlock, James. 1983. "The Library Liaison Program: Building Bridges with Our Users." *Medical Reference Services Quarterly* 2, no. 1 (Spring): 61–65.

Shedlock, James, and Carol Ann Attwood. 2013. "What is an Informationist and What do Informationists Do? An Interview with Terrie R. Wheeler and Keith W. Cogdill." *MLA News* 53, no. 1 (January): 7, 9.

Shipman, Jean P., Diana J. Cunningham, Ruth Holst, and Linda A. Watson. 2002. "The Informationist Conference: Report." *Journal of the Medical Library Association* 90, no. 4 (October): 458–64.

Socha, Yvonne M., Sandra Oelschlegel, Cynthia J. Vaughn, and Martha Earl. 2012. "Improving an Outreach Service by Analyzing the Relationship of Health Information Disparities to Socioeconomic Indicators Using Geographic Information Systems." *Journal of the Medical Library Association* 100, no. 3 (July): 222–25.

Tennant, Michele R. 2005. "Bioinformatics Librarian: Meeting the Information Needs of Genetics and Bioinformatics Researchers." *Reference Services Review* 33, no. 1: 12–19.

Tennant, Michele R., Beth Auten, Cecilia E. Botero et al. 2012. "Changing the Face of Reference: Adapting Biomedical and Health Information Services for the Classroom, Clinic, and Beyond." *Medical Reference Services Quarterly* 31, no. 3 (July–September): 280–301.

Tennant, Michele R., Linda C. Butson, Michelle E. Rezeau, Prudence Tucker, Marion Boyle, and Greg Clayton. 2001."Customizing for Clients: Developing a Library Liaison Program from Need to Plan." *Bulletin of the Medical Library Association* 89, no. 1 (January): 8–20.

Tennant, Michele R., Tara Tobin Cataldo, Pamela Sherwill-Navarro, and Rae Jesano. 2006. "Evaluation of a Liaison Librarian Program: Client and Liaison Perspectives." *Journal of the Medical Library Association* 94, no. 4 (October): 402–9, E201–4.

Tomaszewski, Robert. 2012. "Information Needs and Library Services for Doctoral Students and Postdoctoral Scholars at Georgia State University." *Science & Technology Libraries* 31, no. 4 (November): 442–62.

U.S. Department of Health and Human Services. 2013a. "Healthy People 2020." Washington, DC: HHS. www.healthypeople.gov/2020/default.aspx.

———. 2013b. "National Partnership for Action to End Health Disparities." Washington, DC: HHS. http://minorityhealth.hhs.gov/npa/.

U.S. National Library of Medicine. 2009. "National Library of Medicine Health Disparities Strategic Research Plan and Budget, Fiscal Years 2009–2013." Bethesda, MD: National Library of Medicine. www.nlm.nih.gov/pubs/plan/NLM-FY2009_2013_Health_Disparities_Stratgic_Plan.pdf.

Vucovich, Lee A., Valerie S. Gordon, Nicole Mitchell, and Lisa A. Ennis. 2013. "Is the Time and Effort Worth It? One Library's Evaluation of Using Social Networking Tools for Outreach." *Medical Reference Services Quarterly* 32, no. 1 (January–March): 12–25.

Wakeham, Maurice. 2004. "Marketing and Health Libraries." *Health Information & Libraries Journal* 21, no. 4 (December): 237–44.

Whitmore, Susan C., Suzanne F. Grefsheim, and Jocelyn A. Rankin. 2008. "Informationist Programme in Support of Biomedical Research: A Programme Description and Preliminary Findings of an Evaluation." *Health Information and Libraries Journal* 25, no. 2 (June): 135–41.

Yarfitz, Stuart, and Debra S. Ketchell. 2000. "A Library-based Bioinformatics Services Program." *Bulletin of the Medical Library Association* 88, no. 1 (January): 36–48.

CHAPTER 10

Research Data Management and the Health Sciences Librarian

Andrew Creamer, Elaine R. Martin, and Donna Kafel

INTRODUCTION

As science becomes increasingly characterized by large-scale collaborations and computational **data** sets, researchers face a range of data management challenges and needs. This creates an opportunity for health sciences librarians to offer researchers at their institutions a range of data management strategies and services. By providing **research data management (RDM)** services, librarians connect and collaborate in new ways with the researcher communities within their institutions. But exactly what kinds of RDM services can health sciences librarians offer? How can health sciences librarians engage with biomedical researchers and market these services? These are the questions that current library school students concentrating in health sciences librarianship and practicing health sciences librarians are asking.

The answers are many and varied. Along with actually searching, assigning metadata elements, and curating, preserving, and archiving data sets in digital collections, health sciences librarians are teaching researchers and students about RDM fundamentals, best practices, and assisting them with writing **data management plans (DMPs)**. The librarians who fill these research roles may be called e-science librarians, scientific data curators, research librarians, data librarians, research informationists, or embedded librarians. Whatever the title, these librarians are engaging with the data needs of the health sciences research community. Some health sciences librarians are already participating in RDM activities, whereas others are still examining models to best adopt these emerging services. RDM services require the development, coordination, and synthesis of a range of library and institutional services and programs. This chapter outlines several of these health sciences librarian RDM services and roles, and addresses the following themes.

- What is RDM?
- Why manage research data?

- Common RDM challenges
- RDM services and roles for health sciences librarians
- Librarian RDM skills and competencies
- Librarian RDM tools and resources

Health sciences librarians should explore helping researchers navigate this new data-intensive research environment, including maintaining their relevance and value for the research enterprise, for many powerful reasons. Combined with the needs of researchers to manage the overwhelming amount of data in their research labs, the National Institutes of Health (NIH) and the National Science Foundation (NSF) are requiring data management and data sharing planning to enable and optimize the use, reuse, and sharing of publicly funded research data. On February 22, 2013, the Office of the President directed federal agencies with more than $100 million in research and development expenditures to develop plans to make the published results and supporting data of federally sponsored research freely available to the public within one year of publication, and to require researchers to better account for and manage their data resulting from federally sponsored scientific research (Office of Science and Technology Policy, 2013). Federal research sponsors' prioritizing of sharing data and their DMP mandates are driving health sciences librarians' increased involvement in RDM.

BACKGROUND

The Association of Research Libraries (ARL) took the lead in identifying new roles for librarians in advancing **e-science** and supporting researchers. As early as 2006, ARL had launched its E-Science Task Force. It defined the domain of e-science as "those new methods that are large-scale, data-driven and computationally intense, and often engaging research teams across institutional boundaries" (ARL, 2010). The Task Force's first report highlighted the fundamental changes in the ways in which scientists carried out their work, the tools needed, and the nature of data documentation and data publication.

In 2010, ARL charged a Working Group with the task of raising member libraries' awareness of the professional skills librarians need to address data stewardship, policy development, and the data-publishing environment of scientists. Its report outlined the results of a survey seeking baseline data about institutional and library engagement with these issues. At that time, the data revealed a "professional community experiencing a not-unexpected diversity of approaches and investments," and "a portrait of emerging models" (ARL, 2010).

Davidoff and Florance (2000) proposed that librarians could play information specialist roles. Although many of the subsequent informationist projects were clinically focused, drawing upon the rich history of clinical librarianship as a model, the emerging informationist role is the librarian embedded on a biomedical research team (Martin, 2013). The **research informationist** reinforces the concept of "immersion" into the culture and workplace of the clinicians and scientists being supported (Florance, 2013).

In 2013, the National Library of Medicine (NLM) began sponsoring a new support program at NIH: The NLM Administrative Supplements for Informationist Services in NIH-funded Research Projects. This program specifically requested proposals from NIH-funded research teams requiring research informationists as part of their teams; the scope of the grant particularly focused on the health sciences librarian's role in data management. NIH granted eight awards, and although the librarian roles and projects varied, each application emphasized the librarian's added value to the researchers' data management needs (Martin, 2013). In this age of big data, community, clinical and translational science awards, human genomics, bioinformatics, and the electronic health record (EHR), the possibilities for health sciences librarian involvement with managing data seem boundless.

The embedded informationist role is a new one for my library, yet it appears to be a type of service it needs to invest in for the future. Becoming integrated into a research team gives the informationist, and thus the library, opportunities to become more involved and, ultimately, more valued by the researcher community. The informationist can bring library and information services a greater depth than those offered via traditional support roles.

Sally Gore, MS, MS LIS, embedded research librarian and informationist, Lamar Soutter Library, University of Massachusetts Medical School, Worcester

WHAT IS RDM?

The University of Edinburgh Data Library (2011) describes research **data** as unique information products that are "collected, observed, or created for purposes of analysis to produce original research results." In other words, a single datum represents information in isolation, disconnected. However, through a human or a machine's processing, contextualizing, and interpretation of data, meaning emerges. Replicating this meaning provides evidence to confirm or refute hypotheses, ask new questions, and cultivate new knowledge, new discoveries. Commonly cited types of research data are:

- data derived from observations;
- data derived from experiments, such as measurements taken by scientific instruments under varying and constant conditions;
- data derived from simulations and models, such as models used to predict epidemics and changes in climate; and
- data derived from already existing data that scientists can reexamine, repurpose, and build upon to derive original discoveries. (University of Virginia, 2012)

Because research data can take so many forms, it is logical for them to be recorded and stored in many types of digital file formats. There are competing digital file formats for spreadsheets, text documents, audio, video, and image files. Thus, many tenets of records management inform RDM: being aware of the types of data that a project produces; following standards for labeling and appraising data; being aware of the formats that are best suited for making data discoverable, accessible, and reusable by others; and being aware of the digital file formats that are best suited for the long-term preservation of those data (Creamer, 2013a).

WHY MANAGE RESEARCH DATA?

"The activities that keep data secure, accessible, and useable comprise research data management; it is a fundamental part of good research practice" (McLeod, Childs, and Lomas, 2013: 71). DataONE (2013) describes RDM as necessary for "making data easier to find, use, analyze, share and reuse." Managing research data is not just something that may be required of a researcher by an institution or a research funding body; it is an important part of the research process. In 2011, Julie McLeod developed one of the first courses aimed specifically at teaching RDM to health sciences postgraduate researchers; she argues that RDM is an integral part of Research Methods (Creamer, 2013a).

Many practical benefits come from having a DMP and following it. Researchers will have no duplication of efforts; they will save time, energy, and resources. Each person on the lab team will know what he or she needs to do in order to manage, document, and protect the integrity of the project's data. Researchers will be able to locate and share data easily among team members; everyone will have the documentation to understand and interpret the data. Researchers will be able to analyze and publish data with the confidence that they are well organized, appropriately formatted, and documented. Additional reasons for managing research data are:

- comply with sponsor/institution/publisher policies;
- comply with ethical and legal requirements;
- enable reuse and new discoveries;
- increase organization and efficiency; and
- meet professional standards and ensure data integrity. (McLeod, Childs, and Lomas, 2013: 74)

Integrity of Scientific Research

In several high-profile instances, published journal articles have been retracted because of falsified or missing data. "Reports of data loss, security breaches, and lack of data authentication are not uncommon and ultimately erode both the sharing of data and access to them" (Hswe, 2012: 117). Sponsors, institutions, publishers, the scientific community, and the public should be able to verify the integrity of published scientific findings. Data managed well can be more easily stored, discovered, shared, accessed, interpreted, and scrutinized. Robin Rice and Stuart Macdonald, data librarians at the University of Edinburgh, observed that a researcher will be more willing to share well-managed data if he or she feels confident about their integrity (Creamer, 2012). **Data sharing** is important in the health sciences because **data reuse** and repurposing may help foster new research, new discoveries, and better health outcomes (Institute of Medicine, 2011).

Mechanisms are increasing for authors to share and publish the data that underlie the results of their published articles. In 2009, scientists at the National Academy of Sciences (NAS) recommended that research data be managed and made accessible to help ensure proper professional conduct and data integrity. This report put the onus for managing data on the researcher:

> Ensuring the integrity of research data is essential for advancing scientific, engineering, and medical knowledge and for maintaining public trust in the research enterprise. Although other stakeholders in the research enterprise have important roles to play, researchers themselves are ultimately responsible for ensuring the integrity of research data. (NAS, 2009: 4)

This report was followed by a series of editorials in leading scientific journals calling on research institutions to do more to provide their scientists with the appropriate support and tools for managing and sharing their research data (*Nature Neuroscience* Editorial, 2009).

In 2011, a group of these scientific journals worked with digital repositories such as Dryad to write the Joint Data Archiving Policy (JDAP) (Dryad, 2011). It required their authors to make their articles' supporting research data publicly available. Their consensus was that transparency and access to these data are crucial for the public and scientific community to scrutinize a study's overall integrity; thus, research data must be managed well in order to be shared effectively. Research integrity, professionalism, and maintaining the public's trust are powerful incentives for health sciences researchers, librarians, and their institutions to prioritize RDM.

Data as Return-on-Investment

Graham Pryor, editor of the book *Managing Research Data*, argues that data represent a return on public investment. "Surely," he writes, "data produced so expensively should not be treated as spoil, put aside like the waste materials from an intellectual mine" (Pryor, 2012: 4). Pointing out the incredible sums of public money spent on research, Pryor argues that the resulting data can no longer be ignored. He laments that the only intellectual product afforded attention by the academy and public is the resulting publications: "Justifiably, they might also expect that the fruits from such rich endeavors will be afforded the attention necessary to ensure an optimum return on investment" (Pryor, 2012: 1).

Researchers are also reaping dividends from their published data in the form of more frequent citations (Piwowar, 2013). The scientific community is increasingly starting to view data sets as just as important as the publications they underlie (DataCite, 2012). "Data should no longer be abandoned on the workbench like wood shavings in a carpenter's shop; increasingly it is expected to join the finished assembly of scholarly output as a valued and managed component with an extended life and sustained usability" (Pryor, 2012: 4). Although the traditional model of measuring researchers' impact valued only the citation of their articles, now alternative metrics (**altmetrics**) are emerging to measure the impact of a researcher's data and other online output as equally relevant scholarly products (Piwowar).

Compliance

Julie McLeod and Sue Childs found that health sciences researchers recognized that a major incentive for them to prioritize RDM was having the organized documentation and confidence to prove that they conducted their research legally, safely, and ethically, and gathered and managed their subjects' data appropriately (Creamer, 2013a). It has long been the practice of sponsors and institutions to expect scientists to conduct their research within the appropriate legal and ethical frameworks, and comply with institutional, sponsor, and legal policies. These stakeholders have reserved rights to investigate their researchers' conduct and audit materials such as laboratory notebooks, research data, consent forms and administrative documentation, lab animal protocols, and so forth. Researchers working with patient data or with other types of sensitive data have to meet a large number of legal and ethical requirements at the institutional, sponsor, state, and federal levels. From a liability standpoint, researchers have to document that they have followed the required Office for Human Research Protections (OHRP) and Institutional Review Board (IRB) policies, ethics protocols, and procedures for properly collecting, storing, and securing sensitive patient data, and that they have taken the appropriate measures to protect their participants' identities and protected health information (PHI).

Federal Data Management and Sharing Policies

A good reason to manage and share data is that more sponsors are requiring it. The NIH policy states that "all data should be considered for data sharing" and "data should be made as widely and freely available as possible while safeguarding the privacy of participants, and protecting confidential and proprietary data" (U.S. National Institutes of Health, 2007). The NSF policy mandates that researchers include a two-page data management plan as a supplementary document with any proposal for funding. The plan must describe how the proposal will "conform to NSF policy on the dissemination and sharing of research results" (NSF, 2011). The OSTP's memorandum on behalf of the Office of the President to the heads of executive departments and agencies within the federal government states:

> The Administration is committed to ensuring that, to the greatest extent and with the fewest constraints possible and consistent with law and the objectives set out below, the direct results of federally funded scientific research are made available to and useful for the public, industry, and the scientific community. Such results include peer-reviewed publications and digital data. (OSTP, 2013: 1)

The U.S. Department of Health and Human Services (HHS) is currently implementing an Open Government Plan. It has developed the HealthData.gov Platform (HDP) to make health data sets available to the public. "The HDP will deliver greater potential for new data driven insights into complex interactions of health and health care services" (Challenge.gov, 2012). These sponsors' data-sharing initiatives will increase the importance of compliance, and hence the visibility of RDM services on the campuses of universities, hospitals, and research institutes.

COMMON RDM CHALLENGES

Health sciences librarians at New York University created a YouTube video titled *A Data Management Horror Story* (Hanson, Surkis, and Yacobucci, 2012). It features a comical exchange between two cartoon cancer researchers. One researcher is interested in looking at the other's data to repurpose for her research. However, the other researcher reveals that he cannot easily find the project's data files. Eventually he tracks down the files, but then he finds that he can no longer remember the meaning of the field titles that his team used, or the values and parameters. The other researchers in his lab have moved on, and the company that created the software program he used to create the files, which the other researcher would need to open and view the files, has gone bankrupt and closed.

Although entertaining, the health sciences librarians' video highlights the serious issues surrounding RDM and the consequences of mismanagement being the stymieing of data sharing, data reuse, and further discovery. RDM challenges include managing the workflows of team science, getting everyone on the team to follow a DMP, and making RDM a priority. The frequency of students, residents, and postdoctoral students (postdocs) rotating in and out of labs creates challenges as does having data stored in multiple places, and in some cases, multiple research team members spread across the globe (Ferguson, 2013). Most principal investigators (PIs) do not manage the day-to-day aspects of their labs. Graduate students and residents who come and go manage the data. Their practices for the most part are ad hoc. Multiple investigators may be collaborating on the same research but manage their data differently in each of their labs. This makes it difficult to share data within the same project and re-create results.

In 2013, the HHS Office of Research Integrity (ORI) noted several RDM issues for improvement:

- technical data not recorded properly;
- technical data management not supervised by PI;
- data not maintained at the institution;
- financial or administrative data not maintained properly;
- data not stored properly;
- data not held in accordance with retention requirements; and
- data not retained by the institution. (Erickson and Muskavitch, 2013)

A s the health sciences librarian on a research team, I have helped to address several different RDM challenges. The biggest challenge we face is that the team's data exist in lots of different places and different formats. Like many research teams, they have a paper lab notebook with the results of their different experiments, as well as a lot of digital data that go with their experiments. Most of these digital data are images in proprietary systems, and these systems are not connected to each other. The challenge is to figure out how we can get all of these data into one place.

Lisa Federer, MLIS, MA, AHIP, research data informationist at NIH Library, Bethesda, MD

The ORI's issues highlight several problem areas where health sciences librarians are assisting researchers in addressing

- lack of assigned RDM responsibility;
- lack of a DMP;
- issues with records management;
- lack of metadata;
- lack of **data dictionaries**;
- issues with storing, backing up, and securing data;
- issues related to data ownership and intellectual property;
- lack of plans for retaining and appraising data; and
- lack of long-term plan for preserving data. (NECDMC, 2013)

Lack of Assigned RDM Responsibility

As the ORI noted, confusion exists among health sciences researchers regarding who is responsible for RDM. Over the past several years, it has become apparent from librarian surveys and interviews with students that labs do not always have a codified procedure or formal course to teach new students or team members how to manage data; students report having to learn it informally "on the job," from another graduate student, or not at all (Piorun, 2013). The ORI wants students and PIs to know that everyone in the institution bears some responsibility for managing data. By assigning RDM responsibilities and delegating tasks, health sciences researchers will increase the efficiency of their research. Laboratory notebooks, both paper and electronic, can be audited by a researcher's institution or sponsor, such as NIH, and collectively they represent a record of science; therefore, a plan is needed for managing and preserving these notebooks. A plan must also bridge the RDM knowledge of outgoing and incoming students, residents, postdocs, and staff.

Lack of a Data Management Plan (DMP)

Since the NSF began requiring PIs to submit data management and sharing plans with funding proposals, health sciences librarians have published articles, research guides, curricula, and online tools to helping researchers write these plans and understand their value for the research process. According to the NSF, these plans should describe:

- the types of data that will be created;
- who will own, have access to, and be responsible for managing these data;
- the equipment and methods that will be used to capture and process data;
- the metadata that will make these data make sense to others; and
- where the data will be stored during and after the project. (NSF, 2011)

Having a DMP will help researchers account for the day-to-day management of a project's data throughout the life of their projects, and beyond. A **data life cycle** describes when data are created, how they can be managed along the steps of the research process, and how these data can be appraised and archived after a project is complete (Ball, 2012; DataONE, 2012). Julie McLeod and Sue Childs describe such life cycle DMPs as "living documents meant to be revisited, added to, and revised as the project unfolds and situations change" (Creamer, 2013a).

Records Management Issues

Many data management issues are related to locating and making sense of data. Common records management failures include inconsistently labeled data files; unmarked file versions; poorly structured folders; undocumented multiple media storage; undocumented file locations; and inconsistent file formats. Ferguson (2013) looked at a sample of student data files on a set of instruments in a bioscience lab. The file names she saw broke a lot of the "rules" for good file management. She saw file names such as "awesome" with just the year, and another version of the file titled "awesomer." Although humorous, these students' choices for their file names exemplified the need for improvement. The students' file naming conventions did not take into consideration how someone not involved in a project would make sense of what is in the file. Indeed, after some time, these files would probably not even make sense to the person involved in creating the file!

Lack of Metadata and Data Dictionaries

Metadata can help to address several data management related issues.

- How will researchers label, document, describe, and contextualize their data?
- How will they describe the data files to make them more discoverable by others?
- How will someone else make sense of their data during and after the project (e.g., field names, terminology, values, parameters, etc.)?

Many Clinical and Translational Science Award (CTSA) sponsored research groups use a web-based application called REDCap to collect their data. In order to set up its data collection spreadsheet, someone on the team has to create a **data dictionary**—a guide documenting, labeling, and customizing the values and parameters used to describe the data that will be captured. Before collecting any data the researcher would need to label fields and provide adequate documentation (e.g., explain field names, field types, instrumentation, questions, responses, branching logic, etc.). Researchers have to document these details systematically and deliberately in order to record and interpret the data they have captured; these details will help them to make judgments later about which data they will want to analyze, which data will be discarded, and which will be saved or can be shared with others.

Several types of metadata can help to make sense of data. Metadata can be descriptive and give details about the nature of the information in the files: who created it, information about the subject or experiment, where was it created, and when, and so forth. Metadata can describe the file that is storing the data, such as how many bytes, the format, the software used to create the file, the hardware and software needed to open and view it, and the version. Some metadata are structural;

they can help the user to navigate the files and understand which files are associated or linked with other documentation. Metadata can be administrative and communicate if the data are licensed; it can also be technical and relay information about the instrumentation that created it. Over the years certain disciplines have come together to create metadata standards, agreed upon elements that can be used to describe their domain's data.

Storage, Backup, and Security Issues

Properly storing, backing up, and securing data are important responsibilities. Institutions and sponsors want researchers to take these responsibilities seriously to protect and ensure the integrity of their data. The IRB wants to ensure that researchers protect the identities and private information of their human subjects. Before starting a project, researchers need to understand their institutional **data security** policies and their responsibilities for storing and securing data. These policies can address several data management issues.

- How often should research data files be backed up?
- How many copies of the data should researchers have?
- What storage options do they have within the institution?
- How much institutional server space can they get and how much does it cost?
- Are they allowed to use their personal hard drives, portable storage such as USBs, or commercial cloud storage vendors? (NECDMC, 2013)

Data Ownership Issues

Determining the ownership of data deserves attention before anyone begins to collect data. Data ownership can be very situation-dependent. However, a growing number of institutions have data ownership and intellectual property policies. Typically, institutions come from the perspective that they provide the employment and facilities of researchers, and therefore they own any data produced by researchers who are employed by the institution and using institutional resources. Similarly, federal sponsors view the institution as the owner of research data and ultimately responsible for its management. The institution sees the PI and students as stewards of the data. If a

For us, performing outreach in the area of data management has involved leveraging existing liaison relationships while reaching across traditional organizational divisions. A request from a biomedical researcher for information on storage and computing resources at UF led us to meet with the director of UF's High Performance Computing Center. Resultant collaborative campus-wide outreach activities have included an invitation to present on research data management best principles/practice as part of Research Computing Day, membership on the Data Life Cycle Subcommittee, creation and teaching of workshops on best practices in RDM, and formation of the Data Management/Curation Task Force.

Rolando Garcia-Milian, MLS, AHIP, basic biomedical sciences librarian; and Hannah F. Norton, MSIS, AHIP, reference and liaison librarian, UF Health Science Center Library, Gainesville, FL

PI working on a federally sponsored research project were to leave to go to a new institution, the ORI would still expect the PI's former institution to be able to account for the project data even after the PI had left (Erickson and Muskavitch, 2013).

No Plan for the Long Term

Before researchers embark on a research project, it may prove difficult for them to appraise the value of their data or think about **data preservation** before any are produced and recorded. However, regardless of how valuable they might think these data may prove to be, researchers should locate their sponsor's data retention policies and policies within their institution issued by stakeholders such as the IRB, Office of Responsible Conduct of Research or Intellectual Property, and the library, which could one day be the archive for these data. The regulatory framework for retaining and destroying data is complex, and researchers or their institution may be called upon to produce data, even if it has been years after a project has ended.

Regulations for retention can overlap, depending on the type of research, the nature of the data, and the sponsors of the research. For example, with human subjects' data or other sensitive data, the regulations are specific regarding the collection, storing, sharing, publishing, and archiving (or destroying) of these data. On top of the institutional and sponsor retention guidelines, state and federal laws might apply as well. Thus, many health sciences researchers are interested in locating information about retention because they want to be in compliance. If questions or allegations arise concerning the validity of a health sciences researcher's data or conduct, then he or she would want to retain all data and supporting documents until the investigations have been resolved.

RDM SERVICES AND ROLES FOR
HEALTH SCIENCES LIBRARIANS

In 2012, the Association of College and Research Libraries (ACRL) identified **data curation** as a top trend and highlighted academic libraries' research data services models. These models depend on the following services:

- information and researcher services (e.g., conducting **data interviews** and consulting on researchers' DMPs);
- metadata services (e.g., **annotating and describing data**, creating records for data, **linking publications with data sets**, etc.);
- reference support services (e.g., finding and citing data);
- educational services (e.g., developing subject guides or websites, teaching **data literacy**, RDM best practices);
- technical support for **data repositories** (e.g., **ingesting data sets** and building digital collections and **assigning persistent identifiers**); and
- **digital curation** services (adding value by preserving data and access to data for the long term). (ACRL Research Planning and Review Committee, 2012)

In the face of fiscal constraints, many academic health sciences libraries cannot afford to hire and designate a single librarian to offer RDM instruction and consultation services; the trend has been to create a working group of librarians from various library departments to share their expertise and cooperate to provide RDM services. Within smaller health sciences and hospital libraries, clinical and subject liaison librarians have chosen to upskill and add RDM services to their support services.

Overall, health sciences librarians' involvement in RDM services is quite idiosyncratic. It is a reflection of the librarians' personal RDM competencies, the level of library and institutional administrative support they receive, as well as the resource and budget capacity of their libraries to support their RDM services (Creamer et al., 2012). In addition, they reflect the nature of their researcher communities' RDM requests made in the context of their institutions and the frequency of these demands. The librarians and their administrators must also envision how they see these circumstances and trends evolving in the future (Piorun, 2013). It may mean that for a library or librarian to add or strengthen a RDM service, they will have to reduce or end other services (Cox, Verbaan, and Sen, 2012).

The emerging RDM roles for health sciences librarians blend a variety of traditional and new skill sets and incorporate aspects from a range of the library's services: public access, reference and instruction, research and scholarly communications, technical services, archives and records management, and collections. These roles include:

- participating in institutional data policy making;
- providing expertise on scholarly communications;
- managing an institutional data repository;
- teaching RDM best practices;
- providing instruction on using RDM-related tools and resources;
- providing RDM reference and consulting;
- offering advice on disciplinary metadata standards and repositories;
- helping researchers to annotate and apply metadata to their data sets;
- offering advice on data ownership, copyright, licensing, and intellectual property;
- helping researchers to locate and cite research data sets;
- creating RDM guidance websites, subject guides, and learning materials;
- archiving and preserving data sets in open formats; and
- partnering with researchers and embedding on research teams.

Instruction and Access

From an instructional and reference perspective, health sciences librarians offer instruction to student and faculty researchers about the value of RDM, and the best practices, tools, and resources for managing and curating their research data (Federer, 2013). Health sciences librarians are stepping outside of the library to offer RDM consulting. They conduct reference-style data interviews with their institutions' researchers to assist with planning and managing their data throughout the life cycle of their research projects, and to write DMPs required or encouraged by a research funder.

Collection Development

From a collection development and archives perspective, health sciences librarians create and manage collections of research data (Kochi, Chatterjee, and Rizk-Jackson, 2013). They help researchers, even in the planning phases of their projects, to appraise and think about the archival and preservation options for their data, as well as the potential for sharing their data. Librarians help researchers to take the appropriate steps to make their data sets more accessible and to provide an adequate amount of metadata to make their data both discoverable and meaningful to other researchers (Higgins, 2012). Health sciences librarians assist researchers at the end of their projects to locate, evaluate, and ingest their data into an appropriate institutional or disciplinary repository. These roles involve being aware of a variety of factors affecting the sharing of data such as institutional policies related to intellectual property, and institutional and research funders' open access and open data sharing policies.

It is never too soon for researchers to consult health sciences librarians about their plans for publishing and sharing data, and appraising and preserving data. Many serendipitous scientific discoveries are out there waiting to happen, and the federal government wants to make publicly funded research data publicly available in the hope that it can spur future innovation. Repositories and data archives play important roles in sharing and preserving data, but they are not the only options. Researchers can self-archive or self-publish their data, place their data in their institution's data archive or repository, place their data in an open data repository, or place them in a national or international data archive or repository.

Health sciences libraries support data sharing and the building of digital collections by providing data repositories, guidance on open file formats, assigning persistent identifiers to digital objects, and by teaching **data citation** practices. Depositing in a repository is not always the same as preserving data; although some data archives' mission is to maintain and preserve data for the future, other repositories may simply be a place to access and store data—no active preservation over time will maintain its integrity. Health sciences librarians help researchers to understand this and the scope and policies of a repository or archive before they submit data.

Scholarly Communications

The stewardship of data described above also has become increasingly important to scholarly communications as the U.S. government and its research funders such as NIH and NSF have continued to mandate and encourage researchers receiving a certain level of public funds to make their resulting publications, and soon their underlying data, publicly available. Simultaneously, the academy is also evolving to see scholars' products of research, including their research data and online output, as equally valuable contributions alongside their publications. Health sciences librarians involved in RDM recognize that they and their libraries have a role in helping to implement and bring about these paradigm shifts in scholarly communications within the cultures of their institutions (Palmer, 2013).

Health sciences librarians help researchers to locate and use open file formats and to obtain persistent identifiers for their data sets such as DOIs. Persistent identifiers make data sets or an associated publication easier to find online, and they are used to measure the citation impact of research data sets. Papers that published data sets are cited more often (Piwowar, 2013). Thus health sciences librarians teach researchers about the emerging conventions for citing the data they use or repurpose for their own research.

RDM Guidance

RDM services from health sciences librarians seem to expand daily, but one of the core services is still providing their researcher communities with the best and most timely information about managing their data. The most visible ways to accomplish this are by creating an online presence for RDM at the library, and by teaching and creating educational materials to support student and faculty researchers (Crummet, 2013). Over the past few years, health sciences librarians have begun to write RDM guidance web pages, and to create online subject and research guides on a variety of RDM topics. Health sciences libraries provide their researcher communities with an online overview of RDM, tutorials, information about the research and data life cycles, and subject guides for tools and resources that support their RDM planning. These may include the conventions for naming their files and structuring folders to house these files, or guidance on writing DMPs. Health sciences librarians have created checklists, templates, and authoring tools to help their researchers write DMPs, and some librarians have even compiled the different data management and data sharing policies and requirements from major research funding bodies so their researchers can have all of this information at hand. Lastly, these library tutorials point researchers to the support services available at their own institutions. A common set of guidance topics includes:

- selecting open file formats, file and folder naming conventions, versioning control, and folder structuring;
- best practices for data security, storage, and backup;
- information on intellectual property, copyright, and data licensing;
- publishing data;
- citing data;
- disciplinary and generic metadata for data sets;
- data analysis tools;
- anonymizing/de-identifying patient data;
- sharing data; and
- information on ethical and legal issues.

RDM Instruction

Another highly visible role and important RDM service that health sciences librarians provide is teaching (Crummet, 2013; Hanson and Surkis, 2013; Norton et al., 2013). The library can be a logical venue for researcher communities to learn about RDM best practices, DMP resources and tools, and institution-specific research support services, policies, and resources. These formal in-person or online courses complement many of the courses that librarians are already providing, such as locating research funding and writing grant proposals, support for writing a dissertation, copyright and publishing, and tutorials on searching PubMed, Evidence-Based Medicine, and using citation management tools.

Librarians in academic health sciences libraries have had to customize RDM teaching models to meet the needs and time demands of their researcher communities: integrating RDM into their lab management curricula and courses on research methods; collaborating with other instructors to present RDM lectures in their courses, or to the members of a research group; offering RDM library workshops for students during postgraduate induction periods; and creating online course modules (Kafel et al., 2013; Creamer, 2012; Creamer, 2013a).

Data Management Consulting

Writing DMPs also requires that health sciences librarians build up a certain level of knowledge about the research being conducted in their institution, the institution's data management and sharing policies, and the support services available to researchers. This equips the health sciences librarians with the knowledge to identify strategies for the types of data being produced, and they will be able to offer institutional-level advice for managing, storing, securing, backing up, and describing these data, and the local or disciplinary repository options available for archiving the data after the project is finished.

Data management consulting requires health sciences librarians to keep current on the policies affecting health sciences research. Although best practices for RDM apply across all disciplines, some disciplines, such as the health sciences, have unique regulatory considerations when it comes to helping researchers manage and share their data. For example, some policies have an impact on how data can be managed and shared in a clinical trial (ClinicalTrials.gov, 2013). Federal laws such as HIPAA regulate the collection, retention, and use of patient data, www.hhs.gov/ocr/privacy/. Institutional polices such as those overseen by the IRB regulate research using human subjects. These policies affect the types and amount of identifying information that can be used in a data set; the amount of time that data and laboratory records are required to be maintained; the procedures for storing, securing, or destroying data; and which data, if any, can be shared or made publicly available.

Creating Data Repositories

Many large academic health sciences libraries have their own repositories for researchers to submit their publications and their data sets (Kochi et al., 2013; Palmer, 2013). When it comes to ingesting data into a repository, unique considerations include the size and formats of the files, core metadata, and the appraisal methods necessary to determine which data should be preserved. Health sciences librarians consult with researchers interested in placing their data into a repository about the types and amount of core metadata to use that will make their data meaningful to others.

Health sciences librarians develop and curate repositories and collections of research data. In addition to institutional repositories, health sciences librarians assist researchers with uploading their data to disciplinary repositories required by sponsors. For example, NIH funds a number of data-sharing repositories. Health sciences librarians create persistent identifiers for data sets and link publications to their underlying data, and keep abreast of the evolving conventions for creating data citations.

The ability to appropriately cite data is professionally important for health sciences researchers for a number of reasons. They may have reused data and want to responsibly cite others' data in their own research. They also want to receive credit from other researchers who have reused their data sets. The ability to document the number of times others have downloaded and cited their data could be of use in defense of their promotion and tenure by demonstrating how their data have increased the impact of their research (Piwowar, 2013). Organizations such as Data-Cite, www.datacite.org; Impact Story, www.impactstory.org; and Orcid, www.orcid .org, are working to increase the acceptance of a researcher's data and online works as equally legitimate scholarly contributions alongside their publications. Health sciences librarians are an important part of this paradigm shift because they help researchers to locate and cite data sets, and to publish their own data (Palmer, 2013).

Championing Public Access to Data

Health sciences librarians help researchers to see the value in publicly and openly sharing their data. Some types of health sciences data certainly cannot and should not be shared, such as sensitive or patient identifying data. But within the health sciences library community it is accepted that transparency in the research process (open science) and universal access (open access) to health information such as research data will benefit the health of a society by leading to better research and better health outcomes (HealthData.gov, 2013). The research community's inability to share, access, or reuse data results in "missed opportunities in economic, social and scientific advancements" (Pryor, 2012: 1). Health sciences librarians create guidance web pages and research guides to help their researchers learn about open access, open science, and open data; how to avoid the use of proprietary file formats; how to prepare and submit their data to open repositories; how to locate and search for data sets within open repositories; and how appropriately to repurpose and cite the data they find (Hanson et al., 2013).

In recent years, NYU Health Sciences Libraries has been building a suite of data management services. To help evaluate potential new data services, my colleague and I are partnering with a research team seeking to acquire new data sets to merge with grant-generated data from their previous studies. In light of the team's need to support the introduction of external data sets into its core data set, we are evaluating and restructuring their data model and data entry tools.

Karen Hanson, MLIS, knowledge systems librarian, NYU Health Sciences Libraries, New York

Data Management and Sharing Policies

Health sciences librarians shape their institutions' policies regulating the management and sharing of their researchers' data. Data management and data sharing policies not only outline the standards for data management, the data ownership, and intellectual property rights of the researchers and institutions, they also set the bar for each department's RDM roles and responsibilities, including the library (Creamer, 2013b). Health sciences librarians are on the committees that craft and implement these policies because they understand that these policies can officially recognize the responsibility of the library to support the institution's research enterprise. This recognition formalizes the role and the many efforts that libraries have pursued to offer RDM services. These policies directly impact the work of libraries to organize, build, and disseminate local collections of data and their mission to ensure that information is preserved and accessible to their users.

LIBRARIAN RDM SKILLS AND COMPETENCIES

Some health sciences librarians want to know if they need to have a background in science or have conducted scientific research to get involved with RDM (Creamer et al., 2012; Gore, 2012). Although this question has no definitive answer, health sciences librarians offering RDM services seek out professional development opportunities to learn more about science and the research process (Kafel, 2012). Corral (2012) found that the library and information science schools that have data curation programs use the data life cycle and **research life cycle** as a foundation for their curricula and many require practical field experience to engage students with the research process. Higgins's (2012) data life cycle outlines the relevant data management and preservation considerations that may arise at each of these steps.

Health sciences librarians embedded into research teams help to manage and preserve their projects' data from the outset, coordinating database design and knowledge mapping (Martin, 2013). Librarians need to build on their core information science knowledge base and expand that base to include technology, informatics, and outreach skills (Corral, 2012; Cox, Verbaan, and Sen, 2012; Creamer et al., 2012; Gore, 2012). Specific skills such as database management, database design, information searching, research methods, and digital preservation are traditional librarian skill sets. Data literacy, being able to communicate and solve problems, having an entrepreneurial spirit, a willingness to take risks, confidence, and working as part of a team are skills that librarians may be less familiar with (Gore, 2012).

Job postings for librarians involving some aspect of data management appear on a regular basis (Martin, 2012). Sample job titles include director of research data management, scientific data curator, data services manager, and associate director for data science. Selected job duties include:

- being the primary liaison for scientific data management
- developing library services and guidelines for supporting scientific research
- representing the library in institutional policy development
- facilitating the collection, preservation, and access to scientific data
- serving as a consultant for data management plans and practices for campus constituencies

Required qualifications are extensive and may include some or all of the following:

- advanced degree in physical or life sciences, data curation, or related disciplines
- recent graduates of data curation programs
- an understanding of the research process
- demonstrated technical knowledge
- familiarity with metadata
- understanding of institutional repositories
- grant-writing experience (E-science Portal for New England Librarians, 2013)

Creamer et al. (2012) surveyed health sciences librarians about their data management roles and competencies and the types of professional development instruction they felt were needed to offer RDM services. In addition to knowledge about RDM best practices, they needed domain-specific knowledge, data literacy instruction, and additional professional development opportunities to increase their technical competencies. Corrall (2012) found LIS programs teaching RDM skills to their students focused instruction on data literacy and technical skills. However, Cox, Verbaan, and Sen (2012) reported that the challenges to librarians' adopting RDM roles were not technical or data-related, but rather their lack of direct personal experience with research and difficulty balancing the provision of RDM services with their other priorities.

LIBRARIAN RDM TOOLS AND RESOURCES

The Data Interview

The data interview has become the essential tool for librarians to engage a researcher about his or her research practices and RDM needs (Witt and Carlson, 2007). Librarians use this type of interview to help researchers thoughtfully review their project and communicate the essential information about their data needs. This includes information on how the projects produce data, the nature of these data, as well as any challenges their teams may encounter managing these data. The data interview also provides the librarian with a tool to help researchers explore their intentions to preserve and share their data post-project.

The Data Curation Profiles

One of the first tools to build and expand upon the data interview was the Data Curation Profiles Toolkit (Purdue University and University of Illinois Urbana-Champaign, 2010). Librarians use the toolkit to interview researchers and explore the life cycle of a research project and requirements and issues regarding the resulting data. The completed **Data Curation Profiles** also comprise a digital reference collection with detailed information about a specific research project, its methods, and its data.

The DMPTool

Today, online data management planning tools such as the **DMPTool** have become key resources for librarians helping researchers to write DMPs for funders and to plan for their data management over the life cycle of their projects. A service of the University of California Curation Center of the California Digital Library, the DMPTool is an online tool that researchers can use to write their DMPs using customized templates for specific research funders and their data management and sharing requirements (California Digital Library, 2013). Any researcher at any institution can use the DMPTool; however, institutions that become partners of the DMPTool can customize the templates with guidance, resources, and policies specific to their institution.

RDM Professional Development Resources

In 2009, the Lamar Soutter Library at the University of Massachusetts Medical School (UMMS) and the National Network of Libraries of Medicine, New England Region (NN/LM, NER), created a continuing education program to develop RDM roles for health sciences librarians. The program has expanded to include a cadre of data-related professional development and continuing education events, courses, tools, and resources. UMMS hosts a data-related librarian Community of Interest (COI), an annual symposium, an annual boot camp, and an annual librarian professional development workshop, as well as a web portal for librarians, http://esciencelibrary.umassmed.edu/. In 2011, UMMS published a framework for a data management curriculum that included lesson plans, readings, and activities; and, in 2012, it launched a journal to publish health sciences librarians' data-related scholarship (Kafel, 2012).

In 2013, UMMS partnered with several libraries to publish the New England Collaborative Data Management Curriculum (NECDMC), http://library.umassmed.edu/necdmc/index, an online, case-based RDM course intended for use by health sciences librarians to teach RDM best practices to students and researchers. Each of the course modules aligns with NSF's DMP recommendations. The course's growing collection of actual research teaching cases provides discipline-specific context for the content presented in the modules. The teaching cases come from a range of research settings including clinical research, biomedical labs, clinical trials, and a qualitative behavioral health studies.

SUMMARY

RDM will increasingly become a part of health sciences librarianship. Today's health care delivery and research environments use a range of digital technologies to track measurements of patient health indicators and store clinical data. Tools such as EHRs, patient monitoring devices, automated lab instrumentation, and smartphones have become invaluable sources for locating and collecting health care data. The unprecedented volume of clinical and research data is rapidly growing. To ensure that researchers, clinicians, and patients can access these data, they must be appropriately managed, stored, and preserved. The stewardship of data requires a coordination of efforts by multiple players in the research environment—PIs, researchers, clinicians, lab assistants, IT staff, statisticians, funding agencies, and health sciences librarians. The successful use of these data in research and patient care has the potential to transform health care and spur treatments that will drastically improve the quality of human lives (Institute of Medicine, 2011).

The Institute of Medicine (2011) noted: "The successful development of clinical data as an engine for real-time knowledge generation has the potential to transform health and health care in America." However, broader access to and use of health care data requires not only fostering reliable and accessible data systems, but also addressing the issues such as individual data ownership and patient and public perception of clinical data as a carefully stewarded public good. The adaptation of digital technologies in health care delivery holds great promise to spur innovations in detection and treatment of disease and improve patient care. Thus, as operating components of health care and research environments, health sciences libraries are adopting and developing roles in RDM.

This chapter has highlighted emerging RDM roles for health sciences librarians: writing RDM guidance pages, teaching RDM best practices, demonstrating RDM tools and resources, offering RDM consulting and assistance with DMPs, building and managing collections of research data, and embedding within clinical and biomedical research teams. The RDM services offered vary by institution and by librarian. They depend on the number of staff, time, resources, and funds available, as well as the individual experience, skills, and competencies of the librarian. Offering RDM services is an evolving and emerging role for health sciences librarians. No one health sciences librarian can offer the full range of all data services, but he or she can observe best practices, share curricula, cooperate, and learn from colleagues. Retooling and learning new skills (upskilling) are important as few libraries have the funds to hire additional staff. The health sciences librarians undertaking these roles need continued administrative support and professional development. Investing in RDM services is important for health sciences libraries because they will ensure their future relevance.

STUDY QUESTIONS

1. What activities comprise RDM?
2. Why are health sciences librarians teaching researchers how to manage their data?
3. How have the federal government research sponsors' data management and sharing policies affected the roles of librarians?
4. Why do librarians use the research and data life cycles to teach data management?
5. What is the benefit of having a data management plan?
6. What RDM skills would health sciences librarians need to partner with/support researchers?

REFERENCES

ACRL Research Planning and Review Committee. 2012. "2012 Top Ten Trends in Academic Libraries." *College & Research Libraries News* 73, no. 6 (June): 311–20. http://crln.acrl.org/content/73/6/311.full#sec-3.

ARL (Association of Research Libraries). 2010. "E-Science and Data Support Services." August. www.arl.org/storage/documents/publications/escience-report-2010.pdf.

Ball, Alex. 2012. "Review of Data Management Lifecycle Models." February. http://opus.bath.ac.uk/28587/1/redm1rep120110ab10.pdf.

California Digital Library. 2013. "About the DMPTool." DMPTool. Accessed May 21. https://dmp.cdlib.org/about/dmp_about.

Challenge.gov. 2012. "Health Data Platform Metadata Challenge." Office of the National Coordinator for Health Information Technology. Accessed May 21. http://challenge.gov/ONC/374-health-data-platform-metadata-challenge.

ClinicalTrials.gov. 2013. "Protocol Data Element Definitions." Accessed May 21. http://prsinfo.clinicaltrials.gov/definitions.html.

Corral, Sheila. 2012. "Roles and Responsibilities: Libraries, Librarians and Data." In *Managing Research Data*, edited by Graham Pryor, 105–34. London: Facet.

Cox, Andrew, Eddy Verbaan, and Barbara Sen. 2012. "Upskilling Liaison Librarians for Research Data Management." *Ariadne*. December 6. www.ariadne.ac.uk/issue70/cox-et-al.

Creamer, Andrew. 2012. "Creating an Online Research Data Management Course: A Conversation with Data Librarians Robin Rice and Stuart Macdonald." *E-Science Community*. October 9. http://esciencelibrary.umassmed.edu/rice_macdonald_interview.pdf.

———. 2013a. "Crossing That Bridge We Have Come To: Teaching Students How to Manage Qualitative Data. A Conversation with Professor Julie McLeod and Susan Childs about DATUM for Health and DATUM: Research Data Management at Northumbria University." *E-Science Community*. March 19. http://esciencelibrary.umassmed.edu/esci_community_creamer_20130312.pdf.

———. 2013b. "A Seat at the Table: Involving the Library in the Planning of Institutional Research Data Management Policies and Responsibilities. A Conversation with the Iridium Project Team at Newcastle University." *E-Science Community*. May 22. http://esciencelibrary.umassmed.edu/esci_community_creamer_20130312.pdf.

Creamer, Andrew, M. E. Morales, J. Crespo, D. Kafel, and E. R. Martin. 2012. "An Assessment of Needed Competencies to Promote the Data Curation and Management Librarianship of Health Sciences and Science and Technology Librarians in New England." *Journal of eScience Librarianship* 1, no. 1. http://escholarship.umassmed.edu/jeslib/vol1/iss1/4/.

Crummet, Courtney. 2013. "One Academic Library's Response to the Data Dilemma." Contributed paper presented at the annual meeting of the Medical Library Association, Boston, May 6.

DataCite. 2012. "Why Cite Data?" Accessed May 21. www.datacite.org/whycitedata.

DataONE. 2012. "Best Practices." The Data Life Cycle. Accessed May 21. www.dataone.org/best-practices.

———. 2013. "Data Management Guide for Public Participation in Scientific Research." DataONE Public Participation in Scientific Research Working Group. February. www.dataone.org/sites/all/documents/DataONE-PPSR-DataManagementGuide.pdf.

Davidoff, Frank, and Valerie Florance. 2000. "The Informationist: A New Health Profession?" *Annals of Internal Medicine* 132, no. 12 (June): 996–98.

Dryad. 2011. "Joint Data Archiving Policy." Dryad. Reaffirmed April 7. http://datadryad.org/pages/jdap.

Erickson, Stephen, and Karen M.T. Muskavitch. 2013. "Data Management." U.S. Department of Health and Human Services. Office of Research Integrity. http://ori.hhs.gov/education/products/rcradmin/topics/data/open.shtml.

E-science Portal for New England Librarians. 2013. "Career Opportunities." University of Massachusetts. May 28. http://esciencecommunity.umassmed.edu/category/jobs/.

Federer, Lisa. 2013. "All It Takes Is One: Single-Session Data Literacy Instruction." Contributed poster presented at the annual meeting of the Medical Library Association, Boston, May 5.

Ferguson, Jen. 2013. "Lurking in the Lab: Analysis of Data from Molecular Biology Laboratory Instruments." *Journal of eScience Librarianship* 1, no. 3 (March): 148–58. http://escholarship.umassmed.edu/jeslib/vol1/iss3/5/.

Florance, Valerie. 2013. "Informationist Careers for Librarians: A Brief History of NLM's Involvement." *Journal of eScience Librarianship* 2, no. 1 (May): 3–5. http://escholarship.umassmed.edu/jeslib/vol2/iss1/2/.

Gore, Sally. 2012. "Failure to Communicate." *A Librarian by Any Other Name*. September 25. http://librarianhats.net/2012/09/.

Hanson, Karen, Alisa Surkis, and Karen Yacobucci. 2012. "Data Management Snafu in 3 Short Acts." *YouTube*. December 12. www.youtube.com/watch?v=N2zK3sAtr-4.

Hanson, Karen, Theodora A. Bakker, Mario A. Svirsky, Mario A. Neuman, Arlene C. Neuman, and Neil Rambo. 2013. "Informationist Role: Clinical Data Management in Auditory Research." *Journal of eScience Librarianship* 2, no. 1 (May): 24–29. http://escholarship.umassmed.edu/jeslib/vol2/iss1/7/.

Hanson, Karen, and Surkis, Alisa. 2013. "Introducing Researchers to Data Management: Pedagogy and Strategy." Contributed paper presented at the annual meeting of the Medical Library Association, Boston, May 6.

HealthData.gov. 2013. "Unleashing the Power of Data and Innovation to Improve Health." U.S. Department of Health and Human Services. Accessed May 21. www.healthdata.gov/unleashing-power-data-and-innovation-improve-health.

Higgins, Sarah. 2012. "The Lifecycle of Data Management." In *Managing Research Data*, edited by Graham Pryor, 17–45. London: Facet.

Hswe, Patricia. 2012. "Data Management Services in Libraries." In *Special Issues in Data Management*, edited by Norah Xiao and Leah Rae McEwen, 115–28. Washington, DC: American Chemical Society.

Institute of Medicine. 2011. "Clinical Data as the Basic Staple of Health Learning." National Academies. February 3. www.iom.edu/Reports/2011/Clinical-Data-as-the-Basic-Staple-for-Health-Learning.aspx.

Kafel, Donna. 2012. "Activities of Regional Consortia in Planning e-Science Continuing Education Programs for Librarians in New England." In *Special Issues in Data Management*, edited by Norah Xiao and Leah Rae McEwen, 69–96. Washington, DC: American Chemical Society.

Kafel, Donna, M. Piorun, S. Najafi, T. LegerHornby, and E. R. Martin. 2013. "Frameworks for a Data Management Curriculum for Science, Health Sciences, and Engineering Students." Contributed poster presented at the annual meeting of the Medical Library Association, Boston, May 5.

Kochi, Julia K., K. Cameron, A. Chatterjee, and A. Rizk-Jackson. 2013. "DataShare: Facilitating Scientific Data Sharing." Contributed paper presented at the annual meeting of the Medical Library Association, Boston, May 6.

Martin, Elaine R. 2012. "What Do Data Services Librarians Do?" *Journal of eScience Librarianship* 1, no. 3 (March): 1–2. http://escholarship.umassmed.edu/jeslib/vol1/iss3/3/.

———. 2013. "Highlighting the Informationist as a Data Librarian Embedded in a Research Team." *Journal of eScience Librarianship* 2, no. 1 (May): 1–2. http://escholarship.umassmed.edu/jeslib/vol2/iss1/1/.

McLeod, Julie, Sue Childs, and Elizabeth Lomas. 2013. "Research Data Management." In *Research Methods in Information*, 2nd ed., edited by Alison Jane Pickard, 71–86. Chicago: Neal-Schuman Publishers.

NAS (National Academy of Sciences). 2009. "Ensuring the Integrity, Accessibility, and Stewardship of Research Data in the Digital Age." Committee on Science, Engineering, and Public Policy (COSEPUP). http://books.nap.edu/openbook.php?record_id=12615.

Nature Neuroscience Editorial. 2009. "Ensuring Data Integrity." *Nature Neuroscience* 12, no. 1205. www.nature.com/neuro/journal/v12/n10/full/nn1009-1205.html. doi:10.1038/nn1009-1205.

NECDMC (New England Collaborative Data Management Curriculum). 2013. Lamar Soutter Library. University of Massachusetts Medical School. November. http://library.umassmed .edu/necdmc/index.

Norton, H. F., R. Garcia-Milian, M. Tennant, and C. E. Botero. 2013. "Supporting the Local Research Data Environment via Cross-Campus Collaboration and Leveraging of National Expertise." Contributed paper presented at the annual meeting of the Medical Library Association, Boston, May 6.

NSF (National Science Foundation). 2011. "Dissemination and Sharing of Research Results." Accessed May 21. www.nsf.gov/bfa/dias/policy/dmp.jsp.

OSTP (Office of Science and Technology Policy). 2013. "Expanding Public Access to the Results of Federally Funded Research." February 22. www.whitehouse.gov/blog/2013/02/22/ expanding-public-access-results-federally-funded-research.

Palmer, Lisa. 2013. "Article Level Metrics." Contributed paper presented at the annual meeting of the Medical Library Association, Boston, May 5.

Piorun, M. 2013. "The Library's Role in E-Science Programs in Research Universities." Contributed paper presented at the annual meeting of the Medical Library Association, Boston, May 5.

Piwowar, Heather. 2013. "Altmetrics: Value All Research Products." *Nature* 493, no. 159 (January). www.nature.com/nature/journal/v493/n7431/full/493159a.html.

Pryor, Graham. 2012. "Why Manage Research Data?" In *Managing Research Data*, edited by Graham Pryor, 1–16. London: Facet.

Purdue University and University of Illinois, Urbana-Champaign. 2010. "Purpose and Use of the Profiles." Data Curation Profiles. Accessed May 21. http://datacurationprofiles.org/ purpose.

U.S. National Institutes of Health. 2007. "NIH Data Sharing Policy." Office of Extramural Research Grants & Funding. April 17. http://grants.nih.gov/grants/policy/data_sharing/.

University of Edinburgh Data Library. 2011. "Research Data Explained." *MANTRA*. June 20. http://datalib.edina.ac.uk/xerte/play.php?template_id=9.

University of Virginia. 2012. "What is Data: An Introduction to Data Types." University of Virginia Graduate Student Portal. July 9. http://pages.shanti.virginia.edu/SciDaC_Grad_ Training/2012/07/09/observational-data/.

Witt, Michael, and Jake R. Carlson. 2007. "Conducting a Data Interview." Purdue University Libraries Research Publications. December. http://docs.lib.purdue.edu/cgi/viewcontent .cgi?article=1092&context=lib_research.

CHAPTER 11

Instruction in Health Sciences Libraries

Maureen "Molly" Knapp

INTRODUCTION

Instruction has long been an important role for public services librarians in the health sciences. Whether to achieve standards, meet accreditation requirements, or simply demonstrate a resource, educational services—instruction in some form or another—is something most health sciences librarians encounter at some point in their career. Thus, a basic understanding of some of the underlying methods, trends, and environments of instruction in the health sciences is useful to possess. This chapter discusses information literacy standards used in health sciences and higher learning and examines various methods and environments used in health sciences libraries.

HISTORY

Library instruction in the health sciences can be traced back to 1910, the publication year of the Flexner Report, which described the state of medical education in the United States and recommended improvements. The Flexner Report essentially codified medical education in the United States for the next century. The report observed that "certain general considerations affect equally instruction in all these laboratory sciences" and included among the calls for fully staffed medical laboratories, care and quarters for animals, and copious study space, a "reference library in regular receipt of important publications" (Flexner, 1910: 60), as necessary to the core function of the medical school.

As early as 1914, Charles Frankenberger, librarian at Jefferson Medical College, mused:

> Would it not be well for our medical colleges to provide somewhere throughout the course in medicine an opportunity for instruction in the use of the various indexes and

bibliographic reference works so valuable to the medical writer and investigator? Could not this instruction best be given by the one most familiar with the subject, the librarian in each institution? (Frankenberger, 1914: 656)

As the number of books, journals, and resources in the medical literature grew, the need for formal instruction emerged, albeit slowly. In 1931, only one medical library in the United States reported offering formal (e.g., required) library instruction (Runge, 1931). In 1975, a survey of medical libraries in the United States found that of the one hundred libraries responding, only eighteen offered formal course work, with nineteen more planning to do so (Martin, House, and Chandler, 1975). Twenty years later, this survey was repeated, with 75 percent of the fifty-five responding libraries offering formal instruction. "The survey responses reveal the prevalence of required library instruction in medical school curricula, and a broad-scale commitment to the development of lifelong learning skills among future health professionals" (Earl, 1996: 191).

Perhaps the most important standard for instruction librarians today is the *Information Literacy Competency Standards for Higher Education* from the Association of College and Research Libraries (ACRL). The term **information literacy** itself was coined by Paul Zurkowski in 1974 and plays a prominent role in academic library instruction. The ACRL's January 18, 2000, report defined information literacy as "a set of abilities requiring individuals to recognize when information is needed and have the ability to locate, evaluate, and use effectively the needed information" (ACRL, 2000: 4). The ACRL information literacy standards are often used to satisfy accreditation standards in undergraduate education and can be useful to health sciences librarians involved with undergraduate programs such as nursing or allied health.

THE RISE OF INFORMATION LITERACY

The ACRL information literacy standards are used heavily in undergraduate institutions to qualify information-seeking skills in students. A revised edition is forthcoming (Bell, 2013). Information literacy competency standards:

1. The information literate student determines the nature and extent of the information needed.
2. The information literate student accesses needed information effectively and efficiently.
3. The information literate student evaluates information and its sources critically and incorporates selected information into his or her knowledge base and value system.
4. The information literate student, individually or as a member of a group, uses information effectively to accomplish a specific purpose.
5. The information literate student understands many of the economic, legal, and social issues surrounding the use of information and accesses and uses information ethically and legally.

From: ACRL, 2000. *Information Literacy Competency Standards for Higher Education*. Chicago, IL: American Library Association. Used with permission.

The American Nurses Association (ANA) states that all nurses need informatics competencies in computer literacy, information literacy, and professional development to practice with health information technology (Cheeseman, 2013). In 2004, the Technology Informatics Guiding Educational Reform (TIGER) Initiative brought together leaders in the fields of nursing practice, education, and the delivery of patient care to develop strategies for improving the practice of nursing. TIGER's final report incorporated the ACRL information literacy competency standards into its recommendations (Technology Informatics Guiding Education Reform Initiative, 2009). A complete set of information literacy competency standards in nursing was projected to be completed and submitted to ACRL for approval in mid-2013. The goal is to create a common language for nursing faculty and librarians to use when incorporating standards into programs in order to assess student readiness for evidence-based practice. The TIGER initiative has also established a shared understanding of student information literacy competency needs between administration and curriculum committees (Phelps, 2013).

In 1998, the Association of American Medical Colleges (AAMC) introduced the Medical School Objectives Project (MSOP), an initiative "designed to reach general consensus within the medical education community on the skills, attitudes, and knowledge that graduating medical students should possess" (AAMC, 2013). A number of reports discussed contemporary issues in medicine, but the most relevant report for librarians was Report II: Contemporary Issues in Medicine: Medical Informatics and Population Health.

Report II recommended that, at the time of graduation, medical students should be able to "utilize biomedical information for: formulating problems; arriving at strategies for solutions; collecting, critiquing and analyzing information; taking action based on findings; and communicating and documenting these processes and the results" (AAMC, 1998: 4). Interestingly enough, the report does not mention using a librarian to teach these skills.

Likewise, the Liaison Committee on Medical Education (LCME), the nationally recognized accrediting authority for medical education programs leading to the MD degree in the United States and Canada, has standards for library equipment and resources but does not outline specific instruction responsibilities for librarians. The Accreditation Council for Graduate Medical Education (ACGME), which accredits medical residency programs, similarly requires only computers and Internet access for accreditation. Most residency programs also stipulate that a training program must provide access to a major medical library either onsite or at a nearby institution.

The Association of Schools of Public Health, an accrediting agency for graduate-level public health programs, includes information literacy in its 2006 report on core competencies for master's-level public health programs. Interdisciplinary competencies of note include collecting, managing, and organizing data; using information technology to access evaluate and interpret public health data; and applying evidence-based approaches to the development and evaluation of social and behavior sciences interventions (Association of Schools of Public Health Education Committee, 2006).

A 2009 survey of the health sciences librarians in medical education found that although the ability to access, manage, and use information resources is a critical skill for health care providers, "the standards issued by the agencies that accredit theses training programs generally do not recognize the roles and contribution of health sciences librarians" (Schwartz et al., 2009: 283). It is of rising importance to work with faculty and accrediting agencies to ensure validation and recognition of the library's role in health sciences education.

Information literacy standards have seen steady adoption in the health professions since codified by ALA in 2000. A 2012 report by Eldredge et al. generated an inventory of library and information literacy competencies from twenty-seven professional organizations in health care. The report reveals "library/informatics skills and competencies now appear to occur primarily within the context of Evidence-based Practice in health professional education curricula" (Eldredge et al., 2012: 38). The report includes a compendium of library/informatics-related competency statements from professional organizations in health care, with a goal to "provide readers with a starting point for integrating their own library/informatics training into the health profession education programs affiliated with their libraries" (Eldredge et al., 40).

An awareness of library/informatics competencies for health professionals is strongly recommended for any librarian involved in instruction. For academic librarians, it is necessary in order to ensure that accreditation standards are met. For hospital librarians, it is necessary in order to understand the information needs of patrons. Knowing what accrediting agencies expect of medical libraries will ultimately ensure that the library stays on target in terms of patron and stakeholder needs and expectations.

GENERATIONS AND LEARNING

Several generations are at play in the health care world today. A generation is defined as "individuals of a certain age group who share common experiences, values, communities and sense of identity, all of which are shaped by major national & world events or social trends" (Roberts, Newman, and Schwarzstein, 2012: 274). The Silent Generation refers to people born between 1928 and 1945 who shared common experiences such as the Great Depression and World War II. These are the emeritus faculty and retired researchers who may wander into the medical library. Baby Boomers are their children, born roughly between 1945 and 1964; they are currently reaching retirement age. Their lives were shaped by social upheaval, the civil rights movement, and the Vietnam War. Generation X, born between 1964 and 1982, grew up in a time of relative stability and growth in the world economy and are now approaching middle age. Finally, the Millennial Generation (also referred to as "Generation Y" and the "Me" Generation) are individuals born since 1982. The Millennials are the current crop of students in higher education, and the ones causing the most consternation among instructors.

"I like to think of my generation, the class of 2000, as the Millennial Generation. . . . We're the kids who are going to change things" (Howe and Strauss, 2000: 12). So begins Howe and Strauss's influential work, *Millennials Rising: The Next Great Generation*, which sought to define the generation that would turn eighteen and enter college or the adult workforce at the turn of the millennium. Millennials have grown up experiencing a varied amount of environmental and cultural forces including omnipresence of online technology; novel modes of communication, such as e-mail, mobile devices, and texting; a weak global economy; September 11; school shootings; and seemingly endless wars.

Several features of Millennial learning differ from previous generations. Millennials tend to be experiential and exploratory learners, preferring to find a link between classroom content and its real-world application. They are practical and results oriented: When faced with a graded activity, timely feedback is expected. Millennials identify themselves as multitaskers, claiming to able to work on several activities at once. They are the first true **digital natives**—those who have had access to technology such as e-mail, texting, and the Internet all their lives (Prensky, 2001). As such, Millennials expect technology to work properly.

Millennial instruction is most successful when the focus is on active learning. **Active learning** can be defined as "providing students the opportunity to talk and listen, read, write, and reflect" (Sayre, 1999: 31). Group-based activities that work to solve complex, realistic problems will resonate with contemporary learners more than lecture and rote memorization, as will access to resources on demand through learning management systems or subject guides, and an emphasis on cooperative group learning and discussion. Examples of active learning will be explored later in the chapter.

LEARNING PARADIGMS

When thinking about teaching, what should be the focus? Several paradigms exist. Student-centered learning emphasizes the student as an active participant in knowledge building, often through activities that allow students to discuss, listen, read, write, and reflect. Conversely, teacher-centered learning focuses on the teacher— "the sage on the stage." Teacher-centered learning is traditionally what is found in education: the expert in a lecture hall, armed with PowerPoint slides and a long conversation. This section will explore different approaches to student- and teacher-centered learning models.

Teacher-Centered Learning

As any student can attest, sitting through a long lecture on library resources can be torturous, and indeed, library science students interested in instruction should attempt a forty-five-minute lecture on **bibliographic instruction** if only for a practice in masochism. Teacher-centered learning, the basic lecture format that was a paradigm of higher education for most of the twentieth century, must be engaging to be effective.

As an in-classroom technique to enhance learning, audience response systems (popularly called "clickers") have gained popularity in education because of the accountability and interactivity they offer in large lecture environments. These sophisticated systems can be used to take attendance and quiz or assess attitudes, and response data can be collected and recorded in course management systems for grading purposes. In the classroom, informal polling systems that use text

What if a professor or program director gives you forty-five minutes to an hour of your audience's undivided time to discuss library resources?
Best tips:

- Frame your presentation in the context of your audience. Open with a recent study, story, or news item of interest to the group.
- Offer objectives or an overview of what you'll cover at the beginning of the lecture. This also helps you stay focused on what you'll talk about.
- Allow for classroom discussion and questions during the lecture.
- If questions arise, answer them and move on. Sketch a time frame for each objective and stick to it.
- Include the "who, what, when, where, and how" of library resources: hours, contacts, location, interlibrary loan, link resolvers/full text, printing/scanning, and borrowing privileges.
- At the end of the lecture, revisit your objectives or overview and reflect.
- Always emphasize your contact information. We are here to support our patrons.

messaging, Facebook, or a website to respond to questions can be used to keep the audience engaged and break up a long lecture.

Types of Student-Centered Learning

Problem-based learning, team-based learning, and case-based learning are all examples of small group-centered learning that can be used to incorporate information literacy standards into the curriculum while still learning about a larger subject. They are also examples of active learning, which is discussed as a trend in Chapter 3. The key for success in using these techniques is ensuring that the students receive feedback on their performance and that they exhibit learning progress in some way.

Problem-Based Learning

In **problem-based learning (PBL)**, students work in groups on open-ended problems, with minimal instructional intervention. The teacher acts as a facilitator, answering questions, probing opinions, and working toward an answer (Eldredge, 2004). PBL is concerned with both what students learn and how they learn it (Barrows, 1983), and uses specially prepared problems, usually written cases derived from clinical experience, as the basis of the curriculum (Bligh, 1999). An important part of PBL is developing self-directed learning skills, which allow the student to become sensitive to personal learning needs and to locate and use appropriate information resources.

McMaster University in Ontario, Canada, was the first medical school in North America to adopt a PBL medical curriculum. The University of New Mexico was the first medical school in the United States to use PBL, whereas Mercer University School of Medicine in Georgia was the first school in the United States to use PBL as the only curricular offering (Donner and Bickly, 1993). Today, PBL is used in many health sciences disciplines. Librarian involvement in PBL has been embraced by many fields, including medicine (Eldredge et al., 1998), dentistry (Hasman, 2012), nursing (Barnard, Nash, and O'Brien, 2005), and occupational therapy (Vogel, 2012).

The format of PBL usually centers on a case study or a problem or question that does not have one easy answer. For example, at the University of New Mexico School of Medicine, medical students work though a simulated patient case in small tutorial groups, meeting twice a week for three hours per session. The students have no prior reading or lectures to prepare them for the simulated patient. Instead, they call upon the collective wisdom of the group and their reasoning abilities to solve the case. The simulated patient acts as a springboard to identify "learning issues" in the small group sessions, which students research independently, and bring back for discussion at the next small group session. Throughout the small group process, faculty members act as tutors and advisers, actively listening, guiding, and assessing student performance (Eldredge, 2004).

In health sciences libraries, PBL can be used to teach information-seeking skills. Librarians at the University of Toledo College of Medicine (UTCOM) incorporated information literacy PBL into a clinical decision-making course for first-year medical students (Mi, 2011). Learning objectives for the course already included applying scientific knowledge to diagnose clinical problems, identifying learning issues, and selecting references from credible sources to answer clinical questions, so inserting an information literacy component into the curriculum was simple. As part of the course, the librarians provided a one-time large group lecture that included an explanation of question formation and how it is used in the practice of evidence-based medicine. A physician educator demonstrated how to perform the clinical reasoning process, and the librarian overviewed online library resources appropriate for finding answers to clinical questions. An online subject guide with pertinent library resources was also created.

Armed with this information, students proceeded to work on a small group case discussion. Students were taught how to diagnose and treat a clinical case, as well as submit a list of references to back up their clinical decisions. Faculty members facilitated discussion, offering clinical expertise and probing questions to guide students to appropriate answers, and encouraging participation from group members. Librarians participating in the facilitation process found that involvement in PBL cases expanded their role beyond the library and increased collaboration with course directors and medical educators. Students also developed a better awareness of library online resources and information-seeking skills (Mi, 2011).

Working as a small group facilitator or tutor is a one role for librarians involved in PBL. Although not content experts, librarians can provide behavioral modeling to show how to use library resources to answer clinical questions. They can also coach students on where to look for answers in simulated patient systems, or prompt the use of learning activities to accomplish tasks collaboratively (Mi, 2011). Ensuring that the environment promotes all students' learning, guiding students in critically appraising information resources, and encouraging feedback and assessment from group members are all roles a librarian–facilitator can embrace, without the clinical expertise (Eldredge, 2004).

Although many health sciences librarians are involved in PBL, some research has questioned its effectiveness. A randomized controlled trial conducted at the University of Alberta, Canada, found the addition of a librarian had little impact on the students' knowledge and attitudes on evidence-based practice (Koufogiannakis et al., 2005). More recent studies suggest that librarians offering individualized feedback to students during PBL group sessions may protect against the decline of good information retrieval habits over time (Chen et al., 2009) as well as increase the use of resources specifically highlighted during instructional sessions (Rafferty, 2013). Nevertheless, librarian involvement in PBL is likely to continue, and more research on the impact of librarian-led instruction is needed (Dorsch and Perry, 2012).

Case-Based Learning

Case-based learning (CBL) is similar to problem-based learning in that both involve discussing patient cases in small groups. Unlike PBL—in which students are given a problem, then generate "learning issues" to study independently—in CBL, students receive a complete case for study and research prior to class. The subsequent interactive case discussion, directed by the teacher in a tutorial role, combines both student- and teacher-directed learning. The instructor plays a more active role in providing information, rather than being solely a facilitator for self-directed student learning. Srinivasan et al. (2007) provide a detailed comparison of the features of problem-based versus case-based learning.

Examples of the involvement of health sciences librarians in CBL are less prevalent in the literature than they are for PBL. In one instance, librarians at the Indiana University School of Medicine used a case study to introduce first-year medical students to various information resources. A clinical case provided the framework to explain the concepts of foreground and background questions; then, students were divided into small groups for hands-on exploration of resources via a web-based subject guide (Whipple et al., 2009). Another library used LibGuides to create an online portal to facilitate case-based learning (Neves and Dooley, 2011).

Team-Based Learning

Team-based learning (TBL) is a way to engage small group learning in a large group setting. Students review the primary material ahead of time, and use class time to work on small group projects and assignments. TBL was developed in the 1970s by Larry Michealsen, a university instructor at the University of Oklahoma. Michealsen created group-driven assignments to deal with the increasing numbers of students in his lecture-based classes and noticed uncalculated benefits emerging from team activities (Michaelsen, Knight, and Fink, 2002). TBL is useful for library instruction because it offers the opportunity to apply hands-on work with databases to unique projects that resonate with students. Generally, students are presented with a problem or case and are instructed to provide a solution. Faculty or mentors facilitate by asking questions, guiding discussion, handling group dynamics, and keeping the class on schedule. In that respect, it is very similar to PBL and CBL. What differentiates TBL from other active learning techniques is the emphasis on a formalized learning process incorporating individual and group assessment.

COMPONENTS OF TBL—PART 1:
READINESS ASSURANCE PROCESS (RAP)

Step one: Preclass reading assignment
Step two: Individual Readiness Assurance Process Test (iRAT)

- Multiple-choice quiz covering key concepts in the reading, taken individually.
- Purpose: holds students accountable for preclass material.

Step three: Team Readiness Assurance Process Test (tRAT)

- The same multiple-choice quiz, completed in small groups using a scratch-off answer sheet called the Immediate Feedback Assurance Test (IF-AT).
- Purpose: Group discussion and decision making reviews reading, resolves misunderstandings, serves as occasion for peer teaching.

Step four: Appeals

- Compare tRAT and iRAT scores.
- Students appeal incorrect questions.
- Purpose: concept review, specifically focusing on areas of difficulty.

Step five: Mini-lecture

- Focused lecture on concepts most problematic for students is delivered using iRAT scores as a guide to gaps in learning.

Two common phrases encountered in TBL are iRAT and tRAT. These formalized terms refer to assessments at the individual and team level. They are used during the first step in TBL: the Readiness Assurance Process, which ensures that students are held accountable for completing the preclass reading and have the foundational knowledge to work on solving problems together. The sidebar "Components of TBL—Part 1" describes their function and purpose in the TBL process.

Once the Readiness Assurance Process is completed, learners should be prepared to apply course concepts to in-class group activities. "Components of TBL—Parts 2 and 3" explains the four features of successful TBL group activities and feedback methods once the activity is completed. As Sweet notes, the worst task for a TBL exercise is a group paper or presentation. The best task is similar to a courtroom jury: Given a tremendous amount of complex information, groups produce choice and rationale for a decision (Sweet, 2013).

Although TBL is still being adopted as an instructional technique in libraries, early adopters are impressed with the level of learning that occurs. Health sciences librarians at Duke University collaborated with physical therapy faculty to create a TBL for students in a doctoral physical therapy program about locating evidence-based literature. The TBL included an online tutorial preassignment, readiness

COMPONENTS OF TBL—PARTS 2 AND 3: IN-CLASS ACTIVITIES AND FEEDBACK

Part 2: In-class Activities
Purpose: Applies course concepts to larger problems via group application exercises.

Successful group activities employ the four S's of TBL:

1. Address a <u>S</u>ignificant problem that demonstrates a concept's usefulness
2. Make a <u>S</u>pecific choice among clear alternatives
   Examples: What is the most important piece of evidence in support of this concept? Which statement would the author most agree with?
3. Work on the <u>S</u>ame problem as other teams
4. Report their decisions <u>S</u>imultaneously, to explore team differences
   Examples: holding up cards, audience response systems, write solution on board

Part 3: Feedback
Purpose: Holds all team members accountable, contributes to grade

- Mid-course and end-of-course feedback from group members suggested for long-term TBL.
- Should be anonymous.
- Example: group members list one thing they appreciate, and one thing they request for each of their teammates (Sweet, 2013).

assessments, and a team application in class activity. "The team application presented a case and required student groups to form a clinical question; construct a search strategy; and search PubMed, PEDro, and Google Scholar for an answer" (Tuttle and Leonardelli, 2012). In 2013, librarians at Duke expanded their TBL sessions to provide EBM and PubMed instruction for second-year medical students (Schardt and von Isenburg, 2013).

Student-centered, active learning techniques such as PBL, case studies, and TBL are a departure from traditional teaching methods. This can be intimidating because it requires some loss of control, as well as a great deal of time investment preparing course activities, but the payoffs are worth it. Students learn best when they are active in their own learning, and instructors, seeing knowledge from the classroom applied to real-life situations, receive concrete proof of a job well done.

DISRUPTIVE TECHNOLOGY AND HEALTH SCIENCES INSTRUCTION

Disruptive technologies are innovations that shake up the production of a product or the application of a service, and press for changes in the way things are done or made (Premebida, 2010). The Internet and video games are examples of disruptive technologies working their way into contemporary library instruction.

Flipped Classroom

Like it sounds, a **flipped classroom** flips the traditional environment of the classroom. Students do what would usually be included in a class lecture beforehand (such as background readings and listening to lectures), leaving class time devoted to exercises, projects, or discussions about content. "In the flipped classroom, the teacher shifts from being the 'sage on the stage' to the 'guide on the side'" (Parslow, 2012: 337). Lectures are covered at home, and the homework activities are brought to the classroom as active learning activities. The flipped classroom method emerged in 2006 when a hedge-fund manager named Salman Khan started developing and sharing math tutorials with family on YouTube. As his tutorials grew in popularity, Khan left his career to create the Khan Academy, www.khanacademy.org/, now a robust site of more than 4,400 web-based tutorials on a variety of topics.

As an instructor, it is important to know your audience and their immediate need. I tailor my instruction using a scenario or example that provides context to that particular set of learners. Making the session interactive is crucial to deep learning. Even if the instruction is not hands-on, make your learners do the work. I will often provide a brief ten- to fifteen-minute overview of the resource(s), then turn it back to the group to solve a scenario-based question using the covered resource(s). Active peer learning with instructor input engages learners and provides instructor insight into misconceptions.

Sarah Knox Morley, MLS, AHIP, clinical services librarian, University of New Mexico Health Sciences Library & Informatics Center, Albuquerque

As an emergent educational model powered by technology, the flipped classroom has been criticized for teaching only basic skills (Parslow, 2012). The potential application of flipped classrooms in library instruction is intriguing. Online tutorials could provide instruction on information-seeking skills, using class time for hands-on learning activities. For an example of how the flipped classroom model is applied to medical education, see UndergroundMed, http://undergroundmed.net. The site provides interactive videos on clinical topics. The videos are created by medical students and reviewed by experienced medical educators.

Gamification

Gamification can be defined as "application of game-play mechanics in nongame settings" (Danforth, 2011: 84). A nonhealth sciences libraries example of gamification in libraries is the game BiblioBouts, http://bibliobouts.org, an online game designed by the University of Michigan's School of Information and George Mason University's Center for History and New Media to teach information literacy skills. The online game challenges students to identify literature on a preset topic, which is then ranked by peers for use on a research assignment. A forthcoming book, *Designing Information Literacy Games that Students Want to Play*, discusses how to design, develop, deploy, and evaluate the online information literacy games, using BiblioBouts as a case study (Markey, Leeder, and Rieh, 2014).

Although gamification in health sciences library instruction is a relatively new concept, some libraries have incorporated games into their online arsenal. Librarians at the Reed Health Sciences Library, at Lincoln Memorial University in Harrogate, Tennessee, provide a list of freely available interactive games, simulations, tutorials, and quizzes that support the curriculum for undergraduate and graduate health sciences programs (Travis, 2013); others have attempted library scavenger hunts via mobile devices to varying degrees of success (McMunn-Tetangco, 2013).

HOSPITAL LIBRARIES AND INSTRUCTION

Hospital librarians count instruction as one of the many responsibilities they have in running what is usually a smaller staffed library. Consumers, patients, and hospital staff all have varying educational needs, which the hospital library is expected to satisfy. The rise of evidence-based practice has increased the demand for health care practitioners to locate and evaluate research. Hospitals seeking nursing magnet status may see an increased awareness of evidence-based practice and a call for instruction about these techniques (Pappas, 2008).

In 2006, a report by Scherrer, Dorsch, and Weller observed the different approaches to instruction in hospitals versus academia and recognized that "evidence-based practice curricula in health professions colleges will need teaching approaches that are appropriate for instruction of students in a classroom, while the hospital librarian may be looking for point-of-need instructional techniques that would be effective with residents and clinicians" (2006: 163). Hospital librarians may find themselves providing instruction more informally than academic medical librarians.

Educating nurses on information resources and practices is another important feature of instruction in hospital libraries. Most U.S. nurses do not enter the profession with a bachelor of science in nursing, the level where research classes are consistently offered. As a result, many nurses lack familiarity with research concepts (Cyrus et al., 2012).

Hospital libraries offer numerous approaches to nursing instruction. At LSUHSC-Shreveport, librarians provide mobile instruction following the nursing in-service model, traveling to various wards and modeling how to access library resources through the hospital's electronic health record system (Cyrus et al., 2012). Others have used a "survivor" style elimination game (Gage, Peckman, and Greene, 2011) and a menu/buffet theme to evaluate and use hospital staff databases (Polger, 2010). Other examples of hospital library instruction include providing foreign language labs (Whelan, 2006), offering grant and publishing support (Blobaum, 2007; Doyle, 2005), coordinating continuing medical education (Beales, 2002), and distributing patient information (Strube, 2006).

USER EDUCATION AND INSTRUCTIONAL MECHANICS

Health sciences librarians approach classroom instruction in a variety of ways. Instruction may be taught face-to-face in a computer lab or classroom (live synchronous learning), facilitated in real time over the Internet (online synchronous learning), or created for the web to be accessed as needed (asynchronous online learning). In academic settings, health sciences librarians may be a departmental liaison, teaching library introduction classes as they come along, or they may be integrated into a particular program of study. For distance programs, librarians may be asked to develop and facilitate online content and instruction.

Bibliographic instruction is a term often used when discussing user education in libraries. It can be defined as "the systematic nature of the effort to teach a set of principles or search strategies relating to the library, its collections or services, using predetermined methods in order to accomplish a pre-defined set of objectives" (Salony, 1995: 32). The subsequent sections in this chapter will describe a basic approach to explaining the search process in the context of database searching, delve into different formats of library instruction in the health sciences, and explore common subjects of health sciences instruction.

Database Instruction—the Basics

Imagine being tasked with your first instruction session in the health sciences. Where do you start? If a library user doesn't grasp a basic knowledge of search construction, he or she can be frustrated from the beginning. Framing a search as a series of steps clarifies the information needs of the user, targets results, and saves time locating items. Constructing and executing a search includes six basic components, regardless of topic, location, or specialty (see Figure 11.1).

First, and most important, a thesis statement identifying the topic to be searched should be formulated. A bad search example is, "I need articles about sickle cell disease." This is too broad. Does this refer to sickle cell disease in specific populations? Sickle cell disease associated with another ailment? Should the results contain articles for a health professional or a consumer? A thesis statement should be as specific as possible. In the case above, a refined thesis statement could be: "I need research that supports the use of NSAIDS for children with sickle cell disease."

The second step breaks apart the thesis statement into simple phrases or concepts. Using the sickle cell example above, the concepts would be: NSAIDS, children, and sickle cell disease. Another recommendation is to brainstorm synonyms. What acronyms or other phrases are used to describe key concepts? Use this point in instruction to discuss how databases provide controlled vocabularies and automatic term mapping to enhance discovery. Differentiate between a keyword search (terms used in a search engine such as Google) and using subject headings (the controlled vocabularies used by databases to classify the main idea of an article, book, or other work).

The third step introduces Boolean logic to connect, exclude, or expand the search. Ask the class if anyone has heard of Boolean operators, and what they are. Boolean searching is based on an algebraic system of logic formulated by George Boole, a nineteenth-century English mathematician. In a Boolean search, keywords are combined by logic operators AND, OR, and NOT to narrow or expand the search. A good piece of advice to impart to students is to replace prepositions (words such as "in," "about," "for," "according to") with the Boolean operator AND for better results. When that is completed, press the search button and an overwhelming number of results are retrieved.

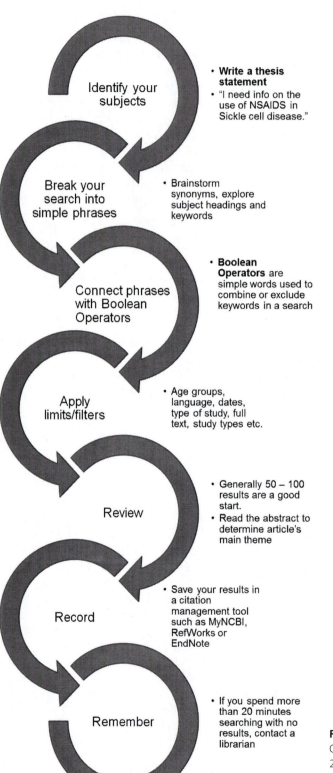

Identify your subjects

- **Write a thesis statement**
- "I need info on the use of NSAIDS in Sickle cell disease."

Break your search into simple phrases

- Brainstorm synonyms, explore subject headings and keywords

Connect phrases with Boolean Operators

- **Boolean Operators** are simple words used to combine or exclude keywords in a search

Apply limits/filters

- Age groups, language, dates, type of study, full text, study types etc.

Review

- Generally 50 – 100 results are a good start.
- Read the abstract to determine article's main theme

Record

- Save your results in a citation management tool such as MyNCBI, RefWorks or EndNote

Remember

- If you spend more than 20 minutes searching with no results, contact a librarian

Figure 11.1. Search Process Outlined. Credit: Copyright 2013 Maureen M. Knapp.

Step four narrows search strategies using filters, limits, or facets. The words vary among databases, but the endpoint is the same: further reducing and refining results using limits such as dates, age groups, populations, journal titles, or publication types. For groups concerned with scientific research, randomized controlled trial is always a useful filter for locating research articles.

Step five reviews the results. To determine an article's relevance, read the abstract of an article and identify whether it is research, editorial, or review. Explain how to mark articles for further review.

Step six records the results. Identify options for e-mailing or exporting articles to a bibliographic citation manager, using that as a springboard for discussion on various citation styles and what information from the abstract is important to record so it can be cited or referenced in a paper.

A final "step" in the basic database instruction session is more of a piece of advice: Remember, if more than twenty minutes are spent on fruitless searching, it's time for the user to contact a librarian.

Library Instruction Formats

One-Shot Session

One-shot instruction sessions are short, generally one hour or less, and focus on a particular assignment. Content varies depending on the assignment, but generally includes basic information about the library and how to use a particular resource to complete an assignment. One-shot sessions differ from library workshops or seminars primarily because they are connected to a single class or course in a program of study.

ONE-SHOT SESSION EXAMPLE—NURSING RESEARCH

A nursing course instructor wants students to receive a review on how to search the database CINAHL: The Cumulative Index to Nursing and Allied Health Literature, prior to writing a pathophysiology paper. The one-shot session covers how to use CINAHL subject headings to identify subjects (as compared to a simple keyword search) and using subheadings such as physiopathology when conducting a subject heading search to find specific pathophysiology research. The session also shows how to obtain the full text of an article and use interlibrary loan when the article is unavailable. A final portion of the class discusses APA style citations.

Course-Integrated Instruction

Course-integrated instruction consists of multiple instruction sessions over a single course. As opposed to focusing on a particular assignment, library topics are worked into the course to demonstrate their usefulness as tools for the health practitioner or student. Course-integrated instruction can be useful in developing closer relationships with faculty and students and meeting accreditation standards in research literacy, but challenges can arise if the class is not required for all students, or the course is reassigned from year to year and the library is not always included.

COURSE-INTEGRATED INSTRUCTION EXAMPLE—RESPIRATORY THERAPY COURSE ON EVIDENCE-BASED PRACTICE

Students enrolled in a respiratory therapy program require instruction on evidence-based practice tools during their course on evidence-based practice. Working with the instructor, librarians designed a three-part series of classes. The first class introduces search methods in evidence-based practice, such as constructing foreground and background questions; PICO; and using PubMed, Medical Subject Headings, and PubMed Clinical Queries. The second session introduces the point-of-care database DynaMed and encourages comparison in discovering evidence-based research in different ways (e.g., searching a literature database versus using a point-of-care tool). The third session reviews RefWorks and discusses using a reference management tool to organize research for a paper.

Curriculum-Integrated Programming

Curriculum-integrated programming, the "gold standard approach to information literacy instruction" (Brower, 2008: 228), refers to multiple instruction sessions over a course of study. It can be defined as "any programming that is consistently integrated into the requisite curriculum of the school" (228). Many health sciences fields have incorporated information literacy standards into accreditation, driving a broader adoption of curriculum-integrated programming.

Curriculum-integrated programming can take various forms and time lines, but four elements of curriculum-integrated programming are constant:

1. It has authority. Curriculum-integrated programming is recognized by the dean or department chair, supported by the library director, and has the general support of the school's faculty.
2. It meets standards. The curriculum meets information skill requirements set forth by the accrediting agency.
3. It has uniformity. All students enrolled in the program are exposed to the same material.
4. It is customized. The course is designed to best meet the information literacy needs of the discipline or school. (Brower, 2008)

CURRICULUM-INTEGRATED PROGRAMMING EXAMPLE— PHYSICAL THERAPY INSTRUCTION

Physical therapy students receive a sixty-minute library introduction in their first semester covering the basics (catalog, finding full-text resources, hours, location, services, and contacts). The next semester, students receive more customized instruction during a Research I class as they begin formulating ideas for their thesis/capstone project. This class covers search construction, subject databases, and search techniques. A final class in the beginning of the second year covers the use of reference management tools so they can organize and cite their research, and offers one-on-one time with the librarian to review search techniques and locate research as the capstone due date approaches.

Curriculum-integrated programming is time consuming and requires a great deal of planning. Identifying educational objectives, mapping them to standards, creating lesson plans, developing online content, and evaluating the results are all important components of the planning process, which will be explored shortly.

INSTRUCTIONAL DESIGN— CREATING YOUR CLASS

Instructional Design Models

Instructional design is the systematic process of creating effective instruction. It incorporates instructional theory, research, and outcomes. It involves creating learning objectives, choosing lecture and presentation strategies, and developing assessment materials. Instructional design has been influenced by a number of disciplines, especially cognitive and behavioral psychology.

Instructional design models have been applied to health sciences instruction with positive results. One example of an instructional design model is ADDIE, which was used by librarians at Weill Cornell Medical College to redesign an evidence-based medicine course for first-year medical students. Using an instructional design model resulted in outcomes-focused instruction relevant to students' needs (Reinbold, 2013).

We work with the school of medicine undergraduate education committee to provide resource instruction to second-year medical students. Four librarians share the responsibilities of providing instruction in multiple, one-hour sessions two weeks prior to group presentations on medical topics. Our instruction targets specific module topics, introducing relevant resources for medical students' educational development. The library curriculum includes assessment of student competencies in evidence-based practice, which follows the ACGME competency assessment of medical residents. Collaboration with school of medicine course coordinators resulted in librarians being included and recognized as important players in curriculum development. For example, I was invited to explain the medical informatics curriculum to the LCME accreditation committee during their site visit.

Kathy Kerdolff, MLIS, AHIP, assistant professor of medical bibliography, Louisiana State University Health Sciences Center Library, New Orleans

The ADDIE model divides the process of instructional design into five steps: Analysis, Design, Development, Implementation, and Evaluation. In the analysis phase, a problem is identified and learning objectives, needs, and goals are composed. The design stage identifies the appropriate instructional strategy and learning environment. The development stage builds the course—perhaps a dry run of the course is tested and reviewed. In the implementation phase, the course is executed and feedback is collected. In the final evaluation stage, evidence collected from the class is assessed and used to further refine future iterations of a course.

Although the ADDIE model is useful to structure courses, it is not without its limitations. One caveat of the model is that it is only a method to design training, not a solution to boring classes. "It is not a guarantee that the training will succeed, as instructor delivery can make a well-designed course succeed or fail" (Reinbold, 2013: 255).

Explaining other instructional design models is beyond the scope of this chapter due to their number and complexity. For more information on other instructional design models in libraries, see Char Booth's *Reflective Teaching, Effective Learning: Instructional Literacy for Library Educators* (Booth, 2011).

Components of Instructional Design

Lesson Plans

A lesson plan can be anything from a scribbled outline to a formalized document. Lesson plans are useful because they provide a framework for conducting a class. They are also convenient in the event you cannot teach a class, because your colleagues will have an outline to use. Finally, lesson plans are useful reminders for classes that may be taught once or twice a year or at irregular intervals.

Generally, lesson plans include a title or subject of the class, notes such as the number of students expected, the time frame to teach and prepare, the class location, whether attendance is counted toward a grade or if the class is in preparation for a particular assignment, learning objectives, class materials, in-class examples, planned activities, and assessment materials. If "winging it" is not your style, consider writing a lesson plan to focus your learning outcomes and activities.

Learning Objectives and Bloom's Taxonomy

Writing down learning objectives before a class helps focus course content. Learning objectives answer the question, what will the students be able to do at the end of the session? Bloom's taxonomy provides useful vocabulary for writing learning objectives and studying which level of learning is engaged during that activity.

Bloom's taxonomy was created in 1956 by a group of educators chaired by Benjamin Bloom, for which the taxonomy was named. The taxonomy is divided into three domains: cognitive, affective, and psychomotor. The cognitive domain is most useful for classroom instruction. The cognitive domain is further separated into six categories, in order from simple to complex: knowledge, comprehension, application, analysis, synthesis, and evaluation. The sidebar shows a breakdown of the cognitive domain of Bloom's taxonomy and suggested action verbs for creating learning objectives.

Evaluation and Assessment

Evaluation and assessment of instruction can be as simple or as complicated as needed. In basic terms, it is nice to know whether you have done a good job and, for the purposes of library statistics, how many people attended the class. Using a sign-in sheet and a simple feedback survey is one way to know whether the students were satisfied with your class on an emotional level. Assessing whether anyone learned anything is another matter. Assessment in library instruction can take different forms.

A 2012 report comparing the methods by which health sciences librarians evaluate educational impact found that evidence is collected in many ways, including measures of performance (tests, portfolios, products), and measures of attitude

BLOOM'S TAXONOMY—THE COGNITIVE DOMAIN

- Knowledge—simple recognition or recall of material
  1. Library example: recognizing the name of the library catalog
  2. Verbs: select, recognize, list, identify, name, locate, define, recite, describe, state, memorize, label
- Comprehension—restating or reorganizing material to show understanding
  1. Library example: explain the purpose of the library catalog (e.g., to find library resources)
  2. Verbs: match, explain, restate, defend, paraphrase, distinguish, rewrite, summarize, give example, interrelate, express, interpret, illustrate, extend
- Application—problem solving or applying ideas in new situations, constructing charts and figures
  1. Library example: using library catalog to find materials other than books
  2. Verbs: organize, sketch, generalize, apply, dramatize, solve, prepare, draw, produce, show, choose, paint
- Analysis—separating ideas into component parts, examining relationships, distinguishing between facts and inferences, identifying organizational structures
  1. Library example: recognize that library catalog is one systemic component of how resources are organized; linking to publishers to get full text
  2. Verbs: compare, differentiate, analyze, subdivide, classify, infer, point out, survey, select, categorize, prioritize
- Synthesis—integrating ideas into a statement or product new to the learner
  1. Library example: search a database for a topic, identify and export references to a bibliographic management system
  2. Verbs: compose, construct, originate, produce, hypothesize, plan, develop, create, invent, combine, organize
- Evaluation—judging by using self-produced criteria or established standards, the ability to critique
  1. Library example: judge the authority of a web page
  2. Verbs: judge, consider, relate, critique, weight, recommend, support, appraise, evaluate, compare

(Verbs adapted from Kennedy, 2007)

(surveys) and behavior (library usage). The review revealed that practical exercises are the most effective to document applied skills, and that students were poor self-judges of their skill level but excellent judges of their attitudes, feelings, beliefs, and perceptions—which were not actually indicative of whether they learned anything. Surprisingly, it also found that online instruction and traditional instruction are comparable in terms of the impact on students' anticipated information usage behaviors and their actual usage behaviors (Schilling and Applegate, 2012). What that largely means is bibliographic instruction can take place face-to-face or online, and students will have learned the same thing.

Two types of assessment are important to instruction. Formative assessment monitors student learning and provides feedback while instruction occurs. It is a way to gauge what the student has learned and what learning gaps still need to be addressed. It is low stakes—not graded or of little point value. An example of formative assessment is the iRAT at the beginning of a team-based learning program.

Summative assessment evaluates student performance. It is high stakes, taking place at the conclusion of instruction. An example of summative assessment would be a final exam, midterm, or graded project. Summative assessment evaluates whether learning occurred and compares it to an outcome measure or learning objective. The sidebar provides an example plan for evaluating learning outcomes in curriculum-integrated programming using summative assessment.

WEB-BASED LEARNING

Web-based learning, also known as e-learning or online learning, can be defined as "teaching and learning supported by the attributes and resources of the Internet" (Smith, 2006: 219). Web-based learning has seen great adoption among medical schools and indeed education in general. Web-based learning can manifest in a number of ways, ranging from accessing readings in a learning management system

---

EXAMPLE OUTCOME MEASURES, COMPETENCY ASSESSMENT, AND EVALUATION USED IN CURRICULUM-ORIENTED INSTRUCTION— SCIENCE AND PRACTICE OF MEDICINE 200 CURRICULUM

- Online competency tests for evidence-based practice skills. Students will be able to:
  1. Recognize primary research studies
     a. Use PubMed to locate primary research studies
        1. Identify type of study design
        2. Critically analyze study for best practice
  2. Identify authoritative Internet sources for information for:
     – Physicians
     – Patients
- Exam questions (item analysis):
  1. Library questions from midterm, quarterly, and final exams
- Examine knowledge gained from clinical forums:
  1. Compare answers with previous second-year classes
- SPM 200 course coordinators examine presentations:
  1. Librarians evaluate quality of student references and presentation quality.
- Evidence-based practice skills evaluated in a longitudinal study:
  1. IRB approval from orientation session
  2. Papers presented at medical education and medical library conferences
  3. Papers written in professional journals
  4. Book chapters in peer-reviewed texts
- Expand library's curriculum model:
  1. Orientation for first-year medical students as introduction to library resources

(Kerdolff, Marix, and Bridgewater, 2012: 19)

to participating in a class via webcam with attendees from all over the world. Some common types of web-based learning are discussed below.

Embedded in Distance Education

Distance education programs provide another outlet for instruction in health sciences libraries. With the advance of technology, health sciences librarians have the opportunity to create and conduct instruction solely on the web. Merriam-Webster Online (2013) defines webinars as "live online educational presentation during which participating viewers can submit questions and comments." Webinars are a form of synchronous education, where the content is delivered live to an online audience. Current common webinar and webcasting software includes Adobe Connect and GoToMeeting. Audience participation will vary depending on the complexity and size of a webinar. In most cases, a chat box is provided for participants to ask questions and offer comments. Sometimes a web camera may offer the ability to view and hear other participants in the event.

Embedded librarianship is a term used to describe academic librarians acting as key collaborators by providing significant integrated support within courses in which they are not the primary instructor (Konieczny, 2010). Health sciences librarians have been embedded in online education for nursing (Schulte, 2008), medicine (Sullo et al., 2012), dentistry (Jeffery, Maggio, and Blanchard, 2009), and physician assistant programs (Kealy, 2011). For librarians involved in distance education, the responsibility of ensuring that off-campus students receive the same library services as those at the main campus falls to them. This may take the form of creating content; designing tutorials and activities around evidence-based practice skills; running a live, synchronous instruction session through webcasting software; monitoring discussion boards; or providing research support via e-mail, chat, and phone.

Factors to consider when involved in online courses include clarifying with the instructor what the librarian's responsibility will be within the course and determining what level of support is desired. The time commitment will vary depending on course needs, class size, and level of librarian involvement. "For a general course that does not require the development of materials customized specifically to meet the class's needs, there is little time commitment involved to upload library content that has been preselected as core links and tutorials for classes" (Konieczny, 2010: 53). Indeed, once library content in the form of tutorials has been created, it is easy to customize and drop them into other classes, as librarians did at Boston University Medical Center (Jeffery, Maggio, and Blanchard, 2009). Working in an online format differs from face-to-face classes. Assignments and expectations must be clear. "One important lesson learned was the librarian must ensure that instructions for activities are as clear as possible and yet provide enough guidance and detail to motivate students to complete the activity satisfactorily" (Schulte, 2008: 167).

Online Courses

Online courses are another distance education tool librarians use. Typically, online courses in library instruction are asynchronous, meaning the librarian creates the content in the form of online tutorials, videos, and links in order to provide on-demand educational material for users. Typical components of a web-based course include a syllabus or course information; an announcements area and calendar; teaching materials such as slides, handouts, articles, and videos; communication via e-mail or discussion board; assessments; student management tools (records, statistics, student tracking); and links to useful websites (e.g., library, online databases, and journals) (McKimm, Jollie, and Cantillon, 2003). Course management systems (CMS) such as the open source products Moodle and Canvas or the proprietary Blackboard provide many of these features.

MOOCs

A massive open online course (MOOC) is an online course aimed at large-scale interactive participation and open access via the web. MOOCs emerged in 2007–2008 from open online courses taught by David Wiley at Utah State University and Alec Couros at the University of Regina. The term MOOC was first used to refer to a course led by George Siemens called "Connectivism and Connective Knowledge," which explored the use of social media and open education (Hill, 2012). The benefit of MOOCs is that they are free and offer the chance to collaborate and learn from a vast and varied learner base. The downside is that there is no real reason to complete the course beyond the desire to learn, so attrition is quite common. Medical librarians delved into MOOCs with the 2011–2012 online course "Get Mobilized: An Introduction to Mobile Resources and Tools in Health Sciences Libraries," https://sites.google.com/site/getmobilizedmla/, which provided continuing education for health sciences librarians interested in trends in mobile apps and devices. In January 2013, the University of California–San Francisco (UCSF) became the first health sciences university in the world to launch a MOOC on evidence-based health sciences content. Course participants were primarily students from outside the United States (Williams, 2013).

LibGuides

LibGuides are a popular product libraries use to create research guides and share knowledge. The tool has features such as commenting tools, assessments, statistics collection, and optimized mobile templates. It is designed to be user friendly, with WYSIWG entry. Health sciences librarians have embraced the use of online portals to enhance content in face-to-face classes (Gerberi, Hawthorne, and Larsen, 2012).

Created in 2007, LibGuides is a product by Springshare LLC, a library web technology vendor. At its most basic, LibGuides is a content management system that decentralizes web content creation, allowing individuals to create customized subject guides, web portals, and course guides. Web 2.0 applications such as RSS, embedded media, and social bookmarking, are integrated as well as a feature to add books from the library catalog. Detailed usage statistics allow tracking of use down to the URL. Commenting and quiz features are available, as well as **widgets** for chat boxes or other content. Pages can be formatted for printing. As of 2013, LibGuides reportedly counts more than 4,000 libraries as subscribers to its service (Springshare.com, 2013). Health sciences libraries count themselves among that number, perhaps more so in academic libraries than hospitals. It is always possible that by the time this book is published, LibGuides may be called something entirely different or not exist at all. However, the need for a list of starting resources for a specific topic—these days often provided as a web page—will likely remain. Lib-Guides are useful for creating customized directories of topics that link to a variety of electronic formats.

As a relatively new product, case studies abound about converting traditional pathfinders into subject guides in academic settings. In the health sciences, Lib-Guides have been used to serve up mobile library content (Gomes and Abate, 2012), provide specialized subject portals (Johnson, Repp and Layton, 2012), and bring a hospital library intranet portal into the cloud (Osterhaus-Trzasko, Farrell, and Rethlefsen, 2012). Some best practices that have emerged from the literature include organize resources by year of program and unit of study, provide mostly electronic resources when available, and include an instant messaging widget to facilitate contact with the library on each guide.

Neves and Dooley (2011) describe how the Dalhousie University Faculty of Medicine in Halifax, Canada, integrated LibGuides into undergraduate evidence-based practice sessions. In previous years, librarians would give a lecture on search skills, followed up with an in-person visit to the student's small group sessions to provide advice and instructional support. Using LibGuides, librarians replaced the didactic session with five webcasts, or "modules," which the students watched independently. Instead of visiting the small group sessions in person, a librarian was available via a chat widget during the small group sessions. The new format revealed several benefits. Students could watch, pause, or replay the videos at their own convenience, which they enjoyed; librarians could serve multiple groups at one time, which addressed staffing problems for the smaller library. Finally, offering online support was less intrusive. Rather than a librarian bursting into the middle of small-group learning sessions, students could ask their questions at the point of need.

Sonsteby and Dejohnge studied the usability of LibGuides at Metropolitan State University, in St. Paul, Minnesota, and found that patrons struggled most when encountering jargon, inconsistent language, and visual clutter. Consistency in naming, labeling, and style is important, as is specificity in guide content and re-source descriptions. In an era of discovery tools, the future of the subject guide was questioned—whether it was an appropriate use of time to create subject-centered guides, which can be time consuming to build and maintain. The research asserted that course guides, "which are designed to align closely with a particular research assignment" (Sonsteby and Dejohnge, 2013: 92), will remain useful, if only because the relevant course material is collected in one place. Accenting online course material with multiple electronic communication methods, such as e-mail addresses and chat widgets, will also facilitate learning.

Integrating library content into learning management systems (LMSs) is one way to enhance access to resources. Many LMSs offer ways to embed simple code in the form of a widget (a small application with limited functionality that can be installed and executed within a web page that links to other data), which management systems such as LibGuides produce automatically. The key to embedding library information is contact with the faculty or department in charge of the LMS, who will be able to load the widget into the course system.

SUMMARY

Compared to its beginnings as a humble suggestion in the pages of *JAMA* a century ago, the scope of instruction in the health sciences today is vast and varied. The rise of information literacy standards in education and the advent of student-centered active learning techniques have increased librarian involvement. Instruction can occur in different environments, and different skills and levels of participation are required. Forming a lesson plan, creating learning objectives, and developing assessments that evaluate whether objectives have been met (and whether learners were satisfied) are critical components of the instruction process. Ultimately, experience and enthusiasm, coupled with a familiarity with the literature, will produce the best learning outcomes.

STUDY QUESTIONS

1. Define teacher-centered and student-centered learning and give an example of each.
2. Explain the difference between a one-shot bibliographic instruction session, course-integrated instruction, and curriculum-integrated programming.
3. Identify three trends currently influencing health sciences library instruction.
4. Explain the difference between formative and summative assessment.
5. Explain the difference between synchronous and asynchronous learning.
6. Define active learning and give an example of active learning in the classroom.
7. Create three learning objectives for a basic bibliographic instruction session.

REFERENCES

AAMC (Association of American Medical Colleges). 1998. *Contemporary Issues in Medicine-Medical Informatics and Population Health: Report II of the Medical School Objectives Project.* https://members.aamc.org/eweb/upload/Contemporary%20Issues%20in%20Med%20Medical%20Informatics%20ReportII.pdf.

———. 2013. "Medical School Objectives Project (MSOP)." Accessed September 23. www.aamc.org/initiatives/msop/.

ACRL (Association of College and Research Libraries). 2000. *Information Literacy Competency Standards for Higher Education.* Chicago: American Library Association. www.ala.org/acrl/sites/ala.org.acrl/files/content/standards/standards.pdf.

Association of Schools of Public Health Education Committee. 2006. "MPH Core Competency Model Version 2.3." August. www.asph.org/publication/MPH_Core_Competency_Model/index.html.

Barnard, Alan, Robyn Nash, and Michael O'Brien. 2005. "Information Literacy: Developing Lifelong Skills through Nursing Education." *Journal of Nursing Education* 44, no. 11: 505–10.

Barrows, Harold S. 1983. "Problem-Based, Self-Directed Learning." *Journal of the American Medical Association* 205, no. 22 (December): 3077–80.

Beales, Donna I. 2002. "Exemplary CME: Putting the 'Library' into CME/Library Specialist." *Journal of Hospital Librarianship* 2, no. 3: 29–38.

Bell, Steven. 2013. "Rethinking ACRL's Information Literacy Standards: The Process Begins." *ACRL Insider* (blog). June 4. www.acrl.ala.org/acrlinsider/archives/7329.

Bligh, John. 1999. "Problem-Based Learning in Medicine an Introduction." In *Handbook of Problem Based Learning*, edited by Jocelyn Rankin, 3–10. New York: Forbes.

Blobaum, Paul. 2007. "The Hospital Grantsmanship Center: A New Role for Hospital Librarians." *Journal of Hospital Librarianship* 7, no. 1: 29–41.

Booth, Char. 2011. *Reflective Teaching, Effective Learning: Instructional Literacy for Library Educators*. Chicago: American Library Association.

Brower, Stewart. 2008. "Information Literacy Education in Health Sciences Libraries." In *Introduction to Health Sciences Librarianship*, edited by M. Sandra Wood, 217–40. New York: Haworth Press.

Cheeseman, Susan. 2013. "Information Literacy: Foundation for Evidence-Based Practice." *Neonatal Network* 32, no. 2 (March): 127–31.

Chen, Huiju C., Josephine P. Tan, Patricia O'Sullivan et al. 2009. "Impact of an Information Retrieval and Management Curriculum on Medical Student Citations." *Academic Medicine* 84, no. 10 (October): S38–S41.

Cyrus, John, David C. Duggar, Julia Esparza, Mararia Adams, Montie' Dobbins, and Kimberly Pullen. 2012. "Connecting with Hospital Nurses through MINE." *Journal of Hospital Librarianship* 12, no. 2: 142–53.

Danforth, Liz. 2011. "Gamification and Libraries." *Library Journal* 136, no. 3 (February): 84.

Donner, Robert S., and Harmon Bickley. 1993. "Problem-Based Learning in American Medical Education: An Overview." *Bulletin of the Medical Library Association* 81, no. 3 (July): 294–98.

Dorsch, Josephine L., and Gerald (Jerry) Perry. 2012. "Evidence Based Medicine at the Intersection of Research Interests Between Academic Health Sciences Librarians and Medical Educators: A Review of the Literature." *Journal of the Medical Library Association* 100, no. 4 (October): 251–57.

Doyle, Jacqueline D. 2005. "Teaching the Publishing Process to Researchers and Other Potential Authors in a Hospital System." *Journal of Hospital Librarianship* 5, no. 1: 63–70.

Earl, Martha F. 1996. "Library Instruction in the Medical School Curriculum: A Survey of Medical College Libraries." *Bulletin of the Medical Library Association* 84, no. 2 (April): 191–95.

Eldredge, Jonathan D. 2004. "The Librarian as Tutor/Facilitator in a Problem-based Learning (PBL) Curriculum." *Reference Services Review* 32, no. 1 (January): 54–59.

Eldredge, Jonathan D., Sarah K. Morley, Ingrid C. Hendrix, Richard D. Carr, and Jason Bengtson. 2012. "Library and Informatics Skills Competencies Statements from Major Health Professional Associations." *Medical Reference Services Quarterly* 31, no. 1 (January–March): 34–44.

Eldredge, Jonathan D., Janis Teal, Judith Ducharme et al. 1998. "The Roles of Library Liaisons in a Problem-Based Learning (PBL) Medical School Curriculum: A Case Study from University of New Mexico." *Health Libraries Review* 15, no. 3 (October): 185–94.

Flexner, Abraham. 1910. *Medical Education in the United States and Canada Bulletin Number Four (the Flexner Report)*. New York: Carnegie Foundation for the Advancement of Teaching. www.carnegiefoundation.org/publications/medical-education-united-states-and-canada-bulletin-number-four-flexner-report-0.

Frankenberger, Charles. 1914. "The Value of the Medical College Library to the Student." *Journal of the American Medical Association* 63, no. 8 (August): 655–56.

Gage, Mary P., Gail S. Peckman, and Maureen T. Greene. 2011. "Using a 'Survivor' Style Game to Guide Nursing Research into Practice." *Journal of Hospital Librarianship* 11, no. 1: 94–98.

Gerberi, Dana, Dottie M. Hawthorne, and Karen E. Larsen. 2012. "Rethinking Responsible Literature Searching Using LibGuides." *Medical Reference Services Quarterly* 31, no. 4 (October–December): 355–71.

Gomes, Alexandra, and Laura Abate. 2012. "Rethinking Our Mobility: Supporting Our Patrons Where they Live." *Medical Reference Services Quarterly* 31, no. 2 (April–June): 140–49.

Hasman, Linda. 2012. "Librarian-Facilitated Problem-Based Learning Course in a School of Dental Medicine." *Medical Reference Services Quarterly* 31, no. 3 (July–September): 336–41.

Hill, Phil. 2012. "Online Educational Delivery Models: A Descriptive View." *Educause Review* 47, no. 6 (November/December): 85–97.

Howe, Neil, and William Strauss. 2000. *Millennials Rising: The Next Great Generation.* New York: Vintage.

Jeffery, Keven M., Lauren Maggio, and Mary Blanchard. 2009. "Making Generic Tutorials Content Specific: Recycling Evidence-based Practice (EBP) Tutorials for Two Disciplines." *Medical Reference Services Quarterly* 28, no. 1 (January–March): 1–9.

Johnson, Rienne, Amber Repp, and Beth Layton. 2012. "Systemizing Copyright: A Specialized Library Service." *Journal of Hospital Librarianship* 12, no. 3: 272–80.

Kealy, Shannon. 2011. "Continual Evolution: The Experience Over Three Semesters of a Librarian Embedded in an Online Evidence-Based Medicine Course for Physician Assistant Students." *Medical Reference Services Quarterly* 30, no. 4 (October–December): 411–25.

Kennedy, John M. 2007. "File: Bloom's Rose.png." Wikimedia Commons. August 1. http://commons.wikimedia.org/wiki/File:Bloom%27s_Rose.png.

Kerdolff, Kathy, Mary Marix, and Carolyn Bridgewater. 2012. *LSUHSC Library Resources Instruction—Science and Practice of Medicine 200 Curriculum (2015).* July. www.lsuhsc.edu/no/library/resources/guides/L2Curriculum12-13.pdf.

Konieczny, Alison. 2010. "Experiences as an Embedded Librarian in Online Courses." *Medical Reference Services Quarterly* 29, no. 1 (January–March): 47–57.

Koufogiannakis, Denise, Jeannette Buckingham, Arif Alibhai, and David Rayner. 2005. "Impact of Librarians in First-year Medical and Dental Student Problem-based Learning (PBL) Groups: A Controlled Study." *Health Information and Libraries Journal* 22, no. 3 (September): 189–95.

Markey, Karen, Chris Leeder, and Soo Young Rieh. 2014. *Designing Online Information Literacy Games Students Will Want to Play.* Lanham, MD: Rowman & Littlefield Publishers.

Martin, Jess A., David L. House Jr., and Harold R. Chandler. 1975. "Teaching of Formal Courses by Medical Librarians." *Journal of Medical Education* 50, no. 9 (September): 883–86.

McKimm, Judy, Carol Jollie, and Peter Cantillon. 2003. "Web Based Learning." *British Medical Journal* 326, no. 7394 (April): 870–73.

McMunn-Tetangco, Elizabeth. 2013. "If You Build It . . .? One Campus' Firsthand Account of Gamification in the Academic Library." *College & Research Libraries News* 74, no. 4 (April): 208–10.

Merriam-Webster Online. 2013. "Webinar." Accessed October 26. www.merriam-webster.com/dictionary/webinar.

Mi, Misa. 2011. "Renewed Roles for Librarians in Problem-Based Learning in the Medical Curriculum." *Medical Reference Services Quarterly* 30, no. 3 (July–September): 269–82.

Michaelsen, Larry K., Arletta Bauman Knight, and L. Dee Fink. 2002. *Team-Based Learning: A Transformative Use of Small Groups.* Westport, CT: Praeger.

Neves, Karen, and Sarah Jane Dooley. 2011. "Using LibGuides to Offer Library Service to Undergraduate Medical Students Based on the Case-Oriented Problem Solving Curriculum Model." *Journal of the Medical Library Association* 99, no. 1 (January): 94–97.

Osterhaus-Trzasko, Leah C., Ann M. Farrell, and Melissa L. Rethlefsen. 2012. "Converting an Intranet Site to the Cloud: Using CampusGuides to Refresh a Library Portal." *Medical Reference Services Quarterly* 31, no. 3 (July–September): 245–57.

Pappas, Cleo. 2008. "Hospital Librarians' Perceptions Related to Evidence-Based Health Care." *Journal of the Medical Library Association* 96, no. 3 (July): 235–38.

Parslow, Graham R. 2012. "Commentary: The Khan Academy and the Day-night Flipped Classroom." *Biochemistry and Molecular Biology Education* 40, no. 5 (August): 337–38.

Phelps, Sue F. 2013. "Designing the Information Literacy Competency Standards for Nursing." *Medical Reference Services Quarterly* 32, no. 1 (January–March): 111–18.

Polger, Mark A. 2010. "Information Takeout and Delivery: A Case Study Exploring Different Library Service Delivery Models." *Journal of Hospital Librarianship* 10, no. 1: 3–22.

Premebida, Adriano. 2010. "Disruptive Technology." In *Encyclopedia of Nanoscience and Society*, edited by David H. Guston, 167–69. Thousand Oaks, CA: Sage. doi: http://dx.doi.org/10.4135/9781412972093.n94.

Prensky, Marc. 2001. "Digital Natives, Digital Immigrants." *On the Horizon* 9, no. 5 (October): 1–6.

Rafferty, Ryan. 2013. "The Impact of Library Instruction: Do First-year Medical Students Use Library Resources Specifically Highlighted during Instructional Sessions?" *Journal of the Medical Library Association* 101, no. 3 (July): 213–17.

Reinbold, Sarah. 2013. "Using the ADDIE Model in Designing Library Instruction." *Medical Reference Services Quarterly* 32, no. 3 (July–September): 244–56.

Roberts, David H., Lori R. Newman, and Richard M. Schwartzstein. 2012. "Twelve Tips for Facilitating Millennials' Learning." *Medical Teacher* 34, no. 4 (December): 274–78.

Runge, Elizabeth D. 1931. "Teaching the Use of the Library." *Bulletin of the Medical Library Association* 20, no. 1 (July): 14–15.

Salony, Mary F. 1995. "The History of Bibliographic Instruction: Changing Trends from Books to the Electronic World." *The Reference Librarian* 24, no. 51–52 (January): 31–51.

Sayre, Jean Williams. 1999. "Active Learning Models in Medical School Curricula." In *Handbook of Problem Based Learning*, edited by Jocelyn Rankin, 31–43. New York: Forbes.

Schardt, Connie, and Megan von Isenberg. 2013. "Team-Based Learning: Creating a Better Learning Experience for PubMed Instruction." Contributed paper presented at the annual meeting of the Medical Library Association, Boston, May 7.

Scherrer, Carol S., Josephine L. Dorsch, and Ann C. Weller. 2006. "An Evaluation of a Collaborative Model for Preparing Evidence-based Medicine Teachers." *Journal of the Medical Library Association* 94, no. 2 (April): 159–65.

Schilling, Katherine, and Rachel Applegate. 2012. "Best Methods for Evaluating Educational Impact: A Comparison of the Efficacy of Commonly Used Measures of Library Instruction." *Journal of the Medical Library Association* 100, no. 4 (October): 258–70.

Schulte, Stephanie. 2008. "Integrating Information Literacy into an Online Undergraduate Nursing Informatics Course: The Librarian's Role in the Design and Teaching of the Course." *Medical Reference Services Quarterly* 27, no. 2 (Summer): 158–72.

Schwartz, Diane G., Paul M. Blobaum, Jean P. Shipman, Linda G. Markwell, and Joanne G. Marshall. 2009. "The Health Sciences Librarian in Medical Education: A Vital Pathways Project Task Force." *Journal of the Medical Library Association* 97, no. 4 (October): 283.

Siemens, George. 2004. "Connectivism: A Learning Theory for the Digital Age." Elearnspace. December 12. www.elearnspace.org/Articles/connectivism.htm.

Smith, Susan S. 2006. *Web-based Instruction: A Guide for Libraries*, 2nd ed. Chicago: American Library Association.

Sonsteby, Alec, and Jennifer DeJonghe. 2013. "Usability Testing, User-Centered Design, and LibGuides Subject Guides: A Case Study." *Journal of Web Librarianship* 7, no. 1 (September): 83–94.

Springshare.com. 2013. "LibGuides: The Next Generation!" *Springshare Support Blog*. June 26. http://support.springshare.com/2013/06/26/libguides-the-next-generation/.

Srinivasan, Malathi, Michael Wilkes, Frazier Stevenson, Thuan Nguyen, and Stuart Slavin. 2007. "Comparing Problem-Based Learning with Case-Based Learning: Effects of a Major Curricular Shift at Two Institutions." *Academic Medicine* 82, no. 1 (January): 74–82.

Strube, Kathleen. 2006. "Patient Information Rounds in a Hospital System." *Journal of Hospital Librarianship* 6, no. 4: 13–28.

Sullo, Elaine, Tom Harrod, Gisela Butera, and Alexandra Gomes. 2012. "Rethinking Library Service to Distance Education Students: Analyzing the Embedded Librarian Model." *Medical Reference Services Quarterly* 31, no. 1 (January–March): 25–33.

Sweet, Michael. 2013. "The Least You Need to Know about Team-Based Learning." Accessed July 9. www.missouriwestern.edu/appliedlearning/documents/LeastToKnow TBLMichaelsen2011.pdf.

Technology Informatics Guiding Education Reform Initiative. 2009. *Informatics Competencies for Every Practicing Nurse: Recommendations from the TIGER Collaborative.* August. www .thetigerinitiative.org/docs/TigerReport_InformaticsCompetencies_001.pdf.

Travis, Lisa D. 2013. "Creating Interdependency between the Curriculum and the Library Website." Contributed poster presented at the annual meeting of the Medical Library Association, Boston, May 6.

Tuttle, Brandi, and Adrianne Leonardelli. 2012. "Bringing New Methods into Library Instruction: A Case Study in Team-Based Learning." Contributed paper presented at the annual meeting of the Medical Library Association, Seattle, May 21.

Vogel, Kimberly A. 2012. "Librarians and Occupational Therapy Faculty: A Collaboration for Teaching Evidence-Based Practice." *Journal of Allied Health* 41, no. 1 (Spring): e15–20.

Whelan, Julia S. 2006. "Hospital Library Foreign Language Labs: The Experience of Two Hospital Libraries." *Medical Reference Services Quarterly* 25, no. 2 (Summer): 81–95.

Whipple, Elizabeth C., Margaret (Peggy) W. Richwine, Kellie N. Kaneshiro, and Frances A. Brahmi. 2009. "Teaching First-year Medical Students Where to Go First: Connecting Information Needs to e-Resources." *Medical Reference Services Quarterly* 28, no. 2 (April–June): 180–86.

Williams, Steven. 2013. "Reaching a Global Audience of Medical Students and Professionals with Massive Open Online Courses (MOOCs)." Contributed paper presented at the annual meeting of the Medical Library Association, Boston, May 5.

CHAPTER 12

Access Services: Circulation, Course Reserves, and Interlibrary Loan in Health Sciences Libraries

Everly Brown, Na Lin, and Megan Wolff

INTRODUCTION

This chapter explores the ways in which health sciences libraries provide information resources to their user populations. An access services department's mission is to ensure that those resources, whether digital or print, on-site or remote, are easily accessible at the point of need.

Access services departments in today's health sciences libraries are concerned with providing access to both electronic and print resources. The variety of digital resources and the complexities of handling them are challenging these units as they seek to provide an excellent patron experience. Patrons can be overwhelmed by the array of information health sciences libraries place at their fingertips. Access services staff can mediate the patron's need to have to check multiple places for information and know which database to search in (Sievert et al., 2011). Access services help to gather and disseminate information directly to a patron's tablet or e-mail in-box, create course reserve pages with links gathered on one course page, locate and deliver material not owned by the library, and troubleshoot complicated questions about access to e-resources.

ACCESS SERVICES

Health sciences libraries usually have an access services department to handle circulation, electronic reserves, and stacks maintenance. Interlibrary loan may be included, but it can often be a part of technical services (Breeding, 2013) or even part of reference services. The department is typically headed by a librarian with an MLS degree, but it can also be led by a paraprofessional working under the supervision of a librarian. The department's duties traditionally include lending and receiving materials, registering patrons, working with the library's ILS (integrated library system),

303

answering directional and ready reference
questions, opening and closing the library,
handling fines and notices, shelving and
shelf reading, collecting statistics, processing electronic reserves requests, and enforc-
ing library policies and procedures (ALA,
2010).

Although a separate service desk for circulation and reference remains the norm,
one trend is toward combining the two
desks and cross-training staff to create a
more streamlined experience for the patron
(Schulte, 2011). Other library services may
also participate in this model of consoli-
dation—for instance, integrating the help
desk for technical support (Zabel, 2005).

> When working in public services,
> every day brings opportunities
> to be creative and innovative. Whether
> librarians are inventing a new type of
> technology-enhanced study space,
> redesigning a new reference staffing
> model, or smoothing the way for easy
> access to library resources, the mission
> remains the same—to provide excel-
> lent service.
>
> *Alexa Mayo, MLS, associate director for
> services, University of Maryland, Baltimore*

The mission of an access services department is to ensure that the library's materials are accessible, the library's space is available, and that this is achieved using skilled staff who provide the best possible customer service experience for the
patron.

CIRCULATION SERVICES

Physical Access

The role of the library as a physical space continues to evolve. No question, access to the hard copy collection is declining. The Association of Academic Health
Sciences Libraries (AAHSL) statistics for FY2008 and FY2012 show a 13.7 percent
decline in the gate count and a 45.7 percent decline in total circulation over all the
libraries that participated (Byrd, 2010; Squires, 2013). Despite the move away from
using a print collection, patrons continue to use health sciences libraries in both
traditional ways and in new ones. As the Library of Congress's Deanna Marcum
predicted, "The library will certainly change. And its need for space may significantly shrink. But the digital era, far from ending the physical library, may free it
to facilitate learning rather than to house shelves—and may free those who work
within the library spaces to do less book processing and more learning facilitation"
(Folkenberg, 2005: 4–5).

Amid the change, health sciences library buildings continue to provide space
for quiet individual study and collaborative group work, access to the minority
of material still only available in print, and a place to ask for information and
guidance from expert staff. Public computers in libraries remain necessary, as not
everyone has access to them or wishes to carry one. Additionally, access to an Internet connection is not universal. Some developing uses of health sciences libraries' physical space include sharing space with other campus units such as writing
and counseling centers, offering specialized services such as presentation practice
studios, and grant writing and copyright expertise at merged service desks (Rempel,

Hussong-Christian, and Mellinger, 2011). Health sciences libraries remain access points for research, reflection, and professional assistance and instruction regardless of the format or location of the information they offer.

Access for the Disabled

Health sciences libraries should consider access for the disabled (ALA, 2001). They should have a written policy detailing how they will accommodate providing access to their resources and services. Additionally, the library's space should be designed to accommodate persons with disabilities. For example, the preferred clearance between aisles in library stacks is forty-two inches to allow for easy wheelchair accessibility (ALA, 2013). Speaking to a local office of disability services or center for independent living can give valuable information to the library about how best to accommodate access for the disabled (Willis, 2012).

Public Access

Individual libraries' policies vary, but most health sciences libraries do allow the general public in-house access to their print and digital collections. They may even tailor parts of them toward consumer health in an effort to serve this population (Shipman and Funk, 2009). Licenses with vendors of electronic materials generally do not allow off-site access for those not affiliated with the library as the cost to the library would be prohibitive. Steering those without full access to **open source** and free resources is one way to accommodate these patrons.

Borrowing

Borrowing privileges at health sciences libraries are characteristically extended to those affiliated with the institution. Faculty, staff, students, admitting physicians, residents, **emeritus** faculty, visiting scholars, and volunteer faculty are some of those who may be allowed to borrow. Loan periods are usually shorter than those at regular academic libraries. Health sciences libraries loan periods tend to vary between fourteen and twenty-eight days, whereas many academic libraries may lend for up to a full semester, especially for faculty. Reference and reserve books and journals usually do not circulate outside the library.

Hours

Patrons of health sciences libraries consistently press for longer hours. Medical necessity at hospital libraries and student needs at academic health sciences libraries mean that the more hours a library is open, the more satisfied its patrons. Even with a mostly digital collection, a library's physical space remains highly valued. Many have converted stack and study spaces into areas where users can gather for collaborative work in an electronic environment (Drake, 2010). Well-designed and technologically current facilities have noted increased usage of their space (Ludwig, 2010). Some academic health sciences libraries are able to provide 24/5 or 24/7 access. As funding tightens, however, a significant number have been forced instead to decrease hours (McGowan, 2012).

Security

Library security is often under the supervision of the access services department. Typical issues that arise are noncompliance with library policies and theft and mutilation of materials. Library administration may set policies, but it is frequently up to access services staff to implement them and ensure that they are adhered to. A security guard may be present to control entry into the library and to support enforcement of library policies by staff.

Other security measures include security gates that alarm when material is taken beyond them without having been checked out. Libraries typically use magnetic strips adhered to material or radio frequency identification tags (RFID) to accomplish this (Ayre, 2012). Locks on physical equipment such as photocopiers and printers ensure that paper remains secure, stamps or stickers let patrons know that material belongs to the library, and electronic access systems restrict who can enter the building at select times.

Libraries should have robust policies in place to deal with security violations. Stolen material, disruptive patrons, policy violators, and the like are common concerns that need to be documented and tracked to ensure that access to the library's space and collections is unrestricted.

Books

Books at hospital libraries and academic health sciences libraries are typically arranged using the National Library of Medicine's (NLM) classification scheme. NLM's Medical Subject Headings (MeSH) are applied to each item's record in the online catalog to categorize the collection. Academic health sciences libraries with a social services component to support, such as a school of social work, may use the Library of Congress classification system, both its subject headings and MeSH headings, to ensure that this area of their collections is properly described.

Call number classification allows works on a similar topic to be shelved near one another, facilitating browsing. Under the NLM classification system, QV indicates pharmacology, the practice of medicine falls under WB, and nursing is located at WY; a patron can easily peruse the stacks to find related materials.

Journals

The journal collection at a health sciences library is usually much larger than its monograph collection. Hospital and academic health sciences library patrons are often looking for journal articles as they frequently need the most current information on a given topic (Tenopir, King, and Bush, 2004). Journal articles are more current because the publication process is shorter than that for monographs. Patrons of health sciences libraries are usually looking for specific information and will want to go directly to an article of interest.

Most of a library's journal titles will be in electronic format and accessed through a database, the online catalog, or an A–Z list of titles. Print journals are generally arranged in alphabetical order by title. A browsing collection of a small number of high profile titles such as *Nature* or *JAMA* may be there for the convenience of patrons (Kirk, 2010).

Media and Equipment

Audiovisual materials at health sciences libraries encompass a variety of formats. They may be cataloged and stored as an independent media collection or stored with other print material that they support—for example, a textbook with an accompanying CD. Many libraries provide special areas for viewing and interacting with audiovisual materials such as technology labs and collaboration spaces with computers and software to support the collection.

Supporting devices such as headphones, charging devices, and connecting cables are typically available to check out. Other equipment such as iPads, Kindles, and laptops are being provided to lend support to mobile access of the library's collections (Yelton, 2012).

Remote Storage

Space remains an issue at health sciences libraries, even with the rise of electronic books and journals. Most libraries have large **back files** of print journals and full historical book holdings. Weeding and removing print materials, which can be a politically charged situation, must be accomplished slowly and deliberately as people may react emotionally if they perceive that good information is being *thrown away*.

The solution for some libraries is to house older and less-used parts of their collections in off-site storage or in a **closed stacks** area of the library. Patrons can still request the material, but retrieving it for them may involve a small delay. **Compact stacks** are also used to increase space by storing the books in mobile shelving units that can be opened and closed as needed. Even these solutions can cause controversy, as the New York Public Library found in 2012 when it announced a plan to move many of its three million books to remote storage, which set off a heated debate with researchers who use the collection (Howard, 2012).

Challenges and Opportunities

The switch from print to electronic resources has profoundly changed the concerns occupying access services staff as they work to provide access to these materials. Print materials need to be shelved in correct call number order in order to be located easily. Electronic materials bring with them a new set of access challenges as they rely on stable networks and servers to maintain them. Access services staff find themselves troubleshooting access inquiries when patrons cannot get to material. Forgotten passwords, network interruptions, browser issues, and missing content from publishers are just a few of the challenges of providing electronic content.

Another challenge is the pressure to provide universal free access to library content. As universities and hospitals expand their partnerships and initiatives, they bring along loosely affiliated groups that often expect full access to library materials. Such access is not always covered by the licenses libraries sign with vendors. Health sciences libraries cannot ignore these licenses without opening themselves to legal inquiries. It can be difficult for staff to parse who should and should not have access and to make all parties understand this. Firm policies and a cohesive message from all library staff make this process easier to navigate.

COURSE RESERVES

General Information and Policies

Academic health sciences libraries have traditionally placed hard copies of course materials on reserve for short, in-library loans. Today's course reserves include these items along with remotely accessible digital files, such as links to articles, e-books, and multimedia resources. Faculty members submit reserve requests over e-mail, through online request forms, or on paper. Some health sciences libraries require that faculty send a separate request for each individual reserve item, note if each item is available in the library, and attach copies of documents to be scanned. Other libraries ask for only a reading list of citations or a print or digital syllabus. Digital syllabuses may take the form of electronic versions of their traditional print counterparts, or they may incorporate features such as hyperlinks and media files (Maurino, 2005–2006). Digital syllabuses also have the benefit of being easily modified, interactive, searchable, potentially ADA compliant, and environmentally friendly. Faculty may be tempted to upload documents or add links to readings directly to their course web page or interactive syllabus. This can result in access issues, if **permalinks** and a proxy are not used, and in copyright violations (McCaslin, 2008). A library's course reserve service can avoid these problems, as well as handle copyright requests, generate document usage statistics, provide 24/7 access to digital readings, and supply readings not owned by the library or faculty member. These advantages, along with general convenience, may be mentioned when marketing library course reserve services.

E-Reserve Systems

Electronic course reserve systems available for academic libraries include proprietary software, such as Docutek's ERes and Atlas Systems' Ares; as well as free, open source programs, including ReservesDirect. Other institutions use homegrown systems customized to their specific needs, or have reserve staff add links and upload PDFs directly into their campus's **course management system (CMS)**, such as Blackboard, Sakai, and Moodle (Li and Demers, 2010). Electronic course reserve systems give library reserve staff a single place to upload and manage reserve materials, track copyright, calculate statistics, and hold existing reserve pages for reuse in future semesters. Students can search the system for their courses, find documents and other course materials, and find call numbers for items on reserve. Students may access e-reserve pages by searching the system or through a direct link. Electronic reserves that can be integrated into course management systems generally increase ease of use for students and faculty (Clumpner, Burgmeier, and Gillespie, 2011). Without integration, students may need to be authenticated before accessing the materials and to log in to multiple systems. An e-reserve system integrated into the CMS, with materials supplied by library staff, may also lower the number of faculty uploading readings on their own.

Accessibility of course materials is another benefit of digital course reserves, as some e-reserve management software and course management systems are designed with Americans with Disabilities Act (ADA) compliance in mind. For instance, Blackboard is both Section 508 standard compliant and follows the World Wide Web Consortium's Web Content Accessibility Guidelines (WCAG) 2.0 standards (Blackboard, 2013). Library staff can also take the time to add ALT text to uploaded images and to create ADA compliant, OCR-readable PDFs when scanning documents for digital reserves.

Challenges and Opportunities

Copyright permissions may be necessary for digital or print versions of reserve readings not available through a library's licensed electronic databases. Libraries should keep up with changes to copyright law and have a written copyright policy in place, possibly developed after consulting with university legal counsel (Hansen, Cross, and Edwards, 2013). The TEACH Act is useful in making copyright decisions for distance education. General recommended procedures include making the reserve page or readings password-protected, attaching a copyright notice and agreement to the documents and/or reserve page, and making readings available only to students enrolled in the course and only for the length of the semester. Permissions are obtained and paid for by contacting either the Copyright Clearance Center or individual publishers. Deciding exactly which items need permissions can be a complicated matter. **Fair use** analysis includes the following four factors: purpose and character of the use, the nature of the copyrighted work, amount and substantiality of the portion of the work, and effect on the potential market for or value of the work (U.S. Copyright Office, 2012). The task of weighing these factors for a document can be placed on either the faculty member submitting readings or library staff (Wagner, 2008). Rather than evaluating reserve items using the fair use checklist to make copyright decisions, some academic libraries pay for copyright permissions for nearly every reading used in e-reserve, or only request permissions if an article is used in one course for multiple semesters, equating first-time use with fair use (Wagner, 2008). The recent ruling in a legal case involving Georgia State University's e-reserve copyright policy may encourage academic libraries to reevaluate their copyright policies (Pike, 2012). The judge in this case made no mention of first-time use but did place limits on the amount of material that can be reproduced from a single book (not more than 10 percent or one chapter of a book, not more than two to three articles from one issue of a journal). This opens the doors for nonprofit, academic libraries to take a more liberal view of fair use.

Academic institutions have not escaped the effects of the recent economic downturn. Budgetary constraints create a challenge for libraries to cut costs without impacting service. To keep up with reserve work during hiring freezes or staff cuts, libraries may consider interdepartmental cross-training. Student workers can also be trained in certain tasks, such as scanning reserve documents (McCaslin, 2010). When a library is forced to cancel subscriptions to e-journals, the number of scanned articles requiring copyright permissions can increase. Libraries with previously conservative copyright policies may reevaluate their stance on fair use (McCaslin, 2010). Limiting the amount of money the library is willing to pay for copyright per article is another option. For instance, if copyright permissions for a single article go over $50, a library may offer a print copy for a lower cost, discuss removing the article from reserves, or have faculty negotiate with the copyright holder (Wagner, 2008). The ever-increasing cost of textbooks can also be an issue. Rather than purchasing new editions each year, a course reserve department may place faculty members' personal copies on reserve, or not place required textbooks on reserve at all, leaving students to purchase texts (Pollitz, Christie, and Middleton, 2009). Other libraries place only required books and articles on reserve, rather than including recommended and supplemental readings. Although commercial e-reserve software streamlines the reserve process, budget concerns may encourage libraries to switch to homegrown or open source systems, or to add reserve items directly into the campus's existing CMS (Pollitz, Christie, and Middleton, 2009).

INTERLIBRARY LOAN AND DOCUMENT DELIVERY

For more than a century, libraries have been sharing resources with one another through interlibrary loan service (ILL) to supplement their collections (Chudnov, 2007). Libraries borrow materials from other libraries on behalf of their patrons, and also lend materials in their collections to other libraries. ILL materials include returnables such as books and multimedia and nonreturnable journal articles, the latter being more prevalent in health sciences libraries. Although the term "document delivery" often encompasses ILL, in most library operations, ILL is defined as a transaction to lend to or borrow from other libraries' materials, and document delivery is a service that supplies materials from in-house collections to the library's patrons.

Most health sciences libraries in academic institutions have a dedicated department or function for ILL service headed by a librarian. But it can also be led by a paraprofessional working under the supervision of a librarian. Some libraries may also employ student workers. Hospitals, on the other hand, may only have a one-person library operation to cover the service.

Resource Sharing Networks

Many national and regional networks are servicing interlibrary loans; health sciences libraries usually join DOCLINE, OCLC, and/or their local consortia to share resources.

DOCLINE

DOCLINE was created by the National Library of Medicine (NLM) to provide a platform for libraries in the United States, Canada, and Mexico to communicate with one another for rapid delivery of requested materials including articles and books. The DOCLINE system is managed by eight Regional Medical Libraries (RMLs). Each geographic region has a National Network of Libraries of Medicine

(NN/LM) office that manages the participating libraries. Membership is free. To date, more than 3,000 libraries have joined DOCLINE, with a pool of more than 1.6 million serials holdings records (Collins, 2010).

Through automation, members jointly maintain material holdings. DOCLINE routes borrowing requests quickly to the first library that has the holding for fulfillment. The system also allows libraries to specify their preferred lenders in their profiles. Urgent patient care requests are to be filled within two hours before moving on to the next available library. Print copies are scanned, in color if requested, and delivered through e-mail or transmission systems such as Odyssey, www.atlas-sys.com/odyssey/, or Ariel, www.infotrieve.com/ariel-interlibrary-loan-software. Facsimile transmission has become less used, and postal mail remains the least used delivery option (Collins, 2010).

Each member library specifies its service charges for filling a request. Billing and payment can be done through Electronic Fund Transfer System (EFTS), www.uchc.edu/, a system created by NLM and the University of Connecticut Health Center (UCHC) to automate the payment process.

Integrated within DOCLINE is the Loansome Doc service. Loansome Doc enables individual users to order documents found in PubMed within the PubMed interface. It is available to users worldwide. A user registers in Loansome Doc and establishes an agreement with a preferred supplying library(ies). The supplying library processes requests via DOCLINE and provides articles either from its own collection or via other libraries. Although some libraries use the service for their primary clientele, many offer it exclusively to unaffiliated users such as health care professionals and individual consumers for a fee. More information on NLM, DOCLINE, and Loansome Doc can be found on NLM's website, www.nlm.nih.gov/.

> DOCLINE is the ILL librarian's best friend and it predates Google, Amazon, and FedEx. You can search and find out which library has the journal or book you want, how much you will be charged, or if you can get the full-text article free. Best of all, the wonderful staff of the lending library will gladly rush your requested article electronically; it makes your customer service outstanding.
>
> *Joanna Lin, MS, MLS, chief, library service, VA Maryland Health Care System, Baltimore*

OCLC WorldShare Interlibrary Loan Service

In addition to DOCLINE, many health sciences libraries also join OCLC WorldShare Interlibrary Loan service to further expand their resource pool and support interdisciplinary studies. Membership is through a fee-based subscription, which provides access to more than one billion holdings of print and digital resources owned by more than 7,000 libraries through WorldCat database search (OCLC, 2011). The holdings data allow libraries to select potential lenders for items they wish to obtain. In 2010, OCLC introduced a new feature in the WorldCat knowledge base, www.oclc.org/us/en/knowledgebase/default.htm, that combines the lending library's electronic resources and licensing data to facilitate the lending process through its linking features.

OCLC Policies Directory provides contact information and lending policies such as fees and loan periods of WorldShare ILL participants. In addition to holdings data, lending policies allow a prospective borrowing library to weigh its options. To expedite the ILL cycle on both ends, a lending library can also set up automatic deflections in the Policies Directory to bypass requests it cannot fill, such as e-books, allowing the borrowing request to skip the deflecting lender and move on to the next lender.

Billing and payment for ILL transactions can be done through OCLC's ILL Fee Management Services (IFM). Payments can also be made by International Federation of Library Associations (IFLA) vouchers that can be purchased at OCLC. More payment information can be found at the OCLC website, www.oclc.org/us/en/resourcesharing/features/default.htm.

Consortia

Health sciences libraries may also explore the option of joining other ILL networks for benefits that may not be realized elsewhere. Through respective regional medical libraries (RML), a health sciences library may join various consortia for free reciprocal ILL service. FreeShare, a cross-regional DOCLINE library group, provides free-of-charge service to its members on a reciprocal basis, http://nnlm.gov/rsdd/freeshare/. Similarly, the Basic Health Sciences Library Network (BHSL) provides free reciprocal interlibrary loans among member libraries in the Mid-Atlantic and New England regions. In the south central region, the South Central Academic Medical Libraries Consortium (SCAMeL), www.tulane.edu/~scamel/index.htm, services both in and out of region medical libraries. The maximum charge for in-region libraries is one dollar, and these libraries may form free reciprocal ILL among themselves.

Smaller or subject-oriented consortia can also operate efficiently. RapidILL, for example, is a system for article ILL designed by Colorado State University that has more than 200 academic library memberships nationwide, http://rapidill.org/. It operates by "pods," which are groups of specific types of libraries. Health sciences and hospital libraries have a pod. Although it requires initial setup and annual membership fees, articles are supplied at no charge. This pod-based paradigm enables high fill rate and makes the twenty-four-hour turnaround time commitment achievable. It is especially attractive to libraries with a high volume of ILL requests because it brings down the overall cost. Regional or university system consortial ILL may also provide health sciences libraries with greater access to interdisciplinary resources in an economical fashion. Many university consortia have established agreements to provide member libraries with loans at low or no cost within a specified turnaround period. Participating in a mission-specific **consortium** also provides the possibility for sharing more journal resources with lower or zero fees. For example, facing the common problem of library space reduction, academic libraries in Maryland created a distributed repository of print holdings. Each participating library retains print runs of selected titles for use by the constituents of the partnering libraries. Equal access to the distributed collection is provided, primarily through the use of electronic document delivery at no cost.

Document Delivery

Document delivery service provides users with materials from in-house collections and, in some libraries, open access materials from the Internet. Document delivery tasks include locating the materials from the library's print or digital collections, scanning and/or making copies, and delivering them to users, predominantly in electronic formats. Because the materials are in-house, the turnaround time is usually shorter than ILL borrowing. The practice of filling requests with content available online differs among libraries. Some health sciences libraries provide the service regardless of the content format, whereas others may do so only for faculty/practitioners, and teach students to retrieve online materials for themselves. Document delivery service is considered by many to be one of the most essential services of a health sciences library.

Systems and Tools

ILL networks such as DOCLINE, OCLC WordShare Interlibrary Loan Service, and RapidILL can each operate as stand-alones. However, many health sciences libraries, especially those with multiple memberships with these networks, use ILLiad to bring incoming requests together onto a single platform for processing.

ILLiad

ILLiad Resource Sharing Management software, designed by Atlas, www.atlas-sys .com/illiad/, and distributed by OCLC, manages ILL and document delivery requests through a single Windows-based interface. ILLiad connects with DOCLINE, OCLC, and RapidILL to bring lending requests in, process them, and post updates back into these systems. Users place requests through a web form that transports the request into ILLiad to be sorted into borrowing or document delivery. Borrowing requests are then sent to appropriate supplying libraries. ILLiad is highly configurable. Based on their operational procedures, libraries design workflows through creating routing rules, triggers for actions, and language for user notifications. Add-ons, or software widgets, for invoking search engines/discovery tools, online bookstores, library catalogs, and full-text linking tools can be added in ILLiad to optimize request processing. The ILLiad statistical module provides canned reports including fill rates, most requested journals, and turnaround time, which can assist in collection management and process improvement. The customer searching feature allows for ad-hoc queries or customized reports. ILLiad Billing Manager generates invoices for libraries not participating in EFTS or IFM and for individual borrowers. Although IFM credits and debits library accounts automatically in OCLC, EFTS requires libraries to generate DOCLINE lending data through Billing Manager and manually upload them to EFTS in order to credit their accounts. Another module of the ILLiad system is Odyssey, which delivers and receives scanned articles in PDF or TIF format and subsequently updates ILLiad transactions.

ILLiad is distributed and supported by OCLC, and can be installed locally or hosted by OCLC.

Delivery Systems

Loans are delivered to borrowers in a number of ways. Postal mail or courier services remain the primary method for delivering returnable items such as books and multimedia items. As technology evolves, electronic delivery has become a predominant method for nonreturnable materials in digital form. Besides using e-mail systems, secured transmission systems such as Ariel and Odyssey are commonly used to deliver and receive digital materials. Relais Express by Relais International Inc., www.relais-intl.com, provides automatic document scanning and transmission. RapidILL's delivery system RapidX allows lending libraries to deliver the articles regardless of whether the borrower libraries receive them via Ariel, Odyssey, or Relais. A borrowing library may check a received material first before sending it to the user, or opt to have it delivered to the user directly. The user can then pick up the material from a secured location.

Cloud computing has become a cost-effective way for electronic document delivery. It does not require customers to invest in hardware and software, and it can be accessed by any type of computer. Services such as Dropbox, Microsoft's SkyDrive, and Google Drive (formerly, Google Docs) provide secured storage for and access to customer files at no or low cost. To ease the internal server load, many libraries use these services to temporarily store documents before delivering them to users. Although the cloud extends server storage space, another positive outcome is that it streamlines document upload and retrieval to and from the cloud in ILL processing. OCLC's Article Exchange is a cloud-based document delivery service embedded in its WorldShare ILL workflow. It is also integrated into the ILLiad process. It provides a single, secure location where lending libraries can place—and borrowing libraries or users can retrieve—materials obtained from ILL (OCLC, 2013). Innovative Interfaces' ArticleReach Direct, www.iii.com/, offers integrated support for Odyssey, Ariel, and Dropbox. All three options offer centralized sending and receiving of articles, automatically update interlibrary loan requests as "filled," and then notify patrons when requested articles are available on the web.

The niche market of ILL delivery systems has been expanding. In addition to those long-established library solution vendors, other industry players have also turned attention to libraries. For example, scanner manufacturers have developed software to integrate their products with ILL products. Among them are ImageAccess Inc.'s BSCAN ILL family of scanners, www.imageaccess.com/ and Xerox's Xerox BookCentre, http://xeroxbookcentre.com/. Both can be integrated with ILLiad, Odyssey, and Article Exchange to scan and deliver documents and update transactions in ILLiad.

Integration with Library Solutions and Other Applications

One of the crucial factors in continuously improving ILL service and user experience is to integrate ILL seamlessly with other information service solutions. Interoperability has become a key requirement in the deployment of library applications including ILL. Standards have also been established to steer product development in this direction.

NCIP (NISO Circulation Interchange Protocol, also known as Z39.83), a North American standard, has been around for a decade. It facilitates task automation and data exchange between Circulation and ILL through messaging-based communication. To make it work, both the ILL and ILS systems need to be NICP compatible. A variety of ILS products by vendors, including Exlibris, www.exlibrisgroup.com/; SirsiDynix, www.sirsidynix.com/; and Innovative Interfaces, www.iii.com/, have NCIP enabled in their circulation module. Once the two systems are connected, circulation processes can be performed within the ILL environment. For example, ILLiad, equipped with an NCIP add-on, allows staff members to track items received from borrowers and return them to lending libraries. On the lending side, staff can check loan items in and out of the local catalog. OCLC WorldShare Interlibrary Loan Service is also planning to release NCIP functionality in the future.

GIST (Getting It System Toolkit), http://idsproject.org/tools/gist.aspx, is an open source tool to integrate and optimize acquisitions and the ILL service. It was developed by the Information Delivery Services Project (IDS), a group of libraries in the New York State University, in partnership with Atlas System and OCLC. GIST enables a user to initiate book/media purchasing requests through connectivity to OCLC Worldcat, Google Books, Index Data, and Amazon. It merges acquisitions and ILL request workflows using one interface, ILLiad, and hence, achieves coordinated collection development. A library formulates policies regarding whether a GIST request should be processed in ILL or acquisitions. Based on the policies, the requests are transferred between ILL and acquisitions for fulfillment (Bowersox et al., 2011).

In library management systems (LMS), ILL and other fulfillment functions such as e-reserves and circulation can be integrated in several ways: fully embedded within the LMS, or through interoperability based on standard communication protocols including NICP. For example, ExLibris's Alma product provides a built-in resource-sharing fulfillment function to manage ILL that is threaded in with other functional processes in Alma. But it can also be set up to connect to ILL systems such as OCLC, ILLiad, and Relais to manage internal ILL workflows within Alma, leaving the ILL systems between the borrowing and lending libraries to conduct ILL transactions as usual. OCLC WorldShare Interlibrary Loan, on the other hand, interoperates with other applications such as the Policies Directory to display lender fees and library catalogs in WorldCat Local to display the holdings inventory. Library users will use familiar WorldCat.org-based services for discovery and to place requests (OCLC, 2012). Innovative Interfaces' consortium borrowing system ArticleReach, www.iii.com/products/article_reach.shtml, uses a consortium catalog to evaluate library holdings, verify citations, identify sources, and deliver requests to the appropriate supplier. When the system receives an article electronically, it posts the document to a web server for retrieval.

OpenURL-based linking technology (NISO ANSI Z39.88) provides databases and discovery tools with full-text linking capability. It has also enhanced user experience in requesting materials through ILL. With resource data and holdings information exposed to databases and discovery tools, OpenURL allows a citation to be automatically populated in the ILL request form. It also functions as a gatekeeper in mediated and unmediated ILL processes, in that it ensures that only materials not internally available are requested from external libraries.

Interoperability between ILL and discovery systems remains desirable at this point—for example, the ability to bring in additional information such as call numbers from the discovery tool on the fly. A discovery tool user in a session would be able to see the similar requests he or she has placed already to avoid submitting a duplicate one.

Identity management through **single sign-on** (SSO) continues to be a way for academics and hospitals to enhance security measures and user experience. It allows users to log onto systems across the institution with a single credential. Although ILL systems such as ILLiad offer this capability, the challenge often lies in the implementation, which can encompass resources, expertise, and competing priorities within an organization. In an enterprise-wide SSO implementation, health sciences libraries need to advocate for the inclusion of the ILL system, conduct data cleanup, and collaborate with campus IT to, for example, classify users in identity directories.

Copyright

ILL is subject to the limitations and conditions of various copyright exceptions, most notably fair use and Section 108 of the U.S. Copyright Act. In addition, the National Commission on New Technological Uses of Copyrighted Works (CONTU) promulgated guidelines to help further define Section 108 and specify what can and cannot be copied for ILL.

Copyright Law

The copyright law of the United States governs the making of photocopies or other reproductions of copyrighted material. The fair use doctrine in section 107 (*17 U.S.C*), 1 www.copyright.gov/title17/92chap1.html#107, permits limited use of copyrighted material without acquiring permission from the rights holders. Section 108 (*17 U.S.C. 108*), www.copyright.gov/title17/92chap1.html#108, in which nothing "in any way affects the right of fair use as provided by section 107," expands the rights of libraries and archives by allowing them to furnish a photocopy or other reproduction to their users or qualifying libraries through interlibrary loan transactions. Section 108 dictates a set of rules and conditions regarding library reproduction. One of these specified conditions is that the photocopy or reproduction is not to be "used for any purpose other than private study, scholarship, or research." Because the rules are tightly phrased, they are easier for libraries to follow than the fair use doctrine in section 107, which only offers some guidance in determining when the principles of the doctrine apply. In ILL and document delivery practices, libraries often need to ask themselves if a particular group of users should be served or a type of request should be filled under the copyright law. Dr. Matthew Dames at Syracuse University advises, "Section 107 and Section 108 coexist synergistically, and should be deployed in a very specific way: try to qualify for Section 108 first, and if you cannot qualify for Section 108, then use fair use as your safety net" (Dames, 2012). ILL librarians need to familiarize themselves with these copyright provisions, and when unclear, libraries should consult with their legal counsel.

CONTU

Section 108 allows libraries to engage in ILL arrangements, so long as the library does not receive and distribute copies "in such aggregate quantities as to substitute for a subscription to or purchase of such work." However, it does not define the limit at which the library should purchase its own copy of the work instead of relying on ILL. In 1978, the National Commission on New Technological Uses of Copyrighted Works (CONTU), http://digital-law-online.info/CONTU/contu24.html, published guidelines to address this gap. The guidelines allow a library to receive, in one year, up to five copies of articles from the most recent five years of a journal title. Borrowing (or receiving) libraries are responsible for paying copyright permission and royalty fees starting with the sixth copy. When submitting requests to lending libraries, borrowing libraries must display the copyright notice on the request form, along with a compliance statement of copyright law and CONTU guidelines. For each copy supplied, lending libraries must include the original copyright notice or a standard notice if the original is not available.

These guidelines were never enacted into law, but they were accepted by the library, publishing, and author communities as reasonable accommodations for everyday use. Because CONTU guidelines were established in the 1970s prior to electronic publications, they do not address the use of digital content (Copyright Clearance Center, 2007).

Licensing and ILL

A license is a grant of rights by a publisher who owns or has rightful possession of a property (Carroll, 2007). Although fair use principles and Section 108 apply to print publications, they do not apply to electronic content if they are not incorporated into the license. In other words, license agreements take precedence over copyright law. Nevertheless, many publishers include Section 108, the fair use clause and, often, CONTU in their licenses. ILL articles included in license agreements unanimously forbid commercial use. Other terms of use such as eligibility, Loansome Doc use, geographic restriction, and the delivery method of ILL copies may vary depending on publishers and often on negotiations between a library and publisher. ILL staff members need to have access to these licenses in order to determine if a lending request should be honored. As more health sciences libraries transition to electronic subscriptions, it is imperative that acquisitions librarians seek input from ILL staff and negotiate ILL rights to sustain the ILL enterprise.

Challenges and Opportunities

The interlibrary loan environment in health sciences libraries, as with their peers in other environments, is undergoing changes. Advances in technology, new breeds of publishing, and Google have affected the traditional way of conducting ILL service. Information is abundant, yet not always completely available. Users can easily find citations from anywhere, no matter how obscure or rare the materials may be, and they want the full text delivered fast, electronically, and free (Posner, 2007). In addition, budget constraints may stimulate a higher volume of ILL requests stemming from limited electronic resources and shrinking print stacks due to space reduction. In 2011, NLM eliminated the national maximum charge by resource libraries for DOCLINE requests. As a result, some libraries increased service charges for lending requests to ease their budget pressures, which added additional financial burden to borrowing libraries.

These challenges, on the other hand, also present opportunities for ILL service. Since the birth of electronic resources, libraries have put more focus on providing access to resources through licensing rather than owning those resources. In this paradigm, ILL has rapidly assumed the role of an essential function necessary to maintain a library's viability (Smith, 2006). To effectively assume this role is to facilitate faster turnaround and a higher fill rate in an economic manner. It requires ILL staff to expand process capabilities, develop skill sets, adopt and use new products and services creatively, and work collaboratively with other library functions such as collection development and acquisitions.

Pay per View

Pay per view, a per-article purchasing model publishers offer, has been adopted by ILL since the 1990s to respond to the problem of rising subscription prices and the resulting tension between the need to cancel journal subscriptions and still provide access to needed items (Chamberlain and MacAlpine, 2008). The cost-per-use for on-demand articles is cheaper than seldom-used subscriptions. It may also be a solution to space problems because it incurs no storage cost. A variation of this model is "token access" by publishers such as Wiley, www.wiley.com, in which a library pays for articles with prepurchased tokens from the publisher. Pay per view is usually done through direct purchase from publishers or a document delivery service such as Infotrieve, www.infotrieve.com/document-delivery-service. In 2010, the Copyright Clearance Center rolled out Get It Now, a 24/7 pay-per-view service available to academic libraries, www.copyright.com/content/cc3/en/toolbar/products AndSolutions/getitnow.html. Get It Now provides immediate fulfillment of full-text articles from more than nine thousand journals from more than fifty publishers, often at a lower rate than the publisher offers. The process can be integrated into ILL workflow such as ILLiad and/or an institution's OpenURL link resolver. Starting in 2013, libraries purchasing articles through Get It Now can make payments using their IFM account.

Pay-per-view services usually offer both unmediated and mediated options. Libraries, based on their budgets and trial data, decide which option, or if a hybrid of both, will fit them the best. It is important to weigh cost and turnaround time when choosing a pay-per-view service.

Pay per Use (Short-Term Loans)

Pay per use of e-books, often referred to as short-term loans or short-term purchase, provides a "just-in-time" solution for libraries and users as an alternative to interlibrary loan. Unlike ILL for electronic journal articles, it is common for publishers and vendors to prohibit the use of e-books for ILL purposes. According to a survey of 185 libraries Washington State University conducted in 2011, "only 2.4% of respondents indicated that all of their ebook licenses included interlibrary loan rights, while 26.6% responded with a qualified affirmative that some ebook licenses permit interlibrary loans, and 30.8% with a definite negative that no ebook licenses permitted interlibrary loans (Frederiksen et al., 2011: 125). As more libraries opt to purchase e-books over print, ILL staff may face increasing difficulty in finding lenders to fill book requests (Wicht, 2011). This impediment can have a profound impact on urgent patient care for health sciences libraries. The pay-per-use model alleviates the situation by providing instantaneous access to e-books through the purchase of a short-term loan at a fraction of the publisher's purchase price. Loan periods can range from twenty-four hours to twenty-eight days, depending on the e-book vendor. Similarly, the cost per loan varies by vendor and by the length of the loan period. Currently, Ebook Library (EBL), ebrary, EBSCO, and Ingram's MyiLibrary are major players in the market to provide short-term loans for e-books, and are (or are becoming) OCLC's listed lending providers. To take advantage of these services, health sciences libraries need to evaluate each vendor's pricing model and content relevancy in order to accommodate user needs and balance the budget at the same time.

Purchase on Demand

Purchase on demand, also commonly known as demand-driven acquisitions, is another "just-in-time" acquisition of both print and electronic books. Libraries that adopt this model add titles from a book vendor to the online catalog. The purchase is triggered if a title is accessed a certain number of times or browsed for a certain number of pages. Because this type of purchase is unmediated, libraries need to closely monitor spending and adjust purchase plans as needed. Book purchase requests or requests that cannot be filled with traditional ILL, on the other hand, usually go through a mediated process in which staff follow purchasing criteria and acquire the book if the criteria are met. Criteria may include requester status, cost, genre, and publication date (determined by the library).

Purchase on demand may also be an alternative way to obtain out-of-print books. Libraries often hesitate to loan out-of-print books, especially when the books are in poor condition, or they put restrictions on or charge a higher fee when loaning them. Contrary to common perception, out-of-print books, including older and rare books, are often available at a reasonable price from sellers such as Amazon, which holds more than thirty million out-of-print titles (Holley, 2010).

ILL, collection development, and acquisitions need to work together to establish a workflow to streamline the purchase-on-demand process. GIST by SUNY Geneseo facilitates such workflow using ILLiad automatically. Purchase requests are submitted to ILLiad, where a review process determines whether the request should be filled through purchase or ILL or be canceled.

Consortium Purchase

Consortial purchase with pooled money from participating libraries allows the libraries and their users to gain greater purchasing power, deeper discounts, and broader access to content. With the increased buying power comes increased negotiating power on ILL privileges or shared access across the consortium (Wicht, 2011). For example, the Orbis Cascade Alliance, www.orbiscascade.org/, a consortium of thirty-seven academic libraries in Oregon, Washington, and Idaho, has implemented a purchase plan through YBP Library Services, www.ybp.com/, and EBL whereby all e-book titles individual libraries purchase can be shared across the Alliance. Although health sciences libraries may have unique requirements for certain content, they can still leverage consortium purchasing for content of common interest among the members, such as basic sciences or interdisciplinary studies.

The Changing Roles and Responsibilities of ILL Librarians

ILL function is no longer a relatively stand-alone operation as it was in the past. Although it may remain a processing center for getting users the materials they need, the way of doing it has largely changed in response to the transformation in the supply and demand of information. This change has inspired ILL librarians to play a larger role in library services, to take on more responsibilities, and to not only sustain the current service quality, but to advance that service with innovation and collaboration.

To achieve this, ILL librarians continue to expand their knowledge base and skill sets in technology, copyright law, vendor management, analytics and user services, and evolve from being only implementers to also strategists, aligning the service with the library's mission. They become user-centric, cost conscious, and technology savvy, and are continuously looking for opportunities to improve the service in an economical way. This often requires revamping processes, reallocating or repurposing staff resources, providing staff training, and implementing new technologies. They keep a vigilant eye on new products in the market and conduct timely assessments to turn them into new opportunities. Facing limited budgets, they reach out to consortia and peer libraries for free or low-cost ILL reciprocation. To implement a purchase on demand model, they negotiate with vendors to get the best deals. ILL librarians no longer leave "teaching moments" to reference staff for products such as clinical databases or discovery tools, but they often teach users at the same time as they help to locate content or place requests through these tools. They develop key performance indicators to measure ILL service, conduct benchmarks to develop best practices, generate metrics to understand trends, and anticipate and prepare for forthcoming challenges.

Being innovative and tech savvy are requirements for the librarian and staff responsible for ILL/document delivery. Gone are the days of obtaining a photocopy of an article and snail-mailing it or having the user come to the library to pick it up. The e-content revolution has changed the playing field, in some ways making it easier to supply resources, but at the same time making it challenging to understand and use the technology and systems to the best advantage. As systems continue to evolve, the roles of the librarian and support staff need to evolve as well.

Patricia Hinegardner, MLS, AHIP, associate director for resources, Health Sciences and Human Services Library, University of Maryland, Baltimore

At the same time, ILL librarians look beyond the ILL function and play an active role in other aspects of library services. They participate in the evaluation and implementation of products such as discovery tools; assist in collection management;

negotiate ILL rights in licenses; and collaborate with acquisitions to streamline purchase on demand. As library services continue to evolve, so will ILL librarianship.

SUMMARY

The mission of access services departments is to ensure access to materials both physical and digital, both owned by the library and not, in spaces both traditional and virtual. In today's user-driven ecosystem of modern information services, access services staff need to take a broader view beyond their traditional functions and play a leadership role in the evolution of the service to support the overall mission of the library.

STUDY QUESTIONS

1. In what areas can staff members who provide traditional library services such as shelving and photocopying be retrained to provide meaningful work in a modern health sciences library?
2. What might be the strengths and challenges in combining services at one desk?
3. Why is it necessary to educate patrons about copyright compliance? What are some effective ways to do so?
4. In what direction do you see ILL services evolving?
5. What will be the impact of this evolution on ILL librarianship?

REFERENCES

ALA (American Library Association). 2001. "Library Services for People with Disabilities Policy." American Library Association. www.ala.org/ascla/asclaissues/libraryservices.
———. 2010. "Access Services." American Library Association. http://wikis.ala.org/professionaltips/index.php?title=Access_Services.
———. 2013. "ADA and Libraries." American Library Association. www.ala.org/tools/ada-and-libraries.
Ayre, Lori. 2012. "Library RFID Systems for Identification, Security, and Materials Handling." *Library Technology Reports* 48, no. 5: 9–16.
Blackboard. 2013. "Commitment to Accessibility." Accessed March 13. www.blackboard.com/Platforms/Learn/Resources/Accessibility.aspx.
Bowersox, Tim, Cyril Oberlander, Kate Pitcher, and Mark Sullivan. 2011. "GIST: Getting It System Toolkit a Remix of Acquisitions, Collection Development, Discovery, Interlibrary Loan, and Technical Services." Contributed paper presented at the annual ILLiad conference, Virginia Beach, VA. March 24.
Breeding, Marshall. 2013. "Introduction to Resource Sharing." *Library Technology Reports* 49, no. 1: 5–11.
Byrd, Gary, ed. 2010. *2008–2009 Annual Statistics of Medical School Libraries in the United States and Canada*, 32nd ed. Seattle: Association of Academic Health Sciences Libraries.
Carroll, Diane. 2007. "Electronic Resource Management: Licensing and Interlibrary Loan." Washington State University. Research Exchange. https://research.wsulibs.wsu.edu:8443/xmlui/handle/2376/1081.

Chamberlain, Clint, and Barbara MacAlpine. 2008. "Pay-per-view Article Access: A Viable Replacement for Subscriptions?" *Serials* 21, no.1 (March): 30–34.

Chudnov, Daniel. 2007. "The History of Interlibrary Loan." Accessed January 7. http://old .onebiglibrary.net/mit/web.mit.edu/dchud/www/p2p-talk-slides/p2p-hist-ill.html.

Clumpner, K. E., M. Burgmeier, and T. J. Gillespie. 2011. "Embedded Course Reserves: Piecing the Puzzle Together." *Computers in Libraries* 31, no. 4 (May): 10–14. *CINAHL with Full Text, EBSCOhost.*

Collins, Maria. 2010. "Emergency Access Initiative and DOCLINE Update." Contributed paper presented at the annual meeting of the Medical Library Association, Washington, DC. May 21.

Copyright Clearance Center, 2007. "Interlibrary Loan Copyright Guidelines and Best Practices." www.copyright.com/media/pdfs/ILL-Brochure.pdf.

Dames, K. Matthew. 2012. "HathiTrust: Authors Guild Claims Libraries Ineligible for Fair Use." http://copyright.syr.edu/authors-guild-claims-libraries-ineligible-for-fair-use/.

Drake, Miriam. 2010. "Academic Library Challenges." *Searcher* 18, no. 9 (November): 16–53.

Folkenberg, Judith. 2005. "Libraries in the Digital Age." *NLM Newsline* 60 (Spring Special). www.nlm.nih.gov/archive/20120906/pubs/nlmnews/spring05/60sp_newsline.pdf.

Frederiksen, Linda, Joel Cummings, Lara Cummings, and Diane Carroll. 2011. "Ebooks and Interlibrary Loan: Licensed to Fill?" *Journal of Interlibrary Loan, Document Delivery & Electronic Reserve* 21, no. 3: 117–31.

Hansen, David R., William M. Cross, and Phillip M. Edwards. 2013. "Copyright Policy and Practice in Electronic Reserves among ARL Libraries." *College & Research Libraries* 74, no. 1 (January): 69–84. http://crl.acrl.org/content /74/1/69.full.pdf+html.

Holley, Robert. 2010. "Buying Library Materials on the Out-of-Print Book Market." ALCTS. Association for Library Collections & Technical Services. www.ala.org/alcts/confevents/ upcoming/webinar/coll/100610oop.

Howard, Jennifer. 2012. "Debate at N.Y. Public Library Raises Questions: Can Off-Site Storage Work for Researchers?" *Chronicle of Higher Education* 58, no. 34. https://chronicle.com/ article/Debate-at-NY-Public-Library-/131615/.

Kirk, Tom. 2010. "What Has Happened to Browsing Collections in Academic Libraries?" *Library Issues* 30, no. 5: 1–4.

Li, Xiaohua, and David Demers. 2010. "Improving Electronic Reserve Services: A Collaborative Effort." *Journal of Interlibrary Loan, Document Delivery & Electronic Reserves* 20, no. 4 (September/October): 263–69. doi:10.1080/ 1072303X.2010.507134.

Ludwig, Logan. 2010. "Health Sciences Libraries Building Survey, 1999–2009." *Journal of the Medical Library Association* 98, no. 2: 105–34. doi:10.3163/1536-5050.98.2.004.

Maurino, Paula San Millan. 2005–2006. "Syllabi as Cybergenre." *Journal of Educational Technology Systems* 34, no. 2: 223–40. *Professional Development Collection, EBSCOhost.*

McCaslin, David J. 2008. "Processing Electronic Reserves in a Large Academic Library System." *Journal of Interlibrary Loan, Document Delivery & Electronic Reserves* 18, no. 3: 335–46. doi:10.1080/10723030802186348.

———. 2010. "What Are the Expectations of Interlibrary Loan and Electronic Reserves During an Economic Crisis?" *Journal of Interlibrary Loan, Document Delivery & Electronic Reserves* 20, no. 4: 227–31. doi:10.1080/1072303X.2010.507722.

McGowan, Julie J. 2012. "Tomorrow's Academic Health Sciences Library Today." *Journal of the Medical Library Association* 100, no. 1: 43–46. doi:10.3163/1536-5050.100.1.008.

OCLC. 2011. "WorldCat Resource Sharing User Guide." www.oclc.org/support/ documentation/resourcesharing/using/userguide/WCRS_UserGuide.pdf.

———. 2012. "OCLC WorldShare™ Interlibrary Loan." www.oclc.org/services/brochures/ 214781usf_WorldShare_ILL.pdf.

———. 2013. "Article Exchange: Secure, Copyright-compliant Delivery of Documents." Accessed January 2. www.oclc.org/resourcesharing/features/articleexchange/default.htm.

Pike, George H. 2012. "The Verdict in the GSU Case." *Information Today* 29, no. 7 (July/August): 10. *Academic Search Premier, EBSCOhost.*

Pollitz, John H., A. Christie, and C. Middleton. 2009. "Management of Library Course Reserves and the Textbook Affordability Crisis." *Journal of Access Services* 6: 459–84. doi:10.1080/15367960903149268.

Posner, Beth. 2007. "Library Resource Sharing in the Early Age of Google." *Library Philosophy and Practice* 9, no. 3 (Summer): 1–10.

Rempel, Hannah Gascho, Uta Hussong-Christian, and Margaret Mellinger. 2011. "Graduate Student Space and Service Needs: A Recommendation for a Cross-Campus Solution." *Journal of Academic Librarianship* 37, no. 6: 480–87. doi:10.1016/j.acalib.2011.07.004.

Schulte, Stephanie J. 2011. "Eliminating Traditional Reference Services in an Academic Health Sciences Library: A Case Study." *Journal of the Medical Library Association* 99, no. 4: 273–79. doi:10.3163/1536-5050.99.4.004.

Shipman, Jean, and Carla Funk. 2009. "The Health Information Literacy Research Project." *Journal of the Medical Library Association* 97, no. 4: 292–301. doi:10.3163/1536-5050.97.4.014.

Sievert, MaryEllen; Dirk Burhans, Deborah Ward et al. 2011. "Value of Health Sciences Library Resources and Services to Health Care Providers in Medium and Large Communities Across Two Mid-Continental States." *Journal of Hospital Librarianship* 11, no. 2: 140–57. doi:10.1080/15323269.2011.558882.

Smith, Jane. 2006. "The RAPIDly Changing World of Interlibrary Loan." *Technical Services Quarterly* 23, no. 4: 17–25.

Squires, Steven J., ed. 2013. *2011–2012 Annual Statistics of Medical School Libraries in the United States and Canada*, 35th ed. Seattle: Association of Academic Health Sciences Libraries.

Tenopir, Carol, Donald W. King, and Amy Bush. 2004. "Medical Faculty's Use of Print and Electronic Journals: Changes Over Time and in Comparison with Scientists." *Journal of the Medical Library Association* 92, no. 2: 233–41.

U.S. Copyright Office. 2012. "Fair Use." www.copyright.gov/fls/fl102.html.

Wagner, Victoria H. 2008. "Processing Reserves, Seeking Permissions and Engaging the Campus: How the Library Serves as the Copyright Touchstone." *Journal of Interlibrary Loan, Document Delivery & Electronic Reserves* 18, no. 2: 247–54. doi:10.1080/10723030802099970.

Wicht, H. 2011. "The Evolution of E-books." *Collaborative Librarianship* 3, no. 4: 205–11.

Willis, Christine A. 2012. "Library Services for Persons with Disabilities: Twentieth Anniversary Update." *Medical Reference Services Quarterly* 31, no. 1 (January–March): 92–104. doi:10.1080/02763869.2012.641855.

Yelton, Andromeda. 2012. "Expanding Access to Devices, Collections, and Services." *Library Technology Reports* 48, no. 1: 19–24.

Zabel, Diane. 2005. "Trends in Reference and Public Services Librarianship and the Role of RUSA Part One." *Reference & User Services Quarterly* 45, no. 1: 7–10.

CHAPTER 13

Consumer Health Information Services

Kay Hogan Smith

INTRODUCTION

This chapter will describe the purpose and scope, as well as a brief history, of **consumer health information services** in libraries or involving librarians. The first section will cover the definition and general background of consumer health information services, including historical trends and current influences on the field. The second half of the chapter will provide practical guidance in setting up and managing a consumer health information service, whatever model libraries may choose to follow. Consumer health librarianship is an exciting and rewarding career path for any librarian, hopefully one the reader will consider after reading this chapter!

OVERVIEW OF CONSUMER HEALTH INFORMATION SERVICES

Definition of Consumer Health Information Service

What does it mean to provide consumer health information services? What do these services comprise typically? The Medical Library Association's (MLA) Consumer and Patient Health Information Section (CAPHIS) defines consumer health information as "an umbrella term encompassing the continuum extending from the specific information needs of patients to the broader provision of health information for the lay person" (CAPHIS, 2013). So, a library that includes consumer health information services among its offerings would make sure its policies and collections reflected the personal or family health information needs of the community it serves. Traditionally, a distinction has been drawn between the provision of general health information for consumers and that provided as part of patient education delivery in a health care setting. This distinction helped librarians determine where to draw the line in setting up their policies for consumer health information services, as patient education was determined to be the province of health care professionals, not librarians (Quist, 1994). More and more, however, as hospital librarians especially become involved in patient education committees, functions of the library overlap in serving both consumers and patients (Beschnett and Bulger, 2013).

Brief History of Consumer Health Information Services in Libraries

Consumer health information services in libraries have their roots in the consumer movements of the 1960s and 1970s in the United States, although a few libraries for hospital patients have been in existence since the nineteenth century (Perryman, 2006). Along with all the other social movements that marked a shift in attitudes toward authority figures and institutions, this period in medicine was distinguished by a transition in the doctor-patient relationship from a largely paternalistic, authoritarian pattern to one where patients began to adopt a more assertive role as partner in their own health care (Timmermans and Oh, 2010). This newfound patient empowerment led to a growing desire to learn more about their bodies and health conditions on their own as well as through the teaching of health care professionals. Self-help books and magazine articles focused on health and wellness were increasingly produced to meet this demand from consumers, although consumer health book publication has leveled off in recent years. Still, librarians, especially public librarians, were hesitant about providing health information services to clients beyond the basics such as referring them to a medical dictionary or encyclopedia in their collections. Gradually, however, these professional attitudes began to change as demand for such information grew. Librarians began to develop policies to allow them to help their users access reliable health information while avoiding the pitfalls of providing medical advice. These special services to consumers, however, were mostly driven by medical libraries in the 1970s and 1980s (Rees, 2013).

In 1996, Alan Rees chaired a task force of CAPHIS, which drafted a policy statement on "The Librarian's Role in the Provision of Consumer Health Information and Patient Education." This statement, approved by the Medical Library Association, clarified the roles librarians might play in providing health information for consumers toward the societal goal of a healthy community, cautioning that "[the librarian] cannot be held responsible for the scientific accuracy or currency of all materials in the collection" (CAPHIS, 2010). The American Library Association also produced guidelines around this time related to medical, legal, and business reference queries (RUSA, 2001). Thus, the old trepidation about overstepping the library's traditional boundaries was largely mitigated, and a period of notable growth in library-based consumer health information services ensued.

Of course, consumerism was not the only trend driving the growth of consumer health information services in libraries. The technological advances of the latter part of the twentieth century, especially the growth of the Internet and World Wide Web from 1993 onward, helped fuel the demand for readily accessible, understandable, and cheap—if not free—health information for the public.

The explosive growth of online resources for health information came with its own set of challenges, one of which was the information overload so apparent today (Lindberg and Humphreys, 2008). Another challenge that soon became evident to librarians was that of encouraging critical evaluation skills among users of health information. This last issue continues as a professional concern, with Pew studies indicating decreasing attention to cite quality details among health information seekers (Fox, 2006).

Current State of Consumer Health Information Services in the United States and Canada

Consumer health information services come in many forms today. For the purposes of this book, which is intended for librarians, the range of health information services covered will focus on those involving libraries of some kind.

In truth, there is no one example of a "traditional" consumer health library. As noted, these services take many forms in many configurations, from basic print collections and reference services in a single library setting, to collaborative setups, to online resources only. Following are a few representative examples.

Planetree Health Resource Centers

Planetree, http://planetree.org, is a non-profit organization partnering with health care organizations across the continuum of care to create and nurture a patient-centered culture. Planetree's approach is devoted to educating, empowering, and engaging patients and families to take full part in decision making about their health and care. To that end, the celebrated Planetree Health Resource Centers (HRCs) were created to enable easy access to medical and health information on a variety of levels and on a wide range of subjects for consumers and providers alike, setting the standard for consumer health libraries everywhere. Today, a number of Planetree HRCs exist in the more than 500 Planetree member health care organizations, though not all Planetree health care organizations have libraries. These HRC services include not only print collections arranged via the Planetree consumer health classification system, http://planetree.org/?page_id=148, but referral services for health-related organizations, support groups, and practitioners in the relevant areas, as well as access to online resources. Community education and informational programs and community partnerships are another hallmark of Planetree HRCs.

Consumer health information technology includes a broad array of apps, resources, services, and electronic devices that have the potential to empower consumers with information. Self-tracking and using data are part of a new movement called Quantified Self (QS). Quantified Self does not have a generally accepted definition; however, Wikipedia states that QS "is a movement to incorporate technology into data acquisition on aspects of a person's daily life in terms of inputs (e.g., food consumed, quality of surrounding air), states (e.g., mood, arousal, blood oxygen levels), and performance (mental and physical)" (Wikipedia, 2013). This movement creates new opportunities to promote consumer engagement in health and wellness. Although these technologies are not currently widely adopted, they have the potential to change the level and depth of questions librarians receive from consumers.

Gabe Rios, MLIS, director,
Ruth Lilly Medical Library,
Indiana University, Indianapolis

Healthnet (Connecticut)

Healthnet is an example of a program begun in an academic medical library—University of Connecticut (UC) Lyman Maynard Stowe Library in Farmington—as an outreach service to not only consumers but also other libraries, especially public libraries. Begun in 1985 with Library Services and Construction Act (LSCA) funding, the collaboration quickly spread throughout the state's public libraries (Rees, 1991). Public librarians appreciated the effort by the UC health center library to provide training and collection development consultation in consumer health services to their staffs, and the network relied on the public libraries' strengths as a known and trustworthy community resource. Since its beginnings as one of the earliest collaborative library networks devoted to consumer health information service, Healthnet has made only modest changes over the years. It still provides a prime example of a stable and workable partnership among multi-type libraries, each drawing on its own strengths. Its example, as well as that of similar pioneers in the field, has provided inspiration for many other consumer health information services in multilibrary networks through the years.

NC Health Info

Another collaborative effort, NC Health Info, www.nchealthinfo.org/index.cfm, was also begun in an academic medical library (Health Sciences Library, University of North Carolina at Chapel Hill). The Health Sciences Library (HSL) provides reference services to the public in person and online, or through text, chat, or phone. The website, however, is its main product. In 2002, NC Health Info was launched as the pilot program for the National Library of Medicine's MedlinePlus "Go Local" program (see section on "National Library of Medicine"

They say, "The times, they are a-changin'." Although that is true, some things endure, such as an individual's need to understand the context and meaning of significant life events, oftentimes a personal health imperative. Planetree Health Resource Center changes with the times and yet endures because it is fundamentally about connecting individuals to the resources, tools, and new skills needed to help guide their health care journey.

Michele Spatz, MS, former Planetree Health Resource Center director; currently, consultant, Planetree

"I want all the information you have on heart valve surgery." These "all the information you have" questions happen frequently in an active consumer health information service. Many years ago, when health information was not so readily available, they were relatively easy to answer. Now, with so many information sources out there, these questions can be extremely time consuming. If we step back, however, and ask ourselves, "What is the person really looking for?," or, better yet, ask the person looking for the information to be more specific about the information he wants, the task can be much simpler.

Alberta Richetelle, MLS, MPH, program director, Healthnet

below). HSL librarians initiated the creation of Go Local and the organization of a large, statewide database of health services. In 2006, NC Health Info added links to easy-to-understand, reliable health information of particular interest to the people of North Carolina (Silbajoris, 2013). This website has been continually maintained by the North Carolina librarians associated with the project and is one of only a few former Go Local sites that continued in existence beyond the National Library of Medicine's withdrawal of support for the service in 2010.

Recent Developments

The Internet is changing rapidly from its earliest days of static websites and e-mail, and online health resources are no exception (Mayer, Smith, and Rios, 2008). In fact, some estimates indicate that 72 percent of American adults go online specifically to find health information for themselves or loved ones (Fox and Duggan, 2013), so health consumers may be

The Health Sciences Library continues to respond to the ever-changing needs of consumers and the rapidly evolving health care system environment. At the time of this writing, the library is planning another extreme makeover of NC Health Info that will emphasize the availability and assistance medical librarians can provide. The goal is to build upon a service the library already provides—the provision of health information that empowers patients to make informed decisions—to more fully engage patients and assist them in becoming effective, contributory partners in their health care.

Christie Silbajoris, MSLS, AHIP, consumer health & patient education librarian; director, NC Health Info, Health Sciences Library, UNC-Chapel Hil

a potential driver of many of the innovations in web technology. In recent years, many of these innovations have centered around the social networking capabilities of consumer-directed content, such as that evident in sites such as YouTube and Facebook, as well as health-specific sites such as HealthGrades and medical blogs. Mobile technology is also playing an increasing role in health innovations, particularly in rural and "resource-poor" areas. Public health practitioners are very interested in the possibilities of mHealth, which involves mobile and wireless technology as a means of promoting health objectives. Many people—currently about one in five—use a mobile "app" to track health criteria such as calories or exercise (Fox and Duggan, 2012). The jury is still out regarding both the consumer participation in social networking-based health sites such as HealthGrades (Fox, 2011) and peer-to-peer health care sites such as PatientsLikeMe.com as well as the evidence of effectiveness of mHealth solutions to health issues (mHealth, 2013). But these trends could easily change as the technology—and consumers—evolve. Consumer health librarians should try to keep abreast of these trends and keep up with new health applications and technology.

In addition, health policy is evolving in ways that might, at least indirectly, affect the practice of consumer health librarianship. **HIPAA**, or the **Health Insurance Portability and Accountability Act**, passed in 1996, may have implications for consumer health library policies, such as that of sharing information on a user's medical information request with other family members without the user's express consent. More information about HIPAA can be found at www.hhs.gov/ocr/privacy/ hipaa/understanding/index.html. The **Affordable Care Act (ACA)** passed in 2010 was landmark legislation designed to increase health insurance and health care accessibility to all (or most) Americans. Although the ACA is still facing some uncertain issues such as Medicaid expansion, many of its provisions may have implications for librarians. In particular, the incentives in the law to promote comparative effectiveness research in medicine may well give rise to a new category of consumer interest in health care quality as this research is produced and reported in the popular media. The Kaiser Family Foundation produces a wealth of information about the ACA on its website at http://healthreform.kff.org/; the U.S. Health and Human Services Department produces a consumer-friendly site on the new legislation and its implications at www.healthcare.gov/.

National Library of Medicine

The National Library of Medicine (NLM) began to expand its focus from just serving health care professionals to the public in 1998 with the launch of the MedlinePlus consumer health website that year. Currently, MedlinePlus, www .medlineplus.gov, covers almost 1,000 disease and wellness topics. It also provides healthcheck tools such as an Interactive Sleep Quiz and a Colorectal Cancer Risk Assessment Tool, as well as numerous videos and interactive tutorials on various procedures and conditions. MedlinePlus was designed as a gateway to reliable online health information, especially that available from government sources such as the National Institutes of Health and CDC. These links are vetted by the site staff at the National Library of Medicine. Its linking policies are available at www.nlm .nih.gov/medlineplus/criteria.html. The site is optimized for mobile access as well, http://m.medlineplus.gov/.

In 2002, NLM began pointing users to local health services in North Carolina via the latter's NC Health Info site (see above). This marked the beginnings of the MedlinePlus "Go Local" experiment, which attempted to connect users to relevant local health services from the Health Topics pages and other points on the site. Eventually, more than thirty local sites linked to MedlinePlus via the Go Local program. However, disappointing usage of the service and other considerations forced NLM to rethink its commitment to this program, and Go Local support ceased in 2010.

MedlinePlus Connect was introduced in 2010 as a means of connecting the information for consumers on the site to electronic health records. The information links are produced by any of the codes included in standard patient record documentation such as ICD-9 (International Classification of Diseases, 9th ed.), NDC (National Drug Code), and LOINC (Logical Observational Identifiers Names and Codes) (U.S. National Library of Medicine, 2012).

Health Literacy

Health literacy is an issue that threads through any discussion of consumer health information. It is defined by the National Institutes of Health (NIH) as the "capacity to obtain, process and understand basic health information and services needed to make appropriate health decisions" (U.S. Department of Health and

Human Services, 2013). There has long been a growing awareness that medical information purportedly produced for the general public is written (or narrated) at a higher reading level than the average person can understand easily. With the publication of *Health Literacy: A Prescription to End Confusion* (Institute of Medicine, 2004), the issue of health literacy gained nationwide prominence among health care providers, educators, and, of course, librarians. Studies indicate that although most adults in the United States read at an eighth- or ninth-grade level, most health-related materials for them are still written at a tenth-grade level or above (NPSF, 2013). But the issue involves more than reading ability. The decision-making skills the U.S. health care system requires are made more difficult by the complexity of that same system for even the most proficient reader—whose literacy skills are likely to diminish when he or she isn't feeling well or has been given bad news (Clancy, 2010). Because the preferred outcome of any health-related message is "appropriate health decisions," it is necessary to keep all these factors in mind in offering health-related materials.

Fortunately, the increased attention to the issue in recent years has led to some improvements, particularly in the production of health-related material featuring plain language and formatting designed to facilitate understanding. Guidelines such as Simply Put, by the Centers for Disease Control (U.S. Dept. of Health and Human Services, Centers for Disease Control and Prevention, 2009), provide clear instructions for health information producers so that the material made available to patients and families is easily understandable. Of course, this is more difficult than it might seem at first, because information about medical conditions and treatments is often so complicated.

> The statistics on the number of people with limited health literacy are sobering: Only 12 percent of U.S. adults are able to understand and navigate our health care system. The Institute for Healthcare Advancement (IHA) operates in that space where solutions to problems are learned, shared, and implemented. Our annual continuing education health literacy conference teaches hands-on skills, so those people can go back to their jobs and make health information more accessible and usable for patients. I am so proud to work for a nonprofit company that makes a difference.
>
> *Michael Villaire, MSLM, chief operating officer, Institute for Healthcare Advancement, La Habra, CA*

The movement to simplify the patient's navigation of the health care system itself has seen less advancement, although not for lack of interest in this area. Recent publications such as the Health Literacy Universal Precautions Toolkit (DeWalt et al., 2010) encourage health care institutions and providers to take stock of their patient care environments and practices to see where they can make their patients' experiences more easily manageable. The Toolkit, www.ahrq.gov/legacy/qual/literacy/healthliteracytoolkit.pdf, is easy to navigate, with Quick Start Guides to help even the most time-challenged provider make improvements in its practices. Still, moving toward such a "patient-centered practice" goal for health care is by no means easily accomplished, as the generally slow progress in this area demonstrates (Parker and Ratzan, 2010).

For a list of "Health Literacy Resources" and more information about health literacy in the United States, go to www.healthinfonet.org/Pages/Librarians.aspx. Click on the link at the bottom of the page to locate a bibliography of resources— including publishers of easy-to-read health materials and tools.

ESTABLISHING AND MANAGING A CONSUMER HEALTH INFORMATION SERVICE

The preceding section focused on the history, background issues, and current status of consumer health information systems. This section will provide practical guidelines for setting up and managing a consumer health information service in a library setting.

Community Needs Assessment and Strategic Planning

The first step toward establishing any new library service is assessing the need, if any, for that service. In the process of determining the need, the assessment may also help the librarian understand the actual or potential clientele better. As noted in the Finding Health and Wellness @ the Library toolkit, www.library.ca.gov/lds/docs/HealthToolkit.pdf, the first "core competency" for providing consumer health information services is that of knowing the community. This includes not only knowing the broad outlines of the community (e.g., its demographics, socioeconomic makeup, etc.), but also more subtle cultural aspects and other population features that may encourage or discourage use of a service devoted to self-education about health issues. As such, the librarian may start with basic census data (for a geographic area or an institution such as a hospital), but he or she should not stop there. The librarian may need to commission a survey or some other assessment method to determine the need for this new service. However, he or she should be aware up front that a survey is more than a random list of questions on a page or a website. Survey creation requires skill and training. It takes careful consideration to create a survey tool that is valid and reliable, while at the same time respectful of the respondent in terms of its length. Anything less diminishes the reliability of the results and wastes time.

The library may be a part of a hospital, municipality, library system, or other entity that has ready access to data supporting this need as part of its patient/citizen/client satisfaction or other regular surveys. If these types of data are not already collected, the librarian will have to go to some trouble and maybe expense to quantify the need. However, the investment is almost always worthwhile, and it is possible to keep the cost of the assessment (both in time and money) to a minimum if necessary.

The target users of the service are of primary importance in guiding the assessment. If the library is focusing the potential consumer health information services within a hospital, for example, the librarian should probably focus the assessment on current patients and family members. If the community the library wishes to serve is broader, however, it will be necessary to survey at least a good representative sample of the wider community.

Before diving into the assessment process, take stock of available resources. Those resources should include the following:

- People/partners to help with the assessment
- Tools available, including technology
- Funding

People/Partners

Other people or agencies may be interested in working with the library to assess the population, either in conjunction with a related effort or on its behalf. For instance, in a university setting a survey research unit may provide student assistance in conducting an assessment or expert advice in setting up the survey.

Tools

Technological advances such as Survey Monkey, www.surveymonkey.com, have made online surveys much easier to post, and collect and analyze results. However, online surveys are not appropriate in all situations. The first consideration is to determine whether the target respondents are likely to see the posted survey, and, if so, are they likely to respond? Because this type of survey is almost always a convenience sample (i.e., limited to those who volunteer to take the survey), it is subject to biased results. However, it is certainly cheaper and less time-consuming than other methods such as telephone and face-to-face survey methods. The librarian must make the judgment whether the potential pitfalls of online surveying are outweighed by its convenience.

Funding

Almost all assessment efforts involve some financial cost, in staff time if nothing else. For instance, a license to Survey Monkey is not free, and more rigorous methods such as focus groups or telephone surveys can be expensive, even if conducted by a partner agency. Some funding will likely be necessary to complete the assessment successfully. If the institutional budget will not allow for expenses related to assessment, the librarian should look for external sources of funding for this important planning effort. The sidebar lists potential external sources of funding for this and other efforts related to establishing a new consumer health information service.

The result of the assessment process, hopefully, will be a better idea of who might use the consumer health information services and how much. Armed with this knowledge, the librarian can press ahead in planning this new service.

Library Policies and Procedures for Consumer Health Information Services

Like all policies, library policies and procedures regarding a consumer health information service provide the framework and boundaries for the service. They may even help the library sidestep any potential legal issues that might arise. In

POTENTIAL FUNDING SOURCES

It is always a good idea to keep an eye on additional sources of funding to support consumer health information services, even if one's institution is willing to fully fund all aspects of the service. A few potential funding resources for librarians to consider in planning for the service are:

- American Library Association
- National Network of Libraries of Medicine
- Other regional/state/local library associations
- Federal government funding (LSTA)—see www.ala.org/advocacy/advleg/federal legislation/lsta#funding
- Universities
- State/local government
- Medical/health professional associations
- Pharmaceutical companies (especially those with a state or local presence)
- Family and community foundations

Other resources (searchable funding opportunities databases) include:

- Grants.gov government funding opportunities—available free online at http://grants .gov/applicants/find_grant_opportunities.jsp
- Foundation Center private funding opportunities—some information available free online at http://foundationcenter.org/findfunders/. (Foundation Center also offers subscriptions to its Foundation Directory Online and other proprietary resources at its website.)
- SPIN Funding Opportunities—available for subscription at http://infoedglobal.com/ solutions/grants-contracts/spin-funding-opportunities/

Remember:

- In searching funding opportunity databases (or individual foundation websites), use broadly relevant keywords, such as "health" or "libraries" or "education," in order to obtain all related funding opportunities. Don't use too many keywords either; one or two will suffice.
- Use personal networks! Especially if the consumer health information service has an advisory board, use the contacts made available through that network of active community volunteers—one of them may know someone in a position to help fund the service.

preparing the consumer health information service policies and procedures, be sure to address the following:

- Who may use the service—hospital/clinic patients, family members, community members, some combination of these?
- Any charges associated with the service—printing, mailing, remote access to licensed resources, registration fees?
- What services are included—circulating collection, information packets, telephone reference, community health services identification, website, social media and e-mail reference? What are the parameters of each service? (For example, how much information will the library provide over the telephone?)
- Hours
- Circulation policies
- What about **disclaimers**?—Policies and wording of any disclaimers to be attached to promotional materials, included in information packets, should be included.
- Privacy/confidentiality policies
- Other relevant limits—guidelines for staff in determining limits of the librarian role in providing health information

The "Consumer Health Information and Librarian Roles" page of the HealthInfo Iowa website, www.healthinfoiowa.org/librarians, has more information. Additionally, appendix A contains a sample CHIS policy.

Collaborative Consumer Health Information Service Arrangements

A number of multi-institutional collaborative arrangements exist for consumer health information services in which libraries are involved. For example, Health InfoNet of Alabama, www.healthinfonet.org, is a cooperative service of the state's medical and public libraries. Other collaborations may involve hospital libraries as well as academic medical or public libraries, health and health care organizations, foundations, faith-based groups, insurance companies, or any combination thereof. Any multi-institutional collaboration offers potential opportunities and potential pitfalls. It is important to observe the best practices of stakeholder engagement in order to promote the opportunities while avoiding the pitfalls.

This chapter will not go into detail about building and maintaining successful collaborations except to refer the reader to other resources for information on this important task. In particular, some characteristics of successful coalitions and methods of creating and maintaining them have been identified by Dr. Frances Butterfoss in her chapter on "Building and Sustaining Coalitions" in *Community Health Education Methods: A Practical Guide*, 3rd ed. (2008). Refer to this guide for more information.

Is it necessary to create a coalition in order to have a successful consumer health information service? Absolutely not! In certain cases, forming an extensive community coalition would be, at best, an unnecessary effort expenditure; and, at worst, it would be counterproductive. For example, a consumer health information service based within a health care organization and focused on serving the patients and family members within that institution would not likely be well-served by establishing a formal coalition to guide the service. However, the guidelines presented in Butterfoss's book chapter are also helpful in forming steering committees of stakeholders within an organization. This type of stakeholder involvement—including, for example, hospital/clinic administration, clinicians, health educators, and patient advocates—is likely to be an advantage in promoting the success of any consumer health information service. The involvement of multiple perspectives on the issue of health information literacy among any target population is vital in preventing the tunnel vision that may arise from forging ahead with a project without input from other stakeholders.

Staff Training

Conducting regular staff training in providing a consumer health information service is the best way to both alleviate staff anxiety about responding to health questions and prevent any inappropriate performance in this realm—for example, offering personal recommendations of health services or failing to honor a client's privacy. Fortunately, resources are available to help with this training, espe-

In collaborating with public libraries, whether in Tennessee or South Africa, Preston Medical Library has endeavored to provide current, relevant, and scientifically valid health information to the consumers we serve. People come to their public libraries asking questions. The formats may change but not the questions. We work with our public library colleagues to provide the training, knowledge of resources, and collection development guidance requested to answer those questions. Our goal remains the same: to empower the consumer at point of need.

The value and role of both medical and public libraries remain strong. Public librarians may not feel as qualified to answer complex consumer questions without consultation with specialist librarians. We found this in both countries and consistently in the literature. Public librarians are like primary care providers who rely on medical librarians for referral and consultation.

Martha Earl, MSLS, AHIP, assistant director,
Preston Medical Library,
University of Tennessee, Knoxville

cially those from the National Network of Libraries of Medicine (NN/LM). NN/LM offers numerous courses by trained instructors on a variety of topics related to consumer health information service and outreach. A regularly updated list of such courses is available at http://nnlm.gov/training/. Both in-person and virtual courses are provided, and often the regional medical library (which provides the bulk of the services offered by NN/LM) will send the instructor(s) to the local libraries in its area to teach the courses, if an in-person workshop is preferred. Local and state library associations are other readily available resources for continuing education for library staff. Finally, there are books aimed at librarians about providing consumer health information; one excellent example is Michele Spatz's *Answering Consumer Health Questions: The Medical Library Association Guide for Reference Librarians* (2008).

Any staff training on providing consumer health information in libraries should include the following components:

- Reference interviewing for health questions—Training should cover communication techniques, such as asking open questions (i.e., those requiring something other than a yes or no response), confirming information (especially medical terms provided by the consumer), and helping users to refine their requests when necessary. For more information about reference interviewing in a health reference transaction, see http://nnlm.gov/outreach/consumer/ethics.html.
- Critical evaluation of health information sources, both print and online—Training should include guidelines for verifying the accuracy, authority, and currency of medical information as well as assessing any potential for biased presentation of facts. For additional guidance, see the MedlinePlus Health Topics Page on "Evaluating Health Information" at www.nlm.nih.gov/medlineplus/evaluatinghealthinformation.html.
- Background information about medical research, because librarians may need to help users evaluate the evidence for a particular treatment or practice.
- Respecting the privacy and confidentiality of the user.
- Dealing with situations such as conditions with a poor prognosis and/or an emotional client—This is where training and role playing can be especially helpful for library staff.
- Clarifying the role of the library staff, for themselves and their clients—This is important in observing the ethical and legal boundaries of the librarian's role. See www.ala.org/rusa/resources/guidelines/guidelinesmedical for more guidance.
- Special procedures, such as the inclusion of a library-specific disclaimer with materials and instructions on responding to health questions via telephone or e-mail/chat/social media, and so forth.

Staff training is an essential, ongoing commitment on the part of library administration. It is key to the success of any consumer health information service.

Marketing on a Shoestring

Marketing the consumer health information service is another key element for its success, yet libraries rarely have extensive marketing budgets on hand for this purpose. So, it is necessary to be creative as well as opportunistic in marketing this service.

The American Library Association (ALA) has created a nationwide marketing campaign, the @Your Library campaign, www.ala.org/advocacy/advleg/publicawareness/campaign@yourlibrary, to help guide librarians in marketing their services. Among the tools provided to libraries as part of this campaign is a marketing guidebook (ALA, 2007). This book advises librarians to craft a marketing plan prior to forging ahead piecemeal with efforts to promote the service. The suggestions include:

- Assessing the environment for introducing the service. This may involve a SWOT analysis (i.e., assessing the Strengths, Weaknesses, Opportunities, and Threats relevant to the introduction of the service).
- Stipulating the goals for the marketing campaign. These should naturally be related to the overall goals for the library.
- Spelling out campaign objectives. These should be SMART objectives (i.e., Specific, Measurable, Attainable, Relevant, and Time-bound, or completed within a certain time frame).
- Identifying the primary audience(s) for the service and the marketing campaign, and prioritizing them.
- Developing key messages for the campaign. This is the point at which the most important aspects of the service—those features of the library health information service that should be highlighted the most, and the most often—are identified and key phrases to describe them are produced. For example, the Health InfoNet of Alabama information service has the tagline "We're Your Health Information Experts—And We're in Your Neighborhood" (see Figure 13.1.) This message highlights the information-seeking expertise of the library staff; the "In Your Neighborhood" reference recalls the fact that the participating public libraries have branches in close proximity to most target users. These key messages should be repeated regularly in multiple outlets as part of the overall campaign.
- Outlets/strategies for presenting the message(s). This is the point at which any and all media outlets or presentation formats are identified for broadcasting the messages about the service. These outlets may be as mundane as the library's newsletter or as exciting as a radio or television spot. However, all potential outlets should be taken advantage of, as funding will undoubtedly limit the availability of most mass media promotions. Do not forget the interpersonal "outlets" available in day-to-day interactions—prepare and practice that "elevator speech" (i.e., the short impromptu description of the service that might be proffered to someone in an elevator).
- Consider collaborating with other organizations to extend the promotions reach in the target audience. See Figure 13.2 for an example of a collaborative marketing effort between Health InfoNet of Alabama and the local 211 service.
- Develop means to measure the success or failure of promotional efforts. Include process evaluation measures—such as numbers of presentations, articles, health fairs, and other campaign efforts—as well as outcome measures—such as numbers of questions received, follow-up surveys, or website analytics.

Planning the promotional objectives and campaign will increase the chances for success, both for the campaign and for the health information service.

Collection Development

Consumer health collections in libraries require special attention because medical information may become outdated quickly, and thereby useless or even potentially hazardous to consumers. Health information can also be biased, especially in areas where experts disagree or authors have a financial stake in the treatments or

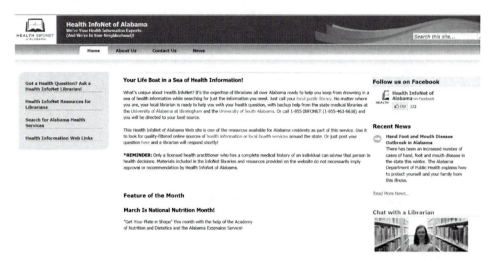

Figure 13.1. Health InfoNet of Alabama Home Page (www.healthinfonet.org).

practices they discuss. Thus, it is important for librarians to carefully evaluate health collection purchases (or licenses) and even free online resource referrals for their clients. Criteria for collection development in health collections should include:

- Author/responsible party qualifications—Who is the author? What are his or her credentials? If the work is produced by an agency, is it a well-known, respected entity?
- Evidence-based recommendations—The evidence for any recommendations in a consumer health resource should be identified through thorough documentation of sources. At least some of the sources cited should be from mainstream medical literature, and the bibliography should include fairly recent citations.
- Balance in presenting all sides of a medical controversy—If this cannot be found within a single source, consider purchasing works on both (or all) sides of the controversy.
- Cultural/literacy considerations—This is where the importance of knowing the service's users or potential users comes in. The items in the health collection should reflect any ethnic or cultural aspects of the community in any illustrations or photographs included in the works. In addition, the librarian should, if possible, determine the reading level of the materials up front to make sure it is not too high for the majority of the users. Many medical works are written at a fairly high reading level, so this may take some investigation. Some publishers, such as Krames Staywell, provide health materials for people with low reading skills.

Weeding is another important aspect of collection development, particularly with health collections. It is generally better to have nothing in the collection on a particular health topic than to have a work that is out of date or of poor quality. The rule of thumb in health collections is to consider anything more than five years

Figure 13.2. Billboard Promoting Both Health InfoNet of Alabama and Local 2-1-1 Service in Birmingham, 2009.

old as a potential candidate for weeding. For some areas of intensive research, such as HIV/AIDS or prescription drugs, that time limit may be narrower. Note that a few classics, such as Kübler-Ross's works on death and dying, may be maintained beyond the five-year limit, but these "keepers" are relatively rare. In addition, librarians should keep abreast of advances in medical science sufficiently to be aware when a particular medical regimen has been debunked by the scientific evidence, and to weed out any materials that promote the debunked regimen. Resources for keeping up with medical science include:

- MedlinePlus—MedlinePlus has a Health and Medical News feed, www.nlm.nih .gov/medlineplus/healthnews.html, that provides continual updates on the latest health news from the popular press.
- PubMed Health—PubMed Health, www.ncbi.nlm.nih.gov/pubmedhealth/, provides summaries of "reviews of effectiveness" of treatments and prevention measures especially for consumers (as well as clinicians). It is designed to answer the question, "What works?" In addition, the "Behind the News" feature in PubMed Health is an excellent resource for helping users make sense of medical headlines as they apply to their own lives and those of their loved ones.
- Guidelines.gov—Another evidence-based clinical effectiveness research tool is the National Guideline Clearinghouse database, www.guidelines.gov/, which is an initiative of the Agency for Healthcare Research and Quality (AHRQ). Because clinical practice guidelines are produced by numerous professional and official organizations, this research includes a handy "Compare Guidelines" feature as well.

Where should librarians look for good health information resources? Many of the primary collection development resources such as *Library Journal* include sections on health materials, both print and nonprint. Noted consumer health librarian Barbara Bibel produces a regular "Best of Consumer Health" column for *Library Journal*. In addition, the Consumer and Patient Health Information Section (CAPHIS) of the Medical Library Association provides book reviews of consumer health works in its newsletter, *CAPHIS Connections*, available at http://caphis.mlanet.org/publications/newsletter.html. CAPHIS also has a "Collection Development" section on its website, http://caphis.mlanet.org/chis/collection.html, which includes bibliographies of recommended materials for health collections produced by member librarians.

In summary, consumer health collections require vigilance and industry in keeping up with advances in medicine and health care. However, such attentiveness is key to providing access to reliable information for the library's clients.

Online Resources

Given the frequent rapid changes in availability of resources, this chapter will not attempt to provide a comprehensive bibliography of consumer health information sources on the Internet. Many links are likely to change by the time this work is published. Instead, this section highlights a few of the most reliable and stable gateway sites for health information, along with tips for searching for additional resources and evaluating online resources. The sidebar contains a core recommended list of sites; most of them include a mirror site in Spanish, with the exception of PubMed Health.

As noted previously, these are just a sampling of the many excellent online resources available on the Internet to help librarians respond to health questions from users. These sites are intended as a starting point for consumer health research, and in most cases the user will find relevant information there to suit his or her needs. However, at times the librarian may have to look further afield to find the specific information requested by the user. In such cases, it is helpful to become practiced in searching the medical literature via databases such as PubMed, as well as web searching via search engines such as Google.

PubMed, www.pubmed.gov—which is not the same as PubMed Health—is a major bibliographic database of the biomedical literature from around the world incorporating more than twenty-two million citations from MEDLINE, life science journals, and online books. Although most of the items indexed are intended for health care providers, and so are not easy to read, they can be very useful especially for very specific health queries not served by more general consumer health sites. PubMed does support keyword searching as well as Medical Subject Headings (MeSH, a controlled vocabulary) searching. The Advanced search interface allows easy combinations of concepts, and filters such as human subject, age ranges, language, and date limits help sharpen your results. Note also the availability of search filters such as those specific to certain topics (e.g., Complementary Medicine) and Clinical Queries for evidence-based research results. Other databases specific to a discipline, such as PsycINFO for mental health issues, might also serve some requests.

Finally, look at Google as well as other web search engines. Fortunately, most librarians are skilled at selecting the right search engine and using its features as well as common devices such as truncation symbols or phrase searching to hone the results.

For more help in searching Google, look at Princeton University Library's Libguide on using Google at http://libguides.princeton .edu/google.

The main thing to remember in using search engines is that they do not provide any quality filtering of the results they provide in a search. So, it is up to the librarian to stress the importance of critically evaluating those results, and to teach the user how to do so. The main criteria for evaluation of online resources are:

- Authority—Try to find out (usually via the About Us section) who is responsible for the website, and how reliable they are.
- Bias—Is there a potential conflict of interest? Is the site supported by commercial interests? Does the author or supporting organization have an agenda that might prejudice any recommendations?
- Currency—Because medical information is updated constantly according to new research results (see Weeding discussion under Collection Development above), with few exceptions information available online should be no more than five years old.

Other evaluation guides, such as those included in the MedlinePlus Evaluating Health Information health topic page, include criteria such as cultural sensitivity, privacy considerations, and resource documentation as clues to its basis in evidence rather than opinion (U.S. National Library of Medicine, 2013). All of these criteria are helpful in determining the site's reliability as an information source.

The Oakland Public Library serves a very diverse population of more than 400,000 people in Northern California. We also provide library service for two adjacent cities, Emeryville and Piedmont. The population includes people from many countries who speak many languages. We buy books in Spanish, Russian, Amharic, Tigrinya, Arabic, Chinese, Vietnamese, Japanese, Korean, Lao, Khmer, Tagalog, Hindi, and Guajarati. We also buy books on several reading levels, because many of our patrons are English learners and/or educationally disadvantaged. This is especially important for providing consumer health information, because patrons need to understand it. We get a wide variety of questions about anatomy and physiology, specific diseases, drugs, nutrition, and fitness. Those come from students with assignments, those who have seen stories in the media, and those seeking information for themselves or a loved one. Helping these people find the right information is rewarding. It is one of the few jobs that allows you to feel that you have done something good at work.

Barbara M. Bibel, MLS, reference librarian/ consumer health information specialist, Oakland Public Library, Oakland, CA

Evaluation

Evaluating the successes or failures of a consumer health information service starts with an evaluation plan. This plan should be prepared along with the plans for implementing the consumer health information service. It is informed by the community assessment conducted at the beginning of the project, as well as the

RECOMMENDED STARTING SITES FOR CONSUMER HEALTH INFORMATION QUERIES

- MedlinePlus, www.medlineplus.gov—The National Library of Medicine's award-winning gateway site for consumers, with quality-filtered links to reliable full-text resources online for hundreds of health and prevention topics. See "Current State of CHIS—National Library of Medicine" above.
- Centers for Disease Control, www.cdc.gov—The CDC site is a powerhouse of resources for information on all types of conditions and injuries, as well as government policy and programs (e.g., Healthy People). Updated daily, it includes current information on travelers' health, workplace safety, and emergency preparedness as well as disease outbreaks and health statistics.
- National Center for Complementary and Alternative Medicine, http://nccam.nih.gov/—Another excellent (and free) government-supported gateway site for health information focused on complementary medicine. NCCAM is the National Institutes of Health's leading center for research into "health care systems, practices and products that are not generally considered part of conventional medicine." Note that because many CAM devotees may be suspicious of information the government provides, librarians may need to provide other evidence-based information sources for complementary medicine, such as Natural Standard, another excellent (but not free) resource. For more information on subscribing to Natural Standard, see www.naturalstandard.com/.
- KidsHealth.org, http://kidshealth.org—Produced by the Nemours Foundation, this site provides distinct portals for children, teens, parents, and educators. Information is reliable, up-to-date, and reviewed by experts. In addition, it is easy to understand by the age group for whom it is intended, with a minimum of medical jargon, if any.
- PubMed Health, www.ncbi.nlm.nih.gov/pubmedhealth/—As noted above (see "Collection Development"), PubMed Health is a terrific resource for "clinical effectiveness research" summaries to help users determine the evidence basis for any treatment or prevention protocol.

mission and goals for the service, thus providing the Who, What, and Why answers to guide the evaluation. The strategic plans and logic models that were (hopefully) created will also help tremendously in providing short-term and long-term outcomes to measure.

According to Burroughs's *Measuring the Difference: Guide to Planning and Evaluating Health Information Outreach* (2000), the evaluation plan should include:

- Evaluation objectives (related to program objectives)
- Implementation plans
- Questions to be answered by evaluation
- Data considered relevant to provide meaningful answers to those questions (e.g., door counts, web analytics, survey responses or comment cards)
- Evaluation design(s)
- Data collection plan
- Resources (staff, funding, technical resources, etc.)
- Time frame

Establishing meaningful outcomes and measures of those outcomes for any library service is difficult, and a consumer health information service in the library is no exception. Keep in mind that the library's resources may not allow for all relevant questions to be answered; it may be necessary to prioritize those evaluation questions that are the most important in measuring service success. Again, involve the stakeholders in determining the most relevant objectives and measures for the evaluation.

It is not within the scope of this chapter to go into details of evaluation methods as they relate to consumer health information services, but it is important for coordinators of these services to be aware of them. Refer to Burroughs's *Measuring the Difference* (2000) for more information.

SUMMARY

Consumer health information is a natural service for libraries to provide for their users, especially in medical and public libraries. By now libraries have a wealth of experience in planning and producing such programs, much of which is available for consultation through professional organizations such as the Consumer and Patient Health Information Section of the Medical Library Association. This chapter has provided an overview of the history of such health information services in libraries, as well as practical suggestions for how to start and run a consumer health information service. Be sure to check out the appendix and references, included with this chapter, as well as the glossary at the end of the book, for more information.

STUDY QUESTIONS

1. What are the three main criteria to use in evaluating the reliability of health information?
2. Name one of the topics to address in a library's consumer health information service policies.
3. What is the rule of thumb regarding the age of materials in library health collections—that is, at what age should an item be considered for weeding?
4. Name one key subject to cover in a library's consumer health information service staff training.

REFERENCES

ALA (American Library Association). 2007. "Marketing @ Your Library: The Campaign for America's Libraries: Simple Steps that Will Help You Create an @ Your Library Campaign." American Library Association. www.ala.org/advocacy/sites/ala.org.advocacy/files/content/advleg/publicawareness/campaign@yourlibrary/prtools/marketing_wkbk.pdf.

Beschnett, Anne, and Jim Bulger. 2013. "Patient Education and the Hospital Library: Opportunities for Involvement." *Journal of Hospital Librarianship* 13: 42–46.

Burroughs, Catherine M. 2000. *Measuring the Difference: Guide to Planning and Evaluating Health Information Outreach*. Bethesda, MD: National Network of Libraries of Medicine. http://nnlm.gov/evaluation/guide/.

Butterfoss, Frances. 2008. "Building and Sustaining Coalitions." In *Community Health Education Methods: A Practitioner's Guide*, 3rd ed., edited by Robert J. Bensley and Jodi Brookins-Fisher. Sudbury, MA: Jones and Bartlett Publishers.

CAPHIS (Consumer and Patient Health Information Section). 2010. "The Librarian's Role in the Provision of Consumer Health Information and Patient Education." Medical Library Association Policy Statement. Approved February 1996, updated March 24. http://caphis.mlanet.org/chis/librarian.html.

———. 2013. "Purpose." Medical Library Association. Last updated March 7. http://caphis.mlanet.org/organization/membership.html.

Clancy, Carolyn M. 2010. "Improving Your Health Literacy." Agency for Healthcare Research and Quality. September 7. www.ahrq.gov/news/columns/navigating-the-health-care-system/090710.html.

DeWalt, D. A., L. F. Callahan, V. H. Hawk et al. 2010. *Health Literacy Universal Precautions Toolkit*. Rockville, MD: Agency for Healthcare Research and Quality. April. www.ahrq.gov/legacy/qual/literacy/healthliteracytoolkit.pdf.

Fox, Susannah. 2006. "Online Health Search 2006." *Pew Internet & American Life Project*. October 29. www.pewinternet.org/Reports/2006/Online-Health-Search-2006/05-Eroding-Attention-to-the-Details-of-Information-Quality/01-Threequarters-do-not-consistently-check-the-source-and-date-of-online-health-information.aspx.

———. 2011. "The Social Life of Health Information." *Pew Internet & American Life Project*. May 12. http://pewinternet.org/Reports/2011/Social-Life-of-Health-Info.aspx.

Fox, Susannah, and Maeve Duggan. 2012. "Mobile Health 2012." *Pew Internet & American Life Project*. November. http://pewinternet.org/Reports/2012/Mobile-Health.aspx.

———. 2013. "Health Online 2013." *Pew Internet & American Life Project*. January 15. http://pewinternet.org/Reports/2013/Health-online.aspx.

Institute of Medicine. 2004. *Health Literacy: A Prescription to End Confusion*, edited by the Institute of Medicine, Committee on Health Literacy. April 4. www.iom.edu/Reports/2004/Health-Literacy-A-Prescription-to-End-Confusion.aspx.

Lindberg, Donald A. B., and Betsy L. Humphreys. 2008. "Rising Expectations: Access to Biomedical Information." *Yearbook of Medical Informatics* 3, no. 1: 165–72. www.ncbi.nlm.nih.gov/pmc/articles/PMC2441483/pdf/nihms-44688.pdf.

Mayer, Susan, Kay Hogan Smith, and Gabriel Rios. 2008. "Consumer Health Information Services 2.0." *Journal of Consumer Health on the Internet* 12, no. 3: 187–99.

"mHealth." 2013. "DRAFT: mHealth: Emerging High-impact Practices for Family Planning," *FHI 360/PROGRESS and the Johns Hopkins Bloomberg School of Public Health/Knowledge for Health Project*. Accessed August 7. www.mhealthworkinggroup.org/sites/mhealthwg.org/files/draft_mhealth_fp_hip.pdf.

NPSF (National Patient Safety Foundation). 2013. "Health Literacy: Statistics at-a-Glance." Accessed August 7. www.npsf.org/wp-content/uploads/2011/12/AskMe3_Stats_English.pdf.

Parker, Ruth, and Scott C. Ratzan. 2010. "Health Literacy: A Second Decade of Distinction for Americans." *Journal of Health Communications* 15 (supplement 2): 20–33.

Perryman, Carol. 2006. "Medicus Deus: A Review of Factors Affecting Hospital Library Services to Patients Between 1790–1950." *Journal of the Medical Library Association* 94, no. 3 (July): 263–70.

Quist, Sharon. Unpublished manual. 1994.

Rees, Alan M., ed. 1991. *Managing Consumer Health Information Services*. Phoenix: Oryx Press, 39–49.

———. 2003. *Consumer Health Information Soucebook*, 7th ed. Westport, CT: Greenwood Press, 10.

RUSA (Reference and User Services Association). American Library Association. 2001. "Guidelines for Medical, Legal, and Business Responses." Approved 1992, rev. and updated 2000 and 2001. June. www.ala.org/rusa/resources/guidelines/guidelinesmedical.

Silbajoris, Christie. E-mail message to author. May 15, 2013.

Spatz, Michele. 2008. *Answering Consumer Health Questions: The Medical Library Association Guide for Reference Librarians*. New York: Neal-Schuman Publishers.

Thompson, Nancy, Michelle C. Kegler, and David R. Holtgrave. 2006. "Program Evaluation." In *Research Methods in Health Promotion*, edited by Richard A. Crosby, Ralph J. DiClemente, and Laura F. Salazar, 199–225. San Francisco: Jossey-Bass.

Timmermans, Stefan, and Hyeyoung Oh. 2010. "The Continued Social Transformation of the Medical Profession." *Journal of Health and Social Behavior* 51: S94–S106. http://hsb.sagepub.com/content/51/1_suppl/S94.

U.S. Department of Health and Human Services. 2013. "Quick Guide to Health Literacy." U.S. Department of Health and Human Services, Office of Disease Prevention and Health Promotion. Accessed August 7. www.health.gov/communication/literacy/quickguide/factsbasic.htm.

U.S. Department of Health and Human Services. Centers for Disease Control and Prevention. 2009. *Simply Put: A Guide for Creating Easy-to-Understand Materials*, 3rd ed. Atlanta: Centers for Disease Control and Prevention. www.cdc.gov/healthliteracy/pdf/simply_put.pdf.

U.S. National Library of Medicine. 2012. "MedlinePlus Connect." U.S. National Library of Medicine and National Institutes of Health. Updated October 11. www.nlm.nih.gov/medlineplus/connect/overview.html.

———. 2013. "Evaluating Health Information." U.S. National Library of Medicine and National Institutes of Health. Updated July 17. www.nlm.nih.gov/medlineplus/evaluatinghealthinformation.html.

Wikipedia. 2013. "Quantified Self." *Wikipedia*. Last updated August 18. http://en.wikipedia.org/wiki/Quantified_Self.

PART IV

Administrative Services

CHAPTER 14

Library Administration in Health Sciences Libraries

Diana J. Cunningham

INTRODUCTION

The term *library administration* in the health sciences library environment includes a broad sweep of functions and titles: director, administrator, manager, leader, organizer, personnel, coach, mentor, facilitator, advocate, fund-raiser, grant-writer, problem solver, and even actor or actress. On any given day, one role or function may be predominant depending on the situation. Or, a new one may be added: for example, archivist! Library management is another term that is often used and can be large scale, small scale, or a one-person operation wherein the manager is responsible for all functions. What makes the health sciences library different from other libraries is the focus on providing quality health information to enable clinical or research decision making, the need for evidence-based information, and timely access at the point of care. The library brings value by providing the best evidence, enables diagnoses, better treatment decisions, and shorter lengths of stay. Recent studies—for example, the so-called Rochester Studies—have proven the value of the library on clinical decision making, which will be discussed later in this chapter (Marshall, 1992; Marshall et al., 2013).

Not everyone seeks the role of library director. Rachel Singer Gordon's 2008 book, *The Accidental Library Manager*, is based on the premise that any librarian who spends time in the profession will become a library manager without any planning or training. This chapter includes: definitions of a library administrator; some management theories and tools; institutional organization and structure; the organization's vision and how the library plays a supporting role toward fulfilling that vision; director competencies; managing up, down, and out; the role of standards and accreditation and strategic planning; benchmarking and assessment; management models; advocacy and generating support; and, saving the best for last—getting money. Library administration is complex, with no cookbook or recipe to follow. This is important for new or potential administrators to know: Start where you are, recognize it as a beginning, listen well, be ready to learn from others, look for constant change, and be prepared to collaborate with others.

WHAT IS A LIBRARY ADMINISTRATOR OR MANAGER?

What does it mean to be a library administrator? The subject of how to manage or lead is well represented in the general literature but not necessarily in the health sciences library literature. Approaches and tools are many, and this chapter will present a beginning menu of management models and tools. Each person comes with a unique set of knowledge and skills, and each organization may seem to be unique. In the end, each person in this function must define his or her own role, style, and practice within the organizational context in which he or she serves. And, lifelong learning and continuing education are basic requirements to hone knowledge and skills.

Some definitions of terms referencing the Oxford English Dictionary (OED) Online follow (OED, 2013). The word *director* is defined as "one who directs, rules, guides, conducts, or has authority over others." The *administrator* is defined as "generally any person engaged in carrying out or over-

In preparation for my interview, now more than two years ago, I spent months talking to managers at conferences and meetings. I did so with the goal of preparation for the interview, but I discovered quickly that those were very rich conversations. I was thirty-six years old when I became the director, and I am certain that as a "wannabe" library director I looked forward to the "old guard" leaving because I felt sure it was time for change. But corporate memory and lessons learned are extremely valuable, and most managers are happy to share their stories. So I guess my advice might be to seek out those conversations as networking opportunities.

Lee-Anne Ufholz, directrice/director, Bibliothèque des sciences de la santé/Health Sciences Library, University of Ottawa, Canada

seeing the tasks necessary to run an organization." The term *manager* is "one who organizes, directs, regulates or deploys resources, a person skilled in controlling or regulating finances and expenditures, or managing an organization with an executive or supervisory function." For some, this term has a negative connotation as it implies controlling people. By contrast, the *leader* is "one who conducts, guides others in action or opinion, and is followed by disciples or adherents." The literature contains a lot about defining leadership, but explaining how to lead is not straightforward. According to Bennis and Nanus, "The exact nature of leadership skills remains elusive. . . . There is no simple formula, no rigorous science, no cookbooks that lead inexorably to successful leadership" (1985: 223). *Personnel* refers to people, managing, directing, inspiring, coaching, or disciplining them to assure that the functions of the library organization are done well; *human resources* is another term

for managing people. Human resources can be described as "managing talent" (Oakes, Tompson, and Lykins, 2010: 108). Generating financial support is an important component and may be performed through fund-raising, grant writing, and budgeting. *Finance* refers to money: planning or requesting, often referred to as budgeting, spending, or managing expenditures.

Learn all you can, and do not be afraid to work outside or beyond your job description.

Joe Swanson Jr., MSLS, director, MSM Library, Morehouse School of Medicine, Atlanta, GA

Accountability is a major issue when dealing with an organization's finances. Evaluating how well or effectively it was spent closes the cycle; *assessment* and *evaluation* go together. In this chapter, all of these terms or functions together comprise *library administration*. Although the term *library director* will be used frequently, assume for the most part that the information provided may apply to any manager or supervisor at any level in his or her library or those who aim at some point to direct, manage, or lead a library function.

Directing or managing is never done alone; it is always in context with others above, adjacent, or below in the organizational structure. Someone always is above the library director: a higher-level director, dean, vice president, board, or the public. In sum, the role of the director must be defined within the culture of the institution served.

SOME MANAGEMENT THEORIES OR TOOLS

Libraries are people organizations whose principal product is services; they are managed by people who serve as intermediaries between customers or patrons and the information they need. Management is done through people. Only people can lead: technology cannot, strategy cannot, and organizations cannot (Kouzes and Posner, 2010). Knowing and applying various management theories and tools (Harvard Business School, 2004) can be helpful. Directors, managers, or supervisors may choose one over the other based upon the issues at hand. Some may call this a contingency model. A few of the major approaches are listed below.

1. **Benevolent Neglect**. This is less a deliberate theory than a style of management. Gordon describes this theory as one that grows over time due to "managerial laziness or fear of confrontation," wherein the manager takes little interest in the daily activities, leaving the staff to go their own way (Gordon, 2008: 262). Essentially, this style assumes that if you leave people alone, things will resolve themselves. This approach is not well regarded. The approach is problematic, but it can work well where there is clear direction, expectations, and trust that the best have been hired. Taking deliberate actions, making decisions, and solving problems are still part of the charge of the director or manager. The premise in this theory is if you hire the brightest people and trust them to perform at their best, then the director's role is to open doors for staff so they can do good work.

2. **Herzberg Theory of Motivation**. In the 1950s, Herzberg asserted that people are motivated by their work environment and job satisfaction. Achievement, recognition, the work itself, responsibility, and growth are important factors. "People are motivated by interesting work that lets them grow and learn while still serving organizational goals" (Gordon, 2008: 266). Many health sciences librarians enter the profession already highly motivated by the work itself. This theory lets motivated people do what they do best. Motivation theory may be considered when staff members show signs of poor morale, and the director needs to step in and provide motivation.

3. **Lead by Example**. Leading by example shows a willingness to step in, to show staff you understand and can do the work. Using this approach, managers need to

show they understand and respect the work that their staff members are doing—enough so they are willing to do it, too. Modeling the best professional ethics and practices will, in turn, encourage and inspire staff to do the same.

4. **Learning Organizations**. Peter Senge, author of *The Fifth Discipline* (1994), inspired many management experts to believe in a "culture of learning." The so-called *learning organization* functions as a single system or brain, with staff who are innovative and communal in their networking, and driven by a desire for quality and continuous improvement (Sullivan, 2003). Leadership from the top is key, the organization's values are aligned, and staff have a deep commitment to improve performance. The five learning disciplines that form the basis of this theory include:

> Never be afraid of hiring people who are smarter than you are, or who are better at their job than you would be. They will make you—and the library—look good. The library director should function like the cowcatcher on an old-fashioned locomotive. Our job is to ride at the front of the train to sweep away the debris and obstacles that prevent our staff from performing at the highest possible level.
>
> *Barbara Epstein, MSLS, director, University of Pittsburgh, Health Sciences Library System, Pittsburgh PA*

1. personal mastery (continually clarifying and deepening personal vision)
2. mental models (testing assumptions)
3. shared vision (collaboration)
4. team learning (sum is greater than the parts)
5. systems thinking (seeing the whole picture)

Senge asserts that learning organizations are premised on strong communication, team learning, shared vision, and a goal to decentralize decision making. Reportedly, many library organizations do their very best work under a decentralized or less authoritarian, team-based structure. Some examples of team charges might include improving the work environment of the library building, improving reference services, or managing orientations and outreach opportunities. Each team might write a report or draft a white paper describing a problem (e.g., faulty HVAC or lack of acoustics) and outlining for the director recommended solutions.

5. **Management by Objectives**. Management by objectives (MBO) "emphasizes results, laying out specific organizational goals and focusing organizational efforts to achieve those goals" (Gordon, 2008: 268). Individual goals and objectives are then created based upon the department's goals, and specific action steps with target dates are set. Everyone knows everyone else's roles and the direction the library is headed. Performance review is then based on the extent to which the objectives are reached. Strategic planning is relevant to the emphasis on goal setting.

6. **Management by Walking Around**. Although it is not really a high-level concept, some library directors espouse the importance of managing by walking around. They feel the best approach is to learn firsthand their library's needs and staff needs by listening to their thoughts regularly on a one-to-one basis. It also includes walking around and talking to library patrons to learn firsthand what their needs are. Every morning some directors go throughout the library, greeting staff and finding out

about concerns, generally by listening to their thoughts and plans for the day. Some directors routinely take breaks with individual staff, bring doughnuts or pizza, or have coffee or lunch with staff in a collegial fashion. Some believe the communication and harmony that result among the staff is well worth the time spent. Walking around allows you to see firsthand the users and any facility or systems problems.

7. **Participatory Management.** Participatory management is built on getting everyone involved in library decision making, including all line staff, not just supervisors. That is, rather than the director or manager making all plans and decisions, he or she includes all staff at various levels in the decision-making process. Participative management relies on various committees, functional or ad hoc, to resolve issues in a collaborative environment. Strategic planning (see below and later) is also part of the participatory management process and reflects a bottom-up effort via annual staff retreats and/or shared goal setting. For example, setting aside one staff development day or retreat whereby staff identify highlights of the previous academic year or outline and prioritize issues for the upcoming year are indicators of a participatory management environment.

8. **Strategic Management.** The strategic management approach creates a vision of the future, sets objectives, and lays out the day-to-day activities needed to reach this vision. Communicating the vision to others is critical, involving staff in the process and inspiring them to see a vision and help make it happen. Developing a strategic plan is the result of this management approach, which will be discussed below.

For centuries, libraries were defined by their collections, but today's key resource is the people who make things happen. Select and retain the best, both to accomplish your mission and to reflect well on you as a director. As Niccolo Machiavelli said in 1532 in *The Prince*: "The choice of a prince's [director's] ministers [key staff] is a matter of no little importance; they are either good or not according to the prudence of the prince. The first impression that one gets of a ruler and of his brains is from seeing the men [or women] that he has about him."

Rick Forsman, MLS, retired, former director, University of Colorado Health Sciences Center Library, Boulder

This list is far from comprehensive, and none of the theories is mutually exclusive, but the list is intended to provide a flavor of the approaches and models available.

INSTITUTIONAL ORGANIZATION AND STRUCTURE

Health sciences organizations can vary from institution to institution and between types of libraries (e.g., academic health sciences library versus hospital library), and the structures used to organize their libraries reflect these institutional differences. Organizations may be freestanding institutions, or part of a larger university, hospital, or health consortium. Not all health sciences libraries are strictly medical in their focus; they may focus on public health, nursing, or physical therapy, just to name a few (see Chapter 1). However, most academic health sciences libraries supporting educational programs include support for affiliated clinical or teaching sites that are organizationally separate from the library's parent institution. Historically, medical schools owned their own hospitals, and hospitals sponsored their own nursing or physical therapy programs. Today, these relationships are often defined by affiliation contracts; examples include Metropolitan Hospital and New York Medical College or New York Hospital and Weill Cornell Medical College. From time to time, affiliated sites may separate from their partners and join another academic sponsor or health system. As a result, the library's user community also changes to reflect new organizational structures.

Every academic health sciences library that serves a school of medicine, nursing, dentistry, or physical therapy, and so on, will also serve a host of clinical teaching sites: hospitals, clinics, community centers, or preceptor offices. Generally, it is expected that the library serve these locations at some level. This includes working in collaboration with peer hospital or clinical librarians. Together, this library team works out responsibility for collections and services so that users are connected to the information they need to do their clinical work.

Within the academic organizational structure, the library director or manager may report to one or more health center deans, an information technology manager (academic computing director or the chief information officer [CIO]), or to the university librarian or dean at a main campus.

Within the hospital organization, the library director or manager may report to a chief of staff, risk manager, nurse educator, or human resources director. The library staff is comparatively smaller or may be a solo librarian position, wherein the hospital librarian does it all, with perhaps only volunteers to help.

The library's place in the organizational structure often tells a story. The higher the level of reporting, the higher the library may be valued and supported. Presumably, the higher this level of reporting, the more management skills are expected on the job.

Although all libraries may provide access, resources, and services, each health sciences organization may group functions differently. In addition, some health sciences libraries will be responsible for educational media, audiovisual support, poster printing, or academic computing. Hospital libraries may also be responsible for services such as risk management and continuing medical education.

Generally, the more knowledge the library director has of the institution, the better to plan the services and resources necessary to satisfy the information needs of the local community. Useful information about an organization may be found on the organization's website, internal and external reports, or the institution's strategic plan—especially the vision, mission, and objectives. Scrutinizing the organization's plan, if it has one, should be primary reading for the interviewee applying for a library director's job, and the second step upon appointment. Identifying how and where to contribute to the overall organization may get you the job. It is always impressive to interview someone who has taken the time before the interview to learn about the organization.

The organization chart is a picture of the structure of the organization and a vision of who, where, and how functions and departments are organized and relate to each other. Finding the library director or manager on a chart can be helpful in identifying the library's position within the organization. The organization chart answers the question of whether the library is a department or a subunit, and shows the library's designated peers, superiors, and support staff. A vertical chart generally indicates top-down management, whereas a so-called flatter organization (more boxes on the same level) may reflect more participatory management. Peers identified by the organization chart can be potential partners or collaborators with the library, especially in terms of advocating for new programs or getting more funding.

MANAGEMENT COMPETENCIES

Competencies are the knowledge and skills a person needs to do the job. There are many lists of management competencies. In 2002, Kouzes and Posner identified 225 different values, traits, and characteristics important for leaders, including honest, forward-looking, inspiring, and competent. By 2010, Kouzes and Posner developed a model, distilled down from other lists to five practices of exemplary leadership:

1. model the way
2. inspire a shared vision
3. challenge the process
4. enable others to act
5. encourage the heart

In other words, leaders should model the behavior they espouse, get people excited about the future, think outside the box, get a team to help, and recognize the contributions of others. For library-specific manager competencies, Gordon surveyed 343 library staff in 2006 soliciting views of their library manager's qualities or competencies. Both negative and positive results emerged in "the seven deadly sins (and desirable strategies) for library managers." The desirable strategies sound very similar to the list above, including:

1. encourage growth outside the box
2. provide autonomy
3. look out for staff
4. lead by example
5. communicate and listen in an open environment
6. provide leadership and vision
7. articulate goals (Gordon, 2006)

The American Library Association (ALA) highlights thirteen skills or competencies that library directors or managers need. They include: serving the library's user community; developing new or revise systems, procedures, and workflow; exercising initiative and independent judgment; preparing comprehensive reports and presenting ideas clearly and concisely in written and oral form; making administrative decisions, interpreting policies, and supervising staff; having knowledge and skills in management techniques, notably in directing, planning, organizing, staffing coordinating, budgeting; and evaluating the library's operation—just to list a few.

PROFESSIONAL COMPETENCIES FOR HEALTH SCIENCES LIBRARIANS

Competency 2: "Know and understand the application of leadership, finance, communication, and management theory and techniques."

- Understanding the institution's mission and planning processes and the role of the library in the institution;
- Forging and maintaining alliances with universities, public libraries, public health services, community-based organizations, and others to meet users' information needs;
- Human resources management including recruitment, retention, staff development, and mentoring;
- Facilities planning and space allocation;
- Budgeting, cost analyses, and fund-raising;
- Public relations, marketing, and advertising;
- Library programs and services administration.

Source: Medical Library Association, www.mlanet.org/education/policy/.

Far more important and applicable are *The Medical Library Association Competencies for Lifelong Learning and Professional Success* (2007). This well-honed educational policy statement was adopted in 2007 and includes seven professional competencies for health sciences librarians. Competency number two deals with library management and outlines specific knowledge and skills to attain this competency (see sidebar).

Basic to these is the expectation that a medical library director will be able to apply library and information science principles; specific knowledge and skills in leadership, finance, and communication; and management theory and techniques to the management of health information resources. Management is addressed in terms of managing health information resources as well as technology and systems. Every medical librarian should become familiar with this MLA list of competencies, including the description of personal attributes that contribute to success. Doyle and Wellik provide an interpretation of these MLA competencies in more specific terms (see sidebar on p. 357).

MANAGING THE ENVIRONMENT

Volatility is perhaps the best word to describe the dynamic health care environment in which health sciences librarians work. With transforming organizations, new technologies mandate new priorities and competencies: managing different types of users, remote or distant, and now generations of students, faculty, and staff who cannot remember a time without the Internet and Google. Leading a change management requires knowing where you are going and knowing how best to lead

MANAGEMENT OF INFORMATION SERVICES

Leadership in the application of library and information science to the handling of health information resources in complex institutional environments requires specialized knowledge, skill, and understanding of management, including:

1. the institution's mission and the specific mission of the information resource center;
2. institutional functional planning processes;
3. decision-making strategies;
4. human resources management and labor relations;
5. staff development, project and program management and evaluation;
6. organizational structure and behavior;
7. inter-institutional relations;
8. numerical literacy and computational proficiency;
9. finance and budgeting, cost analysis and price setting;
10. skills in fund-raising and proposal writing;
11. public relations and marketing;
12. facilities planning and space allocation;
13. oral and written communications; and
14. interpersonal relations.

Source: Doyle and Wellik, 2011: 36.

others to get there. Leading with a so-called *light hand* is recommended—that is, encouraging others and creating more flexible, self-managed work teams with clear directions. Jenkins (2011) envisions this as "soaring on the winds of digital speed." In the fifth century B.C. Heraclitus noted, "Nothing endures but change." About the same time, Chinese philosopher Lao Tsu reportedly said: "A leader is best when people barely know he exists, of a good leader, who talks little, when his work is done, his aim fulfilled, they will say, 'We did this ourselves.'" Less is more in leadership. In sum, managing change is as important now as it has always been—a constant, and as such, is central to leadership competencies.

Planning, and Doing It Strategically

Goodstein describes strategic planning as "a leadership imperative" (2010: 43) and adds Peter Drucker's belief that "the two most important tasks leaders needed to perform were to establish a strategic plan and to select managers to execute that plan." Developing a strategic plan is important. Generally, institutions will require a plan from all units. When doing so, the plan's process is defined including the time frame, who should be included in the planning process (staff, users), and the report's structure and deadline. Social networking and technological changes mandate a continuous process; that is, the plan is never finished, yet continuously validated and revised according to the evolving needs of the library. Historically, strategic plans looked forward five years, and sometimes twenty, but no more. Today, three years may be as far ahead as any organization can look.

Creating a vision and marshaling a strategic planning process to complete it is a basic competency for all managers. Distilling the library's vision and mission with the overall vision and mission of the parent organization is critical along with outlining broad goals, specific objectives, and expected outcomes. Strategic planning is really setting clear priorities, developing specific action steps with staff assignments, and defining accountability measures, dates, or outcomes. Often new priorities or projects emerge from the planning process (e.g., a health organization may expand with new facilities and consequent stress on resources, need more of the library's space, or receive unexpected donations that enable new institutional projects or programs). A new joint academic program or degree may require new or better support from the library, and the library's priorities need to be flexible enough to accommodate any of these changes.

There are many ways to begin the strategic planning process, but all library staff and appropriate leadership within the organization should be involved. As a customer service organization, the library needs to include representative stakeholders. The model usually begins with an environmental scan—an assessment of the external forces on the library organization; often the strengths, weaknesses, opportunities, and threats (SWOT) in grid format will guide the process. Next steps include clarifying the library's organizational values, its vision, and its mission or purpose as noted earlier.

The strategic planning process can be done internally or externally. Many libraries find it easiest to hire an external consultant to work with the planning team, rather than do it by themselves. Or the process can be done internally, relying on the planning team and key players within the institution. Often, an institutional leader who carries the title of vice president or director of strategic planning can lead the library's planning process. A good strategy is to review strategic plans of similar libraries to gather ideas and view how those libraries have approached their plan. The sidebar provides some links to strategic plans of several academic health sciences libraries.

EXAMPLES OF STRATEGIC PLANS OF ACADEMIC HEALTH SCIENCES LIBRARIES

- Duke University Medical Center Library: https://mclibrary.duke.edu/sites/eno.duhs.duke.edu/files/public/about/strategic%20plan%202011-2014%20FINAL.pdf
- New York Medical College's Health Sciences Library: http://library.nymc.edu/Information/goals1213.cfm
- New York University Medical Center's Ehrman Medical Library (sample interim or bridging plan): http://hsl.med.nyu.edu/strategic-plan
- University of Pittsburgh's Health Sciences Library System: http://files.hsls.pitt.edu/files/long-range-plan.pdf
- University of South Carolina School of Medicine Library: http://uscm.med.sc.edu/School%20of%20Medicine%20Library%20Strategic%20Plan%202013-14.pdf

Managing Human Resources

Understanding organizational structure is critical, and making it work with staff is an ongoing process. Every library director or manager inherits an existing structure, sometimes with professionals as well as support staff charged with both broad and specific areas of responsibility relative to their jobs. It is important to understand clearly what each individual is charged to do, and their understanding of their jobs. Periodically, feedback is needed along with an evaluation of the extent to which jobs are done; as new or different needs arise, jobs and objectives may need to be redefined. Each time a job opening occurs, it is an opportunity to assess what knowledge and skills are needed to support the current and potentially new evolving environment. As a new library director or manager, one helpful technique is to ask staff to write their current job description and responsibilities, compare it to the official ones, and then consider how to rethink jobs for the future.

> Realize that you will be spending more of your time managing the people rather than the tasks.
>
> *Jane Bridges, ML, AHIP, associate director, Savannah Campus, Health Sciences Library, Mercer University School of Medicine, Savannah, GA*

Historically, the library was organized around public or technical services. Newer models include electronic resources and technology-related services. New roles for medical libraries may result in upgraded positions such as **informationist**, content management librarian, data curation specialist, web-based resources librarian, or translational medicine librarian. For example, the more traditional job title of acquisition librarian may now be called electronic resources management librarian. Similarly, the former associate director of collection development may become the network systems manager, because technology expertise is needed to manage the new cloud-hosted integrated library system. In some places, the reference and circulation desks have been streamlined into a single service desk called access services, with a triage system wherein staff call the reference librarian for questions or searches that are too complicated for their level of training. So, the reference desk may have been replaced by online consults, chats, or webinars. Even the term "reference" may have been replaced, by user support, education and research services department USERS for short! Reviewing online job descriptions reveals many new ways of describing jobs. These changed functions and job titles have been discussed in more detail in earlier chapters in this book.

ROLES OF THE DIRECTOR: UP, DOWN, AND OUT

The library director or manager must manage others within the organization. That is, the manager needs to manage up (to superiors and higher administrators), down (to library staff—direct and indirect reports, if any), sideways (to peers such as other department heads), and out (to external or community relationships). All should be viewed as collaborators and potential partners.

Managing Up

The director must be able to manage up, that is, to the person the director reports and to other institutional higher administration (e.g., a direct supervisor, dean, associate or assistant dean, chief financial officer, or president). The library director's role may include serving on institutional committees, ad-hoc teams, or advocating for the needs of the overall institution as well as the library itself. In managing up, the library director becomes a team player. Through committee work and related activities, the library director demonstrates to his or her boss an understanding of the broader impact of the library within the life of the institution. Getting additional library staff involved on institutional committees, such as the institutional review board, may bring the talents of the staff to the attention of administration as well as give visibility for the library itself.

It is even more important for a solo librarian to become part of the institutional "team" in order to show visibility and willing participation. This new teamwork may involve reordering priorities or obtaining temporary or volunteer coverage so that the solo librarian may participate. If the organization is part of a multisite network, library participation may also be requested. At the most basic level, managing your supervisor is critical in terms of capitalizing on his or her ability to increase the library's budget, provide more staff, or smooth out library problems (e.g., defending the library's position on an issue such as copyright and intellectual property).

Develop a high tolerance for ambiguity. You will need it in dealing with deans, vice chancellors, provosts, vice presidents, chancellors, and presidents. Many situations in higher education administration are characterized by uncertainty and incomplete information, and you must be prepared to move forward with decisions and action in spite of this ambiguity.

Ruth A. Riley, MS, AHIP, assistant dean for executive affairs and director of library services, School of Medicine, University of South Carolina, Columbia

Further, the library director or manager must learn his or her supervisor's personal style (e.g., communication preferences—e-mail, personal meetings, telephone chats, etc.). In sum, the director or manager must be seen as helping the supervisor do his or her job, and in the style and format he or she prefers. On any given day, the supervisor may change, due to resignations or re-organization; so the library director needs to be nimble and flexible enough to change to reflect what is needed by the organization. And it is the director's job to mobilize the library team to help get the superior's job done.

Managing Down

Managing down involves supervision; it means making the best use of your own resources—staff, money, and space. As noted above, the library director serves as change agent as well as maintains the status quo. On any given day, the director must guide staff to embrace the vision of the plan and maintain a stable, positive work environment. One way to do this is through the library's strategic plan, which will set goals and objectives for the staff (see earlier section in this chapter). For example, create a firm list of the library's own information competencies that includes the goal that the library will foster and teach, internally and externally, and will become competent in using new web-based skills and tools, for example, http://library.nymc.edu/Information/goals1213.cfm. That will keep staff working toward a common purpose. Managing staff members consumes the greater part of any director's day.

As people-based organizations, medical libraries provide resources and services based upon health information needs. Finding the best staff—recruiting, hiring, orienting, training, assigning, and evaluating—are all part of the director's responsibility. Creating the optimal organizational structure and understanding specific functions and staff roles are a manager's responsibility: who does what, how, why, and when. Jim Collins (2001; 2006) in his "Good to Great" concept notes that building a great organization involves four basic stages: disciplined people, disciplined thought, disciplined action, and building greatness to last. Leaders must be ambitious and resolve to do what it takes to make good on their vision and then have the right people "on the bus" and "in the right seats on the bus" to get the organization to where it needs to be. In other words, until you find the right person, leave the position vacant. The process involves a step-by-step journey that can adapt along the way to changing needs. A diagnostic tool to assess how and where staff view the bus ride is available at www.jimcollins.com/tools/diagnostic-tool.pdf.

Developing New Leaders

Creating new managers is also an ongoing part of a library director or manager's responsibility. Becoming a manager should not be "accidental," as Gordon is quoted in the introduction to this chapter. Raising the knowledge and expertise of staff is a basic charge. Promoting from within when possible improves the motivation of everyone on the staff, and makes the staff performance continue to grow. Mentoring and programs to develop new leaders are interrelated. The best directors assign mentors to mentees as well as provide targeted orientation and training. Several excellent programs can aid new or "wannabe" directors or managers, though not all of them are specifically for health sciences librarians:

- The American Library Association (ALA) *Emerging Leaders Program*, www.ala. org/educationcareers/leadership/emergingleaders. This program is designed for those relatively new to the library field. Selectees work in groups to create projects, learn about ALA, and are exposed to leadership and development opportunities (Akbar-Williams, 2012).
- American Society for Training and Development (ASTD), Certified Professional in Learning and Performance (CPLP), www.ala.org/educationcareers/leadership/emergingleaders. CPLP is a certificate program in workplace learning and performance professionals, with an entire array of conference, workshop opportunities, and training tools. If time were no problem, every potential manager should explore relevant leadership and management courses offered by ASTD.
- Association of Academic Health Sciences Libraries (AAHSL), www.aahsl .org/index.php?option=com_content&view=article&id=21. AAHSL provides

leadership scholarships, a new directors' symposium, and a Leadership Fellows program. The Leadership Fellows one-year program is offered in cooperation with the National Library of Medicine, wherein Fellows are assigned a mentor, attend an Association of American Medical College (AAMC) annual meeting, and visit the mentor's home library. A New Directors Symposium is scheduled as part of the AAMC annual meeting. Although this program focuses on individuals who want to be in leadership positions, anyone may apply with approval of their directors. Not everyone who participates as a Fellow ends up as a director, yet the leadership exposure and experience will enrich the competencies and skills of the participants. Symposium topics include managing financial resources; developing high-performance staff; understanding the environment, technology, and the library; emerging new roles; and the life of the director (Lipscomb, 2013).

- AAMC Group on Information Resources (GIR), leadership development program, www.aamc.org/members/gir/leadership_institute/.
- Frye Leadership Institute, calling itself The Leading Change Institute, is another resource; www.leadingchangeinstitute.org/.
- Harvard University's Leadership Institute for Academic Librarians, www.gse.harvard.edu/ppe/programs/higher-education/portfolio/leadership-academic-librarians.html.

Training new leaders is a widespread need. Many national, regional, and local professional organizations (such as the Medical Library Association or other nonmedical associations) provide continuing education on managing, directing, and leading. Scholarships or funding may be available based upon justification and job responsibilities.

In addition, the library administrator's own organization may provide seminars or sessions, and some even offer tuition remission to attend formal management classes. State libraries, library associations, and the National Network of Libraries of Medicine (NN/NLM) Regional Medical Library program all support continuing professional education.

Mentoring

Mentoring is another important aspect of managing staff. It may occur informally without an official program, or it may be part of a formal program such as the Medical Library Association (MLA), www.

The NLM/AAHSL Leadership Fellows Program is an amazing opportunity. I learned so much about the essentials of leadership, strategies for dealing with change and developing strong collaborations with colleagues within and external to the library, and surprising (to me) roles the library director plays. Our capstone event provided access to leaders and decision makers in the national libraries as well as library- and health-related professional associations. Most importantly, as a Fellow, I became part of a lasting network whose members (mentors and Fellows) serve as sounding boards, idea generators, and true colleagues.

Michele R. Tennant, PhD, MLIS, AHIP, assistant director, Health Science Center Libraries; and bioinformatics librarian, UF Genetics Institute, University of Florida, Gainesville mlanet.org/mentor/index.html. Following specific guidelines, the MLA program searches the entire MLA database to identify the best match for mentoring given the career goals of the mentee. Experienced librarians volunteer to mentor new medical librarians, who in turn are matched with individual MLA members who participate in the program. Some MLA chapters assign mentors or "buddies" for new or first-time attendees at the chapter's annual conference. Some managers may consider all current and former employees as their mentees and seek to help them move along in their career. In addition, the AAHSL/New Leader Fellows program mentioned above is also a mentorship program; each fellow is assigned a mentor with whom he or she works closely during the year of the program (AAHSL, 2013a).

Managing Personnel Issues

As mentioned earlier, managing people is by far the most time-consuming part of a library director job. Respecting each individual's background, affiliations, gender, race, and more will strengthen the library as a whole. Diversity is a rainbow of strength. Building relationships with staff at each level is essential, and knowing how to motivate and acknowledge the work of others is a part of the director's role. Rewarding staff for a job well done may be a public or private "thank you," or a memo confirming quality work. Performance appraisals may highlight demonstrated quality performance, and in some cases may justify a higher-level position. A job could be rewritten to expand a person's area of responsibility, preferably with an equivalent salary increase, bonus, or merit raise. Basically, the leader can and should acknowledge and reward high performing employees at every opportunity. Not only will the employee be encouraged, but others may follow suit.

Some issues are not under the library director's or manager's control. Staff members are human and will bring all sorts of personal issues to the work environment. These issues may be pressures at home, conflicting personalities, interpersonal conflicts, or personal attitudes. Generally, in any group, at least one person just cannot be positive—he or she may not know how. Negative thinking can be contagious, so the goal is to motivate everyone to work together, contribute to the best of their abilities, and get the job done. Managers need to understand and learn about their employees as individuals, to empathize with differing points of view and show that they care about employees' progress. Gordon (2008) asserts that most employees quit their managers, not their jobs.

When hiring, it is critical to find the best employee with the knowledge and skills needed for the job. Beyond the requisite skills in the job description, the person's attitude, ability to learn and fit into the library's culture, and the new talents he or she can bring to the library environment may be *more* important than having the knowledge and skills on day one. As a rule, new employees should know only one-third of what the experienced person knows; the job should be a learning experience. Interviewing is the process of finding a good fit between a potential employee and the existing staff; many tools are available to guide managers about interview skills. One of the best is Falcone's text published by the American Management Association, titled *96 Great Interview Questions to Ask Before You Hire* (2007). The questions are designed to learn more about the candidate; none of them has a perfect answer.

From time to time, it is necessary to discipline an employee who cannot seem to change negative behaviors and performance into positive ones. Despite coaching sessions, the employee shows no positive movement. If this is the case, it involves a potential legal issue, so working with the human resources department is necessary. The library director or manager needs to report the problem and develop a corrective plan. Generally, a performance review identifies shortcomings. If an issue does surface as a major problem, policies require coaching sessions and a corrective plan of action for the employee to follow. When the steps are followed and documented but the employee does not demonstrate positive change in performance, dismissal will occur. Terminating staff can become a legal issue, and the terms of termination often have financial payouts tied to them. Termination proceedings are stressful, but the library director's responsibility is to create a positive work environment.

Managing Out (aka Collaboration)

Managing out (or sideways) means working with peers within the institution, being involved with institutional priorities in the community, and networking with libraries and librarian colleagues—in other words, collaborating individually and as the library's representative. Libraries and librarians naturally collaborate—over the years, that is how libraries have maintained resources and services to meet their users' needs. It is up to the library to take the lead in networking activities.

Managing Sideways within the Institution

Internally, the library director may have natural colleagues or partners (e.g., department heads, nurse educators, chief residents or fellows, clerkship directors, residency coordinators, or information technology [IT] staff). New library directors should look for key individuals in the institution who will champion library causes. These can be heads of the instructional programs or researchers with major grants; they will be heavy information users who recognize the value of the library.

Participation in institutional committees and task forces keeps the library director and staff apprised of institutional priorities and helps to stay attuned to the "climate" of change. By making connections, the librarian often becomes involved in projects by serendipity. For example, a special research initiative might be in need of help with research design, and the library director can volunteer the help of a staff member who has the required knowledge and skills the project team needs. The library director must be able to work closely with other department heads. For example, close coordination with the "help desk" or IT department is required to facilitate special projects or initiatives involving electronic resources or the library's website, which will improve access to information. If part of a health system, working with affiliated librarians may be a powerful way to manage information resources.

Most health care and academic institutions consider service to the community as part of their mission. The library director should seek opportunities to be involved in such activities, and should involve library staff, as appropriate. For example, if the organization agrees to cosponsor an American Heart Foundation campaign, the library director might well serve as team leader in organizing the fund-raising campaign. If the organization cosponsors a health fair, a historical event, faculty author reception, alumni reunion, or regional scientific society event, the library director can use these as opportunities to network with the outside organizations and perhaps open new doors for the library.

Managing Outside the Institution

The library director or manager leads the way in external networking activities. The visibility of the library externally enhances the institution. Nonlibrary administrators seem amazed at how well librarians network with others—not knowing that before electronic resources, librarians always shared and valued shared sources of information. With limited funds for resources and services, librarians are natural collaborators. Given the economics of licensing electronic resources, many library directors have become members of regional cooperatives or statewide purchasing groups (e.g., New England Research Libraries [NERL]; the New York State Higher Education Initiative [NYSHEI]; or the Health Sciences Libraries of New Jersey [HSLNJ]).

In today's environment, social media have facilitated collaboration. Generally, librarians have been quick to adopt new social tools (e.g., web tools, Google, Listservs, Facebook, and Twitter) and use them advantageously for collaborative projects. Organizational or professional Listservs may bring together library directors, reference librarians, catalogers, serials librarians, or other peer groups that provide networking or collaboration to resolve management or technical issues. Listservs are excellent sources for managing issues and collaborating to solve problems; heavily used lists include the Association of Academic Health Sciences Libraries (AAHSL) director list, MEDLIB-L, MLA's Hospital Libraries Services Section, as well as the other MLA chapters, sections, and regional or local networks. Every MLA section and chapter has its own Listserv; each state and regional library association has a management section (e.g., NYLINE or METRO for New York State). Although primarily for academic health sciences library directors, the AAHSL Listserv may include associate or assistant directors, depending on the approval of the appropriate library director. AAHSL's mission statement may say it best: "AAHSL promotes the success of its members through relevant programming and services; benchmarking; advocacy; partnerships with like-minded organizations; and the development of a community of colleagues" (AAHSL, 2013b). Social media may also facilitate work with peers via private groups through LinkedIn, Facebook, or Twitter.

As a library director, management activities include managing budgets, people, programs, and projects up and down the institution's hierarchy. It is a more multifaceted role than just managing up or down, however. It takes a commitment to managing diagonally to identify the key stakeholders, champions, and leaders who can exist anywhere in your institution.

Heidi A. Heilemann, MLS, MLA, AHIP, associate dean for knowledge management and director, Lane Medical Library & Knowledge Management Center, Stanford University, Stanford, CA

Professional Networking

Professional organizations can be a powerful way to network with colleagues. Participation in professional organizations, such as MLA, can provide the director and all staff with opportunities to practice presenting, leading or facilitating groups, recruiting resources, and practice serving as a mentor or mentee with more experienced colleagues. Often the continuing education opportunities can lead to a credential, such as AHIP, or open doors to new opportunities. Attending professional meetings connects health sciences librarians with vendors, state-of-the-art practices in the profession, and can be a place to interview or be interviewed for a better position. Volunteering to host library school students or interns, fellows, or mentees can be a real boost to the library in terms of meeting some of the project objectives included in the library's strategic plan.

ROLE OF STANDARDS AND ACCREDITATION

Standards and accreditation are important in the management of health care organizations and academic institutions. Standards guide the development of programs, and accreditation confirms that standards have been met. If institutions fail to measure up to the relevant standards, they may not be qualified to treat patients or award degrees or certificates. Peer review and self-study are formal components of the accreditation process. Participation as part of an institutional professional peer review is a special role for the library and the library director. Every professional license or degree-granting institution has its own peer review process.

Implementing or meeting accrediting standards is an important responsibility of the library director. For libraries that serve schools of medicine, the Association of American Medical Colleges (AAMC) Liaison Committee for Medical Education (LCME) standards titled *Functions and Structure of a Medical School: LCME Accreditation Standards* (2012) apply; www.lcme.org/functions.pdf. Specifically, objective MS-37 addresses adequate learning environments including study space, and ER-11-14 addresses library and information resources. In 2013, the LCME distributed new consolidated standards for review and comment with implementation expected by the end of 2014, whereby the Library Resources/Staff section is rewritten and renumbered as follows:

> 5.8 [formerly ER-11/ER-12]. LIBRARY RESOURCES/STAFF. An institution that sponsors a medical education program provides ready access to well-maintained library facilities sufficient in size, breadth of holdings, and technology to support its educational and other missions; the library services are supervised by a professional staff that is familiar with regional and national information resources and data systems and responsive to the needs of the medical students, faculty members, and others associated with the institution. www.lcme.org/

The Joint Commission (TJC, formerly Joint Commission on the Accreditation of Hospital Organizations or JCAHO) performs a similar role for hospitals, www .jcrinc.com/Joint-Commission-Requirements/. TJC accredits hospitals and health care systems, but it does not address the library per se except in terms of access to knowledge-based information resources. The 2013 Hospital Accreditation Standards information management section (IM.03.01.01) mandates that "knowledge-based information (KBI) resources are available, current and authoritative (TJC). Further, 24/7 access is mandatory and the hospital shall make cooperative arrangements with other institutions to provide KBI resources not otherwise available on site" (Joint Commission, 2013). It is no longer a requirement to have a librarian on-site—much to the distress of hospital librarians who see their roles undermined. However, in 2007, the MLA Hospital Library Section (HLS) updated its earlier set of eleven standards that are intended to fill the void with a goal to serve as a guide for hospital administrators, staff, and accreditation bodies (Bandy, Doyle, and Fladger, 2008). HLS requirements assert that there should be a separate library department with its own budget, managed by a qualified librarian serving as department head.

Many other professions have respective accreditation standards. For medical residencies and fellowship programs, the Accreditation Council for Graduate Medical Education (ACGME) serves this function, www.acgme.org/acgmeweb/tabid/89/Publications.aspx. Similarly, the Council on Education for Public Health (CEPH) accredits schools and programs for the Association of Schools of Public Health, http://ceph.org/, and the National League for Nursing Accrediting Commission serves a similar function for nursing, www.nlnac.org/home.htm.

Other professional health organizations follow peer review practice, with a designated organization or association legally responsible for monitoring the respective profession. The best way to identify which organizations accredit your own organization is to scrutinize the main website and description of professional programs sponsored. This information is important to recruiting efforts; many potential students would not consider applying to a nonaccredited program. The more accreditation organizations identified, the stronger the programs; and, for the most part, strong educational and research support from the library is required by all. A poor review of library services could be good news for the director if the organization then commits financial resources to fix the problem. The sidebar contains a short list of general professional standards for libraries.

EVALUATION AND ASSESSMENT

Evaluation and assessment are critical components of library management. Dudden defines *evaluation* as "assigning merit, value or worth to the findings"; and *assessment* as "the gathering of meaningful or purposeful data that will provide information

PROFESSIONAL STANDARDS FOR LIBRARIES

- Association of College and Research Libraries (ACRL) *Standards for Libraries on Higher Education* (2004): www.ala.org/acrl/standards
- American Library Association standards: ww.ala.org/acrl/standards/standardslibraries
- Association of Academic Health Sciences Libraries (AAHSL) *Challenge to Action*, written in 1987; updated in 2003 by *Building on Success: Charting the Future of Knowledge Management within Academic Health Centers*: www.aahsl.org/assets/documents/Building-On-Success.pdf
- The Hospital Library Section of the Medical Library Association's *Standards for Hospital Libraries* 2007, noted above: www.ncbi.nlm.nih.gov/pmc/articles/PMC2268237/

that informs, improves, or confirms" (Dudden, 2011: 100). Often these terms are used interchangeably. Evaluation generally brings to closure the goals or plans that have been set into motion. Documenting the worth of the information at the point of need is the rationale behind having a health sciences library. Knowledge is power and has value; assuring that it is correct, timely, and complete requires continuously communicating to library users.

Communicating value is one form of assessment. It can be a simple annual report, or a more complex research study. One of the early research studies proving the impact or value of the hospital library on clinical decision making was the Rochester study, completed in 1992 and updated in 2013. This landmark study provided evidence that, as a result of having clinical information available from the hospital library, physicians changed their diagnosis (29 percent of the time), changed their choice of tests (51 percent) and choice of drugs (45 percent), reduced length of stay (19 percent), and altered advice given to the patient (72 percent) (Marshall, 1992). In 2013, this study was repeated on a larger scale with similar results that confirmed the value of the library and information services to clinicians (Marshall et al., 2013). The 2013 study was updated and expanded to a national level and funded by the National Network of Libraries of Medicine Middle Atlantic Region (NN/LM-MAR, 2013). A summary of this and other recent studies proving the value of the health sciences library were promoted broadly in the health sciences literature by Sollenberger and Holloway (2013) in the *Journal of the American Medical Association*. The research results are evidence-based and may be used to carry the value of libraries message.

Assessing quality is another approach: Whether it is called total quality management (TQM), continuous quality improvement (CQI), quality improvement (QI), or just a quality initiative, it all has to do with what quality is and how it can be measured. Dudden has done a great deal of work in assessment and describes the health sciences environment as a "culture of assessment"—with an emphasis on creating systems that are based on continuous assessment (Dudden, 2011: 102). One example is the FOCUS-PDCA tool, which outlines steps to quality improvement

THE FOCUS-PDCA CYCLE

F   Find a process to improve
O   Organize a team
C   Clarify the current process
U   Understand the causes of variations to the process
S   Select a process improvement approach

Then:

P   Plan the process improvement
D   Do the process improvement
C   Check it
A   Act to improve the process further

Source: Dudden, 2011: 115.

(see the sidebar). This is the learning culture in action. It documents improvements, largely in patient care outcomes (as noted above). TJC standards are premised on quality improvement and assessment.

Another assessment approach uses evidence-based practice. For hospital or academic health sciences libraries, it means using the best available evidence in the literature to create programs, services, or staffing. For example, if the literature identifies a single-service desk as the best use of staffing, then library managers may feel justified applying a similar approach. Further, the logic model helps librarians plan and carry out evaluation. The National Network of Libraries of Medicine (NN/LM) uses a basic logic template that includes the goal, the resources (inputs), the activities, the outputs, and the outcomes. The NN/LM provides a detailed guide on how to use the model at http://nnlm.gov/outreach/community/logicmodel.html. See Chapter 3 for further information about evidence-based practice.

One of the most frequently used assessment tools of health sciences library managers is needs assessment. As a customer service organization, library managers need to completely and totally understand the needs of their users. The needs-assessment tool is frequently a survey, but it could also be a focus group, with or without structured questions. This is often part of the strategic planning process or part of the environmental scan of the users. Survey Monkey and Zoomerang are two relatively easy-to-use software tools that enable a user needs assessment survey. Careful selection of questions or open-ended questions is important to glean unbiased results. Other forms of assessment include observation of user behavior, usability studies (e.g., observing use of a website), one-on-one interviews, and capturing electronic usage of resources. Assessment of the library's resources is covered in Chapter 4.

Benchmarking

Benchmarking deserves mention. Benchmarking may be based on performance (comparative data), process (methods and practices), or strategy (systematic review of best practices). Dudden's *How To Do It Manual* on benchmarking (2008) is a major resource for directors or managers interested in doing assessment using logic models, planning a project, selecting measurements and/or methods. In addition, Dudden's entire chapter titled "Evaluation and Improvement Management" in *The Medical Library Association's Guide to Managing Health Care Libraries*, 2nd ed., is a must-read for beginning managers (Dudden, 2011).

Benchmarking in relation to peer libraries and/or institutions provides value to the decision makers in the organization or externally. National averages may be helpful measures, but often specific hospitals or universities have selected peer groups with which to measure or compete for students and staff. Or, the individual library may benchmark itself against the national average (e.g., using the AAHSL online data). Additional benchmarking tools include the following:

- Association of Academic Health Sciences Libraries (AAHSL) has collected statistics from its members since the mid-1970s. By 2013, the annual compilation statistics permit benchmarking specific peers and survey questions over time, www.aahsl.org/annual-statistics.

- MLA benchmarking interactive report site as well as links to the MLA Benchmarking Network is another site for hospital library benchmarks. Although now somewhat dated (2004), it can be a useful resource.
- Association of Research Libraries LibQual+ initiative presents an assessment tool that does multiple things including benchmarking within the survey cohort. As ACRL's Value of Academic Libraries project, ACRL has selected seventy-five institutional teams to participate in the first year of Assessment in Action: Academic Libraries and Student Success (AiA). This is sponsored by the Institute of Museum and Library Services and carried out in partnership with the Association for Institutional Research, www.acrl.ala.org/value/.

GENERATING SUPPORT

Generating support includes a wide range of topics, including financial planning, budgeting, writing grant proposals, soliciting donations, creating a community of advocates, and generating revenues from the sale of services to hire or purchase resources. Financial management is the means to achieve the ends. As Prottsman explains, "The financial plan describes the library's anticipated accomplishments and identifies the resources necessary to make them happen" (Prottsman, 2011: 63). The end result is getting money to do the things that need to be done.

The AAHSL *Annual Statistics* is perhaps the most recognizable achievement of the Association of Academic Health Sciences Libraries. The collective annual volumes since 1978 tell a story in numbers about health sciences libraries in the United States and Canada. That story includes the transition to more and more electronic resources and services, and the changes and continuities in library collections, expenditures, personnel, and services during the past thirty-four years. Libraries repeatedly report that reliable and valid comparable data are useful for all manner of management analysis, decisions, and library promotion. Though the kind of data about library inputs and outputs AAHSL collects is not the whole story about library value, it is an essential part. AAHSL can be proud of its contribution in this regard.

Steven J. Squires, MSLS, editor,
AAHSL Statistics and Assessment
and Research Services librarian,
UNC-CH Health Sciences Library,
University of North Carolina at Chapel Hill

Managing Finances

Library directors must be able to manage money. They don't need to be accountants, but they do need to understand how to read revenue and expense reports. Gordon asserts that it doesn't take high-level skills to manage finances: "Any library manager . . . can master the math and numerical understanding needed . . . managing money requires common sense and a willingness to look at numbers in the context of what they really mean for the institution" (2008: 203). Library managers also need to understand the generally accepted accounting standards (GAAS) used by their institution, how to work within the institution's budget constraints, and know how to loosen those constraints so that the necessary services can be provided to the library's users.

Most institutions use either cash-based or accrual-based accounting. Cash-based accounting records expenses when actually paid out and revenue when received. Accrual-based accounting records expenses when items are purchased, and revenue is billed no matter when it is received. Accrual-based accounting also spreads the value of the assets across their useful life, rather than just reporting the value of the purchase in the year of purchase as in cash-based accounting. Essentially, this means that for library subscriptions purchased during a fiscal year (July to June or September to August), expenses will be spread over the twelve months of the term of the subscriptions. If the vendor uses a calendar year, no doubt the library's budget will be charged at two different rates.

Budgeting

Budgeting estimates the costs of library activities over a given period, usually one year; it can be a calendar year, an academic year, or a fiscal year. Once the institution sets the budget, the manager is responsible for staying within the limits of the money allocated. Prottsman (2011) superbly identifies various approaches to justifying budgets: needs assessment and cost estimates, cost-benefit analysis, and cost/use calculations. Generally, salary-related expenses are separated from nonpersonnel expenses (referred to as OTPS); they are usually locked in and set by the institution. Fringe benefits are generally handled separate from OTPS.

Budgets come in different types: operational or operating, capital (equipment or large-ticket items), grant award budgets, donations, or revenue generated from sales or services. Whatever the source of the money, the library must follow the terms of the funding source. If a National Network of Libraries of Medicine awards a subcontract through the regional medical library program, the budget set by the grant must be followed. Strategic planning often guides budgeting. But if a budget cannot keep up with the vendor rates of inflation, then appropriate cuts must be made to stay within the relevant budget. The alternative is some assessment and/or justification to increase the money allocated to the library.

The library director generally has overall responsibility for the library's budget, although assistant directors or others responsible for resource purchasing may have this delegated responsibility. Some larger medical libraries will have separate assigned staff to handle the library's financial operations.

Generally, the institution mandates the type of the library's budget. It can be a lump sum, with little instruction or requirements for how it should be spent. This type is rare. It can be a formula budget that allocates the library budget based upon the number of staff per users served, or departments served. Some institutions charge back their academic and clinical departments based upon the services rendered the previous year. Line-item budget is another type, and perhaps the most common. This budget type assigns dollar amounts to each line of the budget (e.g., books and periodicals, contractual services, or databases/software). Program budget is another type, which allocates money spent on a service or program directly to an organizational goal, showing the resources needed, including staff time and materials. Finally, a zero-based budget may be used, which essentially starts from nothing and builds the budget based upon current costs and expected revenue. Many non-profit organizations budget their conferences in this way, with revenues expected to cover all projected expenses.

A new library director needs to investigate immediately the institutional accounting method, the actual budget or budgets and sources, and the process in place to request money. Often, if vendors levy cost increases and the library's budget remains flat at last year's level, the urgency is either to get more funding, or to cut resources and do more with less. The latter has been the practice, as more libraries are not getting funding increases from year to year. More information about budgeting for purchase of resources can be found in Chapter 4.

Raising Revenues

Because of budget shortfalls, many libraries have looked to new ways to generate revenue. Options include fund-raising, creating Friends of the Library groups, creating special membership programs, or submitting proposals to organizations such as the National Network of Libraries of Medicine (NN/LM) to take advantages of the many award programs offered via the eight regional medical library sites, http://nnlm.gov.

NN/LM is a primary source of awards for member health sciences libraries. A library must be a member to receive these awards, but membership is free. The regional networks offer funding for outreach, pilot projects, regional symposia, technology improvement, health information services, assessment and planning, professional development, exhibiting, and training. Each of the eight regional centers manages awards for its respective geographic region.

Some grant funding agencies require matching or a portion of the funding from the institution. However, the opportunity to get more money may look cost-effective to them, especially if the project is one the institution would have to do anyway. Another source of revenue may be joining purchasing consortiums to share costs. Adding a fee-for-service program may be another option. For example, two deans at New York Medical College approached the library director with a proposal: If they purchased a poster printer, could the library provide poster printing services to students at a low cost? Since the service began, it has generated more money every year than any other service and continues to cover the shortfalls in the regular operating budget.

Soliciting Donations

Working with local offices of institutional advancement or alumni relations, the library may be the favorite place to designate donations. Generally, institutions prefer unrestricted donations, but former students, staff, or faculty often remember the library with fondness and designate the library as the recipient of their donation. Often medical staff in a hospital may have a special "library fund" to which they donate to thank their local library or librarian. Many a renovation project has been accomplished with alumni or patient donations (e.g., computer labs, new furniture, or complete facilities upgrades). Library directors should work with an institution's development office to garner support from potential donors.

Creating Support Groups

Journal clubs, a Friends of the Library group, or medical staff support groups all help the library advocate and/or generate additional revenue. Working through the institution's development staff, donations can be officially acknowledged as federal or state income tax deductions. Membership rates, or levels of memberships with meaningful benefits such as attending special meetings, events, and/or library access, may result in increased income for the library. All of these efforts can be time-consuming, so the director needs to assess which options for generating revenue will be cost-effective.

SUMMARY

The literature of library administration is complex. Even as the range of roles and competencies is growing, so are applicable tools and resources that may be applied from other disciplines. The terminology is daunting. The competencies are critical, but lists upon lists of them exist, and all must be selected and used within the context of the information needs of the specific institution and the expectations of both library patrons and higher administration. This chapter is only a starting point, and references to other excellent resources, noted throughout, must be pursued.

As the spokesperson for the library, the library director must lead, guide, administer, inspire, and manage up, down, and outward—providing value culturally, clinically, and economically—and do so with passion. Recent health sciences library research has validated the library's worth. Opportunities abound to make a difference. The knowledge and skills in strategic planning will clarify the library's direction and help develop a working implementation plan. Today is the best time to be a library leader: Making a difference was never more important or valued. Manage to direct a difference.

STUDY QUESTIONS

1. Describe your own personal style of management and how you might describe your library's environment during an interview for a prospective librarian.
2. Outline the strategic planning process and why it is important, and identify some tools to use with staff.
3. Why are accreditation standards important, and how might you, as a library manager, participate in the institutional process?
4. Describe at least three assessment tools and how and why you chose them.

REFERENCES

Akbar-Williams, Tahirah. 2012. "In Order to Lead, You Have to Know What Direction You Are Going; Cultivating Well-rounded Leaders in Staking a Claim on Our Future." *College & Research Libraries News* 73, no. 10 (November): 606–7.

AAHSL (Association of Academic Health Sciences Library Directors). 2013a. "AAHSL Leadership Scholarships." www.aahsl.org/index.php?option=com_content&view=article&id=21.

———. 2013b. "Strategic Plan. 2012–2014." www.aahsl.org/index.php?option=com_content&view=article&id=145.

Bandy, Margaret, Jacqueline Donaldson Doyle, Anne Fladger et al. 2008. "Standards for Hospital Libraries 2007." *Journal of the Medical Library Association* 96, no. 2 (April 2008): 162–69.

Bennis, Warren, and Burt Nanus. 1985. *Leaders: The Strategies for Taking Charge.* New York: Harper & Row.

Collins, Jim. 2001. *Good to Great: Why Some Companies Make the Leap and Others Don't.* New York: HarperCollins.

———. 2006. "Where Are You on Your Journey?" From *Good to Great, Industrial Worksheet Packet.* www.jimcollins.com/tools/diagnostic-tool.pdf.

Doyle, Jacqueline Donaldson, and Kay K. Wellik. 2011. "Topics in Management." In *The Medical Library Association Guide to Managing Health Care Libraries,* 2nd ed., edited by Margaret Moylan Bandy and Rosalind Farnam Dudden, 35–62. New York: Neal-Schuman and Medical Library Association.

Dudden, Rosalind F. 2008. *Using Benchmarking, Needs Assessment, Quality Improvement, Outcome Measurement, and Library Standards: A How-To-Do-It Manual for Librarians.* Chicago: Neal-Schuman and Medical Library Association.

———. 2011. "Evaluation and Improvement Management." In *The Medical Library Association Guide to Managing Health Care Libraries,"* 2nd ed., edited by Margaret Moylan Bandy and Rosalind Farnam Dudden, 99–134. New York: Neal-Schuman and Medical Library Association.

Falcone, Paul. 1997. *96 Great Interview Questions to Ask Before You Hire.* New York: American Management Association.

Goodstein, Leonard D. 2010. "Strategic Planning: A Leadership Imperative." In *The ASTD Leadership Handbook,* edited by Elaine Biech, 43–54. Alexandria, VA: ASTD.

Gordon, Rachel Singer. 2006. "Seven Deadly Sins (and Desirable Strategies) for Library Managers." *FreePint* 196 (January 5). https://web.freepint.com.

———. 2008. *The Accidental Library Manager.* Medford, NJ: Information Today.

Harvard Business School. 2004. *Manager's Toolkit: The 13 Skills Managers Need to Succeed.* Cambridge, MA: Harvard Business School Press.

Jenkins, Farley W. 2011. "The Role of Leadership in Library Administration." *Library Student Journal* (November). Accessed April 3, 2013. www.librarystudentjournal.org/index.php/lsj/article/view/278/316#introduction.

The Joint Commission. 2013. *Hospital Accreditation Standards: Accreditation Policies, Standards, Intents.* Oakbrook Terrace, IL: The Commission.

Kouzes, James M., and Barry Z. Posner. 2002. *The Leadership Challenge,* 3rd ed. San Francisco: Jossey-Bass.

———. 2010. "The Five Practices of Exemplary Leadership." In *The ASTD Leadership Handbook,* edited by Elaine Biech. Alexandria, VA: ASTD.

LCME (Liaison Committee for Medical Education). 2012. *Functions and Structure of a Medical School; Standards for Accreditation of Medical Education Programs Leading to the M.D. Degree.* (May). www.lcme.org/functions.pdf.

Lipscomb, Caroline. 2013. Personal e-mail. May 14.

Marshall, Joanne G. 1992. "Impact of the Hospital Library on Clinical Decision-Making: The Rochester Study." *Bulletin of the Medical Library Association* 80, no. 2 (April): 169–78.

Marshall, Joanne Gard, Julia Sollenberger., Sharon Easterby-Gannett et al. 2013. "The Value of Library and Information Services in Patient Care: Results of a Multisite Study." *Journal of the Medical Library Association* 101, no. 1 (January): 38–46.

Medical Library Association. 2007. "Competencies for Lifelong Learning and Professional Success: The Educational Policy Statement of the Medical Library Association." www.mlanet.org/education/policy/.

NN/LM-MAR (National Network of Libraries of Medicine Middle Atlantic Region). 2013. "Value of Library and Information Services in Patient Care Study." http://nnlm.gov/mar/about/value.html.

Oakes, Kevin, Holly Tompson, and Lorrie Lykins. 2010. "Managing Talent." In *The ASTD Leadership Handbook*, edited by Elaine Biech, 103–22. Alexandria, VA: ASTD.

OED (Oxford English Dictionary). Accessed April 13. www.oed.com/.

Prottsman, Mary Fran. 2011. "Financial Management." In *The Medical Library Association Guide to Managing Health Care Libraries*, 2nd ed., edited by Margaret Moylan Bandy and Rosalind Farnam Dudden, 63–78. New York: Neal-Schuman Publishers.

Senge, Peter. 1994. *Fifth Discipline: Fieldbook*. New York: Doubleday.

Sollengerger, Julia F., and Robert G. Holloway. 2013. "The Evolving Role and Value of Libraries and Librarians in Health Care." *Journal of the American Medical Association* 320, no. 12: 1231–32.

Sullivan, Maureen. 2003. *Creating a Culture of Learning; A Workshop for the Medical Sciences Library at New York Medical College*. June 9. Valhalla, NY.

CHAPTER 15

Physical Space in Health Sciences Libraries

Stewart M. Brower

INTRODUCTION

Health sciences libraries have reaped considerable benefits over the past twenty-plus years of the Internet. Large, cumbersome print indexes are being replaced with exhaustive bibliographic databases and slick, powerful search engines. Vast collections of printed, bound journals are ignored in favor of the ubiquity and feature-richness of their electronic counterparts. Books, long a staple of medical education, now come in electronic form as well, and are available on an array of portable devices.

These changes have ancillary effects as well. Interlibrary loan, once a vital means of getting obscure materials for medical researchers, has been scaled back dramatically in recent years as library users find other means of getting what they need. For example, the National Library of Medicine (NLM) interlibrary loan system DOCLINE statistics show a 46 percent drop in interlibrary loan requests from 2002 to 2011 (U.S. National Library of Medicine, 2013).

Reference librarians' roles have also shifted, from waiting for questions behind a desk to embedding themselves more directly into the operations of the departments they serve. The number of reference transactions taking place at a traditional desk, staffed by full-time librarians, has fallen off significantly. Medical librarians, like librarians from many other disciplines, have discovered that they best serve their user populations by having a regular, continuous presence at the physical point of need of their users. Some medical librarians are now being hired as clinical informationists who go on rounds with physicians and health care teams and provide evidence-based medical literature on demand. In nonclinical settings, library liaisons conduct office hours in the colleges and departments they serve. Collectively, these new service models have changed the way library reference work is done in a health sciences setting.

Circulation statistics for printed materials decrease as electronic usage increases. With activity in the physical book stacks dwindling, library operations related to the selection, procurement, cataloging, shelving, binding, and circulation of physical materials no longer have the impact on staffing and budget that they used to have. Many libraries now look to off-site storage of physical collections or the elimination of the print collection in its entirety. These changes, inevitable in the face of a new electronic age of information, have forced administrators to ask challenging questions about the use of space by libraries.

This chapter will focus on the challenges faced in library space planning in the electronic age, and making use of space in a way that improves the value of health sciences libraries to their constituencies and their administrators. In short, this chapter will try to answer the question, "What is the value of a health library's physical space in an electronic world?"

FACTORS IN SPACE PLANNING AND DESIGN

According to a 2009 survey, more than twenty new medical libraries were constructed in the previous ten years and many more were renovated (Ludwig, 2010). Although the likelihood of any librarian getting the opportunity to participate in a major new construction project might be somewhat limited, many, if not most, librarians will have a hand in either a renovation project or a space-planning project during the course of their careers. Additionally, many trends that have been recognized in the library literature should be noted. Although the scope of this chapter is somewhat limited in this regard (and dozens of books are available on the subject), these elements and trends should be defined and discussed to help the reader better understand what follows.

Space planning is a ubiquitous term, albeit a misleading one: Space planning requires a detailed examination of the intended function of a space, while mapping out the physical impression and value of the space itself. In other words, space planning is as much a consideration of function as form, and this chapter will return to that concept repeatedly. This examination of space planning will look at what would be needed for a large-scale plan—for example, renovating a floor of a larger library or moving a hospital library to a larger space. These recommendations could be scaled back for smaller projects—an office move, for example—but should give an impression of the variables involved in any new space plan.

Preplanning

It can be difficult to say exactly when and where a decision to change or build new physical library space starts. Perhaps a site-accreditation team mentions the need for a larger library, or a potential donor likes the thought of her name over a new history of medicine collection, or possibly student complaints about the lack of computers finally reach the administration. The reasons for library space planning can vary widely, sometimes coming from the users, sometimes from the librarians, and sometimes from the administration, but optimally any such "seed" would be recognized by all parties as a needed change. Often, at this early stage, a **project owner** is identified who will be the lead coordinator of the project and the individual who will be responsible for the decisions that follow.

Preplanning efforts often begin with a collection of the library's own stakeholders—those librarians and staff who are most affected by the intended function of the space. A committee of library staffers might be selected by the project owner to plan some office moves, or to plan a relocation for the journal collection, or something similar. However, sometimes these planning teams can forget to include other key stakeholders—the library's users and administration. A planning team should form around the objective of making the space serve the functions for which it is intended, and the library users are those who are often most affected by these changes. The institutional administration must be able to provide oversight and approvals for various stages of the project, so they should be included as part of the planning team. A good space plan will try to involve all key stakeholders and their diverse points of view.

For some projects, outside consultants are beneficial or even necessary to develop a successful space plan. Architects and interior designers, contractors, engineers, electricians, information technology (IT) specialists, plumbers, masons, landscapers, carpenters, and other specialists may need to be consulted or actively employed in a project to see it through to completion. Architects, in particular, should be brought in early on any major library space initiative. A licensed and credentialed architect should have expert-level knowledge of how human beings engage with constructed spaces such as buildings and offices, and should use that knowledge to help his clients create the kinds of spaces they need (American Institute of Architects, 2013). Additionally, architects understand and have extensive knowledge of the building codes that might affect a space planning or construction project, and can work to be sure that a project is completed with no violations. An architect should help the client work with the other stakeholders and consultants to craft elegant solutions to tricky problems. Optimally, an architect would be consulted for any library space plan, no matter how minor, but realistically, that is rarely feasible.

Space Planning

Once a planning team is set, a **space program** can be developed, either by the leadership of the space planning team, or by the whole team. A space program is a foundational document, one that details what work is being proposed, how it should be done, and why. Space programming requires careful examination and measurement of the space available for a project, who will be using the space and for what purposes, what kinds of furnishings and technologies might be needed, the overall anticipated time frame, and what budget is available for the project. Other supporting documents—user surveys, budget worksheets, quotes for labor and materials, diagrams and drawings—should be included as evidence of the need for the project and its likely success. Lastly, this document will be shared with administrators who need to approve the project, and so an executive summary of all the above items should be provided.

One planning document that may be included as a part of the space planning is the **blocking map**. This is particularly true of projects that include the renovation of existing space or the development of new space. Blocking is the activity of taking a floor plan or similar map and dividing it into sections by their intended functions. An example might be an office plan for three different departments, each blocked out on a floor plan to show its general location. Blocking allows the planners to maximize their use of the allocated space through the placement and configuration of blocked off areas. As an exercise, blocking helps define certain planned functions or areas within a larger space, without fully committing to a furniture plan. At the same time, however, general square footage allocations can be made, accounting for factors such as foot traffic, width of aisles, distance to entrances and exits, distances and adjacencies of the various blocks to each other, and locations of utilities and services within the floor plan (see Figure 15.1).

Once the team has been formed, the space has been blocked, the program approved, the budget secured, and all appropriate consultants brought in for the project, the planning moves to a more formal stage. Architects and furniture planners and other designers may begin drafting formal plans for approval. The planners begin listing and accounting for the locations of existing resources such as electricity or network ports, fire exits and other safety features, traffic patterns of library users, and staff who will occupy the space. Many other factors such as lighting, colors, and textures become part of the overall discussion, as well as furniture design and selection of interior finishes. The project may have artificial constraints, such as an imposed time frame for completion, or elements required by ranking administrators, all of which need to be included in the plan. Requests for building permits and other official documentation and approvals may need to be secured, project items may need to be sent out for bids, and contractors or construction specialists may need to be selected and hired.

A budget for a space-planning project can usually be broken down into two major categories: construction and "FF&E," which stands for **furniture, fixtures, and equipment** (Wikipedia, 2013a). The budget for construction is for the entirety of the work and materials needed to complete the physical creation of the space, whereas FF&E includes all the items that are being moved into and installed in the constructed space. Generally, in budgeting for a new build or renovation, the architect or contractor will work with a budget estimate, then have subcontractors bid for the individual work items—electrical, plumbing, steel, rough and finish carpentry, IT, and so forth. Once the bids are received and the budget finalized, the project owner may be presented with a final fixed project cost that is higher than the budget will accommodate. The project team may then engage in **value engineering,** an examination of the anticipated function of the space with an eye toward cost reductions by eliminating items that are not essential (Wikipedia, 2013d). Understandably, the FF&E budget is often targeted during any value engineering process; less-expensive options may be substituted for these items, which can be an easy way to save money. This process can also undercut the intended function of the new

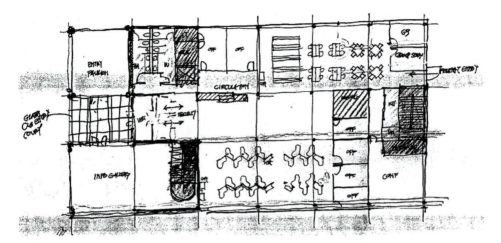

Figure 15.1. Blocking: Early drawings such as this floor plan can identify major elements without requiring details or specifications about the space being used.

space, so it should be treated with all due consideration. Additional funding may need to be secured as well.

Overseeing a major space-planning project, such as the construction of a new library building, can be the equivalent of a full-time job for the project owner. A "routine" renovation to existing space can take from several months to a couple of years, depending on the project. A single new building project, from preplanning through planning and construction and installation of furniture and equipment, can take several years to complete. Careful attention to planning will help ensure that the final product meets the expectations of the institution, and will keep the project owner and team on track.

Other Concepts and Trends

The two previous sections provide a very brief and generalized overview of the major concepts of space planning. A few other major concepts should be introduced before moving on to health sciences libraries and their physical spaces, some of which capture the current best thinking in planning for library space.

Flexibility as a design concept suggests that the more adaptive and open the spaces that are being created, the easier it will be for those spaces to be remodeled and reused in the future. For libraries, flexibility might mean larger unbroken areas to be adapted for storing collections and providing study spaces for our users. It can also be adapted to suggest the kinds of furnishings that best suit library users.

Modular design essentially breaks larger furnishings down into smaller ones designed to accommodate each other with greater flexibility (Wikipedia, 2013b). An example of this might be study tables that only seat one or two users, but that have casters on the legs and can be pushed together to seat larger numbers. Such a design would accommodate individuals, small groups, or larger groups for their study needs using the same furnishings, saving money for the library and maximizing the return on the use of the furniture and the study space itself.

Flexibility also gives rise to the concept of **future-proofing**. Future-proofing is the purposeful effort to develop infrastructure to support technologies that do not exist yet. Older library spaces, in particular, often pose challenges when being configured for the use of technology. Poured concrete floors may need to have channels cut into them with chisels and jackhammers in order to lay new wiring. Ceiling and wall spaces may be likewise inaccessible in older libraries. Note that technologies for a building might not always mean computer and information technology; sometimes plumbing or heating/air conditioning systems might be difficult to upgrade or repair because of initial planning that did not take into account new developments that might occur.

By and large, successful future-proofing takes on many of the forms of advance planning and modular design in new buildings. Floors are poured with under-floor channel systems already in place to allow easy access to cabling for networking and power. Walls are designed to be easily accessible from the ceiling, so that new wiring may be dropped or relocated as needed. Of course, wireless access to the network has become essential and should be installed in any institutional space so as to make access as ubiquitous as possible.

Building mechanical systems should be located in easily accessible areas as well. Often, electrical closets and networking/IT cabinets will be **stacked**, or placed above each other from floor to floor, for ease of maintenance and to have utilities hook up to the building at the same access points. The same is often true of plumbing. Although health sciences libraries will not typically have elaborate plumbing systems, they will have access to water and drainage for bathrooms, water fountains, fire suppression systems, and possibly lawn and landscaping. Keeping the access to water in a single area of the building, stacking the bathrooms from floor to floor, and planning for additional building drainage even in areas where the need for water is not anticipated, all can help future-proof the building against new plumbing developments.

A major future-proofing in designing any user space, particularly locations where computer use is anticipated, is access to electricity. Wall outlets are the most common kind of electrical access point, and in the United States these outlets are generally designed to accommodate a three-wire grounded plug. New USB (universal serial bus) outlets are also available on the market, allowing a user to charge a device directly from the USB port in a wall-mounted fixture, but the future viability of the USB standard might not justify the installation of these outlets in a library space. Knowing the right choice to make in these situations can be challenging, particularly when librarians and many users appreciate new technologies—but those technologies may only be transitional in nature. (Even USB has gone through more than one standard since its introduction in 1996 [USB Implementers Forum, 2013].)

Another significant trend in new construction is **sustainability**, or the potential for a new building to interact with the environment in a way that has minimal negative impact, or even ongoing positive impact (Wikipedia, 2013c). Examples of this kind of sustainability might include water-saving and energy-saving features, recycled building materials, or the installation of solar panels or other alternative energy systems.

Some new libraries have achieved recognition for their sustainability through certification. **Leadership in Energy and Environmental Design**, more commonly known as **LEED**, is a voluntary certification program developed by the United States Green Building Council (U.S. Green Building Council, 2013). Examples of health sciences libraries in the United States with LEED certification include the Eccles Health Sciences Education Building at the University of Utah and the College of Medicine-Phoenix of the University of Arizona. LEED certification is based on criteria judged in six categories: sustainable site, water efficiency, energy and atmosphere, materials and resources, indoor environmental quality, and innovation and design process.

An ongoing criticism of LEED certification has been the initial cost of sustainable design and construction compared with standard building costs. Although some early LEED projects came with a hefty price tag, the value of sustainable and energy-reducing construction practice over the lifetime of a building can make up for the initial investment. Moreover, as the techniques and materials for sustainable design have become more commonplace, the economics have begun to shift. It is now estimated that the cost per square foot of a new LEED-certified construction project is only 2 percent higher than standard construction costs, or about three to five dollars per square foot on average (Miller, Spivey, and Florance, 2008).

SPACE NEEDS OF DIFFERENT TYPES OF HEALTH SCIENCES LIBRARIES

When thinking of a health sciences library, specifically the physical presence of the library and its space, many potential images come to mind. In practical terms, however, health sciences libraries follow a few standard types.

The academic health sciences library caters to the students, staff, and faculty of a given health sciences or medical campus. Often, if the primary focus of the library is the support of medical education, it will be referred to as an "academic medical library." Such a library is intended to support academic centers and campuses, with their general missions of education and research, and, often, practice of the health sciences. That is to say, an academic health sciences library always has a mission to support the educational practices of the campus, but often it will find itself connected to a teaching hospital or similar setting where the practice of medicine is part of the educational backdrop.

It should be noted that some academic centers have begun adapting campuses and programs once reserved for the health sciences disciplines exclusively to serve multiple disciplines that are not always directly health-related. An academic library supporting programs in medicine, nursing, and pharmacy might also be asked to support programs in social work, health business administration, genetics, biological sciences, and more. Some such libraries even support programs as diverse as architecture, education, engineering, psychology, and human relations. The definition of the academic health sciences library has been changing over time, but generally speaking, if the scope of the library's operations includes teaching and research in health-related disciplines, then that library is considered a health sciences library.

An academic health sciences library requires enough space for services and a collection suitable for the educational and research needs of its campus. In the past, that usually meant a sizable collection of print materials, a nonprint media area, significant space for reference services, and enough computer workstations to meet user needs. Additionally, significant space would be used for staff offices and processing areas, particularly for collection management or historical materials. Other common features would include group study rooms, conference rooms, study carrels, and similar spaces.

When someone imagines a general academic library—as part of a four-year liberal arts school, for example—the imaginer might conjure up images of a lush, verdant campus, with stately buildings and distinct ornamentation. Although certainly some health sciences libraries are to be found in settings just like that—the Harvard Medical School quad comes to mind as such an example—many academic medical centers are actually based in large urban settings and have a more modern architectural style. As a result of building primarily in congested urban centers, these campuses have historically found themselves with little room for expansion, and free space for new development is often at a premium.

This is a common refrain with hospital libraries as well. The hospital library is eponymous—the function of such a library is to serve the hospital. The history of hospital libraries is tied to the medical staff who require access to the medical literature, but over time many hospital libraries have expanded their roles to encompass services for all hospital employees, including nurses, pharmacists, technicians, and administrators. The hospital library generally requires enough space for a core collection of journals and books, as well as study space and computers, and office space for the librarian. Many hospital libraries have been efficiently run by minimal staff, and one-person hospital libraries are common.

In 2007, the Hospital Libraries Section of the Medical Library Association developed a standard that mirrors this general description in more exacting language:

> **Standard 10**: The physical library will be large enough to accommodate the library staff, the in-house collection, an appropriate amount and selection of personal computers and other information technology (IT) hardware, and seating for an appropriate number of users. A separate office will be provided for at least the professional library staff.

> **Intent.** A library that cannot comfortably accommodate staff, users, equipment, and collection is likely to be underutilized. Separate areas for staff enable privacy of communication among library staff and with persons requesting information. (Bandy et al., 2008: 166)

Hospitals are found in all manner of settings—urban, suburban, rural—but they tend to share one common trait: being landlocked. Most people have shared the unnerving experience of walking into a hospital and trying to get directions to a specific department or room; hospitals are typically confusing in their layout and byzantine in their traffic patterns. By and large, the potential for growing a hospital with new buildings rests in finding unused bits and pieces of land inside already densely overbuilt space and adding on to it.

Because of this, the space used for hospital libraries often has to be justified to administrators, or else it will be claimed and cannibalized for offices, labs, or even waiting rooms. The statement of "intent" given above in justification of Standard 10 explains the need exceptionally well. If a library is not sizable enough to be comfortable and accommodate the materials and people using them, it probably will not get much use. In terms of form following function, the hospital library must develop and support valuable services to justify the allocation of space. Likewise, without adequate space, the hospital library will most likely find its services being underused.

Although academic health libraries and hospital libraries make up the majority of health sciences libraries, other types do exist. Consumer health libraries are intended for the use of general populations to help them identify and use quality health information. Many possible configurations occur for consumer health library operations, including being a part of a larger academic health sciences library or even a hospital library, or being a part of a public library system. A consumer health library might be a designated area in a larger library, or a separate enclosed space in a hospital or clinic, or might take on any number of other configurations. Some larger hospitals have libraries that are dedicated to serving their patients, providing not just medical information, but also books and DVDs for long-term patients, and coffee and workshops for their family members.

Because the potential needs and configurations of consumer health libraries can vary so widely, it is difficult to identify their common space needs. Generally speaking, such a library would need space for the librarian such as a desk or office; some collection space for books, magazines, and DVDs; computer workstations for their users; and general reading or lounge spaces. If such a library caters to children, some features and fixtures might be devoted to their particular needs, including video game stations, smaller furniture, and perhaps casual reading materials for different age groups.

Other libraries with particular focus on the health sciences include libraries for health-related corporations and research groups, including pharmacy, medical technology, biochemical research, and even cosmetics and food sciences. These libraries might be private or public, large or small, modern or traditional—the definition of a health sciences library can include a great many types of libraries, serving many types of users.

If one thought becomes clear in reading through these various types of libraries, it should be this: The purpose and work of the library should determine what space is needed and how it is used. This is not always the case, but it calls to mind again the old adage that "form follows function," and when space planning for any health sciences library, you have to first know what the functions of that library really are.

FUNCTIONS AND SPACE NEEDS
OF HEALTH SCIENCES LIBRARIES

Health sciences libraries—whether they are academic, or hospital, or something else—function much as any other library might. They all help bring people together with useful information, and they require certain materials and services to achieve that goal.

In many respects, academic health sciences libraries are much like any other academic library. They have collections and spaces for their users, service areas, and workspaces for staff. Although they have much in common with general academic libraries, health sciences libraries often have specialized, discipline-specific materials and collections, services that blend academic and clinical practice in nuanced ways, and computer and simulation laboratories for students to apply what they learn in a controlled environment.

Hospital libraries, in contrast, tend to be much smaller and therefore have fewer such amenities, but they are very service-oriented. No other kinds of libraries compare easily to the traditional hospital library. The emphasis on service can take precedence sometimes over other space needs. Workspace for staff might be very small and awkward, favoring larger spaces for their patrons. Still, space for collections, technology, and staff workspaces must be considered as well, even in environments that favor the needs of the user.

In this section, the various functions of the health sciences library will be examined relevant to their space needs. This section is in no way meant to be a comprehensive list of such needs, but it should give a sense of the complexity and range of demands placed on space in any given health sciences library.

Space for Collections

Printed materials require shelving to provide options for storage and retrieval as well as collection organization. In health sciences libraries, the standard for organizing monographs and journals is according to the classification schema of the National Library of Medicine (NLM). Typically, monographs will be classified with call numbers according to the NLM classification, whereas journals will be shelved separately, arranged in alphabetical order by title.

For a collection, each stack of shelves is a **shelving unit**. Shelving types for health sciences library collections vary greatly in both form and function. Selection of shelving for a collection is often based on a few key factors, including capacity, shelving height, shelving depth, aisle width, available space, and price of materials.

Capacity refers to the volume and mass of the items being shelved and the ability of the shelving units to handle the size and weight of those items. Medical books and journals tend to be thicker and taller, on average, than materials shelved in other libraries. Librarians should plan, generally, for no more than six to eight volumes per linear foot for a health sciences library.

As an example of measuring capacity, if a single-sided shelving unit is thirty-six inches wide, and holds six shelves, the number of volumes it can potentially hold might be calculated like this:

7 volumes per foot × 3 linear feet per shelf × 6 shelves per unit = 126 volumes

In this example, six shelves per shelving unit is an arbitrary number; it might only be five shelves per unit, or it could be seven or eight. **Shelving height** determines the number of shelves per unit. **Shelf depth** for medical and health sciences books and journals needs to be generous; these materials tend to be large. The use of twelve-inch-deep shelves is common for health sciences collections, with sixteen-inch shelves available for oversized materials such as medical atlases and anatomy books.

Aisle width is the space between rows of shelving units. The shelving units themselves are configured into **shelving ranges**, the length and configuration of which are determined by the floor space available. Ranges are configured as either single-facing, such as would be mounted on a wall, or double-facing, the most common shelving configuration. The aisle width, then, must be factored into space planning for collections to allow clearance for patrons and staff to enter the collection area and retrieve materials. Accordingly, it must meet requirements for wheelchair access as directed by the **Americans with Disabilities Act (ADA)**. Minimum clearance between stacks to meet ADA requirements is thirty-six inches between ranges of shelving units, with no individual range longer than seven stack sections (twenty-one feet) without a cross aisle provided to break up the stacks. Main aisles that provide access to the collection itself must meet a minimum of forty-four inches in width. ADA requirements are minimums; some states such as California have imposed stricter standards. An organizational safety officer or ergonomics specialist should be consulted if meeting these requirements prompts concerns.

An option for library collections that require larger volumes of material to be contained in limited space is **compact mobile shelving**. Also known as high-density or movable aisle systems, compact mobile shelving systems possess the same characteristics as standard shelving systems but are installed on rails and are able to be moved. The major benefit of compact mobile shelving is to maximize floor space by limiting the number of aisles. Instead of having an aisle for every range of shelves, a group of ranges might have one aisle, and that aisle is opened up to the user by physically moving the ranges to the left or the right. Space savings of up to 60 or 70 percent of the floor area can be delivered by the use of these systems, making them very attractive options for libraries that need to downsize their collection space.

The mechanical properties of compact mobile systems are variable. Many compact mobile systems are motorized, requiring electricity to function; others are manual and use a simple hand crank to move the units. Installation of these systems sometimes requires the construction of a secondary floor in which to place the rails, or the addition of electrical wiring and panels. Mobile shelves can place additional stress on the structure of the floors beneath them. The weight-bearing load of the floors should be examined carefully before considering compact mobile shelving, and a structural engineer should be consulted on any installation.

Another common option for large collections that have significantly low use is **off-site storage and retrieval**. Typically, this means the rental or construction of a separate facility for warehousing of low-use materials. Off-site storage has become a viable option for libraries that do not wish to eliminate large amounts of print materials but feel that library space might be better used for other purposes. This can be an expensive solution for many libraries, so some institutions will work in partnership to construct and maintain off-site storage and retrieval for multiple libraries. An example of this is the Library Storage Facility at the Pickle Research Campus in Austin, which services both the University of Texas and Texas Tech.

Other specialized collection areas include special collections, archives, and historical collections. Such collections often have rare or unusual items that would be hard to replace and require more advanced storage requirements than a general use collection might. In the case of health sciences libraries, these collections might include such items as radiographs and X-rays, medical and surgical equipment, skeletons and human models of various types, artwork, medical atlases, and many other kinds of rare books and antiquities.

Specialists in the care and handling of these materials should be included in any discussions of space planning for the storage of these kinds of materials. Environmental controls for these collections are typically more exacting than those found for general collections, particularly for temperature and humidity, and exposure to various light sources is more rigorously controlled. Additionally, security and fire suppression systems will often be given greater forethought than those for a general health sciences collection.

Traditional Spaces for Library Users

People who use health sciences libraries are not that different from those who use other libraries; only their need for health information distinguishes them. In academic health sciences centers, faculty, staff, and students are the primary library clientele. Their interests in health information usually take the form of research, education, or clinical care. Because health information is so valued by communities at large, academic libraries that open their doors to the public might also find lawyers and legal aides seeking information for cases that involve medical care, or unaffiliated health care workers who are seeking an answer to a unique medical question, or even laypeople looking for information about their own medical conditions.

Hospital libraries, by comparison, typically have very defined user populations. For most, only employees of the hospital—doctors, nurses, pharmacists, hospital executives, and others—may have access to the library and its collection. If it is a teaching hospital, medical residents and students might be common users. For some hospitals, the library might also be open to patients and their families. Rarer still are the hospital libraries that allow access to the general public.

With the breadth of people who use the health sciences library, it may come as little surprise that the space needs for these users likewise are broad and complex, and that "user space" is a far from ubiquitous concept. What follows is an examination of the various types of space configurations to be found in a health sciences library, but not a comprehensive analysis.

In very general terms, students and users who need space, comfort, and quiet to conduct their work do so in study areas. A study area can range from a collection of tables and chairs, to a small conversational area with couches and low tables, to specialized study carrels and desks. Additionally, different users have different preferences for these kinds of spaces. Some prefer the seclusion of a study carrel for individual study, whereas others need large tables and chairs to gather around and conduct work in groups. The modern library often uses a combination of these kinds of configurations, if space is sufficient to support them all, to meet the needs of the majority of their users. Flexible, modular furniture helps make these study areas more adaptable for growth and future needs (see Figure 15.2).

The concept of modular design can be extended to other study areas as well. Among the highest demand user spaces in a health sciences library are the computer workstations, sometimes referred to as public access computers. A computer workstation, in library space planning, refers not only to the computer equipment being made available to the user, but also any desk on which it is mounted, the chair being used, and the space available to the user for working on the computer.

Ergonomics is also a significant factor in designing and planning for computer workstations. The height of the desk can either reduce or increase strain on the user's forearms and wrists from using the keyboard. Modern task chairs feature a pneumatic lift to adjust the height of the seat, lumbar supports to better relieve strain on the back during longer work sessions, and caster wheels to make it possible to reposition the chair while seated. Additionally, workstation areas should include a minimum of forty square feet of space for the user. Any furniture design plan should be coordinated with a public safety officer or other ergonomics specialist to ensure best practices are followed.

In addition to workstation space requirements, the overall adaptability of the workstation area should be a factor in library space planning. Computer workstations generally require both electricity and networking, which often means that wiring for these needs has to extend from beyond the walls of an area to its interior. Options for this kind of wiring include **multiservice poles** that allow cables and wires to be dropped from the ceiling, or **under-floor duct systems** (i.e., Walker duct) that offer easy access to wiring from the floor. Multiservice poles break up the space, sometimes in unwelcome ways, and under-floor wiring is often preferred for this reason.

Library Spaces for Teaching and Learning

Wiring configurations can be a significant factor in the design of other library spaces that have computers for the students. One such category of user space is instructional space, such as a classroom or instruction lab. Although traditional classrooms can be used for library instruction, instructional spaces in health sciences libraries tend to include the significant availability of technology. Classrooms with computer workstations are sometimes referred to as **e-classrooms**. Health sciences libraries commonly use such instruction spaces for information literacy education, but e-classrooms may also double as computer lab space when not being used for classes, or may be made available to others for their use as a service the library provides. Such e-classrooms vary from being quite small and seating only a few, to being large enough to seat whole course sections. An e-classroom may

Figure 15.2. Modular Design: Furniture plan juxtaposed against a photo of the actual furniture in the reading area.

have either computer workstations in fixed positions, similar to the workstations described above, or may use laptop computers and modular furniture to provide a more dynamic learning environment. Projection equipment is fairly standard in these settings, although large flat panel monitors (LCD, LED, or plasma) are also common. Ceilings in e-classrooms should be somewhat higher than those found in a general office setting, particularly if the classroom has raised seating as found in a theater or auditorium. An instructor workstation for such a classroom may be a podium or another desk, and can include equipment such as handheld remotes or touch-panel displays to control audio, video, lighting, and other environmental or technological aspects of the room.

Planning for an e-classroom requires careful evaluation and analysis of the kinds of instruction the library provides, as well as common class sizes, seating orientation, wired or wireless network access, and the need for distance education or videoconferencing, as well as workflow factors such as reservations and technical support. Designing an e-classroom for a library setting is a complex undertaking, requiring concerted effort and coordination of the teaching librarians, information technology specialists, budget officers, security and operations personnel, and space planners to achieve the best outcomes.

Somewhat less complex, but vitally important to many library users, are group study rooms. Many library users are either students who need to work together on class projects, or health professionals needing a space to meet and plan. Although group study rooms can vary somewhat in size and features, these spaces generally provide a comfortable enclosed space in which groups can get work done.

The emphasis on team learning in health sciences programs makes group study rooms particularly valuable to students (Adamson and Bunnett, 2002). Programs in nursing, pharmacy, allied health, and public health professions routinely assign projects to teams of students, and those students often look to the library to provide space and resources to accomplish this work. Group study rooms are popular for this reason, but they come with some significant operational concerns, including policies for use, room scheduling and asset management, maintenance, and housekeeping. Additionally, when the rooms are not needed during lulls in the academic cycle, the floor space cannot be repurposed. But the demand for group study rooms is consistently high, and health sciences libraries have documented the conversion of space once used for collections into group study spaces.

Outfitting group study rooms varies from library to library, but generally they are outfitted as miniature conference rooms. Some seat only a few; others can seat a dozen or more. This variability is usually most welcome, as the student teams come in many sizes. Group study rooms often include whiteboards, either wall-mounted or on easels. Flat-screen monitors with cabling for both USB and video input allow students to work with their laptops and other technologies more easily. Some libraries have installed room schedulers, small touch-screen panels that show the schedule for each room and allow users to make ad hoc or advance reservations (see Figure 15.3). Room schedulers such as these can be tied to standard calendar software, such as Microsoft Outlook, for easier tracking of room reservations.

Innovative and Nontraditional Library Spaces

The popularity of group study spaces in the library and the tendency toward team learning in general has led to the development of other collaborative learning

Figure 15.3. Room Scheduler: This small touch-screen panel, mounted directly outside a group study room at the Schusterman Library, University of Oklahoma-Tulsa, lights up green when the room is available, or red when the room is in use.

technologies. **Collaborative media furniture** can take many different forms, and it is often designed with modular principles in mind. Generally speaking, these collaborative furnishings will include a table with either chairs or bench seating, and large-screen monitors mounted to a panel at one end of the table. This allows a group to gather around a single table and all use the same monitor for their work. Groups can then view presentations, sketch or take notes, browse websites, and share data and images, all from a single unenclosed space. Common features include power supplies and media switches to allow multiple laptops to plug in and use the monitor. Other options available with some collaborative furniture include videoconferencing and surface-mounted touch screens for additional functionality (see Figure 15.4).

Both student groups and busy health professionals often find themselves without much flexibility in their schedules. In particular, medical students and residents, who put in long hours in the classroom and the hospital, often appreciate being able to access library spaces and some services during nontraditional hours. For libraries, keeping the doors open and services running at full capacity around

Figure 15.4. Media:Scape Collaboration Furniture: From the University of Michigan Medical School Learning Resource Center, this collaboration suite features couch seating with elevated desks mounted behind. Source: Photo from Flickr, by University of Michigan MSIS, used under Creative Commons license (www.flickr.com/photos/umich-msis/6443294375/in/set-72157628251587097).

the clock would be a daunting prospect in terms of staff hours and utilities. Because of these reasons, many twenty-four-hour access library solutions end up being a compromise of some kind. For hospital libraries, the compromise might involve who is allowed access, and what kind of security protocols are used to make certain the privilege is not abused. As an example, doctors and residents may be allowed after-hours access, but not other hospital employees. For academic health sciences libraries, often a computer lab or other common study space is identified and made accessible, but the rest of the library including the print collection is closed off and secure. This can be a very challenging space planning effort to execute successfully, particularly when the library building itself was not designed with a twenty-four-hour access model in mind. Elaborate motorized gates and enclosures may be required to limit access to collections while still enabling access to computers and restrooms, and procedures for appropriate staffing and security can become complex. Typically, these twenty-four-hour spaces require the use of identification cards and swipe readers to allow access to individuals, plus keeping a log of who accessed the space and at what times.

Many of the user spaces discussed above require the planning and coordination of key institutional stakeholders. Perhaps the most demanding of all such planning efforts is that of the **library commons**, sometimes known as the information commons or learning commons. Generally, a commons is a space designed to be shared and used by members of the library's primary patron base, where multiple library-based and nonlibrary-based services and resources combine to provide the best research and learning outcomes for the patrons. For example, a commons in an academic health sciences library might share space among the library reference librarians and writing tutors, the information technology help desk, student affairs personnel, and other stakeholders.

The literature on innovation demonstrates the value of creating physical spaces where people with different areas of expertise and differing perspectives can come together to share ideas in informal ways. Many of the most significant innovations of the past century have their roots in the accidental collisions that can result in such spaces. That is why you see so many organizations—companies and universities— focused on fostering innovation, trying to build them. That is what UAB is trying to do with The Edge of Chaos, housed on the top floor of the Lister Hill Library.

T. Scott Plutchak, MA, AHIP, director,
Lister Hill Library; and interim director,
The Edge of Chaos, University of
Alabama at Birmingham

In many ways, the library commons is an expression, a commentary about the potential for library and information services and their application in any given environment, more so than being only a physical space. In a health sciences library, this can mean that the commons blends aspects of reference and instruction with nonprint media, scanning and image services, computer labs, group study facilities—in essence, any of a number of services from within the library itself—alongside other student services from campus stakeholders. As an expression of library potential, the commons gives voice to a complex and valuable base of services for health sciences students.

Equipping and outfitting a library commons requires planning and an understanding of what services are to be provided. Most commons include a combination of computer workstations and group study spaces, but many variations and configurations are possible. Library commons may also include collaborative media furniture, individual study tables and carrels, soft furnishings of various types, and various types of consumer electronics and equipment such as cameras, scanners, laptops, and tablets. Whiteboards and other work surfaces may be added to allow students to record their notes easily, and most all furniture and equipment is optimized for mobility and flexibility of use.

Additionally, the library commons, again, as an expression of the potential of information services, may include cutting-edge technologies and user spaces. An example of this kind of expression is The Edge of Chaos, a collaborative workspace the University of Alabama Birmingham (UAB) School of Public Health developed in conjunction with the UAB Lister Hill Library where it is housed. The Edge of Chaos is a kind of "innovation commons," constructed for the forging of collaborative relationships between community leadership; business leadership; and the faculty, researchers, and students of the university. The space itself is broken into structured and unstructured units, using mobile modular furnishings that allow for multiple configurations and chalkboard walls for easy documentation of problems and ideas. In keeping with the nontraditional naming of the space, the mission of The Edge of Chaos is to tackle "Wicked Problems," challenges that include many contributing factors that can be hard to diagnose, let alone solve. Although not directed as a "library space," The Edge of Chaos places a functioning creative, collaborative workspace directly within the library walls and increases library visibility on the UAB campus.

A library commons can help draw users into the library, and it is often tied to other services inside and outside the library. As rules about food and drink have been made less restrictive over time, many health sciences libraries have added cafés or coffee shops inside the library. Space requirements for such cafés varies considerably, but all such operations must meet both fire safety and food-handling codes, require access to plumbing and electricity, and need significant storage available to them for stocking various supplies, as well as needing some seating and tables.

Although not as common as cafés, another role for the health sciences library, both in terms of service and space, is the **simulation lab**, or sim lab as it is sometimes known. Only a few libraries currently have a role in managing simulation space, but this is an area of some interest and ongoing discussion. Sim labs contain various types of simulators that students use in the health sciences to better learn procedures before employing these procedures on patients. Simulators might take the form of software, such as 3-D anatomy and virtual dissection tools, or physical exam models and manikins for injection and venipuncture procedures, simulated catheterizations, or resuscitation training (see Figure 15.5). In many academic centers, individual departments might maintain their own simulation labs, just like computer labs or other student learning spaces. However, the models themselves and their use do not differ significantly between the various disciplines, and costs are generally higher to maintain independent sim labs.

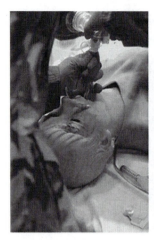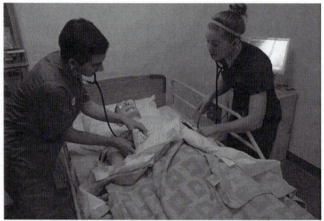

Figure 15.5. Examples of Medical Simulators: Two examples of manikins being used for medical simulation as part of a training exercise. The one on the left is an intubation model, and the image on the right shows nursing students in a simulated hospital room environment. Source: Photos from Flickr, from the Ohio National Guard and the University of Frasier Valley Nursing Program, used under Creative Commons license (www.flickr.com/photos/thenationalguard/3278079904/in/photostream/. www.flickr.com/photos/ufv/8241940521/).

Health sciences libraries have been known to have some simulators and anatomy models in their collections, but a move to centralize sim labs across academic health sciences campuses can lead administrators naturally to look to the library as a possible space for shared sim labs. Some libraries, such as the Hardin Library at the University of Iowa, manage a simulation center, www.lib.uiowa.edu/hardin/simulation/, as part of their service to the health sciences campus. Other libraries purchase and manage simulators as a part of their nonprint media collections. In terms of user space, most sim labs require small to medium-size simulation rooms where individual students or teams can work a specific simulation to satisfy the requirements of a class or exam. Sometimes these rooms may be mocked up to approximate the spaces where these procedures will be used after graduation—a patient room in a hospital, an exam table in an emergency room, or a doctor's office. These lab spaces, the equipment checkout and return policies, expert staffing, and acquisition of new simulators are some of the factors a library would need to consider in managing a sim lab, but it is a service very much in keeping with the scope of a health library's mission.

Points of Service

In any health sciences library, the provision of services to users is critical to the library's success. These services generally include assistance in locating and using information correctly, requesting articles and books from other sources, checking books and other materials in and out of the collection, and assisting with specialized library resources. Traditionally, these services have been provided at specific places in the library as points of service.

One of the most traditional such points of service is the circulation desk. The role of a circulation desk for a health sciences library is not significantly different from that of any other library. Generally, the circulation desk is the primary service point for the checking in and out of library books and other materials, but depending on the service model for the library, this desk may also be responsible for library and course reserves, interlibrary loan, security, stacks maintenance, and even some reference and instruction.

A common setup for such a desk is that of a bi-level counter, similar to a front desk at a hotel, where the staff assist patrons who are standing while they themselves are either seated or standing behind the desk. Counter surface area for a circulation desk needs to be sufficient to include a computer workstation and printer, phone, standard office supplies such as staplers and tape dispensers, and additional equipment specific to circulating materials, such as barcode scanners, magnetic sensitizer/desensitizers, or readers and pads for RFID-based systems. Many times the circulation desk also handles library announcements (via public address system) and financial transactions, which could require a cash register or credit card reader. Generally, circulation desks and counters tend to be large work areas, found near the library entrance(s), capable of accommodating a wide array of library functions from a single service point. Circulation services were discussed in Chapter 12.

The reference desk is another traditional library point of service that looks about the same in a health sciences library as it does in any other library. Reference desks, sometimes labeled information desks or similar, are intended to be a place where patrons can get their questions answered. In the past, the reference desk would often be accompanied by a small but vital reference collection, including dictionaries, encyclopedias, directories, and other reference materials. With the viability of the Internet as a primary reference tool, these collections have been winnowed down from occupying a few ranges of shelving, often to no more than a handful of directories and writing manuals tucked behind the desk. In fact, the ubiquity of the Internet has taken a toll on the traditional reference desk as a service point. Many users are unwilling to come to a specific desk to get help with their queries because they can often look up the information themselves on Google.

That being said, many reference librarians provide consultation with health sciences researchers and students, or assist clinicians in their immediate need for evidence-based health information. These services, not always tied to a specific desk or physical location in the library, make up part of the information services described in full in Chapters 7 and 8.

Some point-of-need services that the reference desk once provided have been transferred to others. A service desk in a health sciences library commons may take responsibility for assisting with logging onto computers, printing and scanning of materials, and many other routine activities. These services may also be blended into the circulation desk or other spaces in the library. Referring back to the concept of form following function, a service desk should not take up vital library space if it is not serving an equally vital role in the library service model. To this end, many health sciences libraries have abandoned the traditional reference desk in favor of other solutions. One such solution of note is the *single-point-of-service* model, which is discussed in-depth in Chapter 7.

Staff Workspaces

Health sciences library staff generally are found working in the library space itself, although this is not always the case (e.g., see embedded librarians and informationists, discussed in Chapter 9). Primarily, library staff workspaces take on similar appearances to other generalizable office configurations, with some significant exceptions.

Smaller libraries such as hospital libraries might only include a relative handful of offices to accommodate what is typically a much smaller staff. Larger libraries generally have to allocate more space for staff because of their larger operations.

The work that is done by a health sciences librarian requires a certain amount of space in which to accomplish that work. Librarians need computers on which to do their work; telephones for communicating with patrons and others; some file storage and bookshelves; and open, flat desk space for spreading out papers and materials for various projects. Librarians often meet with other people—patrons, administrators, and other librarians—in their offices and need to accommodate those visitors. The demands of a librarian for appropriate office space, and for offices of standard size in which to accomplish their work, are no less than any other office worker. Sometimes those demands are even greater.

That being said, offices do not come in "standard" sizes. Depending on the number of staff, the work being done, the anticipated traffic in and out of an office setting, and the dimensions of the furniture and equipment being placed, offices can range from being quite small (around sixty square feet) to quite large (several hundred square feet). General offices for individual librarians should be large enough to easily accommodate a good-sized work surface, a computer desk with workstation and printer, office chair, file cabinets, and at least two guest chairs (see Figure 15.6). A 120- to 140-square-foot office would provide a comfortable space to accommodate this furniture configuration. Additional furniture, such as a small worktable and chairs, a sofa or couch, or a wardrobe, would require even more square footage.

Shared offices, of course, put even greater demands on space but can also offer certain benefits. Because they can house different numbers of staff, shared offices are more flexible than individual offices. Office mates can share resources and therefore reduce overall expenses for outfitting that space. Printers, telephones, work surfaces, and even refrigerators and coffeemakers can be shared among office mates. Additionally, though, some workflows and processes can be improved by having staff members of the same department or operation sharing an office. For example, if staff members responsible for processing serials work in the same office, they can communicate and cross-train with each other more effectively. This can lead

Figure 15.6. Example of a Librarian Office: In this example, two furniture plans that occupy the same square footage are presented, alongside a photo of an office at the Schusterman Library, University of Oklahoma-Tulsa.

to improvements in overall work output as well as coverage when an employee is absent from work.

Furniture for a shared office space, as well as utilities such as electrical and network access, requires careful planning and forethought (see Figure 15.7). If electricity and network ports are inset in the office walls, desks will need to be arranged to face those walls, leaving center floor space unused. Alternatively, if office cubicle walls are to be installed in the center of a large shared office to provide some privacy for the individual staff desks, this may facilitate the need for either under-floor wiring or multiservice poles.

Shared offices in technical services operations are not uncommon, partly for the reasons outlined above. Because technical services in a health sciences library is often responsible for the processing of physical items, including books and journals, their offices need space to do this work. Processing space for a large academic health sciences library might include tables or countertops for spreading out and working with significant numbers of materials. Space might be needed for shipping and receiving, for book cleaning and binding repair, for scanning and printing of materials, and for working with oversized or historic or archival materials. The development of digitized objects—including cameras, stands, lighting, tripods, turntables, and various types of flatbed and planetary scanners—requires space for equipment and staff alike. Many times this equipment requires stable, flat workspaces of specific height to allow a staff member to work comfortably. For example, an interlibrary loan staff member who needs to do significant amounts of scanning will need the scanner to be on a stable work surface similar to a desk, low enough that he can sit in a chair and comfortably scan materials, but high enough to provide clearance for his legs. Sometimes this can be accomplished

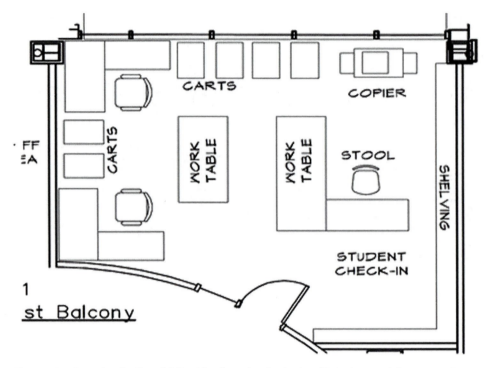

Figure 15.7. Example of a Shared Office: This floor plan for the Interlibrary Loan and Digitization Center, Schusterman Library, University of Oklahoma-Tulsa, exemplifies a shared workspace.

with existing furniture, but sometimes these library processes and equipment require custom-built furniture or cabinetry.

A conference room, appropriately sized for the library and its staff, can be used for meetings and workshops. Correctly outfitting and furnishing a conference room will largely depend on its intended functions. Most conference rooms should include at least a speakerphone for taking conference calls or teleconferences, but a facility that has significant need for meeting with people who are off-site should consider installing videoconferencing equipment instead. Videoconferencing equipment usually can handle standard telephonic communications as well. Many conference rooms have either a projector and screen or a large monitor for displaying PowerPoint slides, webinars, or other computer-based presentations. In many instances, a conference room can also double as a classroom, or even a place for staff to take their lunches and breaks. When a conference room is expected to serve multiple functions, it can sometimes be referred to as a multipurpose room. Standard conference room furniture often consists of a large conference-style table with seating all around the perimeter, whereas furniture for a multipurpose conference room will often be modular, with smaller tables being used to set the room in various ways. This may allow the room to be set as one

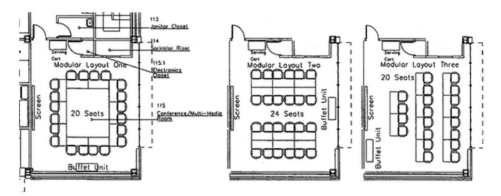

Figure 15.8. Multipurpose Room Furniture Plan: Examples of three different furniture layouts using the same furniture in the same space, including use as a general conference room, or for two smaller groups, or for instruction. Photo by author.

large shared table, in rows for a presentation or workshop, or in small groups for lunches and social events (see Figure 15.8).

Large hospital libraries might include shelving for collections, spaces for the users, offices for the staff, and even conference rooms or classrooms for meeting and instruction. But even the largest hospital library typically will be contained within the larger hospital facility, so many common utility spaces will be shared with other departments and staff (Bridges, 2009). The academic health sciences library, however, is often its own building, meaning that it will have features standard to other academic facilities, including bathrooms, mail rooms, storage rooms, entryways and atriums, utility closets, staff lounges, and sometimes even kitchens.

Responsibilities for these kinds of spaces vary depending on campus policies and are sometimes shared with the library staff. At times, an individual on the library staff is identified as **building manager**, who assumes responsibility for ordering maintenance and repair for the building, and its equipment and furnishings. The building manager issues work orders for electrical, painting, plumbing, carpentry, landscaping, air handling, and similar matters. This can be a large responsibility, and is traditionally tied to library administration or budget officers.

THE NEED FOR SPACE

The value of the physical health sciences library should be clearer following the discussions in this chapter. The need for spaces for library collections, for library patrons, and for the librarians and other staff members continues to hold true even in this era of electronically-dominant information. If librarians serve as a bridge between patrons and the information they need, surely it is reasonable to dedicate physical space toward that purpose.

However, this has not kept many health sciences libraries from making, or being forced to make, significant changes to their space in recent years. Several case studies in the literature point out that as reliance on printed materials has been reduced, and off-site options for storage and retrieval have been created, administration often looks to the library for opportunities to redevelop the space in ways that provide greater benefit to the institution. The hope is to approach these situations as opportunities for partnership with the institutional community.

Even under positive circumstances, these changes often are referred to as a "space crisis," suggesting that the situation has moved outside of the library's own control and requires extensive political and strategic finesse from the library leadership to maintain some say in the future use of the library's own space. Many times, the voices of librarians cannot be heard over the call to repurpose space for the betterment of the institution, which sometimes can lead to very undesirable outcomes for the library itself. For example, after having been forced into a lengthy and difficult process to refit its fourth floor as a classroom, the University of Arizona's Health Sciences Library discovered that the newly crafted space was not being used.

SUMMARY

In the final analysis, all health sciences libraries, whether hospital-based or part of an academic center, are not independent entities but are part of a larger institution. Taken in that context, any health library could face a crisis of space one day. If the premise that "form follows function" is accurate, then this becomes a reasonable concern as the need for large areas devoted

We learned that when faced with the loss of library space, it is best to make the most of it. Look for repurposing of space that will enhance the library's mission and continue to make the library a vibrant and highly visible place on campus. Some examples are learning commons, collaborative learning spaces, student study areas, and academic partnerships.

Rajia Tobia, AMLS, AHIP, director;
and Jonquil Feldman, MALS, AHIP,
associate director for public services,
University of Texas Health
Sciences Center, San Antonio Library

We were especially disappointed when, after two semesters, faculty members found other teaching spaces they preferred. The college considered renovating the space for other uses, but the high ceilings; four light switches for the entire floor; heating, ventilation, and air conditioning designed for stacks; and odd location (top floor of the building) made it an expensive space to renovate. For several years, the floor became an open, impromptu study space. However, noisy groups would bother others trying to find a quiet space to study. Recently, with some financial support from the College of Medicine, we have been able to add to the floor forty-eight six-foot-square study cubicles and more than twenty study tables, making it an attractive and, we hope, functional study space.

Gary Freiburger, MLS, director,
Arizona Health Sciences Library,
University of Arizona, Tucson

to print collections has understandably diminished over the past few years. If the sole function of a library is to warehouse printed materials, then spaces are likely to be taken from libraries for more important institutional needs, and probably should be.

However, if the function of a library is truly to provide connections and opportunities for learning and understanding, then the need for appropriate space becomes paramount, as does the need for strong collaborative ties with the library's institution and its leadership. The value of a library can only be enhanced through the thoughtful and balanced application of space, furniture, information, and technology; and the health sciences librarian should play a significant role in determining the purpose and planning of institutional spaces.

STUDY QUESTIONS

1. Can you name three challenges an administrator might make against the need for library space?
2. What is the difference between future-proofing and flexibility as it relates to space planning? Can you give three examples of future-proofing in a library space plan?
3. What does it mean when new construction is designed to be "sustainable?" What is the standard for sustainable architecture? What are the costs of sustainable design compared with standard construction?
4. Explain the need for collaborative work spaces within the health sciences library. What equipment or technologies might assist library users to collaborate on their work?

REFERENCES

Adamson, Martha C., and Brian P. Bunnett. 2002. "Planning Library Spaces to Encourage Collaboration." *Journal of the Medical Library Association* 90, no. 4 (October): 437–41.

American Institute of Architects. 2013. *The Value of an Architect.* www.aia.org/value/index.htm.

Bandy, Margaret, Jacqueline Donaldson Doyle, Anne Fladger et al. 2008. "Standards for Hospital Libraries 2007: Hospital Libraries Section Standards Committee." *Journal of the Medical Library Association* no. 96, no. 2: 162–69. doi:10.3163/1536-5050.96.2.162.

Bridges, Jane. 2009. "Moving a Hospital Library." *Medical Reference Services Quarterly* 28, no. 1 (January–March): 77–87. doi:10.1080/02763860802616094.

Ludwig, Logan. 2010. "Health Sciences Libraries Building Survey, 1999–2009." *Journal of the Medical Library Association* 98, no. 2 (April): 105–34. doi:10.3163/1536-5050.98.2.004.

Miller, Norm, Jay Spivey, and Andy Florance. 2008. *Does Green Pay Off?* City of Auburn Hills. www.auburnhills.org/departments/community_development/green_building_design/index.php.

USB Implementers Forum. 2013. *USB Developers Documents.* www.usb.org/developers/docs/.

U.S. Green Building Council. 2013. *LEED.* http://new.usgbc.org/leed.

U.S. National Library of Medicine. 2013. *DOCLINE Presentations*. www.nlm.nih.gov/docline/
    doclinepresentations.html.
Wikipedia. 2013a. "Furniture, Fixtures and Equipment (Accounting)." http://en.wikipedia
    .org/wiki/Furniture,_Fixtures_and_Equipment.
———. 2013b. "Modular Design." http://en.wikipedia.org/wiki/Modular_design.
———. 2013c. "Sustainable Architecture." http://en.wikipedia.org/wiki/Sustainable_architecture.
———. 2013d. "Value Engineering." http://en.wikipedia.org/wiki/Value_engineering.

CHAPTER 16

New Roles and New Horizons for Health Sciences Librarians and Libraries

Margaret E. Henderson

INTRODUCTION

Health care, technology, and education are changing dramatically, and health sciences librarians and libraries must continue to adapt to keep up with the needs of patrons. Health sciences librarians moved beyond the role of information gatekeeper even before web searching was commonplace, working as clinical medical librarians starting in the 1970s (Cimpl, 1985). In the 1990s, many libraries started moving to single-service desks staffed by paraprofessionals rather than reference librarians (Lubker et al., 2010; Moore, McGraw, and Shaw-Kokot, 2001; Murphy et al., 2008), leaving health sciences librarians more time to work on other new services inside and outside of the library building. These are only a few of the ways that health sciences librarians have adapted services to meet the changing needs of their patrons. In today's climate of change, it is not enough just to react and respond to those changes; health sciences librarians need to learn to spot trends, anticipate the needs of their patrons, and proactively find new roles that will help the mission of their organization. Health sciences libraries and librarians can stay relevant by linking goals and activities to the institutional goals for research, patient care, and education.

In order to take on new roles, reskilling (Auckland 2012), upskilling (Plutchak, 2012), and continuous professional development have become the norm for health sciences librarians; and library administrators need to factor time and money for continuing education into budgets. As T. Scott Plutchak noted in his 2011 Janet Doe lecture (2012), librarians need to focus on their skills and activities rather than on their libraries. Plutchak also says that health sciences librarians may be doing things that have never before been associated with a library. Once skills are separated from a specific place, be it a hospital or an academic institution, it is easier to consider new roles and services in a variety of locations. Health librarians also need to consider their nonlibrarian education and teaching as they look for new roles and activities to advance their organization's mission (Reed, 2009). Health sciences librarians need to be open to any niche that opens up as new technologies and new institutional goals bring to light possible roles for information professionals. Finally, professional development activities must be actively pursued if health sciences librarians are to be considered partners and colleagues of collaborators outside of the library (Gore, 2013a) and keep libraries and librarians relevant. This chapter will cover some of the new roles for health sciences librarians that have recently appeared in the literature and job announcements, and consider some new roles that are appearing when health sciences librarians collaborate with institutional leadership and initiate new roles.

TRANSFORMATION OF HEALTH SCIENCES LIBRARIANSHIP

In 2005, Lindberg and Humphreys predicted that the jobs and functions of health sciences librarians would change by 2015. This transformation already has begun.

> It is common to find librarians working as part of health care teams, writing grant proposals, serving on institutional review boards, working as bioinformatics database specialists within science departments, serving as faculty members in evidence-based medicine courses, and being involved in multilingual health-literacy programs and community partnerships. (Lindberg and Humphreys, 2005: 1069)

In academic libraries today, health sciences librarians are ahead of most librarians when it comes to being embedded in the research and teaching activities of their organizations. An Association of Research Libraries report suggests that liaison librarians will need to build teams of library experts to advance client research, and librarians need to divest themselves of some work to take on emerging roles (Jaguszewski and Williams, 2013). Specifically, Trend 2 in the report suggests a hybrid model combining the roles of liaison and functional specialist or expert. This role should sound familiar to anyone in health sciences libraries. Clinical informationists, consumer health specialists, and bioinformatics librarians all combine a subject specialty with outreach to a specific community or group that uses the library. Interestingly, the video interview that accompanies this report is with a clinical liaison librarian, indicating the advanced nature of health sciences librarianship (Association of Research Libraries, 2013).

Finding New Roles

The October 2013 issue of the *Journal of the Medical Library Association* (*JMLA*) was a special issue, "New Roles for Health Science Librarians." In the editorial for the issue, Elaine Martin (2013b) points out that health sciences librarians can be more than just the keepers of the literature at the end of the research; librarians can contribute to the entire scholarly communication process. Martin isn't just speaking futuristically. Under her leadership, the Lamar Soutter Library at the University of Massachusetts Medical School has accepted that the work of health sciences librarians is increasing in volume and becoming more complex and technology focused.

The library is removing the reference desk and moving to a consultation model of reference as more librarians work outside the library.

A pair of articles in the *JMLA* special issue looks at new roles for health sciences and biomedical librarians using a survey (Crum and Cooper, 2013) and a systematic review of the literature and job ads (Cooper and Crum, 2013). The systematic review identifies among the new roles various embedded roles: liaison librarian, informationist, clinical informationist, bioinformationist, public health informationist, and disaster information specialist. Among the new activities are participating in systematic reviews; finding and teaching emerging technologies (which includes user experience librarian); and involvement with continuing medical education, grants development, and data management (Cooper and Crum, 2013). This list is similar to the most common added or planned roles from the survey paper:

- support for systematic reviews
- support for social media
- analysis/enhancement of user experience
- help for faculty/staff with authorship issues
- help for institutional authors to comply with National Institutes of Health (NIH) public access policy
- implementation/support for researcher profiling/collaboration tools
- embedded librarian
- help for authors/department/administrators to comply with funder mandates

Many of these roles deal with the research enterprise of an institution, and Crum and Cooper note that hospital librarians are less likely than their academic counterparts to take on new roles.

Finding new ways to learn about what users need is one way to develop new roles for health sciences librarians. Symplur lists more than 104 Tweet Chats, www. symplur.com/healthcare-hashtags/tweet-chats/, in the health care stream, and many of these can provide service ideas. One such chat is covered in the blog *Emerging Technologies Librarian*, which summarizes the Healthcare Leaders group discussing the future of medical librarians (Anderson, 2013). Health care providers would like librarians who can provide reliable, accurate information via new technological formats, but who can also act as interpreters to digest data and communicate the information. Quite a few doctors mention that librarians should help patients with apps, and even help doctors and health care providers find evidence supporting the use of technology. Social media allow librarians a new level of interaction with users and can give insights into the world at large. Judiciously reading Twitter or blogs or even looking at the mobile apps pinned on the **Pinterest** board of a patient or doctor for later study could give health sciences librarians an idea of what must be done to help users get the information they need.

EXPANDED ROLES IN RESEARCH

The importance of information literacy and health information literacy for students and consumers has enhanced the importance of health sciences librarians in the curriculum. Many academic health sciences librarians have moved beyond basic orientation sessions and are teaching throughout the curriculum in schools of medicine, dentistry, nursing, pharmacy, and other health professions. For example, the Bibliothèque de la santé at Université de Montréal has numerous curriculum-integrated workshops throughout its biomedical undergraduate and graduate programs, as well as a specialized class in patents and genetic databases, virtual classes that have allowed the health sciences librarians to reach more than 3,500 attendees in the 2011–2012 academic year (Clairoux et al., 2013). Now, health sciences librarians need to focus on becoming part of the institutional research enterprise. Research grant dollars are an important part of the income of many institutions, and the prestige of a well-cited research program is sought after by many institutions. At his keynote talk at the 2013 Association of Southeastern Research Libraries (ASERL) Summertime Summit, Sayeed Choudhury, associate dean for research data management, Johns Hopkins University Sheridan Libraries, encouraged librarians to promote themselves as providing research support, not just a library service (Choudhury, 2013).

Reaching Out to the Research Community

In order to expand research services, some health sciences libraries have relied on the expertise of a specific librarian or hire properly qualified librarians or nonlibrarians to develop support for a particular research need. This is especially true for bioinformatics services, where an individual with a graduate degree and/or practical research experience is essential to providing good support. With the proper personnel and support, a bioinformatics program that provides training, consultation, and software access can be a key part of integrating a health sciences library into the research process (Li, Chen, and Clintworth, 2013). As seen in Chapter 10, health sciences librarians with data expertise can help with research data management teaching and data management plans for grants. Alternatively, health sciences librarians can evaluate the skills and expertise of existing staff and develop a suite of skills that can help researchers throughout the research life cycle. Effective marketing and outreach, and input from researchers, were found to be most important when the librarians at the Health Science Library, University of North Carolina at Chapel Hill, developed a research life cycle model for library services (Vaughan et al., 2013).

As large, interdisciplinary research teams realize that they do not know the literature of the multiple fields of research covered by a project and that they have data and information to organize from multiple experiments from different groups, they will begin to recognize the need for knowledge management. Health sciences librarians must have an understanding of the research process and recognize the importance of the research enterprise to their institution to help with these new projects. Health sciences librarians must also seek out opportunities to find and meet researchers. When University of Florida (UF) health sciences librarians learned that more than 2,000 UF researchers were on ResearchGate, www.researchgate.net, they began providing asynchronous reference services through the network. By using an existing social network for researchers, the health sciences librarians were able to answer questions and come in contact with more researchers at the university (Lessick et al., 2013). As Clifford Lynch has pointed out, it is necessary to go beyond pure research when deciding on services. Sometimes you need to work with real researchers to make progress (Lynch, 2014).

Informationists

The role of informationist is covered in Chapter 9, but the combination of specialized knowledge of a subject and information management, plus the model of paying for some part of the time of a health sciences librarian, should be considered further. Health sciences librarians working as informationists have been shown to be of great value at the National Institutes of Health (Grefsheim et al., 2010), so the National Library of Medicine awarded eight "NLM Administrative Supplements for Informationist Services in NIH-funded Research Projects" grants in 2012 to further promote health sciences librarians as informationists.

Early reports from the health sciences libraries that received the awards have been generally positive. Being integrated into a research team gives the informationist and the health sciences library opportunities to become more involved and valued by the research community at the institution. The informationists have found the work to include many new tasks that require specialized subject knowledge, such as creating a **data dictionary**. That, in turn, allowed all team members to discuss and request data efficiently (Gore, 2013b), recommending tools and **workflows** to help with the collection of data and specimens (Surkis et al., 2013), filtering and appraising studies (Goode and Anton, 2013), and helping with data management and curation (Federer, 2013; Hanson et al., 2013). More traditional tasks such as conducting systematic reviews, teaching citation management and sharing, and helping with publishing issues have also been found to be part of the informationist's role on a research team (Hasman, Berryman, and McIntosh, 2013). A concern was raised with balancing the amount of time needed for the research project with the other duties of the informationists (Whipple et al., 2013).

Greyson and colleagues (2013) describe the similar role of research-embedded health librarian (REHL). The REHL is defined as a librarian who "participates in a research team(s) rather than focusing on traditional library management and services and provides tailored, intensive information services to a health research team with which she or he is integrated" (Greyson et al., 2013: 288). REHLs help with current awareness, search the literature for a research team, and summarize and analyze the literature. REHLs also need to write and edit; and manage, extract, and analyze data. The REHL role depends heavily on the educational background and continuing education of the librarian.

The education and funding of informationists raises some interesting questions about the future of health sciences librarians and libraries. Should health sciences library managers work to get salaries for informationists and data librarians included in grants, or as separate grants? What will happen to the neutrality of libraries and library services if some people start paying to get more service? When researchers realize what informationists can do, will they hire them away from libraries? If research teams are asked to pay for informationists, will instructional teams be asked to pay for embedded librarians? Will informationists need to have dual degrees to be accepted on a research team? These questions do not have easy answers, but

THE MANY NAMES OF AN INFORMATIONIST

- bioinformationist
- clinical informationist
- clinical librarian
- clinical medical librarian
- embedded clinical librarian
- information specialist in context (ISIC)
- public health informationist
- research embedded health librarian (REHL)
- research informationist
- research librarian

health sciences librarians and library managers will need to consider these questions as they strive to provide the best possible service to their communities.

Research Assessment

Faculty members often turn to librarians for help when searching for citation counts to help with promotion and tenure documentation. The amount of author, journal, and institutional level citation information available to study impact at multiple levels of an organization has increased, making health librarians useful partners in assessment. Health sciences librarians can help by learning about all the new methods of assessment and collecting the various measures. Educating researchers and faculty about these methods of assessment is equally important and should start with teaching about author disambiguation. Faculty and researchers need to know how to set up profiles in multiple systems and how to link their profiles and output. If researchers and funders are going to value all output, as suggested by Heather Piwowar (2013), they will need to keep up with more than just citations to articles. Citations to online lab notebooks, patents, contributions to a software library, bookmarks to data sets from content-sharing sites such as Pinterest and **Delicious**, and other forms of scholarly impact will need to be followed, and the skills of health sciences librarians will be of great help.

Research on Health Sciences Libraries

Health librarians also need to conduct research to assess themselves and their libraries. Crum and Cooper (2013) found that analysis/enhancement of user experience was one of the roles that many libraries had planned for future positions. Hospital librarians, as mentioned above, need to be aware of the need to assess not only their services but also their value to the organization. The reduction in knowledge-based information access standards from the Joint Commission on Accreditation of Healthcare Organizations (Klein-Fedyshin, 2010); the space needs of new, lucrative hospital departments; and the increasing push for health care to be cost-effective have left little in the budget for hospital libraries. Health sciences librarians, like all librarians, must be aware of the need to advocate for their library and their role in the institution. One model, the contributions of library and information services (CLIS) approach, involves linking library services to the specific goals of the organization and finding measures of library services that will show the impact of the library on that goal, and hence to the organization (Abels, Cogdill, and Zach, 2004). The Medical Library Association (MLA) Research Section is using the questions developed from its Research Agenda study to organize groups to conduct systematic reviews that will give health librarians some evidence for their value (Eldredge et al., 2012).

CLINICAL LIBRARIANS AND HOSPITAL LIBRARIES

Academic health sciences libraries have had to give up certain traditional roles and services in order to focus on new goals (Allee et al., 2014), and the same is true for hospital libraries. Some hospital libraries have given up physical library space in favor of a virtual library, and have found that literature search requests have increased and librarians are now able to regularly participate in rounds, which has also increased

One of the most enjoyable parts of my job is working with researchers to help them enhance the impact of their work. Cathy Sarli and I included strategies for investigators to enhance the impact of their research as part of the Becker Model for Assessing the Impact of Research, https://becker.wustl.edu/impact-assessment. Repetition, consistency, and an awareness of the intended audience form the basis of most of the strategies, which are divided into three categories: Preparing for Publication, Dissemination, and Keeping Track of Your Research. The strategies provide guidelines to help individuals optimize discoverability of their research to enhance its visibility and impact. We teach workshops on campus and provide in-person consultation services for our investigators, enhancing the visibility of the library in the process.

Kristi L. Holmes, PhD, director,
Galter Health Sciences Library,
Northwestern University, Chicago, IL

search requests (Waddell, Harkness, and Cohen, 2014). Recent studies show the value of hospital libraries (Health Libraries Inc. and ALIA Health Libraries Australia, 2013; Marshall et al., 2013). But hospital librarians must consider doing their own research to prove their value to administrators and the institutional bottom line—and should think about new activities that can help secure the place of the hospital library in the institution (Kraft, 2013). One way to do this is for hospital librarians to explore opportunities to support research being done in hospitals. Any hospital that has or wants **Magnet Recognition Program** status (American Nurses Credentialing Center, 2013) needs to support nurses doing research. Colglazier and Henderson (2008) provided literature search support for nurses as well as setting up a collaborative workspace on the hospital intranet for the nurses to share ideas and work on research projects. The nurses of the Virginia Commonwealth University Health System (VCUHS) are always doing research to keep their Magnet status. The liaison librarian from the health sciences library works with the nurses to help them understand and improve the process of evidence-based practice at the bedside, and has developed classes and educational tools, including a Search Process Checklist, that takes them through all the steps involved in researching a problem. Approaching the chief nursing officer and members of the nursing research committee has allowed the liaison to reach nurses throughout the hospital (Brown, 2013).

Clinical librarians, whether they are based in a hospital library or an academic health sciences library, need to combine subject knowledge with information science, similar to informationists. Besides understanding clinical terminology, knowledge of electronic health records and other advances in clinical care are useful additions to the skills of clinical librarians. Helping with infobuttons or evidence-based practice by finding guidelines is a necessary skill for clinical librarians if they are to contribute to the clinical decision-making process (Hardiker, Dundon, and McGowan, 2012).

Hospital and clinical librarians should also make a point of learning about patient-centered outcomes research and the grants being awarded by the Patient Centered Outcomes Research Institute PCORI, www.pcori.org/, and other groups interested in outcomes research. Any medical center with a community engagement program or a focus on patient outcome measures will be interested in learning how its activities could be funded. Investigating free bibliographic citation tools to help hospital employees with reports, articles, and other projects, and providing instructional sessions or consultations on preparing bibliographies are other useful services. Traditional services, such as alerting administrators about funding opportunities or new articles; and expert services, such as systematic reviews on community health issues, can combine to make the hospital librarian invaluable to the organization.

COLLABORATIONS

As trusted partners, health librarians can help faculty, researchers, staff, students, and others find out about the different, sometimes competing, resources on campus or educate them about the best ways to measure the impact of their work. Even when the research office of an institution provides a listing of core facilities for researchers to use, often groups outside of the funded cores can help with research or teaching.

Collaborative Workspaces

Departments have become siloed at many institutions, and the library is often the commonality, giving librarians the chance

When the University of Virginia established a Bioinformatics Core in late 2011, our library had several conversations with the incoming director about enhancing our support for PIs and other researchers. One idea generated was to provide researchers with a technology-enabled collaborative workspace. Most of the library's computing environment was designed to support curricular needs, and we wanted to differentiate a space for research. For us, it was a symbolic step in stating that this library is interested in providing deeper research support services, and we are willing to invest in that future. As suspected, the BioConnector Collaboration Environment is heavily used by a variety of patrons for purposes that support not only the research mission, but clinical and educational missions as well.

Bart Ragon, associate director for knowledge integration, research, & technology, Claude Moore Health Science Library, University of Virginia, Charlottesville

to pull groups together. The library as a place can help as well, bringing collaborators together in a neutral place with the technology and collaboration tools that will facilitate research partnerships, or housing tools that multiple groups on campus need, such as simulation models or large-format printers and specialized software. Health sciences libraries can also provide hands-on experience with new technology and software for users who want to experiment before buying. Laptops and iPads are on loan in many libraries, with a selection of apps for testing. Computers with media software or statistical packages and 3-D cameras make it easy for students, researchers, and health care workers to create presentations and reports or try new things without purchasing their own equipment.

The health sciences library can also act as a location for equipment that multiple groups need. Housing a distance education room or computer lab that can be booked by other groups is common, but it can be especially useful for hospital groups when patient services that bring in revenue for a hospital take over the training room in a hospital. Health sciences libraries that house anatomy models or collaborative equipment in their study rooms can make these more visible and available by providing a room scheduler on the library website that includes room contents so students and researchers know which room to book.

Collaborations with Campus Partners

The clinical and translational science program is a good place to form partnerships at a university, but health sciences librarians must seek out other opportunities and institutional gaps that will allow them to become integrated into the institutional community. The Medical Center Library at Duke University, for example, helps manage compliance with the NIH Public Access Policy for the university.

Other funder or government requirements can act as a foot in the door for health sciences libraries. The Medical Library Association has a special interest group for librarians who work with the Institutional Animal Care and Use Committee (IACUC) at their institutions, and many librarians participate in Institutional Review Boards (IRB) covering research on human subjects.

As the manager for the Hardin Library Simulation Center, I keep track of the different curricular uses of the models housed in the library and keep our list of simulation centers on campus as up-to-date as possible. In addition, I serve as the head of our simulation center advisory committee, which still includes representatives from each of the health sciences colleges on campus. This advisory committee discusses issues surrounding the use of simulation to support health sciences education and interprofessional education goals as well as issues related to the models and simulators housed at Hardin Library.

Day-to-day responsibilities for managing the Hardin Library Simulation Center include the creation and modification of policies and procedures regarding the delivery and circulation of the models the library houses. I am also responsible for ensuring that the models are clean, well maintained, and not missing consumables, such as silicone oil to lubricate different parts, catheters, syringes, and so forth. This means that I have to be familiar to a certain extent with how the models function.

Amy Blevins, clinical education librarian,
Hardin Library for the Health Science,
University of Iowa, Iowa City

Librarian oversight of background searching for IACUC or IRB protocols is one way to become integrated into the research community of an institution. Data management plans and sharing mandates from the NIH and National Science Foundation (NSF), and data and publication access mandated by the Office of Science and Technology Policy (OSTP) in February 2013, allow opportunities for health sciences librarians to insert themselves into the research enterprise of an institution that receives government funding. Other funding agencies will soon have similar open access or sharing requirements that health sciences librarians can help with if they learn about these mandates and plan for services that will help researchers comply.

The Taubman Library at the University of Michigan has taken collaboration beyond the institutional or national level. With the new Global Health program, the Taubman Library brings together global health units throughout the health sciences campus by helping with information resources, cultivating partnerships, finding grant and funding opportunities, helping with research, and collaborating with faculty to lessen health disparities (Allee et al., 2014).

Through informal discussions with the director of the Duke Office of Clinical Research (DOCR), I obtained an eRA Commons account in late 2012. Soon after, we learned that NIH planned to enforce the public access policy and realized that the library could have a role in supporting compliance. I have access to download reports from the NIH Compliance Monitor and do so periodically. We have formed a team of librarians who are trained in the process of ensuring compliance. Together, we have notified more than 700 of our PIs and guided our faculty from a compliance rate of 74 percent to 93 percent in six months.

Emily Mazure, biomedical research liaison librarian, Duke Medical Center Library, Durham, NC

ALTERNATIVE ROLES AND ACTIVITIES

Health Organizations

Working for a health association or professional organization library outside of the usual hospital or academic library has always been an option for health sciences librarians, but a recent survey found those that positions are changing as well (Dunikowski et al., 2013). The number and complexity of services in association libraries are increasing, and they support the association in nontraditional ways as well. Archives, publications support, advocacy, records management, and website help are the most reported services.

Institutional Archives

Involvement with the institutional archives offers another opportunity for health sciences librarians to expand their roles within the institution. One project at the Eskind Biomedical Library at Vanderbilt University Medical Center (VUMC) aligned the library's strategic plan with the community-centered goals of the institution to create the website "VUMC Through Time: A Photographic Archive" (Giuse et al., 2013). The website team collaborated with the alumni, public affairs, and news offices, and members of the community can add photos and comments, increasing the community awareness of the library. The Rex Healthcare Medical Library in Raleigh, North Carolina, created a digital archive of its hospital and nursing school (Sorrell and Ender, 2011). Ready-made PDFs and PowerPoint slides make it easy for interested staff to include historical references in their presentations.

Expanding Opportunities for Health Science Librarians

Health sciences librarians should also be aware of positions outside of the health sciences library, especially those that require knowledge and skills in education, data, open access, institutional repositories, or scholarly communication. These areas span the institution; and because health sciences and biomedical research is at the forefront in many of these areas, health sciences librarians are well positioned to move to more global positions. Health sciences librarians direct continuing education in hospitals; hold data management, assessment, or education positions in the clinical and translational science programs at universities; have become directors of information technology for an institution; and have moved into higher administration positions such as associate vice president for academic affairs in an academic health sciences center.

THE CHANGING HEALTH SCIENCES LIBRARY ORGANIZATION

The Taubman Library at the University of Michigan (Allee et al., 2014), like the Lamar Soutter Library (Martin 2013a), has made some major changes in staffing and library organization to reflect the new roles

As information resources supervisor for the Oncology Nursing Society, I provide information services to staff—especially those in the education, publishing, and research departments—and members (currently more than 35,000), especially those who serve on project teams such as our Putting Evidence Into Practice (PEP) or edit/write for the books and journals we publish.

Mark Vrabel, information resources supervisor, Oncology Nursing Society, Pittsburgh, PA

In 2012, I was promoted from a middle management position in a health sciences library to assistant director of university libraries within a large ARL library system. To make that transition, I certainly called on my knowledge of librarianship and information science, and had innovated in some strategic areas. However, a data-driven orientation, knowledge of research metrics, or technological aptitude pale in comparison to the skills derived from **emotional intelligence**. Having high emotional intelligence will distinguish you in a pool of applicants, ensure a smooth transition into a new environment, and allow you optimally to perform your new job with aplomb.

Dean Hendrix, assistant director of university libraries, University at Buffalo, The State University of New York, Buffalo

of health librarians. The position title of nonsupervisory librarian involved in academic, research, and clinical activities has been changed to "informationist." In some ways, it doesn't matter what terms are used to describe a position, because the positions all require more expertise than can be crammed into a two-year master's program, which is one of the reasons multiple institutions are now offering fellowship programs. Clinical research teams responding to an NIH survey viewed science and medicine education as key to the preparation of informationists (Grefsheim et al., 2010). In addition to the subject background of health science librarians is the need to respond to changes in education, health care, and technology. AAMC objectives include lifelong learning for medical students (AAMC and Medical School Objectives Project, 1998) so it is not unreasonable to expect the same of the librarians who are teaching and helping health care students, doctors, nurses, and the other members of the health care team.

Health sciences librarians and libraries can learn from health care organizations that have had to become learning organizations to keep up with the changes in electronic health records (EHRs) and new health care expectations because of the Affordable Care Act (ACA). Kaiser Permanente leaders developed a system for continuous improvement in their hospital systems (Schilling et al., 2011) by creating a learning organization that includes six building blocks to make a transition:

1. real-time sharing of meaningful performance data
2. formal training in problem-solving methodology
3. workforce engagement and informal knowledge sharing
4. leadership structures, beliefs, and behaviors
5. internal and external benchmarking
6. technical knowledge sharing

These building blocks help improve team learning; build a shared vision; practice learning at personal, work unit, and organizational levels; and build and share knowledge throughout the organization. Workforce engagement and uptake of technologies will bring challenges, but the organization can move forward, knowing that a learning organization has the capability to improve.

Health sciences library managers need to look outside of the library for direction. A survey of health sciences library directors found that libraries need to align with the institutional mission, and librarians need to "become more involved in the fabric of the institution so that they can anticipate where unique skill sets might be required to foster an evidence-rich environment" (McGowan, 2012: 44). Additional credentialing or continuing education beyond the MLS may be needed to keep up with new institutional goals and the constant changes in technology and increases in available information. Membership in the Academy of Health Information Professionals (AHIP) is one way health librarians can show their commitment to professional development.

SUMMARY

It is easy to get caught up in the excitement of new roles and interesting research ventures; but without administrative support, taking on new activities can bring problems. Cox, Verbann, and Sen saw problems with the many new roles librarians are being asked to fill with all the changes in health and education: "After all, librarians are already busy. Liaison librarians, for example, have a range of existing roles, such as in collection development, information literacy training, enquiry handling, marketing, committee work, informal networking and management roles" (2012). And Jake Carlson (2013), looking at the role of librarians in data services, finds that "libraries must reconsider their organizational structures and cultures to be able to take on data management and other innovative service areas successfully." Health sciences library managers must find a balance between the time needed for extra training and professional development and the new and existing roles that health sciences librarians are being asked to take on to support their organizations.

Future roles for health sciences librarians offer no shortage of ideas. The challenge will be to find managers and administrators who are willing to see a larger role for health sciences librarians and libraries in the research, clinical, and educational enterprise of their institutions. Health sciences librarians will need to be flexible and curious in order to fill the new roles that arise as education and research change in response to technological and societal pressures. Two years of postgraduate education will not be enough for librarians to take on the emerging roles in health libraries. Graduates will need to come into library science programs with health science-related degrees and experience; or they will need to be willing to pursue additional subject-related continuing education classes; or they may choose to work as fellows or interns for one or two years to acquire the skills necessary to fill the new roles health sciences librarians are taking on. Professional development will be critical for all health sciences librarians because of advances in technology, educational models, and health sciences research. All health sciences librarians must learn to live in a world of constant change.

STUDY QUESTIONS

1. Which new roles for health sciences librarians would you pursue if you were a library director, and how would you introduce those roles to your existing staff?
2. Which professional development activities would you recommend for health sciences librarians who want to take on new roles?
3. What research could hospital or clinical librarians conduct to show the value of their services?
4. Study the organizational structure of an academic institution, research organization, or hospital, and list the groups and departments that could use or support health sciences librarians.

REFERENCES

AAMC and Medical School Objectives Project. 1998. *Report 1: Learning Objectives for Medical Student Education: Guidelines for Medical Schools.* https://members.aamc.org/eweb/upload/Learning%20Objectives%20for%20Medical%20Student%20Educ%20Report%20I.pdf.

Abels, Eileen G., Keith W. Cogdill, and Lisl Zach. 2004. "Identifying and Communicating the Contributions of Library and Information Services in Hospitals and Academic Health Sciences Centers." *Journal of the Medical Library Association* 92, no. 1 (January): 46–55.

Allee, Nancy J., Jane Blumenthal, Karen Jordan et al. 2014. "One Institution's Experience in Transforming the Health Sciences Library of the Future." *Medical Reference Services Quarterly* 33, no. 1 (January–March): 1–16.

American Nurses Credentialing Center. 2013. "ANCC Magnet Recognition Program." www.nursecredentialing.org/Magnet.aspx.

Anderson, Patricia F. 2013. "Hashtags of the Week (HOTW): Healthcare Leaders on the Future of Medical Librarians (Week of September 2, 2013)." *Emerging Technologies Librarian* (blog). http://etechlib.wordpress.com/2013/09/06/hashtags-of-the-week-hotw-healthcare-leaders-on-the-future-of-medical-librarians-week-of-september-2-2013/.

Association of Research Libraries. 2013. *New Roles for New Times: Transforming Liaison Roles in Research Libraries with Jonathan Koffel.* www.youtube.com/watch?v=Y0cxdS-EYpU&feature=share&list=UU81MgM4v-scw34Q6zLWYCwg.

Auckland, Mary. 2012. *Reskilling for Research: An Investigation into the Role and Skills of Subject and Liaison Librarians Required to Effectively Support the Evolving Information Needs of Researchers.* Research Libraries UK (RLUK). www.rluk.ac.uk/files/RLUK%20Re-skilling.pdf.

Brown, Roy. Personal communication. 2013.

Carlson, Jake R. 2013. "Opportunities and Barriers for Librarians in Exploring Data: Observations from the Data Curation Profile Workshops." *Journal of eScience Librarianship* 2, no. 2: article 2.

Choudhury, Sayeed. 2013. "Open Access & Data Management Are Do-Able through Partnerships." Keynote speaker at Association of Southeastern Research Libraries, Summertime Summit, Atlanta, ASERL, August 6.

Cimpl, K. 1985. "Clinical Medical Librarianship: A Review of the Literature." *Bulletin of the Medical Library Association* 73, no. 1 (January): 21–28.

Clairoux, Natalie, Sylvie Desbiens, Monique Clar, Patrice Dupont, and Monique St-Jean. 2013. "Integrating Information Literacy in Health Sciences Curricula: A Case Study from Quebec." *Health Information and Libraries Journal* 30, no. 3: 201–11. doi:10.1111/hir.12025; 10.1111/hir.12025.

Colglazier, Merle, and Margaret Henderson. 2008. "Helping Nurses Reach for Magnet Status: Facilitating Collaboration and Information Sharing." Poster presented at the Mid-Atlantic Chapter of the Medical Library Association, Morgantown, WV, October 20–22.

Cooper, I. Diane, and Janet A. Crum. 2013. "New Activities and Changing Roles of Health Sciences Librarians: A Systematic Review, 1990–2012." *Journal of the Medical Library Association* 101, no. 4 (October): 268–77.

Cox, Andrew, Eddy Verbaan, and Barbara Sen. 2012. "Upskilling Liaison Librarians for Research Data Management." *Ariadne: A Web & Print Magazine of Internet Issues for Librarians & Information Specialists* 70. www.ariadne.ac.uk/issue70/cox-et-al.

Crum, Janet A., and I. Diane Cooper. 2013. "Emerging Roles for Biomedical Librarians: A Survey of Current Practice, Challenges, and Changes." *Journal of the Medical Library Association* 101, no. 4 (October): 278–86.

Dunikowski, Lynn G., Aleta C. Embrey, Warren G. Hawkes, Jean E. Riedlinger, Marian G. Taliaferro, and Pamela M. Van Hine. 2013. "The Health Association Libraries Section Survey: Finding Clues to Changing Roles." *Journal of the Medical Library Association* 101, no. 4 (October): 318–22.

Eldredge, Jonathan D., Marie T. Ascher, Heather N. Holmes, and Martha R. Harris. 2012. "The New Medical Library Association Research Agenda: Final Results from a Three-Phase Delphi Study." *Journal of the Medical Library Association: JMLA* 100, no. 3 (July): 214–18. doi:10.3163/1536-5050.100.3.012; 10.3163/1536-5050.100.3.012.

Federer, Lisa. 2013. "The Librarian as Research Informationist: A Case Study." *Journal of the Medical Library Association* 101, no. 4 (October): 298–302.

Giuse, Nunzia B., Shelia V. Kusnoor, Taneya Y. Koonce et al. 2013. "Strategically Aligning a Mandala of Competencies to Advance a Transformative Vision." *Journal of the Medical Library Association* 101, no. 4 (October): 261–67.

Goode, Victoria H., and Blair Anton. 2013. "Welch Informationist Collaboration with the Johns Hopkins Medicine Department of Radiology." *Journal of eScience Librarianship* 2, no. 1: article 5. doi:http://dx.doi.org/10.7191/jeslib.2013.1033.

Gore, Sally A. 2013a. "The Talented Mr. Ripley in the Library with the Candlestick." *A Librarian by Any Other Name* (blog). http://librarianhats.net/2013/09/25/mr_ripley/.

———. 2013b. "A Librarian by Any Other Name: The Role of the Informationist on a Clinical Research Team." *Journal of eScience Librarianship* 2, no. 1: article 6. doi:http://dx.doi.org/10.7191/jeslib.2013.104.

Grefsheim, Suzanne F., Susan C. Whitmore, Barbara A. Rapp, Jocelyn A. Rankin, Rex R. Robison, and Candace C. Canto. 2010. "The Informationist: Building Evidence for an Emerging Health Profession." *Journal of the Medical Library Association* 98, no. 2 (April): 147–56.

Greyson, Devon, Soleil Surette, Liz Dennett, and Trish Chatterley. 2013. "'You're Just One of the Group When You're Embedded': Report from a Mixed-Method Investigation of the Research-Embedded Health Librarian Experience." *Journal of the Medical Library Association* 101, no. 4 (October): 287–97.

Hanson, Karen L., Theodora A. Bakker, Mario A. Svirsky, Arlene C. Neuman, and Neil Rambo. 2013. "Informationist Role: Clinical Data Management in Auditory Research." *Journal of eScience Librarianship* 2, no. 1: article 7. doi:http://dx.doi.org/10.7191/jeslib.2013.1030.

Hardiker, Nicholas R., Joanna Dundon, and Jessie McGowan. 2012. "Changing Technology to Meet Clinicians' Information Needs." In *Changing Roles and Contexts for Health Library and Information Professionals*, edited by Alison Brettle and Christine Urquhart, 39–50. London: Facet Publishing.

Hasman, Linda, Donna Berryman, and Scott McIntosh. 2013. "NLM Informationist Grant—Web Assisted Tobacco Intervention for Community College Students." *Journal of eScience Librarianship* 2, no. 1: article 8.

Health Libraries Inc and ALIA Health Libraries Australia. 2013. *Worth Every Cent and More: An Independent Assessment of the Return on Investment of Health Libraries in Australia.* Canberra ACT, Australian Library and Information Association. www.alia.org.au/sites/default/files/Worth-Every-Cent-and-More-FULL-REPORT.pdf.

Jaguszewski, Janice M., and Karen Williams. 2013. *New Roles for New Times: Transforming Liaison Roles in Research Libraries.* Association of Research Libraries. www.arl.org/storage/documents/publications/NRNT-Liaison-Roles-final.pdf.

Klein-Fedyshin, Michele. 2010. "It Was the Worst of Times, It was the Best of Times: Positive Trends Influencing Hospital Libraries." *Journal of the Medical Library Association* 98, no. 3 (July): 196–99.

Kraft, Michelle. 2013. "Australian Healthcare Orgs Gain $9 for Every $1 Spent on Their Health Libraries." Abstract. http://kraftylibrarian.com/?p=2509.

Lessick, Susan, Eric Rumsey, Donald S. Pearson et al. 2013. "Moving beyond the Bookshelves." *Journal of the Medical Library Association* 101, no. 4 (October): 239–43.

Li, Meng, Yi-Bu Chen, and William A. Clintworth. 2013. "Expanding Roles in a Library-Based Bioinformatics Service Program: A Case Study." *Journal of the Medical Library Association* 101, no. 4 (October): 303–9.

Lindberg, Donald A. B., and Betsy L. Humphreys. 2005. "2015—the Future of Medical Libraries." *New England Journal of Medicine* 352, no. 11: 1067–70.

Lubker, Irene M., Margaret E. Henderson, Catherine S. Canevari, and Barbara A. Wright. 2010. "Refocusing Reference Services Outside the Library Building: One Library's Experience." *Medical Reference Services Quarterly* 29, no. 3 (July–September): 218–28.

Lynch, Clifford. 2014. "The Next Generation of Challenges in the Curation of Scholarly Data." In *Research Data Management: Practical Strategies for Information Professionals*, edited by Joyce M. Ray, 395–408. West Lafayette, IN: Purdue University Press.

Marshall, Joanne G., Julia Sollenberger, Sharon Easterby-Gannett et al. 2013. "The Value of Library and Information Services in Patient Care: Results of a Multisite Study." *Journal of the Medical Library Association* 101, no. 1 (January): 38–46.

Martin, Elaine R. 2013a. "The Four R's: The Future of the Library (Reject, Rethink, Redo, Rejuvenate: A New Model for Academic Health Sciences Libraries)." SlideShare presentation. www.slideshare.net/ElaineMartin1/social-media-slides-4-rs.

———. 2013b. "Shaping Opportunities for the New Health Sciences Librarian." *Journal of the Medical Library Association* 101, no. 4 (October): 252–53.

McGowan, J. J. 2012. "Tomorrow's Academic Health Sciences Library Today." *Journal of the Medical Library Association* 100, no. 1 (January): 43–46.

Moore, Margaret E., Kathleen A. McGraw, and Julia Shaw-Kokot. 2001. "Preparing Staff to Work at a Single Service Desk." *Medical Reference Services Quarterly* 20, no. 1 (Spring): 79–86.

Murphy, Beverly, Richard A. Peterson, Hattie Vines et al. 2008. "Revolution at the Library Service Desk." *Medical Reference Services Quarterly* 27, no. 4 (Winter): 379–93.

Piwowar, Heather. 2013. "Altmetrics: Value all Research Products." *Nature* 493, no. 7431: 159.

Plutchak, T. S. 2012. "Breaking the Barriers of Time and Space: The Dawning of the Great Age of Librarians." *Journal of the Medical Library Association* 100, no. 1: 10–19.

Reed, Andrea D. 2009. "Skill Check: Utilizing Your Nontraditional Library Education." *Info Career Trends*. March 2. http://lisjobs.com/career_trends/?p=523.

Schilling, Lisa, James W. Dearing, Paul Staley, Patti Harvey, Linda Fahey, and Francesca Kuruppu. 2011. "Kaiser Permanente's Performance Improvement System, Part 4: Creating a Learning Organization." *Joint Commission Journal on Quality and Patient Safety/Joint Commission Resources* 37, no. 12: 532–43.

Sorrell, Melanie, and Deniz Ender. 2011. "Rex History Project: Looking Back to Capitalize on Our Progress." Poster presented at the Mid-Atlantic Chapter of the Medical Library Association, Richmond, VA, October.

Surkis, Alisa, Aileen McCrillis, Richard McGowan et al. 2013. "Informationist Support for a Study of the Role of Proteases and Peptides in Cancer Pain." *Journal of eScience Librarianship* 2, no. 1: article 9.

Vaughan, K. T., Barrie E. Hayes, Rachel C. Lerner et al. 2013. "Development of the Research Lifecycle Model for Library Services." *Journal of the Medical Library Association* 101, no. 4: 310–14.

Waddell, Stacie, Amy Harkness, and Mark L. Cohen. 2014. "The Road to Virtual: The Sauls Memorial Virtual Library's Journey." *Medical Reference Services Quarterly* 33, no. 1 (January–March): 92–101.

Whipple, Elizabeth C., Jere D. Odell, Rick K. Ralston, and Gilbert C. Liu. 2013. "When Informationists Get Involved: The CHICA-GIS Project." *Journal of eScience Librarianship* 2, no. 1: article 10. doi:http://dx.doi.org/10.7191/jeslib.2013.1035.

Glossary

AACR2: Anglo-American Cataloguing Rules Second Edition—the second edition of a national cataloging code designed for use in the construction of catalogs and other lists in general libraries of all sizes. First published in 1967 as the *Anglo American Cataloguing Rules*, it is published jointly by the American Library Association, the Canadian Library Association, and the Chartered Institute of Library and Information Professionals in the UK. (Adapted from *Wikipedia*)

Active learning—instruction styles that focus the responsibility of learning on the learner. Often includes group-based, learner-centered activities that work to solve complex, realistic problems and provide students the opportunity to talk and listen, read, write, and reflect.

Administrative metadata—metadata used in managing and administering information resources (e.g., location or donor information). Includes rights and access information, data on the creation and preservation of the digital object. http://library.csun.edu/mwoodley/DublinCore/glossary.shtml.

Affordable Care Act—a federal law (complete title, the Patient Protection and Affordable Care Act) passed in 2010 designed to reform existing health insurance rules and expand access to coverage through a mix of mandates and subsidies for individuals and employers, as well as insurance market regulations. Also known as "Obamacare."

Aisle width—the space between rows of shelves, in inches. Minimally, the aisle width must be thirty-six inches to accommodate wheelchair access according to the Americans with Disabilities Act.

Algorithm—a set of steps that are followed in order to solve a mathematical problem or to complete a computer process. (Merriam-Webster online)

Altmetrics—alternative metrics, or "altmetrics," represent new ways to measure engagement with research products. (esciencelibrary)

Americans with Disabilities Act (ADA)—enacted into federal law in 1990, the act establishes a clear and comprehensive prohibition of discrimination based on disability. Title III of the ADA addresses accommodations in public facilities, including libraries.

Approval plan—refers to a customized profile of subject areas, publisher and format preferences, and depth of collection (e.g., standard, research, etc.) in each subject area.

Assigning identifiers to data—assigning identifiers to data helps to provide a method of persistent identification of research data collections and data sets that are global, standardized, and widely used in the digital environment. (esciencelibrary)

Association of Academic Health Sciences Libraries (AAHSL)—an association composed of academic health sciences libraries whose medical schools hold member or associate member status in the Association of American Medical Colleges.

Asynchronous reference—a digital or virtual reference transaction that does not occur in real time. E-mail reference would be asynchronous, as the patron is unlikely to expect an immediate reply. Text reference would likely be asynchronous.

Authority control—a process that organizes library catalog and bibliographic information using a single, distinct name for each topic. These one-of-a-kind headings are applied consistently throughout the catalog, and they work with other organizing data such as linkages and cross-references. (*Wikipedia*)

Authority record—an indexical record of all decisions made by catalogers in a given library or consortium that catalogers consult when making or revising decisions about headings. The records contain documentation about sources used to establish a particular preferred heading, and may contain information discovered while researching the heading that may be useful. (*Wikipedia*)

Back files—older editions of journals. Digital back files can be purchased to allow a library to save space.

Benchmarking—a method of comparing specific measures of performance to determine how good one is compared with another.

BIBCO (Monographic Bibliographic Record Program of the PCC)—BIBCO participants contribute bibliographic records to international databases, meeting or exceeding the elements of the BIBCO Standard Record. BIBCO records include headings backed by complete authority work, both descriptive and subject. (Library of Congress)

Bibliographic control—the process by which information resources are described so that users are able to find and select that information resource (also known as information organization or bibliographic organization). (*Wikipedia*)

Bibliographic instruction—the systematic effort to teach a set of principles or search strategies relating to the library, its collections or services, using predetermined methods in order to accomplish a predefined set of objectives.

Big science—large-scale projects requiring significant funding, often at the national or international level, conducted by teams of researchers in pursuit of a major goal. Examples of big science include NASA missions to the Moon and Mars, the Human Genome Project, the War on Cancer, and large-scale multi-institutional epidemiological studies involving thousands of study participants.

Bioinformatics—the use of computational methods to solve biological problems, very often at the molecular (DNA, RNA, protein) level. The National Center for Biotechnology Information provides numerous freely available, online molecular databases and analysis tools that can be used to support bioinformatics. A number of biomedical libraries provide outreach to molecular and other basic science researchers.

Blocking map—in space planning, a rough document that visually describes spaces by their proposed functions, defining those spaces and general foot traffic in a library without requiring details and specifications about the space being used.

Brandeis model—see "tiered reference service."

Building manager—an individual library staff member who has responsibility for maintenance and repair of the building, including equipment and furniture.

Capacity—the physical volume and mass of materials being shelved by a library. May also refer to the ability of a library's shelving system to accommodate those materials.

Case-based learning—an instructional format in which students receive a clinical case and reading assignment prior to class, then use class time for an interactive case discussion, with the instructor acting as a guide and facilitator.

Classification scheme—in metadata, a classification scheme is a hierarchical arrangement of kinds of things (classes) or groups of kinds of things. Typically, it is accompanied by descriptive information of the classes or groups. A classification scheme is intended to be used for an arrangement or division of individual objects into the classes or groups. The classes or groups are based on characteristics the objects (members) have in common. (*Wikipedia*)

Closed stacks—books and other items that are not available for viewing or browsing by the public, limiting retrieval to professionally trained library staff. (*Wikipedia*)

Collaborative media furniture—furniture with electronic components integrated into their design to optimize the work of small groups of library users.

Compact mobile shelving—also known as high-density shelving, a system of shelving ranges that are installed on rails and can be moved, thereby using less floor space than standard freestanding shelves.

Compact stacks—special shelving units that move on tracks to allow access. These stacks can be closed, so they save space and allow for a higher volume of items to be stored in a small space.

Competency—demonstrated knowledge or skill needed to perform a certain function.

Computerized physician order entry (CPOE)—electronic entry of medical practitioner instructions for the treatment of patients (particularly hospitalized patients) under the practitioner's care. (*Wikipedia*)

Concurrent user—refers to the number of patrons who can access the same platform, database, material (e.g., book or article) at the same time.

CONSER: Cooperative Serials Program of the PCC—an authoritative source for bibliographic records, documentation, and training materials for serials cataloging. CONSER members work together in an atmosphere of collegiality and trust to promulgate standards related to serials and are a voice for serials in the library community. (Library of Congress)

Consortium—an agreement, combination, or group (as of companies) formed to undertake an enterprise beyond the resources of any one member. (Merriam-Webster online)

Consultations—scheduled or unscheduled one-on-one meetings between a library patron and librarian in order to meet an information need or instruct on the use of library and information resources.

Consumer health information service (CHIS)—any information service specifically focused on the provision of information about health and health care services for lay users. This type of service is often provided by a library or library network, but also by pharmaceutical companies, nonprofits, health care systems, and insurance companies, among others.

Controlled vocabulary—a carefully selected list of words and phrases that are used to tag units of information (document or work) so they may be more easily retrieved by a search. (*Wikipedia*)

Copy cataloging—adaptation of a preexisting bibliographic record . . . to fit the characteristics of the item in hand, with modifications to correct obvious errors and minor adjustments to reflect locally accepted cataloging practice. (Reitz, ODLIS)

Course-integrated instruction—multiple library instruction sessions over a single course.

Course management system (CMS)—a software application for the administration, documentation, tracking, reporting, and delivery of e-learning education courses or training programs. (*Wikipedia*)

Critical appraisal—the third step in both the evidence-based practice (EBP) and evidence-based library and information practice (EBLIP) processes when decision makers sort through the best available evidence to determine which evidence has greatest applicability and highest quality.

Curriculum-integrated programming—multiple instruction sessions over a course of study or degree program. The "gold standard" of library instruction.

Data—data used for research can be defined as the recorded factual material that is commonly accepted in the scientific community as information that is required to validate research findings. (esciencelibrary)

Data citation—provides attribution to research data sources to allow for easier access to research data within journals and on the Internet. (esciencelibrary)

Data curation profiles—completed data curation profiles can be searched to provide research data management reference assistance to librarians or researchers looking for information or prescriptive steps on managing and curating data practices in a specific discipline/research methodology. (esciencelibrary)

Data dictionary—a data dictionary is a centralized repository that provides information about specific data such as meaning, relationships to other data, origin, usage, and format. (esciencelibrary)

Data interview—a process that involves a librarian interviewing a researcher to draw out information that needs to be considered in order to construct a data curation profile or data management plan. (esciencelibrary)

Data life cycle—the data life cycle represents all of the stages of data throughout its life from its creation for a study to its distribution and reuse. (esciencelibrary)

Data literacy—in the sciences, can be described as the "knowledge and skills involved in collecting, processing, managing, evaluating, and using data for scientific inquiry." (esciencelibrary)

Data management plan (DMP)—a data management plan grows out of an understanding of how data should be collected, normalized, processed, analyzed, preserved, used, and reused over their lifetime. (esciencelibrary)

Data preservation—consists of a series of managed activities necessary to ensure continued access to data for as long as necessary. (esciencelibrary)

Data repository—a place that holds data, makes data available to use, and organizes data in a logical manner. (esciencelibrary)

Data reuse—a concept that involves using research data for a research activity or purpose other than that for which it was originally intended. (esciencelibrary)

Data security—the ways that data are kept safe from harm, alteration, or unauthorized access during gathering, analysis, storage, and transmission. (esciencelibrary)

Data sharing—the practice of making data used for scholarly research available to other investigators. (esciencelibrary)

Delicious—a free online service that allows the saving, tagging, and sharing of web links. https://delicious.com/.

Delphi method—enables groups of peers to reach consensus on issues. Peers often are selected for their special expertise or perspectives on the issues. Facilitators guide the group asynchronously (e.g., via e-mail or social media) to vote upon or rank preferences through procedures intended to prevent any individual from dominating the process.

Describing and annotating data—describing and annotating data sets provides an avenue for data to be better understood across borders and sectors. (esciencelibrary)

Descriptive metadata—describes a resource for purposes such as discovery and identification. It can include elements such as title, abstract, author, and keywords. (NISO)

Digital curation—the management and preservation of digital data over the long term. (esciencelibrary)

Directional questions—information contacts about the logistical use of the library and facilities that do not involve knowledge resources.

Disaggregated content—the practice of publishers and content producers to make available unbundled pieces of information (e.g., an article from a journal issue or a song from an album).

Disclaimer—a brief statement clarifying the intent of a product, such that legal responsibility for misuse is denied. In the context of health information websites, disclaimers usually make a statement to the effect that the information provided is for general purposes and is not intended to take the place of a health care provider's advice to an individual.

Disintermediation—refers to the current state of information acquisition in which a consumer has little to no interaction with the information provider (e.g., interlibrary loan will acquire and send an article electronically, therefore having no dialog with the patron).

Disruptive technology—innovations that shake up the production of a product or the application of a service, or that press for changes in the way things are done or made.

DMPTool—allows researchers to create ready-to-use data management plans for specific funding agencies. (esciencelibrary)

Dublin Core—the Dublin Core Metadata Element Set is a vocabulary of fifteen properties for use in resource description. (DCMI)

Dublin Core Metadata Initiative (DCMI)—an open organization that supports shared innovation in metadata design and best practices across a broad range of purposes and business models. (DCMI)

e-classrooms—generally, an instructional space that is outfitted with computers for students and instructors to use.

e-science—the use of networked, high-powered computers to support any research endeavor requiring extensive data support. E-science serves both big science and other research projects whenever these involve special computational or large file sets.

Electronic health record (EHR) or electronic medical record (EMR)—an electronic record of patient health information generated by one or more encounters in a health care setting. The record includes patient demographics, progress notes, problems, medications, vital signs, past medical history, immunizations, laboratory data, and radiology reports. (Healthcare Information and Management Systems Society)

Embargo—refers to the time lapse between the date a journal is published and when content access begins. Embargo dates can be six months, one year, or longer. Embargoes can be from date published or "rolling" from current date.

Embedded librarian—a librarian who may or may not have in-depth domain knowledge but is embedded in some way into the workings of a client group (e.g., physically in the client's department or unit, or virtually in a course management system).

Emeritus—a former officeholder, especially a college professor who is retired but is allowed to retain his or her title as an honor. (Adapted from Google definition)

Emotional intelligence—the ability to reason with emotions and perceive the emotions of others to help with social relationships. www.unh.edu/emotional_intelligence/.

Entrez Program Utilities (E-utilities)—a set of eight server-side programs that provide a stable interface into the Entrez query and database system at the National Center for Biotechnology Information (NCBI). The E-utilities use a fixed URL syntax that translates a standard set of input parameters into the values necessary for various NCBI software components to search for and retrieve the requested data. (NCBI)

Ergonomics—the practice of providing a comfortable work environment designed to reduce physical stress and fatigue while maximizing productivity.

Evidence-based health care—the conscientious, explicit, and judicious use of current best evidence in making decisions about the care of individual patients. (Adapted from Sackett et al.)

Evidence-based library and information practice (EBLIP)—a process for integrating the best available evidence into making important decisions. The practitioner uses the best available evidence while informed by experience and critical-thinking skills, and modulated by the affected user population's values or preferences.

Evidence-based practice (EBP)—a sequential process used by professionals to reach informed decisions. EBP offers a way to reconcile the need for sound decisions with exponential growth of applied research knowledge.

Fair use—falls under U.S. copyright law www.copyright.gov/fls/fl102.html and refers to the ability to use published material for education, scholarly work, or research.

File transfer protocol (FTP)—is a standard that allows the transmission of data files between computers. (Ince, 2013)

Flexibility—in space planning, the concept of keeping spaces adaptive for different kinds of use.

Flipped classroom—an instructional model that requires review of course content ahead of time, usually incorporating streaming media of lectures and required reading; then, uses class time to complete active learning assignments or projects that would traditionally be considered homework.

Furniture, Fixtures, and Equipment (FF&E)—in space planning, a major budgetary category that includes all items being purchased and installed in a constructed area. FF&E is calculated separately from construction costs but included in the overall budget.

Future-proofing—in space planning, an effort to design infrastructure in a way that accommodates technologies that do not exist yet.

Grey literature—reports or other intellectual products that are not part of the peer-reviewed published professional literature. National or regional associations also generate speeches, contributed papers, and posters that report findings to the profession. These grey literature sources sometimes include abstracts that are readily accessible even when the texts for the original speeches no longer exist.

Gross Domestic Product (GDP)—the value of a country's goods and services for a given period.

Health Insurance Portability and Accountability Act of 1996 (HIPAA)—a federal law designed to improve continuity of health insurance but known mostly for the "privacy rules" for health care providers and insurance companies regarding who may access personal health information.

Health literacy—the "capacity to obtain, communicate, process, and understand basic health information and services to make appropriate health decisions." (Affordable Care Act, 2010; see definition above)

Hype Cycle—a popular conceptual framework for organizations to track the emergence, peak, decline, and eventual plateau of successful new information technology adaptation. The Hype Cycle reveals that even information technologies that become widespread fail to deliver their initial hyped promises. www.gartner.com/technology/research/hype-cycles/.

Indemnification—refers to the agreement between parties to hold each other blameless in event of a license breech and to hold one party harmless from claims alleged from a third party.

In-depth questions—research type questions that involve more time, usually multiple resources, and/or the development of a search strategy.

Informationist—an information professional who provides in-depth customized information services, residing within a clinical, research, educational, or administrative context. By strictest definition, informationists embody both domain and information knowledge. Unlike embedded librarians or liaisons, they are often integrated at the team or project level.

Information management competencies—the competencies or set of skills needed to find, evaluate, use, and communicate information.

Ingesting data sets—the process of ingesting data sets into an institutional repository. (esciencelibrary)

Institutional repository—an online locus for collecting, preserving, and disseminating—in digital form—the intellectual output of an institution, particularly a research institution. (*Wikipedia*)

Integrated library system (ILS)—also known as a library management system (LMS), is an enterprise resource planning system for a library, used to track items owned, orders made, bills paid, and patrons who have borrowed. An ILS usually comprises a relational database, software to interact with that database, and two graphical user interfaces (one for patrons, one for staff). Most ILSs separate software functions into discrete programs called modules, each integrated with a unified interface. Examples of modules are acquisitions, cataloging, circulation, serials, and the OPAC (public interface for users). (*Wikipedia*)

Internet Protocol (IP) address—a unique number that identifies a computer (or other networked device) and the subnetwork it resides on. Internet Protocol version 6 (IPv6) is a new standard that will support the ever-increasing number of networked devices as well as authentication and data encryption. (Ince, 2013)

Knowledge base or knowledgebase (also KB or kb)—a special kind of database for knowledge management. A knowledge base is an information repository that provides a means for information to be collected, organized, shared, searched, and used. It can be either machine-readable or intended for human use. (*Wikipedia*)

Leadership in Energy and Environmental Design (LEED)—a voluntary certification program developed by the U.S. Green Building Council to demonstrate sustainability in construction of new spaces.

Levels of evidence—serve as a guide rather than a strict prescription for critical appraisal. The quality of an individual research study takes precedence within the levels of evidence. A research design such as a randomized controlled trial (a type of experiment) implemented correctly resides near the top of the levels of evidence in answering an Intervention question, for example.

LibQUAL+ survey—survey offered by the Association of Research Libraries aimed at identifying gaps between user minimal expectations, desired expectations, and actual perceptions of experiences. www.libqual.org/.

Library commons—a space designed to include multiple functions and services to be shared by all library patrons.

Library of Congress Subject Headings (LCSH)—comprise a thesaurus (a controlled vocabulary) of subject headings, maintained by the U.S. Library of Congress, for use in bibliographic records. (*Wikipedia*)

Linked data—describes a method of publishing structured data so that it can be interlinked and become more useful. It builds upon standard web technologies such as HTTP and URIs, but rather than using them to serve web pages for human readers, it extends them to share information in a way that computers can read them automatically. (*Wikipedia*)

Linking data to publications—involves creating links between academic publications and their underlying associated data sets. (esciencelibrary)

Link resolver—software that accepts and parses properly formed OpenURL data and uses these data to direct users to holdings at their respective institutions. (Adapted from Drupal, http://drupal.org/project/link_resolver)

Magnet Recognition Program—advances three goals within health care organizations: to promote quality in a setting that supports professional practice; to identify excellence in the delivery of nursing services to patients/residents; to disseminate best practices in nursing services. www.nursecredentialing.org/Magnet/ProgramOverview.

MARC (Machine Readable Cataloging)—defines a data format that emerged from a Library of Congress-led initiative that began nearly forty years ago. It provides the mechanism by which computers exchange, use, and interpret bibliographic information, and its data elements make up the foundation of most library catalogs used today. MARC became USMARC in the 1980s and MARC 21 in the late 1990s. (Library of Congress)

Medical Subject Headings **(MeSH) thesaurus**—a controlled vocabulary produced by the National Library of Medicine and used for indexing, cataloging, and searching for biomedical and health-related information and documents. (U.S. National Library of Medicine)

Meta-analysis—a statistical analysis of data from several studies that usually results in an overall weighted average of results; this helps the reader determine the preponderance of evidence to support a conclusion, especially when individual studies offer different or conflicting results; often reported as part of a systematic review.

Metadata—structured information that describes, explains, locates, or otherwise makes it easier to retrieve, use, or manage an information resource. (NISO)

Minimum Viable Product (MVP)—provides a framework for developing a modestly scaled information technology application quickly and without seeking high levels of perfection. MVP seeks to determine, from the producer perspective, whether users might want or need an information resource. Or, MVP can be used by an organization trying to adapt the technology on the consumer side.

Modular design—in space planning, the concept of having furnishings that are smaller and adaptive.

Multiservice poles—narrow conduits for dropping wires from a ceiling grid into the interior of a large space to provide electrical and networking access.

Name Authority Cooperative Program (NACO)—through this program, participants contribute authority records for personal, corporate, and jurisdictional names; uniform titles; and series headings to the LC/NACO Authority File. (Library of Congress)

National Information Standards Organization (NISO)—nonprofit association accredited by the American National Standards Institute (ANSI); identifies, develops, maintains, and publishes technical standards to manage information in our changing and ever-more digital environment. (NISO)

OCLC: Online Computer Library Center, Inc.—a nonprofit membership computer library service and research organization dedicated to the public purposes of furthering access to the world's information and reducing information costs. (*Wikipedia*)

Off-site storage and retrieval—in space planning, a facility located away from the original library where lower-use materials are warehoused and some access is provided.

Omics—scientific disciplines that involve the complete complements of particular molecule types that end in the suffix "ome." For example, genomics is the study of the entire genome (genetic makeup) of an organism or an individual. Similarly, proteomics is the study of the proteome (proteins); and metabolomics is the study of the metabolome (metabolites).

One-shot session—a single library instruction session, generally one hour or less, that focuses on a particular assignment and/or gives basic information about the library.

Online public access catalog (OPAC)—a database composed of bibliographic records describing the books and other materials a library or library system owns. One module of an integrated library system (ILS), it is the public interface for users, known simply as the "library catalog." Most online catalogs are searchable by author, title, subject, and keywords. (Reitz, ODLIS)

Ontology—formal representation of knowledge as a set of concepts within a domain, and the relationships between those concepts. Ontologies are the structural frameworks for organizing information. (*Wikipedia*)

Open Archives Initiative Protocol for Metadata Harvesting (OAI-PMH)—a low-barrier mechanism for repository interoperability. *Data providers* are repositories that expose structured metadata via OAI-PMH. *Service providers* then make OAI-PMH service requests to harvest that metadata. OAI-PMH is a set of six verbs or services that are invoked within HTTP. (Open Archives Initiative, www.openarchives.org/pmh/)

Open source—refers to a program in which the source code is available to the public for use and/or modification from its original design. Open source code is typically created as a collaborative effort in which programmers improve upon the code and share the changes within the community. (*Wikipedia*)

OpenURL—URLs containing bibliographic metadata, enabling direct links to full-text articles, journals, books, chapters, dissertations, following NISO standard Z39.88. (Trainor and Price, 2010)

Overlap—refers to having access to the same title from more than one provider. A library may have four instances of a journal from four providers, but each platform offers different dates.

Patient-centered medical home (PCMH)—model of health care delivery that emphasizes a primary point of care and the coordination of health care around the needs of the patient.

Patient Protection and Affordable Care Act (PPACA)—See Affordable Care Act.

Patron-driven acquisition (PDA)—the practice of seeding the catalog with preapproved electronic monograph records and setting a purchase threshold based on user visits to the record.

Permalink—a permanent static hyperlink to a particular web page or entry in a blog. (Google definition)

Perpetual access—the right to ongoing access to electronic materials. In situations where digital materials are licensed, access to these materials is often lost after the licensing agreement has expired. (*Wikipedia*)

Pinterest—a free online service that allows the saving, tagging, and sharing of images and videos from the web. www.pinterest.com/.

Principal investigator (PI)—the lead scientist who has responsibility for the completion of a research project. Depending on the venue, the PI may have a number of additional roles. In academic institutions, such individuals are often faculty members who lead not only a project but an entire laboratory, lead cohesive research programs in a particular area of interest, mentor graduate students and postdoctoral associates, and may have formal teaching responsibilities.

Problem-based learning—an active learning method that involves small groups of five to seven students normally led by a faculty facilitator/tutor. The students work through a simulated patient case or other critical-thinking exercise using inductive logic to define the core issues. Students engage in self-directed learning, frequently involving the pursuit of library research, to understand the cases.

Program for Cooperative Cataloging (PCC)—an international cooperative effort aimed at expanding access to library collections by providing useful, timely, and cost-effective cataloging that meets mutually accepted standards of libraries around the world. (Library of Congress)

Project owner—in space planning, the lead coordinator of the project with responsibility and administrative authority to make decisions on behalf of the institution.

Proximity operators—symbols used in a keyword search to specify that two terms must be within a certain distance of each other in the text field of the document being searched.

Ready reference questions—questions that are information/knowledge-based but are quickly answered, such as holdings information or quick facts.

Reference interview—a short interview intended to determine what the user really wants to know so that the reference staff can locate information to answer the user's question.

Remote access—refers to the ability of authorized users to use the resource in question from off-site via a proxy server or another authentication scheme.

Research data management (RDM)—a concept used to describe the managing, sharing, and archiving of research data to make them more accessible to the broader research community. (esciencelibrary)

Research informationist—a medical or health sciences librarian who also has a subject-specific background in a biomedical discipline that serves as part of a clinical or biomedical research team. (esciencelibrary)

Research life cycle—the process a researcher takes to complete a project or study from its inception to its completion. (esciencelibrary)

Residency training—in the health sciences, typically, postdoctoral clinical training resulting in specialization; in medicine, internship refers to the first year of residency; and house staff is a term applied to all residents, referring to an earlier time when new doctors lived in the hospital; postresidency fellowships result in further specialization, sometimes referred to as subspecialization.

Resource description and access (RDA)—a standard for cataloging that provides instructions and guidelines on formulating data for resource description and discovery. (*Wikipedia*)

Resource description framework (RDF)—a language for representing information about resources on the World Wide Web. It is particularly intended for

representing metadata about web resources, such as the title, author, and modification date of a web page, copyright and licensing information about a web
document, or the availability schedule for some shared resource. (W3C [World
Wide Web Consortium], www.w3.org/TR/rdf-primer/)

Roving reference—reference service that happens, by design, away from the reference desk.

Semantic—relationship-driven or meaning-driven (when used with searching or
searches).

Semantic Web—the extension of the World Wide Web that enables people to share
content beyond the boundaries of applications and websites. (Semantic Web,
http://semanticweb.org/wiki/Main_Page)

Seminal—having a strong influence on ideas, works, events, and so forth, that come
later: very important and influential. (Merriam-Webster online)

Shelf depth—the depth of an individual shelving unit, measured in inches.

Shelf-ready—the delivery to the library of books ready to place on the shelf. The
books can have Tattle Tape, property stamps, dust jackets, bar codes, etc., already
prepared when they arrive on-site.

Shelving height—the height of an individual shelving unit, measured either in
inches or by number of shelves per unit.

Shelving range—a row of shelving units.

Shelving unit—a single stack of bookshelves.

Simulation lab—in academic health centers, a teaching environment designed to
allow students to learn procedures in a no-risk setting using models or manikins
and other simulators.

Single sign-on (SSO)—a property of access control of multiple related but independent software systems. With this property, a user logs in once and gains access to
all systems without being prompted to log in again to each of them. (*Wikipedia*)

Space program—in space planning, a foundational document cataloging what
work is being proposed, how it will be done, and for what purpose. A space
program provides the starting point for any major space planning initiative.

Stacking—in space planning, the intentional placement of mechanical systems in
the same location from floor to floor for easier access and maintenance.

Structural metadata—in digital library community usage, structural metadata describes the intellectual or physical elements of a digital object. For a file that
represents a single page as a compound document (e.g., a JPEG 2000 jpm file),
the structural metadata may include information on page layout. In a multifile
digital object (e.g., a scanned book with many page images), structural metadata
describes the object's components and their relationships: pages, chapters, table
of contents, index, and so forth. Such metadata can support sophisticated search
and retrieval actions as well as the navigation and presentation of digital objects.
(FADGI [Federal Agencies Digitization Guidelines Initiative], www.digitization
guidelines.gov/term.php?term=metadatastructural)

Sustainability—in space planning, the concept of designing buildings and other
spaces to have minimal negative impact on the surrounding environment,
including the conservation of power and water, or use of alternative energy
sources.

Synchronous reference—a digital or virtual reference transaction that occurs in real time. Chat reference allows for immediate real-time response and conversation between the librarian and the user and would be an example of synchronous reference.

Systematic review—a literature review focused on a research question that tries to identify, appraise, select, and synthesize all high-quality research evidence relevant to that question. (*Wikipedia*)

Team-based learning—a formalized active learning technique that incorporates into the instruction process preassignments, individual and group assessments, in-class group activities, and peer and instructor feedback.

Technical questions—questions that do not pertain directly to the information resources of the library, but rather to the computers and tools that are used to access, manage, or communicate information.

Tiered reference service—a model of service whereby the public service desk in the library is staffed by trained paraprofessionals or graduate students who **triage** questions based upon level of difficulty of the questions and their ability to answer them.

Translational science—incorporates research results into health care practice in a timely manner. Type I translational science is the migration of laboratory or clinical research from "bench to bedside"; Type II translational science is migration to wider "bedside to community" practice.

Triage—in medicine, triage is the process of determining which patients to treat first based on the severity of their condition. In a tiered reference service, it is the determination of which questions can be answered by a paraprofessional at an information desk and which need to be referred to a reference or subject-specialist librarian.

Truncation operators—symbols used in keyword searches to find word variants containing the root. The character replaces one or more letters in the word. Also called wild-card operators.

Under-floor duct systems—conduits under existing flooring that allow access to wiring for networking and electricity. A common under-floor system is known as Walker duct.

Value engineering—when budgeting for space planning, a cost-reduction method that targets nonessential items while still preserving the overall function and intended use of the space.

Virtual International Authority File (VIAF)—implemented and hosted by OCLC; a joint project of several national libraries plus selected regional and transnational library agencies. The project's goal is to lower the cost and increase the use of library authority files by matching and linking widely used authority files and making that information available on the web. (VIAF: The Virtual International Authority File, http://viaf.org/)

Virtual reference services—virtual reference or digital reference services occur using digital technologies such as e-mail, instant message, text, or other technologies that allow reference service via computer.

Web-based learning—teaching and learning supported by the attributes and resources of the Internet. Also known as e-learning or online learning.

Web-scale discovery system—a service capable of searching across a vast range of preharvested and indexed content quickly and seamlessly (Jason Vaughan. 2011. "Web Scale Discovery: What and Why?" *Library Technology Reports* 47: Services, no. 1 [January]: 6. *MasterFile Premier*)

Widget—a small application with limited functionality that can be installed and executed within a web page that links to other data.

Workflow—the sequence of steps that need to be followed to complete a task, care for a patient, conduct an experiment, and so on.

Z39.50—the Z39.50 information retrieval protocol defines the way computers communicate for the purpose of information retrieval. Z39.50 can allow a user to search multiple systems seamlessly (e.g., searching multiple library catalogs). (NISO)

SOURCES

DCMI (Dublin Core Metadata Initiative). http://dublincore.org/documents/dces/.

eScience Thesaurus. http://esciencelibrary.umassmed.edu/thesaurus.

Google definition. http://google.com.

Healthcare Information and Management Systems Society. 2013. *Electronic Health Records.* www.himss.org/library/ehr/?navItemNumber=13261.

Ince, Darrel, ed. 2013. *A Dictionary of the Internet,* 3rd ed. Oxford University Press. www.oxfordreference.com/.

Library of Congress. www.loc.gov/.

Merriam-Webster online. www.merriam-webster.com/.

NCBI (National Center for Biotechnology Information). www.ncbi.nlm.nih.gov/.

NISO (National Information Standards Organization). www.niso.org/.

Reitz, Joan M. 2013. *Online Dictionary for Library and Information Science.* ABC-CLIO. www.abc-clio.com/ODLIS/odlis_A.aspx.

Sackett, D. L., W. M. Rosenberg, J. A. Gray, R. B. Haynes, and W. S. Richardson. 1996. "Evidence Based Medicine: What It Is and What It Isn't." *BMJ* no. 312 (7023): 71–72.

Trainor, Cindi, and Jason Price. 2010. "Rethinking Library Linking: Breathing New Life into OpenURL." *Library Technology Reports* 46, no. 7 (October).

U.S. National Library of Medicine. www.nlm.nih.gov/.

Wikipedia, The Free Encyclopedia. http://en.wikipedia.org/.

Index

Key:
page numbers in Italics = figure or table
page number in bold = vignette

3-D printers, 160
6S model, 210–11

AACR2. *See* Anglo-American Cataloging
   Rules (AACR2)
academic health sciences libraries, 6, 8, 354;
   space needs, 382–83; strategic plans, 358
Academy of Health Information
   Professionals (AHIP), 10, 16, 414. *See
   also* Medical Library Association (MLA)
access services, 303–4. *See also* circulation
   services; course reserves; interlibrary
   loan/document delivery
AccessMedicine, 219
acquisitions, 116–19; monographs, 117–18;
   serials and databases, 119
active learning, 65–71, 279
ADDIE, 291
administration, *See* library administration
administrative staff, 178
Affordable Care Act (ACA), 32, 329, 414
allied health, 41
altmetrics, 207
American Library Association, 20–21, 161;
   Code of Ethics, 5–6; competencies for
   directors, 355; Emerging Leadership
   Program, 361; marketing, 336–37; RUSA
   guidelines, 172–73, 325
American Medical Informatics Association
   (AMIA), 21

American Recovery and Reinvestment Act
   (ARRA), 38
American Society for Training and
   Development, 361
Americans with Disabilities Act (ADA), 309,
   386. *See also* disabled
Anderson, Max, **160**
Anglo-American Cataloging Rules (AACR2),
   122–24
animal care: support for, 215–17
Antikythera computer, 75–76
approval plans, 105
Ariel, 314
Association for Information Science &
   Technology (ASIS&T), 21
Association of Academic Health Sciences
   Libraries (AAHSL), 18–20; advocacy, 19;
   annual meetings, 19; annual statistics,
   18, 61, *108*, *111*, 178, 180, 304, 369;
   leadership program, 18–19, 361–62;
   listserv, 365; Matheson Lecture, 19–20;
   mission, 18
Association of American Medical Colleges
   (AAMC): accrediting standards, 366;
   Group on Information Resources (GIR),
   19, 362; Medical School Objectives
   Project (MSOP), 277, 414
Association of College and Research
   Libraries (ACRL): *Information Literacy
   Competency Standards for Higher
   Education*, 276–77
Association of Research Libraries (ARL):
   benchmarking, 370; E-Science Task
   Force, 253; statistics, 178, *179*, 182. *See
   also* LibQUAL+

authentication, 151

authority control, 124–28; Library of Congress Subject Headings (LCSH), 127–28; Medical Subject Headings (MeSH), 124–26

Bandy, Margaret, **8**

Banks, Marcus, **213**

basic science graduate students, 234–35

Bass, Wilma, **122**

benchmarking, 369–70

benevolent neglect, 351

BIBCO (Monographic Bibliographic Record Program), 120

Bibel, Barbara M., **341**

BIBFRAME, 130–33

bibliographic control, 122

bibliographic instruction. *See* library instruction

big science, 71–72

bioinformatics research: support for, 232–34. *See also* biomedical research

Biological Abstracts, *203*

biomedical research, 46–50; funding for, 47–48; information needs, 197; innovative collaborations, 71–75; outreach to, 232–34; publishing, 48–50; research process, 46–47; searching databases, 197–210

Blevins, Amy, **411**

Bloom's taxonomy, 292–93

Brandeis model, 184

Brandon-Hill list, 106

budgeting, 108–13, 371–72; budget types, 109; for resources, 108–13; for space planning, 379; funding services, 109–10; managing finances, 370–71; planning and monitoring, 110–12; prioritizing, 113; raising revenues, 370; soliciting donations, 372

Butson, Linda, **241**

case-based learning (CBL), 282

cataloging. *See* collection organization

cataloging standards, 122–24; Anglo-American Cataloging Rules (AACR2), 122–24; evolution of, *123*; Name Authority Cooperative Program (NACO), 122–24; RDA: Resource Description and Access, 122–24, 127

Centers for Disease Control and Prevention (CDC), 50; website, 342

Chattopadhyay, Ansuman, **233**

CINAHL, 61, 202–3

circulation services, 304–8; access for disabled, 305; borrowing, 305; challenges/opportunities, 307–8; circulation of books, 306; circulation of journals, 306–7; circulation of media, 307; desk, 395; hours, 305–6; physical access, 304–5; public access, 305; remote storage, 307; security, 306

Clark, Ann Marie, **127**

Clinical and Translational Science Awards, 74–75; MLA special interest group, 74–75; outreach to researchers/institutes, 236–37; REDCap, 260

Clinical Decision Support Systems (CDSS), 152, 211

clinical librarians, 5, 409–10

Clinical Queries, 201

ClinicalKey, 219

ClinicalTrials.gov, 13

clinicians, 177–78

cloud computing, 314

Cochrane Library, 204–5, 210

Cogdill, Keith W., **23**

Coghill, Jeffrey G., **97**

collaborations, 233, 364–66, 410–12; outside the institution, 365; with campus partners, 411–12; with researchers, 71–75, 406–7; with translational sciences, 74–75; within the institution, 364–65; workspaces, 410–11

collaborative furniture, 391–92

collection development, 87–115; budgeting for, 108–13; database evaluation, 106–7; defined, 87; deselection, 97; disaggregated content, 88; disintermediated access, 89; electronic resources licensing, 98–101; electronic resources product evaluation, 101–8; free resources evaluation, 107–8; in research data management, 264; keeping current, 113; journal evaluation, 102, 104–5; monograph evaluation, 105–6; of consumer health information, 337–40; policies, 90–97; Research Libraries Group Conspectus, 91–92, 95, 96

collection organization, 119–39; authority control (MeSH), 124–27; cataloging standards, 122–24; discoverability,

133–34; Library of Congress Subject Headings (LCSH), 127–28; link resolvers, 134–37; linked data, 137–39, 140; MARC/BIBFRAME/Dublin Core, 130–33; metadata, 130; National Library of Medicine Classification System, 128–29; resources management and access, 119–22; Semantic Web, 137–39

communication, 152–54

compact shelving, 307, 386

competency-based education, 44

computerized provider order entry (CPOE) systems, 211

concurrent use, 98–99

conference rooms, 398–99

CONSER (Cooperative Online Serials Program), 120

consortiums: interlibrary loan, 312; licensing, 101; purchasing, 319–20

consultation services, 188

consumer health information, 324–45; collaboration, 334–35; collection development, 337–40; current state of, 326–28; definition of, 324–25; evaluation, 341–43; funding sources, 333; health literacy, 329–31; Healthnet, 327; history of, 325–26; library space needs, 384; managing a consumer health information service, 331–43; marketing, 336–37; National Library of Medicine role, 329; NC Health Info, 327–28, 329; needs assessment/planning, 331–32; online resources, 340–41, 342; policies/procedures, 332, 334; Planetree Health Resource Centers, 326; recent developments, 328–29; staff training, 335–36

CONTU, 316–17

copyright, 316–17; and licensing, 317; CONTU, 316–17; fair use, 99–100, 309, 310

Copyright Clearance Center, 309, 318

COUNTER-compliant statistics, 102

course-integrated instruction, 289–90

course management systems, 308–9

course reserves, 308–10; challenges/opportunities, 309–10; course management systems, 308–9; e-reserve systems, 308–10; policies, 308

culture of medicine, 9–10

curriculum-integrated programming, 289–91

data: as return-on-investment, 256; defined, 254–55; integrity of, 255–56; public access to, 267. *See also* research data management

data curation, 262; profiles, 269

data interview, 269

data management consulting, 266

data repositories, 266–67

database searching, 197–210; expert searching, 212–17; full-text search engines, 209–10; instruction, 287, *288*, 289; managing references, 217–18; staying current, 220–21 systematic reviews, 214-215; trends, 218–21

Delphi method, 60

demand-driven acquisition, 118–19

deselection, 97, 338–39

Dewey, John, 65–66

digital curation, 133

digital natives, 279

Directory of Open Access Journals (DOAJ), 107–8

disabled: access for, 305, 309

disaggregated content, 88

disaster plans, 149

discovery services: discoverability, 133–34; discovery tools, 120, 315–16

disintermediated access, 89

disruptive technologies, 284–86; flipped classroom, 285; gamification, 285–86

distance education, 295

DMPTool, 269–70

DOCLINE, 12, 310–11, 317–18; Loansome Doc, 311, 317

document delivery. *See* interlibrary loan/document delivery

Doody's Review Service, 106

Dublin Core, 132–33

DynaMed, 211–12

e-books, 118; portals, 219–20

e-classrooms, 388-390

e-learnin. *See* web-based learning

e-mail, 53

e-reserve systems, 308-9

e-science, 72–73

Earl, Matrha, **335**

EBSCO MEDLINE. *See* MEDLINE/PubMed

EDUCAUSE, 21, 162

Eigenfactor, 208

electronic health records, 38–39, 145, 149–50, 151–52

electronic resources: authorized users, 98–99, 100; consortial licensing, 101; database evaluation, 106–7; delivery and access, 100; free resources evaluation, 107–8; journal evaluation, 102, 104–5; legal issues, 100–1; licensing, 98–101; monograph evaluation, 105–6; product evaluation, 101–8; sharing, 99–100; statistics, 102; trials, 102
Electronic Resources Management (ERM) systems, 112
Elias, Marie, **150**
EMBASE, *203*
embedded librarians, 5, 226, 228–29, 295, 407
emerging technologies, 160
emerging trends: in health sciences librarianship, 57–83; staying current, 77. *See also* trend
Epocrates, 204
ergonomics, 388
Esparza, Julia M., **39**
evaluation: criteria for weeding, 97; of consumer health information services, 341–43; of electronic resources, 101–8; of library instruction, 292–94; of library services, 367–70; of reference services, 178–83
evidence-based library and information practice (EBLIP), 60–65; levels of evidence, *62*
evidence-based medicine (EBM), 36–37
evidence-based practice (EBP), 36–37, 58–65; critical appraisal, 59, 62–63; origins, 64–65; research support, 210–12
Evidence Updates, 220
experiential education, 65–66
expert searches, 212–17

faculty, 177
Faculty of 1000, 220
fair use. *See* copyright
federal data management, 257
Federer, Lisa, **258**
Fellows. *See* residents
Ferreti, Stephanie, **134**
firewalls, 150
Flexner Report, 40, 42, 275
flipped classroom, 285
FOCUS-PDCA Cycle, 368
Forsman, Rick, **353**

Fowler, Susan, **216**
Freiburger, Gary, **400**
Friends of the Library groups, 373
FTP, 150
full-text search engines, 209–10
Fulton, Stephanie, **36**

gamification, 285–86
Garcia-Milian, Rolando, 261
Genbank, 72
general medical librarian, 230–31
genomic medicine, 34–35
global health, 50–51
Goodell, Jon, **107**
Google, 340–41
Google Scholar, 209–10
GoPubMed, 202
Gore, Sally, **254**
GPEP Report, 42–43
grey literature, 61, 212–13
Guidelines.gov, 339

h-index, 207, 210
Hanson, Karen, **267**
Harvard University's Leadership Institute for Academic Librarians, 362
health, 50
health care: business of, 31–32; delivery of, 33–36; electronic health records, 38–39; in the U.S., 30–39; information technology in, 38–39; interdisciplinary teams, 35–36; patient-centered, 33–35; quality improvement, 37–38; quality of, 32–33
health care informatics, 45–46
Health Insurance Portability and Accountability Ace (HIPAA), 38, 144, 149, 328–29
health literacy, 33, 329–31
health professionals: education, 39–46
health sciences environment, 30–56; managing, 356–59
health sciences librarians: alternative roles, 412–13; collaborations, 410–12; creating data repositories, 266–67; data management counseling, 266; new roles for, 403–18; RDM guidance, 265; RDM instruction, 263, 265–66; RDM skills/competencies, 268–69; RDM tools/resources, 269–70; roles in research, 405–9; roles in research data management, 262–68

health sciences librarianship, 3–29; education for, 21–23, 415; environments, 6, 8–10; ethics, 5–6, 7; hiring process, 23–24, *24*; job opportunities, 23–24; journals, *26*; profession, 3–6; professional involvement/keeping current, 24–26; seeking a position, *24*; terminology, 4; transformation of, 404–5; trends in, 57–83

health sciences libraries: borrowing, 305, 306–7; changing organization, 413–14; hours, 305–6; new roles for, 403–9; patron types, *91*; physical space, 376–402; public access, 305; research on, 408–9; security, 306; staff workplaces, 396–99; types of, 6, 8–9; users of, 174–78. *See also* hospital libraries

Healthnet, 327

Healthy People, 50

Heilemann, Heidi A., **365**

Hendler, Gail Y., **154**

Hendrix, Dean, **413**

Herzberg Theory of Motivation, 351

Hinegardner, Patricia, **320**

HIPPA. *See* Health Insurance Portability and Accountability Act (HIPAA)

Holmes, Carolyn, **201**

Holmes, Heather N., **190**

Holmes, Kristi L., **73, 236, 409**

Homan, J. Michael, **10, 51**

hospital libraries, 6, 8, 354, 409–10; instruction in, 286; space needs, 383–84, 399

Human Genome Project, 72

human resources: managing, 359, 363–64

Hype Cycle, 76

indemnification, 100–1

Index Medicus, 48, 144

information literacy: defined, 276; standards, 276–78. *See also* library instruction

information management competencies, 175–76

information services. *See* reference services

information specialists in context (ISIC). *See* informationists

informationists, 5, 229–34, 253–54, 407–8

Institutional Animal Care and Use Committees (IACUC), 48, 215–17, 237, 411

Institutional archives, 412–13

institutional repositories, 132

Institutional Review Boards (IRB), 48, 237, 411–12

Instruction. *See* library instruction

instructional design, 291–94; ADDIE, 201; Bloom's taxonomy, 292–93; components, 292–94; models, 291–92

integrated library systems (ILS), 112, 120–21, 155–56

integrity of scientific research, 255–56

interdisciplinary teams, 35–36

interlibrary loan/document delivery, 310–21; challenges/opportunities, 307–8, 309–10, 317–21; consortia, 312; CONTU, 316–17; copyright, 316–17; DOCLINE, 310–11; document delivery, 313; ILLiad, 313, 316; integration with library systems, 314–16; licensing, 317; OCLC WorldShare Interlibrary Loan Service, 311–12; pay per view, 318; pay per use, 318–19; purchase on demand, 319; resource sharing networks, 310–12; roles/responsibilities of interlibrary loan librarian, 320–21; systems/tools for, 313–16

International Federation of Library Associations and Institutions (IFLA), 92; RLG Conspectus, 91–92, 95, 96

Interprofessional Education Collaborative (IPEC), 36

intranets, 151

IP addresses, 150

Iwema, Carrie, **233**

The Joint Commission (TJC), 166–67

Journal Citation Reports, 207–8

Journal Impact Factors, 207

Katz, Linda M. G., **161**

Katz classification, 182

Kerdolff, Kathy, **291**

KidsHealth.org, 342

Kolb, David, 66

Kuntz, Gretchen, **231**

Lexicomp Online, 204

lead by example, 351–52

Leadership in Energy and Environmental Design (LEED), 382

leadership programs, 361–62

learning organizations, 352
levels of evidence, 62
liaison librarians, 184, 188, 226–29, 409–10
LibAnswers, 180–81, 183, 191–92
LibGuides, 296–97
LibQUAL+, 187, 370
library administration, 349–75; budgeting, 371–72; defined, 349–51; evaluation, 367–70;
generating support, 370–73; institutional organization/structure, 353–55; management competencies, 355–56; management theories/tools, 351–53; managing finances, 370–71; managing human resources, 359; managing the environment, 356–59; roles of the director, 359–66; standards/accreditation, implementing, 366–67; strategic planning, 357–58. *See also* library directors
library commons, 392–93
library directors: managing down, 360–64; managing out (collaboration), 364–66; managing up, 360; roles of, 359–66
library instruction, 275–302; ADDIE, 291; Bloom's taxonomy, 292–93; case-based learning, 282; course-integrated instruction, 289–90; curriculum-integrated programming, 289–91; database instruction, 287, *288*, 289; disruptive technologies, 284–86; evaluation, 292–94; flipped classroom, 285; gamification, 285–86; generations and learning, 278–79; history of, 275–78; in hospital libraries, 286; in research data management, 263, 265–66; instruction mechanics, 286–91; instructional design, 291–94; instructional formats, 289–91; learning paradigms, 279–84; one-shot session, 289; problem-based learning, 280–82; student-centered learning, 280–84; teacher-centered learning, 279–80; team-based learning, 282–84; web-based learning, 294–97
library journals, *26*, 161
library management systems, 315
Library of Congress: LC Subject Headings (LCSH), 127–28
licensing: and interlibrary loan, 317; consortiums, 101; of electronic resources, 98–101

Lin, Joanna, **311**
link resolvers, 120, 134–37, 157
linked data, 137–39, 140
LinkOut, 136-137
Lister Hill National Center for Biomedical Communications (LHC), 13
Loansome Doc, 311, 317. *See also* DOCLINE
long tail of resources, 88–89
Lyon, Jennifer A., **239**

Machine Readable Cataloging *see* MARC (Machine Readable Cataloging)
Magnet Recognition Program, 409–10
management by objectives, 352
management by walking around, 352–53
management competencies, 355–56
management theories, 351–53
MARC (Machine Readable Cataloging), 119, 130–33
marketing, 244–45; consumer health information services, 336–37
Matheson, Nina, 19–20
Mayo, Alexa, **304**
Mazure, Emily, **412**
McKelvy, Dina, **152**
Medicaid. *See* Medicare and Medicaid
medical education, 40–44; competency-based, 43–44; history, 40–42; reform, 42–44. *See also* health professionals
Medical Library Assistance Act (MLAA), 13–14
Medical Library Association (MLA), 15–18, 161–62; Academy of Health Information Professionals (AHIP), 10, 16, 414; advocacy, 17; benchmarking, 370; CAPHIS, 324, 325, 340; Code of Ethics, 6, 7; Consumer Health Information Specialization, 16–17; continuing education, 10; Disaster Information Specialization, 16; Hospital Libraries Section, 383; international work, 51; listserv, 365; Librarians without Borders, 51; organization of, 15–16; professional competencies, 356; programs and services, 16, 17; publications, 17–18; Research Section, 408; Translational Sciences Collaboration Special Interest Group, 74–75. *See also* Academy of Health Information Professionals (AHIP)

Medical Subject Headings (MeSH), 94, 124–26, 199

Medicare and Medicaid, 31

MEDLARS, 144–45

MEDLINE / PubMed, 12, 61, 144–45, 340; about, 199; GoPubMed, 202; PubMed Central, 13, 48, 202; PubMed Health, 201–2, 339, 342; PubMed LinkOut, 136–37; searching, 199–202

MedlinePlus, 12, 339, 342; Connect, 329; Go Local, 327–28, 329

Medscape, 220

mentoring, 362–63

meta-analyses, 49–50

metadata, 122, 130, 260–61

Micromedex, 204

minimum viable product (MVP), 77

mobile technologies, 158–60

MOOCs, 148, 296

Morley, Sarah Knox, **44, 285**

Name Authority Cooperative Program (NACO), 122–24

National Center for Biomedical Information (NCBI), 13

National Center for Complementary and Alternative Medicine (NCCAM), 342

National Information Standards Organization (NISO), 130

National Institutes of Health, 11; as funding source, 47; data plans, 72, 257; Public Access policy, 238, 257, 411; publication of funded research, 48, 253

National Library of Medicine, 10–15; and disasters, 51; and consumer health information, 329; classification system, 94, 128–29; collection development manual, 11–12, 94; databases, 12–13, 72; DOCLINE, 12, 310–11; exhibits, 243; Lister Hill National Center for Biomedical Communications (LHC), 13; MeSH, 124–26; mission, 11; National Center for Biomedical Information (NCBI), 13; NLM Administrative Supplements for Informationist Services to NIH-funded Research Projects, 234, 254, 407; services, 12–15. *See also* MEDLINE/PubMed and specific databases

National Network of Libraries of Medicine (NN/LM), 13–14; and CHI staff training, 335; awards, 372; DOCLINE, 310–11; funded projects, 241–42

National Science Foundation (NSF), 72; policy, 257

Natural Medicines Comprehensive Database, 204

Natural Standard, 204

NC Health Info, 327–28

Networking. *See* professional networking

new technologies, 75–77

Nitecki, Danuta A., **192**

OCLC, 131; Article Exchange, 314; EZproxy, 151; ILLIAD, 313, 314; WebJunction, 147; Worldshare Interlibrary Loan service, 311–12

off-site storage. *See* remote storage

office space, 396–99

omics, 232

One Health, 51

one-shot session, 289

online courses, 295–96

OPAC (Online Public Access Catalog), 120, 155

open source system, 156

OpenURL, 135–36, 157, 315

organizing references *see* reference managers

outreach services, 226–51; external outreach, 238–42; informationists, 229–34 internal outreach, 226–38; liaison librarians, 226 -29; marketing and communication, 244–45; to basic science graduate students, 234–35; to clinical and translational science researchers, 236–37; to committees and task forces, 237–38; to dental public health professionals, 240; to health care consumers, 240–41; to high school students, 240; to offices of research, 238; to patients, 241–42; to postdoctoral associates, 235–36; to senior citizens, 239; successful outreach, 245–46; visibility, 242–46

participatory management, 353

patient-centered care, 33–35

Patient Centered Outcome Research Institute (PCORI), 410

Patient Protection and Affordable Care Act (PPCA). *See* Affordable Care Act (ACA)

patron-driven acquisition, 106

pay per use, 318–19
pay per view, 318
personnel. *See* human resources
Phyillaier, Cynthia, **121**
physical space, 376–402; academic health
    sciences libraries, 382–83; by function
    in health sciences libraries, 385–99; by
    type of health sciences library, 382–84;
    consumer health libraries, 384; for
    collections, 385–87; for library users,
    387–88; for service points, 394–96; for
    staff workplaces, 396–99; for teaching,
    388–90; hospital libraries, 383–84;
    innovative/nontraditional space, 390–94;
    library commons, 392–93; repurposing
    space, 399–400; simulation labs, 393–
    94. *See also* space planning
Planetree Health Resource Centers, 326
Planning. *See* strategic planning
Plutchak, T. Scott, **392**
postdoctoral associates, 235–36
problem-based learning (PBL), 66–67,
    280–82
professional networking, 366
professional standards: for health
    organizations, 367; for librarians, 367
Program for Cooperative Cataloging (PCC),
    120
Project SHARE, 240–241
PsycINFO, *203*
public health, 41–42
PubMed. See MEDLINE / PubMed
PubMed Central, 13, 48, 202
PubMed Health, 201–2, 339, 342
PubMed LinkOut, 136–37
purchase on demand, 319

quality improvement, 37–38
Quertle, 202

Ragon, Bart, **410**
Ratajeski, Melissa, **217**
RDA (Resource Descriptor and Access),
    122–34, 127, 130–32
RDF (Resource Descriptor Framework), 131,
    137–39
READ scale, 182–83
REDCap, 260
reference interview, 173–74
reference managers, 217–18

reference services, 171–95; and health
    sciences users, 174–78; consultation
    services, 188, *189*; defined, 171–72;
    evaluation, 178–83; functions, 172–73;
    interview, 173–74; LibQUAL+, 187;
    reference desk, 183, 185–87, 395;
    reference transaction flowchart, *189*;
    roving reference, 190; scheduling
    and staffing, 183–90; service points,
    184; single-service desk, 183, 186–87;
    statistics, 178–83; triage, 183, 187–88;
    virtual reference, 184, 191–92
regional medical libraries, 14
remote access, 100
remote storage, 307, 386–87
research assessment, 408
research collaborations. *See* collaborations;
    researchers, collaboration with
research data management, 252–74;
    challenges, 258–62; compliance, 257;
    data management plans, 252–53, 259–
    60; data ownership, 261–62; defined,
    254–55; federal data management, 257;
    integrity, 255–56; librarian RDM skills/
    competencies, 268–69; long-term plan,
    262; metadata, lack of, 260–61; need
    for, 255–57; RDM responsibility, 259;
    records management issues, 260; roles
    for health sciences librarians, 262–68;
    storage, backup, security issues, 261–62;
    tools/resources, 269–70
research informationists. *See* informationists
Research Libraries Group (RLG), 91;
    Conspectus, 91–92, 95, *96*
research life cycle, 268, 406
research services, 196–225
researchers: collaboration with, 71–75,
    406–7; information needs, 197. *See also*
    biomedical research
residents, 176–77
Richetelle, Alberta, **327**
Riley, Ruth A., **360**
Rios, Gabe, **326**
roving reference, 190

Sarli, Cathy C., **237**
Schaefer, Nancy, **186**
scholarly communications: role for health
    sciences librarians, 264–65
scientific research: integrity of, 255–56

Scopus, 205, *206*, 207–8; journal analytics, 208

search process, *289*

security, 149–51; authentication, 151; firewalls, 150; intranets, 151

Semantic Web, 121, 137–39

Shared Electronic Resource Understanding (SERU), 100

Sheffer, Rena, **135**

Shipman, Jean P., **14**

Siebert, Jean L., **105**

Silbajoris, Christie, **328**

simulation labs, 393–94

single-service desk, 183, 186–87

social media, 25, 162, 296, 405

space planning, 377–82; budget, 379; future-proofing, 381; modular design, 380–81; planning documents, 379; preplanning, 377–78; space program, 378–79; sustainability, 381–82. *See also* physical space

Spatz, Michele, **327**

special libraries, 9

Special Libraries Association (SLA), 20

Special-Topics Queries, 201

Squires, Steven J., **370**

statistics: reference, 178–83

strategic management, 353

strategic planning, 357–58

student-centered learning, 280–84; case-based learning (CBL), 282; problem-based learning (PBL), 280–82; team-based learning (TBL), 282–84

students, 175–76

SUSHI protocol, 102

Swanson, Joe, Jr., **350**

systematic reviews, 48–49, 63, 214–15

Tatro, Anna L., **241**

TEACH Act, 309

teacher-centered learning, 279–80

team-based learning (TBL), 282–84

technology services, 143–68; authentication, 151; communication, 152–54; disaster plans, 149; e-mail, 153; educational support, 154–55; emerging technologies, 160; firewalls, 150; intranets, 151; keeping current, 161–63; link resolvers, 157; mobile technologies, 158–60; open source systems, 156; planning, 145–49; security, 149–51; systems, 155–58; technology plans, 146–49; virtual reference, 153–54; Voice-over IP (VoIP), 153; Web 2.0, 157–58; web-scale discovery, 156; websites, 157

Tennant, Michele R., **362**

Timm, Craig, **70**

Tobia, Rajia, **400**

Tooey, M.J., **17**

translational sciences, 73–75

trend: defined, 57–58

triaged service, 187–88

Ufholz, Lee-Anne, **350**

update services, 220–21

UpToDate, 211–12

U.S. health care, 30–39; as a business, 31–32; evidence-based practice, 36–37; influences on, 33–39; information technology and, 38–39; interdisciplinary teams, 35–36; quality of, 32–33, 37–38. *See also* health care

value engineering, 379–80

Villaire, Michael, **330**

Virtual International Authority File (VIAF), 127

virtual private networks (VPN), 151

virtual reference, 153–54

Voice-over IP (VoIP), 153

Vrabel, Mark, **313**

Warner classification, 183

Web 2.0, 157–58

Web of Science, 205, *206*, 207–8

web-based learning, 294–97; embedded librarians, 295; LibGuides, 296–97; MOOCs, 296; online courses, 295–96

web-scale discovery, 133–34, 156, 218–19

websites, 157

weeding. *See* deselection

Zipperer, Lorri, **90**

About the Editor and Authors

M. Sandra Wood, MLS, MBA, AHIP, FMLA, is librarian emerita, Penn State University Libraries. She was a librarian at the George T. Harrell Library, the Milton S. Hershey Medical Center, College of Medicine, Pennsylvania State University, Hershey, for more than thirty-five years, specializing in reference and educational and database services. Ms. Wood is a Fellow of the Medical Library Association, where she was a founding member, chairman, and section council representative of the Reference Services Section (now Public Services Section); served on numerous MLA committees; and served as a member of MLA's Board of Directors. Ms. Wood is founding and current editor of *Medical Reference Services Quarterly*, now in its thirty-fourth volume. She also was founding editor of the *Journal of Consumer Health on the Internet* and the *Journal of Electronic Resources in Medical Libraries*, serving as editor/coeditor of both journals through 2011; she is the author or editor of numerous books and journal articles. Ms. Wood received an MLS from Indiana University and MBA from the University of Maryland.

Marie T. Ascher, MS, AHIP, is associate director for user support, education and research (USER) services at the Health Sciences Library at New York Medical College (NYMC) in Valhalla. Ms. Ascher has worked in public services, primarily in academic health sciences libraries, for the past twenty years since graduating from the Drexel University College of Information Studies in 1993. Ms. Ascher is active in the Medical Library Association, currently as a member of the Research Agenda Committee of the Research and chair of the PH/HA Core Journals Project. She was the founding editor of the Grey Literature Report, has led information outreach projects in New York City, and is responsible for the restructuring of the liaison program and development and deployment of local information management competencies at NYMC. She received the 2013 Katy Nesbit award for exemplary service from the UNYOC Chapter of MLA.

Stewart M. Brower, MLIS, AHIP, is director of the Schusterman Library, University of Oklahoma-Tulsa, where he was responsible for the construction of a brand-new 22,000-square-foot library facility, which was completed in 2011. Additionally, Mr. Brower is cofounder and editor of *Communications in Information Literacy*, serves on multiple editorial boards, and was recognized for his contributions to the South

Central Chapter of the Medical Library Association by being named Librarian of the Year in 2013.

Everly Brown, MLIS, is the head of information services at the University of Maryland, Baltimore's Health Sciences and Human Services Library in Baltimore. She has worked in access services for more than ten years in both circulation and course reserves. In 2012 Ms. Brown took on the additional responsibility of heading the reference department. She completed her MLIS degree at the University of Texas, Austin.

Andrew Creamer, MAEd, MSLIS, coordinates research data management (RDM) education initiatives for the Lamar Soutter Library of the University of Massachusetts Medical School. He works on a variety of the library's science, eScience, and research data management outreach projects, including the New England Data Management Curriculum (NECDMC). He has also been involved with the library's international outreach projects, including the rehabilitation of the University of Liberia's medical college library. Mr. Creamer joined the library staff in 2009 as an intern on the Science Portal project. He teaches research data management at Simmons College and for the Center for Clinical and Translational Sciences at the University of Massachusetts. Mr. Creamer holds a degree in biology and is a graduate of Virginia Tech's Graduate School of Education and Simmons College Graduate School of Library and Information Science. His research interests include international library models for teaching research data management and providing RDM services.

Diana J. Cunningham, MLS, MPH, AHIP Distinguished, is associate dean and Lillian Hetrick Huber Endowed Director at the Health Sciences Library of New York Medical College, Valhalla. Ms. Cunningham has served as director for more than twenty years, and received an MPH in Health Policy and Management in 2000. She received the academic excellence award, and has been a principal investigator on five National Network of Libraries of Medicine subcontracts addressing public health competencies, health literacy, and developing tools and strategies for health professionals, as well as enhancing reference services. After five years working with a national team of pediatric experts, Ms. Cunningham was coauthor on the results of their efforts. Ms. Cunningham has been active in the Medical Library Association as well as the New York-New Jersey and UNYOC chapters, currently serving as treasurer and 2014 conference cochair.

Megan Del Baglivo, MLS, is the serials metadata librarian at the Health Sciences and Human Services Library of the University of Maryland, Baltimore. She has a BA from Rutgers University with a major in zoology, and her MLS is from Southern Connecticut State University. Ms. Del Baglivo has more than seventeen years of experience working in several different areas of technical services.

C. Steven Douglas, MA, MLS, AHIP, is head of collection management, University of Maryland Health Sciences and Human Services Library, Baltimore. He received an MA from the University of Alabama, Tuscaloosa, and an MLS from the University of Maryland, College Park. As head of collection management, Mr. Douglas oversees

the work of selecting, acquiring, and providing access to the HS/HSL's information resources.

Jonathan D. Eldredge, MLS, PhD, is associate professor at the University of New Mexico. His primary appointment is in the Health Sciences Library and Informatics Center with a secondary appointment in the Department of Family & Community Medicine. Dr. Eldredge received his BA with honors from Beloit College, his MLS from the University of Michigan's School of Information, and his MA and PhD from the University of New Mexico. For years he has enjoyed the challenges of tackling increasingly complex projects. He has an active research program with more than forty articles published in peer-reviewed journals. Dr. Eldredge codirects the three-year longitudinal evidence-based practice course for all medical students at UNM and coteaches required courses for clinical research, public health, and physician assistant graduate students.

Nancy R. Glassman, MLS, is assistant director for informatics at the D. Samuel Gottesman Library of the Albert Einstein College of Medicine, Bronx, New York. She received her BA from Cleveland State University and MLS from Kent State University. She was coeditor of *MLA News* Technology and Internet Resources columns, from 2010 to 2013; and currently edits the Mobile Computing in the Library column in the *Journal of Electronic Resources in Medical Libraries*.

Gale G. Hannigan, MLS, MPH, PhD, AHIP-D, is currently a research professor at the University of New Mexico Health Sciences Library and Informatics Center. She obtained the MLS from UC Berkeley, the MPH from the University of Texas, and a PhD in information science from the University of North Texas. She is a Distinguished Member of MLA's Academy of Health Information Professionals. Dr. Hannigan has been a medical librarian since 1977.

Margaret E. Henderson, BSc, MLIS, AHIP, is director, research data management, VCU Libraries, Virginia Commonwealth University, Richmond. She obtained her BSc and MLIS from the University of Western Ontario, and a graduate certificate in biomedical informatics from Oregon Health and Sciences University. Ms. Henderson has also been the database manager for the Department of Anatomy and Neurobiology, School of Medicine, VCU; a library consultant for the Bon Secours Richmond Health System; and the director of libraries and archives, Cold Spring Harbor Laboratory, Cold Spring Harbor, New York.

Donna Kafel, RN, MLIS, is the project coordinator for the eScience program at the Soutter Library at the University of Massachusetts Medical School. In this role, Ms. Kafel manages multiple eScience professional development events and resources for librarians in the New England region, including the annual University of Massachusetts and New England Area Librarian eScience Symposium, the eScience Portal for New England Librarians, Science Boot Camp, and professional development days. She coordinated the planning phase "Frameworks for a Data Management Curriculum," which preceded the development of the New England Collaborative Data Management Curriculum (NECDMC), and served as a coeditor and co-coordinator for NECDMC. She is an adjunct co-instructor at Simmons GSLIS, teaching scientific research data management. Prior to library school, Ms. Kafel worked as a registered nurse in a variety of inpatient hospital settings.

Maureen "Molly" Knapp, MA, AHIP, is a research support and education librarian at the Rudolph Matas Library of the Health Sciences at Tulane University, New Orleans. A librarian with more than a decade of experience, she received her master of library and information science degree from the University of South Florida (Tampa) in 2002. Ms. Knapp is a Distinguished Member of the Medical Library Association's Academy of Health Information Professionals, and a 2010 NLM Fellow in medical informatics at the Marine Biological Laboratory in Woods Hole, Massachusetts. An enthusiastic pedagogue, Ms. Knapp received the 2012 Librarian of the Year award from the South Central Chapter of MLA for her development of the online class "Get Mobilized: An Introduction to Mobile Resources and Tools in Health Sciences Libraries." Her research interests include online education, hashtag communities, and digitization projects in health sciences libraries.

Na Lin, MLS, is the head of digital archive and resource sharing at the Health Sciences and Human Services Library, University of Maryland, Baltimore. She received her MLS from Rutgers. She recently published "Discovering the Present, Preserving the Past: The Development of a Digital Archive at the University of Maryland" (*Journal of Electronic Resources in Medical Libraries*, 2012; coauthored with P. Hinegardner), and she coauthors a column on ERM for the *Journal of Electronic Resources Librarianship*.

Elaine Russo Martin, MSLS, DA, is director of the Lamar Soutter Library of the University of Massachusetts Medical School and associate professor in the Department for Family and Community Medicine. The library serves under contract by the National Library of Medicine as the Regional Medical Library for the six New England states, and Dr. Martin also serves as the director of that program. Before joining UMass, Dr. Martin was director of the health sciences library at the University of Illinois at Chicago and served in various other professional positions in medical school libraries in Virginia, Washington, D.C., and Washington State. Dr. Martin received her MSLS from the Catholic University of America, Washington, D.C., and her doctorate in library science administration from Simmons College, Boston. Dr. Martin's research interests include biomedical informatics; consumer health informatics; assessing the information needs of public health workforce; evidence-based public health; eScience librarianship, and organizational development, in particular leadership and teamwork as they apply to medical libraries. She is an adjunct professor of practice at Simmons College Graduate School of Library and Information Sciences, Boston, where she teaches courses in medical librarianship, library management, and scientific research data management.

Holly E. Phillips, MILS, MS, AHIP, is the director of planning and administrative services at the College of University Libraries and Learning Sciences at the University of New Mexico (UNM). She received her MILS from the University of Arizona in 2003. In addition to other responsibilities such as strategic planning, project management, human resources, and operating budget, Ms. Phillips is responsible for collection budget oversight. Prior to joining the main campus libraries in 2011, she was coordinator of resource access and delivery at the Health Sciences Library and Informatics Center at UNM. She has served as webmaster for the collection development section of the Medical Library Association (MLA), is on the Editorial Board of the *Journal of the Medical Library Association*, has held many positions in the South Central Chapter of MLA, served on the SCAMeL Collection Development Committee, and has taught a number of MLA accredited continuing education courses including Managing Electronic Resources Management Systems (ERMS). She is a member of MLA and SCC/MLA among other professional associations.

María Milagros Pinkas, MLS, is metadata management librarian, Health Sciences and Human Services Library (HS/HSL), University of Maryland, Baltimore. She received her MLS from Escuela Graduada de Bibliotecología y Ciencias de la Información, Río Piedras, Puerto Rico. Her responsibilities include overseeing the cataloging activities and the assignment of metadata for the University of Maryland digital archive. She has also played a leadership role in the implementation of a web-scale discovery service for HS/HSL.

James Shedlock, AMLS, AHIP-DM, FMLA, is a consultant in health sciences library management and operations including space planning. The former director (retired) of the Galter Health Sciences Library, Feinberg School of Medicine, Northwestern University, Mr. Shedlock has more than thirty years of experience as a health sciences librarian since graduating from the University of Michigan School of Information in 1977. His career output includes numerous articles, opinion pieces, papers, and posters. He has held several leadership positions in the Medical Library Association, including service on the Board of Directors, and the Association of Academic Health Sciences Libraries. Mr. Shedlock's previous positions at Northwestern, the University of North Carolina at Chapel Hill, Wayne State University, and St. Joseph Mercy Hospital in Pontiac, Michigan, concentrated on user services and database searching.

Kay Hogan Smith, MLS, MPH, CHES, is community services librarian at the University of Alabama at Birmingham Lister Hill Library of the Health Sciences. She also initiated the Health InfoNet of Alabama consumer health information service for state residents in 1999, and has directed the project ever since. Kay is a Distinguished Member of the Academy of Health Information Professionals.

Michele R. Tennant, MLIS, PhD, AHIP, is assistant director of the Health Science Center Library and Bioinformatics Librarian for the Genetics Institute at the University of Florida. Michele received her BS in biological sciences from the University of Southern California, her PhD in biology from Wayne State University, and her MLIS from the University of California, Los Angeles. At the HSCL, Michele is head of the biomedical and health information services (BHIS) department, which encompasses the library's liaison, instruction, and outreach activities. BHIS liaisons are deeply integrated into the curricula for the colleges they serve (Dentistry, Medicine, Nursing, Pharmacy, Public Health and Health Professions, Veterinary Medicine), as well as in coursework for PhD and undergraduate science students; provide outreach to clinicians through rounding services and to patients through the internal medicine clinic; and develop numerous services for researchers including those related to bioinformatics, data, public access, and other areas of interest.

Lee A. Vucovich, MS, MLS, AHIP, is the assistant director for reference services at Lister Hill Library of the Health Sciences at University of Alabama at Birmingham. She received her masters of library science degree from Indiana University in 2001 and has an MS in organic chemistry from the University of Michigan. Currently, Ms. Vucovich serves as library liaison to the Joint Health Sciences Departments and the Center for Clinical and Translational Science and works with research faculty in the School of Medicine.

Megan Wolff, MS, is an instructional technology specialist with the University of Maryland, Baltimore's School of Nursing. She formerly worked as a library reserve associate in the UMB Health Sciences and Human Services Library. Ms. Wolff holds a master of science degree in instructional technology and a postbaccalaureate certificate in interactive media design from Towson University.